Handbook of Research on Inclusive and Innovative Architecture and the Built Environment

Ng Foong Peng
Taylor's University, Malaysia

Ungku Norani Sonet
Taylor's University, Malaysia

A volume in the Advances in Civil and Industrial Engineering (ACIE) Book Series

Published in the United States of America by
    IGI Global
    Engineering Science Reference (an imprint of IGI Global)
    701 E. Chocolate Avenue
    Hershey PA, USA 17033
    Tel: 717-533-8845
    Fax: 717-533-8661
    E-mail: cust@igi-global.com
    Web site: http://www.igi-global.com

Library of Congress Cataloging-in-Publication Data

Names: Ng Foong Peng, Veronica, editor. | Sonet, Ungku Norani, DATE-
    editor.
Title: Handbook of research on inclusive and innovative architecture and
    the built environment / edited by Ng Foong Peng, and Ungku Norani Sonet.
Description: Hershey, PA : Engineering Science Reference, [2023] | Includes
    bibliographical references and index. | Summary: "The Handbook of
    Research on Inclusive and Innovative Architecture and the Built
    Environment discusses inclusive and innovative approaches to providing
    socio-cultural value within architecture and the built environment. It
    focuses on issues of diversity, sustainability, resilient designs, and
    more. Further, the book expands the knowledge and awareness of
    architecture and the built environment towards inclusivity in design
    development and emerging advanced technology. Covering topics such as
    architectural challenges, global health, and urban morphology, this
    major reference work is an excellent resource for architects, government
    officials, urban planners, practitioners, students and educators of
    higher education, researchers, and academicians"-- Provided by
    publisher.
Identifiers: LCCN 2022062293 (print) | LCCN 2022062294 (ebook) | ISBN
    9781668482537 (hardcover) | ISBN 9781668482544 (ebook)
Subjects: LCSH: Architecture and society. | Architecture--Environmental
    aspects.
Classification: LCC NA2543.S6 H367 2023 (print) | LCC NA2543.S6 (ebook) |
    DDC 720.1/03--dc23/eng/20230103
LC record available at https://lccn.loc.gov/2022062293
LC ebook record available at https://lccn.loc.gov/2022062294

This book is published in the IGI Global book series Advances in Civil and Industrial Engineering (ACIE) (ISSN: 2326-6139; eISSN: 2326-6155)

British Cataloguing in Publication Data
A Cataloguing in Publication record for this book is available from the British Library.

All work contributed to this book is new, previously-unpublished material. The views expressed in this book are those of the authors, but not necessarily of the publisher.

For electronic access to this publication, please contact: eresources@igi-global.com.

Advances in Civil and Industrial Engineering (ACIE) Book Series

Ioan Constantin Dima
University Valahia of Târgovişte, Romania

ISSN:2326-6139
EISSN:2326-6155

MISSION

Private and public sector infrastructures begin to age, or require change in the face of developing technologies, the fields of civil and industrial engineering have become increasingly important as a method to mitigate and manage these changes. As governments and the public at large begin to grapple with climate change and growing populations, civil engineering has become more interdisciplinary and the need for publications that discuss the rapid changes and advancements in the field have become more in-demand. Additionally, private corporations and companies are facing similar changes and challenges, with the pressure for new and innovative methods being placed on those involved in industrial engineering.

The **Advances in Civil and Industrial Engineering (ACIE) Book Series** aims to present research and methodology that will provide solutions and discussions to meet such needs. The latest methodologies, applications, tools, and analysis will be published through the books included in **ACIE** in order to keep the available research in civil and industrial engineering as current and timely as possible.

COVERAGE

- Materials Management
- Urban Engineering
- Ergonomics
- Hydraulic Engineering
- Optimization Techniques
- Transportation Engineering
- Structural Engineering
- Productivity
- Coastal Engineering
- Construction Engineering

IGI Global is currently accepting manuscripts for publication within this series. To submit a proposal for a volume in this series, please contact our Acquisition Editors at Acquisitions@igi-global.com or visit: http://www.igi-global.com/publish/.

Titles in this Series

For a list of additional titles in this series, please visit: www.igi-global.com/book-series

Global Science's Cooperation Opportunities, Challenges, and Good Practices
Mohamed Moussaoui (Abdelmalek Essaadi University, Morocco)
Engineering Science Reference • copyright 2023 • 300pp • H/C (ISBN: 9781668478745) • US $245.00 (our price)

Artificial Intelligence and Machine Learning Techniques for Civil Engineering
Vagelis Plevris (Qatar University, Qatar) Afaq Ahmad (University of Engineering and Technology, Taxila, Pakistan) and Nikos D. Lagaros (National Technical University of Athens, Greece)
Engineering Science Reference • copyright 2023 • 385pp • H/C (ISBN: 9781668456439) • US $250.00 (our price)

Geoinformatics in Support of Urban Politics and the Development of Civil Engineering
Sérgio António Neves Lousada (University of Madeira, Portugal)
Engineering Science Reference • copyright 2023 • 263pp • H/C (ISBN: 9781668464496) • US $250.00 (our price)

Implications of Digital Systems on Mobility as a Service
John M. Easton (University of Birmingham, UK)
Engineering Science Reference • copyright 2023 • 335pp • H/C (ISBN: 9781799841388) • US $250.00 (our price)

Impact of Digital Twins in Smart Cities Development
Ingrid Vasiliu-Feltes (University of Miami, USA)
Engineering Science Reference • copyright 2023 • 314pp • H/C (ISBN: 9781668438336) • US $260.00 (our price)

AI Techniques for Renewable Source Integration and Battery Charging Methods in Electric Vehicle Applications
S. Angalaeswari (Vellore Institute of Technology, India) T. Deepa (Vellore Institute of Technology, India) and L. Ashok Kumar (PSG College of Technology, India)
Engineering Science Reference • copyright 2023 • 288pp • H/C (ISBN: 9781668488164) • US $260.00 (our price)

Urban Life and the Ambient in Smart Cities, Learning Cities, and Future Cities
H. Patricia McKenna (AmbientEase, Canada)
Engineering Science Reference • copyright 2023 • 261pp • H/C (ISBN: 9781668440964) • US $215.00 (our price)

Remapping Urban Heat Island Atlases in Regenerative Cities
Hisham Abusaada (Housing and Building National Research Center, Egypt) Abeer Elshater (Ain Shams University, Egypt) and Marwa Khalifa (Ain Shams University, Egypt)
Engineering Science Reference • copyright 2022 • 267pp • H/C (ISBN: 9781668424629) • US $250.00 (our price)

701 East Chocolate Avenue, Hershey, PA 17033, USA
Tel: 717-533-8845 x100 • Fax: 717-533-8661
E-Mail: cust@igi-global.com • www.igi-global.com

List of Contributors

Table of Contents

Section 2
Sustainability, Technology, and Built Environment Education

Section 5
Built Environment Wellbeing

Section 6
Culture, Place Experience, and the Everyday Spaces

Detailed Table of Contents

Section 1
Technology and the Metaverse

Chapter 1

    Kenn Jhun Kam, Taylor's University, Malaysia
    Lim Jun Wei, Taylor's University, Malaysia
    Tze Shwan Lim, Taylor's University, Malaysia
    Habizah Sheikh Ilmi, Taylor's University, Malaysia
    Lam Tatt Soon, Taylor's University, Malaysia

It is an undeniable fact that by implementing smart home technology (SHT), the quality of life for the occupants within can be improved for different aspects such as safety, leisure, comfort, and healthcare. However, it is discovered that Malaysians are highly reluctant in adopting SHT in their house. The research approach undertaken was quantitative method by sending questionnaire through emails. This research found the main key features of SHT are that they have high helpfulness level in improving the occupants' quality of life; the chapter lays out the main factors affecting the home buyers to adopt SHT and the main challenges exist staying in a smart home. Moreover, attractiveness and clear interface are both main factors affecting the smart homeowners to adopt SHT from the smart home users' perspective. However, poor operationality is rated as the most challenging limitation faced by the smart home users themselves. Also, poor operationality has the most significant influence on the smart home user's overall satisfaction level toward the smart home system.

Chapter 2

    Lam Tatt Soon, Taylor's University, Malaysia
    Hsien Shien Goh, Taylor's University, Malaysia
    Tze Shwan Lim, Taylor's University, Malaysia
    Boon Tik Leong, Taylor's University, Malaysia
    W. T. Hong, Heriot-Watt University, Malaysia
    Kenn Jhun Kam, Taylor's University, Malaysia

The adoption of 3D modelling in construction has contributed many benefits to the industry, yet some of the construction players are still either unfamiliar with the software or not utilizing the software to its fullest potential. The objectives of this research are to determine the challenges faced in 3D modelling software, to postulate the solutions based on the identified challenges in 3D modelling software, and to investigate the strategies of 3D modelling in the QS profession. A qualitative method of research will be carried out to acquire the data and opinions from the quantity surveyors in the construction sector. Based on the findings, financial issues are the most significant challenges on 3D modelling, whereas training for construction staff and enforcement from the government is the most impactful solution and strategy. This study can boost the construction players' confidence in integrating 3D modelling in the construction industry. It also brings higher efficiency in daily operations and helps to improve the productivity of workers.

Chapter 3

The pandemic has certainly become a paradigm shift in multiple sectors and industries, including the built environment. Therefore, this chapter highlights one of the methods which was adopted during the pandemic in continuing the architecture, engineering, and construction (AEC) practice without disregarding the site assessment due to the pandemic circumstances. This chapter is to discuss the potential of adopting 3D laser scanning and 3D photogrammetry in the making of a virtual site and building model for various purposes, including building inspections, virtual visits, and defect inspections. The case study of six projects is used to demonstrate the usage of the two methods: 1) 3D laser scanning, and 2) 3D photogrammetry. The results show the potential for the site and building assessment in adopting virtual advanced technologies pertaining to the post pandemic COVID-19 and various future circumstances and challenges in the field of the built environment.

Chapter 4

The term metaverse was first used in the novel 'Snow Crash.' However, it has come into people's lives with the development of 3D design and visual techniques, machine computations, blockchain, and the internet. Companies and communities worldwide are launching their metaverse platform with diverse functions like trading, gaming, and socialization. The virtual spaces are designed, and virtual buildings or reconstructions of existing ones can be seen. The facts and laws of the universe that people live in directly affect their understanding, so developers generally tend to implement these into their virtual environments. However, the factors which shape and govern the real world are not valid in virtual environments. Thus, there are diverse possibilities in the metaverse. This chapter presents the metaverse and its platforms with definitions, usage, interfaces, and problems. It explores the facts of the universe and discusses gaps and lack of designing spaces and buildings in virtual environments by thinking about the possibilities in the metaverse.

Sujatavani Gunasagaran, Taylor's University, Malaysia
TamilSalvi Mari, Taylor's University, Malaysia
Nik Syazwan Shawn Nik Ab. Wahab, Taylor's University, Malaysia
Azim Sulaiman, Taylor's University, Malaysia
Khairool Aizat Ahmad Jamal, Taylor's University, Malaysia

The use of mobile apps for learning is not common in learning of technical modules in architecture, but studies have been advocated to learn its potential two decades ago. E-learning has supplemented traditional learning in Malaysian Universities since 2004. The Covid-19 pandemic forced education to be conducted virtually. Lecturers with knowledge of blended learning were able to switch to virtual learning but had challenges. The challenge of this module is access to environmental lab and data loggers that would need travelling and sharing of devices. Apps for measuring weather data led to minor adjustment in teaching and learning without altering the learning outcome. The students' perception of learning was captured in a survey with 114 responses. The result evidenced that students had a good learning experience by reporting high mean value for all the items. All Pearson's Correlation values showed positive with moderate to very high correlation between the factors. Post-pandemic teaching and learning in universities need to explore the potential of m-learning.

Salmiah Aziz, Faculty of Innovative and Design Technology, Universiti Sultan Zainal Abidin
(UNISZA), Malaysia & Architectural Technology and Management Group, Faculty of
Architecture and Ekistics, Universiti Malaysia Kelantan (UMK), Malaysia & Institute
for Artificial Intelligenice and Big Data (AIBIg), Office of Deputy Vice Chancellor
(Research and Innovation), Universiti Malaysia Kelantan, Malaysia
Siti Nuratirah Che Mohd Nasir, Architectural Technology and Management Group, Faculty
of Architecture and Ekistics, Universiti Malaysia Kelantan (UMK), Malaysia
Nor Diyana Mustapa, Human Centered Design Group, Faculty of Architecture and Ekistics,
Universiti Malaysia Kelantan (UMK), Malaysia
Nik Nurul Hana Hanafi, Architectural Technology and Management Group, Faculty of
Architecture and Ekistics, Universiti Malaysia Kelantan (UMK), Malaysia
Noorul Huda Mohd Razali, Architectural Technology and Management Group, Faculty of
Architecture and Ekistics, Universiti Malaysia Kelantan (UMK), Malaysia
Mohammed Fadzli Maharimi, Architectural Technology and Management Group, Faculty of
Architecture and Ekistics, Universiti Malaysia Kelantan (UMK), Malaysia

The advancement of new technologies into our daily lives has resulted in a significant increase in the use of information and communication technology (ICT) in education in recent years. The research objectives were to identify the possibility of blogging amongst architectural design students for the future of schooling (blended-learning) and to formulate the best practice of ICTs knowledge management practice through blended-learning for the architectural design students. The data collected through reviewing the literature by other authors (secondary sources) on the subject of digitalisation, digital construction, and digital education. The research could significantly affect the future of education in producing young tech-savvy generations in terms of technologically advanced classrooms; new option of blogging platform for the architectural design students to practice design communication through e-learning known as TACblog as a digital education formulation.

Chapter 7
   Lam Tatt Soon, Taylor's University, Malaysia
   Kai Kong Chow, Taylor's University, Malaysia
   Hai Chen Tan, Heriot-Watt University, Malaysia
   Myzatul Aishah Kamarazaly, Taylor's University, Malaysia
   Tze Shwan Lim, Taylor's University, Malaysia

In the construction-related course, there is a lot of knowledge that is tough to verbalize or teach, especially understanding building details through imagination without experiencing or seeing the construction elements in reality. Visual reality (VR) enables users to visualize the complexity of buildings. The research method used in this research is qualitative method in which interviews were conducted in this research. The interviewees were invited to try the VR technology and data was collected. Throughout the whole research, the workflow of converting a 3D model to a VR model is developed, the constraints of adopting VR are identified and strategies are recommended. The results in the findings showed that all the interviewees need guidance when using the VR technology and some of them suffer from motion sickness. The findings of this research serve as a reference for universities that are interested in adopting VR technology in education to enhance knowledge of VR technology and provide better understanding in the classes.

Chapter 8
   Azrina Binti Md Yaakob, Taylor's University, Malaysia
   Myzatul Aishah Kamarazaly, Taylor's University, Malaysia
   Yee Shi Lee, Taylor's University, Malaysia

There are two types of online learning, which are online learning and hybrid. COVID-19 pandemic, coining the term "new normal" has impacted, directly and indirectly, the global economy, including shaking up the education sector. The education system completely shifted the learning method from traditional face-to-face classes to an online learning system. This situation has posed an extreme challenge to the education community and forced the educators to shift their teaching mode overnight. Taylor's University had constantly applied traditional learning in quantity surveying education has been exposed to the new changes as well. This pandemic has highlighted the need for more online technology training and evolution. However, the online learning trend in quantity surveying education remained undervalued due to the familiarity of students with traditional face-to-face classes. Hence, the objective of this research is to identify the differences in students' attitudes, to identify the differences in students' achievement and to provide strategies to improve online learning and hybrid learning.

This research examines architecture graduates' perceptions of their proficiency in 21st-century skills. A quantitative methodology was employed for this study. The data was obtained through a structured questionnaire, which 141 architecture graduates completed. The online survey assessed the graduates' 21st-century skills. The collected data was analyzed using SPSS version 25. The findings show that the graduates' level of proficiency in 21st-century skills is generally moderate, with information; media and technology skills; and life and career skills being the most prominent. The graduates rated their learning and innovation skills the highest (M=3.76), followed by moderate scores for both life and career skills (M=3.60) and information, media, and technology skills (M= 3.04). The study adds to the existing literature on 21st-century skills by providing a student perspective on the topic, which has not been widely explored in published research.

Section 3
Innovative Building Materials

Glue-laminated timber (GLT) and closely related cross-laminated timber (CLT) represent a technological shift that has brought about new possibilities for architects to employ as part of their design toolkits. In temperate climate zones and industrial countries, GLT and CLT have seen a recent surge in their application. Its popularity has increased in response to favourable changes in building regulations and due to the increasing importance of certifiable sustainability in the built environment. In Malaysia, the adoption of GLT has been very limited to date. This study examines which factors influence Malaysian architects with regard to the use of GLT/CLT as a building material. From the Malaysian architects surveyed for this research, it is evident that there is a significant interest in using GLT and CLT in future projects. Most respondents stated that they had previously considered using GLT and/or CLT but abandoned the idea due to the absence of local supply and the resulting high cost of importing GLT/CLT.

Chapter 11

Tze Shwan Lim, Taylor's University, Malaysia
Yee Lin Lee, Tunku Abdul Rahman University of Management and Technology, Malaysia
Yin Xi Goh, Tunku Abdul Rahman University of Management and Technology, Malaysia
Kenn Jhun Kam, Taylor's University, Malaysia
Lam Tatt Soon, Taylor's University, Malaysia

The impact of the construction industry on the environment has made people more and more aware that it is necessary to adopt a sustainable and responsible attitude to the current construction practices. Increasing attention has prompted the Malaysian government and professional institutions to alleviate this problem more actively without restricting development needs. The objective of this study includes identifying the types of green materials adopted in buildings, comparing the differences between green materials and common materials, and investigating the challenges of using green materials in buildings in Malaysia. A quantitative method with a questionnaire has been adopted in this study and analysis of the study is conducted by descriptive method, inferential method, and ANOVA method. Through intensive literature study, it has brought a better understanding of the types of green building materials adopted.

Section 4
Challenges in the Construction Industry

Chapter 12

Chin Ai Ling Shirley, Taylor's University, Malaysia
Myzatul Aishah Kamarazaly, Taylor's University, Malaysia
Naseem Ameer Ali, Massey University, New Zealand
Ali Moossajee, Taylor's University, Malaysia

The Construction Industry Payment and Adjudication Act 2012 (CIPAA 2012) has redefined how construction disputes are resolved in Malaysia. The Chartered Institute of Arbitrators (CIArb) in Kenya has long provided Adjudication Rules for the Construction Industry 2003. According Muigua and Muigua, it is not commonly used to resolve commercial disputes in Kenya. This research fills the gap to address curiosity. The chapter studies the trend of contractual adjudication in Kenya, and the potential challenges of implementing statutory adjudication in Kenya for construction payment disputes. The results revealed that QS in Kenya usually are involved in contractual disputes nevertheless commonly refer to negotiation and arbitration. The findings also indicate that adjudication is not a preferred choice of ADR due to cost, time and lack of provisions in the standard form of contract in Kenya. But the findings proved that most QS's will propose adjudication as the preferred method due to the structured manner the rules will be provided in backed by the parliament.

    Kenn Jhun Kam, Taylor's University, Malaysia
    Xiao Jing Lim, Taylor's University, Malaysia
    Tze Shwan Lim, Taylor's University, Malaysia
    Lam Tatt Soon, Taylor's University, Malaysia

Competitive and fast-track construction environments with quantity without quality lead to the occurrence of building failure and defective works. The necessity of building inspection and rectification of the defect figure is becoming predominant in the vacant possession of new residential buildings. This paper study on cost involvement and worthiness of building inspection and building defects rectification from the contractors' and house buyers' perspectives to resolve the arising problem of building failure and defective works. The research is a mixed-method approach, it comprises qualitative and quantitative methods. Interviews were conducted with contractors, whereas a questionnaire survey was carried out with house buyers as targeted respondents of this study to obtain data and information. Both contractors and house buyers' perspectives on building inspection and building defect rectification have been observed. From this study, everyone can better understand the cost involvement of the common defects and have their standard to measure the worthiness of building inspection.

    Myzatul Aishah Kamarazaly, Taylor's University, Malaysia
    Tze Yee Angeline Tay, Taylor's University, Malaysia
    Azrina Md Yaakob, Taylor's University, Malaysia
    Lam Tatt Soon, Taylor's University, Malaysia
    Hasmawati Harun, Universiti Teknologi MARA, Malaysia

Choosing the proper formwork had become challenging, especially in the immediate aftermath of the Covid 19 pandemic. Various formwork materials, including wood, plastic, aluminium, steel, magnesium, and fabric, are available today. The purpose of each formwork is the same, but various properties are displayed. Formwork made of steel and timber is frequently used in Malaysia. Several factors, including resource availability, transportation, time constraints, and labour costs, influenced the contractors' preference for formwork materials. Therefore, this research aimed to determine whether contractors' preferred formwork was appropriate before and after the pandemic. Consequently, essential factors, including cost and preferences, were discussed when choosing formwork materials. Only steel and timber formwork were studied for this particular paper. The G7 contractors involved in various project types were interviewed as part of the qualitative methodology used in this study, which also included document analysis based on previous project reports. The cost was the determining factor before the pandemic, and resource availability held the top spot during the recovery stage, according to the first finding. The importance of transport remained at level 5 throughout both eras. In addition, the second finding revealed that all costs, including labour, transportation, and material, had increased for both timber and steel formwork, primarily as a result.

Section 5
Built Environment Wellbeing

Chapter 15

TamilSalvi Mari, Taylor's University, Malaysia
Tan Wei Sen, Taylor's University, Malaysia
Ng Veronica, Taylor's University, Malaysia
Sujatavani Gunasagaran, Taylor's University, Malaysia
Sivaraman Kuppusamy, Reading University of Malaysia, Malaysia

The stress and mental health risks associated with living and working in cities have increased the importance of designing urban spaces. It is, therefore, crucial to prioritize the mental wellbeing of city residents. Research indicates that people's perception of their wellbeing is influenced by various factors, such as their environment and the people around them. Office workers spend significant time in their workspace, so a well-designed office can positively impact their wellbeing. Biophilic design, which incorporates natural elements into office spaces, has become increasingly popular, and studies have shown that workplace greenery can improve employees' wellbeing and job performance. A study conducted in Kuala Lumpur used a quantitative method to investigate whether incorporating restorative environments into offices could enhance employees' mental wellbeing. The study found that restorative environments within the office space were positively associated with office workers' self-perceived mental wellbeing.

Chapter 16

Xiang Loon Lee, Taylor's University, Malaysia
Sucharita Srirangam, Taylor's University, Malaysia

Affluent high-rise residential developments are booming in Mont Kiara and the City Centre of Kuala Lumpur, Malaysia. However, upscale high life subjects to social alienation issues. Research indicates that social spaces promote human health, but their integration in vertical living is still insignificant. This study investigates challenges with social space design in luxury high-rise buildings in Kuala Lumpur from designers' perspectives. Interviews were conducted with three architectural firms on the challenges they faced in implementation. Findings revealed challenges with synergistic relationships, architectural branding, spatial order, private-public articulation, space design, space optimisation, and space psychology. Subsequently, three characteristics of challenges on culture, impact, and communication were discussed for designers to respond to. On this basis, it is recommended that aspiring designers develop an awareness of these concerns in future designs and examine more challenges to identify tailored solutions to address these issues.

Chapter 17

Siti Nuratirah Che Mohd Nasir, Universiti Malaysia Kelantan, Malaysia & Universiti Sultan Zainal Abidin, Malaysia

Nur Haizal Mat Yaacob Ariffin, Universiti Sultan Zainal Abidin, Malaysia

Najah Md Alwi, Sustainability and Urban Design Group, Faculty of Architecture and Ekistics, Universiti Malaysia Kelantan, Malaysia

Salmiah Aziz, Architectural Technology and Management Group, Faculty of Architecture and Ekistics, Universiti Malaysia Kelantan, Malaysia

Nur 'Izzati Mohd Amin, Human Centered Design Group, Faculty of Architecture and Ekistics, Universiti Malaysia Kelantan, Malaysia

Mohammed Fadzli Maharimi, Architectural Technology and Management Group, Faculty of Architecture and Ekistics, Universiti Malaysia Kelantan, Malaysia

The topic of health is becoming more of a crucial element in today's life particularly due to the COVID-19 crisis. This research was conducted to point out an eco-friendly building material focusing on interior environment towards better quality of life. The method adopted incorporates deeper literature study and interview sessions with expertise in the built environment mainly in eco-friendly and sustainable houses. The results show that there is a long list of available local eco-friendly material mainly timber, brick, concrete, and bamboo that can be used in producing a healthy home. This research concludes that people need to gain more understanding of these materials and demand from our construction players will help to push more interest for these healthier options products. The data collected could be seen as important in the wake of recent endemic COVID-19 that involved wellbeing inside the house. This would be beneficial to the policy maker, enlightened building industry players and homeowners to highlight the significance of practicing a healthy environment.

Section 6
Culture, Place Experience, and the Everyday Spaces

Chapter 18

Najah Md. Alwi, Universiti Malaysia Kelantan, Malaysia

Ida Marlina Mazlan, UCSI University, Malaysia

Although Malaysia is traditionally a tea-drinking nation, the global coffee culture has become an integral part of a "third" space in the country's urban and rural areas. The study highlights the shared qualities and cultural elements that shape the design and atmosphere of Malaysian coffee places, providing insights into their role as important social tools in the country. By exploring the spatial design and social meaning of these coffee places, this research contributes to a deeper understanding of the relationship between architecture, cultural identity, and everyday life experiences in Malaysia. However, this study focuses on a limited number of selected coffee houses in specific regions of Malaysia. The findings should be interpreted within this context and may not capture the full diversity of coffee places across the country. The findings contribute to the growing body of knowledge on the intersection of architecture, culture, and social interactions, serving as a foundation for further exploration and appreciation of Malaysia's unique coffee culture.

Chapter 19

This chapter attempts to rediscover and envision the revitalization idea of Kedai Pati, a gastronomic urban node in Kota Bharu, Kelantan. More than 50 years ago, Kedai Pati likely existed and acted as a local third place, whereby people tend to drop in for a quick snack before going to work or elsewhere. Kedai Pati is perceived as a valuable space for the local working men to informally attend on the regular or irregularly. At the present day, Kedai Pati still survives with its signature theatrical-service pantry operation, and seller-buyer social setting, which is part of a unique ambiance considered Kelantan's cultural heritage. These nodal gastronomic places around Kota Bharu town have been mapped to indicate their current location and studies on reimagining and rebranding the Kedai Pati itself have been made to promote and reintroduce its existence. Varieties of design proposals have then been put forward as it may indicate a new pop-up cart style for Kedai Pati.

Chapter 20

This study investigates the virtual place experience (VPE) approach, using 360° images in Google Street View (GSV), to help learners attain a sense of place. It examines their experience and attitude in the virtual setting of the place of knowledge inquiry. Interpretive phenomenological analysis (IPA) was adopted to examine learners' cognitive learning of place identity, interpretation of place meanings, and attitudes toward the place. Findings indicate that learners developed their sense of presence in VPE through visual elements reflecting the place identity. Place attribute learning requires additional research to understand place identity. Place meanings in the virtual setting were interpreted through the sense of community and historical evidence. Positive affection towards the place was identified, leading to motivation to visit the real place. The study provides insight into how learners' experience with the virtual place phenomenon may contribute to constructing their sense of place, which shall guide their design cognition in future design exercises.

The design of public parks is a vital aspect of urban planning. To ensure that public parks are designed to cater to the needs and preferences of communities, it is important to consider public perception and participation. Therefore, the aim of this study is to evaluate people's perception of public participation in designing public parks in Malaysia. The questionnaire design is mainly derived from the theories of public awareness of public participation exercises in designing public parks in Malaysia. This study adopted quantitative survey questionnaire method. The respondents of the study are users of two public parks in Johor Bahru. In total, there were 383 data collected and analysed. The findings show that civil society in general has a collective interest in participating in public participation exercises in designing public parks in Malaysia.

Chapter 22

Public participation in cultural heritage, with particular regard to conservation, has been a concern ever since the Venice Charter, and it still is to this day. This approach has also been highlighted in World Heritage documents. The Faro Convention adopted a shift in focus from the conservation of cultural heritage values to the value of cultural heritage for society. Accordingly, cultural heritage institutions inevitably have to apply a participatory approach in order to achieve sustainable conservation. Moreover, a number of papers have focused on the importance of public participation in heritage conservation and tourism management. This chapter studies the concept of people's participation in cultural heritage conservation and management in international charters and documents. It also takes into account various methods and approaches in Human-Computer Interaction studies, which have valuable resources for user engagement in designing services by people for people, in order to propose an effective, applicable people-participation approach to cultural heritage management.

Chapter 23

The most important step in the tendency of human beings to change their natural environment is urbanization. Cities are in constant change with re-adaptation of different parts, which developed spontaneously or consciously planned under different socio-economic, natural, religious, and political conditions. Anatolian cities are the simplest and most modest reflections of traditional Turkish-Islamic life. Kastamonu, one of these cities, blends its structure built on this Turkish-Islamic life system with the topography of the region, climatic data, cultural layers, lifestyle, and architectural features of the local people and becomes original with its own internal dynamics. In this study, urbanization, and settlement features of Kastamonu city in the historical process are discussed. Kastamonu historical city center and historical bazaar area were examined by discussing how the main axes shaped in line with unchangeable natural data became subjectivized by human hands and the components of the traditional urban texture in the context of the border, and the morphological inputs of these components were mentioned.

Preface

The *Handbook of Research on Inclusive and Innovative Architecture and the Built Environment* responds to the urgent need to emphasize inclusivity in architecture and the built environment. Innovative technologies within the field of architecture are being developed to enhance inclusivity in architectural approaches and development processes. It is essential to research inclusivity in architecture and the built environment toward holistic sustainable development.

The book discusses inclusive and innovative approaches to providing socio-cultural value within architecture and the built environment. It focuses on issues of diversity, sustainability, resilient designs, and more. Further, the book expands the knowledge and awareness of architecture and the built environment towards inclusivity in design development and emerging advanced technology. Covering topics such as architectural challenges, global health, and urban morphology, this major reference work is an excellent resource for architects, government officials, urban planners, practitioners, students and educators of higher education, researchers, and academicians.

The book is curated based on six themes: Technology and the Metaverse (Chapters 1-4); Sustainability, Technology, and Built Environment Education (Chapters 5-9); Innovative Building Materials (Chapters 10-11); Challenges in the Construction Industry (Chapters 12-14); Built Environment Wellbeing (Chapters 15-17); and Culture, Place Experience, and the Everyday Spaces (Chapters 18-23).

The first theme, 'Technology and the Metaverse', is explored in Chapters 1-4. Chapter 1 studies the adoption of Smart Home Technologies (SHT) among homeowners in Malaysia. Through a quantitative study, the chapter argues that SHT has a high level of helpfulness in improving the occupants' quality of life. Attractiveness and clear interface are both main factors affecting the Smart Homeowners to adopt SHT from the Smart Home users' perspective. Contrastingly, poor operationality is rated as the most challenging limitation faced by the Smart Home users themselves. Also, poor operationality has the most significant influence on the Smart Home user's overall satisfaction level toward the Smart Home system.

Chapter 2 seeks to determine the challenges faced in 3D modelling software, to postulate the solutions based on the identified challenges in 3D modelling software, and to investigate the strategies of 3D modelling in the Quantity Surveying profession. Through a qualitative method, the findings suggest that financial issues are the most significant challenges on 3D modelling, whereas training for construction staff and enforcement from the government is the most impactful solution and strategy. This study supports the integration of 3D modelling in the construction industry.

Chapter 3 discusses the potential of adopting 3D laser scanning and 3D photogrammetry in the making of a virtual site and building model for various purposes including building inspection, virtual visit, and defect inspection. Through six case studies, the results show the potential for the site and building assessment in adopting virtual advance technologies pertaining to the post pandemic COVID-19 and various future circumstances and challenges in the field of the built environment.

Chapter 4 presents the Metaverse and its platforms with definitions, usage, interfaces, and problems. It explores the facts of the universe and discusses gaps and lack of designing spaces and buildings in virtual environments by thinking about the possibilities in Metaverse.

The second theme 'Sustainability, Technology, and Built Environment Education', is framed in Chapters 5-9. Chapter 5 explores the use of mobile apps for learning in a module called Architecture and Environment. The challenge of this module is access to Environmental Lab and data loggers that would need travelling and sharing of devices. Apps for measuring weather data led to minor adjustment in teaching and learning without altering the learning outcome. Results from a survey of 114 students show that the students had a positive learning experience.

Chapter 6 seeks to identify the possibility of blogging amongst architectural design students for the future of schooling (blended-learning) and to formulate the best practice of ICTs knowledge management practice through blended-learning for the architectural design students. The study advocates for the new option of blogging platform for the architectural design students to practice design communication through e-Learning known as TACblog as a digital education formulation.

Chapter 7 examines the use of Virtual Reality (VR) Technology in construction education. Rather than relying on the lengthy knowledge to be gained by the students, Visual Reality (VR) enables users to visualize the complexity of buildings. Throughout the whole research, the workflow of converting a 3D model to a VR model is developed, the constraints of adopting VR are identified and strategies are recommended. Adopting a qualitative method, the results showed that all the interviewees need guidance when using the VR technology and some of them suffer from motion sickness.

Chapter 8 is a case study analyzing the online and hybrid learning trends in a Quantity Surveying education from the pandemic. It uses the case of Taylor's University, which had constantly applied traditional learning in quantity surveying education has been exposed to the new changes as well. This pandemic has highlighted the need for more online technology training and evolution. However, the online learning trend in quantity surveying education remained undervalued due to the familiarity of students with traditional face-to-face classes. Hence, the objective of this research is to identify the differences in students' attitudes, to identify the differences in students' achievement and to provide strategies to improve online learning and hybrid learning.

Chapter 9 focusses on Work Based Learning as a catalyst for sustainability through a study on Architecture students' 21st century skills. This research examines architecture graduates' perceptions of their proficiency in 21st-century skills. Adopting a quantitative methodology was employed for this study, the online survey was completed by 141 architecture graduates. The findings show that the graduates' level of proficiency in 21st-century skills is generally moderate, with Information, Media, and Technology skills and Life and Career skills being the most prominent. The graduates rated their Learning and Innovation skills the highest, followed by moderate scores for both Life and Career skills and Information, Media, and Technology Skills.

The third theme, 'Innovative Building Materials', is covered in Chapters 10-11. Chapter 10 investigates key factors influencing Malaysian architects' use of glue-laminated timber (GLT) and its closely related cross-laminated timber (CLT). In temperate climate zones and industrial countries, GLT and CLT have seen a recent surge in their application. Its popularity has increased in response to favorable changes in building regulations and due to the increasing importance of certifiable sustainability in the built environment. Recognizing the limited use of this material, this study found that there is a significant interest in using GLT and CLT in future projects. The limited usage was due to absence of local supply and the resulting high Cost of importing GLT/CLT.

Chapter 11 studies the adoption and challenges of green material usage in construction projects. With increasing adoption of sustainable materials in Malaysia, this study identifies the types of green materials adopted in buildings and their comparisons to common materials, and examines the challenges of green material adoption. A quantitative method with a questionnaire has been adopted in this study and analysis of the study is conducted by descriptive method, inferential method, and ANOVA method. Through intensive literature study, it has brought a better understanding of the types of green building materials adopted.

Theme 4, 'Challenges in the Construction Industry', is discussed in Chapter 12-14. Chapter 12 studies the trend of contractual adjudication in Kenya, and the potential challenges of implementing statutory adjudication in Kenya for construction payment disputes. The results reveal that QS in Kenya usually are involved in contractual disputes nevertheless commonly refer to negotiation and arbitration. The findings also indicate that adjudication is not a preferred choice of ADR due to cost, time and lack of provisions in the standard form of contract in Kenya. But the findings prove that most QS's will propose adjudication as the preferred method due to the structured manner the rules will be provided in backed by the parliament.

Chapter 13 studies cost involvement and worthiness of building inspection and building defects rectification from the contractors' and house buyers' perspectives to resolve the arising problem of building failure and defective works. Both contractors and house buyers' perspectives on building inspection and building defect rectification have been observed. From this study, everyone can better understand the cost involvement of the common defects and have their standard to measure the worthiness of building inspection.

Chapter 14 examines whether contractors' preferred formwork was appropriate before and after the pandemic in the context of Sarawak. Consequently, essential factors, including cost and preferences, were discussed when choosing formwork materials. Only steel and timber formwork were studied. The G7 contractors involved in various project types were interviewed as part of the qualitative methodology used in this study. The cost was the determining factor before the pandemic, and resource availability held the top spot during the recovery stage, according to the first finding. In addition, the second finding revealed that all costs, including labor, transportation, and material, had increased for both timber and steel formwork, primarily as a result.

The fifth theme is framed around 'Built Environment Wellbeing'. Chapter 15 studies the impact of restorative environments within the office developments on the mental wellbeing of office workers. This chapter is a study conducted in Kuala Lumpur through a quantitative method to investigate whether incorporating restorative environments into offices could enhance employees' mental wellbeing. The study argues that restorative environments within the office space were positively associated with office workers' self-perceived mental wellbeing.

Chapter 16 discusses the architectural challenges for designing social interactive spaces in luxury high-rise residential buildings in Kuala Lumpur. Through interviews with architects, the findings reveal challenges with synergistic relationships, architectural branding, spatial order, private-public articulation, space design, space optimization, and space psychology. Subsequently, three characteristics of challenges on culture, impact, and communication were discussed for designers to respond to.

Chapter 17 examines pragmatic consideration on eco-friendly building materials for healthy homes. It offers deeper literature study and interview sessions with expertise in the built environment mainly in eco-friendly and sustainable houses. The results show that there is a long list of available local eco-friendly material mainly timber, brick, concrete, and bamboo that can be used in producing a healthy home suggesting construction players to push for more interest for these healthier options.

Theme 6 is 'Culture, Place Experience, and the Everyday Spaces'. Chapter 18, "Architecture and the Everyday," narrates about the shared qualities and cultural elements that shape the design and atmosphere of Malaysia coffee places, reinforcing their role as a 'third space'. Using selected cases of coffee houses in specific regions of Malaysia, the chapter draws the relationship between architecture, cultural identity, and the everyday life experiences.

Using a specific case of 'Kedai Pati', a unique coffee place local to Kelantan, an eastern state of Peninsula Malaysia, Chapter 19 maps the Kedai Pati current location and reimagine and rebrand the Kedai Pati to promote and reintroduce its existence as a cultural heritage. Varieties of design proposals were explored suggesting new pop-up cart style of Kedai Pati as an approach to contemporaries and innovate the heritage environment of the local Kedai Pati.

Chapter 20 is a phenomenological study of learner's Virtual Place Experience (VPE) approach using 360° images in Google Street View (GSV) to help learners attain a sense of place. Interpretive Phenomenological Analysis (IPA) is adopted to examine learners' cognitive learning of place identity, interpretation of place meanings, and attitudes toward the place. Findings indicate that learners developed their sense of presence in VPE through visual elements reflecting the place identity. Positive affection towards the place was identified, leading to motivation to visit the real place. The study provides insight into how learners' experience with the virtual place phenomenon may contribute to constructing their sense of place, which shall guide their design cognition in future design exercises.

Chapter 21 evaluates public perception of public participation in designing public parks in Malaysia. To ensure that public parks are designed to cater to the needs and preferences of communities, it is important to consider public perception and participation. Through a quantitative survey questionnaire in two public parks in Johor, the results suggest that civil society in general has a collective interest in participating in public participation exercises in designing public parks in Malaysia.

Chapter 22 studies the local people's participation in cultural heritage conservation and tourism management. Due to the rising urge for public participatory approach in sustainable heritage, this chapter examines the concept of people's participation in cultural heritage conservation and management in international charters and documents. It also considers various methods and approaches in Human-Computer Interaction studies, which have valuable resources for user engagement in designing services by people for people, to propose an effective, applicable people-participation approach to cultural heritage management.

Chapter 23 investigates the effect of Kastamonu Historical Bazaar Area on urban morphology. In this study, urbanization, and settlement features of Kastamonu city in the historical process are discussed. Kastamonu historical city center and historical bazaar area were examined by discussing how the main axes shaped in line with unchangeable natural data became subjectivized by human hands and the components of the traditional urban texture in the context of the border, and the morphological inputs of these components were mentioned.

Consolidating into six themes and 23 chapters, this book is a platform for international researchers to connect, explore and further the necessities of research inclusivity in architecture and the built environment toward holistic sustainable development. This aligns with the visions of UN's Sustainable Development Goals and IR 5.0.

Ng Foong Peng
Taylor's University, Malaysia

Section 1
Technology and the Metaverse

Chapter 1
A Study on the Adoption of Smart Home Technologies Among the Homeowners in Malaysia

Kenn Jhun Kam

 https://orcid.org/0000-0003-4927-4611
Taylor's University, Malaysia

Lim Jun Wei
Taylor's University, Malaysia

Tze Shwan Lim
Taylor's University, Malaysia

Habizah Sheikh Ilmi
Taylor's University, Malaysia

Lam Tatt Soon
Taylor's University, Malaysia

ABSTRACT

It is an undeniable fact that by implementing smart home technology (SHT), the quality of life for the occupants within can be improved for different aspects such as safety, leisure, comfort, and healthcare. However, it is discovered that Malaysians are highly reluctant in adopting SHT in their house. The research approach undertaken was quantitative method by sending questionnaire through emails. This research found the main key features of SHT are that they have high helpfulness level in improving the occupants' quality of life; the chapter lays out the main factors affecting the home buyers to adopt SHT and the main challenges exist staying in a smart home. Moreover, attractiveness and clear interface are both main factors affecting the smart homeowners to adopt SHT from the smart home users' perspective. However, poor operationality is rated as the most challenging limitation faced by the smart home users themselves. Also, poor operationality has the most significant influence on the smart home user's overall satisfaction level toward the smart home system.

DOI: 10.4018/978-1-6684-8253-7.ch001

INTRODUCTION

In this current era, urbanized areas are rapidly being influenced by advanced technology to promote a more comfortable living environment to level up the quality of life of society. And in response to the above statement, smart home technology (SHT) is an emerging technology that catches the eyes of human civilization nowadays.

SHT incorporates common devices that control features of the home (Amri & Setiawan, 2018). A smart home can monitor the environment within a house and operates independently based on the data collected such as the user's behaviour pattern, the humidity of the surrounding, and the light intensity of the external environment.

SHT concept is only getting attention from the public over the last decade (Baharudin, 2019). The features that exist in a smart home provide equal benefits for people of all ages (Tee Wei, 2019). This technology is much more convenient and beneficial compared with a "traditional home" which needs to operate manually by the users themselves.

In short, the primary objective of SHT is to provide house automation, reduce environmental emissions and provide comfort to the occupants within (Gram-Hanssen & Darby, 2018).

BACKGROUND

Concept of Smart Home

Smart homes are homes that are equipped with sensors working towards monitoring different aspects such as the occupants' behaviour and the surrounding environment of the occupants. According to Kirsten and Sarah (2017), they pointed out that from an occupant's perspective towards a smart home, 'smarting' may be the integration of electrical devices such as lighting, security, and photovoltaic generation to function automatically in a house. According to Essiet, Sun, and Wang (2019), we are expecting the concept of a smart home to be evolving in line with the development of technology.

Key Features of a Smart Home

A smart home must-have features that aim to minimize human interaction and also minimizing the usage of energy to reduce pollutants and waste (Hargreaves, Wilson, and Hauxwell-Baldwin, 2018).

The first key feature is the smart home security feature. A smart home security feature is important as it can notify homeowners of any threats and problems as early as possible (Mohammad & Chad, 2019). With the technology integrated with the smart security feature, it can keep track of the homeowner's behaviour and habit, therefore has the capability of notifying the occupant whenever anything suspicious is being detected by the sensor (Amgad, Hammod, Suliman, 2020).

The next key feature of a smart home is the entertainment feature. The entertainment feature of a smart home provides interactive entertainment such as gaming, Smart TV, and various voice-command-based multimedia features (Bestoun, Miroslav, 2019). Smart entertainment feature does not serve as a mandatory functionality of a smart home, however, it provides excitement and increases the quality of life for the occupants within. (Alam, Khusaro, Naeem, 2017).

Furthermore, healthcare is also another key feature of a smart home. Healthcare is considered a significant part of daily life. Therefore, as technology develops, IoT can be integrated with healthcare appliances in a smart home as well (Lauren & Sherif, 2019). Smart healthcare appliances such as wearable sensors, smart kitchens, and environmental sensors can promote and monitor the health of the occupants within.

Furthermore, energy efficiency is another key feature of a smart home which is extremely beneficial for long-term cost savings for the smart home users themselves (Vishwakarma & Upadhyaya, 2019). By integrating IoT with the electrical appliances in a smart home, motion sensors can be used to detect and turns off electrical appliances automatically whenever someone leaves a room to save energy (Vishwakarma & Upadhyaya, 2019).

The last reviewed smart home's key feature in this research study is IoT based on smart appliances which refer to the integration of IoT with appliances in a smart home varies in types such as cleaning machines, refrigerators, television, robots, and many others (Haidawati, Feuead, Kushsairy, Sheroz, 2018). IoT-based smart appliances can maximize the convenience and comfort of the occupants in a smart home.

Factors Affecting the Adoption of Smart Home Technology Among Homeowners

According to Ng, Baharudin, Hussein, and Hilmi (2019), it is important to identify the factors affecting homeowners in deciding whether to adopt SHT in their homes in Malaysia.

The first main factor will be the attractiveness of SHT revolves around being a powerful tool to harness the power of IoT technology to perform various technological features which attracts the interest of home buyers to adopt SHT (Ng, Ahmad, Lubna, Hilmi, 2019). Some of the attractiveness includes the conveniency provided to the occupants, the cool-looking display feature, and the long-term cost-saving feature.

The next factor affecting the smart homeowner to adopt SHT will be the clear interface of a smart home. According to Fabi, Spigliantiti, and Corganati (2017), a clear, understandable, and simple interface is expected to be included in a smart home which is one of the main intentions of homeowners to adopt SHT in their house. A clear interface can enhance the living experience which is one of the main goals of the SHT (Jacob, 2018).

Furthermore, information accuracy is also one of the factors affecting the home buyers to adopt SHT. Information accuracy is always one of the main factors in determining how well a sensor system of a smart home is (Marco, 2018). Sensors and beacons are the basic elements of a smart home that plays an essential role in detecting and transmitting information throughout the smart home system. For the sensors to possess maximum benefit to the users themselves, they need to be precise and accurate (Mohammad, Yousef, Ahmad, Ismael, 2019). Therefore, information accuracy is one of the factors affecting the homeowners to adopt SHT.

Besides, the self-satisfaction factor is also one of the main factors affecting the home buyers to adopt SHT. According to Debajyoti, Tuul, and Suree (2017), one of the main factors affecting smart homeowners to adopt SHT is the SHT being able to satisfy their desire in improving their quality of life. This is also agreed by Hidayati, Mokhtar & Ismail (2018), stating that most of the occupants are expected the SHT to be able to enhance the quality of their life to their self-satisfaction.

The next factor affecting the intention of home buyers to adopt SHT is perceived security. According to Ng, Baharudin, Hussein, and Hilmi (2019), perceived security is also one of the main factors for the intention of smart homeowners to adopt SHT in their house. As the maturation of security technology keeps advanced for the past few decades, the security system is becoming a huge concern to occupants of smart homes (Mohammad & Chad, 2019).

Lastly, the last factor reviewed in this research study is perceived privacy. Privacy in a smart home focuses on preventing the leakage of personal information of users, such as locations, preferences, identity, photos, videos, and movement (Supriya, Vikas, 2019). Therefore, a good privacy system for a smart home can protect the user's private information. According to Ng, Baharudin, Hussein, and Hilmi (2019), perceived security impacts positively the intention of homeowners to adopt SHT in their houses.

Limitations and Constraints Living in a Smart Home

smart home provides home automation which benefits the occupants a lot in daily life. According to Bernheim, Bongshin, Ratul, Sharad, Stefan, and Colin (2016), the majority of smart homeowners are quite positive about their experience staying in a smart home. However, there are still constraints and challenges met by the occupants while staying in a smart home.

The first challenge reviewed in this research study is the high ownership cost. Smart home costs a great deal at the initial installation stage (James, 20). The monetary cost for the installation of smart homes is relatively higher than normal homes. According to a research study conducted by Bernheim, Bongshin, Ratul, and Sharad (2016), the high initial installation cost is one of the main challenges in the opinion of smart homeowners.

The next challenge is inflexibility. One of the main challenges of living in a smart home is the inflexibility of the smart home systems (Suha & Khalil, 2019). According to Menachem (2019), smart home users are expecting the integration of different brands of appliances in a smart home. Therefore, if there are difficulties in the integration of different brands, it possesses a challenge to the smart home users themselves. Besides, the requirement for structural changes with the SHT installation is also considered one of the inflexibilities of a smart home.

Furthermore, poor operationality is also one of the challenges met staying in a smart home. Regular interaction and maintenance of smart appliances are daily interactions of the smart home users with the SHT itself. According to Asmah, Basarudin, Yusoff, and Dahlan (2019), smart home users are facing various challenges and issues in the daily operation of the smart automation system such as the sudden unresponsiveness of some of the smart appliances themselves. The unpredictable behaviour of smart appliances is a great challenge which is facing by smart home users themselves.

The last challenge of staying in a smart home reviewed in this research study is privacy and security issues. As most smart homes integrate IoT technology as a platform for various smart appliances to be connected, despite the advantages of IoT technology, there are still security limitations and challenges that need to be faced by smart home users. Since the scope of IoT technology is wide, there are a lot of security issues that need to be taken note of in aspects such as data storage, wireless sensor networks, performance, and privacy protection (Joseph, Andreas, Paul, 2016). Therefore, security and privacy issues are also the main challenges that smart home users are facing nowadays.

PROBLEM STATEMENT

SHT is expected to be widely implemented by occupants since it is aimed to maximize the quality of life of occupants. However, according to a study conducted by Leeraphong, Papasratorn & Chongsuphajaisiddhi (2016), the adoption rate of SHT is generally low in developing Asia countries including Malaysia, this survey was done in the year 2020-2022. Most Malaysians are reluctant to implement SHT in their house due to different factors concerning them (Asmah, Basarudin, Zuryati, Nuarral, 2018). According to a study conducted by Mokhtar and Ismail (2018), there are still several questions remaining unsolved regarding the adoption of SHT among homeowners in Malaysia. These questions contribute to the low implementation rate of SHT in Malaysia.

According to Fabi (2017), most Malaysians do not know how well-versed the facilities of a smart home should have to be recognized as a smart home. Currently, in Malaysia, there is still no specific statute stipulating the basic elements of a smart home (Asmah & Baharudin, 2018). Therefore, most home buyers do not know what is the helpfulness level of the key features of a smart home in improving their quality of life.

Next, many homeowners are wondering if it is worth implementing SHT in their homes in this current era (Asmah, Basarudin, Yusoff, Mahathir, & Nuarrual, 2018). The main factors affecting smart homeowners in adopting SHT in Malaysia are not known publicly. Therefore, the majority of house owners are not confident in implementing SHT due to their uncertainty about the satisfactory level of implementation of SHT.

Next, the challenges and limitations that exist when staying in a smart home are not known publicly as well (Tom & Richard, 2017). Therefore, this decreases the confidence level of homeowners in Malaysia to adopt SHT in their houses. It is an undeniable fact that any homeowners that do not experience SHT before will have perceptions and concerns about confidence issues in the implementation of SHT in their homes. An individual will only have confidence in the implementation of SHT after he/she understands all information on the SHT concept. Malaysia still has a lot of room of understanding the perception of occupants before the SHT is widely implemented among homeowners.

AIM, OBJECTIVES, AND HYPOTHESES OF THE STUDY

The primary aim of this research is to study the adoption of SHT among homeowners in Malaysia. According to Mokhtar and Ismail (2018), research and academic studies that explain the adoption of SHT among homeowners are lacking in Malaysia. Therefore, this study intends to fill this gap in the contexts of "helpfulness of SHT", "factors influencing the SHT adoption" and "perception of occupants towards the SHT problems", by carrying out the following objectives below:

This study strives to attain the following objectives:

1. To recognise the helpfulness level of key features in a smart home in improving the quality of life from the user's perspective.
2. To evaluate the factors influencing homeowners to adopt smart home Technology
3. To identify the perception of occupants towards the problems faced after the implementation of smart home Technology in their home

Further from the literature, age was pointed out by many researchers, including Amgad, Hammod, Suliman, (2020), Asmah & Baharudin, (2018). Mokhtar and Ismail (2018), and Fabi (2017), mentioned that age is strongly affecting the users in the operation, installation, and usage of SHT. Therefore, it brings the define of the following hypothesis. The hypotheses that are related to the objectives of this research is as the following:

H1. The higher the age of smart home users, the higher the investment of time is needed to manage and operate the smart home system.

H2. The higher the age of smart home users, the more burdensome and troublesome the user will feel towards the installation process.

H3. The higher the age of smart home users, the lesser they have the knowledge on the usage of the smart home system.

RESEARCH METHODOLOGY

Data Collection Method

The methodological approach used in this research is a quantitative approach. An online survey questionnaire is used to collect the primary data from the target respondents which is the smart homeowners in Malaysia.The sample size of this study is 384 number by using the sample size formula intruduced by Krejcie and Morga (1970). Meanwhile, the target respondents of the study are the smart home end users. Simple random sampling and snowball sampling will be used to collect the data from a predetermined sample size within a fixed deadline of one month for the data collection period.Only close-ended questions were prepared in the questionnaires. Section A is the demographic section, and Sections B, C, and D are sections for questions related to the 1st objective, 2nd objective, and 3rd objective respectively in this research. A 1-10 interval scale format is used for the respondents to indicate their opinion on the questions asked in sections B,C and D. All the questionnaire questions were tested with a pilot study among the students in the campus to develop the following questions. The questions were properly developed to ensure that it could have a acceptable reliability and normality to ensure a significant dataset for all.

Design of Questionnaire

Section B questionnaire focuses on the perception of smart home users towards the helpfulness of key features in a smart home in improving the quality of life. Therefore, in this section, respondents are required to answer several questions that are related to the helpfulness of a smart home's key features in helping them to improve their quality of life. The respondents are required to answer several questions based on 1-10 scale (Not helpful to Very Helpful) to reflect their perception towards the helpfulness of each key feature. There are 15 questions asked in section B and the questions are grouped into 5 categories. The categories namely, Security Features, Entertainment Features, Healthiness Features, Energy Efficient Features, and IoT Based Household Smart Appliances, One example of the survey question for Security Features is written as "A2 - Describe your opinion on helpfulness level of a smart digital door lock". Next, one example of the survey question for Entertainment Features is written as "B1-Describe your opinion on the helpfulness level of a Smart TV". All the other questions, 15 of them in total, can be seen in Table 2 from Key Findings in Relation to Objective 1 subtopic.

Next, section C of the questionnaire focuses on questions that aimed to obtain data on the perception of smart home users towards the factors influencing them to adopt smart home Technology in their house.

Same as In Section B, the respondents are required to answer several questions based on a 1-10 scale (Not agree to Strongly Agree) to indicate which are the factors influencing them the most to stay in a smart home. There are 20 questions asked in section C and the questions are grouped into 6 categories. The categories namely, Attractiveness, Clear Interface, Information Accuracy, Self-Satisfaction, Perceived Security, and Perceived Privacy. One example of the survey question for Attractiveness is written as "F2 - I choose to adopt smart home system due to the high quality of attractive display system". Next, one example of the survey question for Information Accuracy is written as "H1- I choose to adopt smart home system because the environmental sensors give real-time information on the weather condition to me". All the other questions, 20 of them in total, can be seen in Table 4 from Key Findings in Relation to Objective 2 subtopic.

Lastly, section D of the questionnaire focuses on questions that aimed to obtain data on the perception of smart home users towards the challenge and limitations met when staying in a smart home. Same as in Section C, the respondents are required to answer several questions based on a 1-10 scale (Not agree to Strongly Agree) to indicate which are the challenges and limitations that bother them the most when staying in a smart home. There are 14 questions asked in section D and the questions are grouped into 4 categories. The categories namely, High Ownership Cost, Inflexibility, Poor Operationality, and Difficulty in Achieving Privacy and Security. One example of the survey question for High Ownership Cost is written as "M1 – The initial cost of adopting smart home Technology is high". Next, one example of the survey question for Inflexibility is written as "N1 - It is not easy for me to integrate different brands of smart appliances." All the other questions, 14 of them in total, can be seen in Table 5 from Key Findings in Relation to Objective 3 subtopic.

Data Analysis Method

Both descriptive analysis and inferential analysis will be used to analyse the data collected for this research. For descriptive analysis, a comparison of mean and ranking of Relative Importance Index (RII) methods will be used. For inferential analysis, the reliability test, correlation test, and multiple regression test will be used to analyse the relationship between independent variables and dependent variables of this study using statistical software named as Statistical Package for Social Science (SPSS).

FINDINGS

Demographic Profile

A total of 3840 sets of questionnaires were sent out to smart homeowners in Malaysia, a number of 10 times the sample size of the respondents. However, within the defined one-month time frame for the data collection period given to this study,a result 182 participants responded to the questionnaires within the defined time frame.

Key Findings in Relation to Objective 1

Table 2 shows the results on the opinion of the respondents towards the helpfulness level of key features of a smart home in improving their quality of life.

Table 1. Demographic analysis

No.	Demographic	Frequency	Percentage
1	**Gender**		
	Male	93	51%
	Female	89	49%
2	**Age Group**		
	20-30	57	31%
	30-40	53	295
	40-50	55	30%
	50-60	17	10%
3	**Status**		
	Single	50	28%
	Married with child	118	65%
	Married without child	14	7%
4	**No. Years staying in a smart home**		
	Below 1 Year	37	20%
	1-3 Years	98	54%
	4-6 Years	47	26%
5	**Type of smart home system**		
	Hardwired	6	3%
	Wireless	105	58%
	Partial	71	39%

For Security Feature (A), smart digital door lock (A2) and surveillance system (A3) are ranked 1st followed by smart fire detection system (A1) which is ranked 2nd. For Entertainment Feature (B), Smart TV (B1) is ranked 1st followed by smart speaker (B2) and smart display (B3) which are both ranked 2nd. For Healthiness Feature (C), wearable sensor (C1) is ranked 1st followed by environment sensors (C3) which is ranked 2nd and smart kitchen (C2) which is ranked 3rd. For energy-efficient feature (D), the smart AC system (D3) is ranked 1st followed by smart lighting (D1) and smart plugs (D2) which both ranked 2nd. Lastly for IoT-based household smart appliances, the smart coffee maker (E3) is ranked 1st followed by smart robots (E2) which is ranked 2nd and smart refrigerator (E1) which is ranked 3rd.

From the 1-10 scale (Not Helpful to Very Helpful) being rated by the respondents, the energy efficient feature (D) has the highest overall mean value of 9.10 and is ranked 1st among other main key features. This means that in the opinion of the smart home users, the energy efficient feature is the most helpful key feature in improving their quality of life. This is agreed by Vishwakarma and Upadhyaya, Kumari, and Mishra (2019) stating that energy efficiency is one of the most important features which attracts most of smart home users. Especially in Malaysia where the electricity tariff is relatively higher than in other countries such as Singapore, energy-efficient features will be emphasized more by the smart home users.

Next, security feature (A) is ranked 2nd with an overall mean value of 8.67. This means that smart home users think that the security feature is the second most helpful feature in improving their quality of life. This is also supported by Bernheim, Bongshin, Ratul, and Sharad (2016) stating that home buyers

Table 2. Descriptive Analysis on the Helpfulness of Key Features of a smart home in improving the Occupants' Quality of life

	Variables	1-10 Scale (Not Helpful to Very Helpful)					
		N	Mean	RII	Rank	Overall Mean	Overall Ranking
	Key Feature: Security Feature						
A1	Smart Fire Detection System	182	8.31	0.32	2	8.67	2
A2	Smart Digital Door Lock	182	8.80	0.34	1		
A3	Surveillance and Automation System	182	8.90	0.34	1		
	Key Feature: Entertainment Feature						
B1	Smart TV	182	8.51	0.34	1	8.27	3
B2	Smart Speaker	182	8.13	0.33	2		
B3	Smart Display	182	8.17	0.33	2		
	Key Feature: Healthiness Feature						
C1	Wearable Sensors	182	7.19	0.35	1	6.82	5
C2	Smart Kitchen	182	6.43	0.31	3		
C3	Environmental Sensors	182	6.86	0.33	2		
	Key Feature: Energy Efficient Feature						
D1	Smart Lighting	182	9.08	0.33	2	9.10	1
D2	Smart Plugs/ Smart Sockets	182	9.03	0.33	2		
D3	Smart AC system	182	9.18	0.34	1		
	Key Feature: IoT Based Household Smart Appliances						
E1	Smart Refrigerator	182	6.64	0.30	3	7.29	4
E2	Smart Robots	182	7.45	0.34	2		
E3	Smart Coffee Makers	182	7.79	0.36	1		

are emphasizing the security feature of a smart home nowadays. Although Malaysia is a relatively safe country, however by having security features installed in a smart home, the homeowners will feel more secure and relaxed staying in a smart home.

Entertainment feature (B) is ranked 3rd with an overall mean value of 8.27. Entertainment feature comes after energy efficiency and security features as entertainment are just feature that facilitate a better comfortable environment for the smart home users. This is agreed by Bestoun & Miroslav (2019) stating that the entertainment feature is exciting and is expected to be included in a smart home to be more interactive with the homeowners. However, the entertainment feature is not a necessity for all smart home users.

Next, IoT-based household smart appliances (E) is ranked 4th with an overall mean value of 7.29. Smart household appliances is ranked as the second bottom feature due to it being able to be adopted individually. According to Haidawati, Fuead, Kushsairy, and Sheroz (2018), smart appliances such as smart robots or smart cleaning machines are appliances that are commonly being adopted in normal homes. Therefore, smart household appliances are not considered as a peculiar feature of a smart home which is important in improving the quality of life in the opinion of smart home users.

Lastly, the healthiness feature is ranked last (5th) by the respondents with an overall mean value of 6.82. It means that from the perception of smart home users, the healthiness feature is the least helpful key feature in improving their quality of life. This is agreed by Jia, Liu, Jiang, Wu, and Wang (2020) stating that although the smart home system can enhance the healthiness of the users themselves. However, most of the smart home users don't see this as an important feature in a smart home. In the perspective of health, it is important to seek medical advice from the medical doctor instead of relying on the technological tools that are approved by the Ministry of Health. As such, healthiness tools is rather contribute little in assisting the house owners.

Comparison of Overall Mean Value between Male and Female Respondents

The overall mean value of the key feature in a smart home obtained will be analysed and compare between male and female respondents to provide a clearer view of the difference of perception between male and female respondents towards the helpfulness level of smart home key features.

Table 3 shows that the difference in the mean value obtained for Security Feature (A), Energy Efficient Feature (B), and IoT-based Household Smart Appliances (E) are not of a huge difference. This means that both male and female respondents have the same level of opinion regarding the helpfulness level of key features A, B, and E.

For the Entertainment feature (B) and Healthiness feature (C), male respondents have a relatively higher mean value compared to female respondents. This means that the opinion male respondents, they think that both of the mentioned features has a higher level of helpfulness in improving their quality of life compared to the opinion of female respondents. This is agreed with Singh, Pyschoula, Kropf, Hanke, and Holzinger (2018), stating that male smart home users tend to have more interest in adopting high-end technology devices in a smart home. Where this finding is in generally correct, as everyone know men are having higher interest in technology things such as cars, machineries, tools and gadget.

Key Findings in Relation to Objective 2

Table 4 shows the results on the opinion of the respondents regarding their level of agreement towards the factors affecting them to adopt SHT. For attractiveness factor (F), conveniency provided by smart appliances (F1), energy efficiency provide (F4) and long-term cost saving (F5) is ranked 1st followed by good-looking display feature (F2) and high-end technology smart appliances (F3) which are both

Table 3. Comparison of the overall mean value for helpfulness level of key feature of a smart home between male and female respondents

	Key Features of a smart home	Mean Value		Difference of mean
		Male	Female	
A	Security Features	8.59	8.74	(0.15)
B	Entertainment Features	9.64	6.83	2.81
C	Healthiness Features	7.53	6.08	1.45
D	Energy Efficient Feature	9.07	9.12	(0.05)
E	IoT based Household Smart Appliances	7.35	7.23	0.12

Table 4. Descriptive analysis of the factors affecting smart home users in adopting smart home technology

	Variables	1-10 Scale (Not Agree to Strongly Agree)					
		N	Mean	RII	Rank	Overall Mean	Overall Ranking
	Main Factor: Attractiveness					8.94	1
F1	Conveniency provided by smart appliances	182	9.13	0.20	1		
F2	Good-looking display features	182	8.79	0.19	2		
F3	High-end technology smart appliances	182	8.82	0.19	2		
F4	Energy Efficiency provided by smart appliances	182	8.98	0.20	1		
F5	Long term cost saving	182	8.97	0.20	1		
	Main Factor: Clear Interface					8.54	2
G1	Clear interface system for easy understanding	182	8.70	0.25	1		
G2	Multiple system of a house can be displayed at once	182	8.47	0.25	1		
G3	User friendly and saves time	182	8.64	0.25	1		
G4	Flexibility of controlling appliances	182	8.36	0.25	1		
	Main Factor: Information Accuracy					6.67	5
H1	Sensors within a smart home giving a real time information	182	6.14	0.46	2		
H2	Allow user to detect danger or threat immediately	182	7.20	0.54	1		
	Main Factor: Self-Satisfaction					7.87	4
J1	smart home provides a comfort living environment	182	9.08	0.29	1		
J2	Smart appliances saves human effort and time	182	8.88	0.28	2		
J3	Provides convenience to the elderly	182	7.12	0.23	3		
J4	Enhances healthiness of users	182	6.41	0.20	4		
	Main Factor: Perceived Security					8.03	3
K1	smart home sensors can always monitor the surroundings	182	8.14	0.34	2		
K2	smart home Technology network is not easy to be hacked	182	7.52	0.31	3		
K3	Smart Door Lock system maximises the security of occupants	182	8.42	0.35	1		
	Main Factor: Perceived Privacy					5.36	6
L1	User's personal data are protected by the security system of SHT network	182	5.30	0.33	2		
L2	The whereabouts of the users are kept confidential	182	6.03	0.37	1		
L3	All software and appliances controller are password protected	182	4.76	0.30	3		

ranked 2nd. For the Clear Interface factor (G), all 4 items; clear interface system for easy understanding (G1), multiple system of a house can be displayed at once (G2), user friendly and saves time (G3), and flexibility of controlling appliances (G4) are all ranked 1st. For the Information Accuracy factor (H), allowing the user to detect danger or threat immediately (H2) is ranked 1st followed by sensors giving real time information (H1) which is ranked 2nd. For Self-Satisfaction factor (J), smart home provides a comfortable living environment (J1) is ranked 1st, followed by Smart appliances saving human effort and time (J2) which is ranked 2nd, provides conveniency to the elderly (J3) which is ranked 3rd and lastly enhances the healthiness of users (J4) which is ranked 4th. For the Perceived Security factor (K), the smart door lock system maximizes the security of occupants (K3) is ranked 1st, followed by smart home sensors can always monitor the surroundings (K1) which is ranked 2nd, and SHT network is not easy to be hacked which is ranked 3rd. For Perceived Privacy factor (L), the whereabouts of the users are kept confidential (L2) is ranked 1st, followed by user's personal data are protected by the security system of SHT network (L1) which is ranked 2nd and lastly all software and appliances controller are password protected (L3) which is ranked 3rd.

From the 1-10 scale (Not Agree to Strongly Agree) being rated by the respondents, the attractiveness factor (F) is ranked 1st with an overall mean value of 8.94. This means that in the opinion of the smart home users, factor F has the highest level affecting their decision in adopting SHT. This finding is agreed by Ng, Baharudin, Hussein, and Hilmi (2019) stating that the attractiveness of a smart home is its unique feature which is not commonly found in a normal home. Therefore, the finding of attractiveness being the most affecting factor is logical. Product attractiveness in interaction with decision-making style influences purchase intentions. Buyers are using an emotional decision-making style condition, they have higher purchase intentions for the high attractive product than the low attractive product (Francisco, Marcel, Rolando, 2022).

Next, clear interface (G) is ranked 2nd with an overall mean value of 8.54. This means that in the opinion of smart homeowners, a clear interface is the second most affecting factor for the homeowner to adopt SHT. This finding is expected and is agreed by Fabi, Spigliantiti, and Corgnati (2017) stating that smart home users are adopting the smart home system due to its user-friendly interface system.

Next, perceived security (K) is ranked 3rd with an overall mean value of 8.04. This means that security feature is still considered as a high affecting factor for home buyers to adopt SHT.

This finding is agreed by Ng, Baharudin, Hussein, and Hilmi (2019) stating that perceived privacy is one of the main factors for the intention of homeowners to adopt SHT in their house as a good security system installed can make the occupants within to feel more secure.

Next, self-satisfaction (J) is ranked 4th with an overall value of 7.87. This means the respondents have a moderate agreement level on self-satisfaction being their intention to adopt SHT. This finding is logical as stated by Fabi, Spigliantiti, and Corgnati (2017) stating that the mandatory feature of a smart home is to interact with the occupants within instead of just aiming to create a comfortable environment.

Next, information accuracy (H) is ranked 5th with an overall mean value of 6.67. This means that the respondents have a lower level of agreement on information accuracy being their intention to adopt SHT compared to the other factors. This finding is logical as most of homeowners have a higher consideration level for the functionality of a smart home instead of the accuracy of the information conveyed itself.

Lastly, perceived privacy (L) is ranked the last (6th) with an overall mean value of 5.36. This means that from the perspective of smart home users, factor L has the lowest affecting level on their intention to adopt SHT. This finding is agreed by Zheng, Apthorpe, Chetty, and Feamster (2018) stating that most smart home users are not confident with the privacy system of a smart home system. Most of the devices in your smart home will use your router for internet access. If a hacker can break into your router, they can potentially view the data from everything connected to it (Ng, Baharudin, Hussein, and Hilmi, 2019).

Key Findings in Relation to Objective 3

Table 5 shows the results on the opinion of the respondents regarding their level of agreement towards the challenges and limitations of staying in a smart home. For the high ownership cost challenge (M), the low perceived value of smart appliances (M3) is ranked 1st, followed by the huge investment of time

Table 5. Descriptive analysis on the challenges and limitations living in a smart home

	Variables	1-10 Scale (Not Agree to Strongly Agree)					
		N	Mean	RII	Rank	Overall Mean	Overall Ranking
	Main Challenge: High Ownership Cost					5.69	3
M1	High initial cost	182	4.88	0.29	3		
M2	Huge investment of time is needed	182	5.72	0.34	2		
M3	Low perceived value of smart appliances	182	6.47	0.37	1		
	Main Challenge: Inflexibility					5.37	4
N1	Difficulty in integrating different brand of smart appliances	182	5.61	0.26	3		
N2	Structural changes needed	182	3.49	0.16	4		
N3	Complicated installation of appliances	182	6.38	0.30	1		
N4	Lack of knowledge towards the usage of SHT	182	6.02	0.28	2		
	Main Challenge: Poor Operationality					6.27	1
O1	Unexpected responsiveness of the system	182	5.89	0.31	3		
O2	Complex user interfaces	182	6.02	0.32	2		
O3	Expert consultants are needed	182	6.90	0.37	1		
	Main Challenge: Privacy and Security Issue					5.76	2
P1	Presence based access appliances are easily being accessed by anyone	182	5.42	0.24	3		
P2	Privacy data stored in the IoT system is easily being leaked	182	6.05	0.26	2		
P3	Temporary access issue (such as giving temporary access is dangerous)	182	5.40	0.23	4		
P4	Remote access issue (controlling main gate with software is dangerous)	182	6.14	0.27	1		

is needed (M2) which is ranked 2nd, and the high initial cost (M1) which is ranked 3rd. For inflexibility challenge (N), complicated installation of appliances (N3) is ranked 1st, followed by lack of knowledge towards the usage of SHT (N4) which is ranked 2nd, difficulty in integrating different brands of smart appliances which is ranked 3rd and structural changes are needed (N2) which is ranked 4th. For poor operationality challenge (O), Expert consultants are needed (O3) is ranked 1st, followed by complex user interfaces (O2) which is ranked 2nd and unexpected responsiveness of the system (O1) which is ranked 3rd. For privacy and security issue challenge (P), remote access issue (P4) is ranked 1st, followed by privacy data stored in the IoT system is easily being leaked (P2) which is ranked 2nd, presence-based access appliances are easily being accessed by anyone (P1) which is ranked 3rd and temporary access issue (P3) which is ranked 4th.

From the 1-10 scale (Not Agree to Strongly Agree) being rated by the respondents, poor operationality (O) is ranked 1st with the highest overall mean value of 6.90. This means that from the perception of the smart home users, the level of agreement on poor operationality (O) exists as a challenge living in a smart home is the highest compared to other main challenges. This is also agreed by Ibrahim and Khalil (2019) stating that smart homeowners have high expectations on their daily interaction with the smart home system. Therefore, with poor operationality being a daily interaction challenge, it is logical for it to be rated as the biggest challenge of staying in a smart home.

Next, the main challenge which is ranked 2nd is privacy and security issue (P) with an overall mean value of 5.76. This finding is agreed by Bernheim, Bongshin, Ratul, and Sharad (2016) stating that with the current IoT-based smart home system, it is difficult to achieve full privacy and security for the occupants within. Therefore, it is logical as well for privacy and security issue (P) to be ranked as the 2nd highest level of agreement by the respondents towards it being a challenge in a smart home.

Next, the main challenge which is ranked 3rd is high ownership cost (M) with an overall mean value of 5.69. This means that in the opinion of the respondents, they have a lower agreement level on high ownership cost being the main challenge of a smart home. This finding is logical and agreed by James (2020) stating that although the initial installation cost for smart home is high.However, the smart home system provides long-term benefits to the smart home users themselves.

The last main challenge which is ranked 4th is inflexibility (N) which has the lowest overall mean value of 5.37. This means that the respondents have the lowest level of agreement towards inflexibility being the main challenge in staying in a smart home.

With technology nowadays, it is easy to integrate different brands of smart appliances in a smart home (Khalil, Ibrahim, 2019). Meanwhile, with IoT smart home systems being commonly adopted nowadays, structural changes are not needed anymore for the installation of a smart home system. Therefore, it is logical for inflexibility to have the lowest level of agreement of it being a challenge to stay in a smart home.

Comparison of Overall Mean Value Between Hardwired and Wireless Smart Home System

The overall mean value of the main challenges in a smart home obtained will be analysed and compared between hardwired and wireless smart home systems to provide a clearer view of the difference of perception between hardwired and wireless smart home users.

Table 6 shows the difference in overall mean value for poor operationality (0) is small with a slight difference of only 0.30. This means that both hardwired and wireless smart home users have the same level of agreement towards poor operationality (O) being a challenge staying in a smart home.

For high ownership cost (M) and Inflexibility (N), a hardwired system has a higher overall mean value compared with a wireless system. This means that hardwired smart home users have a higher level of agreement towards the main challenge M and N being a challenge staying in a smart home. This finding is logical and agreed by Teddy and Rahmithul (2017) stating that due to the need of installing wires throughout the hardwired smart home system, the cost needed for the installation will be high, and structural changes might be needed for the installation of wire which is inflexible.

Table 6. Comparison of overall mean value for agreement level of challenges staying in a smart home between Hardwired and Wireless System

	Challenges staying in a smart home	Mean Value		Difference of mean
		Hardwired	**Wireless**	
M	High ownership cost	7.50	5.73	1.77
N	Inflexibility	6.79	5.51	1.28
O	Poor Operationality	6.27	6.57	(0.30)
P	Privacy and Security Issue	5.13	6.09	(0.96)

For privacy and security issue (P), a wireless system has a higher overall mean value compared with a hardwired system. This means that wireless smart home users have a higher level of agreement towards privacy and security issue (P) being a challenge staying in a smart home. This finding is logical as stated by Khalil and Suhu (2019), due to the usage of a wireless smart home system, all data are transmitted using SHT network which might cause the leakage of smart home user's personal data.

Hypotheses Testing With Inferential Analysis

Reliability Test

Table 7 shows the result of reliability test for independent variables and dependent variables that will be analysed using correlation and multiple regression test under the later sections. The result shows all Cronbach's Alpha value of independent and dependent variables are above 0.70. Hence, all of the variables are in good reliability.

Normality Test

The normality test was conducted using skewness and kurtosis measurement. It is thus concluded that the data to be used for correlation and regression test are symmetric because the skewnss and kurtosis values are both lesser than +-2.00 for all the dimensional constructs and items of the study (George and Mallery (2010).

Table 7. Reliability test of the variables

Type	Variable	Cronbach's alpha	Reliability
Independent	M1. High initial cost	0.841	Very good
Independent	M2. Huge investment of time	0.795	Good
Independent	M3. Low perceived value of smart appliances	0.805	Very good
Independent	N1. Hard to integrate different brands of appliances	0.809	Very good
Independent	N2. Structural changes needed	0.829	Very good
Independent	N3. Complicated installation of appliances	0.800	Very good
Independent	N4. Lack of knowledge towards the usage of SHT	0.803	Very good
Independent	O1. Unexpected responsiveness of the system	0.843	Very good
Independent	O2. Complex user interface	0.834	Very good
Independent	O3. Expert consultants are needed	0.833	Very good
Independent	P1. Presence based access	0.795	Good
Independent	P2. Privacy data easily being leaked	0.811	Very good
Independent	P3. Temporary access issue	0.794	Good
Independent	P4. Remote access issue	0.799	Good
Dependent	Overall satisfaction level of the usage of smart home	0.833	Very good

Table 8. Normality test with skewness and kurtosis

Variables	Skewness		Kurtosis	
	Statistic	**Sd. Error**	**Statistic**	**Std. Error**
M2	-.241	.180	-1.318	.358
N2	-.449	.180	-.878	.358
N4	-.206	.180	-.920	.358
High Ownership Cost - M	-.031	.180	-.764	.358
Inflexibility – N	-.320	.180	-.562	.358
Poor Operationality – O	.186	.180	.286	.358
Privacy Security - P	-.299	.180	-.384	.358

Correlation Test

A correlation test is being carried out to justify the hypotheses of this research study. The relationship between the age group of smart home users and their level of agreement on items M2, N3, and N4 will be analysed using correlation test.

According to Deng, Deng and Cheong (2021), the higher the Pearson's correlation coefficient, it means that the higher an independent variable correlates with a dependent variable. Table 9 shows the result of the correlation test being carried out to identify the relationship between the age group of respondents and items M2, N3, and N4. According to the results shown, item N3 has the highest Pearson correlation value which is 0.885, followed by item N4 which is 0.869, and lastly which is item M2 which is 0.693.

Item N3 (The installation process is burdensome and trouble) has the steepest corelation line which further justifies the finding obtained in Table 9 which has the highest Pearson correlation value to the age group of respondents. On the contrary, item M2 (Huge investment of time is needed to manage and operate smart home system) has the least steep correlation line which also further justify the finding obtained in Table 9 which shows the lowest Pearson correlation value to the age group of respondents.

The result valuemeans that for every increment of the scale by 1 for the age group of respondents, it will affect 88.5% of item N3, followed by 86.9% for item N4, and lastly 69.3% of item M2. All of the Pearson Correlation is in positive value which means the age of respondents is affecting all 3 items positively. This finding is also agreed by Pal, Funilkul, Vanijja and Papasratorn (2018). According to their research study focusing on analysing the elderly user's adoption towards smart home system, the

Table 9. Correlation test between the age group of respondents & items M2, N3 and N4

		Value
M2: Huge investment of time	Pearson Correlation Significant Value	0.693 <0.001
N3: Complicated installation of appliances	Pearson Correlation Significant Value	0.885 <0.001
N4: Lack of knowledge towards the usage of SHT	Pearson Correlation Significant Value	0.869 <0.001

Table 10. The accepted hypothesis of this research study

	Hypothesis	Status
H1	The higher the age of smart home users, the higher the investment of time is needed to manage and operate the smart home system	Accepted
H2	The higher the age of smart home users, the more burdensome and troublesome the user will feel towards the installation process	Accepted
H3	The higher the age of smart home users, the lesser they have the knowledge on the usage of smart home system	Accepted

outcome conclude that elder users tend to have different difficulties in managing smart home system. Hence, it can be concluded that all 3 hypotheses of this research study are accepted according to Table 10.

Multiple Regression Test

Multiple regression tests will be used to study and analyse on the relationship between the level of agreement on the main challenges of staying in a smart home and the overall satisfaction level of staying in a smart home. Hence, the result is expected to determine which challenge affects the overall satisfaction level of staying in a smart home the most from the smart home users' perspective.

Table 11 shows the results of multiple regression test on the overall satisfaction level of staying in a smart home with the 4 main challenges of staying in a smart home which is high ownership cost (M), inflexibility (N), poor operationality (O) and privacy and security issue (P).

According to the results shown, only poor operationality (O) is accepted and is considered due to its p-value of <0.001. According to Maheswari, Priyanka, Thangavel, Vignesh, and Poongodi (2020), when the p-value is above 0.05, it means that the variable is no longer significant and shall be rejected. Therefore, apart from poor operationality (O), the other 3 independent variables M, N and P are rejected.

For the only independent variable being accepted which is poor operationality (O), the regression coefficient (unstandardized coefficient Beta) of it is positive at 0.410 which means that poor operationality (O) is affecting the overall satisfaction level of staying in a smart home by 41%. This finding is logical and is supported by the research study conducted by Harshal, RPalundarkar, Surve, and Biswas (2018). In their study, they pointed out that any problems arising from the daily usage of smart appliances will directly affect the satisfaction level of smart home users. Hence, where poor operationality (O) is a challenge arising from the daily interaction of the smart home users with the smart home system itself, it is

Table 11. Multiple regression test on the overall satisfaction level of staying in a smart home

	Independent Variable	Unstandardized coefficient Beta	P-Value
	Constant	0.737	0.380
M	High ownership cost	0.095	0.553
N	Inflexibility	0.225	0.133
O	Poor Operationality	0.410	<0.001
P	Privacy & Security Issue	(0.167)	0.064

Dependent Variable: Overall Satisfaction Level

logical for it to be the most affecting challenge towards the overall satisfaction staying in a smart home from the opinion of the smart home users.

CONCLUSION

This study is set out to determine the adoption of SHT from the smart home users' perspective. One of the most significant findings is from the perception of smart home users, the energy-efficient feature has the highest level of helpfulness among other key features in improving their quality of life in a smart home. This means that smart home users in Malaysia are emphasizing the energy efficiency of their smart home.

And from the opinion of male smart home users, rated a higher helpfulness level towards entertainment features and healthiness features compared with female smart home users. This means that male users are usually more attracted to high-end technology appliances such as smart TV or smart wearable sensors.

Next, from the perception of smart home users, the attractiveness of a smart home is the highest level affecting them to adopt SHT. This means that the attractiveness of the smart home features actually attracts the smart home users to adopt SHT which is not commonly found in normal homes.

Next, for the challenges faced staying in a smart home, poor operationality is rated as the biggest challenge faced. This means that if any problem arises from the daily interaction of the smart home users with the smart home system itself, it will create a huge challenge for the smart home users themselves.

The next significant finding is the higher the age group of the smart home users, the higher their level of agreement towards the lack of knowledge on the usage of SHT, the investment of time needed to manage the SHT, and the burdensomeness of the installation of the SHT system. This means that the smart home system can still be improved further to be user-friendly to all age groups of users.

In hypotheses testing to understand the relationship between the users' age towards the investment of time is needed to manage and operate the smart home system, the burdensome and troublesome towards the installation process, the knowledge on the usage of smart home system, are all positively correlated with age of the users.

The last significant finding is poor operationality being the biggest affecting factor to the overall satisfaction level of smart home users staying in a smart home. As mentioned before, poor operationality arises when the smart home users are facing unpleasant experiences during their daily interaction with the smart home system itself. Hence, this finding is meaningful as it proves the importance of the operationality towards the satisfaction level of smart home users staying in a smart home.

ACKNOWLEDGMENT

The researchers of this article would like to appreciate the journal's editors and the anonymous reviewers for their positive feedback and suggestions for the improvement of this journal.

This research received no specific grant from any funding agency in the public, commercial, or not-for-profit sectors.

REFERENCES

Alam, I., Khusaro, S., & Naeem, M. (2017, December). A review of smart TV: Past, present, and future. In *2017 International Conference on Open Source Systems &Technologies (ICOSST)* (pp. 35-41). 10.1109/ICOSST.2017.8279002

Amgad, M., Hamood, A., Suliman, M. (2020). A Smart fire detection system using IoT Technology with Automatic Water Sprinkler. *International Journal of Electrical and Computer Engineering.*

Amri, Y., & Setiawan, M. A. (2018). Improving smart home concept with the internet of things concept using raspberrypi and nodemcu. [). IOP Publishing.]. *IOP Conference Series. Materials Science and Engineering*, *325*(1), 012021. doi:10.1088/1757-899X/325/1/012021

Andreas, J., Joseph, B., & Paul, D. (2016). On Privacy and Security Challenges in Smart Connected Homes. *European Intelligence and Security Informatics Conference.* IEEE. https://ieeexplore.ieee.org/document/7870217

Asmah, L., Basarudin, N., Yusoff, Z., Dahlan, N. (2018). smart home Users Perception on Sustainable Urban Living and Legal Challenges in Malaysia. *The Journal of Social Sciences Research.*

Bernheim, B., Bongshin, L., Ratul, M., & Sharad, A. (2016). *Home Automation in the Wild.* Challenges and Opportunities.

Bestoun, S., & Miroslav, B. (2019). Testing of Smart TV Applications. *Key Ingredients, Challenges and Proposed Solutions.* https://www.researchgate.net/publication/325102886_Testing_of_Smart_TV_Applications_Key_Ingredients_Challenges_and_Proposed_Solutions

Chad, D., & Mohammad, A. (2019). Design and Implementation of an IoT- Based smart home Security System. *Atlantis Press SARL.* https://www.researchgate.net/publication/332667088_Design_and_Implementation_of_an_IoTBased_Smart_Home_Security_System

Debajyoti, P., Tuul, T., & Suree, F. (2017). smart homes and Quality of Life for the Elderly. *IEEE International Symposium.* IEEE.

Deng, J., Deng, Y., & Cheong, K. H. (2021). Combining conflicting evidence based on Pearson correlation coefficient and weighted graph. *International Journal of Intelligent Systems.* https://onlinelibrary.wiley.com/doi/abs/10.1002/int.22593

Essiet, I. O., Sun, Y., & Wang, Z. (2019). Optimized energy consumption model for smart home using improved differential evolution algorithm. *Energy*, *172*, 354–365. https://www.researchgate.net/publication/322201732_Smart_Homes_and_Quality_of_Life_for_the_Elderly_A_Systematic_Review. doi:10.1016/j.energy.2019.01.137

Fabi, V., Spigliantini, G., & Corgnati, S. P. (2017). Insights on smart home concept and occupants' interaction with building controls. *Energy Procedia*, *111*, 759–769. doi:10.1016/j.egypro.2017.03.238

Francisco, L. S., Marcel, Z., & Rolando, D. L. (2022). The Interaction of Product Attractiveness and Decision-Making Style on ConsumerPurchase Intention: A Cultural Moderation Perspective. Journal of International Consumer Marketing.

Haidawati, N., Fuead, A., Kushsairy, K., & Sheroz, K. (2018). The Implementation of IoT Based Smart Refrigerator System. *International Conference on Smart Sensors and Application.* IEEE.

Hargreaves, T., Wilson, C., & Hauxwell-Baldwin, R. (2018). Learning to live in a smart home. *Building Research and Information, 46*(1), 127–139. doi:10.1080/09613218.2017.1286882

Harshal, S., Rpalundarkar, V., Surve,S., Biswas, B. (2018). Internet of Things Based smart home Automation. *International Journal of Scientific Research & Engineering Trends, 4*(1).

Hidayati, W., Mokhtar, W., & Ismail, A. (2018). Adoption of smart home Technologies Features Among the Homeowners in Hulu Hangat, Selangor. *International Journal of Real Estate Studies.* https://www.utm.my/intrest/

Jacob, K. (2018). *It's really complicated to connect the Home of the Future.* The Verge.

James, C. (2020). What is a smart home? *Investopedia.* https://www.investopedia.com/terms/s/smart-home.asp

Jia, Y., Liu, B., Jiang, W., Wu, B., & Wang, C. (2020). Poster: Enhancing Remote Healthiness Attestation for Constrained IoT Devices. In *2020 IEEE 28th International Conference on Network Protocols (ICNP)* (pp. 1-2). IEEE.

Jiang, L., Liu, D. Y., & Yang, B. (2004, August). Smart home research. In Proceedings of 2004 international conference on machine learning and cybernetics (IEEE Cat. No. 04EX826) (*Vol. 2*, pp. 659-663). IEEE. 10.1109/ICMLC.2004.1382266

Khalil, H., Suha Ibrahim, A. (2019). Security Challenges and Limitations in IoT Environments. *International Journal of Computer Science and Network Security.*

Kirsten, G., & Sarah, J. (2017). "Home is where the smart is?" Evaluating smart home research and approaches against the concept of home. *Energy Research & Social Science, 37,* 94–101.

Krejcie, R. V., & Morgan, D. W. (1970). Determining Sample Size for Research Activities. *Educational and Psychological Measurement, 30*(3), 607–610. doi:10.1177/001316447003000308

Lauren, L., Nasibeh, Z., & Sherif, A. (2019). *Health Monitoring in smart homes Utilizing Internet of Things.* Department of Electrical and Computer Engineering.

Leeraphong, A., Papasratorn, B., & Chongsuphajaisiddhi, V. (2016). A study on the Factors Influencing Elderly Intention to use smart home in Thailand. *10th International Conference INCEB2016.* IEEE.

Maheswari, C., Priyanka, E. B., Thangavel, S., Vignesh, S. R., & Poongodi, C. (2020). Multiple regression analysis for the prediction of extraction efficiency in mining industry with industrial IoT. *Production Engineering, 14*(4), 457–471. doi:10.100711740-020-00970-z

Marco, B. (2018). *Sensors in smart homes: A new way of living.* Digital Innovation.

Menachem, D. (2019). *smart home Systems Based on IoT*. Automated and Smart Appliances.

Mohammad, M., Yousef, J., Manasrah, A., & Ismael, J. (2019). Sensors of Smart Devices in the Internet of Everything (IOE) Era. *Big Opportunities and MassiveDoubts*. Hindawi. https://www.hindawi.com/journals/js/2019/6514520/

Ng Tee Wei. (2019). smart home in Malaysia. *Dissertation. University Tunku Abdul Rahman*

Singh, D., Psychoula, I., Kropf, J., Hanke, S., & Holzinger, A. (2018, July). Users' perceptions and attitudes towards smart home technologies. In *International Conference on smart homes and Health Telematics* (pp. 203-214). Springer. 10.1007/978-3-319-94523-1_18

Teddy, S., & Rahmithul, I. (2017). Prototype Design of smart home System using Internet of Things. *Indonesian Journal of Electrical Engineering and Computer Science*, 107–115.

Tee Wei, Ng., Baharudin, A., Hussein, L., & Hilmi, M. (2019). Factors Affecting User's Intention to Adopt smart home in Malaysia. *International Journal of Interactive Mobile Technologies*. https://online-journals.org/index.php/i-jim/article/view/11083

Vikas, S. N. (2019). Evaluating Privacy and Security Threats in IoT-based smart home Environment. International *Journal of Applied Engineering Research*. https://www.ripublication.com/ijaerspl2019/ijaerv14n7spl_18.pdf

Vishwakarma, S. K., Upadhyaya, P., Kumari, B., & Mishra, A. K. (2019, April). Smart energy efficient home automation system using iot. In *2019 4th international conference on internet of things: Smart innovation and usages (IoT-SIU)* (pp. 1-4). IEEE. 10.1109/IoT-SIU.2019.8777607

Zheng, S., Apthorpe, N., Chetty, M., & Feamster, N. (2018). User perceptions of smart home IoT privacy. *Proceedings of the ACM on human-computer interaction, 2(CSCW),* (pp. 1-20). ACM. 10.1145/3274469

KEY TERMS AND DEFINITIONS

Efficiency: Efficiency is the ability to avoid wasting materials, energy, effort, money, and time in doing something or in producing a desired result.

Energy: Power derived from the utilization of physical or chemical resources, especially to provide light and heat or to work machines.

Occupants: A person who resides or is present in a building.

Operationality: The functional skill, capability, and capacity of a person or organization to perform certain duties, tasks, and obligations

Satisfaction: Satisfaction is getting a thing that brings gratification, pleasure, or contentment.

Smart-Home: A home equipped with lighting, heating, and electronic devices that can be controlled remotely by smartphone or computer.

Technology: The application of scientific knowledge for practical purposes, especially in industry.

Chapter 2
The Strategies of 3D Modelling in the QS Profession

Lam Tatt Soon
Taylor's University, Malaysia

Hsien Shien Goh
Taylor's University, Malaysia

Tze Shwan Lim
Taylor's University, Malaysia

Boon Tik Leong
Taylor's University, Malaysia

W. T. Hong
Heriot-Watt University, Malaysia

Kenn Jhun Kam
Taylor's University, Malaysia

ABSTRACT

The adoption of 3D modelling in construction has contributed many benefits to the industry, yet some of the construction players are still either unfamiliar with the software or not utilizing the software to its fullest potential. The objectives of this research are to determine the challenges faced in 3D modelling software, to postulate the solutions based on the identified challenges in 3D modelling software, and to investigate the strategies of 3D modelling in the QS profession. A qualitative method of research will be carried out to acquire the data and opinions from the quantity surveyors in the construction sector. Based on the findings, financial issues are the most significant challenges on 3D modelling, whereas training for construction staff and enforcement from the government is the most impactful solution and strategy. This study can boost the construction players' confidence in integrating 3D modelling in the construction industry. It also brings higher efficiency in daily operations and helps to improve the productivity of workers.

DOI: 10.4018/978-1-6684-8253-7.ch002

INTRODUCTION

Three-dimensional (3D) modelling is one form of technology that has recently had a significant impact on the construction field. Due to the automation of the multidimensional model platform, the adoption of 3D modelling software in the construction industry has brought many benefits to the QS profession, such as reducing arithmetic errors and eliminating many tedious tasks in the traditional approach such as tendering and bill of quantities (BQ) production. Hence, it is undeniable that traditional measurement will soon be replaced by 3D modelling if the Standard Method of Measurement (SMM) can be integrated into software [Tee & Kamal, 2021]. The reason for carrying out this study is to provide a better understanding of 3D modelling software as it helps to increase efficiency and productivity of work, tackle complex projects, and bring flat, 2D ideas to life.

RESEARCH PROBLEMS

In this modern era with the introduction of 3D modelling software, some of the construction players are still adopting the use of traditional paper-based methods due to the difficulty of adopting connected devices. The most significant reason individuals are hesitant to use new technology is the failure to adapt people's behaviour to manage new tools (Zahrizan et al., 2013). 3D modelling software would be a productivity boost that is highly welcomed by a skilled quantity surveyor who is familiar with the concepts and specifications of a building. However, the same application used by a junior quantity surveyor, or undergraduates who do not have the same knowledge, would put them in a different position (Ibrahim, 2007). For those who are not well informed about or proficient in the use of modern technology, the myriad of new construction technology can be intimidating. Virtual reality, wearable technology, and a variety of applications and project management software may be required of those individuals. Many people work in the construction sector because they prefer working with their hands and have a nostalgic sense for older construction methods. It is possible that incorporating technology will be met with resistance. One of the major barriers to technology adoption is whether employees will accept it as a part of their daily work lives (McClone, 2019).

Another challenge faced by quantity surveyors is the lack of professional support. Despite the fact that 3D modelling is known for aiding the cross-border interchange of electronic data, Malaysian professions, trades, and industries are still confined by cultural and geographical limits, as well as political identities. In Malaysia, the Government constraints and mandates the limits of Engineering Consulting Services (ECS) (Zainon et al., 2016). Furthermore, with the exception of the more difficult ventures, the majority of local enterprises are still handled by local personnel who follow local norms. Hence, it has been demonstrated that professionals or consultants with the requisite skills and competence are required to make 3D modelling deployment a success (Zainon et al., 2018).

Technical challenges are also one of the barriers in implementing 3D modelling software. Among the factors are a lack of support system, difficulties understanding advanced software, and scarcity of competent technical workers (Zainon et al., 2018). Furthermore, one contractor has stated that if his information system was not linked with the technology used, they risked losing business and incurring additional costs. As a result, the firm hired an external consultant to ensure that the IT was in sync with the new technology. However, this can be costly, and it may force the organisation to incur ongoing expenses that it cannot afford (Love et al., 2001). There are several compelling reasons why 3D modelling software adoption in Malaysia has lagged behind expectations. In comparison to societal challenges, it is difficult for the industry to adopt new information technology (IT). Among the factors are lack of support system, difficulties understanding advanced software, and scarcity of competent technical workers. As detailed and precise models are necessary to tackle interoperability issues, 3D modelling may have had a low acceptance rate (Zainon et al., 2016). As a result, the research gap has been identified to study the challenges and postulate the solutions in 3D modelling.

Management is also one of the challenges in implementing 3D modelling software. There are currently no precise instructions or orders on the method of executing the 3D modelling. There are no clear instructions on ways to use and apply 3D modelling software in construction practices. Even though several software companies have produced tools to aid in the deployment of 3D modelling software, they have only been able to handle the quantity parts rather than the entire process (Zainon et al., 2018). Prior to the implementation of 3D modelling software, the facilities manager had relatively little say in the building's planning process. They were only able to implement building maintenance techniques after the owner had taken possession of the structure. Hence, this research is targeted to investigate the strategies for implementing 3D modelling in the QS profession.

RESEARCH OBJECTIVES

1.   To determine the challenges faced in 3D modelling software
2.   To postulate the solutions based on the identified challenges in 3D modelling software
3.   To investigate the strategies for implementing 3D modelling in the QS profession

LITERATURE REVIEW

The adoption of 3D modelling software in the construction industry has brought many advantages to the QS profession owing to the automation of the multidimensional model platform, such as reducing arithmetic errors and getting rid of many tedious tasks in the conventional approach, like tendering and bill of quantities (BQ) production. Therefore, it is inevitable that 3D modelling will soon dominate the construction industry if the Standard Method of Measurement (SMM) can be integrated into software (Tee & Kamal, 2021). With 3D modelling software, take-offs, counts, and measurements may be produced straight from a model. This offers a method where information is constant throughout the project and where adjustments are simple to make. The capacity to integrate costing efforts throughout all project phases is provided by building information modelling, which supports the entire project lifecycle. Depending on the project's stage, different models and cost estimates are required, from high-level schematic models during the planning stages to detailed estimates as projects move into the building phase (Nigam et al., 2016).

3D modelling software can benefit the industry in a variety of ways. Realistic representation of the building before prior to its creation is one of the biggest advantages that 3D modelling offers the QS profession. With the help of the built-in motion features of 3D modelling, clients may visualize a project far more successfully than they might with flat drawings. Additionally, using 3D modelling software in the construction industry, including the QS profession, reduces time, mistakes, and costs because 3D models can be swiftly rotated and studied from all sides, making it easier to detect and fix problems before the actual construction process ever starts (Valle, 2021). Additionally, the industry's adoption of 3D modelling software can help guarantee a project's completion date. 3D models could be utilized throughout construction to make sure the project stays on schedule and budget (Tailor, 2022). Although the adoption of 3D modelling can deliver benefits to quantity surveyors, numerous constraints are affecting the 3D modelling implementation. Hence, it is the challenges of adopting 3D modelling notably people, process and technical constraints are investigated.

1. Challenges Faced in Integrating 3D Modelling Software
    a. People Constraint

One of the main challenges to reaching a good level of 3D modelling implementation is the lack of professional support. Malaysian government mandates and imposes restrictions on Engineering Consulting Services (ECS) scope. Even though 3D modelling is recognized to facilitate the exchange of electronic data across borders, Malaysian professions, trades, and industries are still constrained by geographic and cultural boundaries as well as political identities [Zainon et al, 2016]. Furthermore, the bulk of local businesses is still managed by local staff who adhere to local customs. Thus, it has been established that the presence of experts or consultants with the necessary abilities is necessary to ensure the success of the deployment of 3D modelling [Zainon et al, 2018].

Many stakeholders are afraid of change. Clients believe that receiving competitive bids will be impacted if contract terms include 3D models. This may be due to clients' lack of knowledge of new technology and its advantages. Therefore, applying 3D modelling software in the construction industry is difficult without client demand [Memon et al, 2014].

In this modern era, some construction players are still adopting traditional paper-based methods due to the difficulty of adopting connected devices. The most significant reason individuals are hesitant to use new technology is failure to adapt people's behaviour to manage new tools [Martinko et al, 2011]. Some businesses are apprehensive to change their business practices because they believe it would result in higher costs and jeopardize their current practices. Some employees in the company worry about changes, especially when new technology is involved, and that technology would make them obsolete in their roles [Love et al., 2001].

    b. Process Constraint

There are risks involved in preserving and verifying the accuracy of data from 3D modelling software. One of the contractual issues that need to be resolved is regarding who will be in charge of contributing data to the model and being accountable for any errors [Azhar, 2011]. Participants are in a condition of uncertainty as a result of the fact that the legal or contractual concerns pertaining to 3D modelling are still being resolved. Insurers in the sector are having issues due to the uncertainty surrounding legal liability, which has clear implications for businesses that offer services.

Ownership is one of the barriers to the adoption of 3D modelling software. If private design features are used as data input for the model, the ownership issue may become more significant [Morrison, 2010]. The primary objective of ownership is to avoid reserves that would deter participants from adoption [Thompson and Miner, 2007].

Contractors are frequently concerned about the additional cost of using 3D modelling since they see rising labour and material costs as a big problem in the industry. Costs associated with acquisition, implementation, and training will undoubtedly be incurred, necessitating substantial time and financial investments from QS firms. As there are not many 3D modelling software professionals working in the construction industry in Malaysia, firms must allocate both time and money to select the best experts to help them implement this technology [Zainon et al., 2018].

c.   Technical Constraint

The economy in which we live presents one of the major obstacles to interoperability [Criminale & Langar, 2017]. The existence of numerous software manufacturers raises problems that may be challenging to manage. The fact that a large number of software firms are on the market now increases the likelihood that many pieces of software would not work together unless they were created by the same company. Additionally, there have been cases where the data had been lost during transfer [Tulenheimo, 2015]. Given the project context, industry diversity, and stakeholder software preferences, there is a strong likelihood that stakeholders will use diverse software.

One of the main issues encountered by quantity surveyors in the 3D environment is the lack of information presented within 3D models. Design flaws and erroneous estimates are caused by the lack of detail and missing information in 3D modelling software [Stanley & Thurnell, 2013]. Identifying information needs is essential to enhance the cost estimation process [Mayouf et al., 2019]. Quantity surveyors can only cost what has been given, 3D models must include the data that quantity surveyors need to make accurate estimates.

Costs are also one of the problems faced while implementing the use of 3D modelling software. One of the major obstacles to 3D modelling adoption, particularly for small and medium businesses, is the need for software and hardware updates [Stanley and Thurnell, 2014]. Firms are required to upgrade their hardware periodically to run the processing software, this leads to a significant barrier, particularly for small-medium size enterprises. A BIM entry-level software, Building Design Suite Premium, cost US$6,825. At the current currency rate of US$1.0:RM4.41, the price in Malaysia works out to RM30,077.78 (Zainon et al., 2018).

Firms are required to upgrade their hardware to obtain the essential software. To transform a 3D environment into an extensive 3D model, workers should receive training. As it costs money and time for QS firms to train their staff, some construction companies may not be able to afford to install 3D modelling software [Mayouf et al., 2019]. A company must thoroughly understand every aspect of any transition before it can take place.

2.   Solutions to the Identified Challenges

It is necessary to develop a flexible training program for all practitioners. Staff training shall be planned at the time the integrated system was being designed, while current potential and management will be involved in the training. The potential users became more open to the idea of new technologies and felt more comfortable utilizing computers [Stephenson & Blaza, 2001].

Establishing a BIM Fund that integrates government resources is also one solution to the identified challenges. The main goal of the BIM Fund is to improve the services provided by the construction industry by encouraging the adoption of BIM regulations. The Singapore Building and Construction

Authority (BCA) hopes to have BIM widely used on all public projects by the year 2015 [Smith, 2015]. Another effort to promote the use of BIM in the industry is the CORENET e-Plan Check system for development applications. The technology enables architects and engineers to verify the regulatory compliance of buildings created using BIM [Cheng et al., 2015].

People are the primary force behind the deployment of 3D modelling software. This can be achieved by client enforcement and an emphasis on changing the conventional methods for contractor selection. Instead of using low-bid cost criteria, this selection must be made based on lifecycle cost evaluation [Smith & Tardif, 2009; Morrison, 2010]. Getting support from professional organizations such as CIDB, BQSM, and PAM, could possibly solve the challenges faced in integrating software [Jamal et al., 2019]. Every professional construction organization has a charter that aims to improve the members' knowledge, technical expertise, and capability. It would be expected that the professional bodies would carry out or advance initiatives to promote 3D modelling software. For instance, the government may plan a number of motivational and awareness-raising events for different tiers of industry participants, such as seminars and workshops [Haron et al., 2017].

Top management plays a crucial role to enhance the implementation of 3D modelling software in construction projects. Top management in organizations must have an early awareness of the technology to improve the implementation [Sacks et al., 2018; Kymmell, 2008]. This could make it easier for employees to receive software training and for an organization to deploy 3D modelling software.

3.   Strategies to Overcome the Challenges

Many companies have developed and set up their in-house standards. For instance, architects offer standard design manuals to help builders reproduce certain construction elements. According to Zhou et al. (2019), The Ministry of Housing and Urban-Rural Development of the People's Republic of China (MOHURD) also focuses on expediting the implementation of 3D modelling into actual projects [26]. Software vendors can create a version of 3D model-based apps that are considerably simpler. The main ideas of building-related content production and data modelling should be the focus of the condensed version. In most cases, it is preferable to modify the tool to fit the user as opposed to trying to modify the user to fit the tool [Ibrahim, 2007]. As a result, it helps to empower the users by boosting their interest in utilizing 3D modelling software.

Some academic institutions and universities have devoted a lot of resources to BIM-related projects [Zhou et al.,2019]. Undergraduates and postgraduates can have early exposure to 3D modelling through collaboration between practitioners, academics, and researchers. Their collaboration could improve students' knowledge of 3D modelling software and expertise [Latiffi et al., 2015]. It is possible to introduce the fundamentals of 3D modelling into one field before moving on to others, either as a required component of a topic course or through distinct courses [Hietanen & Drogemuller, 2008]. Versions that are more focused and have fewer features should result from a highly careful development process and be relevant to the needs of QS undergraduates [Ibrahim, 2007].

The Malaysian government should offer BIM guidelines to help construction industry participants incorporate BIM in their projects. The guidelines will assist construction players to integrate BIM into construction projects in the proper manner [Latiffi et al., 2015]. In the United State, the General Services Administration (GSA) published a BIM Guide Series to enhance the calibre of design and construction outcomes.

Another strategy to overcome the challenges is consulting an expert for guidance and testing out pilot or previous projects [Mayouf et al., 2019]. The pilot project is an initial small-scale execution designed to demonstrate the viability of a project proposal. A firm can appoint a few employees to try out 3D modelling software on a previous project to help lower the risk of initiatives that do not fit within a life cycle that the implementing organization is familiar with.

Mandating the implementation of 3D modelling software for government projects is one of the primary initiatives the government shall be introducing [Jamal et al., 2019]. The mandatory use of BIM in some private sector projects by 2020 has been advocated by the Construction Industry Development Board (CIDB). According to an article by New Straits Times, Datuk Ahmad Asri Abdul Hamid claimed only a small number of significant businesses were utilizing BIM, whereas, in the public sector, projects costing RM100 million or more were required to utilize BIM [Bernama, 2019].

RESEARCH METHODOLOGY

This study is conducted using the qualitative method as it delivers more content that can be applied in the real world, requires a lower sample size than other research methods, and strongly emphasised on preserving rich meaning when analysing the data (Bhandari, 2022). In this research, the semi-structured interview method is adopted to acquire information and knowledge from the interviewees on the challenges faced in integrating 3D modelling software, the solutions based on the identified challenges in 3D modelling software, as well as the strategies of 3D modelling software in the QS profession. Semi-structured interviews were conducted with five quantity surveyors in Malaysia based on their knowledge, expertise, and experience in the industry. Each interview took around 15 to 30 minutes, their responses were recorded for research purposes. In this study, content analysis is adopted and the coding method is used in organising and labelling the qualitative data to distinguish between various themes and the connections among them (Medelyan, 2021).

RESEARCH FINDINGS

1. General Questions

Most of the respondents used Glodon and only one respondent used Cost-X. Out of five of the respondents, two of them used Glodon and Revit concurrently to carry out their daily tasks. The feedbacks of the respondents on having the implementation of 3D modelling software in the industry is quite positive where all respondents think that it is good to implement 3D modelling software in the industry. However, R3 and R5 stated that although the integration of 3D modelling software in the QS profession is good, there are also some challenges faced in implementing the software, which also leads to objective 1 of this research.

Based on the data collected, R1 and R2 do not consider that the implementation of 3D modelling software in Malaysia is efficient. This is because most of the companies in Malaysia are still unable to adapt to the new technologies and could not fully utilise the software as they are still using the conventional method of measurement. However, R4 and R5 have the opposite opinion and the respondents think that the implementation of 3D modelling software in Malaysia is efficient.

2.   Research Findings on Objective 1

Table 1 summarises the results of the responses from the interviewees based on the challenges faced in integrating 3D modelling. Code 'B' represents the category of challenges, code number '1' represents the first theme which is people constraint, while code 'a' represents the first sub-theme which is lack of professional support. Table 1 is divided into three themes namely people, process and technical constraints. R1, R3, R4, and R5 agree that lack of professional support is one of the challenges faced in integrating 3D modelling software in the QS profession. R1 thinks that professionals are irreplaceable, not even with technology. While for R3, he thinks that professional support cannot be obtained easily in Malaysia unless a permanent software consultant is employed. R1 and R3 have similar opinions and they feel that the presence of proficient consultants or professionals is very important. While for R4 and R5, their opinion on the lack of professional support is towards the cost, where they mentioned that the construction players are required to pay for professional support in return to get the support. However, R2 indicated that professional support can be obtained easily in Malaysia as BIM company such as Glodon which provides quite a number of technicians to assist the practitioners.

Table 1. Coding legend on challenges faced in 3D modelling

Category B	Themes	Sub-Themes	Codes
Challenges faced in integrating 3D modelling software	1. People Constraint	a) Lack of Professional Support	B1a
		b) Client Demand	B1b
		c) Resistance to Change	B1c
	2. Process Constraint	a) Legal or Contractual Issue	B2a
		b) Ownership	B2b
		c) Financial Issue	B2c
	3. Technical Constraint	a) Interoperability	B3a
		b) Lack of Information Presented within 3D Models	B3b
		c) Cost	B3c
		d) Lack of Software Compatibility	B3d

R1, R3, and R4 stated that there is no client request for the use of 3D modelling software currently. R3 and R4 mentioned that they are using the software, however, it is not requested by the client, and they just implement it internally. As for R2 and R5, they highlighted that clients do request the use of 3D modelling software currently. R1, R2, and R5 mentioned that with the integration of software, clients will worry that the final cost of their project will be raised. This statement is supported by the study from Baba (2010), stating that lack of client demand is one of the challenges due to the smaller number of potential bids which may cause an increase in the project's total cost [Baba, 2010].

Furthermore, R2 and R3 think that the quantity surveyors in the industry are unafraid of change as the QSs are still improving and changing to be more digitalized. R1 and R5 have the same thinking as R2 and R3 but it is only applicable to the younger generations as they mentioned that it is difficult for the older age group of quantity surveyors to change as they require to learn all over again to cope with the changes. This statement is supported by the study from Martinko, Zmud, and Henry (2011) where they mentioned that some construction players are still adopting conventional paper-based methods due to the difficulty of implementing linked devices [Martinko et al., 2011].

All respondents from R1 to R5 do not think that there is any legal issue in the firm as they do not encounter or heard of any. While for the issue of ownership, all respondents also mentioned that they did not encounter this problem in their firm. As for the financial issue, all respondents agreed that financial issue is the major challenge in implementing 3D modelling software. R1, R4 and R5 mentioned that training costs, labour costs and material costs are one of the additional costs that the practitioners are concerned about. This statement is supported by the study from Rahim and colleagues (2018) where they stated that the contractors are worried about the additional cost of integrating 3D modelling software as there are not only rising labour and material costs but there are also costs incurred for training [Zainon et al., 2018]. Zainon, et al. (2018) also agreed that firms must consider the additional costs of training employees and even employing new staff who are proficient in utilizing 3D modelling software [Zainon et al., 2016]. Besides that, R3 and R5 also mentioned that the renewal of the license also leads to financial issues, being one of the major challenges in implementing the software.

R1, R2, R3, and R5 think that interoperability is uncommon in the firm in which R1 stated that he had not encountered this in his work. However, R4 has a different point of view where she thinks that interoperability is common in the firm. This statement is supported by the study from Tulenheimo (2015) where he stated that there are more chances that various pieces of software would not function together unless they were produced by the same company as there are too many software companies on the market [Tulenheimo, 2015].

All respondents agreed that the lack of information presented within 3D models may affect the work of a QS. R1 added that he thinks Glodon does not provide 100% accuracy on the information and R3 thinks that even minor items will greatly affect the sum. Meanwhile, R2 also mentioned that she had an experience where the consultant could not provide the information that can be supported by the software. R4 and R5 also highlighted that the incomplete drawing and special design which are unable to be shown in the layout plan are also the issues which lead to the lack of information presented within 3D models. This statement is supported by Stanley & Thurnell (2013), and Smith (2016) who mentioned in their study that lack of detail and missing data in 3D modelling software leads to design faults and inaccurate predictions [Stanley & Thurnell, 2013].

Next, is the initial cost. All respondents agreed that the initial cost of software significantly affects the implementation of 3D modelling. According to R1, they need at least RM13k to invest in one software, if there are two software that needs to be invested, such as Glodon TAS & TRB, it requires at least RM30k. R2 also mentioned that the software and hardware updates are the cause which led to higher initial costs which both the firm and client are needed to pay. This statement is agreed by Stanley & Thurnell (2014) who mentioned in their study that the need for hardware and software updates is one of the main barriers to the adoption of 3D modelling, particularly for small and medium organizations [Stanley & Thurnell, 2014].

Furthermore, lack of software compatibility is also one of the challenges faced in integrating 3D modelling software. R1 stated that hardware needs to be updated every five years to be compatible with the software. R4 also further explained that both hardware and software are required to be updated frequently with which hardware is less than five years and software is even more frequent. This issue was also brought up by Smith (2015) who asserted that to obtain the necessary software for the proper usage of 3D modelling software, firms must upgrade their hardware. However, R2, R3, and R5 think that hardware does not require to be updated frequently whereas R3 and R5 further explained that it depends on the company and the software requirements, as different software has different requirements.

3.   Research Findings on Objective 2

Table 2 summarises the results of the responses from the interviewees based on the solutions to the identified challenges in adopting 3D modelling. Code 'C' represents the category of solutions, code number '1' represents the first theme which is the effort from the company, while code 'a' represents the first sub-theme which is training to construction staff. Table 2 is divided into three themes notably efforts from the company, government, and client. Training construction staff is one of the solutions to the identified challenges in implementing 3D modelling software. All respondents agreed that it is important to provide a training programme for the practitioners, especially the newcomers. As a director and a quantity surveyor in the firm, R1 mentioned that BIM company will provide training to them when they have invested in the software. He also added that he provides training programmes to all the practitioners in his firm so that everyone could be an all-rounder. R2 thinks that training programmes are important as not everyone can learn 3D modelling software at their university. R3 and R5 have the same opinion which they think that training is important as it is beneficial to achieve a standardized method of measurement. While for R4, she thinks that training for construction staff is the most impactful solution where her opinion on this is that the practitioners are able to catch up easily and refresh their knowledge of the software.

Table 2. Coding legend on solutions to the identified challenges

Category	Themes	Sub-Themes	Codes
Solutions to the Identified Challenges	1. Efforts from the Company	a) Training to Construction Staff	C1a
		b) Understanding Among Top Managerial	C1b
	2. Efforts from the Government	a) Establish BIM Fund	C2a
		b) Support from Professional Bodies	C2b
	3. Efforts from the Client	a) Enforcement from the Client	C3a

All respondents think that top management must have a good understanding to implement the software. R3 mentioned that top managers must understand and have an early awareness of the software. This statement can be supported by Sacks et al. (2018) and Kymmell (2008), who agreed that top management is required to have an early awareness of the technology to improve the implementation of 3D modelling software in construction projects.

For the establishment of the BIM Fund where all respondents agreed that this is one of the solutions to the identified challenges in integrating 3D modelling software. R1, R4, and R5 think that integrating resources from the Government is able to encourage the use of 3D modelling software. As for R2 and R3, although they think that it is good to establish BIM Fund from the government, however, R2 stated that this is not a good time to integrate resources from the government and R3 highlighted that it also depends on the company if they are interested to implement the software.

All respondents think that it is necessary to obtain support from professional bodies. R1 thinks that professional support would speed up the implementation. For example, CIDB can enforce the contractor or developer, and BQSM can enforce the quantity surveyors. R2, R3, and R4 mentioned that professional bodies can help by organizing seminars, giving talks, and providing training. R4 also added that professional organizations can provide funds for licenses. This statement is supported by the study from Haron, Soh, and Harun (2017) who stated that the government can organize a variety of motivational and awareness-raising activities, including seminars and workshops. Apart from that, R5 highlighted that getting support from professional organizations is able to improve the knowledge and capability of practitioners.

Besides that, all respondents think that enforcement from the client is one of the solutions to the identified challenges. R3 highlighted that client enforcement can encourage the practitioners to implement the software. R1 and R4 mentioned that client enforcement is important so that the quantity surveyors in the industry will no longer be using the traditional method of measurement. This statement is agreed by Smith & Tardif (2009) who mentioned that practitioners are able to adapt to the technology and realise the benefits of 3D modelling software with client enforcement. R2 stated that it is compulsory to use the software if the client insists, where it is also beneficial to use the software. As for R5, the interviewee thinks that client enforcement is important. However, it also depends on the ability of the company, whether they own the license of the software.

4. Research Findings on Objective 3

Table 3 summarises the results of the responses from the interviewees based on the strategies for the identified challenges in adopting 3D modelling. Code 'D' represents the category of strategies, code number '1' represents the first theme which is company strategy, while code 'a' represents the first sub-theme which is software development. Table 3 is divided into three themes namely company, government, and university strategies. Sub-theme 'a' is regarding software development, where R4 thinks that it is the better option for companies to develop their own software as it is easier for the company to implement it. As for R1, he agrees that it is a good idea to develop their own software. However, the cost will be higher, and it is also not user-friendly for everyone. R2, R3, and R5 do not think that the development of their own software is the better option in which R2 and R3 added that it is better to be standardized instead. As for R5, the respondent thinks that it is not necessary to spend time developing their own software, as the same information will be shared within the project team.

Table 3. Coding legend on strategies to the identified challenges

Category	Themes	Sub-Themes	Codes
Strategies to the Identified Challenges	1. Company	a) Software Development	D1a
		b) Modifying the Workflow of 3D Modelling Software	D1b
		c) Pilot Projects	D1c
	2. Government	a) Publication of BIM Guide Series	D2a
		b) Enforcement from the Government	D2b
	3. University	a) Introducing of 3D Modelling Software in University Curriculum	D3a

Furthermore, all respondents think that it is not preferable to modify the workflow of 3D modelling software. R1, R2, and R4 mentioned that most of the elements are able to measure using 3D modelling software. However, there are still some restrictions as mentioned by R1, R3, and R5 where some small elements, excavation and filling, and structural staircase are not able to be measured using Glodon. By saying so, R1 and R5 added that the sequence of measurement and take-off parameters are the same as the quantity surveyors in the industry are all based on SMM2. Hence, it is unnecessary to modify the workflow of 3D modelling software. Besides that, R3 and R4 also mentioned that it is good to follow the traditional method of workflow as everyone is used to it.

Apart from that, R1, R2, and R4 also think that testing out pilots or previous projects is a good strategy to overcome the challenges. Although the company of R1 and R2 did not organise a pilot project, they still agree that it is a good strategy as R1 mentioned that previous projects have their own measurements, and they are able to make comparisons with the software, while R2 also highlighted that a pilot project is like a demo. This statement is supported by Mayouf et al. (2019) who stated that a comparison between traditional methods can be made with the implementation of pilot projects. As for R4, she mentioned that her company did organise this type of project during her training hence, she thinks that it is a good strategy to test out pilots or previous projects. R3 and R5 have the opposite opinion regarding this matter where they think that testing out a pilot project is a waste of time. R5 also further elaborate that it will only be a good strategy if firms have a particular department to study these.

All respondents except R2 agreed that the publication of the BIM Guide Series is one of the strategies to overcome the challenges in integrating 3D modelling software. R1, R3, R4, and R5 highlighted that the publication of the BIM Guide series is important as it serves as a standard guideline for everyone to follow and assists practitioners to integrate the software in a proper manner. Hence, it is better to be standardized and everyone would have the same knowledge to implement the software. This statement is supported by Latiffi et al. (2015) who mentioned that the guidelines will help construction players integrate BIM into construction projects correctly. As for R2, instead of BIM Guide Series, the respondent thinks that it is preferable to have a company guideline as every company has different policies.

Furthermore, all respondents agreed that enforcement from the government is important as this will encourage other firms to gradually implement the software if the government mandates the construction players to integrate 3D modelling software. This statement is agreed by Latiffi et al. (2015) who think that the enforcement from the government encourages 3D modelling practices in construction projects. R5 also mentioned that the government can initiate the enforcement by mandating 3D modelling software in government projects. This statement is also supported by Jamal et al. (2019) who mentioned that one of the main measures the administration will be proposing is mandating the use of 3D modelling software for government projects. R1 also shared that JKR projects currently use 3D modelling software to carry out their work but not many of the private projects are using the software. However, quite many firms are gradually mastering Glodon, such as Gamuda, and IJM.

Finally, all respondents think that it is compulsory for all the students to learn 3D modelling software in the university curriculum, especially in this new era where everything will be digitalized, R4 added. R1 highlighted that students can implement and catch up easily when they enter the industry. While for R2, she mentioned that with the introduction of 3D modelling software in the university curriculum, students are able to have early exposure to the software and have the chance to collaborate with the practitioners to improve their knowledge of utilising the software. This statement is supported by Latiffi et al. (2015) who stated that through collaboration between professionals, academics, and researchers, undergrads and graduates can gain early exposure to 3D modelling. R3 also stated that although training programmes will be introduced to the fresh graduates when they first join the company, it is also necessary to introduce 3D modelling software in the university. Furthermore, R5 also mentioned that every vacancy should have a requirement of having BIM knowledge which brings an advantage to the practitioners hence, it is necessary to introduce 3D modelling software in the university curriculum in this new era.

CONCLUSION AND RECOMMENDATIONS

In conclusion, not all construction companies in Malaysia are utilizing the 3D modelling software as the industry is still facing challenges regarding 3D modelling. There are unquestionably several foreseen and unforeseen underlying issues. It is recommended that construction practitioners should collaborate and work together to overcome the challenges faced in integrating 3D modelling as it brings a lot of benefits to the industry. These research outcomes serve as references for construction players in integrating 3D modelling to minimise the constraints and avoid unpredictable circumstances while implementing the 3D modelling. Instead of using 2D CAD drawings, 3D modelling implementation also enhanced the visualisation and demonstration of planned landscapes and buildings. As a result, it brings higher efficiency in daily operations and helps to improve the productivity of construction players.

REFERENCES

Azhar, S. (2011, June 15). Building Information Modeling (BIM): Trends, benefits, risks, and challenges for the AEC industry. *Leadership and Management in Engineering: 11*(3). https://ascelibrary.org/doi/1 0.1061/%28ASCE%29LM.1943-5630.0000127

Baba, H. D. (2010, December). *Building information modeling in local construction industry*. UTM. http://eprints.utm.my/id/eprint/15311/4/HammadDaboBabaMFKA2010.pdf

Bernama, N. S. T. (2019, March 18). CIDB recommends mandatory use of BIM in certain private sector projects. *New Straits Time*. https://www.nst.com.my/news/nation/2019/03/470468/cidb-recommends-mandatory-use-bim-certain-private-sector-projects

Bhandari, P. (2022). *What is qualitative research? Methods & examples*. Scribbr. https://www.scribbr.com/methodology/qualitative-research/

Cheng, J. C. P., Lu, Q., & Phil, M. (2015, October). *A Review of the Efforts and Roles of the Public Sector for BIM Adoption Worldwide*. ITcon. https://www.itcon.org/papers/2015_27.content.01088.pdf

Criminale, A., & Langar, S. (2017). *Challenges with BIM implementation: A review of literature*. ResearchGate. https://www.researchgate.net/profile/Sandeep-Langar/publication/317842173_Challenges_with_BIM_Implementation_A_Review_of_Literature/links/594db74caca27248ae3436c2/Challenges-with-BIM-Implementation-A-Review-of-Literature.pdf

Haron, N. A., Soh, R. P. Z. A. R., & Harun, A. (2017). *Implementation of building information modelling (Bim) in malaysia: A review*. ResearchGate. https://www.researchgate.net/publication/318266244_Implementation_of_building_information_modelling_Bim_in_malaysia_A_review

Hietanen, J., & Drogemuller, R. (2008, January). *Approaches to university level BIM education.* ResearchGate. https://www.researchgate.net/publication/233604171_Approaches_to_university_level_BIM_education

Ibrahim, M. (2007). *The challenge of integrating BIM based CAD in today's architectural curricula.* Papers.cumincad.org. http://papers.cumincad.org/data/works/att/ascaad2007_051.content.pdf

Jamal, K. A. A., Mohammad, M. F., Hashim, N., Mohamed, M. R., & Ramlil, M. A. (2019). Challenges of Building Information Modelling (BIM) from the Malaysian Architect's Perspective. *Sci.* https://sci-hub.hkvisa.net/https://doi.org/10.1051/matecconf/201926605003

Kymmell, W. (2008, January). *Building Information Modeling: Planning and managing construction projects with 4D CAD and simulations (McGraw-Hill Construction Series).* Access Engineering. https://www.accessengineeringlibrary.com/content/book/9780071494533

Latiffi, A., Mohd, S., & Rakiman, U. (2015, October). *Potential Improvement of Building Information Modeling (BIM) Implementation in Malaysian Construction Projects.* ResearchGate. https://www.researchgate.net/publication/290443821_Potential_Improvement_of_Building_Information_Modeling_BIM_Implementation_in_Malaysian_Construction_Projects

Love, P., Irani, Z., Li, H., Tse, R., & Cheng, E. W. L. (2001, March). *An empirical analysis of the barriers to implementing e-commerce in small-medium sized construction contractors in the state of Victoria, Australia.* Emerald Insight.

Martinko, M. J., Zmud, R. W., & Henry, J. W. (2011). *An attributional explanation of individual resistance to the introduction of information technologies in the Workplace.* Taylor & Francis. https://www.tandfonline.com/doi/abs/10.1080/014492996120085a

Mayouf, M., Gerges, M., & Cox, S. (2019, February 18). *5D BIM: an investigation into the integration of quantity surveyors within the BIM process.* Emerald Insight. https://sci-hub.se/

McClone, M. C. (2019, September 25). *Top 4 technology challenges in the construction industry.* McClone Insurance Group. https://www.mcclone.com/blog/top-4-technology-challenges-in-the-construction-industry

Medelyan, A. (2021). Coding Qualitative Data: How to Code Qualitative Research. *InSights.* https://getthematic.com/insights/coding-qualitative-data/

Memon, A. H., Rahman, I. A., Memon, I., & Azman, N. I. A. (2014, August 5). BIM in Malaysian Construction Industry: Status, Advantages, Barriers and Strategies to Enhance the Implementation Level. *Research Journal of Applied Sciences, Engineering and Technology.* https://www.airitilibrary.com/Publication/alDetailedMesh?docid=20407467-201408-201502170022-201502170022-606-614

Morrison, C. (2010, October). *Bim 2010: The benefits and barriers for construction contractors in Auckland.* Research Bank Home. https://www.researchbank.ac.nz/handle/10652/1778

Nigam, M., Dixit, A., & Sachan, K. K. (2016). Bim vs traditional quantity surveying and its future mapping. *IJEDR.* https://www.ijedr.org/papers/IJEDR1602222.pdf

Sacks, R., Eastman, C., Lee, G., & Teicholz, P. (2018, July 27). *Bim handbook: A guide to building information modeling for owners, designers, engineers, contractors, and facility managers, 3rd Edition.* Wiley. https://www.wiley.com/en-sg/BIM+Handbook:+A+Guide+to+Building+Information+Modeling+for+Owners,+Designers,+Engineers,+Contractors,+and+Facility+Managers,+3rd+Editi on-p-9781119287537

Smith, D., & Tardif, M. (2009, March). *Building Information Modeling: A Strategic Implementation Guide for Architects, Engineers, Constructors, and Real Estate Asset Managers.* ResearchGate. https://www.researchgate.net/publication/319088001_Building_Information_Modeling_A_Strategic_Imple-mentation_Guide_for_Architects_Engineers_Constructors_and_Real_Estate_Asset_Managers

Smith, P. (2015, September). *BIM & Automated quantities – Implementation Issues for the Australian Quantity Surveying Profession.* icoste.org. https://www.icoste.org/wp-content/uploads/2015/09/Smith-PAQS-Paper.pdf

Stanley, R., & Thurnell, D. (2013, November). *Current and anticipated future impacts of BIM on cost modelling in Auckland.* Research Bank Home. https://www.researchbank.ac.nz/handle/10652/2450

Stanley, R., & Thurnell, D. (2014). *The benefits of, and barriers to, implementation of 5D BIM for quantity surveying in New Zealand.* Search.informit.org. https://search.informit.org/doi/epdf/10.3316/informit.200817347855487

Stephenson, P., & Blaza, S. (2001). *Implementing technological change in construction organisations.* ITC. https://itc.scix.net/pdfs/w78-2001-66.content.pdf

Tailor, J. (2022, February 9). *How 3D Modeling can Benefit Construction Industry?* GharPedia. https://gharpedia.com/blog/how-3d-modeling-can-benefit-construction-industry/

Tee, Y. Y., & Kamal, E. M. (2021, May 18). The Revolution of Quantity Surveying Profession in Building Information Modelling (BIM) Era: The Malaysian Perspective. *Journals of universiti tun hussein onn Malaysia.* https://publisher.uthm.edu.my/ojs/

Thompson, D. B., & Miner, R. G. (2007). *Building information modeling—BIM: Contractual risks are changing with technology.* Aepronet. http://www.aepronet.org/ge/no35.html

Tulenheimo, R. (2015, May 13). *Challenges of implementing new technologies in the world of BIM – case study from construction engineering industry in Finland.* ScienceDirect. https://www.sciencedirect.com/science/article/pii/S2212567115002014

Valle, G. (2021, June 25). *8 benefits of 3D modeling in construction.* BuilderSpace. https://www.build-erspace.com/benefits-of-3d-modeling-in-construction

Zahrizan, Z., Ali, N., Haron, A., Marshall-Ponting, A., & Hamid, Z. (2013, December 20). *Exploring the Barriers and Driving Factors in Implementing Building Information Modelling (BIM) in the Malaysian Construction Industry: A Preliminary Study.* MOAM. https://moam.info/exploring-the-barriers-and-driving-factors-in-implementing-building-_599c2a961723dd09401ad760.html

Zainon, N. Mohd-Rahim, F. Azli, & Salleh, H. (2016, January). *The Rise Of BIM in Malaysia And Its Impact Towards Quantity Surveying Practices.* ResearchGate. https://www.researchgate.net/publication/305309677_The_Rise_Of_BIM_in_Malaysia_And_Its_Impact_Towards_Quantity_Surveying_Practices

Zainon, N., Rahim, F., Aziz, N. M., Kamaruzzaman, S., & Puidin, S. (2018, June). *Catching Up With Building Information Modelling: Challenges and Opportunities for Quantity Surveyors.* researchgate. https://www.researchgate.net/publication/329920573_CATCHING_UP_WITH_BUILDING_INFORMATION_MODELING_CHALLENGES_AND_OPPORTUNITIES_FOR_QUANTITY_SURVEYORS

Zhou, Y., Yang, Y., & Yang, J.-B. (2019). Barriers to BIM implementation strategies in China. *EmeraldInsight.* https://sci-hub.se/https:/doi.org/10.1108/ECAM-04-2018-0158

Chapter 3
Post–Pandemic COVID–19 Virtual Documentation Through 3D Laser Scanning and 3D Photogrammetry for Site and Building Assessment

Ungku Norani Sonet

https://orcid.org/0000-0003-4144-150X

Taylor's University, Malaysia

ABSTRACT

The pandemic has certainly become a paradigm shift in multiple sectors and industries, including the built environment. Therefore, this chapter highlights one of the methods which was adopted during the pandemic in continuing the architecture, engineering, and construction (AEC) practice without disregarding the site assessment due to the pandemic circumstances. This chapter is to discuss the potential of adopting 3D laser scanning and 3D photogrammetry in the making of a virtual site and building model for various purposes, including building inspections, virtual visits, and defect inspections. The case study of six projects is used to demonstrate the usage of the two methods: 1) 3D laser scanning, and 2) 3D photogrammetry. The results show the potential for the site and building assessment in adopting virtual advanced technologies pertaining to the post pandemic COVID-19 and various future circumstances and challenges in the field of the built environment.

INTRODUCTION

The COVID-19 pandemic has had a significant impact on multiple areas, including architecture, engineering and construction (AEC) (Takewaki, 2020). The restrictions and safety measures imposed to control the spread of COVID-19 have complicated project schedules, access to job sites, and supply chains for materials needed for construction (Yahaya et al., 2022). Additionally, many AEC companies have shifted

DOI: 10.4018/978-1-6684-8253-7.ch003

to remote working arrangements which can possibly hinder communication and collaboration between team members (Truong et al., 2021). Despite these challenges, the pandemic has also brought about opportunities for innovation within the AEC industry such as advances in virtual design and construction technologies to aid remote collaboration and communication among team members (Zhang & Chen, 2019). Furthermore, it has highlighted the importance of adaptable and flexible design to accommodate changing circumstances and unexpected events (Widyarko et al., 2020). Moreover, the pandemic has also increased attention to sustainability and healthy building practices (Sa'ed et al., 2022).

Overall, the COVID-19 pandemic has underscored the need for resilience and adaptability in AEC practices, as well as an increased emphasis on innovative technologies and sustainable design principles. The COVID-19 pandemic has proven to have a major impact on various industries including the built environment. Despite the circumstance being observed to cause delayed extension of timeline in the construction of physical development, it has also opened up to various alternatives in the practice. The available advanced technology in mitigating the circumstances during the pandemic including in complimenting the remote working method has been able to take place officially and putting into a possible highlight in its use in order to keep the continuity to the profession. Based on developing data-driven and information-based approaches and digital technologies, the golden era of architecture, engineering, and construction (AEC) sectors will certainly continue (Cheshmehzangi, 2021). However, as shown, the present epidemic of the post COVID-19 pandemic has halted development progress and is likely to result in concrete changes to our policies, practices, and viewpoints. It is anticipated that the emphasis on resilience, health, and/or safety will grow. For example, the application of data science is anticipated to influence the development of new methods to information-based modelling, innovative material design, spatial planning, and integrated design solutions. The COVID-19 outbreak indicates the possibility of new paradigm shifts that are likely to alter our growth patterns, notably in the construction and built environment sectors(Cheshmehzangi, 2021). With the rapid advancement of technology, we are likely to adopt new approaches that will improve our resilience and health in cities and communities.

However, scholarly work on the built environment must extend further, and learning from industry reports might facilitate this expansion at a quicker rate. As a result of this epidemic, it is apparent that the world is becoming increasingly digital; therefore, it is expected that professionals would use new technologies to increase productivity (Ogunnusi et al., 2020). The need for more preparation towards the threat and opportunity posed by risk is essential. The question now is, can there be a review of alternative advanced technology to be formally utilised in the construction industry? Should the work process of documentation to the construction projects be reviewed? Would there be a need for a review of the standard of documentation of work progress? This study discovered the potential of the construction industry in adopting laser scanning and photogrammetry technology for documentation purposes during the COVID-19 pandemic.

The documentation of building and construction sites presents a number of challenges, not only due to the complex nature of the technology involved, but also in terms of the planning, processing, and data delivery of cost-effective solutions (Cabrelles et al., 2009). In addition, given that the processes of deterioration on building are ongoing, the activity of documentation has become an essential step that must be taken in order to record the state of the site at a particular point in time (Cabrelles et al., 2009). This helps to facilitate the decision-making process that must be followed by specialists in order to create a comprehensive 3D documentation of the particular project. Within the realm of architecture, engineering, and construction (AEC), laser scanning is swiftly gaining popularity as a technique for three-dimensional (3D) modelling and analysis (Huber et al., 2010). Laser scanners are now able to acquire range measurements at rates of tens to hundreds of thousands of points per second, at distances of up to a few hundred metres, and with uncertainties on the scale of millimetres to a few centimetres. These capabilities have been made possible by advances in technology. These types of sensors are ideally suited for densely recording the geometry of the interiors and exteriors of buildings, as well as the geometry of processing facilities and infrastructure.

LITERATURE REVIEW

3D Laser Scanning

Three-dimensional (3D) laser scanning is a cutting-edge technology that aims to capture the physical characteristics of an object or surface in three dimensions (Kedzierski et al., 2016).This technology involves the use of laser beams to take precise measurements and create a high-resolution digital image or model of the object (Choi et al., 2018). This technology has wide applications in various fields such as engineering, construction, architecture, and manufacturing. Additionally, 3D laser scanning can also be used to capture information concerning the shape, size, texture, and colour of objects in great detail (Vasilakos et al., 2018). Furthermore, the data obtained through 3D laser scanning can be used to create accurate computer models and simulations that are useful in design and planning processes (Zang et al., 2018). Moreover, the ability to capture 3D data quickly and non-invasively makes this technology a valuable tool in forensic investigations, cultural heritage preservation, and medical imaging (Badenko et al., 2018). Overall, 3D laser scanning is a highly advanced technology that has revolutionised the way organisations approach object and surface measurement, modelling, and analysis.

In contrast to 2D graphics, digital 3D models have access to a greater quantity of information and have a greater resemblance to live things (Cheng & Jin, 2006). Consequently, the production of a 3D model of architecture may richly preserve the structure, shape, and construction style of the building. In addition, it provides the fundamental information required for record file and repair protection. In recent years, a variety of 3D laser scanning systems have been created, and the use of these systems will speed up the level of industrial methods. The technique known as 3D laser scanning allows for very accurate and fully automated scanning in all three dimensions (Cheng & Jin, 2006). Optical, mechanical, electronic, and computer technologies are all included in its make-up. The fundamental idea is to scan the item outline point by point, obtain the spatial coordinates and colour information of the points on the surface, merge the data to simulate the shape on the computer, and ultimately produce the architectural model with precision.

The 3D laser scanning technology is a new surveying method that scans the architecture without causing any damage. This is important for the preservation and repair of architectural structures since not only can it rebuild the original shape, but it can also convert data to a CAD file. At the same time, software tools for processing and analysing 3D point data sets, also known as point clouds, have been improving in their capacity to manage the enormous point clouds produced by laser scanners and to integrate the use of point cloud data into CAD modelling software. Point clouds are also known as point clouds (Huber et al., 2010).

The technology of 3D laser scanning can acquire a 3D point cloud rapidly and with a high degree of accuracy. This satisfies the requirements for the surveying and protection of historical architecture. In the field of surveying historical buildings, 3D laser scanning technology has the potential to fully supplant traditional measuring methods. The 3D point cloud can be acquired through the use of a laser scanner, which can then be used to generate the 3D model. In addition, the close-range photogrammetry approach, which generates the orthoimage as well as the linear drawing, can be utilised to acquire the vignette and the detail structure. Not only can surveying historical buildings with 3D laser scanning technology cut down on fieldwork and boost productivity, but it can also produce a variety of goods, such as 3D models, CAD construction drawings, and so on. At the moment, 3D laser scanner technology is developing in the direction of high speed, high accuracy, vast range, and multi-information, etc. All of these features will stimulate the application of laser scanning to the surveying and safeguarding of ancient structures.

Laser scanning is a typical land surveying technology for obtaining precise measurements and data from artefacts, structures, buildings, and landscapes (Razali et al., 2022). The aforementioned documents are still needed today by architects or building staff, but analysis is becoming to be done entirely in 3D for a few factors. To start, data sets in 3D are being collected more easily and thoroughly, mostly by terrestrial laser scanners and 3D cameras (Lerma et al., 2011). The second is the accessibility of user-friendly software that can fully render in 3D millions of characteristics including points, point splats, meshes, and textures. Third, satellite-based, image-based, or other types of surveying technology are readily available everywhere.

The process involves performing a scan of the structure to collect a large number of 3D points, which is commonly referred to as a point cloud. Next, the multiple stations of the point cloud are registered, followed by triangulating the data and fitting the surface. Finally, the 3D model is reconstructed. The modelling method consists of a few steps, which are as follows (Cheng & Jin, 2006):

- Data acquisition - Using a 3D laser scanner, the 3D coordinates of the surface of the object are collected. In addition, information regarding the geometry and position, as well as the density of the point cloud, can be acquired.
- Data registration - It is not possible to obtain a complete image of the object using just one scan. Therefore, it requires scans from a variety of stations. The process of data registration involves bringing together the entire point cloud through coordinate transformation.
- Data pre-processing - Evaluating the data and filtering it are both steps in this process. The purpose of data evaluation is to identify areas that were skipped or repeated during scanning and to determine whether additional measurements should be taken. The goal of data filtering is to lessen the impact of noise by resampling and smoothing it down.
- Surface fitting - Reconstructing a surface that is both succinct and accurate is the goal of the surface fitting process. It is impossible for only one to fit the intricate free-surface area. This results in the data from the various segments being collated and utilised to fit each surface before being joined together to form the entire.

This paper provides an overview of six case studies of projects done through the laser scanning and photogrammetry method documentation. One key aspect of this project was the use of advanced sensors, such as laser scanners, and photogrammetry cameras to monitor for errors of the buildings and sites. We discovered some important lessons about utilising laser scanners to model structures while working on this project. First, it is critical to comprehend the workflows for data processing as well as the low-level constraints placed by laser scanners. It can be challenging to distinguish between a minor construction flaw and noisy or ambiguous data without such expertise. Second, many other kinds of analysis can use the idea of comparing what is measured to what is expected. Third, there are limitations to this comparison approach, and there is a big need to support facility modelling in cases where a design model is not accessible. These lessons naturally translated into three different lines of work processes, which included developing modelling and recognition algorithms to support automatic and semi-automatic model construction from laser scan data and improving our understanding of the low-level aspects of laser scanner data.

3D Photogrammetry

Three-dimensional (3D) photogrammetry is a method of measuring geometric properties and creating 3D models of objects or scenes from two-dimensional (2D) photographs (Pejić et al., 2017). This technique involves taking a series of photographs from different angles, and then using specialised software to analyse the images and create a 3D model that accurately replicates the shape, size, and texture of the subject being photographed (Baiker-Sørensen et al., 2020) The process of 3D photogrammetry relies on the principle of triangulation, where measurements are made by identifying corresponding points in multiple images and calculating their relative positions in 3D space (Khalil & Stravoravdis, 2019). The resulting 3D models created through photogrammetry can be used in various fields, including architecture, engineering, surveying, and filmmaking (Kazaz et al., 2021). Additionally, 3D photogrammetry has proven to be a valuable tool in fields such as medicine, where it is used to create accurate models of anatomy and assist in surgical planning (Deli et al., 2013).

The technology of 3D photogrammetry has revolutionised the way we acquire and process spatial data. By utilising overlapping photographs captured from different angles, photogrammetry software is able to create 3D models of objects and environments with incredible accuracy and detail (Sun et al., 2020). This technology has proven to be highly useful across a broad range of disciplines, including architecture, urban planning, archaeology, and civil engineering. Additionally, 3D photogrammetry has provided a cost-effective and efficient method for creating detailed maps and models of areas that are difficult to access or hazardous for humans to explore (Gharechelou et al., 2018). Furthermore, 3D photogrammetry has also found applications in the entertainment industry to create realistic visual effects and virtual reality experiences. Overall, the technology of 3D photogrammetry has opened up new avenues for data acquisition and visualisation, offering a powerful toolset that continues to advance and expand, increasing its potential applications in various fields (Kim & Gratchev, 2021).

Comparison Between 3D Laser Scanning and 3D Photogrammetry

In the field of 3D modelling and measurement, there are two primary technologies that are commonly used: 3D laser scanning and 3D photogrammetry (Hou et al., 2020). While both technologies serve the same purpose - capturing and creating 3D models of objects, structures or environments - there are some key differences between them (Hua et al., 2020). 3D laser scanning captures measurements by emitting a laser beam at the object or environment and measuring the time it takes for the light to bounce back to create a precise point cloud (Yang et al., 2019)).On the other hand, 3D photogrammetry involves capturing multiple images of an object or environment from different angles and processing them to create a point cloud or 3D model (Vasiljević et al., 2021). This method requires special software to analyse the images and extract dimensional data. Overall, the main difference between 3D laser scanning and 3D photogrammetry is in how they collect data: laser scanning achieves it directly, while photogrammetry relies on processing images to derive dimensional data (Sun et al., 2020).

Another significant difference is the level of accuracy: 3D laser scanning can produce more detailed and accurate models with precise measurements, while photogrammetry may have slightly lower accuracy due to factors such as lighting conditions and the quality of images captured. It is important to carefully evaluate the project requirements and expected outcomes when choosing which technology to use (Ton et al., 2022). Additionally, 3D laser scanning tends to be faster and more efficient for capturing large-scale environments or objects with complex geometries, while photogrammetry may be more suitable for smaller objects or environments with simpler shapes (Napolitano et al., 2018). Furthermore, 3D laser scanning is often used in industries such as architecture, engineering and construction for creating accurate measurements of buildings, infrastructure or landscapes. As for 3D photogrammetry, it is commonly used in fields such as archaeology, cultural heritage preservation and entertainment industry for creating high-quality visualisations and reconstructions of objects or environments. In summary, while both 3D laser scanning and 3D photogrammetry serve to create 3D models of objects or environments, their methods of data collection and level of accuracy differ, making each technology better suited for certain types of projects or applications.

The Potential of 3D Laser Scanning and 3D Photogrammetry in the Built Environment

Over the past few decades, 3D laser scanning and photogrammetry technologies have emerged as valuable tools that can be used to improve various operations in the built environment. These technologies have the potential to enhance project planning, construction documentation, facility management and maintenance activities (Ntiyakunze & Inoue, 2023). Furthermore, 3D laser scanning and photogrammetry can assist with identifying potential design conflicts earlier on in the project life cycle, ultimately reducing rework and construction costs. In addition, 3D laser scanning and photogrammetry can be used to capture highly detailed and accurate as-built conditions of existing structures, which is a critical aspect of building renovation and historical preservation projects (Alvanchi & Seyrfar, 2020). Moreover, the use of 3D laser scanning and photogrammetry can significantly improve safety on construction sites by reducing the need for manual measurements performed by workers. Overall, the potential of 3D laser scanning and photogrammetry in the built environment is vast and varied. These technologies have the capacity to revolutionise the construction industry by streamlining various processes, optimising resource utilisation, accelerating project timelines and improving safety. However, it is important to note that while 3D laser scanning and photogrammetry have numerous benefits, their successful implementation requires careful planning and execution to ensure accuracy and reliability of the data produced. Furthermore, the size and complexity of data generated by 3D laser scanning and photogrammetry call for expertise in data processing, management, interpretation, and analysis. In conclusion, the potential of 3D laser scanning and photogrammetry in the built environment is immense, providing numerous benefits to different stakeholders. However, it is crucial to take into account the challenges that may arise during their implementation, such as data management and interpretation (Qureshi et al., 2022). Ultimately, to realise the full potential of these technologies in the built environment, it is imperative that industry professionals receive adequate training and education on their utilisation, and that they continuously adapt to the changing technological landscape.

Method of Research

This paper presents a laser scanning and photogrammetric procedure in virtual building documentation exercise. The study conducted based on the secondary data of minutes meeting reviewed of the six case studies including; 1) Rumah Tangsi, 2) CSF Computer Exchange, 3) Quill, 4) Restoran Nasi Ayam Gemas, 5) Taski Sri Firdaus, and 6) Maahad Tahfiz Hidayatul Mustaqim. The case studies were selected based on the relevance of the project in involving the process in collecting data using 3D Laser Scanning and 3D Photogrammetry in producing the virtual 3D outcome for different objectives and purposes of the specific projects. All of the case studies are based in peninsular Malaysia; therefore, the limitation of the analysis is to include Malaysia tropical geographical context.

CASE STUDY

Table 1 shows the six case studies of the research including; 1) Rumah Tangsi, 2) CSF Computer Exchange, 3) Quill 5, 4) Restoran Nasi Ayam Gemas, 5) Taski Sri Firdaus, and 6)Maahad Tahfiz Hidayatul Mustaqi. Projects that involve many sets of survey devices call for meticulous planning in order to produce proper documentation with the fewest possible resources expended.

The duration of the data collection of each project in general is only one day for all of the case studies.

Table 1. Six case studies of research

Case Study / Year	Rumah Tangsi, Kuala Lumpur	CSF Computer Exchange, Cyberjaya	Quill 5, Cyberjaya	Restoran Nasi Ayam Gemas, Kuantan	Taski Sri Firdaus, Meru	Maahad Tahfiz Hidayatul Mustaqim, Selayang
Location	Kuala Lumpur	Cyberjaya	Cyberjaya	Kuantan	Meru	Selayang
Duration of Data Collection	1 day	1 day	1 day	1 day	1 day	1 day

Case Study 1: Rumah Tangsi

Figure 1 shows the Matterport cloud platform of Rumah Tangsi.

Figure 1. Rumah Tangsi Matterport cloud
(Source: https://my.matterport.com/show/?m=2cNzLAQoKFj)

Case Study 2: CFS Computer Exchange

Figure 2 shows the Matterport cloud platform of CFS Computer Exchange.

Figure 2. CFS Computer Exchange Matterport cloud
(Source: https://mpembed.com/show/?m=fyVut2auA9g&details=1&mdir=2&hdir=3&mdirsearch=1&load inglogo=https://live.staticflickr.com/65535/51587015906_b170270c24_c.jpg&image=https://live.staticflickr. com/65535/51587015906_b170270c24_c.jpg&fadeui=1&minimap=1&minimaptags=1&minimapnopano=1&backgrou nd_color=grey&copyright=SBR%20%20Consultant)

Case Study 3: Quill 5

Figure 3 shows the Matterport cloud platform of Quill 5.

Figure 3. Quill 5 Matterport cloud
(Source: https://mpembed.com/show/?m=E5sYDdCNcfa&details=3&mdir=1&hdir=2&mdirsearch=1&loadinglogo=htt ps://live.staticflickr.com/65535/51587015906_b170270c24_c.jpg&image=https://live.staticflickr.com/65535/51587015906_ b170270c24_c.jpg&minimap=1&minimaptags=1&minimapnopano=1&background_color=grey&copyright=SBR%20%20 Consultant)

Case Study 4: Restoran Nasi Ayam Gemas

Figure 4 shows the Matterport cloud platform of Restoran Nasi Ayam Gemas.

Figure 4. Nasi Ayam Gemas Matterport cloud
(Source: https://my.matterport.com/show/?m=gY2dFQsbZPV)

Case Study 5: Taski Sri Firdaus

Figure 5 shows the Matterport cloud platform of Taski Sri Firdaus.

Figure 5. Taski Sri Firdaus Matterport cloud
(Source: https://my.matterport.com/show/?m=9jcpuEkGqjp)

Case Study 6: Maahad Tahfiz Hidayatul Mustaqim

Figure 6 shows the Matterport cloud platform of Maahad Tahfiz Hidayatul Mustaqim.

Figure 6. Maahad Tahfiz Hidayatul Mustaqim Matterport cloud
(Source: https://my.matterport.com/show/?m=EBrsYo3cn3e)

RESULTS AND DISCUSSION

Table 2 shows the results of the document reviews analysis of the case studies. There are three laser scanner and photogrammetry scanners used for all these six case studies namely; 1) Matterport MC250 Pro 2 3D Mapping Camera, 2) Leica 3D Disto and 3) DJI Enterprise Terra Pro Overseas Perpetual.

The results show that there are mainly two types of technologies used, including 1) 3D laser scanning and 2) 3D photogrammetry. The 3D laser scanning is suitable to be used for outdoor scanning purposes while the 3D photogrammetry technology is suitable for indoor scanning. These two different technologies required different types of instruments in order to achieve the objective of the data collection. In obtaining the outdoor input, the instruments used for 3D laser scanning technologies are Leica 3D Disto and DJI Enterprise Terra Pro Overseas Perpetual. The Leica 3D Disto could capture the data within 40-50 seconds of data processing 360 degrees per shoot. The DJI Enterprise Terra Pro Overseas Perpetual is a drone to capture the heigh beyond the limitations of the Leica 3D Disto.

Whilst for indoor data collection purposes, the Matter port MC2 3D Mapping Camera was used. This instrument could capture within 20 seconds for data processing of 360 degrees per shot which is slightly faster than the Leica 3D Disto.

The data recorded by all these cameras were simultaneously reflected into the Matterport cloud platform which was immediately visible for views. The ability of the data to be instantly developed and present into the cloud platform allows the stakeholders of the project to overview the projects throughout the data collection process. Also, the benefits of Matterport cloud platform has automatically omitted manual stitching processes of the data collected by similar methods by other instruments.

Table 2. Results of document reviews of six case studies

Case Study / Year	Rumah Tangsi, Kuala Lumpur	CSF Computer Exchange, Cyberjaya	Quill 5, Cyberjaya	Restoran Nasi Ayam Gemas, Kuantan	Taski Sri Firdaus, Meru	Maahad Tahfiz Hidayatul Mustaqim, Selayang
Objective	To develop a visual reality dashboard for online visit	To identify defect on the existing building	To identify defect on the existing building	To develop a visual reality dashboard for online visit	To develop a visual reality dashboard for site analysis	To develop a visual reality dashboard for site analysis
Size of Area	-	-	-	-	-	-
Technology	3D Photogrammetry	3D Photogrammetry	3D Photogrammetry	3D Photogrammetry	3D Laser Scanning	3D Laser Scanning
Perimeter	Indoor	Indoor	Indoor	Indoor	Outdoor	Outdoor
Instrument	1. Matterport MC250 Pro2 3D Mapping Camera	1. Matterport MC250 Pro2 3D Mapping Camera	1. Matterport MC250 Pro2 3D Mapping Camera	1. MatterportMC250 Pro2 3D Mapping Camera	1. Leica 3D Disto 2. DJI Enterprise Terra Pro Overseas Perpetual	1. Leica 3D Disto 2. DJI Enterprise Terra Pro Overseas Perpetual
Data Processing 360 degree per shoot	20 seconds	20 seconds	20 seconds	20 seconds	40 – 50 seconds	40 – 50 seconds
Outcome	Matterport Cloud Platform	Matterport Cloud Platform	Matterport Cloud Platform	Matterport Cloud Platform	Matterport Cloud Platform	Matterport Cloud Platform
Length of Work process in collecting the data	1 day	1 day	1 day	1 day	1 day	1 day

Figure 7 shows the data collection process through Matterport MC250 Pro2 3D Mapping Camera. The data collected is immediately accessible on Matterport cloud platform. Therefore, it could simultaneously access the dashboard.

Finding: The Work Process

Laser scanning has been around for decades and is a well-known technology used in various industries. However, its use in the photogrammetry field has only recently become more widespread. Laser scanning is a method of capturing three-dimensional (3D) data through the use of a surveying laser. The laser scanner is attached to a tripod and has lenses that focus the laser onto the object being scanned. As the object moves, the laser beam is reflected back to a sensor in the scanner, which is interpreted by a computer to create a point cloud of the object. This point cloud can then be used to create 3D models of the subject or can be used to create digital surface models that can be used in conjunction with the point cloud.

There are many applications for laser scanning in different industries. It is used primarily in construction and civil engineering to document the progress of construction or survey sites as well as model buildings and other structures for visualisation purposes. It is also commonly used in the entertainment industry to create computer-generated images for use in movies, video games, commercials, and others. It can also be used in the medical field to model organs or other body parts to aid in the development and testing of new medical devices and pharmaceuticals. The possibilities are endless.

Figure 7. Image of a person in charge collecting the data of the case study using the Matterport MC250 Pro2 3D Mapping camera

Typically, laser scanners are mounted on tripods and have a number of lenses to focus the laser beam onto the object being scanned. Once the scan is complete, the point cloud is recorded and stored as a series of points in a three-dimensional coordinate system. The point cloud is then converted into a polygonal mesh by the computer using a process called triangulation. This creates a highly accurate 3D model of the subject that can be used for a variety of purposes.

3D photogrammetry is a safe and accurate method for capturing 3D data about the subject being scanned. However, there are a few things to be aware of before starting a scan. First, it is important to plan your laser scanning project carefully to avoid potential hazards. It is important to ensure that the instrument properly sets up the laser scanner and is within the recommended range before you begin scanning. Ones should also make sure you are wearing proper safety gear and follow all manufacturer instructions for safe operation. It is also important to check for obstructions such as nearby trees or buildings before you start scanning. Avoid scanning during rain or high winds since these conditions can cause unsafe conditions such as lightning strikes or flying debris which could damage your laser scanner or injure you. Ones should also be careful when operating your laser scanner around pets and children to avoid injury to them or your scanner. Finally, it is important to use only approved parts and accessories with your laser scanner. Using unauthorised parts or accessories could void your warranty and could pose a safety risk to you or others.

Once the laser scanner has been set up and is ready to begin scanning, be sure to keep the following in mind: Do not allow children, pets, or bystanders to enter the working area while you are scanning. It is important to keep appropriate distance at all times from the person being scanned to avoid eye injuries and other safety issues. To ensure safety and prevent damage to the device, always operate the laser scanner in a safe, enclosed environment. It is important to obtain knowledge and consent before scanning people or animals. Exercise caution when working with pointed objects like knives to prevent personal injury and damage to the laser scanner. Wear appropriate safety equipment to protect your eyes and skin while using the laser scanner. Lastly, adhere to the manufacturer's guidelines for safe operation and servicing to maintain the laser scanner in optimal working condition.

When operating the laser scanner in a hazardous environment such as chemical factories or laboratories, it is important to take the proper safety precautions to protect your safety and the safety of those around. Wear protective clothing and eyewear to reduce the risk of injury to you or the devices you are working with. The proper procedures must always be followed when performing maintenance and repairs on your laser scanner to avoid causing damage to it or injuring yourself in the process. These precautions will help protect your investment and prevent unnecessary repairs and downtime. Make sure to follow all of the safety procedures provided by the manufacturer for safe operation of your laser scanner. Follow all instructions listed on the user manual for using the laser scanner. Follow the safety guidelines provided with your laser scanner for proper care and maintenance of the unit. Be sure to clean and lubricate the moving parts on a regular basis to keep it functioning properly and avoid damage. Use the recommended replacement parts when performing repairs on the device. Never attempt to perform repairs or modifications to the device unless you are an expert and have the proper tools and equipment to perform the task safely. Ones should always follow the manufacturer's instructions for proper maintenance and operation of your laser scanner to ensure the safety of yourself and others around you. Failure to do so can result in damage to the device and/or injury to yourself or others in the vicinity.

Use protective eye gear when working with lasers - you can risk permanent eye damage. Wear long sleeved shirts, pants and gloves to prevent injury from hot parts of the laser scanner. Do not use the laser scanner in damp environments or while it is raining as humidity can cause malfunctions with the system. Always disconnect the laser scanner from the power source before performing any maintenance or repair procedures on the unit. The study of six case studies of the research has been further developed to a flow of work process in utilising the 3D laser scanning and 3D photogrammetry technologies into site and building assessment.

Figure 8 shows the work process framework of 3D Laser Scanning and 3D Photogrammetry. The sequence of the work process is as below.

1. Project Input

The project input consists of the objective of the project. The objective should reflect the type of outcome required for the project. To initiate a 3D laser scanning project, the first step is to identify the scope of the project and determine which areas or objects need to be scanned. Once the scope of the project is determined, it is important to establish a scanning plan that takes into account factors such as resolution and accuracy requirements.

Figure 8. Work process framework of 3D laser scanning and 3D photogrammetry

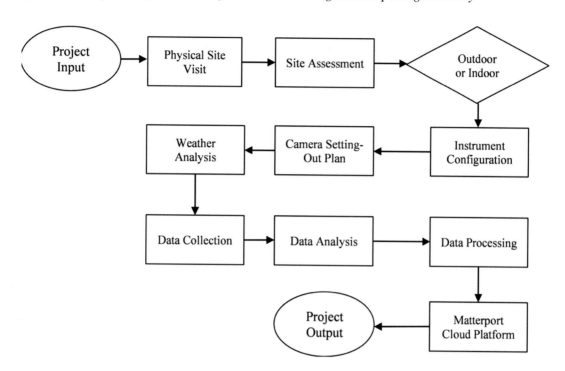

2.   Physical Site Visit

   The physical site visit is to be conducted in analysing the condition of the site and to further investigate the site.

3.   Site Assessment

   The site assessment is to conduct on the site assessment including the appropriateness on the amount of lights received and required. The process of setting up a 3D laser scanning requires a physical site visit. During this visit, the 3D laser scanning technician will assess various factors such as accessibility to areas that need to be scanned, lighting conditions, surface textures, and the presence of any objects that may cause interference with the scanning process.

4.   Outdoor or Indoor

   This stage is to determine between the outdoor or indoor data collection activities. 3D laser scanning is a popular technology that is used in various fields such as engineering, architecture, and construction. For effective 3D laser scanning, it is essential to have an appropriate space for the activity. The type of space required for 3D laser scanning depends on the project specifications and may involve either an indoor or outdoor setting. Indoor spaces are typically used for smaller-scale projects that do not require the scanner to be moved around a lot. On the other hand, outdoor spaces are suitable for large-scale projects that involve scanning of larger objects and environments.

5.   Instrument Configuration

Instrument configuration includes the determination of relevant instruments for the project. 3D laser scanning is a powerful technology that can capture highly detailed and accurate data of the physical world. To ensure optimal data quality and accuracy, it is essential to carefully plan the instrument configuration for 3D laser scanning. This includes factors such as selecting the appropriate laser scanner, determining the scan resolution and range, positioning of control points to ensure proper registration of scans, accounting for environmental factors such as lighting and obstructions, and considering the required level of data precision for the intended application.

6.   Camera Setting-Out Plan

In order to prepare the camera setting-out plan and ensure comprehensive data collection without any missing information, it is necessary to determine the specific location for positioning the camera on-site. To ensure no missing data during the data collection process. In the field of 3D laser scanning, camera settings play a critical role in capturing accurate and precise data. The correct camera settings are dependent on several factors such as the distance to the target, ambient lighting, and desired resolution. A proper setting of the camera in 3D laser scanning is crucial to achieve high-quality, accurate data that can be used for a wide range of applications, including asset inspection, 3D modelling, and construction management.

7.   Weather Analysis

To ensure an appropriate date and day for the data collection process, it is important to determine the suitable timing that aligns with the requirements of the process. This ensures that the data collection day is well-suited for the task at hand. Weather analysis is an important consideration when implementing 3D laser scanning as it can affect the accuracy of the data collected. Factors such as humidity, temperature fluctuations, and precipitation can impact the distance travelled by laser beams, which in turn affects the precision of 3D scans.

8.   Data collection

The data collection process is crucial for 3D laser scanning as it enables the creation of accurate and detailed digital models of physical objects and environments. Before beginning the collection process, it is important to ensure that the scanner being used is appropriate for the desired level of detail and resolution. Once the appropriate scanner has been selected, the first step in the data collection process is to position it at a fixed location and orientation relative to the object or environment being scanned.

9.   Data Analysis

The captured data must be analysed to ensure that a sufficient amount has been collected to cover the entire area. Efficient and accurate data analysis techniques are necessary to process the vast amounts of data obtained through 3D laser scanning. Data analysis for 3D laser scanning involves several steps, including point cloud registration, segmentation, feature extraction, and data filtering. As part of the data analysis process, software tools such as Autodesk ReCap and CloudCompare are typically used to handle large datasets, while also providing advanced visualisation and analysis features.

10.   Data Processing

The data collected through 3D laser scanning needs to be processed in order to eliminate noise and errors, align the scans, and generate a unified point cloud or mesh. This processed data can then be utilized for a wide range of applications. The process of data processing for 3D laser scanning involves a series of steps, including registration, filtering, segmentation, and modelling.

11.   Matterport Cloud Platform

The data will be projected into the Matterport cloud platform. Matterport Cloud allows for centralised storage and management of high-resolution 3D scans, enabling easy access to data across multiple devices and locations. Moreover, Matterport Cloud utilises cutting-edge technology to create immersive virtual walkthroughs that allow users to engage with the scanned environments in a fully interactive and intuitive way, providing an unparalleled level of detail and accuracy. This technology has significantly optimised and streamlined the process of 3D scanning, providing an efficient and cost-effective solution for professionals seeking to capture detailed spatial data in various industries.

12.   Project Output

The end of the project.

CONCLUSION

The method of 3D laser scanning and 3D photogrammetry are advanced in site and building documentation approaches. The study has proven that the methods further complement the present documentation and are able to enhance the built environment industry for a betterment. The site and building assessment are conducted for various reasons and objectives, these technologies offered the alternative method in performing the documentation purposes. When designing a building site for a construction project, consultants have to take into account several factors, such as terrain conditions, existing structures on site, land use and other factors. These factors can affect the time and cost required to construct the building and may even prevent it from being built at all if it is determined to be unsafe. This is where 3D laser scanning and 3D photogrammetry come in. By using these 3D technologies, consultants can accurately assess a site and identify potential hazards and problems before construction begins. By knowing what obstacles are encountered before starting a project, consultants can plan and prepare the site in a way that will prevent these problems from occurring, which will save time and money in the long run. Below we will discuss the benefits of using 3D laser scanning and 3D photogrammetry in assessing a site and building as well as some of the drawbacks associated with these technologies.

There are several benefits of adopting 3D laser scanning and 3D photogrammetry for assessing a site and building. First, these technologies are extremely accurate and can identify potential problems and hazards in a building site that may not be visible to the human eye. This allows consultants to make informed decisions based on accurate data and make the necessary adjustments prior to beginning construction. By implementing these measures, project costs can be reduced, and the risk of project delays caused by unforeseen obstacles and issues can be mitigated. In addition, 3D laser scanning and 3D photogrammetry allow engineers to accurately record and assess the entire site in great detail. This results in more comprehensive data that can be used by architects and designers when designing the building and can help architects to create more efficient floor plans and reduce material waste during construction. Finally, these technologies can be used to record architectural heritage sites and preserve important historical landmarks for future generations. Once recorded, these digital models can be easily shared and stored online and can be easily accessed from anywhere in the world.

Despite their many advantages, 3D laser scanning and 3D photogrammetry have certain limitations that must be considered when planning to use these technologies for a project. One of the main limitations of these technologies is that they are not capable of detecting fine details such as cracks or imperfections in building materials, which may prevent engineers and architects from identifying these issues during the design phase of the project. These details often go unnoticed to the naked eye but can cause serious problems during a construction project if they are not addressed before the work begins. Another issue with these technologies is that they cannot be used to produce reliable measurements when the environment is too noisy. For example, if there is too much interference from the nearby construction site, the data produced by 3D laser scanning and 3D photogrammetry may be inaccurate or incomplete. For this reason, it is important to ensure that the area is free from noise and that workers are focused on their work and not chatting or socialising during data collection sessions. Despite these limitations, 3D laser scanning and 3D photogrammetry are invaluable tools for the construction industry and can be used to improve the efficiency of the design process and help to ensure the success of construction projects.

As more buildings are being designed with sustainability in mind, the need for technologies that can help reduce waste, cut costs, and increase energy efficiency is more important than ever. 3D laser scanning and 3D photogrammetry can be used to make high-quality, detailed models of buildings that can be used to design more efficient floor plans and optimise material usage during construction. These models can then be used by architects and engineers to perform pre-construction analysis and to predict potential problems that could arise during a building project. This information can be used to ensure that major construction activities are carried out in a safe manner to prevent injuries and accidents and minimise the risk of delays and other setbacks that may disrupt the construction process. This can help to improve the overall efficiency of a construction project and reduce the cost and environmental impact of materials used during the process. Construction projects are extremely complex and require careful planning and attention to detail in order to ensure that they are completed on time with minimal disruption to the surrounding environment. Managing such large-scale projects can be challenging and time-consuming and requires extensive experience and skill in order to minimise the potential risks and avoid common errors that can delay or even derail a project.

ACKNOWLEDGMENT

I would like to express my heartfelt gratitude to Ar Azizul Azwar Abd Aziz for his invaluable contribution to this study.

REFERENCES

Alvanchi, A., & Seyrfar, A. (2020). Improving facility management of public hospitals in Iran using building information modeling. *Scientia Iranica*, *27*(6), 2817–2829.

Badenko, V., Fedotov, A., & Zotov, D. (2018). Extracting features from laser scanning point cloud. SHS Web of Conferences, Baiker-Sørensen, M., Herlaar, K., Keereweer, I., Pauw-Vugts, P., & Visser, R. (2020). Interpol review of shoe and tool marks 2016-2019. *Forensic Science International. Synergy*, *2*, 521–539.

Cabrelles, M., Galcerá, S., Navarro, S., Lerma, J. L., Akasheh, T., & Haddad, N. (2009). Integration of 3D laser scanning, photogrammetry and thermography to record architectural monuments. Proc. of the 22nd International CIPA Symposium, .

Cheng, X., & Jin, W. (2006). Study on reverse engineering of historical architecture based on 3D laser scanner. *Journal of Physics: Conference Series*.

Cheshmehzangi, A. (2021). Revisiting the built environment: 10 potential development changes and paradigm shifts due to COVID-19. *Journal of Urban Management*, *10*(2), 166–175.

Choi, S.-H., Koh, K., Lee, K.-J., Hwang, C.-J., & Cha, J.-Y. (2018). Analysis of the morphological characteristics of the palatal rugae for three-dimensional superimposition of digital models in Korean subjects. *BioMed Research International*, *2018*, 2018. doi:10.1155/2018/3936918 PMID:30598994

Deli, R., Galantucci, L. M., Laino, A., D'Alessio, R., Di Gioia, E., Savastano, C., Lavecchia, F., & Percoco, G. (2013). Three-dimensional methodology for photogrammetric acquisition of the soft tissues of the face: A new clinical-instrumental protocol. *Progress in Orthodontics*, *14*(1), 1–15. doi:10.1186/2196-1042-14-32 PMID:24325783

Gharechelou, S., Tateishi, R., & Johnson, A. (1711). B. (2018). A simple method for the parameterization of surface roughness from microwave remote sensing. *Remote Sensing*, *10*(11). Advance online publication. doi:10.3390/rs10111711

Hua, W., Qiao, Y., & Hou, M. (2020). The great wall 3d documentation and application based on multi-source data fusion–a case study of no. 15 enemy tower of the new guangwu great wall. *The International Archives of the Photogrammetry, Remote Sensing and Spatial Information Sciences*, *43*, 1465–1470. doi:10.5194/isprs-archives-XLIII-B2-2020-1465-2020

Huber, D., Akinci, B., Tang, P., Adan, A., Okorn, B., & Xiong, X. (2010). Using laser scanners for modeling and analysis in architecture, engineering, and construction. 2010 44th Annual Conference on Information Sciences and Systems (CISS). ISS.

Kazaz, B., Poddar, S., Arabi, S., Perez, M. A., Sharma, A., & Whitman, J. B. (2021). Deep Learning-Based Object Detection for Unmanned Aerial Systems (UASs)-Based Inspections of Construction Stormwater Practices. *Sensors (Basel)*, *21*(8), 2834.

Kedzierski, M., Wierzbicki, D., Fryskowska, A., & Chlebowska, B. (2016). Analysis Of The Possibilities Of Using Low-Cost Scanning System In 3d Modeling. *The International Archives of the Photogrammetry, Remote Sensing and Spatial Information Sciences*, *41*.

Khalil, A., & Stravoravdis, S. (2019). H-BIM and the domains of data investigations of heritage buildings current state of the art. 2nd International Conference of Geomatics and Restoration (GEORES 2019), .

Kim, D.-H., & Gratchev, I. (2021). Application of optical flow technique and photogrammetry for rockfall dynamics: A case study on a field test. *Remote Sensing, 13*(20), 4124.

Lerma, J. L., Navarro, S., Cabrelles, M., Seguí, A. E., Haddad, N., & Akasheh, T. (2011). Integration of laser scanning and imagery for photorealistic 3D architectural documentation. *Laser scanning, theory and applications*, 414-430.

Napolitano, R., Blyth, A., & Glisic, B. (2018). Virtual environments for visualizing structural health monitoring sensor networks, data, and metadata. *Sensors (Basel), 18*(1), 243. doi:10.339018010243 PMID:29337877

Ntiyakunze, J., & Inoue, T. (2023). Segmentation of Structural Elements from 3D Point Cloud Using Spatial Dependencies for Sustainability Studies. *Sensors (Basel), 23*(4), 1924. doi:10.339023041924 PMID:36850520

Ogunnusi, M., Hamma-Adama, M., Salman, H., & Kouider, T. (2020). COVID-19 pandemic: the effects and prospects in the construction industry. *International journal of real estate studies, 14*(Special Issue 2).

Pejić, P., Krasić, S., Krstić, H., Dragović, M., & Akbiyik, Y. (2017). 3D virtual modelling of existing objects by terrestrial photogrammetric methods-Case study of Barutana. *Tehnicki Vjesnik (Strojarski Fakultet), 24*(Supplement 1), 233–239.

Qureshi, A. H., Alaloul, W., Murtiyoso, A., Hussain, S., Saad, S., & Oad, V. K. (2022). Evaluation of 3D model of rebar for quantitative parameters. *The International Archives of the Photogrammetry, Remote Sensing and Spatial Information Sciences, 48*, 215–220. doi:10.5194/isprs-archives-XLVIII-2-W1-2022-215-2022

Razali, M., Idris, A., Razali, M., & Syafuan, W. (2022). Quality Assessment of 3D Point Clouds on the Different Surface Materials Generated from iPhone LiDAR Sensor. *International Journal of Geoinformatics, 18*(4), 51–59.

Sa'ed, H. Z., Koni, A., Al-Jabi, S. W., Amer, R., Shakhshir, M., Al Subu, R., Salameh, H., Odeh, R., Musleh, S., & Abushamma, F. (2022). Current global research landscape on COVID-19 and cancer: Bibliometric and visualization analysis. *World Journal of Clinical Oncology, 13*(10), 835–847. doi:10.5306/wjco.v13.i10.835 PMID:36337308

Sun, H., Xu, Z., Yao, L., Zhong, R., Du, L., & Wu, H. (2020). Tunnel monitoring and measuring system using mobile laser scanning: Design and deployment. *Remote Sensing (Basel), 12*(4), 730. doi:10.3390/rs12040730

Takewaki, I. (2020). New architectural viewpoint for enhancing society's resilience for multiple risks including emerging COVID-19. *Frontiers in Built Environment, 6*, 143. doi:10.3389/fbuil.2020.00143

Ton, B., Ahmed, F., & Linssen, J. (2022). Semantic Segmentation of Terrestrial Laser Scans of Railway Catenary Arches: A Use Case Perspective. *Sensors (Basel), 23*(1), 222. doi:10.339023010222 PMID:36616820

Truong, P., Hölttä-Otto, K., Becerril, P., Turtiainen, R., & Siltanen, S. (2021). Multi-user virtual reality for remote collaboration in construction projects.

Vasilakos, C., Chatzistamatis, S., Roussou, O., & Soulakellis, N. (2018). Terrestrial photogrammetry vs laser scanning for rapid earthquake damage assessment. *The International Archives of the Photogrammetry, Remote Sensing and Spatial Information Sciences, 42*(W4), 527–533. doi:10.5194/isprs-archives-XLII-3-W4-527-2018

Vasiljević, I., Obradović, R., Đurić, I., Popkonstantinović, B., Budak, I., Kulić, L., & Milojević, Z. (2021). Copyright protection of 3D digitized artistic sculptures by adding unique local inconspicuous errors by sculptors. *Applied Sciences (Basel, Switzerland), 11*(16), 7481. doi:10.3390/app11167481

Yang, J., Wang, X., Wu, C., & Bai, C. (2019). Regularized reconstruction of grid system for traditional chinese timber structure building in HBIM. *The International Archives of the Photogrammetry, Remote Sensing and Spatial Information Sciences, 42*(W15), 1229–1233. doi:10.5194/isprs-archives-XLII-2-W15-1229-2019

Zang, Y., Yang, B., Liang, F., & Xiao, X. (2018). Novel adaptive laser scanning method for point clouds of free-form objects. *Sensors (Basel), 18*(7), 2239. doi:10.339018072239 PMID:29997374

Zhang, C., & Chen, B. (2019). Enhancing Learning and Teaching for Architectural Engineering Students Using Virtual Building Design and Construction. *Higher Education Studies, 9*(2), 45–56. doi:10.5539/hes.v9n2p45

Chapter 4

Explorative Analyses and Discussions to Compose Design Principles of Building and Spaces:
Facts of the Universe and Possibilities of Metaverse

Ekrem Bahadır Çalışkan

ⓘ https://orcid.org/0000-0002-5258-2976

Ankara Yıldırım Beyazıt University, Turkey

ABSTRACT

The term metaverse was first used in the novel 'Snow Crash.' However, it has come into people's lives with the development of 3D design and visual techniques, machine computations, blockchain, and the internet. Companies and communities worldwide are launching their metaverse platform with diverse functions like trading, gaming, and socialization. The virtual spaces are designed, and virtual buildings or reconstructions of existing ones can be seen. The facts and laws of the universe that people live in directly affect their understanding, so developers generally tend to implement these into their virtual environments. However, the factors which shape and govern the real world are not valid in virtual environments. Thus, there are diverse possibilities in the metaverse. This chapter presents the metaverse and its platforms with definitions, usage, interfaces, and problems. It explores the facts of the universe and discusses gaps and lack of designing spaces and buildings in virtual environments by thinking about the possibilities in the metaverse.

DOI: 10.4018/978-1-6684-8253-7.ch004

INTRODUCTION

3D modeling of buildings has been made for 50 years in the virtual environment to enrich the sights of objects before construction in the real world. Spaces, buildings, and some urban areas are geometrically constructed in the virtual world and used for different purposes. By exploring the relation, structural or electromechanical calculations are made, and it is tried to analyze the objects and relations. Furthermore, project stakeholders use diverse 3d rendering technology and methodology to reflect and evaluate the spaces and buildings. With the improvement in technology, especially in Building Information Modelling, semantic knowledge is related to geometrical objects of the 3D model, which makes advanced-level simulation or analysis possible (Li, Wu, Shen, Wang, & Teng, 2017). It is not only technology change but process change by enabling a virtual building represented by intelligent objects that carry detailed information; it alters all of the key processes involved in putting together (Eastman, Teicholz, Sacks, & Liston, 2008). Scheduling, cost calculations, energy analyses, light and life cycle simulations, and experiences with virtual or augmented reality are some possibilities that designers and industry consider. With initial and essential fact, the spaces or buildings developed and created in the virtual environment are somehow copies or twins of designed objects for the real world. These digital twins can monitor, simulate, predict, or optimize (Tao, Xiao, Qi, Cheng, & Ji, 2022). In other explanations, these buildings are tried to be designed for the real world actually or experimentally due to the primary laws and principles of Earth. For example, gravity, the reaction of forces, the scale of human or living beings, physical needs of living beings, and perception in the real world. In this manner, the copies or twins in the virtual environment naturally have features or behaviors parallel to the real world. In addition, all the calculations, semantical relations, and algorithms are to create the same or similar situations in the human world.

In the last decades, improvements and investments in creating virtual environments have dramatically increased. Various companies try to create their virtual universe /metaverse /multiverse and explore and develop the methods and principles to implement real-world experiences. In parallel with massive growth in the internet from the 1990s until now, various innovative technologies have been created to bring users breathtaking experiences with more virtual interactions (Huynh-The et al., 2022). Exchange of lands, formation of public spaces, collaboration environments, and construction of virtual offices started. This virtual environment is to be called Metaverse, which was first used in the novel 'Snow Crash' by Stephenson in 1992. To be related to the real world, digital copies of existing buildings and public areas were transferred into the virtual environment, and some examples of newly designed spaces and buildings took part. The industry and researchers have essential activities to develop principles for ownership and existence of these artifacts by some technologies, for example, NFT (non-fungible token).

Significant designers designed NFT houses, offices, and villas; there are commercially sold examples. However, by looking into these examples, chairs standing on the floor, roofs supported by vertical structural elements, floors, facades for boundaries, or vertical circulation elements could be seen. This situation brings essential questions: Does a chair need a floor to stand on, or does a person need to sit? How can a roof be carried without any vertical circulation structural elements, or should a roof be carried? Are there any necessities to create floors and façades, or how are the spaces created? Should the building need a vertical circulation or any circulation? These result from the reflections of spaces and buildings from the real world. The facts, scale, and universal principles are invalid in the virtual environment. So, the possibilities for creating objects, spaces, and buildings are limitless. Suppose there is no conceptual, functional, or scientific ground for design activities; how design rationale or principles can be formed? It is an upcoming problem to be worked on for years, and the community and principles that will develop the context will be explored. This study aims to open and bring the situation in front by explorative analyses and discussions exploring the facts. The facts and design principles of the natural world: gravity forces in a structural manner, the scale of living beings in space generation, boundaries for circulation and distinction of spaces, and physical needs for functional sights. Human beings have captured the knowledge of these facts for thousands of years and direct all the activities like space and building design. The formation of the multiverse is limitless, but the perception of people is the same. Discussing these real-world principles through their primary causes and effects may enlighten the era to compose design principles for virtual environments.

In this research, firstly, the Metaverse is explored with its definition, usage, problems, interface, and issues related to digital twins and virtual reality. Then, the present metaverse platforms investigated from literature and web survey are conducted. Some contemporary examples of designing spaces in the Metaverse are given. The last part of the chapter presents the facts and principles of designing spaces and buildings in the real world. The author discusses weather-related rationales, sensation, perception, transportation and circulation, boundaries of spaces, functional needs, and force-related principles that affect real-world buildings' design to evaluate their existence and interpretation in the Metaverse. The studies about the 3D environment and their relation and contribution to the AEC industry are convenient and conducted in the community; however, space and building design in metaverse platforms have not been handled enough yet. The reasons could be stated as; not enough contribution from the AEC industry and being developed by programming experts. This research tends to open discussion of areas related to building and space design to be further evaluated by conducting available limited literature and web survey.

BACKGROUND: METAVERSE

The term metaverse was first used in the novel 'Snow Crash' by Stephenson Neal in 1992 (Ball, 2022; Chandra & Leenders, 2012; Clemens, 2022; Dwivedi et al., 2022; Huynh-The et al., 2022; Lv, Qiao, Li, Yuan, & Wang, 2022; Zallio & John Clarkson, 2022; Zhao et al., 2022). Last 30 years, Metaverses have transformed from chats and messages to vivid networks and virtual worlds affecting nations and economies (Ball, 2022). It has many opportunities and possibilities for communities, services, and industries. On the other hand, it needs a scientific ground and agreed on standards to develop and spread worldwide. There is no consensus on the definition and progress of Metaverse by developers and academicians yet. As an example, Roblox ('Roblox', 2023) is a game platform without developed 3D virtual scenes. However, it is stated as one of the important metaverse platforms with interaction and usage rank of users ('10 Best Metaverse Platforms That You Can Try In 2022 - 101 Blockchains', 2022; '12 Best Metaverse Platforms to Play & Invest in November 2022', 2022; '14 Metaverse Platforms You Can Already Enter in 2022', 2022; Jatinder Palaha, 2022). In addition, Roblox as a virtual world provides a more realistic depiction of what the Metaverse appears like, though it is not the Metaverse itself (Clemens, 2022). Minecraft ('Minecraft', 2022) is another virtual world that children like in which they can design their avatars and construct anything they like (Clemens, 2022). Second Life ('Second Life', 2023) is one of the initial platforms in that users can build artifacts, gain clothes, and weapons, offer meeting and conference services, develop buildings, and own all the intellectual property rights to their virtual properties (Chandra & Leenders, 2012). The platform, published in 2003, has millions of residents and their own currency called linden dollar. While thinking there are so many advertorial media for the platforms that have not been published yet, it is a significant situation for using Second Life Platform for 19 years. The virtual games, sports games, estates, and individual or semi-centralized environments exist for many metaverse platforms; however, the things and the facts that direct these platforms are important.

What Is the Metaverse?

The Metaverse is a virtual world that combines the physical and digital worlds, which is still in the early stage of development (Clemens, 2022). Apart from being only a 3D representation or digital twin of the objects or scenes of the real world, the Metaverse offers an inclusive virtual world where users can interact, live and have rights to things. There is no common consensus about the definition and specification of the Metaverse, though the researchers are trying to develop and explore the issue. For an important definition, the Metaverse is 'A massively scaled and interoperable network of real-time renders 3D virtual worlds that can be experienced synchronously and persistently by an effectively unlimited number of users with an individual sense of presence, and with continuity of data, such as identity, history, entitlement, objects, communications, and payments' (Ball, 2022). Ball (2022) explores in his book the definition, necessities, relations, and effects of a metaverse in precise detail.

Zhao (2022) shows the visual construction and exploration of the Metaverse in Figure 1. The scene is the virtual environment that non-player characters (NPC) and users' avatars experience. Avatar is the virtual identity of players, which users can create and customize within the context of the metaverse platform. Diverse 3d graphics techniques, software, and engines are used for the three objects and scenes of the Metaverse. With visualization and interaction techniques, users' interaction and awareness tried to be assured in the real-world context. The environment in the Metaverse, including objects and scenes, the interface for users like head-mounted displays or motion input devices, interaction scenarios and cases, and security/privacy, are essential components of metaverse experiences.

Figure 1. Metaverse: visual construction and exploration
Source: Zhao et al., 2022

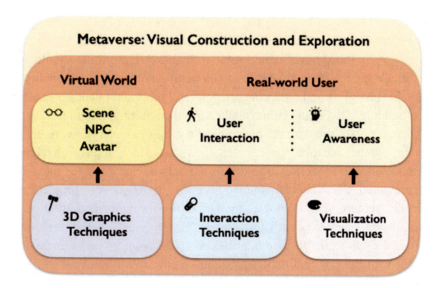

The metaverse applications can be classified in two: Metaverse as a tool to solve difficulties and problems in the real world and Metaverse as a stand-alone target and highly dependent on the virtual environment (Figure 2). Shows the applications of the Metaverse as a tool and as a target. Whether the platform serves as a tool to increase communication and collaboration in the office or make it possible for social meetings, or be a target platform for the game, business, or real estate, the users' expectations are getting more significant in terms of perceptual experience, interaction and discovering new possibilities than the real world.

Figure 2. Applications of the metaverse as a tool and as a target
Source: Dwivedi et al., 2022

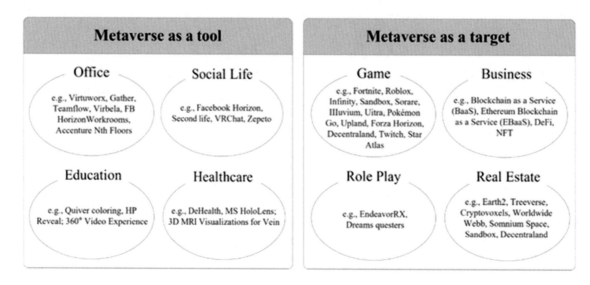

Digital Twin, 3D, and Virtual Reality

Metaverse's existence comes from being in the virtual environment of human beings and interacting with the virtually built context in textual, 2D, and 3D platforms. Although in different dimensions, 3D is a critical specification for the Metaverse platforms (Ball, 2022). Everything should not need to be 3D in the Metaverse, but for the real-world experience and putting it instead of the quality and integrity of 3D is so important. 3D modeling and rendering are powerful tools and talent for industry practitioners to prepare objects, buildings, and living beings in the virtual environment to represent and simulate the facts due to the given context. The manufacturing industry, AEC industry, commercial business, film and animation sector, health, education services, and other industries and research communities use and benefit from 3D modeling and rendering. The details are defined and arranged due to necessities, and integration and representative relations are assured according to business or project core objectives. A digital twin is one of the emerging technologies for digital transformation and intelligent upgrades used for monitoring, simulation, prediction, and optimization (Tao et al., 2022). The virtual model represents not only the object of the real world but also inquiries about the relations and semantic data. It has two-way communication with the physical entity, providing feedback for analysis, optimization, control, and data analysis (Wang, Kang, & Chen, 2022). For example, for the simulation and evaluation of the cities in a smart way, it is used to monitor, analyze and control city infrastructure, transportation, or energy consumption. (Huang, Zhang, & Zeng, 2022). The virtual entity and physical entity connect in two directions: physical to virtual and virtual to physical (Bönsch, Elstermann, Kimmig, & Ovtcharova, 2022). By these, the simultaneous and iterative information transfer is assured to evaluate and experience the entity in the virtual world considering the entity in the real world. However, for the metaverse platforms, the situation is far from these connections regarding human perception and representation. The objects, scenes, and buildings are not designed and modeled mostly to represent physical entities from the real world. The creators and developers tend to design the virtual entities as like entities from the real world to better users (humans) of platform perception. By the lifetime of any human, there is a level of perception and knowledge to conceive the world. So, with the implementation of equipment that increases the level of perception, there is a seeking of the world that people become familiar with.

Virtual reality is a revolutionary technique that can transform human activities and works and perhaps fall in the love future (Clemens, 2022). In principle, virtual reality can immerse the user in a completely simulated world where details can be integrated into arousing particular emotions (Dozio et al., 2022). Augmented reality is another concept that makes users perceive the real world by implementing the virtual world created by the platform. The equipment for augmented reality is developing continuously to remove the borders of real and virtual worlds. According to many contributors to the era, augmented reality will be a core ability and trigger activity for the Metaverse if the equipment as an interface develops to process properly with the connection of the real and virtual world.

Equipment and Interface

The metaverse interface allows the user to interact with virtual environments. The equipment's features used as an interface between the user and Metaverse directly affect the interaction and two-way connections. Some platforms are established to use only computer screens for the interface, and some need to be developed virtual glass to get into the platforms. Primarily VR headsets are used for the metaverse platform (Ball, 2022). Thus, the metaverse companies invest in developing hardware technologies parallel to the software and platform establishments. Motion controllers, lighthouse, tracker, omnidirectional treadmill, haptic glove, and suits are some of the critical equipment that makes humans possibly perceive the virtual world by senses. Figure 3 illustrates this hardware in exact order.

Figure 3. VR equipment
Source: Dincelli & Yayla, 2022

Beyond the 3D glasses and equipment mentioned above, there is significant technology research to link the human and virtual worlds with sensors that can initiate neural activities (Ball, 2022). Through these sensors and neural links, human beings can feel all physical senses as an ultimate called, like in the film 'Matrix', which was in the theatres in 1999. To carry the real-life dimensions into the Metaverse could be only possible by using present technologies now; however, in 10 or 20 years, the dramatic changes may be by simultaneous inventions connecting humans to virtual worlds. Briefly, the metaverse platforms could be used from simple screens like tablets, computers, or big-size Led screens to VR headsets or motion input devices.

Usage and Potential

The purpose of the virtual world can be classified into game-like, to win or score, and non-game, which is for educational, commercial, socializing, or other purposes (Ball, 2022). The game can also be an educational or commercial business, implementing these objectives in virtual environments. The potential of a metaverse platform is generally from the ability to do impossible or hard things in the real world. Time, budget, physical limits, and distance between participants make initiating many activities in the real world very difficult. Thus, metaverse platforms and the virtual world become an alternative or new way and medium to do these services. Education, lifestyle business, entertainment, fashion, and advertisement industry use the platforms (Ball, 2022). Military education and simulations, shopping, healthcare, tourism, use as a workplace, and reviving history are important parts of the metaverse future (Clemens, 2022). Metaverse platforms are also used for real estate, business, role play, digital marketing, and social Life (Dwivedi et al., 2022). Communication, simulations, and evaluation of environments generating interaction of people could also be stated as important metaverse potential. The abilities to remove boundaries, work neglecting distances, live without a true identity, and operate beyond the limitless physical entities can expand the activities and potential of metaverse platforms.

ISSUES AND PROBLEMS

The metaverse development is still in the early stage, and there are gaps in the framework for the visual construction and exploration of the Metaverse (Clemens, 2022). The lack comes from the interaction of users, visual representation techniques, and the absence of common standards and principles. Every company design and publish its virtual environments due to their acceptance and technology. A common ground could not be established. An accepted common issue is using blockchain technology to manage ownership and trade. Since all Metaverse produces values like land, buildings, artifacts, and digital assets, the preservation and protection of ownership are vital. A non-fungible token is one alternative for this issue, but some platforms were constructed on present cryptos. The relation of ownership with the governments' legislations and laws should be discussed and established.

The differences in interfaces are another problem since the interaction and perception change according to information and knowledge transfer capability from the virtual world to the user and vice versa. Sustainability is another issue that should be taken into consideration. To maintain sustainability, the metaverse environment must operate with many users (Dwivedi et al., 2022). Sustainability could be related in two perspectives: use of sources and user participation. The system uses a wide range of bandwidth, electrical energy, and processors. The computer processes (central or local) need to be arranged into low consumption of sources by development in frameworks. The other issue has related to the contribution and participation of real users in platforms. Continuity of enrollments and online time could be assured by not only entertainment. Social interaction benefits from real-life services or activities, and awareness of people should be established.

There are lots of services and activities held on metaverse platforms. What are the generic rules for arranging, serving, or buying them? Every Metaverse creates its own rules for users. However, the activity rules demand a generic approach for all Metaverse due to service typology. It is crystal clear that metaverse platforms are designed, created, and launched day by day. With the development of platforms, the increase in the number of users, and the value of currencies, public authorities and communities will take responsibility for writing the rules and governing the system. However, at the moment, there exist so many issues and problems that should be taken into consideration, and only some of them are underlined in this research, the academicians and developers will have valuable attempts and scientific works for exploring and generating more secure and valid metaverse frameworks.

METAVERSE PLATFORMS

Various companies and communities have developed metaverse platforms for different objectives like gaming, education, real estate, experience in virtual Life, *etc*. Figure 4 shows the metaverse platform's development with significant events. The birth of the internet in 1991, the first usage of the metaverse term in 1992, and the start of the second life platform in 2003 can be stated as important events near the millennium. Roblox was released in 2006 after Bitcoin and blockchain technology were initiated, which were the ancestor of a non-fungible token. NFT technology, which is very new in blockchain technology, guarantees the ownership of virtual assets (Clemens, 2022). Platforms develop and use their NFT or make connections to present cryptocurrency to rule and manage virtual ownership and trade in the Metaverse. This is also an important issue for commercial business, so many platforms could be found that serve as a trade or commercial arena as a core objective.

Figure 4. Metaverse development involving primary events from 1991 to 2001
Source: Huynh-The et al., 2022

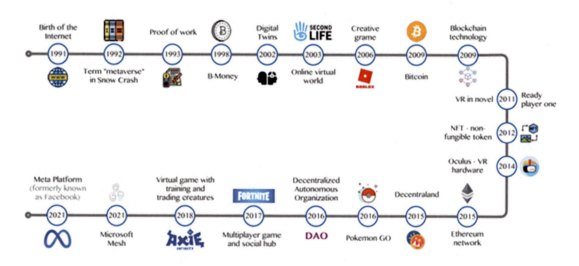

In 2014, the widely used VR headset Oculus was in the market, and many metaverse platforms like Decentraland, Fortnite, Microsoft Mesh, and Meta Platform can be seen. The platforms that could be counted as a part metaverse definition are explored briefly without any classification in terms of the game, real estate or any usage, inclusivity, and being platform itself or the developer platform in the following subheadings. This section presents the metaverse platform and developer services with a brief background, whether they are game, real estate, or other purposes in alphabetical order. Thee These are found in the literature, the internet, and advertorial documents. This survey is conducted for (1) Seeking the possibility of creating virtual elements or buildings by users, (2) Presenting an extensive list to have experience, and (3) Figuring out the market response to the area.

Axie Infinity ('Axie Infinity', 2023)

In Axie Infinity, users can play, partially own, and operate with earning and spending AXS tokens. In the battles, the character called axies take the role, and they have various features. With these, there are billions of genetic combinations for playing in which users can build, battle, and hunt for treasure. It is a play to earn platforms, and the axis could be traded in the marketplace.

Battle Infinity ('Battle Infinity (IBAT)', 2023)

Battle infinity is a gaming platform for battle games to play and earn. All the games in the platform are integrated within a metaverse called IBAT battle arena. In the platform, the token is called IBAT. The platform aims for users to enjoy and experience the immersive metaverse world while playing. Users' activities in the platform for wallet, market, store, and gaming are connected to a cloud server.

Bloktopia ('Bloktopia', 2023)

The team of this platform aims to provide an unprecedented VR experience for the crypto community by bringing users into one immersive environment. The platform allows real estate ownership, advertising revenue, playing games, and building networks using non-fungible tokens. The platform's token is Blok, which can be exchanged with others. The platform has its real-time 3D-creating engine.

Decentraland ('Decentraland', 2023)

Decentraland is one of the early released metaverse platforms that bring users into one environment and offer virtual lands. The land parcels are purchased with NFT, and owners can shape their environment, construct buildings, and create games on the platform. It is a digital ecosystem where users can socialize, trade goods, and attend events like real Life.

Everdome ('Everdome', 2023)

Everdome creates a hyper-realistic metaverse in which people and brands can come together. It offers an opportunity for those who want a version of the Metaverse familiar with real Life. Land ownership, marketplace development in the Metaverse, advertising, and event activations are part of the everdome Metaverse.

Ertha ('Ertha', 2023)

Ertha is a gaming platform where users can buy land and get revenue. Their platform advertorial doctrine is that a natural disaster struck the world, and humankind is on the verge of extinction. The lands are precious, and NFT purchases them. The lands could be sold or rented, the ecosystem could be generated in this land, and the community could be ruled.

Hyper Nation ('HyperNation', 2023)

It is a decentralized ecosystem with democracy and an equitable economy. Their manifesto asked that the real world be a fair place. Users become citizens of an ideal country, living with spread consensus and an equitable economy. Hyper Nation Token is used in the universe as a currency. There is a utopic world that is created for the users.

Illuvium ('Illuvium', 2023)

It is a platform for interoperable blockchain games using the Ethereum blockchain. The lands and characters (illuvitars and illuvials) could be traded in the market. The primary goal of the project is to create a fully decentralized game. There are battle arenas, mining and harvesting places, and exchange arenas.

Metahero ('Metahero', 2023)

The important difference in this platform from other metaverse platforms is to be built on a blockchain. Another critical feature of the platform is to create metahero by enabling 3D scanning and modeling specialist. So, players can use avatars created in the origin of their selves in the real world. The company tries to combine virtual and real worlds with exploring new experiences and opportunities.

Meta Horizon Worlds ('Horizon Worlds', 2023)

Horizon worlds are expanding the Metaverse in that users participate with computer and VR Headsets. This social universe offers a meeting with friends and new people, playing games, attend events. There are over 10.000 worlds and experiences to explore. Users can build scenes and worlds, design avatars, and arrange meetings and events.

Microsoft Mesh ('Microsoft Mesh', 2023)

It is an expanding metaverse platform that users connect by engaging with eye contact, facial experiences, and gestures. The users can connect to the platform by computers, HoloLens, VR Headsets, mobile devices, and computers. It is possible to collaborate virtually, train, and design in 3D.

Mines of Dalarnia ('Mines of Dalarnia', 2023)

It is an action-adventure game where players can mine, interact and combine their forces. The year is 11752, in which the game takes part in. The mined minerals are used to upgrade character and skills. The blockchain is used to play and earn. Lands could be owned, and taxes could be collected. The marketplace trades items, lands, mines, and equipment.

Monaverse ('Mona', 2023)

It is a platform where people build spaces, collect and show their art to other users. Creators and developers can build multiplayer experiences and 3D content using the platform. Mona is a fully multiplayer experience supporting thousands of users with features including hyperlinking, voice chat, text chat, fully customizable avatars, and token-gated functionality.

My Neighbor Alice ('My Neighbor Alice', 2023)

At first glance, the platform is like a Farmville, where users can farm, buy, own, and sell virtual islands. It is a blockchain-based multiplayer game where users can build items and meet other users. The games are designed to allow players to own the game by exercising power over the platform.

Nakamoto Games ('Nakamoto Games', 2023)

Nakamoto Games is a platform where users can use many games, and Nakaverse is the Metaverse. They have their currency called NAKA. Users can rich different games and play to earn. Also, in the Nakaverse, land could be bought or traded. The marketplace allows the trading of land, mine, and other elements.

Omiverse (NVIDIA, 2023)

Omniverse is not a Metaverse platform but a platform for creating and operating applications for the Metaverse in a collaborative environment. The platform helps developers and artists build custom 3D pipelines and simulate large-scale virtual worlds.

Polkacity ('Polka City', 2023)

It is a fully autonomous contract-based NFT platform that allows users to invest in virtual asses in a city called Polkacity. Users can trade transportation devices, commercial equipment, retail and residential, and accessories in the marketplace and store.

Roblox ('Roblox', 2023)

Roblox is one of the oldest platforms for kids and adults to play games in their universe. Robux is their current to buy artifacts, characters, or other trading. The platform has millions of games and millions of users. The important difference from other platforms is not being hosted on the blockchain. Another feature is that developers and players could come together on the platform.

Robotera ('RobotEra', 2023)

Robotera is a metaverse project that offers users an experience of its virtual environment called Taro Planet. It is a comparatively new platform in which people buy land by NFT. The cities and planets in the virtual world will be released on the following dates. The users can participate in world creation, constructing buildings, exploring spaces, preparing original works for museum display, or listening to a concert.

Sandbox ('Sandbox', 2023)

It is another important platform on that users can purchase land with blockchain. The platform has millions of registered users who can build world structures through creativity. 3D visuals are important and designed from a cubical perspective for the platform, and users can interact with others through their avatars. Users can track the calendar to seek events and concerts.

Sansar ('Sansar', 2023)

Sansar platform's focus is different from other metaverses. The aim is to attend and organize events. Thus, it is a socializing metaverse platform where users participate with their avatars, build a world, arrange events, and attend concerts.

Second Life ('Second Life', 2023)

Second Life was launched in 2003, so it can be stated as the first inclusive metaverse platform. The user creates their avatar and joins the platform for various experiences. The platform is also a system for ownership, trade currency, and market. Many destinations (virtual environments) can be found that present real-world scenes or virtually created scenes.

Sensorium Galaxy ('The Sensorium Galaxy', 2023)

Sensorium Galaxy is a metaverse platform that tries to bring real-life experiences into a virtual environment. There are different worlds inside the platform. Sensorium Metaverse is a game in which users have a mission to unveil the mysteries of space, and prism world is for entertainment in which DJs and dancers can be on stage. Motion world is for those who want to learn about themselves by exploring the inner world of their body, mind, and soul.

Somnium space ('Somnium Space', 2023)

It is a virtual reality world platform with its economy and currency. The lands could be traded, constructing buildings be enabled, and users could interact with each other. The platform is accessible from computers, mobile devices, or VR headsets. The platform is to create a new virtual world for everyone to do everything, like communication, e-commerce, meetings, and entertainment.

Sorare ('Sorare', 2023)

Sorare is a platform for playing soccer in an interactive environment. The users could be soccer players or managers and interact with other users by implementing real-world game circumstances. The token is in the center of the platform, which is value for trade, win or lose. Now it is not only for soccer but also for basketball and baseball.

Spatial ('Spatial', 2023)

This platform allows users to build their spaces in the Metaverse to share culture. The brands and creators could design beautiful and functional 3D spaces on this platform, and they can share these spaces and sell or rent them to others. The system is enabled for both augmented and virtual reality.

Stageverse ('Stageverse', 2023)

Stageverse is a platform for virtual venues, interactive experiences, meetings, or digital content using VR headsets. The avatars of users could be dressed up with real-world brands. It is a no-code platform for creators and brands to build metaverse venues and host 3D experiences.

Star Atlas ('Star Atlas', 2023)

Star Atlas is a virtual gaming metaverse bases in the year 2620. The game is based on blockchain, space-themed, and video games. Users can get experience in space flight, role-playing, and buying digital assets like ships, crew, and equipment.

Tamadoge ('Tamadoge', 2023)

Tamadoge is both the name of the Metaverse and the currency used in the platform. The platform allows users to create, breed, care for, and battle their Tamadoge pets. It was launched in July 2023 and will be used on a computer and mobile devices.

Uhive ('Oasis | Uhive', 2023)

It is a platform for social networking in the Metaverse. Users can use Uhive like any social media platform with the benefits of free speech, earning revenue by creating, buying, and selling digital assets, and trading virtual real estate. The Uhive Metaverse is called Oasis, in which users can create their own spaces in the virtual world. The aim is to create a unified free virtual world for social integration.

Ultra ('Ultra', 2023)

Ultra is an entertainment platform where users have an immersive experience by entering different gaming industry services under a single roof. Developers and gamers could be part of this era. Thus, the platform aims to bring all games, digital assets, tournaments, and live streams into one place with a single login.

Unity ('Unity', 2023)

Unity is not a metaverse platform. It is one of the important platforms for developers to use for real-time 3D creation. It is used for games, architecture, the automotive industry, film industry simulations, and creating scenes and virtual worlds. Thus, for designing and creating virtual environments for the metaverse platform, Unity is commonly used.

Upland ('Upland', 2023)

Upland is a virtual property strategy game mapped and connected to the real world. The platform allowed users to play, earn, buy, sell, create homes and neighborhoods, and socialize. Confirmed lands and buildings could be bought and traded between users to earn coins.

Verseprop ('Verseprop', 2023)

It is a metaverse platform that focuses on virtual property. The opportunities and sales of digital assets with NFT technology will be found in the platforms. Individuals, collectors, or investors are invited to the platform.

Viverse ('VIVERSE', 2023)

Viverse is an open metaverse platform that connects people from all over the world in diverse activities. It is supported by blockchain and NFT. There are various virtual worlds as part of Viverse so that users can have unique and different experiences.

Voxels ('Voxels', 2023)

Voxels is a metaverse platform where users can play, buy, and sell digital assets. The quality of 3D graphics is far from reality; however, the variation in digital assets like wearables, scenes, avatars, and spaces is so wide.

ARCHITECTURAL DESIGN IN METAVERSE

Buildings and structures are designed and constructed due to these designs, including some documents, drawings, and specification documents. The project stakeholders, like architects, engineers, investors, users, consultants, and the construction team, are part of this process. The information and knowledge in each stage are evaluated and processed to achieve an ultimate project that can ensure the project's goals and requirements. Some of the knowledge affecting the design could be listed as requirements of clients and users, site and environmental issues, regulatory and construction requirements, and design intentions or concepts (Kamara, Anumba, & Evbuomwan, 2002). The buildings and spaces are contextualized uniquely by evaluating the knowledge and realizing the facts of the real world, like gravity, weather, dimensions, and scale. However, virtual environments have limitless visions or borders within the coding capacity. The participation of real-world users/people brings the similarity or proximity issue from real to virtual worlds. For example, users have experienced virtual worlds through their avatars, so they have scale and dimension relations with the virtual space they move, walk, or touch. Alternatively, the ground of land in the Metaverse is designed to be correlated with the Earth's ground that we stand on. The facts and results of the world we sense can be discussed in many sessions from different perspectives. Do they need to be transferred into cyberspaces? What possibilities exist for creating new rationales by converting or rewriting the metaverse rules? Discussions, explorations, or studies about universal consent while designing spaces and buildings may help the developers expand their visions of creating cyberspaces.

There are some studies to explore the approaches in architectural design virtual environment, the interaction of people with visualization, and getting effective virtual reality. For example, the Vitruvian approach of firmitas, utilitas, and venustas is explored and compared with the situation in virtual reality (Ibáñez & Naya, 2012). The correspondences of real-world architecture to virtual environments are overviewed under the terms and how they can result in the tridimensional, immersive, and virtual world. Table 1 shows an important point of view for evaluating facts and consent from real-world and virtual architecture. Looking into the detail of the table, it can be seen that physical laws are optional, and there will be an interaction of architects and programmers instead of building a construction team. The terrain can be designed in the virtual environment due to buildings, and the designers do not need to assess the site and environmental issues for their building's projects. Spaces have no role in shaping the boundaries outside and inside in terms of arranging atmospheric conditions, and energy usage is considered for computers, CPU, or data centers operating rather than adjusting the temperature in spaces.

Material selection due to function, visuality, or budget is unimportant since they are selected due to appearance and perception. Virtual residential and personnel virtual spaces are initiated, so living and security spaces are out of concern. The security is maintained by codes or software instead of physical arrangements or functional design. Tele transport is possible to be or not be anywhere in virtual spaces. Avatar size affects the scale, dimension, and movements. All these examples open a discussion on the facts and possibilities of designing spaces in the virtual environment. Knowledge creation continues in the Metaverse for commercial or computer-based issues and designing spaces in their context. The significant issues encountered in this research will be discussed in detail in the following parts.

Contemporary Examples

Architectural design companies have designed and released some buildings for diverse metaverse platforms. In this section, some of the examples will be explored. These are buildings directly represented or twins of building from the digital world. Figure 5 is a house designed by Andrés Reisinger in which the relation of privacy-publicity and limits of physical and weather lows are reinterpreted. The building in Figure 6 is created as a levitation center for the transition into a digital existence. The color of the building mimics the sun during different times of the day.

PLP Architecture company has designed a NFT collection (Figure 7). The aim is to bridge the gap between users interested in digital and physical real estate. Zaha Hadid Architects have designed some virtual spaces. NFTism Figure 8 is a virtual gallery exploring architecture and social interaction in the Metaverse, and Medical Centre for PUBG Figure 9 mobile is to explore new technologies and has spatial experience.

Table 1. Adapting the vitruvian triad to virtual (Ibáñez & Naya, 2012)

AEDIFICATIO	Related concepts	Real World Architecture	VIRTUALITAS
FIRMITAS	Stability	Application of physical laws.	Physical laws are optional.
		Selection of inner structure and basement.	Building stability is more related to computer stability, avoiding overloading machine and network resources.
		Design of constructive details to stand against external actions.	Protection of design against unauthorized modification.
	Constructive systems and processes	Architect: design. Builder: construction.	Architect: design and construction. Architect and/or Programmer: interaction.
		Complex constructive processes.	Modeling > Texturing> Lighting > Programming interactivity
	Materials selection	Materials selected for visual appeal, protection, and durability.	Material selection based on appearance only. All visual aspects of RW materials can be emulated. New material properties: Mutability, multimedia, and procedurality.
	Terrain	Terrain influences the building design.	Terrain can be designed to fit building needs.
	Durability	Aging, decay, and wearing.	Aging by means of obsolescence, incompatibilities through versions, broken links.
	Protection	Shelter for atmospheric agents.	Unnecessary.
		Security against external aggressions.	Access control. Closure against malicious activities
	Economy	Construction units (number of bricks, cubic meters of concrete,etc.)	Economy of data. Number of vertices, polygons, size of textures, etc.
		Energy (electricity, fuel, manpower).	Bandwidth, CPU and GPU use, cost of modeling and programming.
		Maintenance of materials and systems.	Maintenance of server and network.
UTILITAS	Program	Living.	Virtual residence. Personal space.
		Leisure.	Games. Social casual activities and relationships.
		Business and work.	e-Business, telecommuting.
		Exhibition.	Virtual exhibits and museums.
		Transport.	Tele transport integrated into virtual buildings.
		Public space – Private space.	Public–private–personal spaces.
		Fora.	Meeting places, game lobbies.
	Spatial Organization	Topological qualities of building space: open, closed, centric, directional, articulated, etc.	Same plus new capabilities derived from new geometries, mutability, weightlessness, practically limitless dimensions and teleportation.
		Function – Form relationship.	Empowered by adaptability of shape of building elements to functions, both static and dynamically.
		Anthropometry and Ergonomics.	Avatar sizes not necessarily in the human limits or not necessarily human-like at all. Design to support new actions, i.e., flying.
	Conditioning	Domotics.	Every aspect of the building is intrinsically programmable.
		Installations and systems.	Lighting control. Multimedia control. Data flow control.
	Environment	Relation with landscape.	Construction of landscape.
		Orientation to sun and winds.	Control of Sun and wind.
	Ecology	Environmental and visual impact.	Control of contents exposed. Fitting to in-world local building trends and customs.
		Waste treatment. Recycling.	Control of objects and data left behind by users.
VENUSTAS	Composition rules	Order, proportion, symmetry, modulation, rhythm, etc.	Research of new composition rules and relations.
	Space qualities	Expressivity of materials, light, color, distance, size, direction.	Spaces that produce sensations and feelings through seeing and hearing. Different perception of variables such as close and far, up and down.
	Formal languages. Styles	Expressionism, Rationalism, Postmodernism, Minimalism Deconstructivism,	New emerging concepts: *Liquid Architecture, Transvergence, Cybrid*. Styles still to consolidate.

Source: Ibáñez & Naya, 2012

Figure 5. Glass box by Andrés Reisinger
Source: Metaverse | Dezeen', 2022

Figure 6. A cantilevered house
Source: Metaverse | Dezeen', 2022

Figure 7. NFT skyscraper
Source: 'PLP Architecture', 2022

Figure 8. NFTism
Source: Zaha Hadid Architects, 2022

Weather Related Rationales

The weather activities and facts directly affect the building design in the real world. Climate due to regions is a long-term statically derived picture of the weather. These climates within climates are a particular situation of specific lands, solar radiation, humidity, snowfall, air quality, and air temperature directly affect indoor and outdoor spaces (Grondzik & Kwork, 2014).

Figure 9. Medical Centre
('Zaha Hadid Architects', 2022)
Source: Zaha Hadid Architects, 2022

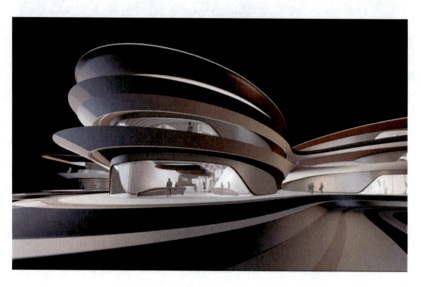

Sun

For anywhere in the world, the sun has a constraint route along a year. Day angles change from sunrise to sunset from January to December. Accessing sunlight, protection from the light, and arranging the sunlight efficiently in spaces are important criteria for designers. For the initial proposals of any building design projects, in the continuity with site analysis orientation, settlement of building and shaping form process is handled. For the development of projects, the zoning of spaces, façade organizing, and energy used for climatization are considered using informal, formal, and computer bases evaluations to design buildings. Considering the virtual environments in metaverse platforms, the sun is an artificial digital asset representing the reality of the Earth. It can be changed from virtual space to another, behaviors of the sun may be changed, and there may be multi suns or no sun. The existence or transferring of the sun to the Metaverse could be thought of by diversifying these to develop principles and rules: The features and behaviors of the sun as a light source, Enlighted objects' reactions (materials, transparency, transmission, *etc.*), and definition of the relation between sun and object.

Climatic Conditions

Climatic conditions like air temperature, atmospheric humidity, and precipitations (rain, hail, snow, *etc.*) influence buildings' design (Philips, 1965). Also, the envelopes, including basement insulation, and façade as vertical surfaces of buildings and roofs are designed due to the climatic conditions of regions. The heat insulations' and water insulations' application and features are determined accordingly. Material selection of building envelopes is always considered with effective weather activities: temperature, precipitation, and humidity (Duggal, 2008). For example, in cold regions, the transparency of outer facades increases the heat loss, or the slope and drainage system of the roofs differ due to the frequency and intensity of rain and snow. In some snowy regions, 30-40% of the roof slope is used, meaning transforming a horizontal surface into almost a vertical surface. These are considered for the durability and maintenance of buildings, building components, and users' comfort in the real world. In virtual environments with no climate and its results, these architectural elements and components that are part of the building definition do not need to be considered. The present building examples of metaverse platforms resemble the features of real-world buildings for people's perception. For a future discussion, it is important to think that if it is a rule or principle to develop and define a climate system for their Metaverse, how do they affect architectural design in a virtual environment? On the other hand, without a climate system, the virtual environment needs a façade or roof for an envelope to ensure indoor and outdoor boundaries.

Wind

The wind is also an act of weather conditions. The power and speed of the wing can change due to regions and altitude. The wind is an important factor in shaping building form in some regions and building typologies. For example, the wind is an important power source for tall buildings that should be considered while designing the form and structural behavior (Günel & Ilgın, 2014). One of the triggering forces of the accepted and perceived visuals of the skyscraper is the effect of the wind on higher levels of buildings. Thus, seeing these kinds of buildings in the Metaverse is normal. However, the effect of wind is not valid in the virtual environment. It is possible to design towers as upside-down positioning of real-world examples.

The world outstands by the universal facts ruling the weather of the regions over the Earth. These rules were written and executed out of human beings' limits in the real world; therefore, the design principles have gathered due to these outcomes. However, the virtual worlds are established by the creators with unlimited possibilities. The rules of weather, if needed so, are to be developed and made related. The crucial thing is the relation and compatibility of created principles between each other and cross-platform. These should be figured out by considering the outcomes of designing spaces and buildings and the users' response based on a grounding scientific approach.

Human Scale

The spaces, space components, furniture, vehicles, toys, and other objects are designed, shaped, and produced due to human scale and dimensions. The height of an entrance door, the height of a railing, the sitting area of a chair, the inside arrangement of a car, or the diameter of a ball are defined for human beings' usage. These relational dimensions and their effects or standards greatly influence practical life and theoretical studies. For example, the related standards are in the book Architect Data (Neufert, 2019). Looking at many published books, research, and standards and observing real Life, the designers understand human relations with their surroundings regarding dimension scale. However, in the Metaverse, the avatar is the generally used digital asset to represent the people. Shaping the avatar with user intentions is an important feature of the Metaverse platform to improve the ownership experience.

Additionally, these avatars' visual appearances and sizes may change due to different scenes and spaces on the platform. Any metaverse user experiences the virtual spaces and interacts with others in this representative avatar. Since the scale can be modified, the perception of the virtual environment changes. This situation should be handled as an important value for the virtual environment to diversify the experiences. It is not a positive or negative factor, but considerations should develop the principles and theories behind establishing any metaverse platform. Some possible metaverse behaviors could be as follows and should be ruled. The ability to change the avatar's scale: Limits, responsibilities, and authorization. Relative change of virtual environments (spaces): Ownership, effects to whom and objectives. Arrangement on digital assets: Correlational relation, perception, and value. Scale is important in considering the perception of an object by the subject. Therefore, the relational ratio of the subject(s) and object(s) will change the values and meanings of the virtual space. A consensus should be generated and structured if users simultaneously need avatars since the design of spaces and buildings is related to users.

Sensation and Perception

The sensation is the process by which people receive information from the environment; these are (1) light-vision, (2) sound-hearing, (3) chemicals-taste and smell, (4) pressure, temperature, and pain-sense of touch, (5) orientation and balance-kinesthetic senses (Alvarado et al., 2011). The environment's information affects the subject (human), and some body parts receive this. Perception is interpreting information from the environment so people can identify the meaning (Alvarado et al., 2011). The meaning sensed information and reaction to this may differ among the receiver due to their background and experiences that bring to the subject today. Interaction and communication are affected directly by sensation and perception. In the real world, in the natural order, a human interacts with the environment with vision, hearing, touch, kinesthetic senses, and taste and smell. The various perceptions of the human to uniquely equal cases result from the routes for interpretation. If a person has a usual perception of an impulse, the same perception may be sustained without an impulse. For example, for the sense of distance and depth, people need two eyes looking. By closing one eye, the distance information cannot be received. However, the known visual relations (change in color, shadow, perspective) of sensing distance make it possible to perceive the distance by looking with one eye. This cause and result relation is commonly used in the perception of metaverse platforms. By only sending the information to visual senses, the users are tried to be affected by kinesthetic senses. Universal consents related to the perception of human beings are widely used for better experiences in the virtual environment.

Interfaces make it possible to enter virtual environments. Computers, mobile devices, and some other devices (VR headsets, haptic devices, neural links) are to activate all senses of the users to perceive the virtual environments. The VR Headsets came at an important level that needs to be developed to make users sense visual and sound. The lens in devices for viewing in 3D by looking 2D screen activates the sense of depth. Acoustic in virtual spaces must be worked on and developed, and the information flow between sender and receiver should be maintained. When the sound devices received from the user and transmitted to the user are developed at a level that can mimic the acoustics of real Life, the experience and interaction will come near. The third issue is the sense of touch. The pressure of impulse, surface patterns, and tissue are important. Vibration on devices commonly used in VR sets begins in this sense. Many technologies invest in developing haptic devices covering only fingers or all of the body. Two directional impulse transfers are carried out for the research: from the virtual world to the user and from the user to the virtual world. The user can sense and perceive the virtual world when seeing scenes or cases in science-fiction movies or books. This will change the rationales and principles in the metaverse platform. Materials, surfaces, and touch movements should be considered. The kinesthetic senses related to orientation and balance are directly related to human body movement. The user entering into a virtual environment tends to be in imitation naturally. However, the movement is limited in real space boundaries and laws. Every movement in a virtual environment cannot be actualized in the real world. The simulation fundamentals of flight or driver education would be a base for developing this sense transfer.

The sense of chemicals by taster and smell is hard to develop in a virtual environment. The complex formula of chemicals makes this harder. However, there is also experimental research to overcome this situation by digital synthesizing. Digitally synthesized smell and taste could make users possibly sense the digital assets chemically, but it seems that there needs time to achieve these devices. Looking at another point of view, all these senses are transmitted from body parts to the brain by neural activities. A way of linking the virtual world directly to the nervous system of users is a solution for sensation. It can be seen as a fictional fact; future achievement may be reached. Considering all the situations among the sensational relation and present devices for interaction should be considered by developers to design spaces in the metaverse platform. Because in the real world, people experience spaces and buildings by using all senses in different ratios. Vision could be considered the most dominant, but the other senses also have a role in perception.

Transportation and Circulation

Transportation is transferring something or somebody from one place to another place. Circulation is a framework of transportation routes in a building or structured environment. By accepting the transportation is made out of the buildings by different vehicles. Motorbikes, cars, buses, trucks, and trains are vehicles on the ground. Planes, helicopters, and drones are used for air transportation at higher speeds. Ships are for sea transportation with diverse sizes and scales. There are also vehicles like bicycles, skates, rollers without any engine, and scooters, electric bikes which use relatively small and assistant engines. In addition, living beings can also transport themselves from one place to another by walking, running, or swimming. These are the general layout of the alternative way to go or transfer anything from the present place to the intended point. Cities, suburbs, and other settlements are established by including the framework of routes for all transportation types. Also, in air and sea, fictional routes make vehicles move in order securely. Implementing these facts to the virtual environment, an important discussion and comparison could be made. Exploring the metaverse examples, there are many transportation outcomes in virtual environments: starships, cars, moving surfaces, *etc.* Do the avatars need to transport or be transported from one place to another, or can they jump from one scene to another at a glance? What are the possible reasons for installing real-world principles into the environment? First, the imitation of real-world activities is used because of the non-existence of any fictional creation instead of transportation. The second reason makes user sense spending time. Because the fast consumption of anything is an important factor for any medium, the creativity of developers will rule the way.

Circulation is the term that building designers use generally. Stairs, escalators, ramps, and moving stairways-walks are used for vertical circulation in buildings (Grondzik & Kwork, 2014). There are important considerations on standards, specifications, and space relations that building project stakeholders should handle while locating and planning these circulation components. Halls, corridors, and doors are part of the horizontal circulation in the same level of buildings. The plan schemas for every building typology consist of spaces and circulating components in which hierarchy, privacy, function, and accessibility are considered.

On the contrary, virtual building spaces do not need vertical and horizontal circulation. If a space is designed with virtual walls as boundaries, they can be disappeared when the user wants the avatar to go in or out. Alternatively, a fictional tele transport opportunity may be implemented in the Metaverse. This will change all planning principles of the virtual environment spaces, which are directly transferred from real-world rationales.

Boundaries of Spaces

Designers plan the spaces due to functional and aesthetical reasons. The space should be defined with some building components, whether the quality or dimension. Walls and glass may be used for vertical boundaries, and visual elements or psychological factors may sometimes be used. The space's horizontal boundaries include floors, ceilings, and roofs. Diverse functions of these components also design open or semi-open spaces. In virtual environments, a copy of this relation is generally used. Fictional walls and roofs and pre-defined floors define some virtual spaces. Obviously, some premise designers of the Metaverse have significant attempts at interpretation. The Glass box example shows that a space is not an opaque boundary for controlling privacy. By this time, the discovery and creation of new ways of defining space boundaries in virtual environments will be seen.

Does the space need a boundary to be defined? It is a crucial question to make discussion in this context. Evaluations on real-life boundaries consider the physical, visual, or psychological. For the virtual environment, the spaces could be dynamic and updatable simultaneously. Therefore, static boundaries will not be valid and can be shaped by users/owners in the platform's framework. However, also, there is a need for a ruled framework that should govern all the creation of spaces by elements or components for boundaries concerning perception. The infrastructure of ownership can be a possible generative attribute for those working on the framework development of boundary principles.

Functional Needs

Every space and building is designed and constructed to provide a system for requirements. Requirement knowledge of a space is the set of significant statements that cover all to their success to design. The requirements of the spaces change and develop due to physiological situations. In the real world, human needs could be organized around these classifications: physiological needs, safety needs, social needs, esteem needs, and self-actualization needs (Maslow & Frager, 1987). The functions of spaces and relations are arranged according to the requirements of users or possible users by evaluating these main needs. These originated the real-world Life of livings beings. The virtual environment is built upon different views. Talking about eating, drinking, sleeping, or security is meaningless. The activities are so different, such as virtually interacting, trade and ownership, experience in virtual spaces, gaming, *etc.* These functions are tried to be ensured at the framework and principles of metaverse platforms. However, the space reflections of this function should be developed orderly. The trade or market space should have properties, or gaming arenas should have different features. The creation of virtual spaces in the Metaverse due to function is one of the competitive actions between platforms, so they are developed at a level of quality.

Functions and requirements of the buildings have been formulated for real life and services. The virtual environment has its value and needs, which have not been written yet. In parallel with the demands and development of virtual activities, space designers should formulate these functions in collaboration with actors in the Metaverse. The objectives and usage of virtual spaces are limitless; however, the users of these spaces come from real Life and are used to actual social interaction, cultural activities, or commercial relations. These behaviors should be transferred to virtual environments by transforming, converting, or redefining.

Force Related Principles

Constructing in the world has universal principles against forces and their effect on structures. Structures should stand against continuous gravity and be resistant to earthquakes. The weight of the buildings is transmitted from the higher part of the building to the lower part and at the end on the ground. All structural approaches are established due to laws of forces and reactions. Masonry, reinforced concrete structures, wooden frames, and steel frame structures use the features of material and possibilities of form to tackle the weights. In addition, spaces frame, shell and cable system, membranes, and pneumatic systems are contemporary structural systems used for buildings. According to the effects of structures on building design and typology, people have common senses to understand and perceive buildings. However, these laws are not in virtual environments and are optional to fictional applications. There are two possible approaches to constructing a virtual environment. First is acceptance of the non-existence of gravity, so the spaces may be designed free of the ground and placed anywhere in virtual space. For these, a new principle to rule the existence of buildings in the virtual environment. The second is to transfer knowledge and behavior of the forces from the real world. The effects and reactions do not need to be the same. However, there should be a common agreement for the activation of laws.

Earthquake is such an important activity that is considered a type of disaster. Although the time and place of this event cannot be known, science has experts and research to explore the zones due to the impact possibilities of earthquakes. According to these statements, the evaluation of earthquakes on buildings is considered differently in different parts of the world; because of these, diverse building structures could be explored in earthquake-free zones or high-risk assessed areas. There are lands and locations representing the world in the Metaverse. Buying, selling, and renting these areas and constructing buildings is possible. Currently, there is no differentiation due to earthquakes in the virtual environment. Whether it should be or should not be are not stated, but awareness of the location feature related to an earthquake is important while transferring the other real-world properties.

FUTURE RESEARCH DIRECTIONS

Based on the findings, explanations, and survey, it can be stated that the metaverse platforms, including all types, somehow represent the perspective of the real world. This structure's reasons are real-life dynamics, human existence, universe facts, rules, and perceptions. Examples of virtual environments which try to break to bond from reality exist; however, their attempts are related to unlinking. The way should be redefined and redesigned in the context. This chapter brings the subject, present situations, and realities of the actual world to develop awareness for further works and create a discussion for figuring bases of frameworks. The findings and suggestions for further work are noted as follows:

- Platforms, communities, or an institution should be founded for tracking, archiving, reporting, discussing, and generating the principles for the market. The scientific community can be invited and support the work.
- Building and space designers are not only part of the design process. Their skills and ability are related to writing the rules of the metaverse creation.

- The rationales of the universe: weather and forces govern the real world. The need' existence of principles in the virtual environment is clear. However, the origin of creation and definition should be related to Earth is open to discussion.
- The sensation and perception of humans are related to types of equipment. Contemporary examples show that it could be assured for visual and sound perception. The developments in other senses will guide the generation of attributes in virtual environments.

CONCLUSION

Metaverse, which comes into our lives with the development of 3D fundamentals and the internet, will significantly affect our way of living. Virtual environments allow transferring the present's real-world activities to the Metaverse and creating new experiences. There are fields to develop, like 3D visual's quality, ownership, interface, and governing principles for the world to make the participation of people in the virtual world more qualified and interactive. This chapter briefly explains the definition, usage, problems, issues, and approximately 35 metaverse platforms. The increasing number of platforms shows the commercial and social value of the metaverses. However, it is observed that direct transferring of real-world principles in terms of space and building design generally exists. The rationales of known spaces and buildings originated from thousand of years of experience and the law of physics. The virtual environments are free of conducting these facts and have the potential to create their own rules for building design. This chapter tried to open discussion and explore the initial outcomes by comparing the real and virtual worlds to be beneficial for future construction.

ACKNOWLEDGMENT

This research received no specific grant from any funding agency in the public, commercial, or not-for-profit sectors.

REFERENCES

101 Blockchains. (2022). *10 Best Metaverse Platforms That You Can Try In 2022*. 101Blockchains. https://101blockchains.com/best-metaverse-platforms/

Alvarado, S., Kanter-Braem, B., Manz, K., Masciopinto, P., Mckenna, E., Nelson, D., & Wozniak, W. (2011). *SENSATION AND PERCEPTION a unit lesson plan for high school psychology teachers*. TOPSS of the American Psychological Association.

Ball, M. (2022). The Metaverse and how it will revolutionize everything. In *Liveright Publishing Corporation*. Liveright. doi:10.1080/15228053.2022.2136927

Battle Infinity (IBAT). (2023). *Home*. IBAT. https://battleinfinity.io/

Bönsch, J., Elstermann, M., Kimmig, A., & Ovtcharova, J. (2022). A subject-oriented reference model for Digital Twins. *Computers & Industrial Engineering*, *172*, 108556. doi:10.1016/j.cie.2022.108556

Buisness2Community. (2022). *12 Best Metaverse Platforms to Play & Invest in February 2023*. Buisness2Community. https://www.business2community.com/cryptocurrency/best-metaverse-platforms

Chandra, Y., & Leenders, M. A. A. M. (2012). User innovation and entrepreneurship in the virtual world: A study of Second Life residents. *Technovation, 32*(7–8), 464–476. doi:10.1016/j.technovation.2012.02.002

Clemens, A. (2022). *Metaverse For Beginners A Guide To Help You Learn About Metaverse, Virtual Reality And Investing In NFTs*.

Dezeen. (2023). *Metaverse*. Dezen. https://www.dezeen.com/tag/metaverse/

Dincelli, E., & Yayla, A. (2022). Immersive virtual reality in the age of the Metaverse: A hybrid-narrative review based on the technology affordance perspective. *The Journal of Strategic Information Systems, 31*(2), 101717. doi:10.1016/j.jsis.2022.101717

Dozio, N., Marcolin, F., Scurati, G. W., Ulrich, L., Nonis, F., Vezzetti, E., Marsocci, G., La Rosa, A., & Ferrise, F. (2022). A design methodology for affective Virtual reality. *International Journal of Human-Computer Studies, 162*, 102791. doi:10.1016/j.ijhcs.2022.102791

Duggal, S. K. (2008). *Building Materials*. New Age International.

Dwivedi, Y. K., Hughes, L., Baabdullah, A. M., Ribeiro-Navarrete, S., Giannakis, M., Al-Debei, M. M., Dennehy, D., Metri, B., Buhalis, D., Cheung, C. M. K., Conboy, K., Doyle, R., Dubey, R., Dutot, V., Felix, R., Goyal, D. P., Gustafsson, A., Hinsch, C., Jebabli, I., & Wamba, S. F. (2022). Metaverse beyond the hype: Multidisciplinary perspectives on emerging challenges, opportunities, and agenda for research, practice and policy. *International Journal of Information Management, 66*, 102542. Advance online publication. doi:10.1016/j.ijinfomgt.2022.102542

Eastman, C., Teicholz, P., Sacks, R., & Liston, K. (2008). *BIM Handbook*. BIM. doi:10.1002/9780470261309

Grondzik, W. T., & Kwork, A. G. (2014). *Mechanical and Electrical Equipment for Buildings*. Wiley. doi:10.5860/CHOICE.29-6058

Günel, H., & Ilgın, H. (2014). *Tall Buildings Structural Systems and Aerodynamic Form*. Routledge. https://doi.org/https://doi.org/10.4324/9781315776521 doi:10.4324/9781315776521

Huang, W., Zhang, Y., & Zeng, W. (2022). Development and application of digital twin technology for integrated regional energy systems in smart cities. *Sustainable Computing: Informatics and Systems, 36*, 100781. doi:10.1016/j.suscom.2022.100781

Huynh-The, T., Pham, Q.-V., Pham, X.-Q., Nguyen, T. T., Han, Z., & Kim, D.-S. (2022). Artificial Intelligence for the Metaverse. *Survey (London, England)*. doi:10.1016/j.engappai.2022.105581

Ibáñez, L. A. H., & Naya, V. B. (2012). Cyberarchitecture: A Vitruvian approach. *Proceedings of the 2012 International Conference on Cyberworlds, Cyberworlds 2012*, 283–289. 10.1109/CW.2012.48

Kamara, J. M., Anumba, C. J., & Evbuomwan, N. F. O. (2002). Capturing Client Requirements in Construction Projects. In Capturing Client Requirements in Construction Projects. doi:10.1680/ccricp.31036

Li, X., Wu, P., Shen, G. Q., Wang, X., & Teng, Y. (2017). Mapping the knowledge domains of Building Information Modeling (BIM): A bibliometric approach. *Automation in Construction*, *84*(July), 195–206. doi:10.1016/j.autcon.2017.09.011

Life, S. (2023). Retrieved 27 February 2023, from https://secondlife.com/

Lv, Z., Qiao, L., Li, Y., Yuan, Y., & Wang, F. Y. (2022). BlockNet: Beyond reliable spatial Digital Twins to Parallel Metaverse. *Patterns (New York, N.Y.)*, *3*(5), 100468. Advance online publication. doi:10.1016/j.patter.2022.100468 PMID:35607617

Maslow, A. H. (Abraham H., & Frager, R. (1987). Motivation and personality. Harper and Row.

Neufert, E. (2019). *Arhitects' data*. John Wiley & Sons Ltd.

NVIDIA. (2023). *Omniverse*. NVDIA. https://www.nvidia.com/en-us/omniverse/

Palaha, J. (2022). 22 Best Metaverse Platforms To Watch Out For in 2022. *Jatinderpalaha*. https://www.jatinderpalaha.com/metaverse-platforms/

Philips, R. O. (1965). Climate as an Influence of Building Design. *Architectural Science Review*, *8*(4), 125–128. doi:10.1080/00038628.1965.9696152

PLP Architecture. (2022). *PLP Architecture and Verse Prop Join Forces to Launch NFT Collection*. PLP Architecture. https://plparchitecture.com/plp-architecture-and-verseprop-join-forces-to-launch-nft-collection/

Tao, F., Xiao, B., Qi, Q., Cheng, J., & Ji, P. (2022, July 1). Digital twin modeling. *Journal of Manufacturing Systems*, *64*, 372–389. Elsevier B.V. doi:10.1016/j.jmsy.2022.06.015

Uhive. (2023). *Oasis*. Uhive. https://www.uhive.com/oasis

Wang, Y., Kang, X., & Chen, Z. (2022). A Survey of Digital Twin Techniques in Smart Manufacturing and Management of Energy Applications. *Green Energy and Intelligent Transportation*, *1*(2), 100014. doi:10.1016/j.geits.2022.100014

Zallio, M., & John Clarkson, P. (2022). Designing the Metaverse: A study on Inclusion, Diversity, Equity, Accessibility and Safety for digital immersive environments. *Telematics and Informatics*, *101909*, 101909. Advance online publication. doi:10.1016/j.tele.2022.101909

Zhao, Y., Jiang, J., Chen, Y., Liu, R., Yang, Y., Xue, X., & Chen, S. (2022). Metaverse: Perspectives from graphics, interactions and visualization. *Visual Informatics*, *6*(1), 56–67. doi:10.1016/j.visinf.2022.03.002

ADDITIONAL READINGS

Ball, M. (2022). The Metaverse and how it will revolutionize everything. In *Liveright Publishing Corporation*. Liveright. doi:10.1080/15228053.2022.213692

Clemens, A. (2022). *Metaverse For Beginners A Guide To Help You Learn About Metaverse, Virtual Reality And Investing In NFTs*.

Dwivedi, Y. K., Hughes, L., Baabdullah, A. M., Ribeiro-Navarrete, S., Giannakis, M., Al-Debei, M. M., Dennehy, D., Metri, B., Buhalis, D., Cheung, C. M. K., Conboy, K., Doyle, R., Dubey, R., Dutot, V., Felix, R., Goyal, D. P., Gustafsson, A., Hinsch, C., Jebabli, I., & Wamba, S. F. (2022). Metaverse beyond the hype: Multidisciplinary perspectives on emerging challenges, opportunities, and agenda for research, practice and policy. *International Journal of Information Management, 66,* 102542. doi:10.1016/j.ijinfomgt.2022.102542

Flachbart, G., & Weibel, P. (Eds.). (2005). *Disappearing Architecture: from real to virtual to quantum.* Walter de Gruyter. doi:10.1007/3-7643-7674-0

Zagalo, N., & Morgado, L. A. B.-V. (2011). Virtual Worlds and Metaverse Platforms : New Communication and Identity Paradigm. IGI Global.

Zallio, M., & John Clarkson, P. (2022). Designing the Metaverse: A study on Inclusion, Diversity, Equity, Accessibility and Safety for digital immersive environments. *Telematics and Informatics, 101909,* 101909. doi:10.1016/j.tele.2022.101909

KEY TERMS AND DEFINITIONS

3D Modeling: Using specialized software to create a three-dimensional representation of an object or scene.

Building Design: Process of planning and creating the layout, appearance, and functionality of a structure or building

Design Principles: Fundamental guidelines that inform the creation of buildings and spaces, considering aspects such as aesthetics, function, sustainability, and context.

Metaverse Platform: Software application or network that enables users to access and interact with the diverse Metaverse.

Metaverse: virtual reality space where users can interact with a computer-generated environment and other users in real time.

Non-Fungible Token (NFT): A unique digital asset that uses blockchain technology to verify ownership and authenticity, often used to represent digital art or collectibles

Virtual Environment: A computer-generated simulation of a physical or imagined space that allows users to interact with and manipulate the environment.

Virtual Reality: A computer-generated simulation of a three-dimensional environment that can be interacted with using specialized equipment such as a headset or gloves, giving the user a sense of immersion and presence.

Section 2
Sustainability, Technology, and Built Environment Education

Chapter 5
Student Acceptance of Using Apps to Achieve Learning Outcomes in Architecture and Environment

Sujatavani Gunasagaran
https://orcid.org/0000-0002-0377-2319
Taylor's University, Malaysia

TamilSalvi Mari
https://orcid.org/0000-0001-5442-3816
Taylor's University, Malaysia

Nik Syazwan Shawn Nik Ab. Wahab
Taylor's University, Malaysia

Azim Sulaiman
Taylor's University, Malaysia

Khairool Aizat Ahmad Jamal
Taylor's University, Malaysia

ABSTRACT

The use of mobile apps for learning is not common in learning of technical modules in architecture, but studies have been advocated to learn its potential two decades ago. E-learning has supplemented traditional learning in Malaysian Universities since 2004. The Covid-19 pandemic forced education to be conducted virtually. Lecturers with knowledge of blended learning were able to switch to virtual learning but had challenges. The challenge of this module is access to environmental lab and data loggers that would need travelling and sharing of devices. Apps for measuring weather data led to minor adjustment in teaching and learning without altering the learning outcome. The students' perception of learning was captured in a survey with 114 responses. The result evidenced that students had a good learning experience by reporting high mean value for all the items. All Pearson's Correlation values showed positive with moderate to very high correlation between the factors. Post-pandemic teaching and learning in universities need to explore the potential of m-learning.

DOI: 10.4018/978-1-6684-8253-7.ch005

INTRODUCTION

The implementation of technology in teaching and learning activities has attracted significant interest from practitioners in higher education institutions in Malaysia. Many higher education institutions have started to adopt and implement information and communication technology solutions, such as electronic learning, as a source for flexible teaching and learning processes either in or outside the classroom (Azizan, 2010). The rapid growth of web-based technology and high internet usage has made teaching and learning online more viable in recent years. Currently, the majority of higher education institutions are equipped for e-learning. Institutions have established information and communication technology infrastructures and a strategic plan to implement online delivery learning in their programme, as e-learning may complement conventional methods of instruction. With the support of the government under the 9th Malaysia Plan (2006-2010), the Malaysian government has prioritised the development of world-class human capital through lifelong education.

Online Learning During the Pandemic, Virtual Learning

COVID-19 was first discovered in the final month of 2019 (Huang et al. 2020). Subsequently, the World Health Organisation (WHO) declared COVID-19 a global pandemic, announcing social distancing as a primary means to curb the spread of the deadly virus (WHO, 2020). As a result, this pandemic has forced the global physical closure of businesses, sports activities, and schools by pushing all institutions to migrate towards online platforms. Globally, over 1.2 billion students are out of the classroom and reverted towards online learning. UNESCO (2020) highlighted that over 1.5 billion learners worldwide could not attend a school or university due to the COVID-19 outbreak as of 4 April 2020. In the context of Malaysia, the government has imposed numerous movement control orders (MCO) to control the spread of the deadly virus nationwide. As a result, the education sector has changed dramatically with the phenomenal rise of e-learning, whereby teaching and learning are undertaken remotely and on digital technology platforms.

Online learning is the use of the internet and some other essential technologies to develop materials for educational purposes, instructional delivery, and program management (Fry, 2001). Tsai et al. (2002) defined online learning as being "associated with content readily accessible either via online or local computer." Hence, such learning content can be effectively disseminated using various digital technologies and platforms such as shared digital media, blogs, cloud-based sharing platforms, video conferencing, social networking tools, applications and other classroom management systems. As for the conduction of classes, Hrastinski (2008) stated that there are two types of online learning, namely asynchronous and synchronous online learning, which is majorly compared, but for online learning to be effective and efficient, there is a need for instructors, organisations, and institutions to have a comprehensive understanding of the benefits and limitations. The learning approach often provided from a physical classroom focusing on distant learning necessitates relevant skills and dependency on electronic media and devices. Several researchers discussed the numerous advantages of online learning over traditional learning methods. Despite its benefits, online learning implementation probes several challenges to existing learning. Adedoyin and Soykan (2020) highlighted social-economic, technological, and digital competence among the salient challenges of online learning during the pandemic.

Student Learning and Engagement Online

The COVID-19 pandemic has tremendously changed how students and teachers interact. Undoubtedly, online learning is a good initiative for carrying on teaching and educational programs during this pandemic but not without problems adjusting to online classes (Kim, 2020). According to Bomia et al. (1997), student engagement is "students' willingness, need, desire, and compulsion to participate in and be successful in the learning process." Student learning engagement may also be defined as students' level of interest, how they communicate and interact in a course, and their motivation to learn about the topics (Briggs, 2015). Subsequently, in a study by Jaggars (2016), the emphasis on providing quality engagement and interaction within the course activities could positively correlate to the student's grade performance.

A few researchers highlighted that online learning greatly facilitated active engagement, information ease, and prolonged teacher interactions (Cameron, 2006; O'Leary & Ramsden, 2002). Hence, such courses delivered online require implementing specific pedagogical strategies with the objective is to create active and meaningful learning engagement opportunities as much as possible. In an online learning environment, various digital tools are widely available for instructors to gather informal data about student participation in the course. Richardson and Newby (2006) found that as the student gaining experience through online learning would encourage students to become more self-directed and responsible for their learning.

Architecture and Environment

Environmental studies of which the building is to be built, which include understanding its social or cultural context, climatic conditions, land type, and others, is one of the primary steps in architectural design. It can be concluded that architecture and its environment are vastly interdependent. While the environment gives context to its architecture, architecture defines the environment it is in (Kulkarni, 2019). In addition, subject matters such as thermal comfort, sustainable building, and passive cooling are commonly taught in the environmental studies of architecture programs. Nevertheless, environmental studies were taught and learned online due to the pandemic, with several associated mobile applications being introduced.

The widespread COVID-19 pandemic has affected human health and disrupted the education system. Most educational institutions postponed their face-to-face classes for fear of spreading diseases (Azman & Abdullah, 2021). In addition, according to Agarwal and Kaushik (2020), the pandemic has not only impacted human life but also impacted the education system severely in some institutions and countries with fewer technological advancements. With principles of social distancing, the countries with technological advancements, all face-to-face classes were suspended and replaced with virtual classes and online exams.

Nowadays, most university tutors implement e-learning and have developed various e-learning materials. One of the learning supports services that have been developed for online tutorials is widely known as e-learning. The use of e-learning can be classified into two parts: First, using e-learning as the primary instructional medium. Second, the use of e-learning as instructional media support. Thus, this indicates that e-learning is a self-learning process that contributes to learning. E-learning as supporting instructional media should be available and ready to be used at any time by students and is regarded as compensation for face-to-face sessions (Said & Syafik, 2016). Most technologically advanced higher education institutions worldwide, including Malaysia, have already used this system. Harlan et al. (2019), researched handphone applications for learning English and stated that technological advancement has greatly improved the existing setting in the education world in recent years.

Furthermore, the wide use of mobile wireless technologies has created more opportunities to shift the traditional academic environment to mobile learning. Many applications of smartphones, personal digital assistants, Blackberry, iPhone, and android have been widely employed in second language learning. In addition, mobile technologies offer numerous practical uses in language learning while it requires thoughtful integration of second language pedagogy.

Apps and M-Learning

The usability of mobile learning (m-learning) applications (apps) includes features that differ from other computer systems. These include the mobile context, connectivity, screen size, and different display resolutions. These features can influence usability factors such as effectiveness, efficiency, satisfaction, learnability, memorability, errors, and cognitive load (Harrison et al., 2013). Another factor that is affected by m-learning applications is learner performance. A study by Vogel et al. (2007) aimed to explore the impact on learning performance. Their study showed positive support for learner performance enhancement, with support for constructive alignment as a moderate variable for students who use m-learning technology.

Moreover, Hamdan and Ben-Chabane's (2012) study discussed improving students' skills and performance using m-learning applications. Experiments were conducted with Information Technology students at the University of the United Arab Emirates (UAE). The study discovered that when m-learning technology is well integrated and adopted, it can significantly improve students' skills such as organisation, communication, assuming responsibilities, critical reading, and writing, problem-solving, class engagement, increasing learning interest, emphasising community contribution, and self-evaluation. In addition, user satisfaction is influenced by many environmental and individual factors. A study by Hassanein et al. (2010) focused only on factors facilitating student satisfaction with m-learning. The study presented a model of student satisfaction with m-learning, showing that external and internal facilitating factors associated with the mobile learner can influence students' satisfaction with this technology.

The S2P Learning framework developed by Bahji et al. (2013) explains that the focal point that characterises the S2P-LM lies in its interest in the process rather than the content (Process-based rather than Content-based). It aims to foster a dynamic within the learner, arguing that the Content is no longer a problem. In an existing module, Architecture and Environment, with formulated Learning Strategy and Learning Process, minor changes were made to the Learning Platform to accommodate teaching and learning online during the pandemic. The focus of this S2P-LM in Figure 1, ranging from macro (in purple) to micro (in blue) level, remains the learner.

In their study on developing a Framework for Mobile Learning for Improving Learning in Higher Education, Barreh and Abas (2015) cited the example of an "Internet Technology" course as an example of how mobile learning might be utilised to support face-to-face instruction. The authors defined mobile learning as using mobile devices with wireless connectivity, such as mobile phones, smartphones, tablets or other handheld devices that allow learners to enhance their learning experience anywhere and at any time. The authors also used 3 (three) other approaches to define m-learning apart from mobile devices, which are Learners and Learning Experience (learning process, collaborating with peers and teachers, constructing meaning and knowledge), Learning (exploring, communication, flexible, accessible,

Figure 1. Macro level view of the S2P learning model
by Bahji et al. (2013).

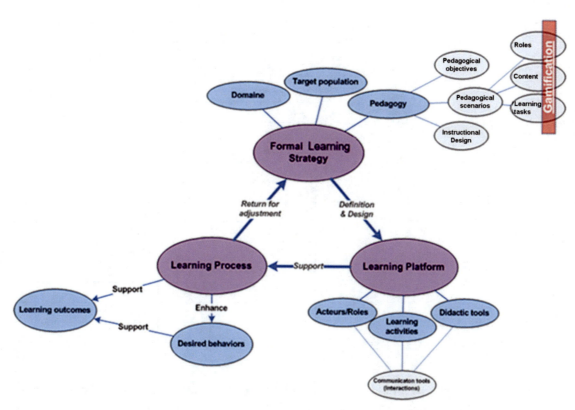

learner-centered), and Combination of Components (e-learning and m-learning). Internet Technology and mobile learning activities were used to supplement face-to-face interaction to enhance the course learning environment. Two main applications were employed: SMS for content and reminders and Facebook for discussions, chats, exercises, videos, and quizzes.

In the Architecture and Environment module, the apps used by the students to complete their learning activities or tasks during the pandemic are for Scientific Measurements and are listed in Table 1 below. Besides that, more apps were also used to communicate and disseminate notes for asynchronous learning, and online synchronous lectures and tutorials have been accomplished via apps like Zoom and Microsoft Teams. Traditionally, the scientific measuring tools or data loggers will be acquired from the Environmental Laboratory, lectures and tutorials are face-to-face and asynchronous learning, communicating, and notes are disseminated using myTIMeS, Facebook and WhatsApp. Applications such as google slides were used as a collaborative tool among group members to present assignment progress during the tutorial sessions via Microsoft Teams. Pre-recorded videos also supplement the virtual lectures. Table 1 also shows applications that perform better using a laptop and those used as m-learning. The administered survey focussed more on using mobile scientific measuring apps to complete the assignment and attain the learning outcome for the module.

Table 1. Apps used during the pandemic to retain the learning outcomes for architecture and environment module

	MOBILE	LAPTOP
Scientific Measurement	Compass	
	Thermometer	
	Humidity Meter	
	Light Meter	
	Sound Meter	
	Wind Meter	
	Weather	
	Calendar	
Communication/ Notes	myTIMeS	myTIMeS
	MS Teams	MS Teams
	WhatsApp	WhatsApp
Collaborative / Teamwork	Google Slides	Google Slides
	Miro Board	Miro Board
Lectures and Tutorials	MS Teams	MS Teams
	Zoom	Zoom

As summarised in Table 1, several useful apps can be used in architecture learning, depending on the modules. The scientific measurement apps listed are commonly utilised for the environmental, green or sustainable modules like Sustainable Design, Policies and Regulations, Energy and Architecture, and Green Strategies for building design.

Generally, these mobile apps can be a valuable resource for architectural students in environmental modules for several reasons:

1. **Accessibility:** Environmental measurement mobile apps are readily available and can be downloaded via smartphones, making them easily accessible for students. This allows them to use the apps at any time, whether in the classroom, at a site or even at home, to get immediate feedback on environmental measurements (Castell et al., 2016).

2. **Convenience:** The interfaces of mobile applications for environmental measurement are designed to be user-friendly and intuitive. Students can instantly learn how to use them and immediately take measurements with minimal training time (Environmental Defense Fund, 2019).

3. **Accuracy:** Environmental measurement mobile apps are often equipped with sensors that can measure various environmental parameters, such as temperature, humidity, and light intensity, among others. These sensors can provide accurate measurements that can be used in the analysis and design of buildings. (Watson et al., 2015).

4. **Data collection:** Environmental measurement mobile apps can collect data over time, providing students with a means to record and analyse environmental measurements more detailed and organised manner. This can be helpful for long-term research projects or the analysis of environmental patterns (Cejudo-Ruíz et al., 2019).

5. **Cost-effective:** Environmental measurement mobile apps are generally inexpensive and sometimes free, making them a cost-effective alternative to traditional environmental measurement equipment, which can be expensive (Gunay et al., 2017).

In summary, environmental measurement mobile apps can benefit architectural students in environmental subjects by providing them with a convenient, accurate, and cost-effective way to measure environmental parameters, collect data, and analyse patterns. This can help them analyse and design buildings more sustainable and responsive to their environmental context.

Poore (2015) noted in her book that it is no longer sustainable to approach educational enterprise as if the teacher is the sole repository of information and knowledge in the classroom because the internet has changed everything, citing that digital technology and social media, in particular, have created new learning potential, as shown in Table 2 below.

Table 2. Old learning vs. new learning potential

Old Learning	New Learning Potential
Teacher-centric	Learner-centric
Passive	Active and Interactive
One-to-many	Individualised learning
Lack of flexibility	Flexible
Monolithic learner	Learning communities
Competition	Sharing and networking
Memorisation	Creativity, discovery, exploration
Separation	Participation and collaboration

(Poore, 2015)

The widespread adoption of smartphones and other mobile devices has led to a significant increase in the use of mobile apps for learning. Apps have revolutionised the learning process by making education more accessible, personalised, and engaging by combining innovative technology and education itself. Teaching and learning of architecture modules have always encouraged peer learning or learning community, active and interactive, learner-centric, sharing and networking, flexible and very much emphasising creativity, especially in architecture design studios. Thus, digital technology would be very suitable if integrated into teaching and learning.

Apps and Mobile Learning in the Post-Pandemic Situation

Mobile learning, or m-learning, is an increasingly popular mode of education that uses mobile devices such as smartphones, tablets, and laptops to access learning materials and participate in educational activities. The COVID post-pandemic has dramatically shifted digital usage, impacting all aspects of work and life learning (Pandey, 2020). Thus, the learning process has been redefined to allow more initiative and improvement in 21st-century working, including driving digitalization, innovation, and mobile working to become much more significant in the future (Peláez, 2021). Kumar (2022) stated that the mobile approach to learning has become particularly significant in architectural education, both during and after the pandemic. Several review articles emphasise this relevance as follows:

1. **Enhancing the future of collaborative learning in architecture education:** Collaborative learning is a required skill in 21st-century learning (Laal, 2012). Online collaborative learning can be defined as a process in which two or more individuals work collaboratively to create meaning, explore a topic, or improve skills. Hence mobile-enabled collaborative learning contributed significantly to increasing mobility and collaboration without regard for time, pace, or location constraints (Makewa et al. 2015). Fu and Hwang (2018) studied collaborative learning facilitated by mobile technologies and discovered that collaborative learning through mobile devices is a fast-emerging study topic that can potentially boost learners' cognitive and metacognitive growth. Mobile learning allows for collaborative learning, where students can collaborate on projects and share their work in real-time. This promotes teamwork, communication, and critical thinking skills essential for success in architecture.

2. **Provide enhancement in interactive and engaging learning experiences**: It is essential to know that education after the Covid-19 pandemic will not be the same as traditional learning, so educational institutions must be ready to implement new strategies, adopt more ICTs equipment and Tech-Ed approaches (Dwivedi, 2020). Mobile learning platforms often incorporate interactive and engaging features, such as videos, animations, simulations, and gamification, to provide enhancement making learning more enjoyable and effective. This can keep students motivated and engaged in their studies.

3. **Flexibility and Adaptations**: Regardless of many limitations in using the m-learning approach, mobile phones and their applications became an essential tool for learning during the pandemic and will continue to be during the post-Covid-19 crisis (Ansi, 2020). The ease of use, mobility, affordability and ability to browse information quickly is the most characteristic of m-learning. In addition, mobile devices are being used as a communication tool through social media, using mobile products such as scanners, printers, videos and cameras to conduct teleconferencing and join cloud learning platforms. Therefore, with the technological advancement of mobile phones and their associated technologies, M-learning expands learning/teaching beyond traditional classroom learning, increasing flexibility and opening many opportunities for learners and educators through online learning environments (Basak, 2018). A study by Said (2021) reported that the rapid shift during the pandemic did not result in a poor learning experience; the m-learning approach is expected to be useful in future learning. This finding was supported by previous studies where a higher satisfaction of students who use m-learning and m-learning was recorded even before the pandemic and is considered a future learning unique tool (Mao, 2014).

Technology Acceptance Model

In Technology Acceptance Model (TAM), the inner tendency is the use beliefs, and the evaluative response is the behavioural intention to use. The two-use belief (PU and PEU) will affect the behavioural intention (BI) to use. The aim of using the technology acceptance model (TAM) presented by Davis (1989) was to explain the user acceptance behaviours for computer technology.

In the universities' communication model (UCOM) and the technology acceptance model, Tawafak et al. (2018) include four factors: academic performance, student satisfaction, effectiveness, and support assessment, simultaneously enhancing student satisfaction and improving the teaching method and academic performance level. The TAM is adopted to measure the level of support assessment and evaluate academic performance improvement using the UCOM model.

Figure 2. UCOM model factors test
by Tawafak et al. (2018).

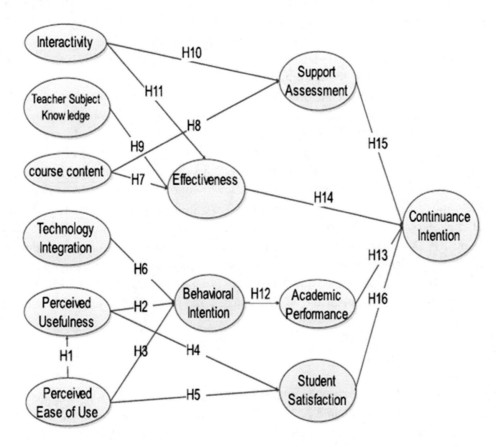

In this study, the TAM model is modified and includes performance, satisfaction and motivation to study the continuance intention to use Mobile Apps in Architectural Studies, illustrated in Figure 3. Previous research stated that the lack of student motivation in using e-learning applications is why e-learning is unsuccessful or does not achieve the desired goal (Bang et al., 2014). Many factors affect motivation in e-learning. Student engagement is the primary mechanism that enables motivational processes to contribute to e-learning and development, according to studies by Furrer and Skinner (2003) and Bahji et al. (2013). Bahji et al. (2013) also stated that few designers had overcome the challenge of designing a learning experience that combines an attractive design quality and effective learning achievement. The authors also emphasised that any aspects should not be compromised for each other.

Meanwhile, Priego and Peralta (2013) stated that student engagement is crucial to succeeding in online formative activities. According to El-Seoud et al. (2009), an interactive feature of e-learning also increases students' motivation. Based on the facts mentioned earlier, it can be concluded that the student's motivation for e-learning applications is worth studying.

Interaction is essential in face-to-face and online learning modalities (Kuo et al., 2013). Many studies have reported that student interactions' quantity and quality are highly correlated with student satisfaction in almost any learning environment. Ke and Kwak (2013) identified five elements of student satisfaction: learner relevance, active learning, authentic learning, learner autonomy, and technological competence. Kuo et al. (2013) determined that learner-instructor interaction and learner-content interaction combined with technology efficacy are valid indicators of students' positive perceptions. However, Battalio (2007), using a criterion approach, argued that a positive course rating requires effective learner-instructor interaction. Dziuban et al. (2015) concluded that satisfaction was most impacted by learning convenience combined with the effectiveness of e-learning tools.

Mobile learning has become an emerging tool that offers a significant learning experience to enhance student learning in higher education institutions. According to Barreh and Abbas (2015), many studies have revealed that mobile learning can support and enhance learning in higher education if adequately designed. However, although m-learning has been used to support a wide range of learning activities, there has been little research done to investigate the students' requirements or understand what types of mobile applications students need to use or examine how mobile educational software can be designed to support learning effectively (Devinder & Zaitun, 2006). Studies on mobile learning provide diverse evidence on the effectiveness of mobile devices on actual academic achievement (Froese et al., 2012). Miller and Cuevas (2017) found no statistically significant effect of mobile learning on academic achievement but found a statistically significant change in students' motivation for learning due to their use of mobile devices. The authors also stated that the students were more confident and excited in their learning and showed a more significant change in their interest and motivation to learn than paper learners.

PROBLEM STATEMENT

The impact of COVID-19, particularly on education, work, the economy, and governance, is immense and unprecedented worldwide (Papapicco, 2020). In education, the crisis has affected students' learning environment on short notice at a large international scale. According to UNESCO (2020), the closure of teaching institutions is believed to be a necessary precautionary measure to influence the spread of the pandemic (Viner et al., 2020). Similarly, the spread of the COVID-19 pandemic has forced the School of Architecture & Building Design of Taylor's university (SABD) to fully adopt the online teaching and learning environment in the March semester of 2020 and August 2020. The closure of the campus and sudden reliance on distance learning disrupted the standard teaching practice and led to innovative learning and teaching methods in supporting students.

While online teaching is not a new pedagogical method and has been used for many years in SABD, the Architecture and Environment module introduced Despite the importance of pedagogical roles, no empirical studies explicitly examine how users' pedagogical role moderates the relationship between their perception of mobile technology and the actual use frequency, as well as how the pedagogical role is associated with learning outcomes (Zhai et al., 2019; Zhai & Shi, 2020).

Although numerous studies have been published on the use of mobile apps in learning, relatively little research has been published on architecture students' acceptability of utilising mobile applications to achieve learning outcomes in architecture and environment modules that need scientific measurements.

The technological leap during the pandemic is said to have accelerated a decade in just two years of the pandemic. Many advantages were found to be beneficial to using mobile learning in teaching and learning. It is easy to use anywhere and anytime, as everyone owns a smartphone nowadays, and frequent use can enhance knowledge and critical thinking. Thus, using apps for teaching and learning architecture post-pandemic would enhance the teaching and learning of the Architecture and Environment module and other modules in architectural studies.

RESEARCH QUESTIONS

This study aims to assess the effectiveness of using mobile applications to teach and learn Architecture and Environment courses without changing learning results during the pandemic and suggest methods for continuing mobile learning after the pandemic.

This study aims to assess the acceptability of mobile applications in architecture students' learning experiences to achieve learning outcomes in the Architecture and Environment module. Following this aim, two specific research questions (RQ) are addressed.:

1. What are the students' perceptions of PU and PEU and their behavioural intention toward using mobile apps in their architectural and environmental studies? PU, PEU, BI
2. What are the students' perceptions of PEU and their satisfaction with using mobile apps in their architectural and environmental studies? PEU, SS
3. What are the student's perceptions of BI and their performance in achieving learning outcomes of the architectural and environmental studies? BI, SP
4. What are the student's perceptions and motivations (SM) towards using mobile apps (BI) to enhance their architectural and environmental studies (SP)? SM/BI/SP

METHOD

To identify the user acceptance of using Apps for learning, the data for this study were collected using a survey questionnaire administered to 114 undergraduate Architecture students from the Jan 2021 intake. Students were instructed in the survey to offer information about their experiences of using Apps and how they impacted their learning during the pandemic. The survey was modified from the Technology Acceptance Model (TAM) constructs, and a five-point Likert scale (1 for strongly disagree to 5 for strongly agree) was used. SPSS application (Version-25) was used to analyse the data. The instrument used for this study was designed based on the objectives of this study. The TAM for this study is illustrated in Figure 3.

The participants of this study consisted of 52.6% of female and 47.4% of male students. Since this course was offered during the short semester, the students enrolled in the course were from various semesters (after semester 1 or 2) and varied in age from 18 to 26 years old.

All students had mobile phones, with 43.8% of them using android phones and 55.3% using IOS phones, while 1 student (0.9%) had both phones. The devices employed for this study are not exclusively mobile learning devices; instead, only scientific data collection was encouraged using smartphones, while additional activities and learning outcomes may require a laptop or tablet. Refer to Table 3 for the sample profile.

Table 3. Sample profile

Characteristics		N	%	Valid %	Cumulative %
Gender	F	60	52.6	52.6	51.6
	M	54	47.4	47.4	100.0
	Total	*114*	*100.0*	*100.0*	
Age	18	9	7.9	7.9	7.9
	19	25	21.9	21.9	29.8
	20	64	56.1	56.1	86.0
	21	10	8.8	8.8	94.7
	22	2	1.8	1.8	96.5
	23	1	.9	.9	97.4
	26	3	2.6	2.6	100.0
	Total	*114*	*100.0*	*100.0*	
The operating system on a Mobile device	Android	50	43.8	43.8	43.8
	both	1	.9	.9	44.7
	IOS	63	55.3	55.3	100.
	Total	*114*	*100.0*	*100.0*	

RESULTS AND DISCUSSION

The reliability statistics of the survey with 25 items Cronbach Alpha (α) value is 0.967. The questionnaire has a high stability rate and can be applied to the research. Mean analyses were performed on the collected data and tabulated in Table 4. The mean score was categorised into three (3) interpretation levels: 1.00 to 2.33 for low or negative perception, 2.34 to 3.66 for medium or neutral perception, and 3.67 to 5.00 for high or positive perception. The participants scored high for all the items in the survey.

Further analysis of Pearson's correlations was performed to the factor of items, and the results were tabulated (Table 5) with the interpretation of the correlation data presented in Table 6. The values of correlation coefficients of the statements of every construct are positive and statistically significant at $p<0.01$ confirming the internal consistency of the items.

All data shows positive and moderate to a very high correlation between the factors.

All Pearson's Correlation values showed positive from a moderate to a very high correlation between the factors.

Table 4. Descriptive statistics

	Items	Mean	Std. Deviation
	Perceived Usefulness (PU)		
PU1	Using apps would improve my learning performance.	4.01	0.897
PU2	Using mobile apps would enhance my academic effectiveness.	4.04	0.921
PU3	Using these apps would increase my productivity (reduce the time required to accomplish the task).	4.11	0.802
PU4	Using these apps can make teaching and learning easier during the pandemic session.	4.32	0.735
PU5	Using these apps can make teaching and learning fun activities during the pandemic session.	3.97	0.897
PU4T	Using these apps can make teaching and learning easier in traditional sessions too.	4.21	0.746
PU5T	Using these apps can make teaching and learning fun in traditional sessions too.	4.18	0.790
	Perceived Ease of Use (PEU)		
PEU1	I found navigating around the Apps screen to be easy.	4.00	0.882
PEU2	Distinguishing the appropriate icon for the application for the needed information is easy.	4.22	0.713
PEU3	The application is user-friendly.	3.96	0.921
	Student Performance (SP)		
P1	Using mobile apps is very useful in completing my assignments.	4.32	0.744
P2	Using mobile apps, my learning skills are enhanced.	4.13	0.747
P3	Using the mobile apps, increased my understanding of thermal comfort.	4.08	0.874
P4	The mobile apps would enable me to perform learning tasks more quickly.	4.28	0.747
	Student Satisfaction (SS)		
S1	Generally, I am satisfied with using Apps for my learning in this module.	4.04	0.906
S2	I will use these mobile apps again for my learning.	3.97	0.917
S3	I will recommend this app to others.	3.88	0.951
	Behavioural Intention (BI)		
B1	I enjoy using these apps.	3.82	0.974
B2	I plan to use these Apps as part of my studies.	3.96	0.916
B3	I will use these apps for my Architecture Design Studio's site analysis.	4.23	0.765
B4	I will use these applications anywhere, for my understanding and not only for site analysis.	4.00	0.831
	Student Motivation (SM)		
M1	I believe that I can improve my skills by using these apps.	4.04	0.886
M2	I believe these apps have helped me to learn new things in Architecture.	4.27	0.768
M3	I like to use apps to learn as much as possible.	3.96	0.882
M4	I will use these apps in my online or traditional learning.	4.09	0.858

1. TAM

TAM has been extensively used and extended to study in an e-learning context. The constant use of the two use beliefs in TAM, perceived usefulness (PU) and perceived ease of use (PEU) were used to explain university students' acceptance of technology in teaching and learning. According to Table 5, a moderate and positive correlation was found between perceived usefulness (PU) and behavioural

Table 5. Pearson's correlations table

		SP	SS	BI	SM	PU	PEU
SP	r	1	.786**	.747**	.707**	.727**	.699**
	p		.000	.000	.000	.000	.000
	N		114	114	114	114	114
SS	r		1	.764**	.704**	.718**	.632**
	p			.000	.000	.000	.000
	N			114	114	114	114
BI	r			1	.823**	.677**	.719**
	p				.000	.000	.000
	N				114	114	114
SM	r				1	.778**	.719**
	p					.000	.000
	N					114	114
PU	r					1	.675**
	p						.000
	N						114
PEU	r						1
	p						
	N						
**. Correlation is significant at the 0.01 level (2-tailed).						

Table 6. Pearson's correlations data interpretation (Hinkle et al., 2003).

Size of Correlation	Interpretation
.90 to 1.00 (-.90 to -1.00)	Very high positive (negative) correlation
.70 to .90 (-.70 to -.90)	High positive (negative) correlation
.50 to .70 -.50 to -.70	Moderate positive (negative) correlation
.30 to .50 (-.30 to -.50)	Low positive (negative) correlation
.00 to .30 (.00 to -.30)	Negligible positive (negative) correlation

intention to use (BI), r = 0.677, p ≤ 0.01. In contrast, the correlation between perceived ease of use (PEU) and behavioural intention to use (BI) was high and positive r = 0.719, p ≤ 0.01. The adoption of m-learning will be adopted when it is easy to use. This finding is consistent with those of Hu et al. (1999) and Gunasagaran et al. (2019), who found that perceived ease of use had a significant effect on attitude towards usage, in contrast to Davis (1989), who found that perceived usefulness has a significantly stronger correlation with user behaviour than perceived ease of use. The correlation between perceived ease of use (PEU) and student motivation (SM) was also strong and positive, r = 0.720, p 0.001. This concludes that the use of apps is easy and will motivate the adoption of use by students for their learning activities. In this study, perceived ease of use (PEU) enhances the perceived usefulness (PU) positively and moderately (r=.675, p ≤ 0.01), similar to a study by Tawafak et al. (2021).

Figure 3. Technology acceptance model for this study with a summary of the "r-value" of Pearson's correlation

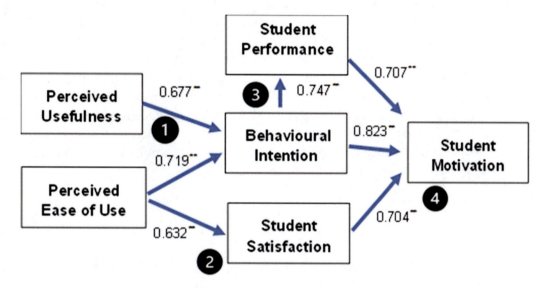

2.   Satisfaction

The lowest correlation for the study, but still positive and moderate, is between the perceived ease of use (PEU) and student satisfaction (SS), r = 0.632, p ≤ 0.01. Students highlighted dissatisfaction over the app's accuracy for scientific measurement. Miao (2012) states that content and perceived usefulness positively influence learner satisfaction with the application. As reported by previous researchers, ease of use, content, and layout design also positively affect m-learners' behaviour. Chaiprasurt (2011) said that students' motivation is influenced by their satisfaction; at the same time, it can affect the relationship between usefulness and performance.

3.   Performance

The correlation between behavioural intention (BI) and student performance (SP) is identified as r = 0.747, p ≤ 0.01. Students perceived that the apps are useful in completing the task quickly, learning skills and their knowledge of thermal comfort are enhanced. Similarly, MacCallum (2009) found that learners are more likely to use mobile technology if they feel it can improve and enhance their performance and proved that motivation significantly impacts how learners use technology for mobile learning. Another study by Gunasagaran et al. (2014) indicated that 80% of students would be able to embrace technology in the Architecture Design Studio, with 93.3% agreeing that they learned new skills followed by analytical skills that improve their performance.

4.   Motivation

In this study, the strongest correlation was found between the learner's behavioural intention (BI) to use and the learner's motivation (SM), r = 0.823, p ≤ 0.01. This indicates that students believe that apps will improve their skills, are easy to use, and can be used anywhere, especially during site visits for architectural design studios. Many factors contribute to successful practice in m-learning applications, and motivation is one of those factors. The correlation between student motivation (SM) and student performance (SP) is positive and high, r = 0.707, p ≤ 0.01. Motivation lies at the heart of successful learning since motivated students are keen to learn. According to Bekele (2010), motivation can be defined as a person's internal needs, desires, and wants and can determine his or her attitude. At the same time, Sha et al. (2012) suggested that students' perceptions might positively impact their engagement in mobile learning in a self-regulated learning process. According to Gunasagaran et al. (2019), using social media as part of e-learning can connect students and instructors, increase learners' motivational levels, and create strong communities of practice for teaching and learning that expand the learning process beyond the boundaries of a traditional classroom.

CONCLUSION

In conclusion, all the correlation between the factor is positive and high. Students' motivation was influenced by their satisfaction; at the same time, it can affect the relationship between usefulness and performance. This study is essential for concluding e-learning from a coerced virtual learning environment and sourcing the necessary resources and devices to aid the teaching and learning of a technical subject in architecture. This study may lead to the future use of apps to assist architects and students in making more informed data-based design decisions considering the interior thermal environment. Therefore, the following are suggested by the study.

- Mobile learning must blend into rich learning environments that co-exist with paper books, classroom experiences, laptops, and tablets.
- Learning with mobile apps during virtual learning environments and traditional learning or face-to-face learning can achieve the same Learning Outcome.
- The potential of using mobile apps must be explored as a blended learning approach to meet the post-pandemic teaching challenges and learn about thermal comfort in Architecture and Environment in higher educational institutions.
- The potential of collaborative applications as a tool for teaching and learning needs to be used and explored more as a learning pedagogy

The use of technology in teaching and learning is highly recommended, particularly m-learning applications, as it can connect students, peers, and instructors, increase learners' motivation levels and create strong communities to advance the learning process in a blended learning approach post-pandemic. The future of Architecture education may also involve learning from the pandemic and doing things differently.

The innovative use of scientific measurement using apps in teaching and learning can be replicated in other studies related to understanding science, weather and climatic conditions, and thermal comfort in various levels, such as primary and secondary schools and higher educational institutions. This learning method promotes experiential learning and critical thinking that helps the learner understand the quantitative data measured, the qualitative environment they have experienced, and the comfort levels according to Malaysian Standards. For example, measuring lighting levels of 200lux – *I can read and write comfortably* off the light and at a measurement of 60 lux, for example – *I have trouble reading.*

The findings suggest that students utilised mobile learning solutions to extend and enrich their learning experience during the pandemic. Therefore, this study suggests that mobile learning needs to blend into rich learning environments, in which they co-exist with paper books, classroom experiences, laptops, and tablets. The insights define that learning with mobile apps during virtual learning environments and traditional learning or face-to-face learning can achieve the same learning outcomes. The potential of using mobile apps must be explored as a blended learning approach to meet the post-pandemic teaching challenges and learn thermal comfort in Architecture and Environment and other modules, notably the Architecture Design Studios in higher educational institutions.

REFERENCES

Adedoyin, O. B., & Soykan, E. (2020). Covid-19 pandemic and online learning: The challenges and opportunities. *Interactive Learning Environments*, 1–13.

Agarwal, S., & Kaushik, J. S. (2020). Student's perception of online learning during covid pandemic. *Indian Journal of Pediatrics*, 87(7), 554–554. doi:10.100712098-020-03327-7 PMID:32385779

Al Ansi, A. M., & Al-Ansi, A. (2020). Future of education post covid-19 pandemic: Reviewing changes in learning environments and latest trends. *Solid State Technology*, 63(6), 201584–201600.

Azizan, F. Z. (2010). Blended learning in higher education institution in Malaysia. In *Proceedings of regional conference on knowledge integration in ICT* (Vol. 10, pp. 454-466). Scientific Research Publishing.

Azman, N., & Abdullah, D. (2021). A Critical Analysis of Malaysian Higher Education Institutions' Response towards COVID-19: Sustaining Academic Program Delivery. *Journal of Sustainability Science and Management*, 16(1), 70–96. doi:10.46754/jssm.2021.01.008

Bahji, S., Lefdaoui, Y., & El Alami, J. (2013). Enhancing motivation and engagement: A top-down approach for the design of a learning experience according to the S2P-LM. [iJET]. *International Journal of Emerging Technologies in Learning*, 8(6), 35–41. doi:10.3991/ijet.v8i6.2955

Bang, M., Wohn, K., & Shi, C. (2014). The Establishment of an e-Learning System Based on SDT. *Olnline Journals, 9*(4), 43-49.

Barreh, K. A., & Abas, Z. W. (2015). A Framework for Mobile Learning for Enhancing Learning in Higher Education. *Malaysian Online Journal of Educational Technology*, 3(3), 1–9.

Battalio, J. (2007). Interaction online: A re-evaluation. *Quarterly Review of Distance Education, 8*(4), 339–352.

Bekele, T. A. (2010). Motivation and satisfaction in Internet-supported learning environments: A review. *Journal of Educational Technology & Society*, 13(2), 116–127.

Bomia, L., Beluzo, L., Demeester, D., Elander, K., Johnson, M., & Sheldon, B. (1997). The impact of teaching strategies on intrinsic motivation. Champaign, IL: ERIC Clearinghouse on Elementary and Early Childhood Education.

Briggs, A. (2015). *Ten ways to overcome barriers to student engagement online*. Online Learning Consortium. https://onlinelearningconsortium.org/news_item/tenways-overcomebarriers-student-engagement-online/

Cameron, L. (2006). Teaching with technology: Using online chat to promote effective in-class discussions. In *Proceedings of the 23rd Annual Conference of the Australasian Society for Computers in Learning in Tertiary Education: Who's Learning*. Ascilite.

Castell, N., Dauge, F. R., Schneider, P., Vogt, M., Lerner, U., Fishbain, B., & Broday, D. M. (2016). Smartphone-based environmental sensing for personal exposure assessment. *Environmental Science & Technology*, *50*(21), 11507–11515.

Cejudo-Ruíz, J. P., García-Pérez, A., González-Velasco, H. M., & García-Zubía, J. (2019). Smartphone-based measurements of light and sound for environmental monitoring applications. *Sensors (Basel)*, *19*(19), 4253. PMID:31575009

Chaiprasurt, C., Esichaikul, V., & Wishart, J. (2011). Designing mobile communication tools: A framework to enhance motivation in an online learning environment, *Proceedings of the 10th World Conference on Mobile and Contextual Learning*, (p. 112–120). Semantic Scholar.

Davis, F. D. (1989). Perceived usefulness, perceived ease of use, and user acceptance of information technology. *Management Information Systems Quarterly*, *13*(3), 319–340. doi:10.2307/249008

Singh, D. & Zaitun A. B. (2006, August). Mobile Learning in Wireless Classrooms [MOJIT]. *Malaysian Online Journal of Instructional Technology*, *3*(2), 26–42.

Dwivedi, Y. K., Hughes, D. L., Coombs, C., Constantiou, I., Duan, Y., Edwards, J. S., Gupta, B., Lal, B., Misra, S., Prashant, P., Raman, R., Rana, N. P., Sharma, S. K., & Upadhyay, N. (2020). Impact of COVID-19 pandemic on information management research and practice: Transforming education, work and life. *International Journal of Information Management*, *55*, 102211. doi:10.1016/j.ijinfomgt.2020.102211

Dziuban, C., Moskal, P., Thompson, J., Kramer, L., DeCantis, G., & Hermsdorfer, A. (2015). Student Satisfaction with Online Learning: Is It a Psychological Contract. *Online Learning : the Official Journal of the Online Learning Consortium*, *19*(2), n2. doi:10.24059/olj.v19i2.496

El Said, G. R. (2021). How did the COVID-19 pandemic affect higher education learning experience? An empirical investigation of learners' academic performance at a university in a developing country. *Advances in Human-Computer Interaction*, *2021*, 1–10. doi:10.1155/2021/6649524

El-Seoud, M. A. S., El-Khouly, M., & Taj-Eddin, I. A. T. F. (2015). Strategies to enhance learner's motivation in e-learning environment. In *Proceedings of 18th International Conference on Interactive Collaborative Learning* (pp. 944–949). 10.1109/ICL.2015.7318154

Environmental Defense Fund. (2019). *Measuring air quality with smartphone sensors: A practical guide for citizen scientists*. EDF. https://www.edf.org/health/measuring-air-quality-smartphone-sensors-practical-guide-citizen-scientists

Froese, A. D., Carpenter, C. N., Inman, D. A., Schooley, J. R., Barnes, R. B., Brecht, P. W., & Chacon, J. D. (2012). Effects of classroom cell phone use on expected and actual learning. *College Student Journal, 46*(2), 323–332.

Fry, K. (2001). E-learning markets and providers: Some issues and prospects. *Education + Training, 43*(4/5), 233–239. doi:10.1108/EUM0000000005484

Fu, Q. K., & Hwang, G. J. (2018). Trends in mobile technology-supported collaborative learning: a systematic review of journal publications from 2007 to 2016. *Computers and Education, 119*(2017), 129–143.

Furrer, C., & Skinner, E. (2003). Sense of relatedness as a factor in children's academic engagement and performance. *Journal of Educational Psychology, 95*(1), 148–162. doi:10.1037/0022-0663.95.1.148

Gunasagaran, S., & Mari, M. (2014). Using Digital Simulation as an E-Learning Tool to Create Dynamic Learning in Architecture Students. *Global Journal of Business and Social Science Review, 2*(3), 61–68. doi:10.35609/gjbssr.2014.2.3(10)

Gunasagaran, S., Mari, M. T., Srirangam, S., & Kuppusamy, S. (2019). Adoption of social media by architecture students in fostering community SERVICE initiative using technology acceptance model. []. IOP Publishing.]. *IOP Conference Series. Materials Science and Engineering, 636*(1), 012015. doi:10.1088/1757-899X/636/1/012015

Gunay, H. B., O'Brien, W., Beausoleil-Morrison, I., & Cui, Y. (2017). Smartphone sensor-based building energy auditing. *Building and Environment, 123*, 152–162.

Hamdan, K., & Ben-Chabane, Y. (2013) An interactive mobile learning method to measure students' performance. *QScience Proceedings, 12th World Conference on Mobile and Contextual Learning (mLearn 2013).* Qatar.

Harlan, H., Badara, A., & Kamaluddin, K. (2019). The use of hand phone application to increase student's ability in learning English vocabulary. *Journal Pendidikan Bahasa, 8*(2), 106–107.

Harrison, R., Flood, D., & Duce, D. (2013). Usability of mobile applications: Literature review and rationale for a new usability model. *Journal of Interaction Science, 1*(1), 1–16. doi:10.1186/2194-0827-1-1

Hassanein, K., Head, M., & Wang, F. (2010). Understanding student satisfaction in a mobile learning environment: the role of internal and external facilitators. *2010 Ninth International Conference on Mobile Business and 2010 Ninth Global Mobility Roundtable* (ICMB-GMR), (pp.289–296). IEEE. 10.1109/ICMB-GMR.2010.38

Hinkle, D. E., Wiersma, W., & Jurs, S. G. (2003). *Applied statistics for the behavioral sciences* (Vol. 663). Houghton Mifflin College Division.

Hrastinski, S. (2008). Asynchronous and synchronous e-learning. *EDUCAUSE Quarterly, 31*(4), 51–55.

Hu, P. J., Chau, P. Y. K., Sheng, O. R. L., & Tam, K. Y. (1999). Examining the technology acceptance model using physician acceptance of telemedicine technology. *Journal of Management Information Systems, 16*(2), 91–112. doi:10.1080/07421222.1999.11518247

Huang, Y., Tu, M., Wang, S., Chen, S., Zhou, W., Chen, D., Zhou, L., Wang, M., Zhao, Y., Zeng, W., Huang, Q., Xu, H., Liu, Z., & Guo, L. (2020). Clinical characteristics of laboratory confirmed positive cases of SARS-CoV-2 infection in Wuhan, China: A retrospective single center analysis. *Travel Medicine and Infectious Disease*, *36*, 101606. doi:10.1016/j.tmaid.2020.101606 PMID:32114074

Jaggars, S. S., & Xu, D. (2016). How do online course design features influence student performance? *Computers & Education*, *95*, 270–284. doi:10.1016/j.compedu.2016.01.014

Ke, F., & Kwak, D. (2013). Constructs of student-centered online learning on learning satisfaction of a diverse online student body: A structural equation modeling approach. *Journal of Educational Computing Research*, *48*(1), 97-122. doi: . e doi:10.2190/EC.48.1

Kulkarni, M. (2019). *10 Things architects learn about in environmental studies in college*. Rethinking The Future. https://www.re-thinkingthefuture.com/rtf-fresh-perspectives/a1693-10-things-architects-learn-about-in-environmental-studies-in-college/

Kuo, Y. C., Walker, A. E., Belland, B. R., & Schroder, K. E. (2013). A predictive study of student satisfaction in online education programs. *International Review of Research in Open and Distance Learning*, *14*(1), 16–39. doi:10.19173/irrodl.v14i1.1338

Laal, M., Laal, M., & Kermanshahi, Z. K. (2012). 21st century learning; learning in collaboration. *Procedia: Social and Behavioral Sciences*, *47*, 1696–1701. doi:10.1016/j.sbspro.2012.06.885

López Peláez, A., Erro-Garcés, A., Pinilla García, F. J., & Kiriakou, D. (2021). Working in the 21st Century. The coronavirus crisis: A driver of digitalization, teleworking, and innovation, with unintended social consequences. *Information (Basel)*, *12*(9), 377. doi:10.3390/info12090377

MacCallum, K. (2009) 'Student characteristics and variables that determine mobile adoption: An initial study', *Proceedings of the Universal College of Learning: Teaching and Learning Conference*, (pp. 1–8). IEEE.

Makewa, L. N., Kuboja, J. M., Yango, M., & Ngussa, B. M. (2014). ICT-integration in higher education and student behavioral change: Observations at university of Arusha, Tanzania. *American Journal of Educational Research*, *2*(11A), 30–38. doi:10.12691/education-2-11A-5

Miao, G. (2012). Interactive design and realization of mobile learning resources through 3G mobile phones, *International Conference on Information Management, Innovation Management and Industrial Engineering* (ICIII), (pp. 56–59). IEEE.

Miller, H. B., & Cuevas, J. A. (2017). Mobile Learning and its Effects on Academic Achievement and Student Motivation in Middle Grades Students. *International Journal for the Scholarship of Technology Enhanced Learning*, *1*(2), 91–110.

O'Leary, R., & Ramsden, A. (2002). *Virtual learning environments. Learning and Teaching Support Network Generic Centre/ALT Guides*. LTSN.

Pandey, N., & Pal, A. (2020). Impact of digital surge during Covid-19 pandemic: A viewpoint on research and practice. *International Journal of Information Management*, *55*, 102171. doi:10.1016/j.ijinfomgt.2020.102171 PMID:32836633

Papapicco, C. (2020). Informative contagion: The coronavirus (COVID-19) in Italian journalism. *Online Journal of Communication and Media Technologies*, *10*(3), e202014. doi:10.29333/ojcmt/7938

Poore, M. (2015). Using social media in the classroom: A best practice guide. *Sage (Atlanta, Ga.)*.

Priego, R. G., & Peralta, A. G. (2013, November). Engagement factors and motivation in e-Learning and blended-learning projects. In *Proceedings of the first international conference on technological ecosystem for enhancing multiculturality* (pp. 453-460). IEEE. 10.1145/2536536.2536606

Richardson, J. C., & Newby, T. (2006). The role of students' cognitive engagement in online learning. *American Journal of Distance Education*, *20*(1), 23–37. doi:10.120715389286ajde2001_3

Said, A. S., & Syafik, E. (2016). The development of online tutorial program design using problem-based learning in open distance learning system. *Journal of Education and Practice*, *7*(18), 222–222.

Sha, L., Looi, C. K., Chen, W., Seow, P., & Wong, L. H. (2012). Recognizing and measuring self-regulated learning in a mobile learning environment. *Computers in Human Behavior*, *28*(2), 718–728. doi:10.1016/j.chb.2011.11.019

Tawafak, R., Malik, S., Mathew, R., Ashfaque, M., Jabbar, J., AlNuaimi, M., ElDow, A., & Alfarsi, G. (2021). A Combined Model for Continuous Intention to Use E-Learning System. *International Journal of Interactive Mobile Technologies*, *15*(3), 113–129. doi:10.3991/ijim.v15i03.18953

Tawafak, R. M., Romli, A. B., & Arshah, R. B. A. (2018). Continued intention to use UCOM: Four factors for integrating with a technology acceptance model to moderate the satisfaction of learning. *IEEE Access : Practical Innovations, Open Solutions*, *6*, 66481–66498. doi:10.1109/ACCESS.2018.2877760

Tsai, S., & Machado, P. (2002). E-learning, online learning, web based learning, or distance learning: Unveiling the ambiguity in current terminology. *Association for Computer Machinery eLearn Magazine*, (7), 3-5.

United Nations Educational, Scientific, and Cultural Organization (UNESCO). (2020). *COVID-19 Educational Disruption and Response*. UNESCO. https://en.unesco.org/themes/education-emergencies/coronavirus-school-closures

Viner, R. M., Russell, S. J., Croker, H., Packer, J., Ward, J., Stansfield, C., Mytton, O., Bonell, C., & Booy, R. (2020). School closure and management practices during coronavirus outbreaks including COVID-19: A rapid systematic review. *The Lancet. Child & Adolescent Health*, *4*(5), 397–404. doi:10.1016/S2352-4642(20)30095-X PMID:32272089

Vogel, D., Kennedy, D., Kuan, K., Kwok, R., & Lai, J. (2007). Do mobile device applications affect learning? *40th Annual Hawaii International Conference on System Sciences* (HICSS'07). IEEE.

Watson, D., Perez, L., & Wing, I. S. (2015). Environmental Monitoring with Smartphones. In Smartphones as Locative Media (pp. 59-73). Palgrave Macmillan, London.

World Health Organization (WHO). (2020). *WHO Director-General's opening remarks at the media briefing on COVID-19*. WHO. https://www.who.int/director-general/speeches/detail/who-director-general-s-opening-remarks-at-the-media-briefing-on-covid-19---20-march-2020

Zhai, X., Li, M., & Chen, S. (2019). Examining the uses of student-led, teacher-led, and collaborative functions of mobile technology and their impacts on physics achievement and interest. *Journal of Science Education and Technology, 28*(4), 310–320. doi:10.100710956-019-9767-3

Zhai, X., & Shi, L. (2020). Understanding how the perceived usefulness of mobile technology impacts physics learning achievement: A pedagogical perspective. *Journal of Science Education and Technology, 29*(6), 743–757. doi:10.100710956-020-09852-6

Chapter 6
Technologically Advanced Classrooms by Customising Blogs (TACblog) Amongst Architectural Design Students for Spotlight and Publication

Salmiah Aziz

Faculty of Innovative and Design Technology, Universiti Sultan Zainal Abidin (UNISZA), Malaysia & Architectural Technology and Management Group, Faculty of Architecture and Ekistics, Universiti Malaysia Kelantan (UMK), Malaysia & Institute for Artificial Intelligenice and Big Data (AIBIg), Office of Deputy Vice Chancellor (Research and Innovation), Universiti Malaysia Kelantan, Malaysia

Siti Nuratirah Che Mohd Nasir

Architectural Technology and Management Group, Faculty of Architecture and Ekistics, Universiti Malaysia Kelantan (UMK), Malaysia

Nor Diyana Mustapa

Human Centered Design Group, Faculty of Architecture and Ekistics, Universiti Malaysia Kelantan (UMK), Malaysia

Nik Nurul Hana Hanafi

Architectural Technology and Management Group, Faculty of Architecture and Ekistics, Universiti Malaysia Kelantan (UMK), Malaysia

Noorul Huda Mohd Razali

Architectural Technology and Management Group, Faculty of Architecture and Ekistics, Universiti Malaysia Kelantan (UMK), Malaysia

Mohammed Fadzli Maharimi

Architectural Technology and Management Group, Faculty of Architecture and Ekistics, Universiti Malaysia Kelantan (UMK), Malaysia

DOI: 10.4018/978-1-6684-8253-7.ch006

ABSTRACT

The advancement of new technologies into our daily lives has resulted in a significant increase in the use of information and communication technology (ICT) in education in recent years. The research objectives were to identify the possibility of blogging amongst architectural design students for the future of schooling (blended-learning) and to formulate the best practice of ICTs knowledge management practice through blended-learning for the architectural design students. The data collected through reviewing the literature by other authors (secondary sources) on the subject of digitalisation, digital construction, and digital education. The research could significantly affect the future of education in producing young tech-savvy generations in terms of technologically advanced classrooms; new option of blogging platform for the architectural design students to practice design communication through e-learning known as TACblog as a digital education formulation.

INTRODUCTION

People in various industries were forced to use digital tools to keep their businesses running during the lockdowns in The New Norm as so-called volatility (V), uncertainty (U), complexity (C), and ambiguity (A) in a short form as VUCA.

Because of this, the pandemic has hastened development across practically all industries, including construction, which has long lagged other sectors in innovation. Construction has a low level of digitalization, a disjointed ecosystem, and a high rate of faults when compared to other industries. The COVID-19 conference has highlighted a change in mindset towards digital tools as well as quicker investment decisions. Modernization and digital transformation are therefore likely to pick up speed and establish themselves as the new industrial norms (Figure 1). Technology adoption was very strong throughout the lockdown periods, and new technologies were integrated into existing designs as part of the reaction to the pandemic. As a result, a digital transformation seems to be well under way in a field that is notorious for being slow to absorb technological advancements.

Figure 1. Aspects of digital transformation
Image: Credit to respective owner

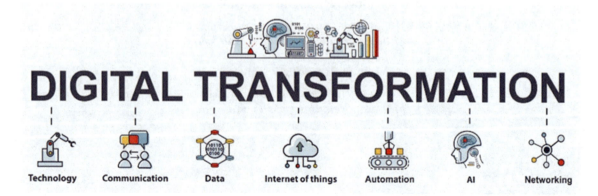

The process of digitising architecture and construction, as well as the built environment in which we all live, necessitates unprecedented cross-domain and cross-industry collaboration. It combines the internet of things, the industrial internet, smart homes and cities, and cloud-based, fully digitised design and manufacturing. And it will take millions of companies to build it because each one focuses on a specific geographic area and type of building. As today's world enters digitization, it's linked to the way of modernization in education, so-called digital learning.

Due to the incorporation of new technologies into everyday life, information and communication technology (ICT) use in education has risen significantly in recent years. ICTs have grown in importance in our society, finding applications in everything from administration to robotics, education, and a variety of businesses. The construction industry is pursuing its revolution, the fourth industrial revolution, with a tidal shift in how the sector addresses difficulties by creating a strong digital basis through cooperative effort. At the intersection of people, new technologies, and innovation, the revolution is a transformation that includes automation, data exchanges, cloud computing, big data, artificial intelligence (AI), the Internet of Things (IoT), and semi-autonomous industrial techniques to realise manufacturing and smart industry objectives (Sa'ar, 2017).

MSC Malaysia, an initiative that has contributed to turning Malaysia into a knowledge-based economy since 1996, will be replaced by Malaysia Digital. The new project aims to improve the country's digital capabilities and advance the digital economy with a new and better framework. The ultimate beneficiaries will be the rakyat, businesses, government, and country. Malaysia Digital will enable Malaysia to better prepare for today's constantly changing scenario and construct the foundation of a digital nation (Corporate Affairs Division, Malaysia Digital Economy Corporation (MDEC), 2022).

Due to the rapid development of the Industrial Revolution (IR) 4.0, the Malaysian Education Institution is transforming the present educational system into the education system of the future 4.0. Due to the consequences of IR 4.0 and the COVID-19 outbreak, the Malaysian Educational Institution has also adopted a new paradigm to guarantee that all lecturers can use ICT in teaching and learning.

Data Analysis (Data From Secondary Sources)

Digital technology, which is described as a sort of technology based on numbers, has an expanding field of application. Digital education is one of the mentioned areas. Education is the area that, surprisingly, lags behind the world's rapid general advancement as we navigate it. According to the WEF Future of Jobs Report 2018, technology advancements are reshaping the global labour market and blurring the line between human jobs and automated machine operations, and most individuals are still ill-equipped to deal with these changes. Table 1 shows the four aspects of digitalisation, such as definition, construction, education, and the issues that existed from the modernization of education, which have impacted the way of future education, as quoted by different authors.

Analysis on Case Studies (Secondary Sources)

Case Study A: Students at Polytechnic Malaysia continue to place a strong preference on digital learning platforms and tools over conventional approaches. Nonetheless, there are several ways that instructors might engage students with digital learning (Bujang et al., 2020).

Table 1. Data analysis of digitalisation aspects in term of definition, construction, education and the issues

No	Definition	Construction	Digitalisation		
			Education	Issues	Research Gap
1	Digitalization is the use of digital technologies to build a company model and new income and value production prospects (Yankn, 2018, p. 9).	400 business leaders were surveyed by McKinsey & Company: 47% were from North America, 39% were from Europe, and 11% were from Asia-Pacific. 75 percent of respondents believed that COVID-19 has expedited the changes and transformation in the construction business, which will be constantly changing over the next five to ten years. 250 managers participated in a Procore Technologies poll that found that 66% of UK businesses implemented new technologies during lockdown, and 94% of those businesses reported improved team performance. Eighty percent of respondents think that working together on an integrated digital platform will be essential for construction work in the future. 52 percent of responders who had enabled online collaboration and implemented productivity technology solutions said that after the lockdown, their teams' safety had improved. Spending on public clouds (and related services) is rising in the Asia-Pacific region at a rate of 25% per year, which is faster than growth in the established economies of the US and Western Europe (Jakarta Globe). The two factors that have been highlighted throughout the crisis, innovation and risk reduction, are stated by 71% of respondents to be the driving forces behind such attitudes.	Information and communication technology (ICT) use in education has grown dramatically over the past few years because of the integration of cutting-edge technology into our daily lives. With a wide range of applications in fields such as entertainment, administration, robotics, education, and all types of organisations, ICTs have grown in significance in today's society. We want to specifically study the effects of ICT use in education in this blog post, but before we do that, let's define ICT. The term "ICT" stands for "information and communication technology." If we had to characterise it, the ideal definition would be "a mix of techniques and devices based on new technological tools and all of the supports and ways of information and communication." This could also include the procedure for acquiring, storing, processing, and transmitting information digitally. ICTs have a sizable impact on society and are being used more and more, which are two variables that cannot be disregarded in the field of education. ICT is quickly becoming a vital tool for novice teachers and students in the classroom. Due to its widespread use in society, ICT shouldn't be utilised less in classrooms and should instead be utilised to the fullest extent possible. However, children must be taught how to use them appropriately and intelligently. The educational system must assume responsibility for gradually integrating all technologies that may in some way support student learning in order to ensure that students are educated to use these tools in a society where they have become an integral part of social and professional life. In the context of e-learning solutions such as Pedagoo, online assessments such as hundreds of examination questions, comprehensive student progress, assessment standardisation, or the establishment of workflows are included. Pedagoo (2020) mentioned a few technological tools that are most frequently used in education, such as: • Blogs and social media sites: These help students organise study groups where they can explore and debate various topics, produce content pertaining to their courses, etc. • Planning with the help of tools: planners and task managers are great for scheduling deliveries, exams, and other tasks like process creation. • The capacity to collaborate and retrieve information from any place or device is made possible by cloud data storage. One or two examples of the applications that make use of this technology are office rooms, storage, and other utilities. • Dynamic tables and electronic whiteboards: Whiteboards allow users to save and/or email the screen as well as project and control images from a computer. Students have the opportunity to interact directly with the surface thanks to the interactive tables. Students' enthusiasm, passion, and interest in the things they are learning have been shown to rise when ICT is used in the classroom. ICT enables the use of state-of-the-art educational resources and the modernization of teaching methodologies, which promotes more student involvement and concurrent technology skill acquisition. ICTs play a key role in the growth of judgement as well. ICT use has a noticeable impact on students' capacity to compare and contrast information from many sources and organise knowledge, two of their most notable new skills. However, there are additional advantages (Pedagoo, 2020): i) The use of tools like movies, the internet, graphics, and games, which liven up traditional courses, boosts students' passion for studying. Engaging and thorough multimedia information is a terrific way to keep students interested in what they are learning. ii) Interactivity: Using technology in the classroom motivates students to engage actively in their education and to perceive themselves as the protagonist. iii) Student cooperation: There is no denying that the use of various digital technologies has increased student cooperation. They can work together more easily, develop team projects, and exchange knowledge. ICT resources support all pupils' initiative and the development of their imagination. Better communication is encouraged among students and teachers via a number of techniques, including more laid-back and spontaneous interactions. Additionally, digital environments allow for up-to-date access to all resources and data, enabling personalization and current content. The materials and tools can also be changed to represent local and surrounding realities (Pedagoo, 2020).	There were problems with implementing electronic educational materials (e-learning) in education, including low adoption rates, bandwidth and connectivity concerns, a digital divide and low computer competence, a dearth of high-quality e-content, difficulties in engaging students online, and language obstacles (Ali P.T., 2013).	Technology Focused Classroom Compared to other periods in history, education is evolving more quickly now. There is a growing understanding among educators and parents that the curriculum of today must change to reflect the realities of the future. Beyond tools and technology, students must learn new abilities to tackle challenging issues, work well in teams, and articulate ideas in novel ways. Google for Education collaborated with a global team of researchers and analysts to look at evidence-based changes in classroom instruction and better comprehend these changes. The eight components of a growing pattern in education are: electronic citizenship, life skills and employment planning, computational thinking, student-driven learning, collaborative classrooms, linking parents and schools, innovative pedagogy, and new technologies (Google for Education).

continued on following page

Table 1. Continued

No	Definition	Digitalisation			
		Construction	Education	Issues	Research Gap
2	Digital technology can be defined as the kind of technology that enables the development of electronic screen devices, gadgets, and machines that transform numerical data into usable, understandable information to simplify the lives of consumers. Digital technology goods serve a variety of new usage scenarios on a daily basis as technology develops, in addition to offering immediate, useful, and common uses once employed. Every day, people's lives are made easier by products like video, cameras, computers, mobile phones, televisions, watches, medical gadgets, laser gauges, electronic culinary utensils, air conditioners, and more that were created or run using digital technology. To take advantage of the opportunities offered by quickly advancing information and communication technologies as well as changing social needs, digitalization is defined as an organisation's comprehensive evolution in human, operational, and technological factors (Demirarslan et al.,2020).	Over the following several decades, the whole digital transformation was anticipated to take place. Robotics, 3D printing, machine learning, and BIM will all eventually be included into construction workflows. Given that COVID-19 appears to have altered the narrative, this may occur sooner than anticipated. Digitalizing project delivery, particularly in the 'post-COVID' world, will at the very least provide the following advantages: • Higher efficiency • Improved collaboration • Building trust • Ensure Occupational Health and Safety (OSH) At present, it appears that some segments of the construction industry are rapidly undergoing a digital transition, and as with any other change, turning digital also requires changing how things are done. Players in the construction value chain must make strategic plans to thrive in the face of expected disruptions in order to embrace this. Following are some proactive measures that members of the construction sector can take, especially now that lockdowns have been released, according to Turner and Townsend: • **Focusing on productivity and outcomes** • **Building digital capability** • **Assured data and analytics** Construction, engineering, and architectural organisations have demonstrated how they can oversee a significant portion of their operations remotely. As an industry, we have the ability and players to continue operating in digital settings that will continue to shape our society for the foreseeable future. The dilemma at hand is how to ensure success in order to successfully carry forth this function of encouraging societal advancement, economic expansion, and environmental responsibility (Constructionplus.Asia, 2020).	To relate, "Design Thinking" has become more well-known in recent years and is now regarded as an innovative new paradigm for tackling issues in fields as diverse as IT, business, education, and medicine. The design research community is challenged by this potential success to offer clear answers to two important questions: "What is the essence of Design Thinking?" and "What may it deliver to practitioners and organisations in other fields?" (Dorst, 2011).	It also showed that the Malaysian government's rules and SOP make the school's existing operation under the new standard time- and energy-intensive. Therefore, installing an intelligent structure system for schools can reduce the amount of extra work and hassle involved in operating the educational facility to comply with the new standard (Yong et al., 2022).	Future educators will have to recognise the fact that pupils will need (and want) to study in a flexible, personalised manner; for some, this may require maintaining an increasingly technologically advanced classroom. Students will anticipate that their educational experience will take into account their time constraints, interests, and academic needs (USCRossier).

continued on following page

Table 1. Continued

No	Definition	Digitalisation			
		Construction	Education	Issues	Research Gap
3	Digitalization is the persistent change in human, useful, and technical elements within an organisation to deliver improved efficiency, effectiveness, support, and consumer happiness according to the opportunities presented by rapidly developing information and communication technology as well as changing social needs. In simple terms, "digital technology" denotes the category of technology that enables the development of electronic screen devices, devices, and equipment whereby numerical data is transformed into usable and intelligible information with the aim of making users' lives easier (Yazar and Yalçın, 2018, p. 613).	The interiors of buildings are expected to change dramatically, but along three major axes of consideration: sustainability, technology, and efficiency. These three transformational impulses will occur concurrently rather than separately, with each influencing and facilitating the other. Cities will hopefully become more sustainable, flexible, and inclusive as a result, though there is still a long way to go.	It is possible to recognise, understand, and internalise the present architecture agenda by incorporating the concepts that differentiate various architectural fields through the lens of technological breakthroughs. The construction of this data infrastructure and interaction setting for architectural design education has undergone constant change because of technological breakthroughs. Architectural design communication (ADC) and its constituent parts must be updated and reevaluated, and fresh communication media that emerged because of technological improvements in architectural design education must be adjusted, monitored, and understood (Akçay Kavakoğlu, 2022). On the other hand, communication is currently a problem in architectural design education. Since the dialogues between the instructor and students and between the students themselves cannot sufficiently develop during the educational process, the quality of the education provided is lower. The process of architectural design is turned into an interactive teaching tool through this dialogue produced by the continually changing ADC language. An architectural design studio serves as the scene for this interaction, where learning occurs through a collection of experiences. The environment of this design office is starting to become both virtual and actual thanks to technological breakthroughs. Online communication platforms are being examined more and more in terms of efficacy, teamwork, and engagement (Rodriguez et al., 2018; Jones et al., 2020; Simoff and Maher, 2000; Gabriel and Maher, 2002; Chiu, 2002). But before these exams have an enormous global effect on architectural design education, it might take until 2020. Due to the COVID-19 pandemic, which caused worldwide adoption of Emergency Remote Teaching (ERT) procedures, almost all design studios moved digital over the 2019–2020 Academic Year Spring term. ERT was immediately implemented at universities with a distance learning infrastructure, while emergency plans were promptly created for institutions without one. Architectural design education has seen a methodological transformation as a result of the COVID-19 epidemic, and online learning has seen a rapid change in communicative interaction. It is especially crucial to organise the common purposes and topics of the ideas and language that will be subject to communication and incorporate them within the list of goals of architectural design education in order to maximise the potential of the virtual classroom (Akçay Kavakoğlu, 2022). The researchers refer to the educational research of Akçay Kavakoğlu (2022) to better understand the current scope of research. The study examines the notion of an ADC to investigate internal dynamics in an online platform for teaching architectural design, according to his research framework. The study assesses the relationships between the ADC elements from the discipline of architectural design curriculum at two institutions in Turkey and Spain, utilising both quantitative and qualitative approaches. According to the paper's hypotheses, a survey is conducted at both campuses. The outcomes of the procedure of analysis are then compared to those of the survey. Through these comparisons, the research intends to identify the association between technology-oriented skills and handmade talents in ADC.	The Malaysian building sector is growing, though more slowly. The nation has just recently begun to embrace the concept of digitalization. The building industry in Malaysia is transitioning from traditional to digital integration. However, the readiness of the stakeholders in regards to finances, models of business, organisational structure strategy, procedure, and maintenance, along with senior management's commitment, is impeding the adoption of digitalization. The digital era has nonetheless arrived, and to grow, people must either adopt the megatrend or risk being left behind (Sa'ar, 2017).	Embedding the newest ICT knowledge for architectural design students in response to Generation Z's interest in the Internet of Things (IoT). The benefits of emphasising the art of digital literacy in the classroom are being emphasised more and more by school administrators, media specialists, and academics since today's youth primarily rely on internet usage as a source of information. Students who are additionally digitally literate know how to find and make use of digital resources. They are adept at creating, sharing, and distributing digital content. Students who are working on their knowledge of digital literacy are aware of the essentials underlying online security, such as setting up secure passwords, understanding and using privacy settings, and knowing what information to publish or not on social networks. They are aware of the dangers of cyberbullying and work to stop current bullies as well as deter others from becoming bullies. The ability to explore, assess, communicate with, and distribute online content efficiently and responsibly is essential for students' futures because practically every career in today's digital world involves some form of digital communication. However, the advantages of giving your pupils instruction in digital literacy start right away in the classroom (Renaissance).

continued on following page

Table 1. Continued

No	Definition	Digitalisation		Issues	Research Gap
		Education	Construction		
4	Data and processes are transformed by digitalization if they are converted through digitization. Digitalization encompasses the ability of contemporary technology to acquire data, spot trends, and make better business decisions, as opposed to merely digitising already-existing data (TruQC).	Schools today may look very different in 20 years due to a variety of factors, such as unforeseen technologies, enormous global impacts, and fundamental changes in how pupils and educators want to learn. In the coming decades of education, teachers will need become more creative, innovative, and entrepreneurial. By then, pupils will be considerably more tech savvy, demanding, confident, and focused as education customers. It is essential to think about what the academic community can do to get ready for the future in order to tackle areas of need right now. Schools should focus on these areas of transformation in order to guarantee that education offers a bright future (USCRossier): • Personalization and Customization • Student Ownership • Enhanced Curricula (Curriculum) • Cutting-Edge Learning Environment • Interconnectivity • Real-World Application Plus Project-Based Learning (PBL) • Technology • Further Examination Future teachers will need to recognise the fact that pupils will need (as well as want) to study in a flexible, personalised style; for others, this may require having an improved, technologically equipped classroom. In order to meet their learning requirements, time constraints, and interests, students will want the learning experience to be flexible (USCRossier).	Over the last decade, the construction industry has prioritised BIM implementation. However, recent efforts in the construction industry's digital transformation have seen the integration of emerging technologies with BIM and the construction process. The construction industry's digital transformation is divided into phases and aspects. This distinguishes it from other industries. This also lends credence to the construction industry's peculiarity, implying that more efforts are required to achieve digital transformation in the construction industry (Adekunle et al., 2021).	Malaysia needs to implement the right policies to boost productivity and economic growth in order to prepare society and the workforce for the digital shift. All of these digital development objectives, meanwhile, would be seen as empty platitudes if the country's digital gap persists. The government has already made a substantial effort to promote digital skills through several initiatives in response to these difficulties. But it seems like the endeavour is still moving at a modest pace. From an economic perspective, it is crucial to hasten the development of digital infrastructure, especially in rural areas. Although well known, rural locations often have lower population densities than metropolitan areas, which may be a factor in the poor adoption of digital infrastructure such as the Internet (Ayob et al., 2022).	To increase the quality of education for the institution's brand and spotlight. According to the consensus reached through interviews and surveys, online education appears to be here to stay now and in the future. Online blended learning has been observed to maximise the advantages of traditional teaching techniques with online learning resources. Additionally, it will increase student access to the curriculum and help professors become more adept at adapting assessments for use online (Shankar Subramaniam Iyer & S.P. Jain, 2021).
5	Information processing, or how digitised data may be utilised to enhance workflows by automating current processes, is at the heart of digitalization. To boost involvement and create new value, digital growth is all about using knowledge and connecting it throughout all business activities. (Monton, 2022).	By applying ICT in education in terms of blogging ability, it may have an impact on student learning outcomes. For casual online postings, businesses and individuals both use blogging extensively. The educational potential of blogs is currently being recognised more and more. Blogs can be used for collaborative projects, peer reviews, and group discussions. Reading about a topic on a blog, though, is more interesting. Through blogging, students can share their "unique voices." They may improve their interpersonal and verbal abilities by responding to comments posted on their blogs or giving feedback on other people's postings. Blog-writing students have a greater probability of being courteous and respectful. Blogging encourages students' analytical abilities and elevates discovering to a higher level, as opposed to just understanding and "remembering." Prior to writing down their ideas, students have to analyse the information and then articulate their ideas. Students must then carefully formulate and maintain their own opinions. Students are urged to consider how readers could interpret and react to their thoughts when they blog. When people create fresh material and design for their blogs, blogging encourages creative expression. Students can use their imagination to personalise the themes, choose pertinent photos or videos, and customise the layout. Students can express themselves visually on this platform. Blogging has the power to make learning enjoyable. Writing is a big part of blogging. Writing abilities do not, however, automatically improve. At the start of the project, instructors need to provide clear instructions on how to write, how to be real, how to support your beliefs, and how to express expectations for the student (Learning and Education Center).	The construction industry is experiencing an increase in demand for major digital dematerialization innovations and technologies such as the Internet of Things, big data, advanced manufacturing, robotics, 3D printing, blockchain technologies, and artificial intelligence. A key driver for digitization is the desire for simplification and transparency in information management, as well as the rationalisation and optimisation of highly fragmented and splintered processes (Daniotti et al., 2020).		The possibility of improved job versatility and student autonomy, which support higher self-regulation, may be the main advantages of digital technology. Not all students, though, might profit from this (Keith J. Topping et al., 2022).

continued on following page

Table 1. Continued

No	Definition	Digitalisation			
		Construction	Education	Issues	Research Gap
6		Because of digitalization, there is more access to customer data, which has improved customization and assisted architects in presenting a variety of design options for customers to choose from. Because of the large number of digitally enabled people in the community, competition is increasing, and architects must come up with increasingly innovative and efficient solutions. Adopting digital practises has enabled architects to create buildings that would have seemed impossible in the past, as well as venture into reducing the building's energy consumption (Patil).	Presently, students can choose how to access the world's knowledge because it is only a few clicks away. With the use of technology, students are now able to create their own learning paths, set their own objectives, and choose how to demonstrate their knowledge, growth, and abilities (Acer for Education, 2017). Likewise, the students can improve their ICT literacy and prepare for the 21st century by using blogging in the classroom to help them build their ICT abilities. Your pupils' ICT skills, including keyboard shortcuts, internet research, and publishing, will advance, giving them more confidence to use technology both within and outside of the classroom (Victoria, 2018).		Especially in this era of expanding educational opportunities, improving the quality of education and training is a crucial concern. ICTs can improve education quality in a number of ways, including by boosting student motivation and engagement, enabling the learning of fundamental skills, and improving teacher preparation. ICTs are transformational resources that, when properly applied, can support the transition to a learner-centred environment (Haddad et al., 2002).
7		Construction industry digitization is progressing. Despite the industry's unique challenges, the construction industry is embracing five key digitization trends. By implementing BIM standards, construction projects are linked across the value chain. A move to digital documentation improves document management and productivity. Construction workers can complete processes on the job site and access project data using mobile-first tools. Process automation expedites construction processes, resulting in a quick return on investment. Furthermore, using data software provides business leaders with a comprehensive picture of processes, allowing them to make better business decisions (Stone, 2022).	Furthermore, more academics are using blogs as e-portfolio platforms as well as for collaboration, discussion, and resource sharing. According to 2013 PBS.org research, 74% of teachers concur that using technology in the classroom encourages students to learn and enables teachers to reinforce academic topics. Additionally, 68 percent said they would want to see more technology in the classroom. Where have we ended up over the past two years? Technology is being used more and more in classrooms. For instance, the number of students taking online courses rose by 4.68 percent between 2013 and 2014. By 2015, according to an earlier study, at least 25 million students, would be enrolled in online courses. Students now engage with computers, iPads, and video chat software more than ever thanks to the advent of technology in the classroom, but blogging is one digital idea that is still making its way into regular classroom settings. Continue reading to find out more about how blogging is being used in classrooms in 2015 (Wallagher, 2015). The advantages of the classroom as mentioned by Wallagher (2015), depending on how a person uses the blog, blogging in the classroom can have a number of advantages. Listed below are a few examples: • Teachers can blog about class events to keep parents up to date, and students can access announcements from anywhere. • Teachers can use blogs to keep lessons online or provide additional resources for student learning. • Teachers can keep up with assignments using blogs, like uploading them electronically for those who are absent or establishing deadlines to ensure all students have access to the syllabus from anywhere. • Teachers may share current students' work with distant parents and family members or upload examples of previous students' work. • Student blogs educate children about writing styles, online publishing, and proper Internet etiquette, all of which they will need in their future employment. • Educators can enable comment sections on blog entries to solicit feedback from parents and the community, as well as spark student debate.		Education is fundamentally about relationships and human connections. While we will never be able to reproduce the magic that occurs when excellent teachers and students connect in person, we should focus on the social aspects of technology to strengthen relationships when teachers and students communicate electronically. It takes a lot more concentration to use technology to enhance teaching and learning in a mixed learning environment that touches children at home and in school (The World Bank, 2021).
		Smart building systems, which integrate several technologies which includes the Internet of Things (IoT), Artificial Intelligence (AI), mechanisms and robotics, and building management systems, allow school administrators to manage schools in compliance with the new standard (Bujang et al., 2020).	The majority of the digital talents were removed and classified into areas such as automation and robotics, communication, design, drafting, and engineering. The developed taxonomy will aid everyone in developing comprehensive and strategic plans for the digital skills that new graduates will need when they enter the workforce. The outcome benefits academics by supporting individuals in developing specialised educational strategies and relevant curriculum changes to address the demand for digital skills (Siddiqui et al., 2022).		The teaching and learning process may be carried out physically and safely in accordance with the new standard by applying smart building technologies. For instance, the new standard will make it easier for teachers and students to teach and learn in physical education (Yong et al., 2022).

continued on following page

Table 1. Continued

No	Definition	Construction	Education	Issues	Research Gap
			Digitalisation		
					Digital skills are not just concerned with using and creating digital programmes or systems; they are also concerned with managing shifting workplace expectations in order to make the best use of technology. The innovation management component needs to be implemented more completely in order to be understood as part of the continuous improvement process. In order for the nation to benefit from a greater pool of talented digital employees, it is vitally necessary to conduct more study into the development of digital curricula in schools (Ayob et al., 2022).

Case Study B: According to a study, schools can operate the physical teaching and learning process safely by utilising smart building technologies. Five schools in Kedah participated in the qualitative method that was used. A secure environment can be established in schools using smart building technologies, and the physical teaching and learning process may be conducted in line with the new standard (Yong et al., 2022).

Results and Discussion

As a result of the analysis of digitalisation areas in relation to digital education, the elaboration is as below in Table 2:

Table 2. Summarization of digitalisation toward modernization in education (digital education)

VUCA and uncertainty	VUCA has highlighted a shift in attitude towards digital tools as well as accelerated investment decisions in new technologies. Modernization and digital transformation are therefore likely to accelerate and establish themselves as industry standards.
Digitalisation's definition	Digitalization is the holistic transformation of an organisation's human, operational, and technological elements for the purpose of delivering more effective, efficient services and user satisfaction in response to opportunities presented by quickly evolving information and communication technologies and shifting social needs.
Digitalisation construction	As a result of digitalization, there is greater access to customer data, which has improved customization and aided architects in presenting a variety of design options for customers to choose from. Competition is increasing due to the large number of digitally enabled people in the community, and architects must come up with increasingly innovative and efficient solutions. By utilising digital techniques, architects are now able to construct structures that previously would have looked unfeasible, as well as test various strategies for lowering the structure's energy usage. School administrators can administer schools in compliance with the new standard thanks to smart building systems that incorporate diverse technologies including the Internet of Things (IoT), Artificial Intelligence (AI), mechanisms and robotics, and building management systems.
Digitalisation education	To underline this, the digital abilities were primarily retrieved and classified into categories such as automation and robotics, communication, design, drafting, and engineering. A thorough and strategic strategy for the digital skills that incoming graduates entering the workforce will need may be made with the help of the developed taxonomy, which will be useful to stakeholders. The use of ICT in the classroom has been shown to boost students' motivation, passion, and engagement in the subjects they are learning. ICT makes it possible to use cutting-edge instructional resources and modernise teaching methods, which increases student engagement and promotes concurrent technological skill learning. ICTs also play a significant role in improving judgements. Two of the most obvious skills that students acquire as a result of utilising ICT are the capacity to arrange knowledge and compare and contrast information from various sources.
Issues	There were problems with implementing digital learning (e-learning) in education, including low adoption rates, bandwidth and connectivity concerns, a digital divide and low computer competence, a dearth of high-quality e-content, difficulties in engaging students online, and language obstacles. In order to get Malaysia's economy and society ready for the digital transformation, the country needs to put the correct policies in place. Meanwhile, if the nation's digital divide persists, all these goals for digital development will be considered meaningless platitudes.
The gap	The digitalisation in construction has impacted the way the students do their learning because of current VUCA as well as to know what the current construction industry is occupied for. Under the new standard, the teaching and learning process can be carried out physically and safely by exploiting smart building technologies. For instance, the new standard eliminates the barrier between educators and students when it comes to physical education and learning.
Summarization	Digitalisation in the construction industry has to be linked with the latest educational methods in order to produce students who are experts in digital literacy because of modernization and the VUCA world.

CONCLUSION

In short, because of the current VUCA, digitalisation in construction has influenced how architectural design students learn as well as what the current construction industry is occupied with. Moreover, because of modernization and the VUCA world, digitalization in the construction industry must be linked with the most up-to-date educational methods in order to produce students who are experts in digital literacy. Students' enthusiasm, passion, and interest in the things they are learning is shown to increase when ICT is used in the classroom. ICT allows for the use of cutting-edge educational materials as well as the modernization of teaching techniques, which results in increased student engagement and the concurrent learning of technology skills. ICTs have a significant impact on how decisions are developed as well. The capacity to structure knowledge and the capacity to compare and contrast information from many sources are two of the most apparent skills that students get as a result of utilising ICT. A new option of a blogging platform for architectural design students to practise design communication through e-learning, known as TACblog, as a digital education formulation, could potentially have a significant impact on the future of education in terms of producing young tech-savvy generations. Students that have the following AIPP capabilities: A (Architectural design), I (IoT and ICTs literacy), P (Publication), and another P (Public Relations: Marketing and Networking) have TACblog knowledge in the subject of architectural design. In contrast, digital learning (e-learning) implementation in education has been troubled by issues such as poor adoption rates, bandwidth and connectivity issues, a digital divide and low computer proficiency, a lack of high-quality e-content, challenges in engaging students online, and language barriers. Malaysia must implement the appropriate policies in order to prepare its society and economy for the digital transformation. All of these objectives for digital development would be seen as empty platitudes if the country's digital divide continued. Incorporating ICT technology into education in the 21st century promotes diversity and the advancement of digital literacy skills. It goes beyond the classroom and the book to broaden education. Finally, it connects instructors and students to new global online communities. This promotes global awareness, which is critical in today's education.

REFERENCES

Acer for Education. (2017, July 5). *How Technology Can Empower Students' Peculiarities*. Acer for Education. https://acerforeducation.acer.com/education-trends/inclusive-education/how-technology-can-empower-students-peculiarities/

Akçay Kavakoğlu, A. G.-C., Güleç Özer, D., Domingo-Callabuig, D., & Bilen, Ö. (2022). Architectural design communication (ADC) in online education during COVID-19 pandemic: A comparison of Turkish and Spanish universities. *Open House International*, *47*(2), 361–384. doi:10.1108/OHI-07-2021-0144

Ali, P. T. (2013). *Issues and Challenge in Implementing E-Learning in Malaysia*. Open University Malaysia Knowledge Repository. http://library.oum.edu.my/repository/145/1/issues_and_challenges.pdf

Ayob, N. H., Aziz, M. A., & Ayob, N. A. (2022). Bridging the Digital Divide: Innovation Policy and Implementation in Malaysia. *International Journal of Academic Research in Business & Social Sciences*, *12*(8), 1373–1389. doi:10.6007/IJARBSS/v12-i8/14554

Bujang, S. D., Selamat, A., Krejcar, O., Maresova, P., & Nguyen, N. T. (2020, April 30). Digital Learning Demand for Future Education 4.0—Case Studies at Malaysia Education Institutions. *Informatics (MDPI)*, *7*(13), 11. doi:10.3390/informatics7020013

Cao, L. (2020, March). What to Expect from Interiors of the Future. *Archdaily.com*. https://www.archdaily.com/935089/what-to-expect-from-interiors-of-the-future

Panith, A. (2020, July 10). *Digital Transformation is the New Normal of Construction*. Construction Plus Asia. https://www.constructionplusasia.com/my/digital-transformation-is-the-new-normal-of-construction/

Corporate Affairs Division, Malaysia Digital Economy Corporation (MDEC). (2022, July 4). *Malaysia Digital is Set To Accelerate Growth of Digital Economy*. MDEC. https://mdec.my/news: https://mdec.my/news/malaysia-digital-is-set-to-accelerate-growth-of-digital-economy

Daniotti, B., Gianinetto, M., & Della Torre, S. (Eds.). (2020). Digital Transformation of the Design, Construction and Management Processes of the Built Environment. Open Acces (Publishing in European Networks). doi:10.1007/978-3-030-33570-0

Dorst, K. (2011, November). The core of 'design thinking' and its application. *Design Studies*, *32*(6), 521–532. doi:10.1016/j.destud.2011.07.006

Google for Education. (n.d.). *Future of the Classroom: Emerging trends in classroom education*. Google for Education. https://edu.google.com/future-of-the-classroom/

Keith, J., & Topping, W. D. (2022, May 10). Effectiveness of online and blended learning from schools: A systematic review. *Review of Education*, *10*(2), 1–41. doi:10.1002/rev3.3353

Learning and Education Center. (n.d.). *NSU Florida*. Learning and Education Center. https://www.nova.edu/lec/This-Week-in-the-LEC/2019/August/Benefits%20of%20Blogging%20in%20Education.html#:~:text=Blogging%20develops%20students'%20analytical%20thinking,their%20thoughts%20about%20the%20subject

Ministry of Finance Malaysia. (2021). *Budget Speech 2022*. Ministry of Finance Malaysia. Percetakan Nasional Malaysia Berhad. https://budget.mof.gov.my/pdf/2022/ucapan/bs22.pdf

Ministry of Finance Malaysia. (2021). *Touchpoints Budget 2022 Measures*. Ministry of Finance Malaysia. Ministry of Finance Malaysia. https://budget.mof.gov.my/pdf/2022/ucapan/bs22.pdf

Monton, A. L. (2022, March 22). *Difference and Similarities: Digitization, Digitalization, and Digital Transformation*. Globalsign by GMO. https://www.globalsign.com/en-sg/blog/difference-and-similarities-digitization-digitalization-and-digital-transformation

Patil, M. (n.d.). *How is digitalization taking over architecture*. Rethinking The Future. https://www.re-thinkingthefuture.com/technology-architecture/a2561-how-is-digitalization-taking-over-architecture/

Pedagoo. (2020, June 20). *What are the uses of ICT in education?* Pedagoo. https://pedagoo.com/uses-of-ict-in-education/?lang=en

Renaissance. (n.d.). *What is digital literacy and why does it matter?* Renaissance. https://www.renaissance.com/2019/02/08/blog-digital-literacy-why-does-it-matter/

Sa'ar, D. C. (2017, December 29). *Digitalisation in Built Environment.* IPM. https://ipm.my: https://ipm.my/digitalisation-built-environment/

Shankar, S. S. & Jain, S. P. (2021). Blended Learning is the future of Education. *The Asian Conference on Education (ACE2021).* Research Gate. https://www.researchgate.net/publication/356557242_Blended_Learning_is_the_future_of_Education

Siddiqui, F., Abdekhodaee, A., & Thaheem, M. (2022). *Taxonomy of Digital Skills Needed in the Construction Industry: A Literature Review.*

Stone, P. (2022, May 19). *5 Key Trends For Digitalization In The Construction Industry.* FlowForma. https://www.flowforma.com/blog/5-key-trends-for-digitalization-in-the-construction-industry

The World Bank. (2021, September 24). *Digital Technologies in Education: The use of information and communication technologies in education can play a crucial role in providing new and innovative forms of support to teachers, students, and the learning process more broadly.* World Bank. https://www.worldbank.org/en/topic/edutech

Tru, Q. C. (n.d.). *Digitization vs. digitalization: Differences, definitions and examples.* TruQC. https://www.truqcapp.com/digitization-vs-digitalization-differences-definitions-and-examples/

USCRossier. (n.d.). *What Will Education Look Like in 20 Years?* USCRossier. https://rossieronline.usc.edu/blog/education-20-years/

Victoria. (2018, June 12). *7 Benefits to Blogging in the Classroom.* Techstarter. https://www.teachstarter.com/us/blog/7-benefits-blogging-classroom-us/

Wallagher, M. (2015, September 8). *How Blogging is Being Used in the Classroom Today: Research Results.* EmergingEdTech. https://www.emergingedtech.com/2015/09/the-state-of-blogging-in-the-classroom/

Yong, L. C., Aziz, N. M., & Mohd-Rahim, F. A. (2022, December 10). Adapting To A New Normal During COVID-19: Leveraging The Smart Building System With BIM Integration for Lifecycle Sustainability. *Planning Malaysia Journal, 20*(5), 209–222. doi:10.21837/pm.v20i24.1198

Chapter 7
Virtual Reality (VR) Technology in Construction Education:
Workflow, Constraints, and Strategies

Lam Tatt Soon
Taylor's University, Malaysia

Kai Kong Chow
Taylor's University, Malaysia

Hai Chen Tan
Heriot-Watt University, Malaysia

Myzatul Aishah Kamarazaly
Taylor's University, Malaysia

Tze Shwan Lim
Taylor's University, Malaysia

ABSTRACT

In the construction-related course, there is a lot of knowledge that is tough to verbalize or teach, especially understanding building details through imagination without experiencing or seeing the construction elements in reality. Visual reality (VR) enables users to visualize the complexity of buildings. The research method used in this research is qualitative method in which interviews were conducted in this research. The interviewees were invited to try the VR technology and data was collected. Throughout the whole research, the workflow of converting a 3D model to a VR model is developed, the constraints of adopting VR are identified and strategies are recommended. The results in the findings showed that all the interviewees need guidance when using the VR technology and some of them suffer from motion sickness. The findings of this research serve as a reference for universities that are interested in adopting VR technology in education to enhance knowledge of VR technology and provide better understanding in the classes.

DOI: 10.4018/978-1-6684-8253-7.ch007

INTRODUCTION

Technology is constantly improving and provides numerous benefits to the majority of people, careers, or job employees throughout the world. The improvement of technology in the construction industry makes the job site safer, saves cost, saves time, and provides new materials or methods (Rhumbix, 2021). Virtual Reality (VR) Technology is able to improve the learning techniques in construction-related education as well. Students can use digital simulations and models to better understand various disciplines (Morison, 2018). VR is used to improve the user's cognition and experience of an object. For example, construction workers are able to learn how to use the construction machinery in a safe area, and so on. Users can interact with this VR environment by picking up tools, manipulating them, and exploring a full range of physical interactions that represent the assembling element (Radianti et al, 2020). The behaviour changes in this work regard improved awareness of industrial safety and increased knowledge on the usage of tools in an industrial setting (Radianti et al, 2020).

In education, virtual reality is expected to improve the learning environment. For example, medical students can learn and practice how to perform surgery before working at the hospital and construction students are able to plan the construction safety management without going to the construction site. Unlike traditional teaching and training methods that rely on static images or 2D drawings, the visual depiction of VR provides a better understanding to the students (Wang et al., 2018). Besides, giving students memorable and engaging experiences that would not be possible otherwise, virtual reality may also enhance education (Immersion VR, 2022). By having VR in construction-related education, students are able to learn more than just from the book or knowledge but with some experience. Using technology nowadays may provide a variety of benefits to everyone, but there are still a number of issues to be addressed. Because no technology is perfect, the computer will eventually fail, the bulb will burn out, the smartphone will be unable to perform some tasks, and so on. Technology is made by sinful human beings living in a sin-cursed world, fighting the Curse, it's no surprise that there is no such thing as the perfect technology (Goff et al., 2016).

RESEARCH PROBLEMS

The design of a building is a complicated combination of abilities, judgment, knowledge, information, and time (Mao et al., 2007). Design, according to Cyon Research (2003), is an iterative process in which a collection of requirements, such as physical, aesthetic, and performance, are creatively altered to produce a design. The architecture and designer must consider numerous difficulties, ideas, and time constraints to come out with a design. Because the construction project's design will be drawn on plain paper, the design will only be viewable in 2D. Before the construction project is completed, we can only have a basic notion or image of what the building would look like by utilizing our imagination. It's tough to develop conceptual estimations by using the imagination because they require the ability to imagine the components rather than count the bricks, windows, doors, and toilet fixtures. Therefore, a strong imagination is needed to have a better understanding of the drawing and be able to study the drawing easily.

The architecture drawing and structural drawings were created by separate individuals, one from the architecture field and the other from engineering. This may cause the sketch design, detailed design, and working drawing production could be easily overlapped (Matipa et al., 2008). Rather than reading traditional drawings, students in architectural education and training can view distinct architectural environments through a 3D object (Wang et al.,2018). As a result, having a 3D or 4D view for everyone to read or check the drawing is preferable to simply looking at the 2D drawing and visualizing how the building would be constructed. To overcome this problem, a system that allows everyone to view the project in an immersive virtual world before it is built is vastly superior to 2D renderings. Additionally, a construction site is an extremely dangerous place which leads the concerned about the site's safety issues as there could be hazards and accidents occurring on the site. The construction industry has the worse rate of fatal accidents than other industries including falls from height, falling objects, exposure to dangerous substances, dust inhalation, working in confined spaces, and being hit in vehicle accidents (Musarat et al., 2022). Thus, it is recommended to improve construction technology to visualise and manage the construction site properly before accidents happen.

Due to the pandemic, all students are required to study at home to reduce the rate of coronavirus transmission. This implies that all students are not permitted to visit the construction site in order to observe how it operates and to become more aware of the dangers present. Even though students can learn about dangers through videos from online classes, they are nevertheless unable to raise their awareness of safety issues on the construction site. This is because students who take online learning classes will often be forced to study challenging topics in the comfort of their own place, without the added stress that comes with traditional academics (Tamm, 2022). As a result, technology makes students become more aware of the dangers of construction sites and improves the construction industry's safety standards at the same time.

Even though we are in the modern era with technology, there are some construction firms or employees who are still utilizing the use of traditional ways to work, which is inefficient compared to using technology. The steep price of a high-end personal computer is the most common reason for not adopting technology in completing their work (Laurell et al., 2019). The product's overall cost is rather high for what it delivers because of the larger research and development potential of the product. Additionally, the valve index data reported that the cost of the primary virtual reality (VR) headset is 999 dollars, while the lowest cost is 249 dollars (Alsop, 2022). As a result, if a student wishes to acquire a VR headset with a high-end personal computer, they still have to pay a significant sum of money in order to enjoy the VR experience.

As a construction project grows increasingly complex and involves multiple building parts, 2D drawings are frequently unable to sufficiently express the design ideas or settle the conflicting issues that interfere with the construction (Wang et al.,2014). The more complicated the construction project, the more likely there will be miscommunication among all parties. Due to miscommunication, misunderstanding, and unawareness, it is hard to let the construction manager manage the whole construction project. The current onsite project management technique has a problem, in which it treats normal construction work tasks as far more independent than they are (Froese, 2010). Due to a variety of complex issues, real construction practices frequently deviate significantly from the plans, resulting in schedule overruns (Wang & Love 2012). As a result, VR technology should be promoted to reduce the construction and educational issues and it is important to develop a workflow for adopting VR technology and identify the VR technology constraints strategies.

RESEARCH OBJECTIVES

1. To explore the workflow of adopting VR technology in education.
2. To identify the constraints of adopting VR technology in education.
3. To propose educational strategies for adopting VR technology.

LITERATURE REVIEW

The Workflow of Adopting the VR Technology in Education

Building Information Modelling (BIM) is the foundation of digital transformation in the architecture, engineering, and construction (AEC) industry. From planning and design to construction and operations, BIM is a process for creating and managing information for a constructed asset throughout its existence. The research conducted by Schiavi et al. (2022) found out there are four (4) steps required to shift the data from the BIM software to the specific AR/VR application:

1. Export the BIM geometry, the authors choose to use the BIM software Autodesk Revit building components contain a variety of available information, and professional drawings can be created automatically once the model is designed.
2. Optimization with 3D modelling software. For example, 3DsMax.
3. Build the application with a 3D game engine. For example, Unity and Unreal Engine. Sometimes additional 3D content was added to the engine. Data from a database such as the safety rules could be added.
4. The AR/VR application needed to be executable with the converted BIM model.

The user will also have to export the BIM metadata to the BIM geometry and metadata defined as all the building objects in the BIM Model. For example, material, geometry, and so on. This is because when the 3D game engine retrieves the metadata it is limited as it takes time to make BIM data compatible with the 3D engine, and to convert the BIM model into 3D geometry (Schiavi et al.,2022). Unity and Unreal Engine has been used in their research as real-time 3D engine and VR 4D Management has been used as VR application.

The Constraints of Adopting VR Technology in Education

VR systems could present educational content in attractive ways and enhance students' motivation, and interest in learning, as well as improve their knowledge. However, some universities, lecturers, or even students are not using the systems and VR technology for some reason and constraints. Cost, experience, health and psychological, and learning issues are the four main constraints in this research.

Cost issues include the hardware of the computer and the gadget cost. In "Virtual Technologies Trends in Education" research by Mora et al. (Mora et al., 2017), it was mentioned that the items that needed to be bought when adopting VR technology in education and three different types of VR headsets. This shows that the cost of adopting VR technology is high. Cook et al. (Cook et al.,2019) mentioned the cost of a personal computer (PC) with a good graphics card and also a reason why a good graphics card is important in adopting VR technology. A graphics card will affect the computing devices to display graphical data including clarity, colour, definition, and overall appearance. In Dunleavy et al. (2009) research, it is noted that technical errors caused by poor hardware caused students' frustration and were identified by teachers as a highly problematic issue.

Additionally, technical issues in adopting VR are affecting the implementation of VR. In Loizides et al. (2014) research, the users have blindfolded issues which they can't see their surroundings and the delay is brought by weak graphics. Besides that, Potter, Carter, and Coghlan (2016) mentioned that some users face difficulty while using VR technology because they are unfamiliar with the technology as there was no instruction in the virtual world. Cook et al. (2019)'s study demonstrated that the wiring which links the headset to the PC restricts user movement and the user is unable to perceive the surroundings in the actual world. In order to download the file and some of the animation content, which may be hosted on a website, the user would require huge file sizes, as well as a strong internet connection (Huerta et al., 2019) as also noted by Schiavi et al. (2022).

Virtual reality sicknesses and motion sicknesses are the most common health and psychological challenges while using VR technology (Chang et al, 2020; Chen et al., 2011). Some of these impacts are temporary, while others might be long-lasting. For instance, it can lead to digital eye strain, musculoskeletal problems, hearing troubles, loss of sleep, and other problems. Most of these problems are caused by the user's addiction to technology use and lack of rest. Although employing VR makes the lesson more engaging, doing so may be harmful to the user's health. In the experiment conducted by Loizides et al. (2014), one-third of the participants felt uncomfortable while using the VR technology and one of the participants stopped using it in the middle of the experiment. Some of the participants shared that they had simulator sickness in the experiment done by Cook et al., (2019). Additionally, Chang et al. (2018) mentioned that the users will feel anxiety, which may lead to alienation between people over time, and they believe that the role of teachers will change in which some positions may be replaced, and students may lose the ability to communicate with one another.

Lastly, Paul (2020) mentioned that new technology has always had a hard time being accepted in a world that defaults to the familiar and causes some problems for users. Magomadov (2020) asserted that it is challenging for teachers who have depended solely on traditional methods to adopt modern technologies. Moreover, technical issue is the most common issue in VR technology as VR content requires a lot of time if it is not done by utilizing efficient design and visualization techniques (Huerta et al., 2019). Cunneen (2021) stated that login, low bandwidth, content glitches, and navigation issues are the issues that users would face while using VR technology. According to Li et al. (2018), academia may not be completely aware of the real constraints and limitations in this field which cause students to lack of knowledge in VR technology.

Educational Strategies for Adopting VR Technology

In order to overcome the motion sickness issues caused by VR technology to the user, Cook et al., (2019) provided a solution by suggesting users to consume ginger candy and use personal mirrors, as well as defining reasonable time limits per person for the in-headset time. In addition, they also mentioned that expensive processing hardware is needed to provide a comfortable experience to the user. However, Fabola et al., (2015) mentioned that some of the participants suggest using smartphone-based VR as a solution for cost. For example, Google Cardboard-type which is able to increase the use of smartphones with the processing power to create stereoscopically 3D interactive instructional content. Furthermore, Akçayır and Akçayır (2017) revealed that it is difficult for students to use VR technology as the technology keeps improving and students will have to study more in order to use the technology easily. Therefore, Cook et al. (2019) suggested that it is advisable to have a training session for the students and faculty because they need a useful introduction to the technology, allowing them to have a positive first experience and recognize the technology. Also, demonstration approaches are also proposed as the solution for presenting the new technology to a variety of university and library community members and showcasing it in a favourable manner (Cook et al., 2019).

Huerta et al. (2019) discovered that it is essential for the proper communication and assignment of activities related to each development stage to have access to crucial information and background experience regarding best practices for training & learning and specific workflows. In addition, they note that storyboarding has also boosted up development and improved the training and learning process all around by helping users to understand and translate user needs into useful design and development insights (Huerta et al., 2019). Hart (1998) also mentioned two ways that practitioners frequently use storyboarding. Lastly, to adopt VR in education, other strategies include exploring the rules of education, building a new teaching mode supported by the technology platform with the help of a VR learning environment, and exploring the integration of a VR learning environment with learning and teaching.

RESEARCH METHODOLOGY

The research technique used in this study is a qualitative research method, an iterative process in which the scientific community gains a better knowledge of the issue being examined by generating new meaningful distinctions. The term "research technique" refers to the methods and equipment that were employed by the researcher to gather the desired data. In a qualitative research approach, there are numerous questions that inquire about "what" and "why," since it is crucial to grasp the interviewees' ideas, experiences, and concepts based on their previous experiences and opinion. Understanding how the audience makes judgments can assist the interviewer in reaching quick conclusions (QuestionPro, 2022). A case study has been adopted in this research to convert a BIM model to a VR 3D model and interviews are conducted to collect the respondents' feedback on the usage of VR technology in construction education. Respondents must give their informed consent in order to participate, and their ages might vary depending on the study's parameters (Mike, 2017). The respondents for this research are students who are studying construction-related courses. This is due to the fact that this research is required to obtain student feedback following their use of VR technology.

Semi-structured interviews are adopted in this study since semi-structured interviews are more adaptable and have a higher level of validity. After the participants have used VR technology, interviews are conducted to elicit their opinions and ideas with prepared interview questions. The interviewees allow the respondents to share more limitations and solutions/strategies for implementing VR technology in education, and the interviewers are allowed to give additional feedback in the interviews. As a result, the interviewee may provide new information or knowledge to the research, which might help to improve the research. The research interview questions are categorised into four sections, namely A, B, and C. Section A is aimed to gather the respondents' background and basic information. After the respondents have experienced VR technology, their comments are collected based on the constraints in adopting VR in section B. Lastly, section C focuses on the respondent's thoughts on the educational strategies for implementing VR technology in the classroom. The interview questions are developed based on the literature reviews collected in the previous chapters. To obtain more precise information from the students without any misunderstanding, each interview will last around 10 to 15 minutes. A recording of the whole interview will be made for future evaluation needs.

After collecting all of the data from the interviewees, content analysis is used in this research to analyse the similar and different points of view from different interviewees. Therefore, coding in qualitative research is adopted to arrange and categorize the qualitative data to distinguish between various themes and connections among all the interviewees (Alyona, 2021). Coding in a qualitative way allows the researcher to identify words or phrases that stand in for significant (and recurrent) themes in each response when the researcher codes consumer feedback. In qualitative research, coding enables the researcher to be rigorous, critical, and self-reflexive about their results. There are just a few ways that, depending on the study goal, are more or less acceptable (Delve et al., 2020). There is no right or incorrect way to code a set of data. This research will be using inductive coding, which is the coding method that starts from the data and from the data comes out with the codes and categories. There will be a few times of qualitative coding to ensure that the data is in the correct codes and categories.

RESEARCH FINDINGS

Six interviewees who took construction-related courses were selected in this case study due to their increased familiarity with the educational benefits of virtual reality technology. Different students will have different concerns, constraints, demands, expectations, and difficulties, regardless if they are in education or using VR technology.

The Workflow of Adopting the VR Technology in Education

A workflow has been established throughout the whole research project. The workflow is quite simple and most importantly a model must be produced. The software that will be used in this case study is Revit and Twinmotion. There will be two different methods to import the model using Direct Link and FBX file method, and both produce a different outcome. After experiencing both different methods, it is concluded that the direct link method is better than FBX file method as the model has been linked and synchronized, so any changes in the Revit will directly change in the Twinmotion as well. It is more convenient and the steps are very easy and simple. However, data loss might happen while using the direct link method but the user will only need to double-check the model every time they synchronize it. The user will also have to make sure that there is extra storage left in the computer to install a plug-in called "Datasmith Exporter". In order to have a better experience in Twinmotion, the user should check their computer hardware to see whether their computer meets the minimum requirement of the software and ensure that the storage is able to install the plug-in "Datasmith Exporter" before using Twinmotion. The table below are the workflow that has been established after experiencing both methods.

The Constraints of Adopting VR Technology in Education

An interview was conducted subsequent to interviewees experiencing the VR technology and data was collected during the interview. All the interviewees are students who study construction-related courses and all of them are ensured to use VR technology for the first time. The interviewees agreed to imple-

Table 1. The workflow of adopting VR from BIM software in the case study

Step 1	Check computer capability to make sure it meets the minimum requirement of the software.
Step 2	Check computer storage.
Step 3	Create a 3D model in Revit
Step 4	Download and install the Datasmith Exporter plugin for Revit
Step 5	Open a 3D view in Revit (Can be the whole model or just a part of the model)
Step 6	Open Twinmotion and click "import" (Do not close Revit)
Step 7	Select "Direct Link", it will automatically detect the Revit file that is opened
Step 8	Choose the Direct Link importing options and click "Import"
Step 9	Go back to Revit and click "synchronize" under the "Datasmith" tab
Step 10	Go back to Twinmotion, the system will automatically link the model from Revit
Step 11	When it shows material conflict, choose "use scene material" and click "ok"
Step 12	The model will appear in Twinmotion and check the model to prevent data lost
Step 13	Go in the model and check whether the room is clear to see or not
Step 14	Link the VR headsets to the Twinmotion
Step 15	Click "Start VR"

ment VR technology as they think that it will help them in education which is supported by Thakkar (2018), who stated VR technology is able to improve certain skills of the students. Besides that, half of them would prefer to have both BIM and VR models in their education, whereas half of them only prefer to have a VR model. However, all of their opinions are similar in which that they agreed VR is able to provide them a better understanding of the building.

Table 2 shows the legend of objective 2 and throughout the interviews, most of the interviewees only have RM 4000 to RM 6000 computer budget, but more investment is needed to have a better computer processor and graphic card to support the VR program. The interviewees were also aware that better VR headset is expensive as well (Experience Crew, 2019; VertigoVisual, 2021). However, half of their budget is low and half of it is high. This is because all the interviewees' demands on VR technology are different.

Furthermore, three out of six interviewees experienced motion sickness while the rest of them did not. Because the level of symptoms varies greatly from person to person, not everyone will have the same symptoms at the same time or for the same duration of time while using it (Coles, 2021). Additionally, two interviewees did not have any psychological issues while using the technology. In terms of safety issues, two of the interviewees felt unsafe when using the VR headset as they could not see their surroundings while wearing it which is supported by Al-Sibai (2022) even though letting the user see the virtual world is the key to the selling point of VR.

The technological constraint is the third group of constraints found in this research. Due to the fact that different people have different demands, there are four constraints in the gadgets issue mentioned by the interviewees. Most of them felt that the controller is hard to use and they are unsatisfied with the teleportation which will cause them to lose track easily. Langbehn et al. (2018) supported this by stating that teleportation had the weakest cognitive mapping. Besides that, half of them felt uncomfortable because of the headsets and felt that they were very heavy. This view is supported by some of the users

Table 2. The constraints of adopting VR from BIM software

Category	Group	Theme	Sub-Theme	Code
Constraints of Adopting VR Technology in Education	1. Financial Constraints	a. Budget of the computer	i) RM 2000 – RM 4000	B-1-a-i
			ii) RM 4000 – RM 6000	B-1-a-ii
		b. Budget of the VR gadgets	i) RM 800 – RM 1500	B-1-b-i
			ii) RM 1500 – RM 3000	B-1-ab-ii
	2. Psychological Constraint	a. Motion sickness	i) Dizzy	B-2-a-i
			ii) Nausea	B-2-a-ii
			iii) Headache	B-2-a-iii
		b. Safety issue	i) Afraid of using in an open space	B-2-b-i
			ii) Afraid of hitting the wall	B-2-b-ii
		c. Does not have any issue	i) Don't have any bad feeling	B-2-c-i
	3. Technological Constraint	a. Gadgets issue	i) Unsatisfied with teleportation	B-3-a-i
			ii) Hard to use the controller	B-3-a-ii
			iii) Uncomfortable caused by the headsets	B-3-a-iii
			iv) Headset is heavy	B-3-a-iv
		b. Computer hardware issue	i) Graphic not that good	B-3-b-i
			ii) Lagging	B-3-b-ii
	4. Familiarity Constraint	a. Unfamiliarity issue	i) Unfamiliar with the technology	B-4-a-i
			ii) No guidance given	B-4-a-ii

in the studies conducted by Nguyen (2022), Nanou (2021), and in VRCover (2022). In addition, four of the interviewees agreed that low graphic provides users to have poor experiences and reduced their motivation on using them. However, two of the interviewees mentioned it was quite lag while using some functions in the software and Ivan (2022) explained that lagging is due to the low quality of the graphics card in the computer.

Some guidance has been given by the lecturer to let the interviewees know where they were and what they could do next. All of them agreed that the guidance given by the lecturer is able to assist and help them while they are using the VR headsets and have a better experience. Barnard (2020) mentioned that the first-time VR user will struggle with the simplest features and functions of the VR. In addition, three of the interviewees stated that they were quite unfamiliar with the technology which caused them to need guidance.

Educational Strategies for Adopting VR Technology in Education

The legend shown in Table 3 above is the strategies collected from the interviewees. In order to reduce the cost of adopting VR technology in education, most of the interviewees agreed that sharing the cost in a group prevents them to pay a very high cost for purchasing the VR gadget. They felt that it is not worth the money to buy hardware that does not meet their demand, and this view is supported by Lang (2021) and it also causes frustration when the computer crashes (Stegner, 2021).

Table 3. Educational strategies for adopting VR technology

Category	Group	Theme	Code
C. Educational Strategies for Adopting VR Technology	1. Cost-Cutting Strategies	a. Share the gadget's cost in a group	C-1-a
		b. Based on software requirement	C-1-b
	2. Safety Strategies	a. Soft surrounding	C-2-a
		b. Enclosed space	C-2-b
		c. Empty space	C-2-c
	3. Learning Strategies	a. Video tutorial	C-3-a
		b. Guidance while using	C-3-b
		c. Lesson class	C-3-c
	4. Change VR Locomotion Method	a. Teleport	C-4-a
		b. Walking-in-place	C-4-b
		c. Joystick	C-4-c

All of the interviewees agreed that using VR technologies in an enclosed space will make the users feel safer as they are blindfolded, and their vision has been covered by the headset of their actual surroundings and it is also asserted by Poore (2021). In addition, Lynch (2021) and Chu (2022) agreed that the greater the space, the better it is for the VR headset experience. Besides that, to increase user safety and trust when using VR technology, placing a soft object on the wall is suggested by one of the interviewees and reiterated by two of the other interviewees. This is supported by Schurman (2019), who also agreed that wall padding is utilized to keep the players safe. Furthermore, half of the interviewees mention having a clear and empty enclosed space to avoid the user from hitting objects or getting injured while using the VR technology will yield better experiences for the user as well.

As previously mentioned, the interviewees faced problems when there was no guidance given. Therefore, all of them strongly agreed that guidance is needed and solutions on what they should do to solve the problems that they are facing should also be provided. A clear direction is capable of assisting the learner in making the best feasible adjustment and assisting the student in devising a strategy for fixing the problem based on the circumstances (EducationTIMES, 2009). Video class is preferred by three of the interviewees in order to prevent first-time users from confusion about ways to use and what to do in the virtual environment. Teng (2015) demonstrated that students used the video tutorial as a performance enhancer and execute it straight away. One of the interviewees agreed with Teng (2015) but two of the interviewees stated that holding a lesson class is good for students who want to learn more about VR technologies. Adopting VR technology in a lesson helps students to become more engaged in the subject matter and to interact with the lecturer to assist them to develop new abilities.

Virtual reality locomotion is the technology that allows the avatar or user to move across the whole virtual environment while only occupying a tiny amount of real-world area (Circuit stream, 2021) and it has various different methods which bring different experiences to the user. Half of the interviewees preferred to use walking-in-place to have a better virtual world experience. One of the interviewees mentioned that it will help to reduce the motion sickness of the user and it is supported by Lee et al. (2018). Besides, two of the interviewees mentioned that teleportation is more than enough for them to use for educational purposes as it only requires a little time to move to the place that they want. Langbehn et al.

(2018) also reiterated the same idea of teleportation which has the least travel time when compared to the other methods. Another method mentioned by most of the interviewees is the joystick method but unfortunately it is the easiest method that causes the user to suffer from motion sickness and it. Coomer et al. (2018) supported this by stating that the joystick approach causes the most motion sickness when compared to the other locomotion methods.

CONCLUSION AND RECOMMENDATIONS

Technology is advancing at a rapid pace, and it is playing an increasingly important role in education. Technology can offer a better understanding of subjects that are complicated and take a lot of imagination. There are a lot of details of the buildings that have to be measured in construction-related courses like architecture and quantity surveyor, and a lot of imagination is required. Therefore, the university should adopt more technology in education to enhance knowledge and provide better understanding in lecture classes. The research involves a single brand of VR headset in the analysis and this might be a limitation of this research study. Varied types of headsets have different designs which could provide different types of experiences to the users. However, due to the limited facilities involvement, respondents in this study only can test the HTC Vive Pro 2 in this research. As a result, it is quite difficult to determine which type of headset is preferred by the student. Experiencing different types of VR headsets will make the research more interesting since several types of VR headsets are available in the market nobility Pico 4, Meta Quest 2, Meta Quest Pro, Valve Index and etc.

The finding of the workflow in adopting VR technology is expected to assist academicians in converting the BIM models to VR models while the constraints and strategies are expected to serve as a reference for academicians who are interested to implement VR in construction education. Based on the findings, the VR locomotion method does affect the overall experience of VR technology. Different locomotion methods may be suitable in various situations, and certain locomotion methods may need the user to use a significant amount of energy to move. Therefore, more research might be undertaken to determine the most appropriate and cost-effective VR locomotion method for educational purposes. Relevant parties can then determine the best locomotion method for students to implement in education. Besides that, Different VR headsets have different costs, designs, functions, and comfort. Trying more different brands of VR headsets to find out which of the headset suits more to the students more to use in education is also very important.

REFERENCES

Akçayır, M., & Akçayır, G. (2017). Advantages and challenges associated with augmented reality for education: A systematic review of the literature. *Educational Research Review*, *20*, 1–11. doi:10.1016/j.edurev.2016.11.002

Al-Sibai, N. (2022, February 1). Virtual reality users keep suffering horrible injuries. *Futurism*. https://futurism.com/neoscope/vr-injuries

Alsop, T. (2022). *Reported price of leading consumer VR headsets 2019*. Statista. https://www.statista.com/statistics/1096886/reported-price-of-leading-consumer-vr-headsets-by-device/

Barnard, D. (2020, November 10). *Guide for training employees in VR (from 1000s of hours of experience)*. Virtual Speech. https://virtualspeech.com/blog/guide-training-employees-vr

Chang, E., Kim, H. T., & Yoo, B. (2020). Virtual reality sickness: A review of causes and Measurements. *International Journal of Human-Computer Interaction*, *36*(17), 1658–1682. doi:10.1080/10447318.2020.1778351

Chang, J., Ren, Q., Han, H., & Xu, L. (2018). Integration and Service Strategy of VR/AR in practical teaching. *IOP Conference Series. Materials Science and Engineering*, *466*, 012109. doi:10.1088/1757-899X/466/1/012109

Chen, W., Chen, J. Z., & So, R. H. Y. (2011). Visually induced motion sickness: Effects of translational visual motion along different axes. *Proceedings of the International Conference on Ergonomics & Human Factors*, (pp. 281–287). IEEE.

Chu, W. (2022, February 24). VR Setup 101: Building a functional room for VR. *Newegg Insider*. New Egg. https://www.newegg.com/insider/vr-setup-101-building-a-functional- room-for-vr/

Circuit stream. (2021, January 12). *VR locomotion: How to move in VR environment*. Circuit Stream. https://circuitstream.com/blog/vr-locomotion/

Coles, J. (2021, September 13). *What causes motion sickness in VR, and how can you avoid it?* Space.com. https://www.space.com/motion-sickness-in-vr

Cook, M., Lischer-Katz, Z., Hall, N., Hardesty, J., Johnson, J., McDonald, R., & Carlisle, T. (2019). Challenges and strategies for Educational Virtual reality. *Information Technology and Libraries*, *38*(4), 25–48. doi:10.6017/ital.v38i4.11075

Coomer, N., Bullard, S., Clinton, W., & Williams-Sanders, B. (2018). Evaluating the effects of four VR locomotion methods. *Proceedings of the 15th ACM Symposium on Applied Perception*. ACM. 10.1145/3225153.3225175

Cover, V. R. (2022, August 16). Ways to make your meta quest 2 more comfortable. *VR Cover*. https://vrcover.com/ways-to-make-your-meta-oculus-quest-2-more- comfortable/

Cunneen, W. (2021, May 4). 5 problems with virtual reality training they don't want you to know. *Roundtable Learning*. https://roundtablelearning.com/5 -problems-with-virtual- reality-training-they-dont-want-you-to-know/

Cyon Research. (2003, February 19). *Architectural automation: Facing the challenges of work-culture*. (A Cyon Research White Paper). http://www.cyonresearch.com/portals/0/files/whitepapers/Cyon%20 Research%20white%20paper %20on%20Work-Culture%20030218%20-%20final%20form.pdf

Dunleavy, M., Dede, C., & Mitchell, R. (2009). Affordances and limitations of immersive participatory augmented reality simulations for teaching and learning. *Journal of Science Education and Technology*, *18*(1), 7–22. doi:10.100710956-008-9119-1

Education Times. (2009, March 16). Importance of guidance. Career, Higher Education & Study Abroad. *Education Times*. https://www.educationtimes.com/article/editors- pick/69574156/importance-of-guidance

Experience Crew. (2019, June 28). *Why is price of VR so high?: Blog: Experience AR/VR Company*. Experience. https://4experience.co/why-is-price-of-vr-so-high

Froese, T. M. (2010). The impact of Emerging Information Technology on project management for Construction. *Automation in Construction, 19*(5), 531–538. doi:10.1016/j.autcon.2009.11.004

Goff, J., Ervin, J., Lorentz, M., & Ring, R. (2016). There's no such thing as Perfect Technology. There's No Such Thing As Perfect Technology.| *Theology of Technology - A Camp Infinity Blog*. https://camp-infinity.com/blog/2016/09/05/truth-3/

Huerta, O., Unver, E., Aslan, R., Kus, A., & Chotrov, D. (2019). Application of VR and AR Tools for Technical Drawing Education. *Proceedings of CAD'19*. CAD Solutions. 10.14733/cadconfP.2019.363-366

Immersion, V. R. (2022) *VR for education - the future of education*. Immersion VR. https://immersionvr.co.uk/about -360vr/vr- for-education/

Ivan. (2022, June 2). *What graphics card do you need for VR in 2022? A short guide*. KommandoTech. https://kommandotech.com/guides/what-graphics-card-do-you-need-for- vr/

Lang, B. (2021, December 3). *How to tell if your PC is VR ready*. Road to VR. https://www.roadtovr.com/how-to-tell-pc-virtual-reality-vr-oculus- rift-htc-vive-steam-vr-compatibility-tool/

Langbehn, E., Lubos, P., & Steinicke, F. (2018). Evaluation of locomotion techniques for room-scale VR. *Proceedings of the Virtual Reality International Conference*. Laval Virtual. 10.1145/3234253.3234291

Laurell, C., Sandström, C., Berthold, A., & Larsson, D. (2019). Exploring barriers to adoption of Virtual Reality through Social Media Analytics and Machine Learning–An assessment of technology, network, price and trialability. *Journal of Business Research, 100*, 469–474. doi:10.1016/j.jbusres.2019.01.017

Lee, J., Ahn, S. C., & Hwang, J.-I. (2018). A walking-in-place method for virtual reality using position and orientation tracking. *Sensors (Basel), 18*(9), 2832. doi:10.339018092832 PMID:30150586

Li, X., Yi, W., Chi, H.-L., Wang, X., & Chan, A. P. C. (2018). A critical review of virtual and augmented reality (VR/AR) applications in Construction Safety. *Automation in Construction, 86*, 150–162. doi:10.1016/j.autcon.2017.11.003

Loizides, F., El Kater, A., Terlikas, C., Lanitis, A., & Michael, D. (2014). Presenting cypriot cultural heritage in virtual reality: A user evaluation. *Progress in Cultural Heritage: Documentation, Preservation, and Protection*, 572–579. Digital Heritage. doi:10.1007/978-3-319-13695-0_57

Lynch, G. (2021, September 13). *How to set up your room for VR*. Space.com. https://www.space.com/how-to-set-up-your-room-for-vr

Magomadov, V. S. (2020). Examining the potential of VR and AR Technologies for Education. *Journal of Physics: Conference Series, 1691*(1), 012160. doi:10.1088/1742-6596/1691/1/012160

Mao, W., Zhu, Y., & Ahmad, I. (2007, July 3). *Applying metadata models to unstructured content of construction documents: A view-based approach*. Automation in Construction. https://www.sciencedirect.com/science/article/pii/S0926580506000203

Matipa, W. M., Kelliher, D., & Keane, M. (2008). How a quantity surveyor can ease cost management at the design stage using a building product model. *Construction Innovation, 8*(3), 164–181. doi:10.1108/14714170810888949

Mike, A. (2017). *The SAGE Encyclopedia of Communication Research Methods.* Sage.

Mora, C. E., Martín-Gutiérrez, J., Añorbe-Díaz, B., & González-Marrero, A. (2017). Virtual Technologies Trends in education. *Eurasia Journal of Mathematics, Science and Technology Education, 13*(2), 469–486. doi:10.12973/eurasia.2017.00626a

Morison, J. (2018, February 24). *8 ways technology improves education.* eLearning Industry. https://elearningindustry.com/technology-improves-education-8-ways

Musarat, M. A., Alaloul, W. S., Irfan, M., Sreenivasan, P., & Rabbani, M. B. A. (2022). Health and safety improvement through Industrial Revolution 4.0: Malaysian construction industry case. *Sustainability (Basel), 15*(1), 201. doi:10.3390u15010201

Nanou, E. (2021, November 14). *The 8 pros and cons to VR Fitness Technology.* MUO. https://www.makeuseof.com/pros-cons-vr-fitness-technology

Nguyen, W. (2022, May 14). *How to make the quest 2 more comfortable (zero pressure).* VR Heaven. https://vrheaven.io/how-to-make-the-oculus-quest-more-comfortable/

Paul, J. (2020, May 20). *Why AR and VR are struggling to break into the classroom.* eLearning Industry. https://elearningindustry.com/ar-and-vr-are-struggling-break-into- classroom.

Poore, S. (2021, October 23). *5 reasons you can't use your VR headset outside (and how to overcome them).* ShaunPoore.com. https://www.shaunpoore.com/vr -headset-outside/

Potter, L. E., Carter, L., & Coghlan, A. (2016). Virtual reality and nature based tourism. *Proceedings of the 28th Australian Conference on Computer-Human Interaction - OzCHI '16.* ACM. 10.1145/3010915.3011854

QuestionPro. (2022, October 13). *What is research - definition, types, methods & examples.* QuestionPro. https://www.questionpro.com/blog/what-is-research/

Radianti, J., Majchrzak, T. A., Fromm, J., & Wohlgenannt, I. (2020). A systematic review of immersive virtual reality applications for higher education: Design elements, lessons learned, and research agenda. *Computers & Education, 147*, 103778. doi:10.1016/j.compedu.2019.103778

Rhumbix. (2021, August 25). *How Technology in Construction is Revolutionizing the Industry.* Rhumbix. com. https://www.rhumbix.com/blog/how-technology-in-construction- is-revolutionizing-the-industry

Schiavi, B., Havard, V., Beddiar, K., & Baudry, D. (2022). Bim data flow architecture with AR/VR Technologies: Use Cases in architecture, engineering and construction. *Automation in Construction, 134*, 104054. doi:10.1016/j.autcon.2021.104054

Schurman, K. (2019, September 25). *Where is wall padding used and what kind?* Greatmats. https://www.greatmats.com/where-should-i-use-wall-padding.php

Stegner, B. (2021, July 7). *5 common PC gaming problems (and how to fix them).* MUO. https://www.makeuseof.com/tag/5 -common-pc-gaming-problems-and- how-to-fix-them/

Tamm, S. (2022*). 10 Biggest Disadvantages of E-Learning*. E-Student. https://e-student.org/disadvantages-of-e-learning/.

Teng, J. (2015, January 1). *The effectiveness of video tutorial and preview on self-efficacy, task performance and learning: An experimental study conducted at a middle school in Shanghai, China*. [Thesis, University Of Twente]. https://essay.utwente.nl/69309/

Thakkar, V. (2018, June 11). *Benefits of VR in Education*. fotonVR. https://fotonvr.com/benefits-of-vr-in- education/

VertigoVisual. (2021, August 4). *Wondering: VR is so expensive? here is why*. VertigoVisual. https://vertigovisual.com/why-is-vr-so-expensive/

Wang, P., Wu, P., Wang, J., Chi, H.-L., & Wang, X. (2018). A critical review of the use of virtual reality in Construction Engineering Education and training. *International Journal of Environmental Research and Public Health, 15*(6), 1204. doi:10.3390/ijerph15061204 PMID:29890627

Wang, W.-C., Weng, S.-W., Wang, S.-H., & Chen, C.-Y. (2014). Integrating building information models with construction process simulations for Project Scheduling Support. *Automation in Construction, 37*, 68–80. doi:10.1016/j.autcon.2013.10.009

Wang, X., & Love, P. E. (2012, March). *Bim + ar: Onsite information sharing and communication via advanced*. Research Gate. https://www.researchgate.net/publication/254039790_BIM_AR_Onsite_information_sharing_and_communication_via_advanced_visualization

Chapter 8

A Case Study to Analyse the Online and Hybrid Learning Trends in Quantity Surveying Education From the COVID–19 Pandemic at Taylor's University

Azrina Binti Md Yaakob
Taylor's University, Malaysia

Myzatul Aishah Kamarazaly
Taylor's University, Malaysia

Yee Shi Lee
Taylor's University, Malaysia

ABSTRACT

There are two types of online learning, which are online learning and hybrid. COVID-19 pandemic, coining the term "new normal" has impacted, directly and indirectly, the global economy, including shaking up the education sector. The education system completely shifted the learning method from traditional face-to-face classes to an online learning system. This situation has posed an extreme challenge to the education community and forced the educators to shift their teaching mode overnight. Taylor's University had constantly applied traditional learning in quantity surveying education has been exposed to the new changes as well. This pandemic has highlighted the need for more online technology training and evolution. However, the online learning trend in quantity surveying education remained undervalued due to the familiarity of students with traditional face-to-face classes. Hence, the objective of this research is to identify the differences in students' attitudes, to identify the differences in students' achievement and to provide strategies to improve online learning and hybrid learning.

DOI: 10.4018/978-1-6684-8253-7.ch008

INTRODUCTION

The rapid development of technology has become one of the essential elements in the 21st century, influencing every aspect of life, including the teaching style in the education sector around the world. Online learning has undeniably become a hot topic of discussion in the education community, particularly in higher education. The percentage of students taking one or more online classes increased from 15.6% in 2004 to 43.1% in 2016 (Bouchrika, 2020). This data has shown that the online learning trend is still evolving and can be increased as there are more people who are willing to adapt to this emerging learning lifestyle.

There are two types of online learning which is fully online learning and hybrid learning. The term 'fully online learning' describes a type of education in which students study in a virtual environment that is supported by the Internet (Prep, n.d.). It is commonly referred to as 'e-learning' among other terms and it is commonly applied in higher education, allowing students to participate and learn at their own pace while earning a degree or certificate. In contrast, hybrid learning is defined as the blending of face-to-face classroom instruction and online learning environments (AlNajdi, 2014). It is frequently used interchangeably with the term blended learning in which students spend at least half of their time learning online and the rest of their time learning in physical classrooms (Daniel, 2021).

Moreover, online learning has become more centric in people's lives since the pandemic (Koksal, 2020). This pandemic has exposed the necessity of technology and has completely shifted Malaysia's typical traditional face-to-face learning environment to an online teaching and learning approach as an alternative teaching method for a better learning experience during this difficult time. Taylor's University which had constantly applied traditional learning in quantity surveying education has been exposed to the new changes as well. This pandemic has also highlighted the need for more online technology training and evolution, as well as giving us the opportunity to be aware and recognize online learning. As a result, the Information and Communication Technologies (ICT) applications enhanced by the Internet have proven to be effective tools and have contributed significantly to the rapid growth of online learning nowadays. However, is online learning and hybrid learning suit the learning environment of quantity surveying education? Hence, this research is expected to investigate the future prospects of online learning and hybrid learning in quantity surveying education.

The Issues

Many students including educators are still hesitant to participate in online courses mainly due to the unfamiliarity and drawbacks that arise in online learning. The issues can range from educators' issues, learners' issues and content issues.

Many educators believe that engaging students and getting them to participate in the teaching-learning process is a challenge because they have not much experience and familiarity with advanced technology tools. It is also difficult for lecturers to switch from offline to online mode by modifying their teaching methods and time management because online learning requires creating and designing content that not only covers the chapters but also engages the students at the same time (Keengwe and T. Kidd, 2010). They are concerned with determining the optimal tools to use for successful learning as well as how to effectively present the concepts for the best student learning outcomes as they believe that the format of online courses challenges or influences student success.

While online learning can be highly effective and productive, it is not a suitable and effective learning environment for students who are more dependent and have poor concentration skills as it requires greater accountability from the students. Moreover, it is challenging for some students to keep up with the pace of online courses due to their weakness in technological knowledge which may face difficulties in identifying the courses materials as well as the assignment submission. Furthermore, collaboration and interaction in online learning remain the major barrier to online learning.

In Malaysia, the online learning trend in education sector is not widely developed before the COVID-19 pandemic. The online learning in quantity surveying education has not been developed and recognized by the community such as The Board of Quantity Surveyors Malaysia (BQSM) these years. In response to the COVID-19 pandemic, BQSM has introduced and developed online learning by promoting an Accreditation Manual for Online Quantity Surveying Programmes, which will serve as a set of standards and guidelines for online platform (BQSM, 2021). Hence, it is clear that online learning in quantity surveying education is still underdeveloped while becoming more common these days and it is important to make sure a consistent practice is being delivered by the education community in a professional manner.

Research Aim and Objective

The aim of this study is to investigate the future prospects of online learning and hybrid learning in quantity surveying education.

The objectives of this study are: -

1. To identify the differences in students' attitudes in face-to-face learning, online learning and hybrid learning
2. To identify the differences in students' achievement in face-to-face learning, online learning and hybrid learning
3. To provide strategies to improve online learning and hybrid learning

Differences in Students' Attitudes

In Face-to-Face Learning

For many years, face-to-face learning has been adopted in Malaysia's education system, where students would have comprehensive attitudes towards the learning environment. According to Mali & Lim (2021), when COVID-19 is not a concern, students prefer face-to-face learning. Students enjoy and prefer the chance to ask questions regarding learning materials and assignments on spot, which they felt more involved in the learning environment.

Moreover, there are students who showed their attitude by expressing that they were able to successfully complete their course in a face-to-face learning environment better due to the continuous guidance and assistance of the lecturer and coursemates in class as a motivation to complete (Headspace, n.d.). This point is supported by Ong et al., (2020), stating that students may feel more natural and easier to reach out to lecturers and coursemates for directions, assistance or advice when they are all in the same physical setting.

In general, the traditional face-to-face learning environment has gained many positive attitudes from the students mainly because of the simplicity that it could provide and it has been the most common and adopted learning method for every youngster. However, the students' attitudes gradually change as a result of the COVID-19 pandemic, which requires them to study in different learning styles in order to prevent the virus from spreading.

In Online Learning

Ullah et al. (2017) once mentioned that students' attitudes are viewed as key aspects in online learning which can cause a significant impact on the adoption of online learning. Aixia & Wang (2011) has further supported this point, indicating that students' attitudes are influenced by the quality and accessibility of using online learning courses and the level of skills they performed in the computer. This is because all these aspects are beneficial in gaining their confidence in using computers, making online learning more enjoyable and appealing.

According to a study conducted by Drennan et al. (2005), positive attitudes towards technology and individualized learning mode enhance students' satisfaction towards online learning. However, different results and experiences will be reacted by different students based on their skill levels and attitudes towards the online learning environment (Hannay & Newvine, 2006). Hence, the outcomes will be highly influenced by students' attitudes towards online learning, which is crucial to the acceptability and adoption of online learning.

However, Gherhes et al. (2021) mentioned that some of the students are dissatisfied with online learning, especially for students who are used to face-to-face learning and subsequently enrolled in online learning courses. Supporting this point, students' previous attitudes toward technology and computer usage may also influence their current attitudes towards online learning (Zhu et al, 2013).

In Hybrid Learning

Sanpanich (2013) revealed that the students who have a favorable attitude towards online learning and flexibility in face-to-face learning are more likely to adapt to hybrid learning. According to both Rovai and Jordan (2004) and Vance (2012), students expressed positive attitudes towards hybrid learning because they appreciated the simplicity of online access combined with the support of face-to-face lecturers when necessary. Likewise, students were more favorable towards hybrid learning over online learning because they valued the freedom of the online format but also desiring for the extra instructional support that a face-to-face learning environment could provide (Senn, 2008).

Furthermore, Zhu (2017) discovered that part-time university students had higher positive attitudes towards hybrid learning. Birbal et al. (2018) indicating that students who working part-time have less time to devote to full-time classes and they appreciate the flexibility that hybrid learning provides, allowing them to participate in a small portion of university life on campus rather than study fully online.

Nevertheless, many students agreed that hybrid learning is very sufficient because technology aids in the fostering of learning activities and the face-to-face classroom methods contribute to social interaction and motivation among students and lecturers which has definitely combined the strength from both online learning and face-to-face learning (Ahmad & Ismail, 2013). Mali & Lim (2021) has also agreed on this opinion, claiming that students showed more positive attitudes towards hybrid learning, especially during the COVID-19 pandemic.

Differences In Students' Achievements

In Face-to-Face Learning

a) Positive Achievement

In a classroom setting, students get to enhance their social skills by interacting with both their lecturers and coursemates. Also, students will be able to develop meaningful relationships and networks with other students as they have the opportunity to meet and interact with them on campus. Every relationship gained is beneficial for the students when they begin their careers (It, 2020). Education Destination Malaysia (2018) stating that students will discover new talents and increase their self-confidence by excelling in any new skill through participating in extracurricular activities provided in offline learning environment.

Besides that, due to the convenience and ease of the face-to-face learning environment provided, students are able to work in groups more easily than in other learning environments. By bringing together everyone's varied ideas and opinions, all of these social ties and linkage can help to generate new ideas and encourage creativity. Lunce (2006) further supported this point, stating that physical simulations allow the students to manipulate variables in an open-ended scenario and evaluate the outcomes.

With the constant pressure provided by the lecturer on the spot, students have to learn to work in high-pressured environments, which is a skill that is transferable to other areas of their lives (McNulty, 2021). It (2020) also mentioned that students can train to be disciplined and punctual throughout their learning experience in face-to-face learning since they must be punctual to class on time regardless of external factors and this good habit can be carried throughout their life.

b) Negative Achievement

Typically, the education cost applied in face-to-face learning is higher as compared to other learning styles. This is because the cost includes maintenance cost, tuition cost, facility cost, miscellaneous cost and others (McNulty, 2021). Additional costs such as transportation fees, accommodation fees, living expenses, food expenses and others are not included in the education cost yet. Hence, students might have issues with the economic pressure when studying in a face-to-face learning environment.

Moreover, while face-to-face learning provided students with a good opportunity to interact with their lecturers, the frequency of interactions may be minimal since face-to-face learning is considered a large group of students studying in the same class (POUDEL, 2019). Hence, it may take a longer time for booking an appointment with their lecturers.

The student requires more time for traveling to and from campus. The amount of time needed is depending on the students' living areas, which can guzzle up gas, time and money. Not to mention the daily traffic jams occurred which will make students feel stressed and burdened (Prout, 2021). According to Makarova (2021), there are students who respond that they felt face-to-face learning is inconvenient for them especially who live far from the university, causing them to spend more time and also money.

In Online Learning

a) Positive Achievement

In an online learning environment, there is no fix or tight schedule to follow, but a flexible schedule instead. Online learning provides students with complete control over when and how they take the course as every classes will be held fully online (Nagrale, 2019). Also, students do not need to waste time getting to and from campus or waiting for a bus or train, especially during peak hours. Similarly, online learning is said to be a method of providing quick delivery of lessons. According to Gupta (2017), this learning mode features a shorter semester as compared to traditional learning, implying that the time required to learn is reduced to 25% to 60% of what is required in traditional learning.

Online learning is redefining the way knowledge is delivered and how it performs in satisfying real market demands since it has emerged as a viable answer to lifelong learning as well as real-life professional training (Mouzakitis et al., 2011). Lifelong learning is defined as a process through which people expand their knowledge, skills and interest throughout their lifetimes as well as learning opportunities (Laal, 2011). Online learning is able to keep students' skills, knowledge, experience and attitudes up to date (Mouzakitis & Tuncay, 2011). In short, learning equals earning as all these lifelong qualities will affect every part of our lives (Ho, 2019).

Moreover, online learning allows students to access and rewind any materials and lecturers an unlimited number of times as every coursework is available online. This is extremely beneficial for students during revision when preparing for an exam (Gupta, 2017). Holley & Oliver (2010) have clarified that students have the opportunity to learn in different ways following their preferences and convenience as long as the academics provide rich and engaging online materials. This is due to the variety of learning styles that can be personalized in a variety of ways to provide the best learning environment according to each student's preferences and needs (Gautam, 2020).

b) Negative Achievement

Online learning is a form of education that involves extensive use of technology over the internet. Without a stable internet connection and strong technology capabilities, any technical issues will turn online learning from a superior to an inferior (Ali, 2004). A study conducted by Sit (2005) also reported that it is stressful and time-consuming for beginners to confront computer technology as compared to the actual learning activities. According to a study by Coman et al. (2020), the majority of students have encountered technical issues such as poor internet connection, signal loss, a lack of adequate digital devices, difficulty signing in to resources etc, all of which have made online learning more burdensome and reduced their learning experience.

It is difficult to engage learners in an online learning environment since it takes a high level of self-motivation, which is often lacking among students. This is because online learning requires motivation to complete tasks, stay engaged and make progress (Ali, 2004). According to Khan et al. (2017), nearly every instructor with varying levels of learning experience expressed anxiety regarding student engagement in online learning, regardless of the number of years they have been teaching online. Unlike in the face-to-face and hybrid learning environment, it is easier for the lecturer to engage students through activities that promote community involvement in order to prevent feelings of isolation (Gautam, 2020).

Nowadays, people are getting the benefits of accessing vast information quickly through the use of the Internet. All personal information is increasingly exposed to a rising number of threats and vulnerabilities as a result of this increased interconnectivity (Chen & He, 2013). For example, students are required to sign up for a variety of applications and software with personal information such as IC number, phone number, email address and others that could be hacked and abused by others (Eldeeb, 2020).

Also, online learning differs from traditional face-to-face learning where the lecturer can give instant feedback in the class. Students can only get in touch with the lecturer through email in online learning, and there is no guarantee that the lecturer would respond as rapidly as they would if they could communicate with the lecturer face-to-face (Firmansyah et al., 2021). Otter et al. (2013) discovered that online students felt more isolated from their lecturer due to the obligated environment in their studies, and the support given by their lecturer was lesser than their lecturer believed.

In Hybrid Learning

a) Positive Achievement

One of the important achievements is definitely the integration of classroom and technology provided by hybrid learning which supports the learning approach through the selection of learning materials, the provision of space for students and lecturers to interact as well as the participation of students and lecturers in virtual life even after the traditional face-to-face classes has ended (Ahmad & Ismail, 2013). Students are able to experience two different types of learning environment which are online and offline at the same time.

Hybrid learning which blends classroom and online learning to provide opportunities for communication, engagement, and multimedia information, has led to students agreeing that they can maintain motivation to study even after the class has ended. Besides, the students are able to achieve and gain knowledge through the improvement of their learning skills in hybrid learning that covers both real and virtual learning environments. According to Ahmad & Ismail (2013), they believe that the additional usage of computers will aid and increase their interest in their learning progress, including the assignments and activities that have been assigned.

Moreover, hybrid learning has the ability to enhance students' learning while also increasing the efficiency of instruction and resource allocation. This is due to the fact that the online section can be completed whenever and wherever the students prefer, whilst the face-to-face section must be completed in a timely manner (Crawford et al., 2014). Illustrating this point, Crawford found that the Northern Arizona University has discovered the students in hybrid learning took roughly one-quarter less time as compared to traditional face-to-face students while attaining the same learning outcomes.

Furthermore, students from hybrid learning environments are able to achieve further skills in a row as a combo at the same time, which is considered a strength when compared to students who solely enrolled in face-to-face learning or online learning. For example, computer skills such as file management, emailing and website navigation gained from hybrid learning are useful and beneficial in the workplace (Giarla, 2021).

b) Negative Achievement

Hybrid learning is considered a newly used term as it is a learning concept that is not widely used in Malaysia's education system. Factors such as inadequate accessibility which may result in resource wastage, technical issues including bad internet connection for online parts and a high maintenance cost are some of the shortcomings in hybrid learning (Oweis, 2018). Some of the students may feel frustrated if the internet connection is lost during ongoing classes or especially during important events such as ongoing exams and presentations (JOHNSON, 2021).

Due to the limited usage of hybrid learning, the number of students enrolled in hybrid learning courses may be lower. This situation may have an impact on the students' experience and interactions with other coursemates, especially for students who develop better when they interact with their peers.

Hence, negative achievements such as lack of interaction, loneliness, feelings of boredom and dullness may arise along with the learning experience (Dean, 2021). Zappia (n.d.) further supported this point indicating that it is difficult for the students to develop friendships and networks due to lack of intellectual and social stimulation environment performed. From this, students are required to adjust their learning methods accordingly, but not everyone is able to do so.

Furthermore, students may experience cognitive load due to the wide range of possibilities provided by the hybrid learning environment, where lecturers may begin to assign more learning activities and content in both practical and online practices (Hunt, 2016). This is because the lecturers tend to prepare and design different activities which fit the face-to-face sections and online sections respectively, allowing students to learn and gain more from different perspectives (Chen & Lu, 2013).

Strategies to Improve Online and Hybrid Learning

Course Design and Structure

The adoption of online learning by students will be boosted by a well-developed online course design and structure. This is because, unlike face-to-face learning, which allows teachers to go off-script, online learning relies more on detailed course content and structure, with all materials pre-set and uploaded to the internet during the planning stages (Team, 2020). Also, it is important to design suitable and comfortable online courses that make use of the Internet in order to improve the students' satisfaction and avoid bad experiences. In short, a high quality course design is able to help ensure that students receive the highest quality experience that online learning and practice can provide (Thomas,2020).

Setup E-Content Development Council

E-learning is a process, while e-content is a product. E-content is typically created to guide students through a large amount of material in order to complete a certain goal. The quality of online learning is determined not only by the manner in which the process is carried out but also by the content learned and the manner in which it is presented (Nachimuthu, 2012). By developing an e-content development council, every piece of material adheres to the learning objectives, ensuring that students do not end up learning the wrong thing without benefits (Hodgson, 2015). Nachimuthu states that there are six phases that must be developed in e-content development aspects: analysis, design, development, testing, implementation, and evaluation. These phases will aid in the planning and design of e-content preparation by assessing the current situation. It also contributes to the actual production of the e-content design with the actual educational field and targeted audience experience in order to satisfy the e-content and its effectiveness for effective e-content delivery. Supporting this point, Ali (2004) agrees that the e-content development council benefits from developing and monitoring e-content standards, promoting knowledge sharing among e-learning providers as well as training and developing e-content experts. Through this action, the quality of online learning and hybrid learning will be strengthened and improved.

Increase Technical Support

Technical support is absolutely important in an online learning environment. The use of technology for learning has long been hampered by technical issues which make the distance learner even more distance. Indeed, it is critical to minimize difficulties as much as possible right from the start of the learning process. An instructor's technical standing is crucial since their level of comfort with technology can be transferred on to their students (Keengwe & Kidd, 2010). It is also important to provide a technical team support standby during office hours to provide technical assistance when the online users run into technical barriers in order to develop an accessible, available and reliable technical support for both leaners and instructors (Shamsy, 2014).

Apply a Variety of Multimedia and Modalities

Since student engagement is an important key in every learning process, students' motivation and interest must be maintained. For example, create a variety of content mediums, such as articles, videos, podcasts, forums, and discussions, so that students can access a variety of materials without getting bored (Team, n.d.). According to Abrami et al. (2012), students can be engaged in online learning by watching instructional videos and interacting with multimedia. Revere & Kovach (2011) also advised that if teachers want their students to be more engaged, they should take attention to the material and content they applied in their courses. For example, they should construct authentic exercises with diverse multimedia or modalities from multiple perspectives in the learning process, rather than simply providing a list of resources. To support this point, a previous study has shown that students feel more involved and engaged in an online section when they participate in a variety of activities that take full advantage of the internet's features (Dixson, 2010).

Provide Substantive Feedback

Since student engagement is an important key in every learning process, students' motivation and interest must be maintained. For example, create a variety of content mediums, such as articles, videos, podcasts, forums, and discussions, so that students can access a variety of materials without getting bored (Team, n.d.). According to Abrami et al. (2012), students can be engaged in online learning by watching instructional videos and interacting with multimedia. Revere & Kovach (2011) also advised that if teachers want their students to be more engaged, they should take attention to the material and content they applied in their courses. For example, they should construct authentic exercises with diverse multimedia or modalities from multiple perspectives in the learning process, rather than simply providing a list of resources. To support this point, a previous study has shown that students feel more involved and engaged in an online section when they participate in a variety of activities that take full advantage of the internet's features (Dixson, 2010).

Increase Interactive Section

One of the most challenging factors in online learning is the sense of isolation students experience in the learning environment as they are put into themselves with the Internet without any face-to-face interactions with their friends and classmates. This is due to the fact that the regular type of communication that occurs in a classroom environment could be hard to replicate in an online learning environment (Barbour & Unger, 2014). According to Keaton & Gilbert (2020), interactions with classmates will benefit students with coursework and social connectedness as they are able to share ideas and resources directly. By implementing online group collaboration activities, it allows students to practice problem-solving with their peers from the interaction section to promote community involvement and prevent feelings of isolation (Pappas, 2016). A research conducted by Hiltz & Turoff (2002) has further agreed that students will be more motivated to actively participate in online sections if the collaboration and interaction sections were largely designed.

Research Methodology

The qualitative research method will be adopted in this study by conducting an online interview with open-ended questions to allow respondents to react to the prepared questions in a variety of ways in order to achieve the nature of the objectives and the data required for this study (Bhat, 2021). A one-on-one conversation will be carried out on five lecturers teaching quantity surveying courses at Taylor's University, selected randomly from the target sampling frame. Figure 1 shows the process of research that will be adopted in this study.

Figure 1. Research process

| **Research Area Selection** |
| Define the research topic |

| **Identification of Research Scope** |
| Define the research problem, aim, objectives, and questions |

| **Literature Review** |
| Studies on related previous literature topic |

| **Research Design** |
| Develop and indentifying the research methodology |

| **Data Collection** |
| Obtain the primary data through semi-structured interviews |

| **Data Analysis** |
| Justify the collected data |

| **Data Summarisation and Conclusion** |
| Report on research findings, recommendations, implications, and conclusion |

The scope of this study shall be limited to viewpoints of lecturers teaching quantity surveying courses and the sampling frame only involves Taylor's University lecturers. Taylor's University has been chosen as a sample university for this research as it has experience all types of learning approach and the lecturers would well-equipped with information and expertise on the research topic by providing their professional inspections and perception.

In terms of interview design, a semi-structured interview will be conducted in this research. Prior to the interview, a defined interview questionnaire on the current online and hybrid learning trend from students' attitudes and achievements gained during the COVID-19 pandemic era, as well as the strategies to improve both learning environments will be prepared, and impromptu questions will be asked in accordance with the interview flow.

Moreover, an open-ended questionnaire will be prepared to allow respondents to react to the prepared questions in a variety of ways which is more comprehensive and significant than just answering a preset answer on a questionnaire.

The outcomes of the data are used as a basis and the findings of this study will be generated through the coding system and reflects the future prospects of online and hybrid learning in quantity surveying education.

Research Framework

Figure 2 illustrates the research framework of this study. It Is necessary for putting the steps taken throughout the research into action. It can be used as a guide for researchers to focus on the scope of their studies. Besides that, doing a research framework is also necessary for presenting readers or future researchers with more organized and clear information about the study conducted.

Findings

Many factors have contributed to the lack of participation in online and hybrid learning from the students in quantity surveying education. Among all the findings collected, most of the respondents agree that a hybrid learning environment enhances the students' learning achievement in a greater way and it should be taken out as a new learning approach even after the pandemic ends. However, the percentage of face-to-face learning shall be higher than online learning, rather than being split in half as it is undeniable that the physical session would enhance students' learning achievements and level of understanding more regardless of the type of learning approach being used.

Also, hybrid learning provides a more freedom and flexible in terms of the learning process while able to obtain what face-to-face and online learning environment has benefited the students (Senn, 2008). For example, it consists fewer constraints and provides more interaction sessions as compared to other learning approaches. Therefore, it is apparent that students are willing to adopt hybrid learning as there are no much differences in the students' attitudes but with greater achievements. Hence, it is important to further promote hybrid learning in the quantity surveying education.

The strategies obtained from the findings can be divided into lecturer's action, student's action and university's action. The lecturer's actions are higher as they are the person who delivers the lectures and it is important for them to improve the way of delivering lectures from time to time such as providing interesting sessions to make the discussion more meaningful (Bedward et al., 2018). Moreover, the students should always provide constant feedback on their learning experience to the lecturers, so

Figure 2. Research framework

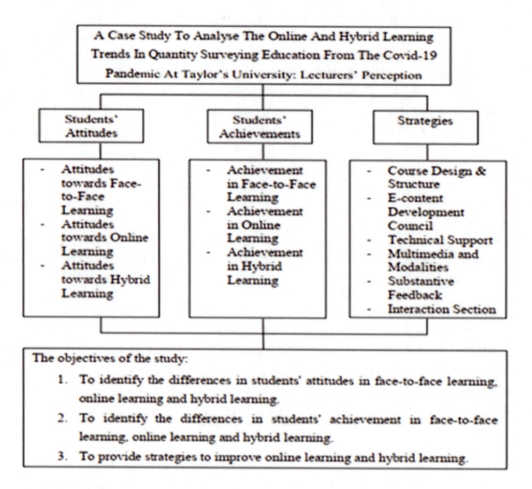

that the lecturers would have a better idea of the way to improve the weaknesses while maintaining the strengths of their teaching approach (Barbour & Unger, 2014). Last but not least, the university shall provide constant training and protocol on the learning tools in order to ensure that the lecturer's skills are updated and they are utilizing the full benefits of online tools for students' better learning experiences.

Additionally, although online and hybrid learning was introduced as a "lifeboat" approach for efficiently delivering knowledge to students during the pandemic time, however it is undeniable that the learning approaches has largely impacted the students' achievement in beneficial way. Hence, it is recommended for future studies to identify the different types of hybrid learning models by determining which model suits the quantity surveying education the best. Also, it should look depth into the pros and cons of hybrid learning as it is not widely adopted in the Malaysian education system, and it is newly introduced in responds to the pandemic outbreak where everyone is still in the process of familiarizing the learning environment.

CONCLUSION

In response to the COVID-19 pandemic, both students and lecturers have been introduced to different learning approaches. It is undeniable that every learning approach has resulted in different advantages and disadvantages from different sectors. Hence, it is important to constantly investigate the learning trend and learning achievements gained from different learning environments in order to adopt the most suitable learning approaches according to the real-time situations.

Finally, this study had a significant impact on achieving all of the study's objectives. It is beneficial to serve as a model or undertake an earlier survey to investigate students' performance in online and hybrid learning environments from various sectors in order to evaluate the learning environment's future prospects and determine whether it is appropriate to be applied in quantity surveying education. Ultimately, this would enhance, modernize and reform the quantity surveying learning environment, especially now that technology has become one of the essential elements in this evolutionary era.

REFERENCES

Abrami, P. C., Bernard, R. M., Bures, E. M., Borokhovski, E., & Tamim, R. M. (2012). Interaction in distance education and online learning: Using evidence and theory to improve practice. In *The next generation of distance education* (pp. 49–69). Springer. doi:10.1007/978-1-4614-1785-9_4

Ahmad, Z., & Ismail, I. Z. (2013). Utilization of hybrid learning in accomplishing learning satisfaction as perceived by university student. International Journal of e-Education, e-Business, e-. *Management Learning*, *3*(2), 98.

Aixia, D., & Wang, D. (2011). Factors influencing learner attitudes toward e-learning and development of e-learning environment based on the integrated e-learning platform. International Journal of e-Education, e-Business, e-. *Management Learning*, *1*(3), 264.

Ali, A. (2004). Issues & challenges in implementing e-learning in Malaysia.

Al Najdi, S. (2014, March). Hybrid learning in higher education. *In Society for Information Technology & Teacher Education International Conference* (pp. 214-220). Association for the Advancement of Computing in Education (AACE).

Barbour, M. K., & Unger, K. L. (2014). Strategies For Overcoming Common Obstacles In The Online Environment. *RealLife Distance Education: Case Studies in Practice*, 21.

Bhat, A. (2021, December 17). *Qualitative Research: Definition, Types, Methods and Examples*. QuestionPro. https://www.questionpro.com/blog/qualitative-research-methods/

Birbal, R., Ramdass, M., & Harripaul, M. C. (2018). Student teachers' attitudes towards blended learning. *Journal of Education and Human Development*, *7*(2), 9–26. doi:10.15640/jehd.v7n2a2

Bouchrika, I. (2020, June 30). *50 Online Education Statistics: 2020/2021 Data on Higher Learning & Corporate Training*. Research.Com. https://research.com/research/online-education-statistics

BQSM. (2021). *Accrediation Manual For Online Quantity Surveying Programmes*. BQSM. https://www.bqsm.gov.my/reference-documents/category/19-accreditation-manual.html

Chen, S., & Lu, Y. (2013, June). The negative effects and control of blended learning in university. In *2013 the International Conference on Education Technology and Information*. Atlantis Press. 10.2991/icetis-13.2013.7

Chen, Y., & He, W. (2013). Security risks and protection in online learning: A survey. *International Review of Research in Open and Distance Learning, 14*(5), 108–127. doi:10.19173/irrodl.v14i5.1632

Coman, C., Țîru, L. G., Meseşan-Schmitz, L., Stanciu, C., & Bularca, M. C. (2020). Online teaching and learning in higher education during the coronavirus pandemic: Students' perspective. *Sustainability (Basel), 12*(24), 10367. doi:10.3390u122410367

Crawford, C., Barker, J., & Seyam, A. A. (2014). The promising role of hybrid learning in community colleges: Looking towards the future.

Daniel, D. (2021, February 9). *What Is Hybrid Learning?* ViewSonic Library. https://www.viewsonic.com/library/education/what-is-hybrid-learning/#What_Is_Hybrid_Learning

Dean. (2021, July 16). *The Pros and Cons of Hybrid Learning*. Dean College. https://www.dean.edu/news-events/dean-college-blog/story/the-pros-and-cons-of-hybrid-learning/#:%7E:text=Limited%20Internet%20Access%20Can%20Be,a%20long%20time%20to%20download

Dixson, M. D. (2010). Creating Effective Student Engagement in Online Courses: What Do Students Find Engaging? *The Journal of Scholarship of Teaching and Learning, 10*(2), 1–13.

Drennan, J., Kennedy, J., & Pisarski, A. (2005). Factors affecting student attitudes toward flexible online learning in management education. *The Journal of Educational Research, 98*(6), 331–338. doi:10.3200/JOER.98.6.331-338

Education Destination Malaysia. (2018, June 29). *5 Benefits of Extracurricular Activities*. Education Destination Malaysia. https://educationdestinationmalaysia.com/blogs/5-benefits-of-extracurricular-activities

Eldeeb, I. (2020, November 16). *Online Learning: 6 Threats Schools and Students Should be Prepared for*. GAT Labs. https://n.gatlabs.com/blogpost/6-online-learning-threats-for-schools/

Firmansyah, R., Putri, D. M., Wicaksono, M. G. S., Putri, S. F., & Arif, A. (2021, July). The University Students' Perspectives on the Advantages and Disadvantages of Online Learning Due to COVID-19. In *Journal of College Science Teaching, 40*(1), 34–40.

Gautam, P. (2020, October 10). *Advantages And Disadvantages Of Online Learning*. ELearning Industry. https://elearningindustry.com/advantages-and-disadvantages-online-learning

Gherheș, V., Stoian, C. E., Fărcaşiu, M. A., & Stanici, M. (2021). E-Learning vs. Face-To-Face Learning: Analyzing Students' Preferences and Behaviors. *Sustainability (Basel), 13*(8), 4381. doi:10.3390u13084381

Giarla, A. (2021, December 29). *The Benefits Of Blended Learning*. TeachThought. https://www.teachthought.com/technology/benefits-of-blended-learning/

Gupta, S. (2017, November 11). *9 Benefits Of eLearning For Students*. ELearning Industry. https://elearningindustry.com/9-benefits-of-elearning-for-students

Hannay, M., & Newvine, T. (2006). Perceptions of distance learning: A comparison of online and traditional learning. *Journal of Online Learning and Teaching, 2*(1), 1–11.

Headspace. (n.d.). Face To Face Vs. Online Learning Options. *headspace*. https://headspace.org.au/explore-topics/for-young-people/face-to-face-vs-online-learning/

Hiltz, S. R., & Turoff, M. (2002). What makes learning networks effective? *Communications of the ACM, 45*(4), 56–59. doi:10.1145/505248.505273

Ho, L. (2019, November 15). *13 Reasons Why Online Learning Is an Effective Way to Learn*. Lifehack. https://www.lifehack.org/856820/online-learning-effective

Hodgson, C. (2015, December 5). *4 Tips To Create High Quality Content In eLearning*. ELearning Industry. https://elearningindustry.com/4-tips-create-high-quality-content-elearning

Holley, D., & Oliver, M. (2010). Student engagement and blended learning: Portraits of risk. *Computers & Education, 54*(3), 693–700. doi:10.1016/j.compedu.2009.08.035

Hunt, V. (2016, December 18). *Pros And Cons Of Blended Learning At College*. ELearning Industry. https://elearningindustry.com/pros-cons-blended-learning-at-college

It, P. (2020, November 17). [*Advantages of Traditional Education*. University of the Potomac. https://potomac.edu/top-advantages-of-traditional-education/]. *Top (Madrid), 6*,.

Jaggars, S. S., & Xu, D. (2016). How do online course design features influence student performance? *Computers & Education, 95*, 270–284. doi:10.1016/j.compedu.2016.01.014

Johnson. N. (2021, August 12). *The effects of blended learning on students in higher education*. Software2. https://www.software2.com/resource-centre/remote-learning/blended-learning-effects

Keaton, W., & Gilbert, A. (2020). Successful Online Learning: What Does Learner Interaction with Peers, Instructors and Parents Look Like? *Journal of Online Learning Research, 6*(2), 129–154.

Keengwe, J., & Kidd, T. T. (2010, June 2). *Towards Best Practices in Online Learning and Teaching in Higher Education*. Merlot. https://jolt.merlot.org/vol6no2/keengwe_0610.pdf

Khan, A., Egbue, O., Palkie, B., & Madden, J. (2017). Active learning: Engaging students to maximize learning in an online course. *Electronic Journal of e-Learning, 15*(2), 107–115.

Koksal, I. (2020, May 2). *The Rise Of Online Learning*. Forbes. https://www.forbes.com/sites/ilkerkoksal/2020/05/02/the-rise-of-online-learning/?sh=125b1ff72f3c

Laal, M. (2011). Lifelong learning: What does it mean? *Procedia: Social and Behavioral Sciences, 28*, 470–474. doi:10.1016/j.sbspro.2011.11.090

Lunce, L. M. (2006). Simulations: Bringing the benefits of situated learning to the traditional classroom. *Journal of Applied Educational Technology, 3*(1), 37–45.

Makarova, E. (2021). Effectiveness of traditional and online learning: comparative analysis from the student perspective. In *SHS Web of Conferences* (Vol. 99, p. 01019). EDP Sciences. 10.1051hsconf/20219901019

Mali, D., & Lim, H. (2021). How do students perceive face-to-face/blended learning as a result of the Covid-19 pandemic? *International Journal of Management Education, 19*(3), 100552. doi:10.1016/j.ijme.2021.100552

McNulty, N. (2021, November 24). *Online education vs traditional education – which one is better and why.* Niall McNulty. https://www.niallmcnulty.com/2021/04/what-is-the-difference-between-online-education-and-traditional-education/#htoc-what-are-the-advantages-of-traditional-education

Mouzakitis, G. S., & Tuncay, N. (2011). E-learning and lifelong learning. *Turkish Online Journal of Distance Education, 12*(1), 166–173.

Nachimuthu, K. (2012). *Need of e-content developments in education. Education Today, An International Journal Of Education & Humanities.* APH Pub.

Nagrale, P. (2019, October 13). *Advantages and Disadvantages of Distance Education.* Sure Job. https://surejob.in/advantages-and-disadvantages-of-distance-education.html

Ong Et Al, J. (2020, December 2). *7 missing pieces: why students prefer in-person over online classes.* University Affairs. https://www.universityaffairs.ca/features/feature-article/7-missing-pieces-why-students-prefer-in-person-over-online-classes/

Otter, R. R., Seipel, S., Graeff, T., Alexander, B., Boraiko, C., Gray, J., & Sadler, K. (2013). Comparing student and faculty perceptions of online and traditional courses. *The Internet and Higher Education, 19*, 27–35. doi:10.1016/j.iheduc.2013.08.001

Oweis, T. I. (2018, November 4). *Effects of Using a Blended Learning Method on Students' Achievement and Motivation to Learn English in Jordan: A Pilot Case Study.* Hindawi. https://www.hindawi.com/journals/edri/2018/7425924/

Pappas, C. (2016, October 5). *Top 8 eLearning Barriers That Inhibit Online Learners Engagement With eLearning Content.* ELearning Industry. https://elearningindustry.com/top-elearning-barriers-that-inhibit-online-learners-engagement-elearning-content

Poudel, D. (2019, September 26). *Pros and Cons of Traditional Schools.* Honest Pros and Cons. https://honestproscons.com/pros-and-cons-of-traditional-schools/

Prep, U. (n.d.). *Introducing Online Education.* Uni-Prep. https://www.uni-prep.com/online-education/introducing-online-education/

Prout, T. (2021, June 15). *Weighing the Pros and Cons of Online vs. In-Person Learning.* National University. https://www.nu.edu/resources/weighing-the-pros-and-cons-of-online-vs-in-person-learning/

Revere, L., & Kovach, J. V. (2011). ONLINE TECHNOLOGIES FOR ENGAGED LEARNING A Meaningful Synthesis for Educators. *Quarterly Review of Distance Education, 12*(2).

Rovai, A. P., & Jordan, H. M. (2004). Blended learning and sense of community: A comparative analysis with traditional and fully online graduate courses. *International Review of Research in Open and Distance Learning*, 5(2), 1–13. doi:10.19173/irrodl.v5i2.192

Sanpanich, N. (2021). Investigating Factors Affecting Students' Attitudes toward Hybrid Learning. *Reflections: The SoL Journal*, 28(2), 208–227.

Shamsy, J. (2014, May). *elearn Magazine: A Balancing Act Part I: Technical Support and the Online Instructor*. ELearnmagazine. https://elearnmag.acm.org/featured.cfm?aid=2627756

Sit, J. W., Chung, J. W., Chow, M. C., & Wong, T. K. (2005). Experiences of online learning: Students' perspective. *Nurse Education Today*, 25(2), 140–147. doi:10.1016/j.nedt.2004.11.004 PMID:15701540

Swan, K. (2002). Building learning communities in online courses: The importance of interaction. *Education Communication and Information*, 2(1), 23–49. doi:10.1080/1463631022000005016

Team, B. (n.d.). *4 Ways to Improve Adoption of Your Digital Education Program*. BenchPrep. https://blog.benchprep.com/4-ways-to-improve-adoption-of-your-digital-education-program

Team, G. (2020, October 5). *Why instructional design is so critical for effective e-learning classes*. Gamelearn: Game-Based Learning Courses for Soft Skills Training. https://www.game-learn.com/en/resources/blog/why-instructional-design-is-so-critical-for-effective-e-learning-classes/

Ullah, O., Khan, W., & Khan, A. (2017). Students' attitude towards online learning at tertiary level. *PUTAJ–Humanities and Social Sciences*, 25(1-2), 63–82.

Vance, L. K. (2012). Do students want web 2.0? An investigation into student instructional preferences. *Journal of Educational Computing Research*, 47(4), 481–493. doi:10.2190/EC.47.4.g

Zappia, S. (n.d.). *Pros & Cons of Hybrid Courses*. Seattlepi. https://education.seattlepi.com/pros-cons-hybrid-courses-3288.html

Zhu, C. (2017). University student satisfaction and perceived effectiveness of a blended learning course. *International Journal of Learning Technology*, 12(1), 66–83. doi:10.1504/IJLT.2017.083996

Zhu, Y., Au, W., & Yates, G. C. (2013). *University Students' Attitudes toward Online Learning in a Blended Course*. Australian Association for Research in Education.

Chapter 9

Work–Based Learning as a Catalyst for Sustainability:
Study of Architecture Students' 21st Century Skills

TamilSalvi Mari
Taylor's University, Malaysia

Veronica Ng
Taylor's University, Malaysia

Sujatavani Gunasagaran
Taylor's University, Malaysia

Sivaraman Kuppusamy
Reading University of Malaysia, Malaysia

ABSTRACT

This research examines architecture graduates' perceptions of their proficiency in 21st-century skills. A quantitative methodology was employed for this study. The data was obtained through a structured question-naire, which 141 architecture graduates completed. The online survey assessed the graduates' 21st-century skills. The collected data was analyzed using SPSS version 25. The findings show that the graduates' level of proficiency in 21st-century skills is generally moderate, with information; media and technology skills; and life and career skills being the most prominent. The graduates rated their learning and innovation skills the highest (M=3.76), followed by moderate scores for both life and career skills (M=3.60) and information, media, and technology skills (M= 3.04). The study adds to the existing literature on 21st-century skills by providing a student perspective on the topic, which has not been widely explored in published research.

INTRODUCTION

Approximately half of the world's population currently resides in cities, and it has been projected that by the year 2030, around three out of every five people will be living in urban areas (Fuller and Gas-

DOI: 10.4018/978-1-6684-8253-7.ch009

ton, 2009). Healthy urban environments are becoming increasingly important because over 50% of the world's population resides in dense urban areas (Dye, 2007). The urban lifestyle is often associated with unsatisfactory working environments, heavy workloads, tight schedules, and extended working hours (Facey et al., 2015). Work-related stress is a significant challenge to both workers' and organizational health, leading to a decline in an individual's physical and mental health, as well as the effectiveness and performance of the organization (WHO, 2011).

White-collar workers, who bear psychosocial work stressors in their working environments, are at a higher risk of developing mental disorders (Stansfeld and Candy, 2006). Job or occupational stress is a harmful emotional and physical response that occurs when the job demands cannot meet the workers' needs or abilities (Centres for Disease Control and Prevention, 2014). In Kuala Lumpur, which is a constantly expanding city, the residents need thoughtfully designed spaces to balance their hectic daily routine, provide relief from mental fatigue and stress, recreation, and offset the negative psychophysiological consequences of living in densely built urban environments (Braubach et al., 2017; Lee et al., 2015; Zhang et al., 2015).

Mental Wellbeing

The Centers for Disease Control and Prevention (CDC) defines mental wellbeing as having positive emotions and moods, such as happiness and contentment and being free from depression, anxiety, or other negative emotions (CDC, 2020). Wellbeing is a multifaceted concept that includes various physical, social, emotional, psychological, and community aspects (Kreitzer, 2014). The definition of mental wellbeing encompasses the hedonic perspective of feeling satisfied and happy and the eudaimonic perspective of self-realization, good relationships with others, and personal growth (Ryan & Deci, 2001). The absence of negative feelings and thoughts and the ability to manage challenging situations are also integral components of mental wellbeing (CABA, n.d.). Good mental health involves not only the absence of mental illness but also the ability to cope with daily stressors, work productively, and contribute to the community (WHO, 2014).

Mental Health Issues Among Office Workers

The concept of restorative environments (RE) within office developments has gained traction in recent years as a potential solution to mitigate the negative effects of office work on mental wellbeing. A RE is a physical space that promotes relaxation, reduces stress, and enhances mental restoration (Ulrich et al., 1991). Features such as natural lighting, greenery, and access to nature have been found to have a positive impact on mental health and cognitive performance (Kaplan, 1995).

However, the COVID-19 pandemic has brought new challenges to the workplace, such as remote work, social isolation, and increased workloads. These challenges have made it difficult for employees to access RE and have increased their risk of developing mental health issues (Chen et al., 2020). As a result, employers must adapt their strategies to promote mental wellbeing in the new normal of remote work and hybrid work environments.

Furthermore, the COVID-19 pandemic has brought new challenges to the workplace, with many employees now working from home. This has resulted in increased social isolation and blurred boundaries between work and personal life, which can contribute to stress and anxiety (Maben & Bridges, 2020). The lack of access to RE within office spaces has also been highlighted as a potential issue, with some employees struggling to find ways to incorporate restorative elements into their home working environment (Bailenson et al., 2021).

Mental health issues among office workers are a significant concern that requires proactive measures from employers. The RE trend has been seen as a potential solution, although challenges have arisen after COVID-19. Employers need to continue to prioritize mental wellbeing in the workplace, whether employees are working from home or in the office, and to incorporate restorative elements where possible.

Problem Statement

The population growth of Malaysia is increasing at a rate of 1.1% per year, resulting in a rise in the workforce, with 15.6 million workers in 2019 and 15.7 million workers in 2020. Of the workers in 2020, 28.2% are highly skilled, while 59.9% are semi-skilled and primarily work in office or indoor environments (Department of Statistics, 2020). Space is becoming more valuable in densely populated urban areas such as Penang, Klang Valley, and Johor. As cities expand and more people work in office spaces, the negative impact of urban living and workplace stress increases exponentially. Office workers spend significant time in stressful environments, leading to deteriorating mental wellbeing.

Occupational stress is caused by a lack of support from colleagues and supervisors, a lack of control over work processes, and poor management practices (WHO). Designers play a vital role in creating workspaces that alleviate work stress and promote mental and physical wellbeing. Many studies have established guidelines and shown the positive impact of RE on mental wellbeing in interior spaces. However, the effects of RE within Malaysian office spaces have not been previously studied or documented (Department of Statistics, 2020). Thus, this study attempted to investigate the current state of workspaces for the presence of RE and their effects on the mental wellbeing of office workers in Malaysia.

Research Questions

1. What are the existing conditions and elements of restorative environments in office spaces within Malaysia?
2. How do the environments within the office space affect the perceived mental wellbeing of office workers in Malaysia?
3. What are the office workers' preferences for restorative environments in their workspace?

BACKGROUND

Indoor Environment Quality and Occupant Wellbeing

Indoor Environmental Quality (IEQ) is an important factor to consider in office spaces in Malaysia, as it can impact the wellbeing and health of occupants. Mallawaarachchi et al. (2012) explain that IEQ measures the performance of the indoor environment and its effects on occupants. Previous studies have shown that various indoor environmental factors, such as lighting, ventilation, acoustics, thermal conditions, furniture, and ergonomics, can positively affect the wellbeing of building occupants when properly designed and implemented (Salonen et al., 2012). To ensure safe and healthy indoor environments, the Centre for Disease Control (CDC) has published an "Indoor Environmental Quality Policy" providing guidelines and procedures for building occupants (CDC, n.d). Architects in Malaysia are also required to follow several clauses in the Malaysian Uniform Building By Law (UBBL), 1984, to ensure the health and safety of occupants (UBBL, 1984).

Restorative Environments (RE)

RE refer to environments, often in natural settings, that can help reduce emotional and psychophysiological stress and rejuvenate or restore depleted attention resources. Such environments are characterized by legibility and elements that offer a break from the daily routine. These environments are based on Attention Restoration Theory and the Psycho-evolutionary Theory, which state that viewing or immersing oneself in natural surroundings can help improve focus and cognitive fatigue (American Psychology Association). According to the Attention Restoration theories (ART) proposed by Kaplan (1989, 1995), the brain's capacity to focus on specific stimuli or tasks is limited, leading to "directed attention fatigue" and mental exhaustion. Mental fatigue can result in various adverse consequences, including irritability, inaccuracy, incivility, and impulsivity.

The COVID-19 pandemic has highlighted the importance of creating RE in office spaces; it promotes stress reduction, psychological restoration, and individual wellbeing (Cairns, 2020). The growing recognition of the link between the physical environment and mental health has fueled this trend. Studies have shown that the built environment can significantly impact individuals' mental health and wellbeing (Kjellgren & Buhrkall, 2010). For example, access to greenery and natural light has been found to reduce stress levels and promote relaxation (Cairns, 2020). Comfortable seating and ergonomic workstations have also been found to improve wellbeing and reduce physical discomfort among workers (Browning et al., 2014).

The COVID-19 pandemic has created new challenges for creating RE in office spaces. One of the main challenges is balancing health and safety concerns with creating welcoming and comfortable workspaces. For example, open-plan offices, which were popular in the past, may need to be redesigned to incorporate barriers or other safety measures (Holtzhausen, 2020). Despite these challenges, the trend towards creating RE in office spaces will likely grow in importance post-COVID-19. This is because the pandemic has highlighted the importance of mental health and wellbeing, and employers are recognizing the need to create supportive and restorative work environments. This trend is likely driven by a desire to attract and retain top talent and promote employee productivity and creativity (Stevenson, 2021).

Importance of Indoor Environment Quality in Workplaces

Previous research has demonstrated the relationship between indoor environmental quality and occupants' physical and psychosocial wellbeing (Dolan et al., 2016). Physical aspects of the indoor environment, such as lighting, noise control, and office furniture and layout, are directly linked to employee stress levels (Vischer, 2007). A field study of six different office spaces with varying features found that physical characteristics such as lighting, acoustics, and cubicle size in open-plan offices can impact work performance and satisfaction (Newsham et al., 2004; Haynes, 2008). There is also evidence that the indoor environment of a workplace can impact a company's operational costs (Heerwagen, 2000).

The indoor workplace environment directly impacts the wellbeing and health of occupants, and buildings that promote their prosperity and happiness contribute to healthy living (Croome, 2013). Architects and the construction industry should focus on creating built environments that foster occupants' health and wellbeing, rather than just meeting the minimum requirements of building regulations and maximizing cost efficiency for profit.

A well-designed and conducive interior work environment can lead to reduced staff turnover rates, fewer sick leaves, increased productivity and job satisfaction, and improved perceived health and wellbeing of the office staff (McGraw-Hill Construction, 2014; US Green Building Council, 2004). The past and current research findings highlight the impact of indoor environmental quality on employee productivity and underscore the importance of good Indoor Environment Quality (IEQ) for the occupants' productivity.

The Effect of Natural Environment on Health and Wellbeing of Individuals

According to Hartig et al. (1996), exposure to natural environments can positively impact the health and wellbeing of individuals compared to urban environments. Stigsdotter et al. (2010) also found empirical evidence of the positive relationship between green outdoor spaces and city dwellers. Studies conducted in the US by Kuo and Sullivan (2001a, 2001b) suggest that exposure to natural environments may reduce anger, frustration, and aggression, potentially leading to decreased aggressive behavior and criminal activity rates.

In addition, Berman et al. (2008) conducted multiple experiments with 50 adults with a mean age of 24.5 and found that short encounters with the natural environment could significantly increase cognitive control. The positive effects of nature on cognitive function and health have also been established by Sanchez et al. (2018). Furthermore, a study conducted in Sweden by Lottrup et al. (2013) found that there were significant relationships between visual and physical access to workplace greenery, decreased stress levels, and a positive workplace attitude among male respondents. These findings highlight the restorative qualities of exposure to nature in an outdoor setting, which have been extensively studied for decades and fall under the branch of study known as RE.

ELEMENTS OF RE AND THEIR BENEFITS

Windows and Views

Various studies have found windows and views of nature positively impact physical and psychological health (Velarde et al., 2007). Research conducted on nurses in hospitals with 12-hour shifts revealed that those with views of nature through windows experienced better stress recovery than those without non-nature views (Pati et al., 2007). In another study, workplaces with views of natural elements positively correlated with high view satisfaction, which correlated with high job satisfaction and work efficiency (Lottrup et al., 2013). A study conducted on a group of workers after a series of written tests and simulations of office workers found that those working in an office with a window view of nature experienced a more restorative heart rate recovery as compared to those without a view or with a nature view displayed through a flatscreen TV (Khan Jr et al., 2008).

Sounds and Sights of Simulated Nature

Using simulated nature, such as murals, paintings, videos, and sounds, has been found to have restorative benefits. Immersive and coherent depictions of nature in murals and paintings can give the observer a sense of being within the environment and increase their perception of being away from their current setting (de Kort et al., 2006). Natural landscapes depicted in murals are aesthetically pleasing and preferred for restoration (Purcell et al., 2001). Large nature murals have been found to provide restorative breaks for university students experiencing attentional fatigue (Flesten, 2009). The addition of natural sounds and large posters of natural landscapes to the waiting room of a student medical center was found to slightly lower the anxiety levels of patients compared to the waiting room with no changes, although the posters did not fully cover the walls (Watts et al., 2016).

Daylighting

Natural lighting has been identified as an essential element of RE. According to Heschong et al. (2002), natural lighting is one of the most important factors in enhancing workers' performance. Research has shown that individuals in urban settings spend 90% of their working hours indoors, leading to a lack of exposure to natural light-dark cycles (McCurdy & Graham, 2003). Office workers' productivity is linked to the distance from windows and the amount of daylight exposure in the workplace, as decreased exposure can lead to decreased productivity and increased sick leave (Boyce, 2006).

However, when workers in daylit, open-plan workplaces are exposed to highly correlated color temperature (CCT) fluorescent lamps, their subjective performance measures, sleep, and productivity improve (Viola et al., 2008). Natural lighting has also been found to be essential for wellbeing (Anderson et al., 2013). The California Energy Commission conducted a study that found workers' efficiency increases with natural lighting in workspaces (Heschong et al., 2003).

Real and Artificial Plants

Using real and artificial plants in indoor environments can have a restorative impact. Patients in a hospital waiting room exposed to real or fake plants reported lower stress levels than those in a control condition (Beukeboom & Dijkstra, 2012). Similarly, the presence of plants and exposure to nature has been positively associated with the productivity and wellbeing of workers, with outdoor plants having better results than indoor and potted plants (Grind & Patil, 2009). Adding green elements to a temporary site office led to better social benefits, such as cooperation and mentoring, and positive psychological effects, such as increased work satisfaction and higher morale, which enhanced users' productivity in handling work-related tasks (Grey & Birrel, 2014).

Timber Office Furniture

According to research, wooden furniture in indoor environments may reduce stress. Studies examining the psychophysiological effects of indoor timber have demonstrated a decrease in autonomic stress responses compared to spaces with little or no timber. In an office furnished with wood, participants showed lower stress levels throughout the study than those in a non-wood office (Bunard & Kutnar, 2015). Increasing the use of timber may be a cost-effective and sustainable way to connect building occupants with the natural environment, as it is perceived as more natural than other materials (Burnard et al., 2017).

METHODS

The study aimed to examine the current state of workspaces for the presence of RE and their effects on the mental wellbeing of office workers in Malaysia. A quantitative approach using survey instruments was used to collect the data from the respondents.

Instruments

In order to accomplish the objective of the study, a survey questionnaire was administered to office workers in office developments throughout Malaysia, utilizing a quantitative research methodology. A quantitative approach was deemed appropriate as the analysis and outcomes needed to be numerical for broader generalization to Malaysia's larger population of office workers. This method was well-suited for the study as it required a comparison among the target group, making any numerical discrepancies easily detectable (Sukamolson, 2007). The study participants were office workers, and the survey questionnaire was specifically created to elicit responses to the research questions.

An online survey questionnaire developed using Google Forms was used to collect data for the study. This method was chosen because it is efficient and time-saving, allowing for instant data collection and analysis through spreadsheets. Participants were briefly introduced to the RE and the study's aim. The survey was conducted over two months and distributed to individuals and their colleagues working in a high-rise or low-rise commercial office units across East and West Malaysia. The survey instrument comprised four main parts, as presented in Table 1.

Respondents of the Study

To ensure the study's accuracy, the participants were randomly selected from the target population of office workers who spend a considerable amount of time working in an office environment. Informed consent was obtained from the participants who met certain inclusion criteria, such as being of a particular age, having a specific level of education, or working full-time. This approach aimed to prevent potential bias in the sample selection (Kothari, 2004).

Part 2 of the questionnaire consists of 6 questions to understand the existing conditions of the respondent's office space and to identify the elements of RE in the office spaces. The elements used in

Table 1. Questionnaire survey aligned to the research questions of the study

Sections	Questions		Research Questions
Part 1	Q1-Q7	Demographics	-
Part 2	Q8-Q13	Identify the presence of elements of Restorative Environments within their current office space	What are the existing conditions or elements of restorative environments in office spaces within Malaysia?
Part 3	Q14-Q24	Assessment of respondents' mental wellbeing using the Warwick Edinburgh Mental Wellbeing Scale (WEMWBS) with a 5-point Likert Scale	How do the environments within the office space affect the perceived mental wellbeing of office workers in Malaysia?
Part 4	Q25-Q30	Preference of RE by respondents using a 5-point Likert scale questionnaire. Participants were to choose from a list of elements that they would prefer to have in future office development or a workplace	What are the office workers' preferences for restorative environments in their workspace?

the questionnaire were identified from the literature reviews (as shown in Table 2). Respondents were given a multiple-choice question to choose the variant for each element.

The third section of the questionnaire included the Warwick Edinburgh Mental Wellbeing Scale (WEMWBS) (Table 3), developed by the universities of Warwick and Edinburgh to assess an individual's mental wellbeing using a 5-point Likert scale. The Likert scale ranges from "1 - None of the time" to "5 - all of the time" and includes positively worded statements covering both functional and emotional aspects of mental wellbeing, making it easily understandable.

This tool has been widely used to evaluate programs and investigate determinants of mental wellbeing nationally and internationally. The WEMWBS scale is self-administered, and the total score is calculated by adding up the scores of all 14 items, ranging from 14-70. The WEMWBS has been compared to the CES-D and has shown a high correlation (.84), with scores of 41-44 indicating possible/mild depression and scores below 41 indicative of probable clinical depression (Stewart-Brown, 2021; Warwick Medical School, n.d.).

Part 4 of the questionnaire is related to the respondents' preferences on the individual elements of RE in their workspace using a 5-point Likert scale, which ranges from "1 - less important" to "5 - most important" (Table 4).

Table 2. Elements of restorative environment identified from literature review

Part 2			
	Variant	**Element**	**Literature Review**
Q8	Presence of windows (views to nature, views to city, no views, no windows)	Windows	(Velarde et al., 2007) (Kaplan, 2001) (Pati et al., 2007) (Lottrup et al, 2013) (Khan Jr et al., 2008)
Q9	Presence of images of natural environments (Paintings/mural arts, photographs, wallpapers, none)	Painting/ Photographs of natural landscapes	(deKort et al., 2006) (Ulrich, 1993; Purcell et al, 2001) (Flesten, 2009) (Watts et al., 2016) (Beernink, 2017)
Q10	Presence of light (more natural light, more artificial light)	Natural light	(Sanchez et al., 2018) (Czeisler et al., 1999) (McCurdy & Graham, 2003) (P. Boyce, 2006) (Viola et al., 2008) (Heschong et al., 2003) (Anderson et al, 2013) (Joarder & Price, 2013)
Q11	Presence of plants (artificial /natural, none)	Plants (artificial / natural)	(Beukeboom & Dijkstra, 2012) (Grinde & Patil, 2009) (Grey & Birrel, 2014) (Sanchez et al., 2018)
Q12	Types of office furniture (timber, non-timber)	Timber furniture	(Bunard & Kutnar, 2015) (Fell, 2010) (Burnard et al., 2017)
Q13	Presence of sounds of nature (sounds of water feature, birds, none)	Sounds of nature	(Watts et al., 2016)

Table 3. Warwick Edinburgh mental wellbeing scale

	Part 3
Q14	I am feeling optimistic towards the future
Q15	I have been feeling useful
Q16	I have been feeling relaxed
Q17	I have had the energy to spare
Q18	I have been dealing with problems well
Q19	I have been thinking clearly
Q20	I have been feeling good about myself
Q21	I have been feeling close to other people
Q22	I have been feeling confident
Q23	I have been able to make up my own mind about things
Q24	I have been feeling loved
Q25	I have been interested in new things
Q26	I have been feeling cheerful

(Source: https://warwick.ac.uk/fac/sci/med/research/platform/wemwbs/using/howto/)

FINDINGS

To assess the potential influence of RE on the perceived mental wellbeing of office workers, the study intends to analyze the WEMWBS scores of each respondent according to the presence of RE elements in their office spaces. The mean and standard deviation of the WEMWBS scores for each variant will be calculated and compared to the average WEMWBS score of the entire target group. This approach aims to determine if the presence of RE elements in office spaces impacts the perceived mental wellbeing of office workers.

- **Presence of Windows**

Respondents working within workplaces with 'Views towards cities' reported a higher mean WEMWBS score than 'Window views to nature'. Both items scored higher (48.28 and 36.50) than the average

Table 4. Preferences of elements restorative environment

	Part 4
Q27	Natural light
Q28	Painting/Photo/Wallpaper of landscapes
Q29	Natural/Artificial plants
Q30	Timber/Wood Furniture
Q31	Windows with views
Q32	Sounds of water features/birds

score of 35.14. As for 'Windows with no views (blocked or translucent glass)' and 'No windows' scored lower than average with 32.50 and 32.68, respectively (See Table 5)

- **Presence of Images of Natural Environments**

Meaning 'Painting/Mural' and 'Wallpaper of Natural Landscape' scored higher than the average score of 35.14 with 38.47 and 38 'Photographs' also scored relatively higher (35.53) than the average, while the item 'None' scored the least (32.93) (Table 5).

- **Presence of Light**

The item 'More natural light' was scored almost close (35.89) to the average, while 'More artificial light' was scored lower (34.55). However, the differences between the items are minimal.

- **Presence of Plants**

Within this RE element, the item 'Natural plants' and 'Artificial plants' were scored above the average with a mean of 36.60 and 35.76, respectively; meanwhile, item 'None' was scored lower (33.08) than average.

- **Type of Office Furniture**

Item 'Timber / wooden tables chairs and shelves' scored higher (38.50) than the average, while 'Non-timber / wooden tables chairs and shelves' scored lower (32.04) than the average.

- **Presence of Sounds of Nature**

Among these RE elements, 'Sounds of water feature/birds' is higher (38.50) than the average, and item 'None' scored lower (33.81) than the average.

The results presented in Table 6 demonstrate the restorative qualities of various elements and their impact on office workers' mental wellbeing. The elements were ranked in ascending order based on their mean WEMWBS score. The study found that 'Views to cities' had the highest mean WEMWBS score (48.28) among all the elements, followed by 'Sounds of water feature and birds' and 'Timber/ wooden tables, chairs, and shelves' with a mean score of 38.50. 'Painting/Mural' (38.47), 'Wallpaper of natural landscape' (38.00), 'Natural plants' (36.60), 'More natural light' (35.89), 'Artificial plants' (35.76), and 'Photographs' (35.53) also scored above average. However, the study found that seven elements scored lower than the average, including 'More artificial light' (34.55), 'No sounds of nature' (33.81), 'No plants' (33.08), 'No images of the natural landscape' (32.93), 'No windows' (32.68), 'Windows but with no views' (blocked or translucent glass) (32.50), and 'Non-timber/ wooden tables, chairs, and shelves' with the lowest mean score (32.04)

Table 5. Restorative elements, sum, Mean, and SD of WEMWBS score

Restorative Elements	Number of Respondents (N= 104)	Sum of WEMWBS Score (N=3655)	Mean of WEMWBS Score AVG: 35.14
Presence of Windows			
Window views of nature	34	1242	36.50 (8.04)
Views to Cities	25	1272	48.28 (7.52)
Windows with no views (blocked or translucent glass)	19	618	32.50 (8.80)
No windows	16	523	32.68 (9.02)
Presence of Images of Natural Environments			
Painting/Mural	19	731	38.47 (7.19)
Wallpaper of natural landscape	13	494	38.00 (6.89)
Photographs	15	553	35.53 (7.48)
None	57	1877	32.93 (8.67)
Presence of Light			
More natural light	46	1651	35.89 (8.67)
More artificial light	58	2004	34.55 (7.78)
Presence of Plants			
Natural plants	45	1647	36.60 (8.71)
Artificial plants	21	751	35.76 (8.08)
None	38	1257	33.08 (7.94)
Type of Office Furniture			
Timber / Wooden tables, chairs and shelves	50	1925	38.5 (6.51)
Non-timber / Wooden tables, chairs, and shelves	54	1730	32.04 (8.59)
Presence of Sounds of Nature			
Sounds of water feature / Birds	29	1119	38.5 (7.56)
None	75	2536	33.81 (7.99)

DISCUSSION

The study aimed to investigate whether incorporating RE in office spaces could improve the mental wellbeing of Malaysian office workers who spend significant time in stressful work environments. The study aimed to identify the presence of RE elements in current office spaces and assess their impact on the mental wellbeing of office workers. Furthermore, the study aimed to determine office users' preferences for RE features and elements in their workplace and identify potential improvements to current workspaces. Previous studies have shown that RE has been linked with allowing the brain to recover from low-stress situations.

The study aimed to investigate how RE in office spaces affects the perceived mental wellbeing of office workers by examining the current conditions of RE elements in office spaces and the preferences of office workers regarding RE. A quantitative method was employed to achieve this, and a survey questionnaire with four sections was distributed to participants using Google Forms. The sections were

Table 6. Elements of RE and mean WEMWBS score against the average score

Restorative Environments	Mean of WEMWBS Score
Views to Cities	48.28
Sounds of water feature / Birds	38.50
Timber / Wooden tables, chairs, and shelves	38.50
Painting/Mural	38.47
Wallpaper of natural landscape	38.00
Natural plants	36.60
Window views of nature	36.50
More natural light	35.89
Artificial plants	35.76
Photographs	35.53
Average	**35.14**
More artificial light	34.55
No sounds of nature	33.81
No plants	33.08
No images of the natural landscape	32.93
No windows	32.68
Windows but with no views (blocked or translucent glass)	32.50
Non-timber / wooden tables, chairs, shelves	32.04

demographics, identification of RE elements in current office spaces, the WEMWBS mental-wellbeing scale, and preferences. The data collected from 104 participants were analyzed using descriptive statistics.

The data on the characteristics of the respondents indicated that most of them were young professionals who had recently started working. Most respondents, 80 (76.9%), were aged between 21 and 30 years, and 71 (68.3%) had worked for less than two years. Less than half of the respondents, 49 (47.1%), worked five days a week, while 18 (17.3%) worked six days a week. This pattern is consistent with a previous study that identified unfavorable work conditions, heavy workloads, tight schedules, and long working hours as common features of urban workplaces (Facey et al., 2015).

The results of the data analysis revealed that respondents who worked in offices with RE (RE) had higher average scores on the WEMWBS mental wellbeing scale than those who worked in offices without RE. These findings support previous research that has suggested that exposure to RE can aid in the recovery from low-stress situations, allowing individuals to relax and unwind (Pati et al., 2007; Fell, 2010; Beukeboom & Dijkstra, 2012). This is because RE possess qualities such as "Being Away," which creates a sense of separation from one's thoughts and worries, and "Fascination," which holds an individual's attention effortlessly, facilitating relaxation and even introspection (Kaplan, 1989).

The presence of RE impacts the perceived mental wellbeing of office spaces, with the data collected indicating a strong correlation with visual qualities. Respondents with more natural lighting in their office spaces had higher WEMWBS scores than those with more artificial lighting (as shown in Table 7), which supports previous studies (Anderson et al., 2013; Joarder & Price, 2013). Natural light connects nature and the outside world, creating a sense of being away from the office space. It also provides good visual qualities and changes throughout the day, essential for regulating circadian rhythms. The importance of natural light to humans was also demonstrated in the study, as it was identified as the most preferred element (77.9%) by the respondents.

View plays an important role in increasing people's sense of wellbeing (Kaplan, 2001). As indicated in previous studies, office workers working in workspaces with views toward natural elements have higher satisfaction (Lottrup et al., 2013). In this study, 'Views toward cityscapes' was identified as having the most potent restorative effect compared to 'Views of nature' (Table 7). Interestingly, this finding correlates with a study that examined office workers from the US, which showed no differences between the wellbeing of office workers who have more natural or more man-made views through their windows.

View features are more important in affecting workers' wellbeing, such as views within a high-rise building overlooking the city or expansive views that offer long-range visibility (Esch et al., 2019). This finding contradicts the study conducted on university students within a campus, which reported that natural elements are more restorative than cityscapes (Fell, 2010). Findings show that artworks, mural arts, and nature photographs have strong restorative effects; however, the effect of these elements is lower compared to the view of real cityscapes from the window. Viewing outside a window, far away from the office space, evokes a sense of fascination and being away, losing one's thoughts and worries. Natural and artificial plant photographs have the same features that reflect outdoor space but are smaller. Therefore, their restorative effects are lower.

According to the data analysis (Table 7), elements of RE that provide immersion have a stronger restorative effect. These elements include views of cities, the sound of water features or birds, timber or wooden furniture, and paintings or murals of natural landscapes. These elements surround office workers spatially and align with the concept of RE, which emphasizes the need for elements that provide a break from routine and evoke fascination and a sense of being away from stressors (American Psychology Association, n.d.). These elements allow users to momentarily disconnect from their worries and concerns, which is a fundamental aspect of RE as proposed by the Kaplans. Even though physical distance is not necessary to achieve this effect, it can enhance it (Daniel, 2014).

RECOMMENDATIONS AND CONCLUSION

Windows and Views

The research indicates that for optimal employee wellbeing, it is recommended that workspaces should be positioned facing windows that avoid glare and excess solar radiation while providing views of wide-open spaces or features where human activities occur. To maximize natural light exposure throughout the day, the windows are suggested to face either North or South. Incorporating nearby public spaces such as parks can be beneficial in the design of office buildings.

Green Indoor Rest Spaces

To improve the quality of relaxation for employees, it is suggested that green spaces featuring plants or nature landscapes be incorporated into the office's rest areas, lounges, or dining areas. This addition will further enhance the restorative qualities of these areas, providing a space for workers to take a break from their work or enjoy their meals in a more relaxing environment.

Table 7. Identified patterns

Patterns	Natural light	Theme
P1	Office workers found to prefer natural lighting in their workspace as compared to artificial lighting	Light - Nature
P2	Natural lighting has a good effect on the mental wellbeing of office workers as compared to artificial lighting	Light - Nature
	Views	
P5	View towards cityscapes and nature have a good effect on the mental wellbeing of office workers	View
P6	Artwork and photographs of natural landscapes have a positive effect on the mental wellbeing of office workers	Views - Nature
P7	Murals and wallpapers of natural landscapes have a higher perceived wellbeing score than photographs and none.	Views - Immersion
P8	Office workers prefer artificial/natural plants compared to no plants at all in the office	Views - Nature
	Immersion	
P6	Artwork and photographs of natural landscapes have a positive effect on the mental wellbeing of office workers	Immersion - Views
P8	Sounds of nature have a positive effect on the perceived wellbeing of the office workers	Immersion - Nature
P10	Office workers prefer timber furniture compared to other materials	Immersion - Nature

Nature Sounds

In conclusion, the study recommends the installation of indoor water features in workplaces to produce soothing sounds during work hours and using speakers to play sounds of the forest or sea in office spaces. Based on the analysis of the mean WEMWBS scores and the elements of RE, there is a positive correlation between these elements and the mental wellbeing of office workers. These findings answer the research question: "How do restorative environments within office spaces impact the perceived mental wellbeing of office workers in Malaysia?"

A good RE for office workers is natural light, views and vistas, and a sense of immersion. These elements enable workers to shift their focus away from their tasks after prolonged periods of work (known as directed attention fatigue) and towards something else that requires less effort (known as effortless attention). This restoration process is based on the Attention Restoration Theory (ART) proposed by Kaplan in 1989 and 1995.

Natural light is important as it provides visual stimulation and allows for changing qualities throughout the day. Views and vistas, whether real or simulated, such as through wallpaper, mural art, or small plants, allow for effortless attention and a break from directed attention. Through mural art, wallpaper, sounds of nature, or timber furniture, immersion provides a sense of escape and relaxation, allowing for a break from work and the restoration of attention to continue focusing on tasks after a brief respite.

In conclusion, creating a RE in office spaces is essential for promoting the wellbeing of office workers. Elements such as natural light, views and vistas, and a sense of immersion can help workers recover from directed attention fatigue, which is common after long work periods. By implementing such features, workers can take breaks and shift their focus away from their tasks, allowing their minds to recharge and reducing stress. The benefits of RE are clear, with research demonstrating the positive correlation between these features and the mental wellbeing of office workers. Thus, employers should prioritize the creation of RE in the workplace to enhance the overall wellbeing of their workforce.

REFERENCES

American Psychology Association. (n.d.). *Restorative Environments*. APA. https://www.apa.org/monitor/2019/03/restorative-environments

Anderson, J., Wojtowicz, M., & Wineman, A. (2013). The impact of daylighting on human health. *Lighting Research & Technology*, *45*(2), 159–175. doi:10.1177/1477153512457607

Anderson, M. D., Carson, D. C., & Grandy, J. (2013). Office light quality and alertness in two office environments. *Journal of Environmental Psychology*, *36*, 94–101.

Bailenson, J. N., Yee, N., & Blascovich, J. (2021). Virtual restorative environments: An immersive technology for personal and planetary health. *Frontiers in Psychology*, *11*, 3583.

Berman, M. G., Jonides, J., & Kaplan, S. (2008). The cognitive benefits of interacting with nature. *Psychological Science*, *19*(12), 1207–1212. doi:10.1111/j.1467-9280.2008.02225.x PMID:19121124

Beukeboom, C. J., & Dijkstra, A. (2012). The effect of plants and fascia on stress-related symptoms and blood pressure in office workers: A randomized, controlled study. *Environmental Health Perspectives*, *120*(3), 377–381.

Boyce, P. (2006). *Human factors in lighting* (2nd ed.). Taylor & Francis.

Braubach, M., Egorov, A. I., Mudu, P., Wolf, T., Ward Thompson, C., & Martuzzi, M. (2017). Effects of urban green space on environmental health, equity and resilience: A scoping review. *Urban Forestry & Urban Greening*, *29*, 310–323.

Browning, W. D., Ryan, C. O., & Clancy, J. O. (2014). *14 Patterns of Biophilic Design*. Terrapin Bright Green LLC. https://www.terrapinbrightgreen.com/wp-content/uploads/2014/06/14-Patterns-of-Biophilic-Design-Terrapin-Bright-Green-2014.pdf

Bunard, D., & Kutnar, A. (2015). The effect of wood on stress responses in office workers. *Forests*, *6*(7), 2336–2352.

Burnard, M., Fragiacomo, M., & Hozjan, T. (2017). Review of the perceptual qualities of timber and timber-based products relevant to sensory evaluation of indoor spaces. *Building and Environment*, *124*, 52–63.

CABA. (n.d.). *What is mental wellbeing?* CABA. https://www.caba.org.uk/help-and-guides/information/what-mental-wellbeing

Cairns, T. (2020). *How to create a restorative environment in the office*. Raconteur. https://www.raconteur.net/sustainability/how-to-create-a-restorative-environment-in-the-office

Centers for Disease Control and Prevention. (2014). *Work-related stress*. National Institute for Occupational Safety and Health.

Centers for Disease Control and Prevention. (2020). *Mental health basics*. CDC. https://www.cdc.gov/mentalhealth/basics/index.htm

Chen, Y., McCabe, O. L., & Hyman, M. R. (2020). Workplace stress and mental health in the era of COVID-19: An urgent need for action. *International Journal of Environmental Research and Public Health*, *17*(19), 7272. doi:10.3390/ijerph17197272 PMID:33027956

Croome, D. (2013). *Creating and managing healthy built environments*. Routledge.

Czeisler, C. A., Duffy, J. F., Shanahan, T. L., Brown, E. N., Mitchell, J. F., Rimmer, D. W., Ronda, J. M., Silva, E. J., Allan, J. S., Emens, J. S., Dijk, D.-J., & Kronauer, R. E. (1999). Stability, precision, and near-24-hour period of the human circadian pacemaker. *Science*, *284*(5423), 2177–2181. doi:10.1126cience.284.5423.2177 PMID:10381883

Daniel, T. C. (2014). Contributions of psychology to an understanding of the restorative environment. In *Biophilic Cities* (pp. 19–31). Island Press.

de Kort, Y. A. W., Meijnders, A. L., Sponselee, A. A. G., & IJsselsteijn, W. A. (2006). What's wrong with virtual trees? Restoring from stress in a mediated environment. *Journal of Environmental Psychology*, *26*(4), 309–320. doi:10.1016/j.jenvp.2006.09.001

Department of Statistics. (2020). *Malaysia Labour Force Statistics in Brief 2020*. DOSM. https://www.dosm.gov.my/v1/index.php?r=column/cthemeByCat&cat=155&bul_id=MGhZUTdVWXpveElUUld MYVhCRWlKQT09&menu_id=L0pheU43NWJwRWVSZklWdzQ4TlhUUT09

Dolan, M., Fullam, R., & Casey, E. (2016). The relationship between indoor environmental quality in Irish offices and occupant perceived health and productivity. *Building and Environment*, *108*, 290–298.

Dye, C. (2007). Health and urban living. *Science*, *318*(5852), 766–769. PMID:18258905

Esch, T., Kim, M. J., Stefano, G. B., Fricchione, G. L., Benson, H., & Kirschbaum, C. (2019). The city versus the country: A cross-sectional study of cortisol and depression in urban and rural areas. *BMC Psychiatry*, *19*(1), 1–9. PMID:30606141

Facey, M. E., Middleton, J., & Griffiths, P. (2015). Managing Employee Stress and Wellness in the New Normal. In E. G. Carayannis & Y. H. Zhao (Eds.), *The Handbook of Stress and Health: A Guide to Research and Practice* (pp. 441–454). Springer. doi:10.1007/978-1-4939-3117-6_25

Facey, M. E., Rees, C. E., & Monrouxe, L. V. (2015). Being 'student-led': Challenging hierarchy in healthcare education and identifying solutions. *Journal of Further and Higher Education*, *39*(2), 248–265.

Fell, D. (2010). *Nature, landscape and natural spaces in universities: Restorative qualities of familiar places for students*. University of Manchester.

Flesten, L. (2009). *The influence of natural views in an office environment on recovery from mental fatigue*. [Bachelor's thesis, Lund University, Lund, Sweden].

Fuller, R. A., & Gaston, K. J. (2009). The scaling of green space coverage in European cities. *Biology Letters*, *5*(3), 352–355. doi:10.1098/rsbl.2009.0010 PMID:19324636

Grey, C. N., & Birrell, C. (2014). Green over grey: The importance of biophilic design in a temporary site office. *Indoor and Built Environment*, *23*(6), 863–877.

Grind, C. C., & Patil, G. G. (2009). The effect of indoor foliage plants on health and discomfort symptoms among office workers. *HortTechnology, 19*(2), 278–282.

Hartig, T., Evans, G. W., Jamner, L. D., Davis, D. S., & Gärling, T. (1996). Tracking restoration in natural and urban field settings. *Journal of Environmental Psychology, 16*(2), 87–101.

Haynes, B. P. (2008). Workplaces and low carbon behaviour. *Building Research and Information, 36*(2), 196–212.

Heerwagen, J. H. (2000). Green buildings, organizational success and occupant productivity. *Building Research and Information, 28*(5-6), 353–367. doi:10.1080/096132100418500

Heschong, L., Heschong, M., & Wright, R. (2003). *Windows and offices: A study of office worker performance and the indoor environment.* California Energy Commission.

Heschong, L., Wright, R. L., Okura, S., & Moule, R. A. Jr. (2002). *Windows and Offices: A Study of Office Worker Performance and the Indoor Environment.* California Energy Commission.

Holtzhausen, D. (2020). *Designing post-pandemic office spaces.* Engineering News. https://www.engineeringnews.co.za/article/designing-post-pandemic-office-spaces-2020-07-10

Joarder, M. A., & Price, A. D. F. (2013). Factors influencing visual quality and occupants' preference in office buildings. *Architectural Science Review, 56*(2), 146–155.

Kaplan, S. (1989). The restorative benefits of nature: Toward an integrative framework. *Journal of Environmental Psychology, 15*(3), 169–182. doi:10.1016/0272-4944(95)90001-2

Kaplan, S. (1995). The restorative environment: Nature and human experience. In J. L. Nasar & A. S. G. Nasar (Eds.), *Environmental aesthetics: Theory, research, and application* (pp. 233–250). Cambridge University Press. doi:10.1017/CBO9780511525599.017

Kaplan, S. (2001). Meditation, restoration, and the management of mental fatigue. *Environment and Behavior, 33*(4), 480–506. doi:10.1177/00139160121973106

Khan, M. M. Jr, Howe, E. T., Chu, A. H., & Nunamaker, J. F. Jr. (2008). *The impact of a nature view on stress reduction of users in a virtual reality simulated office environment. 27th International Conference on Information Systems,* Milwaukee, WI, USA.

Kjellgren, A., & Buhrkall, H. (2010). A comparison of the restorative effect of a natural environment with that of a simulated natural environment. *Journal of Environmental Psychology, 30*(4), 464–472. doi:10.1016/j.jenvp.2010.01.011

Kothari, C. R. (2004). *Research methodology: Methods and techniques.* New Age International.

Kreitzer, M. J. (2014). Well-being concepts. In *Complementary and Integrative Therapies for Mental Health and Aging* (pp. 3–18). Oxford University Press.

Kuo, F. E., & Sullivan, W. C. (2001a). Aggression and violence in the inner city: Effects of environment via mental fatigue. *Environment and Behavior, 33*(4), 543–571. doi:10.1177/00139160121973124

Kuo, F. E., & Sullivan, W. C. (2001b). Environment and crime in the inner city: Does vegetation reduce crime? *Environment and Behavior, 33*(3), 343–367. doi:10.1177/0013916501333002

Lee, A. C. K., Jordan, H. C., Horsley, J., & Value, E. (2015). The health benefits of urban green spaces: A review of the evidence. *Journal of Public Health, 38*(3), e450–e461. PMID:20833671

Lottrup, L., Stigsdotter, U. K., Meilby, H., & Claudi, A. G. (2013). The workplace window view: A determinant of office workers' work ability and job satisfaction. *Landscape Research, 38*(2), 259–267.

Lottrup, L., Stigsdotter, U. K., Meilby, H., & Claudi, A. G. (2013). The workplace window view: A determinant of office workers' work ability and job satisfaction. *Landscape Research, 38*(1), 19–34.

Lottrup, L., Stigsdotter, U. K., Meilby, H., Claudi, A. G., & Grahn, P. (2013). Workplace greenery and perceived level of stress: Benefits of access to a green outdoor environment at the workplace. *Landscape and Urban Planning, 110*, 5–11. doi:10.1016/j.landurbplan.2012.09.002

Maben, J., & Bridges, J. (2020). Covid-19: Supporting nurses' psychological and mental health. *Journal of Clinical Nursing, 29*(15-16), 2742–2750. doi:10.1111/jocn.15307 PMID:32320509

Mallawaarachchi, S., Jayasinghe, J., & Wijesooriya, W. (2012). Indoor environmental quality in green buildings. *Journal of Environmental Protection, 3*(03), 239–248. doi:10.4236/jep.2012.33032

McCurdy, L. E., & Graham, C. (2003). Living in the dark: A study of urban residents' environmental experience in a major North American city. *Journal of Environmental Psychology, 23*(4), 385–398. doi:10.1016/S0272-4944(02)00120-2

Mcgraw-Hill Construction. (2014). *The Drive Toward Healthier Buildings 2014: Tactical Intelligence to Transform Building Design and Construction SmartMarket Report*. McGraw-Hill.

Newsham, G. R., Veitch, J. A., Charles, K. E., & Huang, J. (2004). Effects of daylight and view of nature on office workers' well-being and performance. *Journal of Environmental Psychology, 24*(2), 417–435. doi:10.1016/j.jenvp.2004.08.009

Pati, D., Sahoo, S., & Sagar, R. (2007). Windows with a view: Nurses' stress relief at work. *Journal of Advanced Nursing, 60*(4), 427–432. PMID:17919164

Purcell, T., Peron, E., Berto, R., & Boyle, M. (2001). Why do preferences differ between scene types? *Environment and Behavior, 33*(1), 93–106. doi:10.1177/00139160121972882

Ryan, R. M., & Deci, E. L. (2001). On happiness and human potentials: A review of research on hedonic and eudaimonic well-being. *Annual Review of Psychology, 52*(1), 141–166. doi:10.1146/annurev.psych.52.1.141 PMID:11148302

Salonen, H. J., Lappalainen, S., & Kähkönen, E. (2012). Health and well-being in indoor spaces: A review of recent research. *Indoor and Built Environment, 21*(3), 335–351. doi:10.1177/1420326X11430862

Sanchez, C. A., Hedayati, M., Pielke, R. A. Jr, Anderson, C., & Steiner, A. L. (2018). The influence of greenness on the capacity of green infrastructure to provide multiple ecosystem services. *The Science of the Total Environment, 635*, 1175–1186.

Stansfeld, S. A., & Candy, B. (2006). Psychosocial work environment and mental health—A meta-analytic review. *Scandinavian Journal of Work, Environment & Health*, *32*(6), 443–462. doi:10.5271jweh.1050 PMID:17173201

Stevenson, F. (2021). Restorative environments: the future of office design post-COVID-19. *The Guardian.* https://www.theguardian.com/sustainable-business/2021/mar/25/restorative-environments-the-future-of-office-design-post-covid-19

Stewart-Brown, S. (2021). *Warwick Edinburgh Mental Wellbeing Scale (WEMWBS).* Health and Well-being Services. https://warwick.ac.uk/fac/sci/med/research/platform/wemwbs/

Stigsdotter, U. K., Ekholm, O., Schipperijn, J., Toftager, M., Kamper-Jorgensen, F., & Randrup, T. B. (2010). Health promoting outdoor environments–Associations between green space, and health, health-related quality of life and stress based on a Danish national representative survey. *Scandinavian Journal of Public Health*, *38*(4), 411–417. doi:10.1177/1403494810367468 PMID:20413584

Sukamolson, S. (2007). *Research methodology and data analysis.* Srinakharinwirot University.

Ulrich, R. S., Simons, R. F., Losito, B. D., Fiorito, E., Miles, M. A., & Zelson, M. (1991). Stress recovery during exposure to natural and urban environments. *Journal of Environmental Psychology*, *11*(3), 201–230. doi:10.1016/S0272-4944(05)80184-7

Uniform Building By-Laws (UBBL) Malaysia. (1984). *Uniform Building By-Laws.* Lawnet. http://www.lawnet.gov.my/act/akta-133/

US Green Building Council. (2004). *The business case for green building: A review of the costs and benefits for developers, investors and occupants.* US Green Building Council.

Velarde, M. D., Fry, G., & Tveit, M. (2007). Health effects of viewing landscapes – Landscape types in environmental psychology. *Urban Forestry & Urban Greening*, *6*(4), 199–212. doi:10.1016/j.ufug.2007.07.001

Viola, A. U., James, L. M., Schlangen, L. J., & Dijk, D. J. (2008). Blue-enriched white light in the workplace improves self-reported alertness, performance and sleep quality. *Scandinavian Journal of Work, Environment & Health*, *34*(4), 297–306. doi:10.5271jweh.1268 PMID:18815716

Vischer, J. C. (2007). The effects of the physical environment on job performance: Towards a theoretical model of workspace stress. *Stress and Health*, *23*(3), 175–184. doi:10.1002mi.1134

Warwick Medical School. (n.d.). *Warwick Edinburgh Mental Wellbeing Scale (WEMWBS) scoring.* Warwick Medical School. https://warwick.ac.uk/fac/sci/med/research/platform/wemwbs/using/wemwbs_scoring/

Watts, G., Mills, A. J., & Bullough, S. (2016). Adding nature back to the health service: An evaluation of a natural landscapes and sounds intervention in a student medical centre. *Health Environments Research & Design Journal*, *9*(3), 83–95. PMID:27733656

World Health Organization. (2011). Work-related stress. *Fact Sheet No. 331.* WHO.

World Health Organization. (2014). *Mental health: A state of well-being.* WHO. https://www.who.int/features/factfiles/mental_health/en/

Zhang, J., Wu, X., Chen, F., & Chen, Y. (2015). The effect of forest bathing on residents' perceived anxiety: Based on comparison of two forest types in Beijing. *Forests, 6*(11), 4156–4170. doi:10.3390/f6114156

KEY TERMS AND DEFINITIONS

Attention Restoration Theory: A theory that suggests that mental fatigue and concentration can be improved by time spent in or looking at nature.

Mental Wellbeing: Mental wellbeing refers to a state of being in which an individual can cope with daily life's demands, work towards achieving their goals, and feel a sense of purpose and satisfaction. It is not simply the absence of mental health problems but rather a positive state of wellbeing.

Psycho-evolutionary Theory: The theoretical perspective that suggests that the human mind has evolved to adapt to the demands of the natural environment over time. It posits that the human mind has developed a set of psychological and cognitive mechanisms that have helped our ancestors to survive and reproduce in their specific ecological context.

Restorative Environments: Interior or exterior surroundings that have restorative capabilities.

Restorative Theory: The capacity for natural environments to replenish cognitive resources depleted by everyday activities and to reduce stress levels, according to the Attention Restoration Theory.

Warwick Edinburgh Mental Wellbeing Scale (WEMWBS): This is a self-administered questionnaire with a 5-point Likert scale that measures an individual's mental wellbeing. The scale is intended for the general adult population and was developed in the United Kingdom.

Section 3
Innovative Building Materials

Chapter 10
Investigating Key Factors Influencing Malaysian Architects' Use of Glue–Laminated Timber:
Insights Into the Adoption of an Innovative Building Material

TamilSalvi Mari
Taylor's University, Malaysia

Daniel Rosien
Taylor's University, Malaysia

Veronica Ng
Taylor's University, Malaysia

Sujatavani Gunasagaran
Taylor's University, Malaysia

Sivaraman Kuppusamy
Reading University of Malaysia, Malaysia

ABSTRACT

Glue-laminated timber (GLT) and closely related cross-laminated timber (CLT) represent a technological shift that has brought about new possibilities for architects to employ as part of their design toolkits. In temperate climate zones and industrial countries, GLT and CLT have seen a recent surge in their application. Its popularity has increased in response to favourable changes in building regulations and due to the increasing importance of certifiable sustainability in the built environment. In Malaysia, the adoption of GLT has been very limited to date. This study examines which factors influence Malaysian architects with regard to the use of GLT/CLT as a building material. From the Malaysian architects surveyed for this research, it is evident that there is a significant interest in using GLT and CLT in future projects. Most respondents stated that they had previously considered using GLT and/or CLT but abandoned the idea due to the absence of local supply and the resulting high cost of importing GLT/CLT.

DOI: 10.4018/978-1-6684-8253-7.ch010

INTRODUCTION

While timber construction has been used for centuries, advancements in technology have led to the development of a broader range of timber products known as engineered timber (Basaglia et al., 2015) noted that. These products include sawn timber that has been further processed, such as finger joint-timber profiles and plywood, as well as wood product composites bonded with adhesives. Engineered timber products are increasingly used for non-structural applications such as cladding, decking, and interior design, but also include load-bearing elements such as glue-laminated timber (GLT) beams and columns and cross-laminated timber (CLT) panels that can be used for walls, floors, and roofs.

Forest and Wood Products Australia (FWPA) explained that GLT and CLT are produced by combining smaller timber elements using adhesives, high pressure, and heat in a lamination process. This creates a final product with nearly uniform structural integrity. A case study was conducted that demonstrated the use of GLT and CLT as structural building elements and for the building envelope. The study revealed that the structure and building envelope could make up a significant portion (60-90%) of a building's embodied environmental impacts, highlighting the potential for GLT to serve as an alternative to traditional building methods like reinforced concrete structures and building envelopes made from brick in-fill walls or glass facades.

The use of CLT and GLT for structural purposes is gaining popularity due to their high strength-to-weight ratios, which allow for efficient and sustainable construction. CLT panels, for instance, have been used for walls, floors, roofs, and even bridges. The strength and stability of CLT panels make them ideal for use in tall buildings, providing structural stability and resistance to wind and seismic forces (Ehlbeck et al., 2019). Similarly, due to their high strength and durability, GLT beams and columns are increasingly used as load-bearing elements in buildings, mainly commercial and industrial (Basaglia et al., 2015).

In addition to their structural benefits, CLT and GLT are also being used for finishing purposes, including cladding, decking, and interior design works. The natural aesthetic appeal of wood makes it a desirable material for finishing, and the availability of engineered wood products such as CLT and GLT allows for more efficient and sustainable use of wood in construction. For instance, using CLT for building facades can help reduce the energy required for heating and cooling, as wood is a natural insulator (Brenčič et al., 2017). Using CLT and GLT for structural and finishing purposes represents a significant shift towards more sustainable and efficient building practices. As more research is conducted and more innovative applications are discovered, CLT and GLT will likely continue to gain popularity in the construction industry.

Problem Statement

The urgency for the construction industry to address global challenges, as expressed in the Sustainable Development Goals (SDGs), is becoming increasingly important. The goals of Sustainable Cities and Communities and Responsible Consumption and Production are directly linked to the construction industry, and the adoption of sustainable building materials is a crucial factor in achieving these goals. GLT can potentially be one such material which can address concerns related to the impact, performance, and sustainability of architecture and the construction industry. Despite being a country with a long history of timber construction and a significant forestry and timber production industry, Malaysia has limited adoption of GLT products. However, anecdotal evidence suggests that there has been some recent adoption of GLT in Southeast Asia.

Gap in Research

There is a significant gap in research on using glue laminated timber in Malaysia. While there have been some studies on timber construction in Malaysia, they have primarily focused on traditional timber framing and have not addressed the use of glue laminated timber (GLT) specifically. A study by Mohd Nawi et al. (2018) explored the potential of traditional timber construction methods in Malaysia but did not specifically examine GLT. Similarly, a study by Abdullah et al. (2017) investigated using timber as a sustainable building material in Malaysia but did not focus on GLT.

This gap in research particularly concerns given the potential benefits of GLT in Malaysia. As a country with a significant forestry industry, Malaysia has the potential to use GLT as a sustainable and cost-effective alternative to traditional construction materials. Further research is needed to explore the potential benefits and challenges of using GLT in Malaysia, including its structural properties, environmental impact, and economic feasibility. There is also significant literature regarding the factors influencing architects' decision-making concerning the use of GLT. This area of research is crucial to understand better the barriers to the broader adoption of sustainable building materials like GLT in the construction industry and to develop strategies to overcome them (Global Glue Laminated Timber Market 2018-2020, n.d.; MTC, 2018).

Thus, this study attempted to investigate the critical factors influencing the adoption and use of Glue-laminated timber in projects under the purview of Malaysian Architects. It addresses the lack of insight into factors in the widespread adoption of innovative building materials. The study's primary objectives were to gather factual information on GLT/CLT and determine the key factors influencing architects' decisions regarding their use. Additionally, the study investigated the understanding of Malaysian architects regarding GLT/CLT and identified any obstacles that hinder its increased use in Malaysia.

BACKGROUND

The construction industry contributes much to global carbon emissions and environmental degradation. A large part of the environmental impact of the construction is related to the production and use of concrete and related waste products. According to Jusufi and Capra (2019), energy consumption during the entire life cycle of building materials is essential to sustainable building design. The authors emphasize that traditional materials such as reinforced concrete and steel consume a significant amount of energy during the manufacturing phase, and therefore their use should be minimized. On the other hand, wood and other renewable materials have a low embodied energy, making them a more sustainable alternative.

In a study by Akbari et al. (2020), the embodied energy of different building materials was evaluated to determine their environmental impact. The results show that concrete and steel have the highest embodied energy, while wood has the lowest. The study also highlights that using local and sustainable materials can reduce transportation energy costs and minimize the environmental impact of the construction process. Similarly, a study by Yuce and Turk (2019) investigated the embodied energy and carbon footprint of different building materials in Turkey. The authors found that steel has the highest embodied energy and carbon footprint, while wood and adobe have the lowest. The study recommends using locally sourced and renewable materials to reduce building materials' energy consumption and carbon footprint. For this reason, the last years have seen an intensified quest for alternative materials that can contribute to achieving Sustainable Development Goals rather than jeopardizing them (Basaglia et al., 2015)

One crucial aspect of glue-laminated timber is that it is composed of a renewable source. Smaller timber elements are combined to make up larger members as specifically required. These smaller timber elements are hence easier to produce in the context of sustainable forestry and thus reduce the environmental impact of deforestation, an especially relevant aspect regarding the conservation of rainforests in tropical regions. GLT has a significantly lower carbon footprint compared to other traditional building materials. The manufacturing process of GLT is energy-efficient and produces very little waste, which makes it a sustainable choice for construction (Sulastiningsih et al., 2019).

The production and utilization of glue-laminated timber from sustainably sourced timber have significantly increased. Although the adoption of this construction material has been mainly driven by policies, products, and projects in the Northern Hemisphere's temperate zones, ongoing efforts are to promote it as a viable option for the tropics and other regions. As sustainable forestry practices are gaining importance for preserving tropical rainforests, glue-laminated timber shows promise for use in tropical regions if market entry barriers are overcome, and favourable policy frameworks and building regulations are established (Malaysian Timber Council [MTC], 2018).

CURRENT TRENDS AND ISSUES IN GLT-BASED CONSTRUCTION

In recent years, the breadth of projects in which GLT products have found structural application has grown dramatically. While GLT beams were commonly used to achieve column-free spaces such as indoor sports grounds, warehouses, and market halls until the end of the 20th century, a new application area has been in multi-storey buildings (Global Glue Laminated Timber Market 2018-2020, n.d.). This latest development currently appears to be largely limited to industrialized countries and became possible through a combination of the following factors:

- A higher degree of standardization in product specifications that fulfil structural and fire-resistance requirements and sustainability benchmarks is encapsulated in European regulations such as CEN350, EN15978, EN15804 and ISO 14025:2006 (Bejo, 2014).
- A framework of policies that encourages sustainable products is the Wood First Act in Canada, which mandates that timber products must be used as structural members where it is technically and economically viable (Schoof, 2018).
- Building regulations that enable, encourage and in some cases even mandate the use of timber as a significant building element. Schoof (2018) mentions the examples of Sweden and the United Kingdom, where building regulations have been amended to allow for the broader adoption of timber products as building materials in multi-storey buildings.

Technical Aspects of GLT

Albee (2019) emphasizes the numerous advantages of GLT products, including their superior structural properties in relation to their weight and their environmental benefits resulting from using renewable source materials that sequester carbon emissions. The author also highlights potential economic benefits, such as employment generation and up-skilling labourers, especially relevant to the Malaysian forest and timber industry. In terms of construction, the prefabrication of GLT and CLT products offers the advantage of shorter construction periods and potential cost savings. Additionally, their lower weight compared to reinforced concrete structures allows for smaller foundations, further reducing construction costs and time.

Schoof (2018) reports that proposals for constructing GLT-based buildings that exceed 50 meters in height have received planning permission in several countries, and this trend is expected to continue. To prepare for this, architectural practices worldwide explore realistic scenarios for timber-based highrise constructions. Additionally, many tropical countries with existing forestry and timber-producing sectors are developing GLT products from locally available tropical hardwoods, as shown in studies by Bourreau et al. (2013), Strang and Leardini (2019), and MTC (2018). These studies emphasize the need for higher quality and more standardized specifications for GLT products made from locally grown hardwood species.

Adjustments to the lamination process and adhesives are being researched to make GLT products suitable for tropical climates. However, the higher density of tropical hardwoods can affect the penetration of adhesives, which can result in a less efficient GLT element (Strang & Leardini, 2019). Despite this, the structural properties of hardwoods allow for more efficient member sizing before the glueing process compared to GLT made from softwood (Muraleedharan & Reiterer, 2017). The sustainable growth and harvesting of hardwoods are more time-intensive than softwood, which offsets production efficiency advantages. However, sustainable forestry could still meet the high demand for timber-based building materials, according to a study by Oliver et al. (as cited in Basaglia et al., 2015).

In addition, there is an increasing interest in GLT niche products, such as hybrid structures that combine GLT with steel or other structural reinforcements like fibreglass, as well as glue-laminated bamboo or "glue-bam," which offers potential applications due to its fast-growing raw material with high flexibility and strength (Robertson et al., 2012; Schoof, 2018). Another emerging area of interest is the production of GLT from waste lumber generated by other agricultural activities, such as rubber trees or oil palm, which could have significant environmental and economic benefits (Parra-Serrano et al., 2018).

MATERIAL PROPERTIES AND TECHNICAL ASPECTS GLT AND CLT PRODUCTS

GLT and CLT products are available in standardized sizes and specifications, but they can also be custom-designed as building elements with various shapes, such as curved, straight, and tapered. While individual GLT or CLT elements are typically created by combining timber sections with adhesives and pressure, multiple elements can be joined together on-site using various techniques, including internal steel plates with bolts, external gusset plates, or carpentry joints (Basaglia et al., 2015).

According to Albee (2019), while cross-laminated timber (CLT) and glued laminated timber (GLT) are always prefabricated, they may not be mass-produced. Prefabrication can offer cost advantages by reducing on-site labour and time, but transportation costs can be high depending on the distance between the production site and the building site. Moreover, design and customization processes can offset the benefits of faster on-site processes.

As reported by Schoof (2018), Bejo (2014), and the Glue Laminated Timber Market report 2018-2020 (GLTM, n.d.), GLT products currently meet strict regulations related to fire safety, load-bearing capacity, and long-term structural integrity. This has resulted in increasing multi-storey buildings being approved for construction. Standardization of product quality and specifications (EU, US, and Canada Standards) has enabled wider adoption of GLT and CLT, reducing the need for specialized design and engineering knowledge for individual projects. Typically, GLT and CLT suppliers provide oversight for transportation and on-site installation services, reducing the need for finding local labour with specialized skills.

It is important to note that while GLT and CLT have advantages over conventional building methods in certain areas, such as thermal properties and design possibilities, they may not always be the best option for every project. The choice of building material should be based on a thorough assessment of project requirements, including structural performance, Cost, environmental impact, and local availability.

ARCHITECTURAL CONSIDERATIONS

According to Ramage et al. (2017), the use of timber elements in the construction of tall buildings has increased due to the improvements in fabrication techniques and the emergence of GLT/CLT. This has allowed for the adaptation of timber's unique architectural qualities, such as its aesthetics and feel, and is a material that can be grown to a larger scale.GLT and CLT do not need any extra covering for aesthetic purposes, except when it is necessary for controlling moisture and vapour when used as building envelope components. GLT and CLT have high sound absorption, much like solid timber, which helps to improve indoor quality without requiring specialized sound absorption panels or materials (Strang et al., 2019). GLT and CLT have expanded the possibilities for using timber in scale and building types. GLT is particularly well-suited for large, column-free spaces like halls, gyms, and indoor arenas because the member sizes can be designed to meet specific load requirements. GLT elements can be joined using steel plates, gusset connections, bolts, or various carpentry joints, without compromising structural integrity. This flexibility enables greater design possibilities, such as combining multiple elements to create an extra-wide span beam (Halls, 2018). Overall, GLT and CLT offer architects a new material option that combines innovative design opportunities with well-established material qualities.

Sustainability of GLT

When assessed in terms of Embodied Energy (EE) as an indicator of sustainability, Glue-laminated timber has the potential to be classified as a very sustainable building material. However, this EE performance depends on several factors throughout the production chain and lifecycle of the material. As buildings are designed to be more energy efficient operationally, the amount of embodied energy in the material used to construct the buildings becomes increasingly significant in calculating the lifetime energy balance, which accounts for both the operational and the embodied energy. (Dixit et. al, 2011). This approach appears to offer the most viable approach in determining the degree of sustainability of GLT.

Embodied energy, as a measure of sustainability, encompasses all energy used in the production, transportation, assembly, maintenance, and demolition of construction materials. It covers a timeframe from raw material production through the building's lifetime to the decommissioning of the building, which might end in demolished or salvaged building materials (Bejo 2014).

Basaglia et al. (2015) mentioned that the lifecycle assessment approach (LCA) is a methodology to quantify the environmental impacts of a specific product over its lifecycle. However, different studies employ different system boundaries as the basis for their analysis. The cradle-to-gate approach is the most common approach, which covers the raw-material extraction and construction stages (Robertson et al., 2012). The cradle-to-grave approach encompasses the energy consumed through all stages of the prod-

Figure 1. Performance of laminated timber in categories of lifecycle assessment in comparison to reinforced concrete
(Source: Robertson et al., 2012)

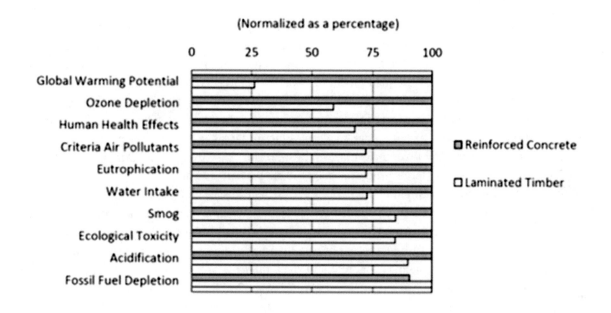

uct/building's lifecycle, starting from raw-material extraction, including the operation and maintenance, end terminating at the end use (which includes options such as recycling, reuse, demolition or disposal).

Bejo (2014) highlights that the limitation of the LCA approach is due to in-depth information not being available for some processes and that the use of different databases and inventories for quantifying embodied energy and the LCA can lead to a wide divergence in results. The literature review conducted by Bejo (2014) concludes that most research into embodied energy supports the notion that timber-based construction fares better than conventional construction using reinforced concrete and/or steel. Additionally, timber-based construction significantly reduces CO_2 emissions compared to steel, brick or concrete-based construction. Even after the energy used in the lamination processes required for GLT products is factored into the EE, the comparison with other building materials is still favourable (Bejo, 2014; Robertson et al., 2012).

Figure 1 illustrates the results of a cradle-to-gate life cycle assessment (LCA) case study conducted by Robertson et al. (2012). The study compares the LCA performance of a scenario that uses GLT with a conventional reinforced concrete scenario. The figure shows that the GLT-based scenario performs significantly better LCA than the reinforced concrete scenario.

Based on the above, GLT can be established as a sustainable building material with a favourable environmental impact. However, as the research above shows, there are requirements in different production stages that need to be met for GLT to be deemed a sustainable material (sustainable forestry, the distance of raw material to the production site and the building site.

Factors Affecting Adoption of Glue-Laminated Timber

Glue-laminated timber (GLT) and cross-laminated timber (CLT) are two building materials that have gained popularity recently due to their sustainability, strength, and versatility. Despite the benefits of using glue-laminated timber (GLT) and cross-laminated timber (CLT), there are still some barriers to their widespread adoption in construction projects globally. One factor influencing architects' use of GLT and CLT is their sustainability. Both materials are environmentally friendly alternatives to traditional building materials because they are made from renewable resources and have a lower carbon footprint than concrete or steel (Buchanan & Honey, 2020). Architects prioritizing sustainability in their designs will likely choose GLT and CLT as building materials. The use of GLT and CLT is also affected is their strength and durability. Both materials are made by glueing layers of lumber together, resulting in a more robust material than solid wood (Ranta-Maunus, 2021). This strength and durability make GLT and CLT suitable for building large structures such as bridges and stadiums.

One of the main issues with using GLT and CLT is their cost. The Cost of GLT and CLT varies depending on factors such as the quality of the wood used, the beams' size, and the project's complexity (Buchanan & Honey, 2020). Architects working on projects with tight budgets may hesitate to use GLT and CLT because they can be more expensive than traditional building materials. Compared to traditional building materials, such as concrete and steel, GLT and CLT can be more expensive due to the manufacturing process and limited suppliers (Wang et al., 2020). The higher Cost may deter architects and builders from using these materials in their designs, especially for projects with a tight budget.

Another barrier to adopting GLT and CLT is the lack of awareness and knowledge among architects and builders. Some architects and builders may not be familiar with these materials or know how to incorporate them properly into their designs (Falk et al., 2020). This can lead to misconceptions about the materials' structural properties and concerns about their durability.

Architects' familiarity with GLT and CLT is also a factor that influences their use. Architects with experience working with these materials are likelier to use them in their designs (Ranta-Maunus, 2021). However, architects unfamiliar with GLT and CLT may hesitate to use them because of concerns about their structural properties or lack of knowledge about their availability in their region.

Finally, the availability of GLT and CLT in a particular region can influence architects' use of these materials. The limited availability of suppliers and manufacturers in certain regions can also create transportation and logistics challenges, increasing the Cost and time required to complete a project. In some regions, GLT and CLT may be readily available, while in others, they may be difficult to obtain (Buchanan & Honey, 2020). Architects who work in regions where GLT and CLT are not readily available may be less likely to use them in their designs.

Additionally, there is a lack of standards and codes for using GLT and CLT in construction. Some building codes have not yet been updated to include GLT and CLT, which can create obstacles for architects and builders who want to use these materials (Wang et al., 2020). The lack of standards and codes can also create uncertainty about the regulatory requirements for GLT and CLT, making it difficult for architects and builders to specify and use the materials confidently.

The shortage of skilled workers is a significant barrier to adopting engineered wood products, including glue-laminated timber (GLT) and cross-laminated timber (CLT). Using these materials requires specialized skills and knowledge that are not always readily available in the construction industry. According to a study by the Wood Products Council (2017), "the biggest challenge for the adoption of mass timber is the availability of skilled labor." The shortage of skilled workers is particularly acute in regions where the construction industry has not traditionally used wood as a primary building material. For example, in the United States, where wood framing is the dominant construction method, mass timber products have been slower to adopt due to the lack of skilled workers trained in wood construction (APA - The Engineered Wood Association, 2020).

Another barrier to adopting GLT and CLT is the lack of client demand. Clients may be unfamiliar with these materials and prefer more traditional construction methods. Additionally, there may be a perception that wood is not as durable or fire-resistant as other materials, which may deter clients from considering wood-based solutions. According to a report by the Building Research Establishment (2018), "the lack of client demand for new and innovative timber-based products is a significant barrier to market growth." This lack of demand can result in a lack of investment in research and development, which can limit the availability and variety of wood-based products in the market.

Several factors influence architects' use of GLT and CLT globally, including sustainability, strength and durability, Cost, familiarity with the material, and availability in their region. Architects who prioritize sustainability, work on large structures, have experience working with GLT and CLT, and have access to the materials are more likely to use them in their designs.

The Current Situation of GLT in Malaysia

Malaysia is a country with a local vernacular that is based on timber construction. Timber houses are still a common sight in rural environments. However, even in those areas, pure timber construction has become increasingly rare, and many building elements that had been timber-based (such as roof rafters, awnings, and decking) have become widely replaced with alternative materials. This shift in materiality is due in large parts to 1) cost, but also due to 2) maintenance issues relating to timber and 3) the required skill becoming scarce (timber grading, carpentry, joinery).

Malaysia is located in the tropics and has a significant forestry and timber industry. However, the industry heavily relies on sourcing raw materials (lumber) from tropical rainforests, with only a small percentage derived from plantation-based timber production. Despite this, recent reports suggest that there has been an increase in plantation-based timber production. Most of Malaysia's timber is used for pulp or paper production, while the local and regional furniture production sector uses solid timber sections, plywood, and veneer. Lower-grade timber that is not pulped is typically used to produce chipboards, fibreboards, or as construction timber (Source: Malaysian Timber Council, 2019)).

Significant activity exists in the local production of engineered timber products, including plywood and composite timber elements. At the same time, there is little documentation about any industry efforts to introduce more sophisticated engineered timber products, including GLT and CLT. There is an absence of plantation-grown timber elements with consistent quality and standards, a prerequisite for the large-scale production of GLT and CLT elements (Bejo, 2014). The Malaysian Timber Council (2019) has promoted GLT made from Malaysian tropical timbers, which has led to a small number of showcase products. From the scale of the buildings and the number of projects, it must be assumed that the GLT elements were custom designed and fabricated as experimental one-of-pieces rather than by an established local supplier of GLT products.

The timber industry in Malaysia has shown a growing interest in developing engineered timber products with higher value-added, which has led to collaboration with the academic sector on industry-focused research. Ismail et al. (2020) reported that current research focuses on developing product standards based on different timber sources and production techniques. This includes optimizing GLT beams by combining medium-density hardwood with softer timbers to increase the strength-to-section ratios and comparing different tree species as GLT and CLT sources to optimize local product development based on availability, suitability, and strength profiles.

The regulatory framework in Malaysia currently restricts the use of timber in buildings beyond individual residential buildings, largely due to fire rating concerns. The Uniform Building Bylaws do not distinguish between solid timber and engineered timber products in fire rating categorization, despite the superior fire rating properties of GLT and CLT. However, there is a lack of documentation on how performance-based approaches to fire safety and approvals can be applied to projects with extensive GLT and CLT elements.

Ismail et al. (2020) document the recent developments in standards for engineering timber products in Malaysia. The paper cites Malaysian standards (MS 544) as a reference that allows for determining mechanical product standards such as bending strengths and other factors related to allowing for the engineered timber to be safely specified as a building material. However, the paper mentions that the standard is not sufficiently developed to address the unique characteristics of GLT and CLT products.

Bourreau et al. (n.d.) and Muraleedharan and Reiterer (2017) noted that using low and medium-density tropical timber for GLT production offers a promising avenue for increased availability of GLT in tropical regions. In Malaysia, this could involve utilizing timber sourced from agricultural by-products such as palm oil and rubber tree plantations. If successful, this approach could provide a sustainable and abundant supply of raw materials for local GLT and CLT production.

Adopting GLT offers many advantages as an innovative building material with attractive architectural properties. However, several considerations are not necessarily within the decision-making realm of architects. For example, the recent boom in adopting GLT and CLT technology for highrise buildings in some industrial countries resulted from changes in policies, regulations, and approval processes. These changes can be influenced and, to some degree, initiated through the workings of the professional architectural community through professional industry networks and advice to policymakers. However, the influence of these regulatory and systemic circumstances does not lie within individual practising architects' scope.

One crucial factor to consider is the growing importance of using sustainable building materials. GLT and CLT can be highly sustainable materials, but achieving sustainability requires a comprehensive effort across the entire supply chain. This includes sustainable timber growth and harvesting, energy-efficient production processes, and proximity to the building site. Architects prioritizing sustainability must use GLT and CLT as building materials to developing a local production and supply chain. With its established timber industry, Malaysia has the potential to develop such a supply chain, although it is still in the early stages. However, the increasing availability of sustainably sourced timber from industrial plantations and ongoing research and development suggest a promising future for GLT and CLT in Malaysian architecture. Table 1 below summarizes the key findings related to these factors.

From the above, it is evident that several factors are required for GLT and CLT to become easily adopted building material choices. The following chapters will investigate the degree of awareness architects practising in Malaysia have with regard to these circumstances and which factors weigh particularly heavily in the Malaysian context.

Table 1. Summary of findings from the review of literature by theme

Area of investigation	Key Findings
Material properties and Technical Aspects of GLT and CLT products	• Product standardization and quality have improved significantly over recent years. • In countries where the regulatory framework has been updated to cater for GLT and CLT and its application even for high-rise projects has seen a significant increase in its use
Architectural considerations	• Laminated timber represents a technological shift which has been able to unlock the architectural attractiveness of timber to be scaled up. • GLT, through customized design and fabrication, allows for the realization of artistic designs and large, column-free projects. • GLT and CLT offer attractive potential as standardized prefabricated products that can help improve project timelines.
Sustainability of GLT/CLT	• In their essential properties, GLT and CLT products are sustainable and largely natural materials (except synthetic adhesives and timber treatments) • More specific analysis is required regarding sustainability on a case-by-case basis, as individual stages of production and end-use can negatively affect the embodied energy and/or life cycle analysis. (Especially sustainable forestry, transport, and energy used in production)
Status quo of GLT/CLT adoption in Malaysia	• As a country with a significant forestry and timber-product sector, Malaysia has the potential to see an increase in local GLT/CLT production and supply. • Product research and development (R&D) is still in its infancy. • Projects in which GLT and/or CLT have been used are still very limited.

METHODOLOGY

This study aims to investigate the factors influencing the adoption of glue-laminated timber (GLT) by architects in Malaysia using a quantitative research approach through a survey questionnaire. The survey questionnaire will be designed to collect data from architects who have experience working with GLT in their designs or have knowledge about the material.

Respondents to the Study

Sampling for this research project will involve selecting a group of professionals who have experience working with GLT and CLT in construction projects.

The study used purposive sampling, which involved selecting participants based on their knowledge, expertise, and experience in the field of study. This method ensures that the participants selected are relevant to the research topic and have valuable insights to share.

The participants, industry associations, and professional organizations specializing in construction and engineering were contacted to identify the potential participants. Online platforms such as LinkedIn were used to search for professionals with experience in glue-laminated or cross-laminated timber projects. Participants were selected based on the following criteria:

- They have experience working with GLT or CLT in construction projects.
- They know the benefits and challenges of using these materials in construction.
- They are willing to share their insights and experiences during the interview.

Once potential participants were identified, they were contacted via email or phone to determine their availability and interest in participating in the study. For participants who agreed to participate, the survey instrument was forwarded to be completed.

The purposive sampling method ensures that the selected participants have the relevant experience and knowledge to provide valuable insights into using GLT or CLT in construction projects.

The Instrument

The survey method most effectively evaluated Malaysian architects' understanding of GLT/CLT and the key factors behind their decisions to use GLT/CLT in projects. The survey helps identify the shifts required to induce a more widespread adoption of GLT/CLT. However, three open-ended and scenario-based questions were included. The comments and responses to the open-ended questions allow a more specific insight. These specific thoughts were also used to corroborate the quantitative data while allowing capturing aspects that might not have crystallized through the quantitative survey questions. The survey was structured to cover four aspects as follows.

i.   The demographics of the respondent
ii. Experience and perceptions of GLT as a building material
iii. Perceptions of sustainability
iv. Malaysia-specific circumstances relating to the use of GLT

Data Collection

The data was collected through a self-administered survey questionnaire. The questionnaire consisted of closed-ended questions with options for participants to select from multiple choices, using a Likert scale and demographic questions. The questionnaire was designed to assess the factors influencing architects' adoption of GLT, such as Cost, knowledge and awareness, availability, and regulatory requirements.

The survey used Google Forms, an online platform. Once the survey was finalized, it was distributed to the target population of architects identified through various channels, such as emails and WhatsApp messages. A date was set as a deadline for completion. To maximize the response rate, clear instructions were provided on completing the survey, and reminder emails and messages were sent to those who had not responded.

Data Analysis

After the data was collected, data were checked for errors or missing responses and cleaned if needed. Statistical software (SPSS) was used to conduct descriptive analyses of the survey data, such as frequency tables and measures of central tendency. Finally, survey findings were interpreted and reported clearly and concisely. The key findings were summarised, conclusions drawn, and recommendations offered for future research or practice related to the use of GLT in architecture.

Limitations

The study's limitations include the non-probability sampling technique, which may limit the generalizability of the findings. The self-reported nature of the data collection may also lead to response biases. Finally, the study's results may be limited to the context of Malaysia and may not be generalizable to other countries or regions.

DATA ANALYSIS

Demographics of Survey Respondents

The survey was primarily distributed to practising architects in Malaysia, but it was acknowledged that architects might not be the sole decision-makers regarding structural materials in some multi-disciplinary companies. Therefore, the survey also included engineers and other consultants with specific expertise. A total of 31 respondents completed the survey, but three entries were excluded due to duplicate entries or insufficient data. Of the valid respondents, 71% were fully qualified architects (LAM III) or graduate architects (LAM II) with at least 5 years of work experience (n=28), while 28.5% were engineers and other consultants working in architectural or multi-disciplinary practices.

Based on the data, the survey respondents are the intended audience for the research. Most respondents are frequently involved in or leading project stages related to project design and material specification. The sample is representative as respondents come from various company sizes, from small practices to large corporations. The largest proportion of respondents (36%) work in companies with 10 to 20 employees. The respondents' companies have a diverse work portfolio that includes all major types of residential, commercial, and mixed-development projects, but fewer are involved in industrial, infrastructure, and public works projects. Additionally, all respondents' companies are engaged in at least one category of project types suitable for GLT/CLT building elements.

Most respondents (91.3%) expressed interest in using GLT/CLT in future projects. The remaining respondents (8.7%) had previous experience using GLT (see response Q5). This highlights the unsatisfactory experience with GLT.

Respondents' Experience With GLT/CLT

A significant proportion of respondents (56%) state that they have previously considered using GLT in a previous project. A smaller number of respondents (12%) responded that to have used GLT in a previous project, while 32% of the respondents had not considered the use of GLT or CLT in any projects yet (Table 2)

The study utilized a Likert scale (ranging from 1 to 5) to investigate the factors that deterred the use of GLT/CLT as a building material after it had been initially considered (Table 3). The reasons were ranked according to the weighted average of the quantitative responses from the participants. Among those who had previously considered GLT/CLT for their project, the most significant factor that prevented its use was the lack of a local supplier, with a weighted average of 3.65. The cost (weighted average of 3.33) and the scarcity of skilled labor (weighted average of 3.11) were the second and third most important factors, respectively. Notably, issues related to authority approvals ranked fourth (2.61), indicating that

Table 2. Experience in GLT/CLT in previous projects indicates a high rate of consideration for use vs a low rate of actual use in projects

Items	%
Have used GLT or CLT in a previous project	12
Have previously considered using GLT or CLT in a previous project	32
Have not considered the use of GLTor CLT in any projects yet	56
Total	100

the decision not to use GLT/CLT was made earlier in the design phase. The finding reinforced that recommendations from other consultants did not significantly affect the decision, which usually occurs later in the project development process.

It must be noted that the sample size of respondents with previous experience in GLT/CLT use is small (12%), which reflects the limited number of projects in Malaysia that have included GLT/CLT, as highlighted in previous studies. With regards to measuring experience with GLT/CLT, the sample size is informative, especially in correlation with the other survey questions but cannot be validated as representative.

In another question (Table 4), respondents were asked reasons for considering GLT/CLT in a project to rank the reasons for using GLT/CLT. The three highest-scored (80%) reasons were "*Bringing the architectural qualities of timber as a building material into larger scale projects*"; this was followed closely by "*the ambition to set new standards in sustainability*" (79%) and "*the materials' characteristic of providing flexibility in structural design*" received a similarly high rating (78%).

Aspects of Sustainability in Choice of Building Materials

Based on the information provided, the perceived sustainability of GLT is a significant motivator for Malaysian architects to consider its adoption as a building material. The high rating of sustainability as a factor is supported by the responses indicating the growing importance of sustainable building materials

Table 3. Factors influencing the decision to not use GLT/CLT as a building material after initial consideration

	Did not influence the decision	Minimal influence on decision	Had some degree of impact on decision	Had major influence on decision	Main reason for not using GLT/CLT	N/A	Weighted Average
Cost	2	2	6	4	4	4	3.33
No local supplier	1	2	4	5	5	5	3.65
The client was against the use	4	4	4	4	1	5	2.65
Considerations of sustainability	5	2	5	3	0	7	2.4
Consultants·recommendation	8	4	4	2	0	4	2
Insufficiently skilled labour (for on-site work)	3	4	3	4	4	4	3.11
Problems relating to authorities and approvals	7	2	3	3	3	4	2.61

Table 4. Reasons for considering the use of GLT/CLT in a project

Reason	%
Adopting the architectural qualities of timber to larger-scale buildings	80
Being able to relate to contextual vernacular	62
Setting new standards for sustainability	79
Flexibility in Structural Design	78
Reaping Benefits of Prefabrication (Construction time, cost reduction, precision, on-site work)	62
Being Innovative/ Experimental	58

and the perceived central role of architects in driving the choice of sustainable materials and construction methods. A frequency of 79% suggests that the architects who responded to the survey feel a high degree of responsibility for selecting sustainable materials and construction methods.

In response to a follow-up question, the survey found that only around one-third of the respondents (32%) rated the importance of sustainability as high when making decisions about building materials. However, most respondents (61%) predicted that the importance of sustainability in building materials would increase significantly over the next five years (Table 5).

Adoption of GLT in Malaysian Projects

The survey results indicate that a significant majority (90%) of the respondents expressed a keen interest in incorporating GLT and/or CLT into their future projects. This positive sentiment towards the potential of GLT/CLT in Malaysia is further evidenced by their responses on which types of projects could benefit from these materials as a primary building element (Table 6). The most popular project type was dentified as Iconic projects such as exhibition centres and museums (83%), followed by Multi-storey buildings up to 5 storeys (65%) and Individual landed residential buildings (65%). This strong interest in using GLT/CLT for iconic projects aligns with the respondents' preference for utilizing these materials to highlight the unique qualities of timber, as indicated in Table 4.

The survey was concluded with a Likert scale analysis (1 to 5) of perceived barriers to the broader adoption of GLT and CLT in Malaysia (Table 7). The results showed that authority approvals are not a significant barrier (scoring the lowest at 2.81) to adopting GLT in the country. Instead, Malaysian architects identified the main challenge in convincing clients (weighted average of 3.43), closely followed by the lack of local or regional suppliers (3.05), as the biggest obstacles to using GLT in Malaysian projects. The findings indicated that climatic suitability and engineering capabilities are not considered significant barriers to using GLT, scoring 3.0 each.

Table 5. Respondents' view regarding the importance of sustainability as a decision-making factor in building elements

	Not important at all	Not very important	Neutral	Somewhat important	Highly important
Currently	0%	9%	27%	32%	**32%**
In 5 years	0%	0%	0%	39%	**61%**

Table 6. Types of projects that respondents regard as suitable for application of GLT/CLT

Types of Projects	n	%
Large-scale highrises > 5 storeys (condominiums, offices ..)	8	35%
Multi-storey buildings up to 5 storeys (commercial)	**15**	**65%**
Multi-storey buildings up to 5 storeys (residential)	13	57%
Large scale mixed developments	5	22%
Special projects such as exhibition centres and museums (Iconic)	**19**	**83%**
Industrial (warehouses, halls)	13	57%
Repetitive housing (landed)	5	22%
Individual residential (landed)	**15**	**65%**
Small scale renovations	10	43%
Infrastructure	5	22%
Public works	9	39%
Other (please specify) Total Respondents: 23	1	4%

Table 7. Perceived barriers to using GLT and CLT more widely in Malaysia

	Strongly Disagree	Disagree	Not sure	Agree	Strongly Agree	SCORE
Climatic suitability	6	2	5	4	5	3.00
Convincing client	4	7	5	4	1	3.43
Engineering Capabilities	6	1	5	5	4	3.00
Authority approvals	4	3	4	5	5	2.81
Local/regional availability	3	8	2	3	5	3.05

FINDINGS AND DISCUSSION

The main reasons cited by Malaysian architects for not using GLT/CLT in their projects after initial consideration were the lack of a local supplier, high cost, and unavailability of skilled labor. However, issues related to authority approvals were not seen as a significant barrier, indicating that the decision not to use GLT/CLT occurred earlier in the design phase. Despite these barriers, Malaysian architects have a high level of interest in using GLT/CLT, particularly for iconic projects such as exhibition centers and museums, as well as multi-storey buildings and individual landed residential buildings.

- **Local supply and cost**

The infancy of the local GLT/CLT product development stage, as highlighted in the literature review. Architects tend to abandon the use of GLT/CLT early in the project stages when they realize that local suppliers are unavailable and the costs are not feasible within the project budget, as reported in the study by Buchanan and Honey (2020).

The cost issue is closely linked to the lack of local supply for GLT/CLT. If architects have to import these elements, it becomes a feasible design option only for high-budget projects with iconic status, such as airports. However, it is unclear at what point the architects surveyed abandoned their interest in GLT/CLT and whether they conducted a thorough cost analysis before making a decision. It is reasonable to assume that GLT/CLT was eliminated from consideration when it became apparent that local supply was unavailable before conducting a costing exercise to evaluate the actual cost of importing GLT/CLT. This finding is consistent with Buchanan and Honey's (2020) study, which suggests that the availability of GLT and CLT in a given region can impact architects' material choice, as it directly increases project cost and time.

The survey results have confirmed that cost is a crucial factor in determining the use of glue-laminated timber (GLT) and material specification overall, which is consistent with earlier studies conducted by Honey (2020) and Wang et al. (2020).

While the research indicates that cost is an important factor in the use of GLT/CLT, a more detailed analysis of cost-sensitivity would require an extensive investigation of micro-economic issues, comparisons between various construction methods and their costs, perceived costs, and trends in construction and material costs. Although the literature review suggests that GLT/CLT can be cost-competitive compared to conventional construction methods, this largely depends on local factors, including supply chains, labour rates, and distances. Conducting a market study and further research into cost sensitivity would provide valuable insights and help drive industry development.

- **Skilled Labor**

The shortage of skilled labor was found to be another major reason why GLT was abandoned as a potential material, which aligns with previous studies by the Wood Products Council (2017) and The Engineered Wood Association (2020). This is a practical concern, as the absence of skilled labour can increase the workload on architects and contractors, leading to a higher opportunity cost, such as time spent on quality control, oversight, training, and project management. This is expected to be an ongoing issue until GLT becomes more widely adopted and training in the construction industry in Malaysia aligns with the demand for GLT/CLT.

Industrial GLT/CLT suppliers often provide specialist construction assistance and support to their clients, including architects and contractors, to ensure the successful implementation of the materials. This assistance can include design and engineering services, detailing and shop drawings, and on-site technical support. Suppliers can help bridge the gap in expertise and experience with GLT/CLT by providing this support, making it more accessible and feasible for architects and contractors.

- **Authority's Approval**

Based on the survey results, it appears that Malaysian architects lack clarity on the issue of authority approval when using GLT. This may be due to the fact that the decision to abandon GLT is made early on before exploring the approval process. However, some qualitative statements from the survey suggest that the current approval processes do not facilitate the adoption of GLT as a primary building material. This finding is consistent with earlier studies by Wang et al. (2020) which suggest that regulations and codes can create uncertainty about the requirements for using GLT and CLT, particularly concerning fire regulations and product standards.

- **Sustainability**

Based on the survey results, Malaysian Architects view the sustainability of building materials as a crucial factor in their decision-making process, with more than 60% of respondents anticipating sustainability becoming highly significant in the next five years. This aligns with previous studies by Buchanan and Honey (2020) and Ranta-Maunus (2021), which suggest that GLT and CLT's perceived sustainability can positively influence their adoption. GLT is perceived as a material that could meet the increasing need for sustainable construction due to its lower carbon footprint, strength, and durability. Therefore, GLT could become more viable as the construction industry shifts towards more sustainable materials and practices.

The survey shows that Malaysian architects believe GLT and CLT can meet the increasing demand for sustainable building materials, but there are concerns about their dependence on sustainable forestry and production location. The respondents feel they need to choose sustainable materials and processes while considering the materials' sustainability in their application. On the technical side, architects are worried about practical issues like the availability of skilled labor for implementing GLT/CLT in their projects. These problems are mainly related to individual project implementation, and the survey indicates that architects overlook the importance of having an enabling framework of regulations and approval processes, as highlighted in the literature review.

CONCLUSION

This study used a survey questionnaire and quantitative research approach to investigate the factors affecting the adoption of GLT by architects in Malaysia. The literature review and survey results indicate that GLT is becoming increasingly popular in Malaysia, but the lack of local suppliers hinders its adoption. However, ongoing local product developments suggest that increased local production of GLT and CLT would meet the overwhelming demand from Malaysian architects. One of the concerns for architects is the sustainability of locally produced GLT/CLT, which is the responsibility of the regulatory and production sector and requires a shift towards more sustainable timber sources. The time needed for this shift significantly impacts how quickly GLT/CLT can gain a foothold in Malaysia. Since there are not enough completed projects using locally produced GLT and CLT, assessing the architects' experience is impossible. An interview-based approach with a small sub-set of GLT-experienced architects in Malaysia could provide further insight to refine the impetus for fabricators, suppliers, and policymakers. In addition, the following research needs to emerge as a follow-up to the findings put forward here:

- Specific amendments to laws, regulations and standards are required to smoothen the process of authority approvals, especially concerning fire regulations.
- Hypothetical Embodied Energy analysis based on locally produced GLT/CLT and comparison with the EE of prevalent local construction materials and methods.
- Continued product R&D involving the timber industry. Architects and academic research focus on developing GLT/CLT product standards of consistent quality based on locally available timber species.

This study provides valuable information about Malaysian architects' perspectives on GLT and highlights various obstacles that must be addressed to promote its adoption. Individual architects can resolve some of these issues, while others require collective efforts from the timber industry and policymakers. However, it is crucial for architects to proactively express their interest in GLT and use their influence through relevant professional and regulatory bodies to remove the barriers preventing its widespread adoption in Malaysia.

REFERENCES

Albee, B. L. (2019). *The Malaysian forest and timber industry: Policies and strategies for sustainable growth*. Routledge.

Basaglia, B., Lewis, K., Shrestha, R., & Crews, K. (2015). A comparative life cycle assessment approach of two innovative long span timber floors with its reinforced concrete equivalent in an Australian context. In *Proceedings of the Second International Conference on Performance-based and Lifecycle Structural Engineering (PLSE 2015)*. eSpace. https://espace.library.uq.edu.au/view/UQ:399256 doi:https://doi.org/10.14264/uql.2016.714

Bejo, L. (2017). Operational vs. Embodied Energy: A Case for Wood Construction. *Drvna Industrija*, *68*(2), 163–172. doi:10.5552/drind.2017.1423

Bourreau, D., Aimene, Y., Beauchêne, J., & Thibaut, B. (2013). (n.d) Feasibility of glued laminated timber beams with tropical hardwoods. *Holz als Roh- und Werkstoff*, *71*(5), 653–662. doi:10.100700107-013-0721-4

Bourreau, M., Aimene, Y., Beachene, S., & Thibaut, B. (2013). From GLT to GLVL: Developing new products for tropical hardwoods. In *Proceedings of the International Conference on Civil, Environmental and Construction Engineering (ICCECE'13)* (pp. 34-38). Paris, France.

Brenčič, M., Bukovec, P., Kryžanowski, A., Kuzman, M. K., & Pavlič, M. (2017). Sustainability aspects of cross-laminated timber facade systems. *Energy and Building*, *151*, 228–237.

Buchanan, A. H., & Honey, T. J. (2020). *Timber: a global survey of mass-timber architecture, engineering and construction*. Thames & Hudson.

Building Research Establishment. (2018). *Barriers to the uptake of innovative construction products and processes in the UK*. BE Group. https://www.bregroup.com/wp-content/uploads/2018/08/Barriers-to-the-uptake-of-innovative-construction-products-and-processes-in-the-UK.pdf

Department of Standards Malaysia. (2013). *MS 544:2013 Portland cement*. Department of Standards Malaysia.

Falk, B., Duinker, P., & Vailshery, L. (2020). Barriers to using cross-laminated timber and glue-laminated timber in North America. *Forests*, *11*(9), 933.

Forest and Wood Products Australia (FWPA). (2017). *WoodSolutions: Cross Laminated Timber (CLT) and Glue Laminated Timber (GLT)*. Wood Solutions. https://www.woodsolutions.com.au/articles/cross-laminated-timber-clt-and-glue-laminated-timber-glt

Research and Markets. (n.d.). Global Glue Laminated Timber Market 2018-2022. *Research and Markets.* https://www.researchandmarkets.com/reports/4618201/global-glue-laminated-timber-market-2018-2022

Hamzah, A. B. (2006). *Guide to fire protection in Malaysia. Kuala Lumpur: The Institute of Fire Engineers.* Malaysia Branch.

Ismail S., Muhammad N., and Ahmad Z. (2020), Bending properties of Mengkulang Gluedlaminated (glulam) timber and laminated veneer lumber (LVL). *International Journal of Basic and Applied Sciences, 20*(02).

Jusufi, I., & Capra, B. (2019). Energy consumption in building materials: Comparison between traditional and innovative materials. *Energy Procedia, 158*, 2094–2099. doi:10.1016/j.egypro.2019.01.550

Laws of Malaysia. (1984). *Uniform building by-laws 1984. Kuala Lumpur: International Law Book.* Services Malaysian Timber Council.

Mohd Nawi, M. N., Mohd Sani, M. R., Md Din, M. F., & Roslan, N. (2018). The potential of traditional timber construction in Malaysia: A review. *Journal of Advanced Research in Materials Science, 44*(1), 9–21.

Muraleedharan, K., & Reiterer, A. (2017). Glue laminated timber (GLT) as an alternative construction material in the tropics. *International Journal of Sustainable Built Environment, 6*(1), 7–17. doi:10.1016/j.ijsbe.2017.02.001

Parra-Serrano, J., Komatsu, K., Inoue, M., Lee, S. H., & Kawai, S. (2018). Performance of glued-laminated timber made from rubber tree and oil palm lumber. *BioResources, 13*(4), 8545–8557.

Ranta-Maunus, A. (2021). Glue-laminated timber in architecture: a review of recent research. *Architectural Engineering and Design Management*, 1-15.

Robertson, A., Lam, F., & Cole, R. (2012). A Comparative Cradle-to-Gate Life Cycle Assessment of Mid-Rise Office Building Construction Alternatives: Laminated Timber or Reinforced Concrete. *Buildings., 2*(3), 245–270. doi:10.3390/buildings2030245

Robertson, A., Lam, F., & Cole, R. (2012). A review of the sustainability of wood buildings in North America. *Wood and Fiber Science, 44*(1), 1–1.

Schoof, U. (2018). *From shacks to skyscrapers: Timber towers hit new heights.* DW Made for Minds. https://www.dw.com/en/from-shacks-to-skyscrapers-timber-towers-hit-new-heights/a-43775847

Strang, T., & Leardini, P. (2019). Opportunities for tropical hardwood glulam in Australia. *International Wood Products Journal, 10*(2), 58–66.

Sulastiningsih, I., Purwanto, A., & Sudjadi, U. (2019). Energy analysis of glue-laminated timber (GLT) production for sustainable building material. *International Journal of Energy Economics and Policy, 9*(1), 132–137. https://www.econjournals.com/index.php/ijeep/article/view/7276/4172

The Engineered Wood Association. (2020). *The Rise of Mass Timber Construction.* APA Wood. https://www.apawood.org/the-rise-of-mass-timber-construction

Wang, X., Zhou, J., Li, X., Li, S., & Gao, Y. (2020). Barriers to promoting the application of CLT (cross-laminated timber) in China. *Forests*, *11*(4), 414.

Wood Products Council. (2017). *Building Tall with Wood: Opportunities and Challenges for 21st Century Wood Construction*. AWC. https://www.awc.org/pdf/education/BUILDING_TALL_WITH_WOOD.pdf

Yuce, B., & Turk, R. (2019). Embodied energy and carbon footprint of building materials in Turkey. *Journal of Building Engineering*, *26*, 100824. doi:10.1016/j.jobe.2019.100824

Chapter 11
The Adoption and Challenges of Using Green Materials in Building Construction Projects

Tze Shwan Lim
Taylor's University, Malaysia

Yee Lin Lee
Tunku Abdul Rahman University of Management and Technology, Malaysia

Yin Xi Goh
Tunku Abdul Rahman University of Management and Technology, Malaysia

Kenn Jhun Kam
Taylor's University, Malaysia

Lam Tatt Soon
Taylor's University, Malaysia

ABSTRACT

The impact of the construction industry on the environment has made people more and more aware that it is necessary to adopt a sustainable and responsible attitude to the current construction practices. Increasing attention has prompted the Malaysian government and professional institutions to alleviate this problem more actively without restricting development needs. The objective of this study includes identifying the types of green materials adopted in buildings, comparing the differences between green materials and common materials, and investigating the challenges of using green materials in buildings in Malaysia. A quantitative method with a questionnaire has been adopted in this study and analysis of the study is conducted by descriptive method, inferential method, and ANOVA method. Through intensive literature study, it has brought a better understanding of the types of green building materials adopted.

DOI: 10.4018/978-1-6684-8253-7.ch011

RESEARCH BACKGROUND

Green building refers to a structure using materials and process that is environmentally responsible and resource-efficient throughout a building's life cycle. Green Building is committed to improving the efficiency of resource use such as water, energy, and materials through better site selection, operation, design, construction, demolition, and maintenance while decreasing the building's impact on human health and the environment in its building life cycle (Darko, Zhang and Chan, 2017). The design and operation of green buildings should lower the overall impact of the built environment on their surroundings. Green buildings are designed to minimize the emission and use of toxic substances (GBI, 2004).

Green building materials are, defined as sustainable materials, qualified by the Life-Cycle Assessment (LCA) methodology during their full life cycle (Franzoni, 2011). The adoption of green materials has become part of the standards in developed countries. Green materials are environmentally responsible for building elements that minimize the consumption of resources in the building's lifecycle (United Nations, 2012). Green building materials improve the overall energy efficiency of the building without a pure architectural design effect. The coverage of energy-efficient buildings is very wide, including walls, floor slabs, roofs, and other indoor products. For example, roof insulation materials can resist sunlight, and lightweight slabs reduce the usage and cost of structural materials (Aathaworld, 2019).

Today, the global construction market is talking about environmental protection and environmental green, and the demand for green building materials is also increasing. The importance of sustainability and sustainable development with the adoption of green building materials has been recognized globally (United Nations, 2012). Due to the government, construction committee, and income tax authorities providing incentives to reward developers for adopting green building materials in building construction, green building materials are becoming more popular, thus increasing the number of green building materials suppliers in Malaysia proposing innovations in the construction application to the users. (GBI, 2004). However, the degree of adoption was not at high success. There is a lack of studies carried out on defining and understanding green materials and the challenges to their adoption. To mitigate this, construction personnel must be able to assess the knowledge and perceptions of the materials as well as the possible challenges, especially as they deal with green design and construction. (Nikyema and Blouin, 2020). As such, the purpose of this study is to investigate 3 main objectives. The first objective is to identify the types of green materials adopted in buildings. The second objective of this research is to compare the differences between green materials and common materials. The third objective is to investigate the challenge of using green materials in buildings.

PROBLEM STATEMENT

Globally, green construction aims to reduce pollution such as noise, vehicle exhaust, waste materials, and the release of pollutants into the ground, water, and atmosphere. In Malaysia, more than six million tonnes of waste have been recorded that was generated, which quarter was produced in the Klang Valley alone. Solid waste issue from construction is one of the biggest environmental problems in Malaysia. The use of housing and industry materials without proper control contributed to environmental problems (Yusoff, 2007). Not only green construction must be incorporated into Malaysia's goals, the green materials selection must be carried out. The adoption of green building materials must achieve a win-win situation for Malaysia's construction industry and the environment without any negative impact. This is because construction project always suffers from problems such as wastage of materials, cost overruns, and produce low-quality products. Therefore, green building materials adoption is important to decrease the environmental impacts in Malaysia's Construction Industry (Reddy, 2009).

However, the rate of adopting green building materials is still low in Malaysia (Aathaworld, 2019). Better strategies are to be adopted to encourage the use and increase the adoption (Tey et. al., 2013). Malaysian construction practitioners such as contractors, suppliers, and developers lack the knowledge of using green building materials and how the common materials will cause the environment. It is supported by Esa et al. (2011) in their research study that, lack of awareness from the consultants, and clients are causing the slow adoption and reluctance in getting involved in green buildings materials. Green building materials must be introduced and promoted not only to the relevant parties in the building industries but also to the general public so that demand and application can be increased. Therefore, this study aims to find out the challenges of green building materials adoption in the Malaysia Construction Industry. This study aims to highlight the differences between green building materials and common materials while addressing the challenges of the adoption, which will be able to assist policymakers, the education industry, and government initiatives to be more apparent in the implementation of green building materials among construction industry stakeholders.

LITERATURE REVIEW

Green Buildings in Malaysia

Malaysia Energy Commission Headquarters

The Suruhanjaya Tenaga (ST) Diamond Building, is also known as Energy Commission's Headquarters. It is a green building landmark in Southeast Asia and aims to showcase the technologies that can reduce energy consumption, stimulate the use of green building materials, and improve indoor environmental quality (Chen et al., 2013). The Suruhanjaya Tenaga (ST) Diamond Tower is the first office building in Malaysia to receive the Platinum rating of the Green Building Index. ST Diamond Tower has also won multiple awards, such as the 2012 ASEAN Energy Award and the 2013 ASHRAE Technology Award, proving that its innovative design has won international recognition (Japheth, 2013).

The thermal insulation concrete roof is adopted to reduce heat absorption in the building, and the top area of the roof is insulated with wooden boards with a thickness of 100mm. The concrete roof is tightly insulated both vertically and horizontally.

The use of sustainable materials and the purpose of building design is also to provide residents with an efficient and healthy working environment. For internal partitions and ceilings, use plasterboard with green labels. This type of gypsum board can recycle 30% of the material, and the emission of volatile organic compounds is low. Floor carpets are also affixed with green labels to reduce VOC emissions and have at least 10% recyclable content. Indoor coatings used in buildings also have low VOC content. The workstation contains materials that can withstand ultraviolet (UV) (The Star, 2011).

Malaysia International Trade and Exhibition Centre (MITEC)

The MITEC building is the largest exhibition center in Malaysia. It derives its unique shape from rubber seeds; a symbol of Malaysia's historical trading business (Sika Malaysia, 2017). The Malaysian International Trade and Exhibition Centre (MITEC) has further enhanced its praise by obtaining the latest success of the Green Building Index (GBI) certification issued by the GBI certification team (MITEC, 2020). MITEC was built with its functional vision as Malaysia's largest trade and exhibition center, but also with strict intentions to ensure that the development project can protect the surrounding environment (Sharen, 2020). MITEC CEO Gunther Beissel said that obtaining GBI status convinced us that we are on the right track in our efforts to leave a positive footprint on the environment (Sika Malaysia, 2017).

MITEC earned its stripes based on 11 winning practices such as the usage of recycled material during construction, installation of a 70% UV repellent glass, rainwater harvesting, Co2 censors and fresh air fans, variable speed drives in the Centre's chiller pumps, the motion sensor in all public toilets, garden watering system based on timers, hand basin in kitchens with censors, building automation system applicable, mold prevention system and no chemicals water treatment for cooling towers.

TYPES OF GREEN MATERIALS

There are different types of green building materials in Malaysia for construction building projects. The unique shape represents the best design method to improve energy efficiency (CRL, 2018).

Autoclaved Aerated Concrete (AAC) blocks contain 27% of post-consumer recyclable components in the AAC blocks. The total energy consumed in the production process is 2 to 3 times lower than other building materials such as burnt bricks. The amount of gas released such as CO, CO, and NOx is also relatively low. By-products of AAC production such as condensate from the autoclaving, hardened AAC waste, and unhardened AAC mixture can be recycled back into the production of AAC. In addition, other industrial wastes such as fly ash and slag may be used as the main raw material (Green Pages Malaysia, 2020). AAC blocks have good thermal insulation properties and require less energy for cooling on AAC buildings. It is breathable, which can effectively reduce moisture content and maintain the correct relative humidity. AAC blocks contain 99% of locally sourced materials, and it is characterized by lightness, durability, heat resistance, fire resistant, sound insulation, breathable, non-toxic, and processable (CRL, 2018).

Low-E glass refers to glass with a low emissivity coating. Low-E glass to be used as windows and panels have gained recent interest as a cost-effective method to improve the energy efficiency of existing windows (Cort, 2013). It reduces heat gain or loss by reflecting long-wave infrared energy (solar heat), therefore decreasing the U-value & solar heat gain and improving the energy efficiency of the glazing. Because of its relative neutrality in appearance and energy efficiency that is suitable for all climates while minimizing energy costs, low-E glass is expected to continue to increase in usage in the coming years (CRL, 2018). The applications of the Low-E glass is mostly used for facades in office and tertiary buildings. In relation to solar energy, solar roof tiles has been introduced. Serving as one of green construction materials, solar roof tiles give an alternative option other than conventional roof tiles. It has the differences as compared to solar panels as this material is being installed on the house roofs with racking system which being part of the building roof. It provides the important function of providing energy for the housing system. With that, it helps to save the energy consumption of fossil fuels what is harmful to our environment. Therefore, solar tiles are considered as local source of renewable energy in applying green building material (Green Pages Malaysia, 2020).

Ecodeck is made of recyclable polyolefin and natural wooden fibers. The product is worn out even if used for a long time. It can be recycled and it is safe for the environment and the human body, which does not contain any chemicals and harmful gases that can damage the endocrine. The natural wooden fibers that are used to make an eco deck are made from sawdust, recycled decks, and waste wood. The choice of materials can minimize gas emissions and save trees as it uses an average of 51% recycled wood flooring (Green Pages Malaysia, 2020). The Ecodeck is made of two components that are the strong and durable inner core and outer sheath are specially designed for excellent weather resistance. The surface design of the eco deck has a natural appearance and color that performs well in the natural environment. For the appearance and texture of the wood, embossed patterns were designed. It is different from natural wood which requires surface treatment and regular maintenance of paint. Ecodeck not only requires low maintenance costs but is also easy to maintain while maintaining its appearance and durability for a long time (CRL, 2018).

Occupants are spending times inside buildings day and night, and are always confronted with the indoor air quality as well as health consequences. This concerns seriously linked to the materials used. Therefore, there are demands in the market for green construction material or products that is low in volatile organic compounds (VOCs) as it is a more safe and non-toxic materials concerning the health risks and indoor air quality awareness. It is popular materials as of low-emitting material credit and lower toxic chemicals. Volatile Organic Compounds (VOCs) in a building material contain carbon molecules which is able to vaporize from material surfaces into air in a building indoor by a process known as off-gassing. This type of green material is recommended green material as VOCs in normal building material can escape into the air that causing allergic and illness to the building occupants. It may creates indoor pollutants to health concerns resulting headaches, nausea, irritation of eye, nose and throat, and other possible health problems. In building materials selection, common used materials such as paints, sealants, treated wood products, and adhesive often release volatile organic compounds into the air (Whole Building Design Guide, 2020). Furthermore, non-VOCs or low VOCs materials is important to serve as green building materials for it's production. In the process of manufacturing building materials, volatile organic compounds are emitted and resulting presence of health concerned indoor air contaminants. With the application of non-VOCs or low VOCs green building materials such as non-VOCs paints, it decreases the reapplication needs and reduces the emission of harmful volatile organic compounds to the environment.

Exxomass Biobrick is an innovative product that has been granted a Malaysian patent by the Malaysian Intellectual Property Corporation (MyIPO). Industrial waste generated by industrial waste generators, the fine quarry dust is transformed to become an innovative, recycled content, energy efficient masonry unit. By harmonizing with the surrounding environment and local climate, it managed to decrease air and dust pollution (Green Pages Malaysia, 2020). Different from traditional bricks, Exxomass Biobrick contains almost no primitive natural resources such as mud, lime, clay, or sand, so its use in Malaysian Green Buildings has ecological and environmental significance. Exxomass Biobrick contains 94% of fine quarry dust as well as a mixture of iron oxide and cement. There is no need for autoclaving, burning, or other heating processes in the production process. The manufacturing process of exomes bio-bricks does not require kiln drying, and the energy consumption is five to ten times lower than clay brick and other bricks. Natural drying and curing processes with less carbon dioxide release can reduce the impact on the environment (CRL, 2018). The thermal conductivity of the exomes bio brick is 7 times lower than concrete and 3 times lower than clay bricks. The size of Exxomass Biobrick is 215mm x 100mm x 64mm and red. It is made of 94 percent pre-consumer recyclable materials and it can save 40 percent on plastering costs compared with clay bricks. It is the first "Eco-Labelled" masonry unit awarded by the Ministry of Energy, Green Technology, and Water in Malaysia (Green Pages Malaysia, 2020).

THE DIFFERENCES BETWEEN GREEN MATERIALS AND COMMON MATERIALS

There are differences identified in comparison between green materials and common materials including energy efficiency, renewable energy, renewable resources, energy conservation, low impact on health, sustainability, and indoor thermal comfort.

According to Hwang and Tan (2010), adopting green materials for green structures bring significant benefits and differences compared with normal/standard materials. It is supported by U.S. Life Cycle Inventory Database that energy effectiveness is the main difference in green material adoption, with lessening energy utilization in building operations (Zuo and Zhao, 2014). For instance, structural insulated panels (SIPs) can be a good green building material to consider when constructing a new home. Sip is a panel with a foam core inside the structural finish. SIPs replace the traditional wooden structure but are manufactured in a factory in a controlled environment, and delivered to the site to form the exterior walls of the house. The insulated foam core provides cool and heat insulation and improves energy efficiency, helping to decrease cooling and heating costs (Green Pages Malaysia, 2020). As such, the advantage of green materials adoption is furthermore identified in helping to reduce the indoor temperature with warm extravagance by various interrelated parts of temperature and humidity from building structures (Zuo and Zhao, 2014).

Green building materials are implemented in the construction process without adversely polluting the environment as the materials can be renewed, reused, or recycled. It alternates the limitation of non-renewable materials with no environmental impact in its production (White and Che, 2011). It is renewable resources that are reusable, renewable, and/or recyclable such as rapidly renewable plant materials like bamboo and straw, recycled stone and recycled metal, or other products such as recycled industrial goods, foundry sand, and demolition debris from construction projects. One of the common renewable resources is bamboo as a construction green material. In contrast to the energy and carbon-intensive steel, bamboo can be regenerated quickly and can sequester carbon. The combination of lightweight, tensile strength, and recyclability make it an ideal substitute for rebar and concrete (CRL, 2018).

In building operations, there is energy consumption for lighting, heating, and cooling purposes. It is important to practice energy conservation for energy-efficient buildings to promote a sustainable environment according to modern sustainability criteria. It can be done by green materials implementation that resulting lesser consumption of electrical resources from burning non-renewable fossil fuel which lowers energy consumption (SBCI, 2007). Studies by Zuo and Zhao (2014) showed that low-energy buildings with green structures and green materials adoption are seemly saving more than 55% of the energy cost as compared with ordinary common materials.

Another difference identified comparing green material with common material is the Renewable energy from green building materials. Solar energy has presently been developed to make full use of clean and rich natural energy that is inexhaustible, for utilization in building operations such as solar energy air-conditioning, solar water heaters, and solar cells (Zhineng, 2017). A solar panel is the paradigm of green building material for renewable energy. Solar panels will absorb the sunlight and convert it into electrical energy, which can be used to power electrical loads (The Economic Times, 2020). Electricity generated by solar panels replacing the electricity generated by fossil fuels is non-renewable and unsustainable which will pollute the environment (Marsh, 2018).

Environmentally friendly materials with minimized impact on health are generally achieved by the selection of non-toxic materials. Indoor air quality is important for occupants' health and Sick Building Syndrome can be minimized if low-toxicity material is used for building finishes. Green building materials can minimize health hazards by not producing a huge amount of toxic chemicals, for instance, Low Volatile Organic Compounds (VOC) paint which is a pigmented liquid that causes a low impact on human health. The particle from low VOC paint can evaporate, but conventional paints consist of high VOC levels that can transfer harmful chemicals into the air and can be a dangerous impact on health concerns (Chemoxy, 2017).

CHALLENGES OF USING GREEN MATERIALS IN CONSTRUCTION BUILDING PROJECTS

Sustainable construction aims to reduce pollution such as waste materials, vehicle exhaust, noise, and the release of pollutants to the atmosphere, water, and ground. Not only must sustainable construction be incorporated into local targets, and also influence the selection of the material (Venkatarama, 2009). Due to the increasing importance of using green building materials in Malaysia's construction industry, construction practitioners and researchers must take action to lower the negative impacts of development and enhance their competitive advantage (Zainul, 2010). The use of green materials is needed to achieve a win-win situation between the global environment and the construction industry. Therefore, this study provides an empirical analysis of the challenges in the adoption of green building materials and aims to achieve its objective by addressing the challenges encountered by project management teams. An extensive review of the literature was conducted and the potential project challenges in green materials adoption were identified. Some of the key challenges identified from the extant review are higher costs of adopting green materials; Budget constraints, insufficient technical skills, and green material information, lack of government support, inadequate awareness; and limited availability of suppliers.

According to Osaily (2010), the limited availability of locally sourced green building materials proved a difficulty for the adoption where materials had to be imported or sourced from elsewhere. In the adoption of green materials, the higher cost is a result of the complexity of the design layout coupled with modeling and green practices (Wu et al., 2019). In the overall cost of building projects, applying green building materials will cost 3-4% more than using traditional common materials (Zhang et al., 2011). As such, government support is one of the key concerns among the challenges. With higher government support promoting the benefits of green materials, there is more access to financial loans and incentives and increases green design project implementation. This in turn increases the demand for green materials and stimulates the manufacture and product availability. Concerning the higher cost of adoption of green material, there is the concern of budget constraint. In most instances, the budget available for construction projects is limited. Once the budget limit has been confirmed, it will have a significant impact on the follow-up design decision such as materials selection. Williams and Dair (2007) observed in a survey of designers involved in housing development plans in England that in many cases, although cost differences have not yet been thoroughly investigated, the designers are convinced that, except for "business as usual", everything else will be more expensive. Speculative architects quickly pointed out that the cost of green buildings is much higher than the standard program, and most people do not believe in the widespread demand for such buildings. It, therefore, becomes a challenge to convince clients and stakeholders for adopting green building materials for sustainable building.

Maintenance concern is one of the challenges for green materials uptake. Studies by Joseph and Tretsiakova-McNally (2010) found that in the mind of construction stakeholders, insisting on using green materials will cause extensive maintenance. Given the customers or clients that are increasingly seeking building maintenance-free, and desire to minimize the operating cost of the building, it is not entirely surprising that maintenance concerns became one of the challenges for green building materials adoption.

Furthermore, insufficient technical skills to adopt green building materials in the construction process challenge the adoption. Silvius et al. (2012) explained that project teams appear to have insufficient or very little knowledge about green materials, and technical skills of sustainable construction methods and processes. Darko et al. (2018) further emphasized these challenges in adoption where insufficient technical skills and unfamiliarity with sustainable technologies adversely affect the overall project outcome and performance. In addition, the lack of green material information which needs to be understood in the building process constitutes a challenge for the adoption (Sch¨oggl et al., 2017).

Opoku et al. (2019) postulated that lack of awareness is a major challenge associated with green building materials adoption. It is due to inadequate public education and sustainability studies concerning the advantages of green materials adoption, specifically on issues concerning indoor environmental conditions, productiveness, and the health of occupants (Darko, 2019). Awareness is the stumbling block that must be conquered in creating a capable and feasible local construction sector (Zainul, 2010). In the construction sector, the willingness of developers and contractors to adopt sustainable materials is still low. There is still a lack knowledge of about using green building materials and how the common materials can cause environmental problems. The transition to the use of green building materials will face major obstacles to existing policies and regulations, existing structures, and the market forces in the Malaysian construction industry.

Time constraints are one of the key challenges affecting the uptake of green materials (Emmitt and Yeomans, 2008). Normally, the customers will require a particular time frame to complete a building, where the amount of time is allocated to the various stages of the construction project. Time is the benchmark for construction project performance including the cost. Regardless of the building size, type of building, and complexity of the design of the building, every project is subject to some form of time constraints (Chan and Kumaraswamy, 2002). When a project has shortened time and needs to be done quickly, it often sticks to the materials previously used in a similar project, thus reducing the time needed to find out sustainable alternatives. Moreover, Graeber (2015) found that the bureaucratic process for adopting new materials in construction projects could increase the project completion time and cause a possible delay due to the sustainability requirements. It involved lengthy processes to seek approval for the construction processes for the projects (Zhang et al., 2011).

RESEARCH METHODOLOGY

A quantitative method was applied in this study. The main data of this study is collected through the questionnaire. The selection of respondents for the research involves selection using the purposive sampling technique. The targeted respondents are the contractors who have adopted green materials in construction projects in Kuala Lumpur Malaysia. There are 124 contractors were chosen from the overall population. The respondents were asked to rate each variable on a five-point Likert scale. Independent Sample t-test and SPSS Statistics are used to analyze the result of the questionnaire. Non-probability sampling technique was adopted. Descriptive statistics and inferential statistics tests generated from SPSS provide a more accurate and detailed analysis of the research.

FINDINGS

Type of Green Materials Adopted in Construction Project

The following descriptive statistics indicate the various types of Green Materials adopted in a construction project.

The result from Table 1 shows that among various type of green materials, autoclaved aerated concrete blocks have the highest adoption mean value which is 3.66 and Standard Deviation is 0.701; whereby solar tiles has the lowest mean value which is 3.09 and Standard Deviation is 1.088. Other than solar tiles which fell under the category of "occasionally" used material in the construction project. The other materials from ranking 1 to ranking 5 are all having a mean score of 3.0. This statistical meaning of it is that the materials were "sometimes" being used in the construction project. . From the finding of the study, it clearly shows that people are paying attention to the various types of green materials adopted in a construction project. Masonry including Autoclaved Aerated Concrete Blocks and Exxomas bio brick is ranked as the first two green materials that are adopted in the construction industry where this statement is also supported by researcher CRL (2018). Masonry plays a major role in building materials and supplies, where masonry covers most of the part of the wall in a building. Following on the third most adopted green material, is Tempered Low-E Glass. Windows are one of the important components of Malaysian buildings, fixed with glass. The application of tempered low-E glass windows can remedy the ultraviolet light that contributes heavily to heat gain in the room where it drastically reduces the amount of heat that enters the home through the windows. The function of assisting to keep the home cooler and more comfortable while also helping to minimize cooling costs has gained the favor of the users. Referring to Green Pages Malaysia, (2020), the new interior design perspective of a residential building is designing their rooms with wood decking or panels. Therefore, the Ecodeck green material is ranked in the top 4 in the finding.

Table 1. Various types of green materials adopted in construction project

Type of green materials	Rank	Mean	Standard Deviation
Autoclaved Aerated Concrete Blocks	1	3.66	.701
Exxomas Biobrick	2	3.56	1.318
Tempered Low-E Glass	3	3.44	.878
Ecodeck	4	3.28	.888
Non-VOC Paint	5	3.22	.975
Sustainable Concrete	5	3.22	1.184
Solar Tiles	6	3.09	1.088

Differences Between Green Building Materials and Common Materials

The respondents opined that there are differences between green materials and common materials. The following descriptive statistics indicate the differences between green materials and common materials and descriptive statistics indicate the various types of Green Materials adopted in the construction projects.

Table 2. Differences between green material and common material

Differences between green material and common material	Rank	Mean	Standard Deviation
Renewable Resources	1	4.00	.762
Renewable Energy	2	3.91	.818
Energy Efficient	3	3.88	.907
Energy Conservation	4	3.81	.693
Low Impact on Health	5	3.75	.762
Reduce Indoor Temperature	6	3.72	.924
Low Maintenance Cost	7	3.59	.756
Long Life of Building	8	3.47	.507

From Table 2 above, the respondents believe that the application of green building materials in the construction industry is usually different from the application of common materials since all the mean values are from 3 (Neither agree nor disagree) to 4 (Agree). In addition, the result above also indicates that renewable resources have the highest mean value which is 4.00, followed by renewable energy, energy efficiency, and energy conservation. The top 4 ranked differences between green materials and common materials are related to the energy concerned in applying green building materials.

The result shows that respondents agreed with the studies that the main differences between green building materials to common materials are their contribution to lessening the impact on the environment concerning' sustainable energy, as building constructions created enormous environmental impact by consuming about 40% of natural resources extraction (Pulselli et. al, 2007). Based on Yu (2008), conventional building construction consumes 40% of the raw natural material used such as stone, gravel, and sand, and 25% of the raw timber which created a significant effect on the entire environment. Furthermore, 65% of the waste has been disposed of in our landfills from building construction (Yudelson, 2008). It supported the results that renewable energy is the main difference between green materials and common materials. In addition, buildings are accountable for the immense amount of harmful emissions, 30% of greenhouse gases in the building operation, and a further 18% induced indirectly due to material transportation and exploitation (Yudelson, 2008; Venkatarama et al., 2003). It supported the results that renewable energy, energy-efficient, and energy conservation are important aspects of green building material selection.

Challenges of Using Green Materials in Construction Building Projects

The following descriptive statistics indicate the challenges of Green Material Applications in the Construction Industry.

Table 3. Challenges of green material application in the construction industry

Challenges of green material adoption	Rank	Mean	Standard Deviation
Limited availability of supplier	1	4.19	.693
High cost of adopting green materials	2	4.13	.660
Budget Constraints	3	3.91	.641
Insufficient technical skill	4	3.84	.847
Maintenance concern	4	3.84	.884
Lack of green material information	5	3.75	.718
Lack of government support	6	3.72	.729
The perception that green materials are low in quality	6	3.72	.924
Lack of awareness	7	3.69	.780
Lack of organization	8	3.66	.902
Aesthetically less pleasing	9	3.59	.911
Low flexibility of alternatives or substitutes	10	3.56	.669
Lack of comprehensive tools and data to compare materials and alternative	11	3.53	.621
Uncertainty in liability of final work	12	3.50	.803
Possible project delay due to sustainability requirement	13	3.44	.878
Time constraints	14	3.34	.701

From Table 3, the results opined that green materials applications in the construction industry are generally facing challenges since all the mean values are above '3' (Neither agree nor disagree) and '4' (agreed). The results indicate that challenges of limited availability of suppliers are ranked 1 with the highest mean; whereby time constraint is ranked last with the lowest mean value. The results find that respondents agreed that the limited availability of suppliers, the high cost of adopting green materials, and budget constraints are the main challenges to green building materials adoption in Malaysia. These three top-ranked challenges are the market-cost-related challenges that cause the slow adoption of green material in the industry. According to Zhang et al. (2011), the use of green building materials costs 3–4% more than common building materials. The exorbitant expenses in the selection of green building materials are one of the key challenges and considerations by the management team as they are accountable for pre-set budget. Hence it is aligned with the findings that the limited availability of suppliers in the market resulting the cost of materials falling on the high side, while the budget will be increased in adopting green building materials. Consequently, the practitioners are facing budget constraints in green materials selections and applications.

CONCLUSION

The rate of adopting green materials in construction projects is low compared to developed countries. In the current Malaysian construction industry, green materials are not widespread. Therefore, an analysis was conducted to identify the types of green materials adopted in buildings. The result shows that the respondents are aware of the types of green material available in Malaysia although the adoption rate is not high, and it explains the previous findings that types of green materials have been adopted in Malaysian buildings. The result concluded that local contractors are active in adopting green materials for building elements of bricks and glasses with above average green materials selection, as to reduce operating energy use, high-efficiency windows and insulation in walls increase the energy efficiency of the building envelope which bring notable impact to the building users in Malaysia.

In comparing the differences between using green materials in buildings to common materials, this research indicates that the significant differences are energy-related differences, which include renewable resources, renewable energy, energy conservation, and energy efficiency. Adopting green building materials in material selection is practicing environmentally responsible and resource-efficient throughout a building's life cycle. The objectives of green buildings are designed to reduce the overall impact of the natural environment and the built environment on human health by efficiently using energy, water, and other resources, and it is aligned with the results. The result strengthens and supports the studies by Marsh (2018) and Chemoxy (2017) on the differences between green materials and common materials.

In addition, the study also identifies the challenges faced by the contractors in green materials adoption. The result of this study shows that the use of green materials in Malaysia's construction industry is challenging. This seems to explain the previous findings that the usage rate of green materials is very low. The result shows that the main challenges faced by the contractor are the limited availability of suppliers, the high cost of adopting green materials, and budget constraints are the most challenging issue. It concluded that market-cost-related challenges are affecting the consideration of green materials adoption by practitioners. It is followed by knowledge and awareness-related challenges. The results are aligned with the studies by Hydes and Creech (2000) that low adoption is perceived from higher costs in green materials selections and is also indirectly affected by the unfamiliarity of the design team and contractors with sustainable construction methods in adopting green materials.

Green building materials adoption is projected to continue growing in Malaysia. This study examined the awareness and understanding of differences between green materials and common materials from the perspective of local contractors. This paper also anticipates highlighting the challenges of green materials adoption in the industry, and hope could give some contributions to the construction participant to increase the adoption of green building materials in Malaysia.

ACKNOWLEDGMENT

The researchers of this article would like to appreciate the journal's editors and the anonymous reviewers for their positive feedback and suggestions for the improvement of this journal.

This research received no specific grant from any funding agency in the public, commercial, or not-for-profit sectors.

REFERENCES

Aathaworld. (2019). *Green building materials Malaysia, design and install.* Aatha World. https://www.aathaworld.com/single-post/Green-Building-Materials-Malaysia-Design-Install

Chan, D. W. M., & Kumaraswamy, M. M. (2002). Compressing construction durations: Lessons learned from Hong Kong building projects. *International Journal of Project Management*, *20*(1), 23–35. doi:10.1016/S0263-7863(00)00032-6

Chemoxy. (2017). *What is low VOC and what are the benefits?* Chemoxy. https://www.chemoxy.com/about-2/knowledge-hub/what-is-low-voc/

Chen, T. L., Eng, P. E. C., Ashrae, F., & Izdihar, A. (2013). *High performing buildings.* Malaysia energy commission headquarters (Diamond Building). HPB Magazine. https://www.hpbmagazine.org/malaysia-energy-commission-headquarters-putrajaya-malaysia

Cort, K. A. (2013). *Low-e Storm Windows: Market Assessment and Pathways to Market Transformation.* Pacific Northwest National Laboratory. doi:10.2172/1095439

CRL. (2018). *7 Sustainable Construction Materials.* CRL. https://c-r-l.com/content-hub/article/sustainable-construction-materials/

Darko, A. (2019). *Adoption of green building technologies in Ghana: Development of a model of green building technologies and issues influencing their adoption.* The Hong Kong Polytechnic University. https://ira.lib.polyu.edu.hk/handle/10397/80543.

Darko, A., Zhang, C., & Chan, A. (2017). Drivers for green building: A review of empirical studies. *Habitat International*, *60*, 34–49. doi:10.1016/j.habitatint.2016.12.007

Emmitt, S., & Yeomans, D. T. (2008). *Specifying buildings: a design management perspective* (2nd ed.). Elsevier. doi:10.4324/9780080569710

Esa, M. E., Marhani, M. A., Yaman, R., Hassan, A. A., Rashid, N. H. N., & Adnan, H. (2011). Obstacles in Implementing Green Building Projects in Malaysia. *Australian Journal of Basic and Applied Sciences*, *10*, 1806–1812.

Franzoni, E. (2011). Materials selection for green buildings: Which tools for engineers and architects? *545. Procedia Engineering*, *21*, 883–890. doi:10.1016/j.proeng.2011.11.2090

GBI. (2004). *What and why green buildings?* Green Building Index. https://www.greenbuildingindex.org/what-and-why-green-buildings

Green Pages Malaysia. (2020). *Directory.* Green pages Malaysia. http://www.greenpagesmalaysia.com/directory/

Hwang, B. G., & Tan, J. S. (2010). Green building project management: Obstacles and solutions for sustainable development. *Sustainable Development*. Advance online publication. doi:10.1002d.492

Hydes, K., & Creech, L. (2000). Reducing mechanical equipment cost: The economics of green design. *Building Research and Information*, *28*(5/6), 403–407. doi:10.1080/096132100418555

Japheth, L. (2013). *St Diamond Building: The green building landmark in Southeast-asia.* JAPHET LIM. http://blog.japhethlim.com/index.php/2013/10/15/st-diamond-building-the-green-building-landmark-in-southeast Asia.

Joseph, P. S., & Tretsiakova-McNally, S. (2010). Sustainable non-metallic building materials. *Sustainability (Basel)*, 2(2), 400–427. doi:10.3390u2020400

Marsh, J. (2018). *What are the main disadvantages of fossil fuels?* Solar News. https://news.energysage.com/disadvantages-fossil- fuels/

MITEC. (2020). *MITEC awarded green building index certification.* MITEC. https://mitec.com.my/press/gbi/

Nikyema, G. A., & Blouin, V. Y. (2020). Barriers to the adoption of green building materials and technologies in developing countries: The case of Burkina Faso. *IOP Conference Series. Earth and Environmental Science*, 410(1), 1–10. doi:10.1088/1755-1315/410/1/012079

Opoku, D. G. J., Ayarkwa, J., & Agyekum, K. (2019). Barriers to environmental sustainability of construction projects. *Smart and Sustainable Built Environment*, 8(4), 292–306. doi:10.1108/SASBE-08-2018-0040

Osaily, N. Z. (2010). *The key barriers to implementing sustainable construction in West Bank.* Prifysgol Cymru University of Wales.

Pulselli, R. M., Simoncini, E., Pulselli, F. M., & Bastianoni, S. (2007). Energy analysis of building manufacturing, maintenance and use: Building indices to evaluate housing sustainability. *Energy and Building*, 39(5), 620–628. doi:10.1016/j.enbuild.2006.10.004

Reddy, B. V. V. (2009). *Sustainable materials for low carbon buildings.* Journal International of Low Carbon Technologies.

SBCI. (2007). Buildings and climate change- status, challenges and opportunities. United Nations Environment Programme.

Sch¨oggl, J. P., Baumgartner, R. J., & Hofer, D. (2017). Improving sustainability performance in early phases of product design: A checklist for sustainable product development tested in the automotive industry. *Journal of Cleaner Production*, 140, 1602–1617. doi:10.1016/j.jclepro.2016.09.195

Sharen, K. (2020). *MITEC Awarded Green Building Index Certification.* New Straits Times. https://www.nst.com.my/property/2020/04/586627/mitec-awarded-green-building-index-certification

Sika Malaysia. (2017). *Malaysia International Trade And Exhibition Centre (MITEC).* Sika Malaysia. https://mys.sika.com/en/project-references/local-projects/malaysia-international-trade-and-exhibition-centre-mitec.html

Suruhjaya Tenaga. (2013). *The energy commission diamond building.* Suruhjaya Tenaga. https://www.st.gov.my/en/details/aboutus/9

Tey, J. S., Goh, K. C., Seow, T. W., & Goh, H. H. (2013). Challenges in adopting sustainable materials in Malaysian construction industry. *International conference on sustainable building asia.* IEEE.

The Economic Times. (2020). *What Is Solar Panel? Definition Of Solar Panel, Solar Panel Meaning.* The Economic Times. https://economictimes.indiatimes.com/definition/solar-panel

The Star. (2011). Diamond Building: A shining example of energy efficiency. *The Star.* https://www.thestar.com.my/lifestyle/features/2011/07/05/diamond-building-a-shining-example-of-energy-efficiency

United Nations. (2012). *Report of the United Nations Conference on Sustainable Development.* United Nations.

Venkatarama, R. B. (2009). Sustainable materials for low carbon buildings. *The International Journal of Low Carbon Technologies, 4*(3), 175–181. doi:10.1093/ijlct/ctp025

Venkatarama-Reddy, B. V., & Jagadish, K. S. (2003). Embodied energy of common and alternative building materials and technologies. *Energy and Building, 35*(2), 129–137. doi:10.1016/S0378-7788(01)00141-4

White, I., & Che, Y. (2011). 3 Is GRC a "Green" Building Material? *Proc. Of The 16th Int. Congress of the GRCA.* Whole Building Design Guide (WBDG). *Evaluating and Selecting Green Products.* https://www.wbdg.org/resources/evaluating-and-selecting-green-products

Williams, K., & Dair, C. (2007). What is stopping sustainable building in England? Barriers experienced by stakeholders in delivering sustainable developments. *Sustainable Development (Bradford), 15*(3), 135–147. doi:10.1002d.308

Wu, Z., Jiang, M., Cai, Y., Wang, H., & Li, S. (2019). What hinders the development of green building? An investigation of China. *International Journal of Environmental Research and Public Health, 16*(17), 3140. doi:10.3390/ijerph16173140 PMID:31466403

Yu, C. (2008). *Environmentally sustainable acoustics in urban residential areas.* [Ph.D. dissertation, University of Sheffield, UK: School of Architecture].

Yudelson, J. (2008). *The green building revolution.* Island Press.

Yusoff, S. (2007). *Sustainable solid waste management: incorporating life cycle assessment as a decision support tool* (Vol. 34). The Ingeniur Board of Engineer Malaysia.

Zainul, A. N. (2010). Investigating the awareness and application of sustainable construction concept by Malaysian developers. *Habitat International, 34*(4), 421–426. doi:10.1016/j.habitatint.2009.11.011

Zhang, X., Platten, A., & Shen, L. (2011). Green property development practice in China: Costs and barriers. *Building and Environment, 46*(11), 2153–2160. doi:10.1016/j.buildenv.2011.04.031

Zhineng, T. (2017). Review of the application of green building and energy saving technology. *IOP Conference Series. Earth and Environmental Science, 100,* 1–4.

Zuo, J., & Zhao, Z. (2014). Green building research–current status and future agenda: A review. *Renewable & Sustainable Energy Reviews, 30,* 271–281. doi:10.1016/j.rser.2013.10.021

KEY TERMS AND DEFINITIONS

Adoption: The action of taking up, following, or using something.

Building: A structure with a roof and walls.

Challenges: A situation that tests the workability.

Construction: The action of building something or a structure.

Environment: The surroundings or conditions of a person or human activity.

Materials: The matter from which a thing is or can be made.

Section 4
Challenges in the Construction Industry

Chapter 12
Resolution of Construction Payment Disputes:
Adjudication in the Kenyan Construction Industry

Chin Ai Ling Shirley
Taylor's University, Malaysia

Myzatul Aishah Kamarazaly
Taylor's University, Malaysia

Naseem Ameer Ali
Massey University, New Zealand

Ali Moossajee
Taylor's University, Malaysia

ABSTRACT

The Construction Industry Payment and Adjudication Act 2012 (CIPAA 2012) has redefined how construction disputes are resolved in Malaysia. The Chartered Institute of Arbitrators (CIArb) in Kenya has long provided Adjudication Rules for the Construction Industry 2003. According Muigua and Muigua, it is not commonly used to resolve commercial disputes in Kenya. This research fills the gap to address curiosity. The chapter studies the trend of contractual adjudication in Kenya, and the potential challenges of implementing statutory adjudication in Kenya for construction payment disputes. The results revealed that QS in Kenya usually are involved in contractual disputes nevertheless commonly refer to negotiation and arbitration. The findings also indicate that adjudication is not a preferred choice of ADR due to cost, time and lack of provisions in the standard form of contract in Kenya. But the findings proved that most QS's will propose adjudication as the preferred method due to the structured manner the rules will be provided in backed by the parliament.

DOI: 10.4018/978-1-6684-8253-7.ch012

INTRODUCTION

The construction industry is no different from any other industry in regard to disagreements. Disagreements arise in this industry for various reasons and can be resolved in many ways. Despite the fact that disagreements are typically amenable to resolution, there are many obstacles and legal considerations that must be taken into account. Employers have disputes with subcontractors, while developers have disputes with investors. Main contractors, numerous consultants, and specialized suppliers throughout the supply chain have disagreed. Regardless of the nature of the dispute, parties would be more receptive to alternative conflict resolution approaches, given their benefits.

ADR is viewed as a viable alternative to litigation in Malaysia for resolving contractual disputes because it is perceived as less expensive, more private, and less likely to result in ill will or animosity. According to Nii and Torgbor (2013), arbitration is the most used alternative dispute resolution method in the construction industry of the United States. The revised standard forms for construction contracts, the Mediation Act, and the Construction Industry Payment and Adjudication Act 2012 (CIPAA 2012) strongly indicate that ADR will be a common feature of construction dispute resolution in Malaysia. The legislature passed CIPAA 2012 on April 15, 2014, and it went into effect on that date. The 'Statutory CIPAA Adjudication' mechanism established by CIPAA 2012 enables aggrieved parties (typically contractors and consultants) to recover unpaid invoices or resolve payment disputes arising from construction contracts. These conflicts may result from non-payment, underpayment, non-certification, or under-certification.

CIPAA follows the "Pay Now, Argue Later" principle. If either party is dissatisfied with the CIPAA Adjudication Decision, it is intended to resolve payment disputes and promptly, efficiently, and summarily facilitate cash flow. Due to the implementation of CIPAA 2012, contractors and consultants who are short on funds will no longer have to wait until the project is completed before bringing legal action against the Main Contractor/Developer.

However, there is a significant contradiction in this ideology in the Kenyan construction industry, with the industry adopting a "Argue Now, Pay Later" mentality, which neither benefits the contractor, who is starving for resources to survive, nor the employer, whose project is stalled and held at ransom by the banks. The various groups in Kenya have established avenues to resolving these disagreements in an amicable "win-win" manner; nevertheless, as Muigua (2011) highlights, parties appear to turn to traditional litigation as a solution, which creates many challenges to the business. It ends up severing relationships between the parties and the employer, having to find another contractor, which becomes even more expensive and time-consuming, compromises the quality of the entire project, and sabotages any future possibility of these two parties working together.

Therefore, this study focuses on "Resolution of Construction Payment Disputes: Adjudication in the Kenyan Construction Industry" to determine whether all parties know their alternatives for settling disputes. Furthermore, the study focused on contractors' understanding of other dispute resolution procedures or their belief that it is their sole option if they refer to litigation. Furthermore, this research investigates whether industry professionals advise their clients and other industry stakeholders on all available dispute-resolution methods and the problems associated with adopting them.

This research is critical in educating individuals in the industry who are unaware that solutions exist for them if they are being mistreated or taken advantage of by their employers over the standard litigation system, which some will avoid resorting to due to the expenses and time involved. This article will be crucial in their comprehension of how to deal with challenges in the future for parties who are aware of adjudication but are unclear on its benefits or why they should use it in their times of need. Thus, it will give contractors the conviction and motivation to undertake more work because they know they can "defend" themselves, which is essential for the Kenyan construction industry.

Problem Statement

A disagreement is unavoidable in any business. As a result, steps have been taken to resolve these disagreements. Conflict management encompasses any process that can lead to resolving a dispute, from informal conversations between the parties to increasing formality and more directive external intervention to a full court hearing involving rigid procedural standards.

According to Muigua (2018), due to the survival of Kenyan customary laws, they must be included in the country's legal structure to defend people's rights. On this basis, federal laws have now recognized and protected traditional dispute resolution processes. The Kenyan construction sector appears to rely on negotiation and litigation more than any other mode of dispute resolution. Negotiation is a non-binding way of resolving disagreements without an outside facilitator. This means neither side is bound to stay in the relationship if they choose to end it. As a result of their frustration, the parties are more inclined to resort to lawsuits. Litigation has various problems, including a lack of privacy and financial and time limits. Despite their availability, contractors and other parties hesitate to adopt effective dispute resolution alternatives.

The Kenyan construction industry's workers must know their options in a dispute. This will enable them to arrive at non-biased and well-informed decisions about addressing the problems. Other proven effective dispute resolution methods must be investigated and these issues addressed if they are not using them. Wasunna (n.d.) has highlighted that the labour force in Kenya has a void in the skills available due to the lack of education available. This study presumes that the following reasons cause a lack of adaptation of adjudication as the preferred method of dispute resolution: lack of awareness and education; wrong/insufficient advice being given; corruption, and lack of resources.

This paper focused on the possibility of implementing statutory adjudication in the Kenyan construction industry. Therefore, the objectives of the research are as follows.

1. To investigate the trend of adjudication in the Kenyan construction industry,
2. To identify the challenges of implementing alternative dispute resolution in Kenya.
3. To propose the application of statutory adjudication in Kenya for construction payment disputes.

Literature Review

According to Biruk et al. (2018), adjudication is a construction contract mechanism that allows the party who has been disputed (typically the contractor or consultant) to recover unpaid invoices or settle a payment dispute such as underpayment, non-certification and non-payment, which are all examples of non-compliance.

According to Mah and Woo (2013), adjudication has a robust judicial component because the adjudicator hears all sides and makes a conclusion. When parties are willing to terminate the contract, arbitration and litigation are usually the last alternative, rather than adjudication, which distinguishes them. Adjudication, conversely, is concerned with resolving typical payment disputes in building projects—a straightforward method and a temporary solution that should not disrupt or postpone the contract or the work.

NECESSITY OF ADJUDICATION

Judgement

Swiftness is exhibited in judging. Due to the 28-day time limit imposed by adjudication procedures, they may not be suitable for complex and highly technical disputes. Even if the parties agree to extend the deadline to 42 days, six weeks is still insufficient to adjudicate a significant claim (Fisher, 2017). There is no risk of having to pay the other side's expenses. Chief Financial Officers (CFOs) will be relieved to learn that if they lose a construction contract dispute, they will not be required to pay the other side's legal fees. Thus, a party with a limited budget can prosecute its claim in a manner that would have been impossible in a court of law (Fisher, 2017).

Privacy

If the technology and construction court reviews the adjudicator's decision, adjudication is private. This makes keeping commercially sensitive information private easier than in a courtroom setting. As an added benefit, it can help protect a company's reputation if its products are not the standard required (Hugh, 2017).

Referrer has Power of Surprise

The referring party has the power of surprise as the referrer. It is possible to issue a Notice of Adjudication fast, which is favourable news for the referrer but unfavourable for the respondent. If referees can make inconvenient decisions, they have a strategic advantage. Advocacy notices can be sent before the respondent has had time to gather information and arrange their response, putting them at a disadvantage (Hugh, 2017).

OBSTACLES IN THE IMPLEMENTATION OF ADJUDICATION

Lack of Legislation and Statutory Force

Ahmad Arzlee et al. (2019) highlighted that when CIPAA 2012 and its statutory rules for adjudication were first drafted, their primary goal was to provide a mechanism for timely payment and effective, speedy, and low-cost dispute resolution, aiming to improve cash flow. Therefore, introducing adjudication was necessary to create a system capable of enforcing decisions and guaranteeing payment. However, adjudication without statutory force is unlikely to be effective, as demonstrated by the experience of other nations with similar regime legislation that requires all parties to comply with adjudication, thereby ensuring that it will have a significant effect.

Lack of Provisions in Standard Form of Contract

In his paper presented at the DRBF 14th Annual International Conference on "Dispute Boards: Realizing the Potential for Dispute Avoidance" at The Fullerton Hotel, Rajoo (2014) highlighted that only contracts written according to the FIDIC model are eligible for the FIDIC—DAB procedure, which has flaws. However, in Malaysia, many contracts, particularly those with lower values and simpler formats, are plagued by disputes over payment. There are no "adjudication" provisions in these contracts that are not FIDIC based (other than the reference of the dispute to the SO). In some instances, customized contracts lack dispute management and resolution clauses.

He further emphasized that the "adjudicator" in disputes between the Contractor and the Employer in the Malaysian JKR 203 Form of Contract is the Superintending Officer, who is the Contract Administrator and a client employee. "adjudicator" in the 1980 Joint Contracts Tribunal Form, where the architect serves as both the contract administrator and an adjudicator when a dispute arises between the employer and the contractor, is similar to this position. Only contracts written following the FIDIC model are eligible for the FIDIC-DAB procedure, which has some shortcomings. However, in Malaysia, payment disputes plague many contracts, particularly those with lower values and simpler formats. They do not have FIDIC-based "adjudication" provisions in these contracts (other than a reference of the dispute to the SO). Custom contracts sometimes lack provisions for resolving disputes or managing claims (Rajoo, 2014).

The Registered and Unregistered Matters for Adjudication

Mazani et al. (2019) further elaborated that the practice of 'pay when paid, pay if paid' is mitigated by establishing a cheaper and faster dispute resolution system in the form of adjudication, which reduces payment defaults. Unless an application to the High Court under Section 16 is made, the parties must abide by the adjudication decision and pay the disputed amount in the interim.

Mazani et al. (2019) found that the CIPAA 2012 is effective and that payment disputes may be addressed promptly using basic adjudication procedures. The statistics for adjudication applications are shown in Table 1. Adjudication, a less costly and faster method of resolving disputes, reduce payment defaults, hence decreasing the "pay when paid, pay if paid" practice. Unless an application is made to the High Court under Section 16, the parties must abide by the adjudication decision and pay the disputed amount.

Table 1. The registered and unregistered matters for adjudication 2014-2018

Timeframe	No. of Registered Matters	No. of Unregistered Matters
As of 31/12/14	29	-
1/1/15 – 31/12/15	181	13
1/1/16 – 31/12/16	447	16
1/1/17 – 31/12/17	704	7
1/1/18 – 15/4/18	224	10
Total	1605	46

(Mazani et al., 2019)

BENEFITS OF THE IMPLEMENTATION OF STATUTORY ADJUDICATION

Timely Payment on Construction Projects

Mazani et al. (2019) stated, concerning the consequences and benefits of CIPAA 2012 on the Malaysian construction industry, that since financial flow plays a crucial role in the completion of work, the primary significance of the new act is to facilitate regular and timely payments of construction projects. In addition, over time, parties become more aware of their financial obligations. Due to CIPAA 2012, construction companies share a common objective: ensuring timely and regular project payments.

Cheaper and Faster Dispute Resolution

In the same study, Mazani et al. (2019) further elaborate that the practice of 'pay when paid, pay if paid' is mitigated by establishing a cheaper and faster dispute resolution system in the form of adjudication, which reduces payment defaults. Except a Section 16 application is made to the High Court, the parties must comply with the adjudication decision and pay the disputed amount in the interim.

Decision is Binding, Unlike Other ADR Methods

In their literature review, Ansary et al. (2017) stated that there has been much success in adjudicating construction disputes through adjudication. Adjudication was first implemented in the UK in 1996 by the Housing Grant, construction, and Regeneration Act (Construction Act) to serve the construction industry better. This helped projects succeed and strengthened the relationships among project team members. In addition, countries such as Singapore, Australia, South Africa, and Malaysia have been included. In contrast to other dispute resolution processes that rely solely on the good conduct of the parties, participants must adhere to the adjudicator's decision because it is final and binding. Due to the ineffectiveness of mediation, adjudication has replaced it.

Application of Statutory Adjudication in African Countries

According to Ansary et al. (2017), construction dispute adjudication has been successful. The Housing Grant (Construction & Regeneration Act) 1996 introduced adjudication in the United Kingdom to better serve the construction industry. This contributed to the success of initiatives and strengthened relationships among project team members. In addition, countries such as Singapore, Australia, South Africa, and Malaysia have been included. In contrast to other dispute resolution processes that rely solely on the good conduct of the parties, participants must adhere to the adjudicator's decision because it is final and binding. Due to the ineffectiveness of mediation, adjudication has replaced it.

Furthermore, in a study to find the significant sources of construction disputes in the construction industry in South Africa, Aigbavboa and Thwala (2014) stated that the five leading causes of claims have been identified because disputes usually arise when a contracting party rejects a claim. Unrealistic expectations, ambiguous contract documents, poor communication between participants, a lack of team spirit, and a failure to respond quickly to changes and expected conditions are some of the reasons.

Promote Adoption of Statutory Adjudication in African Countries

Enforcement of Adjudicator's Decisions

Maritz and Hattingh (2015) highlighted that because of South Africa's courts' vigorous enforcement of adjudicator's decisions and the industry's persistent use of contractual adjudication procedures, a legislative framework could be established to support adjudication practice in the South African construction industry.

The binding nature of adjudication decisions (unless or until appealed) can significantly promote its adoption in the construction industry. South African jurisprudence and the construction industry will benefit greatly from the adoption of the proposed legislative framework for adjudicating disputes in construction contracts on an interim basis and requiring the adjudicators' decisions to be enforced pending the final determination of disputes by arbitration, litigation, or agreement (Maritz & Hattingh, 2015).

Parties in the construction industry will have more confidence in the adjudication procedure if its decisions are upheld. According to the article South Africa Won't Meet the Demand for Adjudicators in the Construction Sector | MDA Law (n.d.), South African courts have supported the adjudication process by repeatedly enforcing adjudicators' decisions by determining that adjudicators' decisions are enforceable as matter of contractual obligation, and by acknowledging that providing notice of dissatisfaction does not prevent enforcement. The parties must comply with and immediately implement the arbitrator's ruling.

Adjudication not being statutory has many gaps compared to adjudication enforced by an act of parliament, which is the greatest selling point of statutory adjudication. Research by Hattingh and Maritz (n.d.) states that South African adjudication has been used extensively since its introduction into the construction industry. However, other countries that have implemented adjudication have found that adjudication without statutory force is not likely to be effective in South Africa.

Research Gaps

After extensive research on adjudication, statutory adjudication, and alternative dispute resolution worldwide, it is evident that little to no research has been carried out on adjudication with a focus on construction payment disputes in Kenya. Although The Chartered Institute of Arbitrators has developed the adjudication rules in Kenya, there is no mention of the proposition of statutory adjudication in the country despite the increase in construction payment disputes referred to litigation, negotiation, or mediation.

The gaps in previous research emphasize the importance of this research study, which will not only raise awareness about adjudication among professionals in the Kenyan construction industry but will pave the way for future research on the topic and possibly the implementation of statutory adjudication in Kenya, which will serve as a lifeline for contractors, subcontractors, and other parties in the event of construction payment disputes.

Research Methodology

According to Indeed (2021), a researcher must make several decisions when developing a study approach. There are several factors to consider when selecting a data approach, such as whether to employ quantitative or qualitative data. Irrespective of the research topic, the collected data will be in the form of numbers or text descriptions, and researchers can opt to collect either numbers or only text descriptions.

Given the subjectivity and opinion-based nature of the research topic and the fact that the questions must be tailored to the interviewee to understand their individual experiences and opinions, the qualitative research method is the most suitable for this research. This chosen research method gives the flexibility necessary to gather as much information as possible from the selected interviewees, as this research paper intends to dive deep into the possibility of statutory adjudication being implemented in Kenya.

In order to acquire the most pertinent data for this study and to obtain a first-hand perspective on the current trends in the disputes and their resolutions faced by contractors in Kenya, this study captured the opinions and experiences of practising consultant Quantity Surveying firms in the Kenyan construction industry in order to comprehend the concepts, opinions, or experiences of the parties, should disputes arise on construction projects, and to discuss the viability of standardized dispute resolution mechanisms.

The sample population for this study is professional quantity surveyors registered with Kenya's Board of Registration of Architects and Quantity Surveyors (BORAQS). To gain a broader perspective on the application of statutory adjudication in Kenya, the targeted audience includes quantity surveyors with varying years of experience to gather the experience of individuals who have a large amount of practical experience in the industry as well as opinions of those who have recently been educated with the latest technologies and modes of practice. The study attempted to include individuals from the commercial and public sectors to compare their points of perspective. Five (5) individuals responded to the authors' invitation to participate in this study.

Given the time difference of five hours between Kenya and Malaysia, the author could not conduct physical interviews with the respondents. Consequently, these respondents were allowed to respond to the interview questions through a virtual Zoom meeting in a semi-structured format or reply to the structured interview document via E-mail or WhatsApp. Thus, two (2) respondents chose a virtual interview, while the remaining three (3) decided to send the completed document by E-mail or WhatsApp. The general information gathered from the participants in this study is presented in Table 1 below:

Research Framework

Figure 1 below shows the systematic flowchart of the framework implemented for this research.

Research Design

To ensure that the interview has a flow and to provide a plan of study that permits accurate assessment, the researcher can make sure that the conclusions are justified. Roopa and Rani (2012) established that the design of interview questions should be given considerable thought. For a questionnaire to be effective, it must be carefully prepared and refined across several phases. These phases are shown in the figure below:

Table 2. Summary of respondents' profiles

No.	Position	Company Type	Sector	Experience
R1	Assistant Quantity Surveyor	Government	Public	5 years
R2	Quantity Surveyor	Consultant	Private	25 Years
R3	Quantity Surveyor	Consultant	Private	6 Years
R4	Quantity Surveyor	Consultant	Private	6 Years
R5	Founder / Managing Director	Consultant	Private	39 Years

Figure 1. Research framework

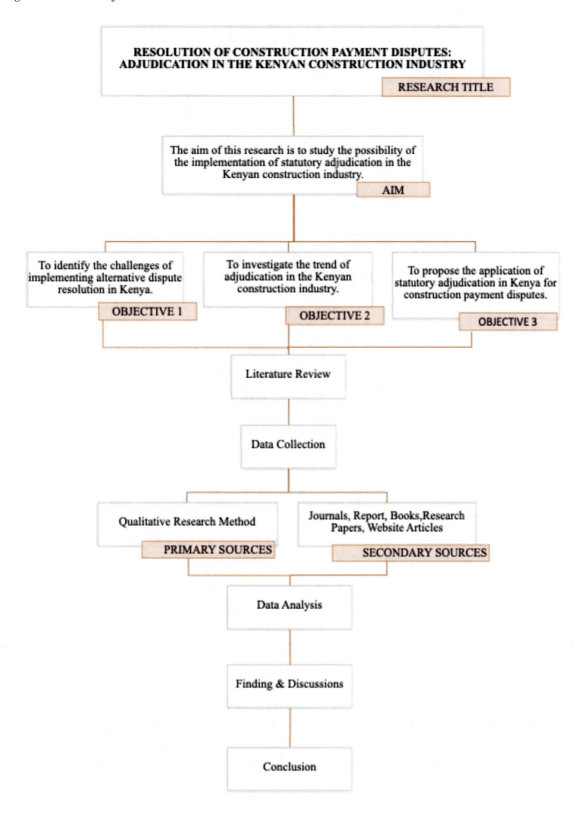

Figure 2. Research design

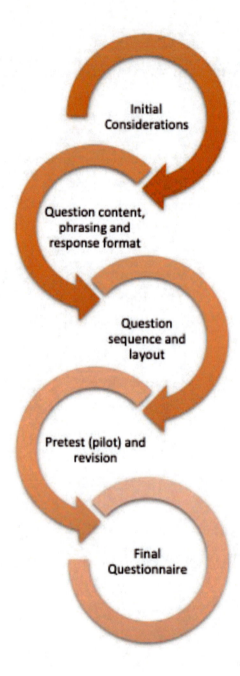

Data Analysis Method

Thorne (2000) describes qualitative research as focusing on inductive reasoning processes to understand and shape the meanings that can be obtained from the data collected. According to Akinyode and Khan (2018), there are numerous approaches to analyzing qualitative data, but the basics are the same. They explained that data should be collected, transcribed, and coded before being analyzed. After the data has been coded, it can be interpreted and classified into themes.

Thematic coding was utilized for analyzing the collected data in this study as it systematically highlights the salient point of the respondents and distinguishes similarities or variations in specific reasoning or argument and opinion.

Ethics

According to Clifford et al. (2010), confidentiality and anonymity are two of the most important ethical concerns. Participants must be assured that all data collected will be kept under lock and key or on a computer database accessible only by a password; that information supplied will remain confidential, and participants will remain anonymous (unless they prefer otherwise); and that participants have the right to withdraw from the research at any time without explanation. Committing to providing participants with an overview of the study findings at the end of the project and then keeping that promise is good research practice.

Orb et al. (2001) elaborated that when conducting an interview, researchers must consider both the potential benefits and risks to the participants, given that this research involves the participants' experiences of disputes and times of conflict, which may have resulted in trauma. For instance, during an interview with a victim of abuse, the interviewer may experience anguish. In this situation, the researcher faces an ethical conundrum: should the interview be prolonged to gain more insight into the subject of study, or should it be terminated to provide guidance or refer the participant to an appropriate therapy or counselling agency?

Findings and Discussion

This section focuses on analyzing responses received from the selected target audience. A qualitative study approach will be utilized to assess respondents' responses to several questions about present adjudication trends, the problems of implementing ADR, and the future implementation of statutory adjudication in Kenya. Data analysis aims to interpret and analyze the collected data to achieve the research aim. The collected data were analyzed and presented in tables so that the findings could be comprehended. Coding was used to categorize and generalize the data by identifying themes and keywords. Thus, each of the study's objectives was related to a topic based on interviewee responses. Additionally, the collected data was analyzed and discussed with reference to the literature review to provide a comprehensive research perspective.

Trend of Adjudication in The Kenyan Construction Industry

This section focuses on the findings of the study. To analyze the trend of adjudication in the Kenyan construction sector' by analyzing the responses from the interviewees. These findings were assigned with thematic codes and presented in tables in the order of the interview questions.

Reasons for the Implementation of ADR in the Kenyan Construction Industry

All five (5) respondents had been involved in disputes while working as Quantity Surveyors on projects in Kenya. All five (5) respondents claimed that the arguments they have been involved in have been over money difficulties. This is congruent with the findings of a study undertaken by Biruk et al. (2018),

Table 3. Causes of construction payment disputes in Kenya

Category A- Trend of Adjudication in the Kenyan Construction Industry						
Coding	Theme	Interviewees				
		R1	R2	R3	R4	R5
A1a	Payment	✓	✓	✓	✓	✓
A1b	Delays		✓		✓	
A1c	Loss & Expense				✓	
A1d	Contract Termination					✓

who indicated that underpayment, non-certification, and non-compliance are all significant causes of payment disputes in the construction business. Respondent R1 explained that these payments could occur at various stages of the construction project. Furthermore, respondent R2 noted that delays are a key factor in Kenya's construction business. Delays can lead to disagreements over awarding extensions of time (EOT) or the amounts billed for liquidated damages, leading to payment conflicts. Respondent R4 claimed that they had similar arguments on delays, which led to payment disputes based on the loss and expense suffered due to these delays when the cause of the delay was the employer. Respondent R5 reported that, in addition to payment concerns, they disagreed about contract termination and the choices available when work on-site has been interrupted.

Awareness Level of the Process of Adjudication

Biruk et al. (2018) defined adjudication as a construction contract procedure that allows the offended party to collect unpaid bills or resolve a payment dispute. In addition, Mah and Woo (2013) assert that this implies that adjudication has a substantial legal component because all parties are heard, and a decision is made.

In comparison, respondent R1 stated that the process involves a third party and that "…the adjudicator is brought in to decide the matter being disputed…" demonstrates that their understanding was fair. Respondent R2, in addition to the previously stated facts, added that the decision is based only on the facts presented to the adjudicator. Although this is most appropriate, there are some exceptions where there can be a call for a hearing or cross-examination, as established by Olswang (2017). Respondent

Table 4. Awareness level of the process of adjudication

Category A- Trend of Adjudication in the Kenyan Construction Industry						
Coding	Theme	Interviewees				
		R1	R2	R3	R4	R5
A4a	Not Aware			✓		
A4b	Involves a Third Party	✓	✓		✓	✓
A4c	Judgement Made by an Adjudicator	✓	✓		✓	✓
A4d	Decision Made Based on Presented Facts		✓		✓	
A4e	Binding Nature of the Decision					✓

R4 had a similar understanding of adjudication, talking about the involvement of a third party, a decision being made, and the basis of the decision being the facts presented to the adjudicator. Respondent R5 contributed further to the discussion of the decision's binding nature. This is a critical factor of adjudication, with the decision being partially binding unless otherwise appealed through arbitration or litigation. Respondent R3 confessed that they were unaware of the adjudication process due to their lack of experience with the ADR method.

Challenges in the Implementation of ADR in Kenya

After understanding the current trend of ADR in Kenya, the next objective of the research paper is to identify the challenges of implementing ADR in Kenya. Section B of the interview focused on questions on the reasons for not adopting adjudication in Kenya, given that none of the respondents had used this method to resolve disputes in the past, the reluctance of parties to adopt the ADR method and the effect of adjudication and arbitration on the relationship between parties in the industry. Finally, based on the findings and literature review, a conclusion was drawn on the effect of adjudication and arbitration on the relationship between the parties.

Reasons not to Adopt Adjudication and Other Methods of ADR.

All five (5) respondents highlighted that the main concern in implementing adjudication as a method of resolving disputes is the cost associated with selecting this ADR method over the other commonly implemented ones, such as negotiation. As analyzed in the questions in category "A", the respondents' primary preference of ADR methods is either negotiation with a zero-cost impact or mediation with relatively minimal costs. The respondents highlighted that they would only consider advising adjudication or arbitration as a last resort if the parties do not agree. The literature review shows that cost is a major factor in the implementation of adjudication. However, Keng and Kah (2018) found that adjudication is the most cost-effective option for the parties compared to arbitration and litigation.

Four respondents stated that the time required to resolve the issue through adjudication is critical to minimize project delays. This contradicts the findings by Keng and Kah (2018), who utilized CIPAA 2012 as an example of a lifeline for contractors, resulting in zero delays. Even within the process, adjudication is the only method of dispute resolution with a definite timeline from application to decision, whereas the other procedures are open-ended.

Table 5. Reasons not to adopt adjudication and other methods of ADR.

Category B - Challenges of implementing alternative dispute resolution in Kenya						
Coding	Theme	Interviewees				
		R1	R2	R3	R4	R5
B1a	Cost	✓	✓	✓	✓	✓
B1b	Time	✓	✓	✓	✓	
B1c	Relationship between parties	✓				
B1d	Not mutually beneficial in outcome		✓			
B1e	Binding nature of decision				✓	

Table 6. Threat level of adjudication to relationship

Category B - Challenges of implementing alternative dispute resolution in Kenya						
Coding	**Theme**	**Interviewees**				
		R1	**R2**	**R3**	**R4**	**R5**
B3a	Significant chance of termination of the relationship	✓	✓	✓		✓
B3b	Unlikely to impact the relationship				✓	

Threat Level of Adjudication and Arbitration on the Relationship Between Client and Contractor

As demonstrated in the preceding summary, most respondents believe that adjudication and arbitration are more likely than negotiation and mediation to dissolve the client-contractor relationship. Respondent R1 stated that regardless of their views on the significant risk, there is less of a threat to the relationship if the dispute is resolved so that both parties benefit something from the outcome, even through adjudication or arbitration. Respondent R5 provided an additional reason for the threat without negotiations between the parties. In these procedures, a third party makes a decision that may be perceived as unjust by the losing party. This is consistent with the research conducted by Spagler (2003), who found that without an "out-of-court" resolution, it is unlikely that a collaborative or integrated solution to the problem will be found in adjudication, as it is a lose-lose situation.

Conversely, respondent R4 believes that adjudication is unlikely to affect the relationship between the client and contractor, even with adjudication and arbitration, in contrast to the highest litigation threat level. The respondent stated in the post-interview discussion that parties in Kenya are open to using ADR methods despite the cost and time involved because they have witnessed the damage that litigation has caused to the relationships between clients and contractors and between contractors and subcontractors involved in previous disputes.

Factors Hindering the Implementation of ADR Methods

Based on the literature review, it has been established that implementing ADR has several challenges. Figure 3 summarises these factors. This question in the interview consists of two parts; the first requires respondents to select the most significant factor impeding the application of ADR in Kenya in terms of people, support, and the process; the second requires respondents to explain, under the same three categories, why they selected this factor as the most significant. The analysis was segmented to determine the respondents' perspectives on each category.

Respondents R1 and R3 both opinioned that the fear of severing the relationship between the client and the contractor is the most significant. Respondents R2 and R5 stated that the parties' lack of expertise and knowledge of the parties on advantages and the process of the options available to them is the hindering factor. Respondent R4, on the other hand, stated that the lack of experience is due to two aspects: the parties do not have sufficient experience in disputes to know what works best and have not investigated every possible option to resolve the dispute to know the significant benefits of using ADR methods.

Respondents R2, R3 and R4 agreed that the most significant factor hindering the implementation of ADR methods in Kenya is the lack of government support and policies. This is consistent with the

Figure 3. Factors hindering the implementation of ADR in Kenya

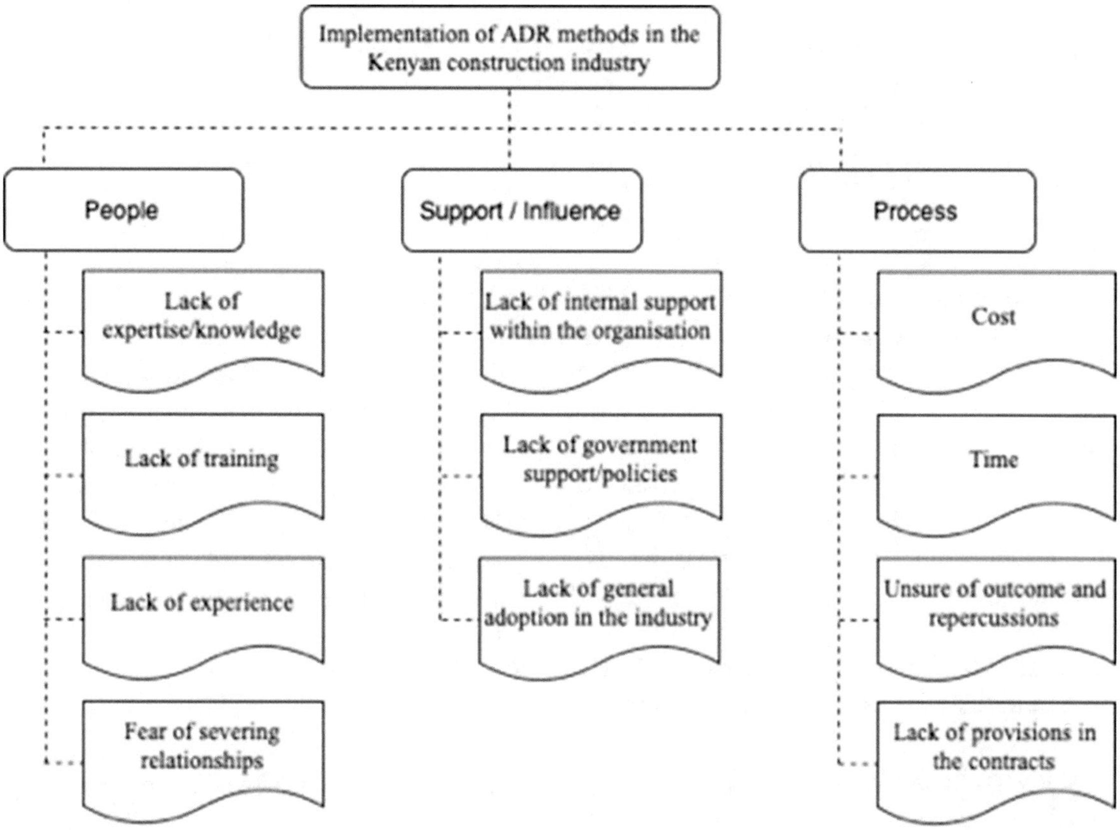

Table 7. Factors concerning people

Coding		Interviewees				
		R1	R2	R3	R4	R5
B4a-1.a	Lack of expertise		✓			✓
B4a-1.b	Lack of training					
B4a-1.c	Lack of experience				✓	
B4a-1.d	Fear of severing relationships	✓		✓		

research done by Rajoo (2014), who stated that only countries whose contracts and policies allow for adjudication and ADR methods to be utilized as an avenue to resolve disputes could use them, but it is ultimately out of the hands of the parties themselves as these policies are made by the government. Respondent R1 stated that the lack of industry adoption is a barrier to adopting ADR applications, which leads back to the issue of the influence of other parties on the use of ADR methods. Respondent R5 pointed out that the organization did not accept using ADR methods due to business culture and policies.

All five (5) respondents cited the uncertainty of the decision's outcome and repercussions as the most significant factor inhibiting the implementation of ADR in Kenya. In contrast to most of the research con-

Table 8. Factors in relation to support

Coding		Interviewees				
		R1	R2	R3	R4	R5
B4a-2. a	Lack of internal support within the organization					✓
B4a-2.b	Lack of government support/policies		✓	✓	✓	
B4a-2.c	Lack of general adoption in the industry	✓				

ducted, such as the study by Mah (2016), there is an increase in the number of cases registered for adjudication, and a contributing factor is that adjudication is "less risky" than litigation and other non-ADR methods.

In addition to this, respondent R1 stated that time is a hindering factor to implementing ADR methods which are in contrast with research conducted where Gould (n.d.) has stated that in the case of adjudication, the process is bound by time frame, whereas litigation it is in the hands of the court. Respondent R3 added that cost is a major factor in selecting ADR methods. Respondent R5 presented a different perspective in which the requirements in the contract in Kenya restrict the application of ADR in Kenya as it cannot be implemented without the essential provisions. This is consistent with Rajoo (2014), who indicated that terms, such as those included in FIDIC contracts, that allow for dispute resolution must be included.

Proposition of the Application of Statutory Adjudication in Kenya for Construction Payment Disputes

This study's third objective is to propose applying statutory adjudication in Kenya for construction payment disputes to comprehend the respondents' views on Kenya's preparation for implementing statutory adjudication and their perspectives on the future of adjudication and ADR in Kenya.

Table 9. Factors in relation to the process

Coding		Interviewees				
		R1	R2	R3	R4	R5
B4a-3.a	Cost			✓		
B4a-3.b	Time	✓		✓		
B4a-3.c	Unsure of outcome and repercussions	✓	✓	✓	✓	✓
B4a-3.d	Lack of provisions in the contract					✓

Table 10. Readiness of parliament to implement statutory adjudication in Kenya

Category C - To propose the application of statutory adjudication in Kenya for construction payment disputes						
Coding	Theme	Interviewees				
		R1	R2	R3	R4	R5
C2a	Ready to implement		✓		✓	
C2b	Not ready to implement			✓		
C2c	Unsure of readiness to implement	✓				✓

Readiness of Parliament to Implement Statutory Adjudication in Kenya

Respondents R2 and R4 believe that the parliament in Kenya is ready to implement statutory adjudication by creating an act of parliament. Respondent R4 stated, " I think the sooner they implement an act for adjudication, the faster adjudication will be used as a common ADR method which will be very good for the construction industry overall". However, according to respondent R3, the Kenyan parliament is unprepared for this. Their reservations were based on the fact that parties in Kenya prefer to settle disputes through "simpler" means, such as negotiations and mediation. This indicates little public demand for the legislature to establish such a law. According to respondent R1, contractors and clients are "set in their ways" and would be difficult to persuade to change. As a result, respondents R1 and R5 questioned the legislature's readiness to implement this act. Respondent R5 contends that imposing obligatory adjudication is not necessary. Even though its implementation benefits the industry, it is unclear whether the legislation is ready.

Action Necessary for the Implementation of Statutory Adjudication in Kenya

All five (5) respondents agreed that the first step towards the adoption of adjudication and other ADR methods is to receive training and workshops from both the government and the institutions on the benefits of each dispute resolution method available as well as the processes and procedures involved so that the consultants can make informed decisions when advising their clients on the best method to pursue based on the specific circumstances. Respondent R3 noted that the specific training they expect to receive from the government should be incorporated into university curricula so that even inexperienced graduates are aware of these opportunities. Respondents R3 and R4 emphasized that the government's formulation of policies on the procedures to resort to ADR methods when confronted with construction payment disputes should be revised to indicate these alternatives, such as in the provisions of Kenya's standard forms of contract. Respondent R5 explained further that Kenyan courts must uphold appealed adjudication decisions. This will enhance the confidence of parties that use adjudication as a means of dispute settlement, and it is congruent with research conducted in a South African case study by Maritz and Hattingh (2015).

Most Practical Method for Solving Construction Disputes in the Future

In addition to adhering to the dispute resolution methods they have experienced in the past and consider to be the most practical for the Kenyan construction industry at present, all five (5) respondents agreed that if statutory adjudication were implemented in Kenya, it would be the preferred method for resolv-

Table 11. Action necessary for the implantation of statutory adjudication in Kenya

Category D - Future of Adjudication and ADR in Kenya						
Coding	**Theme**	**Interviewees**				
		R1	**R2**	**R3**	**R4**	**R5**
D2a	Training and workshops	✓	✓	✓	✓	✓
D2b	ADR training in the university curriculum			✓		
D2c	Formulation of policies by the government			✓	✓	
D2d	Court to uphold decisions made by adjudicators.					✓

Table 12. Most practical method in solving construction disputes in the future

Coding		Interviewees				
		R1	**R2**	**R3**	**R4**	**R5**
D5b.a	Litigation					
D5b.b	Negotiation			✓		
D5b.c	Mediation		✓	✓		✓
D5b.d	Arbitration	✓			✓	
D5b.e	Adjudication	✓	✓	✓	✓	✓

ing future disputes. Respondent R1 expressed his view on statutory adjudication in Kenya by stating, "I believe adjudication can accomplish this more expediently and cost-effectively than arbitration, which is an important factor to consider and may therefore be the future." Other countries have effectively implemented legislation for the construction payment act to resolve these issues (Chian et al., 2016).

CONCLUSION

This research concludes that adjudication is the most practical method for resolving construction disputes in Kenya because it can be implemented faster and cost-effectively than arbitration. Similarly, in countries such as Malaysia, where statutory adjudication has been implemented, the incidence of adjudication in construction disputes has increased substantially, according to the reviewed literature. The review highlights the challenges associated with implementing statutory adjudication and the necessity of overcoming these challenges. Given the prevalence of construction payment disputes on projects, the data acquired from this study's respondents indicate a general interest in the Kenyan construction industry for simplifying payment dispute resolution.

There is a need for the general education of the parties in the industry about the options available to them in resolving disputes and the benefits of each option; therefore, informed decisions can be made rather than relying on standard methods merely because they are comfortable. The research concludes that if statutory adjudication is implemented in the country, many disputes will likely be resolved through adjudication. The ultimate objective of this research paper is to create awareness and educate parties in the industry on adjudication and the alternative dispute resolution methods available for resolving construction payment disputes in Kenya.

Recommendation for Future Studies

Future research should target a more diverse population, including contractors and developers, to determine their perspectives on the issue of statutory adjudication. To gain a broader understanding of the parties in Kenya, the number of respondents to the survey should be re-evaluated. It is recommended that future research should adopt a mixed-method approach to achieve a balance between obtaining in-depth responses on issues and reaching out to the masses to obtain a wider perspective of the parties in the Kenyan construction industry. Future studies should focus on developing a framework for implementing statutory adjudication if it is proved that both parties are willing to use adjudication on a broad scale to resolve construction payment disputes and if the government is interested in assisting this legislation.

REFERENCES

Ahmad, A., Ibrahim Kulliyyah, A., & Ahmad Ibrahim Kulliyyah, M. (n.d.). *Alternative Dispute Resolution in the Malaysian Construction Industry.*

Ahmad Arzlee, H., Hamimah, A., Abdul Izz, M. K., & Noor Aisyah, A. M. (2019). *Challenges against Adjudication Decisions on Payment Disputes within the Construction Industry.* IOP. doi:10.1088/1755-1315/233/2/022035

Aigbavboa, C. O., & Thwala. (2014). *An Exploratory Study of the Major Causes of Construction Disputes in the South African Construction Sector*, 311–318.

Akinyode, B. F., & Khan, T. H. (2018). View of Step by step approach for qualitative data analysis. *International Journal Of Built Environment And Sustainability.* https://ijbes.utm.my/index.php/ijbes/article/view/267/130

Ansary, N., Balogun, O. A., & Thwala, W. D. (2017). *Adjudication and arbitration as a technique in resolving construction industry disputes A literature review View project.* Seek. doi:10.15224/978-1-63248-139-9-55

Appleton, J. V. (1995). Analysing qualitative interview data: Addressing issues of validity andreliability. *Journal of Advanced Nursing, 22*(5), 993–997. doi:10.1111/j.1365-2648.1995.tb02653.x PMID:8568076

Atkinson, D. (2000). The challenges facing statutory adjudication. *Construction News.* https://www.constructionnews.co.uk/archive/the-challenges-facing-statutoryadjudication-30-03-2000/

Bhandari, P. (2020). What is Qualitative Research? *Methods & Examples.* https://www.scribbr.com/methodology/qualitative-research/

Biruk, S., Jakowski, P., Czarnigowska, A., Jiang, W., Wu, W., Wei, M., Hadi, N. A., Othman, K. F., & Dadi, A. M. (2018). The Perception on the Importance of Construction Industry Payment and Adjudication Act (CIPAA) 2012 Towards Remedying Payment Disputes: A Research on Subcontractors in Kuching, Sarawak. *IOP Conference Series. Materials Science and Engineering, 429*(1), 012105. doi:10.1088/1757-899X/429/1/012105

Brand, M. C., & Davenport, P. (n.d.). *A proposal for a "Dual Scheme" of statutory adjudication for the building and construction industry in Australia.*

Bryan, C. Leighton, & Paisner. (2014). *The continued growth of statutory adjudication is good news for a global construction industry.* BCL Plaw. https://www.bclplaw.com/en-US/insights/the-continued-growth-of-statutoryadjudication- is-good-news-for-a-global-construction-industry.html

Cannon, S., & Black, I. (2014). *Statutory Adjudication.* Chartered Institute of Arbitrators.

Chartered Institute of Arbitrators. K. (n.d.). *Adjudication.* CIArb Kenya. https://ciarbkenya.org/adjudication/

Chian, L. K., Tunku, U., & Rahman, A. (2016). *Benefits Of The Construction Industry Payment And Adjudication Act 2012 (Cipaa) And Its Impacts To Payment Problem In Construction.* Cipaa.

Clifford, N. J., French, S., & Valentine, G. (2010). *Key methods in geography.* 545.

Davies, L. (2018). *Adjudication versus other approaches to construction disputes.* Pinset Masons. https://www.pinsentmasons.com/out-law/guides/adjudication-construction-disputes

Desai, N., & Kageni, E. (2022). *Arbitration procedures and practice in Kenya: overview.* Practical Law. https://uk.practicallaw.thomsonreuters.com/5338955?transitionType=Default&contextData=(sc.Default)&firstPage=true

Dona, E., & Elvitigalage Dona, A. (2008). *Women's career advancement and training & development in the construction Industry.* Salford. http://usir.salford.ac.uk/id/eprint/9822/

Ehsan Che Munaaim, M. (2019). *Five years on: A review of statutory adjudication in Malaysia.* HKA. https://www.hka.com/review-of-statutory-adjudication-inmalaysia/

Fisher. (2017). *What Are The Benefits And Risks Of Adjudication?* Fisher Cogginswaters. https://www.fisherscogginswaters.co.uk/blog/article/248/what-are-the-benefits-andrisks- of-adjudication

Gamage, A. (2020). *Alternative Dispute Resolution in Construction Contracts.* Sihela Consultants. https://sihelaconsultants.com/alternative-dispute-resolution-inconstruction/

Gill, P., Stewart, K., Treasure, E., & Chadwick, B. (2008). Methods of data collection in qualitative research: interviews and focus groups. *British Dental Journal 2008, 204*(6), 291–295. doi:10.1038/bdj.2008.192

Gould, N. (n.d.). *Adjudication in Malaysia.* Fenwick Elliott. www.fenwickelliott.co.uk

Harold. (2017). *Statutory Adjudication 101.* HLP Lawyers. https://hlplawyers.com/statutory-adjudication-101/

Harper James Solicitors. (2020). *A Guide To The Adjudication Process.* Harper James Solicitors. https://hjsolicitors.co.uk/article/guide-to-adjudication-in-construction-disputes/

Hattingh, V., & Maritz, M. J. (n.d.). *Should the application and practice of construction adjudication be underpinned by legislative intervention in the South African construction industry?* SCL. www.scl.org.uk

Hugh. (2017). *Construction Adjudication.* Hugh James. https://www.hughjames.com/service/construction/construction-adjudication

Indeed. (2021). *What Is Research Methodology and Why Is it Important?* Indeed.com. https://www.indeed.com/career-advice/career-development/researchmethodology

Iryani Mohamed Nasir, N. I., Ismail, Z., & Muhd Fadhlullah Ng, N. K. (2018). *View of Comparative Analysis On Construction Adjudication Systems Towards Effective Implementation Of Statutory Adjudication In Malaysia.* UTM Journals. https://journals.utm.my/mjce/article/view/16025/7499

Keng, T. Z., & Kah, S. (2018). Effectiveness Of Construction Industry Payment And Adjudication Act (CIPAA) In Remedying Payment Issues Among Sub-Contractors. INTI JOURNAL-BUILT ENVIRON-MENT Faculty of Engineering and Quantity Surveying, 2(5).

Kennedy, P. (2006). Progress of statutory adjudication as a means of resolving disputes in construction in the United Kingdom. *Journal of Professional Issues in Engineering Education and Practice*, *132*(3), 236–247. doi:10.1061/(ASCE)1052-3928(2006)132:3(236)

Leonard, E., & Gardiner, H. (2017). *Statutory adjudication of construction contracts in the UK*. Womble Bond Dickinson. https://www.womblebonddickinson.com/uk/insights/articles-and-briefings/statutory-adjudication- construction-contracts-uk

Lim, C. F. (2016). *Resolution Of Construction Industry Disputes: Arbitration, Statutory Adjudication Or Litigation In The Construction Court?* Mondaq. https://www.mondaq.com/constructionplanning/ 467878/resolution-of-construction-industry-disputes-arbitration-statutoryadjudication- or-litigation-in-the-construction-court

Mah, R. (2016). *Construction Adjudication in Malaysia: Faster and Cheaper Dispute Resolution*. Mahwengkwai. https://mahwengkwai.com/construction-adjudication-inmalaysia-faster-andcheaper/? utm_source=Mondaq&utm_medium=syndication&utm_campaign=Linked In-integration

Mah, R., & Woo, M. (2013). *Construction adjudication in malaysia*. Mahwengkwai. https://mahweng-kwai.com/construction-adjudication-in-malaysia/

Maritz, M. J. (2003). *Adjudication of disputes in the construction industry*. AC. https://www.up.ac.za/media/shared/Legacy/sitefiles/file/44/2163/8121/innovate3/inn bl7879.pdf

Maritz, M. J., & Hattingh, V. (2015a). Adjudication in South African construction industry practice: Towards legislative intervention. *Journal of the South African Institution of Civil Engineering*, *57*(2), 45–49. doi:10.17159/2309-8775/2015/v57n2a6

Maritz, M. J., & Hattingh, V. (2015b). Adjudication in South African construction industry practice: Towards legislative intervention. *Journal of the South African Institution of Civil Engineering*, *57*(2), 45–49. doi:10.17159/2309-8775/2015/v57n2a6

Matende-Omwoma, R. (n.d.). *The Story of Land Adjudication in Kenya: Paradoxes, Uncertainties and Reversionary Tendencies. – Institution of Surveyors of Kenya*. ISK. https://isk.or.ke/2021/01/26/the-story-of-landadjudication-in-kenya-paradoxes-uncertainties-and-reversionary-tendencies/

Mazani, Q. A., Sahab, S. S., & Ismail, Z. (2019). *Trends of Adjudication Cases in Malaysia*. doi:10.1051/ matecconf/2019

MDA Law. (n.d.). *South Africa won't meet the demand for adjudicators in the construction sector*. MDA Law. https://mdalaw.co.za/southafrica-wont-meet-the-demand-for-adjudicators-in-the-construction-sector/

Mewomo, M., & Maritz, M. (2017). The Experts' Views On Factors Influencing The Effective Imple-mentation Of Statutory Adjudication. *Journal of Construction Project Management and Innovation*, *7*(1), 1877–1892.

Mohamed Nasir, N. I. I., Ismail, Z., & Muhd Fadhlullah Ng, N. K. (2018). Comparative Analysis on Construction Adjudication Systems Towards Effective Implementation of Statutory Adjudication in Malaysia. *Malaysian Journal of Civil Engineering, 30*(2), 202–216. doi:10.11113/mjce.v30n2.475

Muigua, K. (2011). *Dealing with Conflicts in Project Management.*

Muigua, K. (2018). *Traditional Dispute Resolution Mechanisms Under Article 159 Of The Constitution Of Kenya 2010 Kariuki Muigua.* Idea. https://www.idea.int/africa/conflict_management_en.cfm,

Muigua, K. (n.d.). *Heralding a New Dawn: Achieving Justice through effective application of Alternative Dispute Resolution Mechanisms (ADR) in Kenya.* Metros.. http://www.metros.ca/amcs/international.htm

Odacc.ca. (n.d.). *Adjudication Process.* ODACC. https://odacc.ca/en/adjudication-process/

Orb, A., Eisenhauer, L., & Wynaden, D. (2001). Ethics in qualitative research. *Journal of Nursing Scholarship, 33*(1), 93–96. doi:10.1111/j.1547-5069.2001.00093.x

Pickavance, J. (2015). *A Practical Guide to Construction Adjudication.* 768. https://books.google.com/books/about/A_Practical_Guide_to_Construction_Adjudi.html?id=ieHNCgAAQBAJ

Rajoo, P. D. S. (2014). *Dispute Boards & Adjudication in Malaysia: An Insight into the Road Ahead by Professor Datuk Sundra Rajoo.* AIAC. https://www.aiac.world/news/108/Dispute-Boards-&-Adjudication-in-Malaysia-:- An-Insight-into-the-Road-Ahead-by-Professor-Datuk-Sundra-Rajoo

Roopa, S., & Rani, M. (2012). Questionnaire Designing for a Survey. *The Journal of Indian Orthodontic Society, 46*(4_suppl1), 273–277. doi:10.1177/0974909820120509S

Shearing, M. (2018a). *A guide to adjudication in construction…* Burnetts Solicitors. https://www.burnetts.co.uk/blog/a-guide-to-adjudication-in-constructioncontracts

Shearing, M. (2018b). *A guide to adjudication in construction contracts.* Burnetts. https://www.burnetts.co.uk/blog/a-guide-to-adjudication-in-construction-contracts

Skaik, S. (2016). *(PDF) Taking statutory adjudication to the next level: a proposal for review mechanism of erroneous determinations.* Research Gate. https://www.researchgate.net/publication/305223084_Taking_statutory_adjudication_to_the_next_level_a_proposal_for_review_mechanism_of_erroneous_determinations

Spagler, B. (2003). Adjudication. *Beyond Intractability.* https://www.beyondintractability.org/essay/adjudication

Thorne, S. (2000). Data analysis in qualitative research. *Evidence-Based Nursing, 3*(3), 68–70. doi:10.1136/ebn.3.3.68

Wasunna, M. K. (n.d.). Kenya has a massive skills gap: how it can fix the problem. *The Conversation.* https://theconversation.com/kenya-has-a-massiveskills-gap-how-it-can-fix-the-problem-91170

Chapter 13
A Study on Building Inspection and Building Defect Rectification From the Contractors' and House Buyers' Sentiments

Kenn Jhun Kam
Taylor's University, Malaysia

Xiao Jing Lim
Taylor's University, Malaysia

Tze Shwan Lim
Taylor's University, Malaysia

Lam Tatt Soon
Taylor's University, Malaysia

ABSTRACT

Competitive and fast-track construction environments with quantity without quality lead to the occurrence of building failure and defective works. The necessity of building inspection and rectification of the defect figure is becoming predominant in the vacant possession of new residential buildings. This paper study on cost involvement and worthiness of building inspection and building defects rectification from the contractors' and house buyers' perspectives to resolve the arising problem of building failure and defective works. The research is a mixed-method approach, it comprises qualitative and quantitative methods. Interviews were conducted with contractors, whereas a questionnaire survey was carried out with house buyers as targeted respondents of this study to obtain data and information. Both contractors and house buyers' perspectives on building inspection and building defect rectification have been observed. From this study, everyone can better understand the cost involvement of the common defects and have their standard to measure the worthiness of building inspection.

DOI: 10.4018/978-1-6684-8253-7.ch013

INTRODUCTION

Over the centuries, the building has had a significant and multipurpose connection worldwide. The primary purpose of a building is to provide an environment with privacy, security, and protection. Occupants would not consider much about the nature of the buildings. However, with civilization development in times, people started to have more and more rigorous requirements towards building construction projects as the building has become one of the basic needs for daily operation. There are numerous different forms of housing in Malaysia, and some other countries have their interpretation of various residential properties ("Types of Residential Properties in Malaysia", 2015).

Increasing the population of people greatly impacts the high demand for residential buildings as residential buildings is one of the basic human necessities. Residential building construction projects play an essential role in Malaysia's economic growth, as it is one of the main pillars of construction that contribute to the country's economy. According to the Department of Statistics Malaysia Official Portal (2022) quarterly construction statistics, the value of completed construction projects contracted to RM29.5 billion in the first quarter of 2022. The residential buildings subsector contributed 24.2 percent to the approximate RM7.14 billion value of construction work done among other subsectors in the quarter. With the increase in the completion of residential buildings, the possibility of defective works found in buildings is also increasing. For instance, the attendance of deficiencies in buildings will raise the need for building inspection and defect rectification.

Defective works can be found in a new residential building or first-hand dwelling even though it is newly constructed. In this research study, a new residential building and first-hand dwelling mainly describe the building's defect liability period (DLP) at vacant possession (VP) within 12 months to 24 months or others stated in the sale and purchase agreement (SPA). It starts from the date the homeowner received delivery of the VP and keys of the property (Teoh, 2021). During this period, the developer is responsible for rectifying any shortcomings in structures that might cause by shoddy workmanship or defective materials.

In construction, there is several aspects that cause the necessity of building inspection. End users' minor involvement in setting functional and quality requirements has cultivated a reputation of inferior quality at consumption. Construction defects can cause an adverse contribution to project performance, time, and cost multiply (Forcada et al., 2015). Rotimi et al. (2015) pointed out that adequate supporting information implies that the number of deficiencies in new residential buildings is substantial and requires careful attention. Additionally, real estate agents and sellers may conceal a potential buyer's inherent fundamental flaws in the property.

What is the purpose of building inspection? Lau (2020) defined building inspection as an assessment carried out by a professional team to investigate the fundamental causes of identified building defects and subsequently provide rectification solutions to ensure the building can remain in service without posing safety hazards to its occupants.

Buildings are assets whose worth fluctuates depending on the quality of the defect rectification undertaken. The value of a building will increase with appropriate rectification and vice versa. Likewise, it would not always be economical to dismantle and restructure to upgrade existing ones (Lateef, 2009). Hong (2016) indicated that if the inspection is done as early as VP, the cost of inspecting and rectifying the building is lower. Hence, remedial works are likely to occur for efficient performance, especially for new residential housing, although the activities incur additional time and cost from a short-term perspective.

In conclusion, a building inspection is essential to identify faulty works; hence, avoiding building defects imposes significant influences on industry and society. Conducting inspections not only to ensure the safety of building residents and occupants, and they should able to discover any faults early on and remedy them to ensure the users' safety and health. As a result, this study aims to study the contractors' perception of building inspection and building defect rectification, the benefits of building inspection and building defect rectification bring to the new house owners, and the possible challenges regarding building defect rectification might faced by the house owners. Lastly, to come out with an analysis of the comparison of building inspection and building defect rectification to show the worthiness of building inspection for a new house.

PROBLEM STATEMENT

In Malaysia, construction deficiencies are a common problem associated with the provision. For residential buildings, it will be very relatable to housing provisions. One of the worst struggles a house buyer may have is defective building issues. However, new houses should ideally be defect-free (Ismail et al., 2015). Ahmad (2004) mentioned that building deficiencies and failures result from a variety of factors. They are still a serious problem that the construction sector must address.

The building inspector discovers defective structures and elements at the building handover. As most developers would like to save their costs by allocating professional building inspectors to check on their completed building development, the developers will instruct the site supervisor or site officer to be the representative to inspect the work done by contractors. In actual practice, developers often rely on their representatives instead of appointing certified building surveyors for a good check on the buildings before a Certificate of Practical Completion is issued to the contractors. Undeniably, some developers appointed building inspectors to inspect the completed buildings (IE, 2015). However, the developers designate them to check on the sample unit. The sample unit will be most likely to comply with the specifications, materials, etc., thoroughly according to the building specifications. Kang (2019) mentioned that "it is common for us property buyers to feel enthralled by the design and quality of work displayed by a show unit. However, the unfortunate reality is that the actual unit delivered could sometimes be very different compared to what we have seen in the exhibition".

Furthermore, fast-track construction projects are becoming more predominant in the construction industry, especially when the builders' completion time is of the essence. Ali and Kam (2011) noticed that recent residential buildings are poorly constructed despite rapid industrial progress. According to Forcada et al. (2014) findings, the most prevalent construction faults are associated with structural stability and improper roof and exterior installation, which are caused by poor craftsmanship rather than the quality of the materials or goods supplied. The builders can efficiently resolve common defects during the defect liability period, but if the element occurs with latent defects, it may pose a safety hazard to the occupants.

In addition, the contractors choose cheaper materials as they are desperate for a low price in return for a high quantity outcome instead of considering the quality measure of the materials. According to Ismail et al. (2015), residential buildings were rapidly being constructed in response to high market demand over other types of buildings. However, the developments suffered from poor building quality. Along with the market competitiveness of the construction industry, it led to an influx of inexperienced labor on-site, regardless of skilled or unskilled labour (Forcada et al., 2012). The only reason for contractors to bring in these labors is to meet project requirements in a short amount of time. However, this results in a noticeable gap between shoddy craftsmanship with the expected quality (Chang, 2021).

Apart from that, certain house buyers lack the knowledge of rights and obligations as property purchasers. One of the problems frequently leads to disagreements and misunderstandings between the developer and the buyer. Seeing that the buyer only chooses to point out the defective and shoddy works when exceeding DLP. In addition, disputes and complaints often arise owing that the home buyers' failure to report the defective works to the developer as soon as they realize the problems before DLP. Moreover, lacking professional knowledge and understanding. Some home buyers prefer to inspect the building on their own and likely rely on visual inspection. Although visual inspection is used in the industry, professional building inspectors will still conduct structural inspections to ensure the evaluation of the building condition is accurately assessed. House buyers depend on self-inspection, which may result in the defects being unidentified and cause the defect to be unrectified.

Despite numerous building inspections and building defect rectification, relevant studies have been conducted by researchers all over the world, but the particular determinants of building inspection and building defect rectification problems in the construction industry in Malaysia are still left with gaps in be completely addressed with following objectives:-

[1] To study contractors' perception of building inspection and building defect rectification.
[2] To study the advantages of building inspection and building defect rectification for new house buyers.
[3] To identify the challenges of house buyers on building defect rectification.
[4] To understand the worthiness of building inspection for a new house.

LITERATURE REVIEW

Advantages of Building Inspection for New House Buyers

Residential building deficiencies are general problems correlative with housing provision in Malaysia (Ismail et al., 2015). It is beneficial for new house buyers to conduct building inspections on their properties. However, they should be clear on the legitimate rights available in Malaysia.

In Malaysia, several government policies are designed for house buyers, especially in building inspection. The Ministry of Urban Wellbeing, Housing, and Local Government's Tribunal for Housing and Strata Management is where a house buyer can ask for assistance, remedy, or reimbursement from the developer or the seller. According to the Housing Development (Control & Licensing) Act of 1966 (Act118) and Regulation, the buyer may seek the remedy of any fault, shrinkage, or other defects discovered with the building during the DLP (CIDB Malaysia, 2017).

Meanwhile, for strata property, house buyers can claim damages with the Strata Management Tribunal through the Ministry of Housing and Local Government for issues such as defects in common properties or the developer's failure to examine defects besides submitting claims with the Tribunal for Homebuyer Claims. The cost of common property rectifications is compensable by the HDA retention sum and an additional retention sum through the Commissioner of Buildings (Choong, 2020).

Mohit et al. (2010) reported that building inspection is crucial to measure the contentment of end-users. This is due to the majority of housing construction errors resulting from shoddy work, which is directly attributed to developers and contractors (Forcada et al., 2012). Therefore, the developer is encouraged to be transparent and accountable for building conditions towards defects before the purchasers decide to secure the properties. Moreover, the findings of a survey conducted by Sulaiman et al. (2012) proved that building work and materials impact customer satisfaction. As a result, building assessment not only safeguards the customer's interests but also enhances the level of workmanship among builders and developers. The presence of high-quality housing is essential since it affects occupants' quality of life. Therefore, buyer interests must be secured (Ahmad et al., 2011; Idrus & Ho, 2008).

Radzuan et al. (2011) study pointed out that a condition survey report serves to examine the building's construction materials and quality. Owing to the majority of new home buyers are ready to settle into their new residence as soon as the property developers release VP. The visual inspection could reveal any construction deficiencies. Che Ani et al. (2014) research revealed that the inspected terrace houses are in poor condition, although the residential buildings were recently completed. Adding on, the general review of shortcomings in this article revealed that recently constructed properties may encounter several deficiencies (Sommerville et al., 2004). Craig in Rotimi et al. (2015) article, underlined that new residential buildings were frequently possessed by new house buyers with extremely high levels of faults, which made them unsatisfied with the overall quality. Therefore, it is significant for house buyers to appoint a building inspector for the quality check, or they may have self-inspection throughout the buildings.

Building inspection enables the house buyers to make good use of the DLP as the defective works are liable under developer and contractor obligations. A building inspection can help the house buyers determine foreseeable defects that might be costly for the buyer to rectify (Lawrence, n.d.). Besides, it ensures the house buyers understand each of their building element's usable life better to stay ahead of maintenance in the future (Robert B. Greene et al., n.d.). House buyers can prevent these costs by bringing awareness to the advice and implementing the necessary precautions. As a result, it can help the house buyer save money by lowering lifecycle costs (Macj, n.d.).

Radzuan et al. (2011) stated that the building assessment report is a detailed document that includes a list of defects, illustrations, a building plan, and suggestions for repair work. The house buyer can utilize the report to monitor the developer or contractor hired to execute the necessary rectification work. This is due to the assessment report being prepared by the professional assessor and it will save a lot of time for the house buyer to determine the defective works accurately. Reifenrath (2020) said that building inspectors work promptly to guarantee the house buyer can receive inspection results faster than expected. Moving on, Macj (n.d.) highlighted that a home inspection service could help a prospective homeowner save time in various ways. To begin with, determining whether the property satisfies the homeowner's needs can take considerable time. Adding on, a home inspector's inspection report can ensure an accurate assessment of the property without squandering time. Besides, the maintenance requirements can be completely outlined in a house inspection report. Therefore, it shortens the time for the homeowner to move into the property.

Robert B. Greene et al. (n.d.) stated that the building condition assessment creates safer resident conditions. Lawrence (n.d.) opined that a housing inspection reveals hazardous conditions in a house, including asbestos, mold, or other dangerous materials, which could result in additional costs for repairs and potential medical expenses that can be prevented. Radzuan et al. (2011) mentioned that the building condition report would state the physical status of the building element and whether the element need for maintenance. Hence, knowing the inherent safety hazards during the inspection could help the house buyer to save money in the long run. A home buyer can also have a clear mind of the element or structure of the building regarding the capacity to meet regulatory and performance requirements. It can ensure that the existence of each component in the space is safe for the occupants to occupy (Radzuan et al., 2011). Referring to Reifenrath's (2020) article, building inspections will advise new buyers on managing all of the property's appliances, such as pipes and cables that lead to the appliances. Therefore, building inspection can assist the house buyer in eliminating buildings in poor safety conditions.

Advantages of Building Defect Rectification for New House Buyers

House buyers shall fully comprehend the current limitations of legal rights available for building defect rectification to recognize the need for the approaches. The practical limitations and rights can educate house buyers on how to avoid financial loss and fulfill their obligations. The Defect Liability Period (DLP) explained as a warranty period where the developer has the liability to fix any defects. It starts from the date the homeowner received delivery of vacant possession and keys of the property (Teoh, 2021). During DLP, the developer is responsible for rectifying any shortcomings in structures that might cause by shoddy workmanship or defective materials. Similarly, Alejo (2012) stated that the DLP or rectification period usually starts from the date of vacant possession (VP). During the DLP, the developer or contractor is deemed to return to the site and rectify the defects. Different terminology is used for the term "Defect Liability Period" in the industry, including the 'defects correction period', 'maintenance period' and 'rectification period' (Pinsent Masons, 2011).

In Malaysia, newly developed houses are protected by the DLP, as specified in Clause 30 of Schedule H of the Housing Development Act (HDA) (Radzuan et al., 2011). The HDA 2015 defined the DLP as the warranty period of recently completed buildings. Under Schedule G and H of the HDA, the DLP is two (2) years, which is twenty-four (24) months from the date the homeowner receives the keys to access the residential building. Schedule G applies to landed buildings, whereas Schedule H refers to high-rise buildings. The homeowner of the building shall inspect for any damage, defects, and faulty workmanship within twenty-four (24) months and report to the developer within the period said. Then, the developer must rectify the defects without extra charges to the homeowner (Choong, 2020). In addition, the DLP in HDA is twenty-four (24) months, however, the exact timeframe of the DLP still depends on the terms that the house buyer had signed in the SPA (REHDA Institute, 2018). Besides, the house buyer must record any construction defects discovered in the Defect Form that the developer delivers during VP. The house buyer needs to hand in the form to the developer for remedial work within thirty (30) days based on the DLP clause in the SPA (Lopez, n.d.).

Patent defects are apparent within DLP, where the defects may be identified in time for the house owner to take action against the developer under the warranty terms and conditions of the housing contract. Therefore, claiming damages for patent defects is generally more straightforward as they have fewer problems. Patent defects are more commonly coped with due to regular inspections. Although it is generally the contractor's responsibility to discover defects and fix or 'snag' the works as they progress, the client is contractually bound to notify the contractor of the defects. Once informed, the contractor must correct them within a reasonable timeframe (Suttling, 2020). In a general contract, the reasonable timeframe is twenty-four (24) months of the DLP after VP.

Latent defects are shortcomings that cannot be found with reasonable care or investigation after some time. In line with Chan (2002), when the relevant limitation period expired and the latent defects become evident, it became challenging to get compensation for loss corresponding to latent defects. Additionally, the latent defects were only discovered after the developers have sold the completed building to the client or house buyers. Besides, Sufian and Rozanah (2008) marked that the DLP is relatively considerable, which may provide buyers with quite reasonable protection; however, there is a problem of latent defects, which may appear only after two years. It is unreasonable for the house buyers to cover the expense of the defects, especially if the defects occur after the defects liability period expired or if the defects are due to the negligence of construction parties (Zolkafli et al., 2014).

The Limitation Act of 1953 specifies in Section 6A, which enables an extension of three years from the date of latent defects discovery to initiate the action with the condition precedent. The conditions include the claim for faults that do not result in personal injury; the action is initiated after the six years limitation from the date of the occurrence of latent defects; the action must be lodged within fifteen years of the occurrence of latent damages following Section 24A.

During the DLP, the house buyer reports any deficiencies to the developer, who determines whether there are defects in the works. If the developer admits that they are defects caused by the contractor, then they may give notice to the contractor to make good the defects within a reasonable time (Designing Buildings, 2021). Choong (2020) suggested that the homeowner shall go around the unit and check every area when the homeowner gets possession of the property and notify the developer as soon as the defects are detected. The homeowner must submit a written complaint to the Developer to arrange for the contractor back to the site to remedy the defective works without any extra charges to the homeowner (Teoh, 2021). At the end of the DLP, the house buyer receives a schedule of defects from the developer, which list the defects that have not yet been remedial and agree with the contractor on the date by which they will be rectified the remaining defect works.

Moreover, renovations should not be conducted by the owner during the DLP because they may exacerbate flaws and developers might decline to compensate for the cost of remedial. To allow the new owner to use the defect liability claim in the event of a property sale during a DLP, the first-hand owner must transfer the right to claim under the DLP to the new owner (Choong, 2020). Besides, the home buyer allows hiring third party to repair the defects if the developer is unresponsive to the submitted defect report. The buyer can claim the rectification cost from the developer's lawyer as there is a retention sum equivalent to 5% of the SPA price (Choong, 2020).

Challenges of House Buyers on Building Defect Rectification

Cost Constraints

Building defect rectification brings cost constraint challenges and financial burdens to the house buyers to treat the damages in the buildings (BCA, 2022). The expenses of addressing the shortcomings are considerable (Rotimi et al., 2015). Hence, past researchers like Chanter and Swallow (2008), Josephson and Hammarlund (1999), and Mills et al. (2009) have shown that the cost of defect rectification could cost the house buyer four to twenty percent or above even though the occupied space is newly completed building. According to Wordsworth (2001), the component's shrinkage rate and the corresponding markup in the cost of rectification are likely without an early response to such a defect. Besides, Anthony in Mok's (2013) report opined that the house buyers would risk incurring significant repair costs and the value of the building will decrease in the future if they choose to overlook defects at the beginning. Moreover, Ali et al. (2010) noticed that rectification costs would impact by the building height or size. The cost of the tools and equipment needed to conduct rectification would increase as the height of the building increased (Skinner, 1982).

Time

Rotimi et al. (2015) pointed out that owners of residential buildings need to pay attention to the occurrence of defective works. The owner requires to allocate some time for the contractor to rectify the defects. This will disrupt the owner's planning, which may get the owner to be frustrated. Besides, delay in executing rectification works at the right time will cause a burden to the occupants. The finding is in line with Narayan (2004), which argued that failure or delay in rectification works at the appropriate time may lead to different consequences.

Weather Conditions

Extreme weather conditions are one of the aspects that influence the workmanship and productivity of construction workers (Dai et al., 2009). This will result in another challenge for the house buyer to tackle due to the delay in the overall planning of the house buyer to occupy the residence. In addition to impacting the quality of the work, an extremely hot environment will also cause cracks in the wall surfaces that expose to high temperatures (Hong, 2016). Hong (2016) further explained that high temperatures would evaporate the moisture and water in the concrete.

Health and Safety

The fact that the house buyer had moved into the residence, he only identified some defects to address. If failed to rectify the defects, the defects may cause health and safety hazards as well as bring a lot of inconveniences to the residents. Therefore, the rectification works shall start as soon as the defects are detected. However, the construction and rectification works may produce biological pollutants, gases, and airborne particles that may endanger the respiratory system of the occupants. Construction projects and restoration activities in indoor environments can unfavorably impact building occupants by emitting airborne particles, biological pollutants, and gases. It is essential to plan and proceed accordingly for indoor environmental quality and avoid exposure during these operations (CDC, 2013).

Gap of Literature Review

Table 1. The gap in previous studies on building inspection and building defect rectification from the contractors' and house buyers' sentiment

Previous Study Title	The gap of Previous Study	Author(s)
Investigate of Defects in New Buildings in Malaysia	To analyse the correlation between defects and costs in new builds.	(Hong, 2016)
Evaluating Defect Reporting in New Residential Buildings in New Zealand	The challenges may be faced by homeowners on rectifying the defects. The cost implications of defects discovered during the handover of new residential structures.	(Rotimi et al., 2015)
The Importance of Building Condition Survey Report for New House Buyers	The quantitative research approach in collecting house buyers' opinions or understanding on the legal binded advantages.	(Radzuan et al., 2011)

RESEARCH METHODOLOGY

Research Process

The flow chart in Figure 1 demonstrates the process from the beginning to the end of the research.

Figure 1. Research process

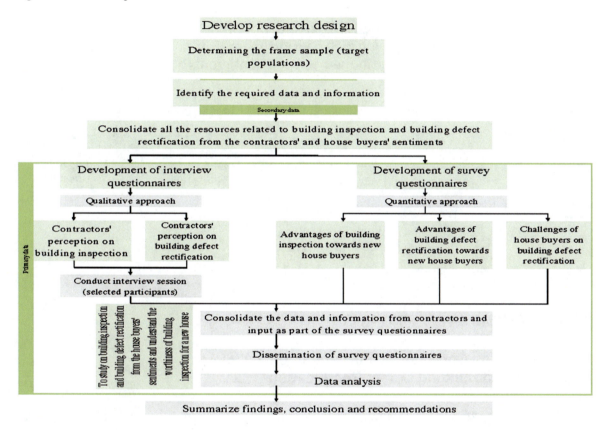

Research Technique

The research technique used in this research study is a mixed-method. It adopts both qualitative and quantitative research approaches, which will be used to determine the outcomes of each of the objectives and aims of the study. The researcher will implement both research approaches to collect primary data and information from two main groups of respondents. This paper will conduct secondary research to gather literature articles from other researchers as well as relevant sources to support and prove documents. In general, open-ended and closed-ended questions will be used to collect statistical and text analysis data. In this study, the researcher will design a similar set of questions for contractors and house buyers for cost analysis and comparison on the worthiness of building inspection, as well as perform the qualitative method for the interview, whereas quantitative method to conduct the survey.

RESEARCH FRAMEWORK

The flow chart in Figure 2 displays the framework of the research plan and enables the researcher to construct and investigate the research problem.

Figure 2. Research framework

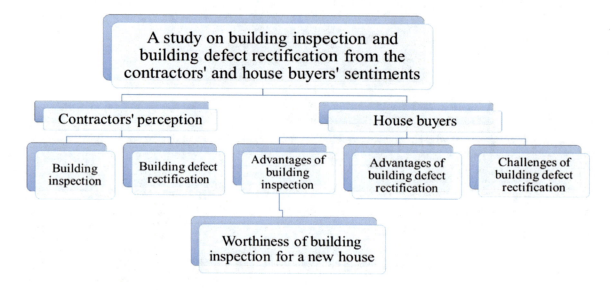

DATA ANALYSIS & KEY FINDINGS

Key Findings on Contractors' Perception on Building Inspection and Building Defect Rectification

From the list of defects shown in Table 2, there are common defects. The common defect is also known as a latent defect. According to Meor Hasan et al. (2016), latent defect is a structural defect that is obvious and foreseeable to a reasonable inspection and is discoverable upon investigation. All the respondents marked that hairline cracks and uneven painting are typical defects the employer (developer) found during the building inspection. In addition, R1 and R2 ranked hairline cracks in 4 scales and 5 scales out of 5 scales, which hairline cracks are often common and very common to be found during building inspection out of other defects listed above. Next, uneven paint is ranked 1 scale, 2 scales, and 5 scales out of 5 scales, which is ranked R3, R1, and R2, respectively. Furthermore, R1 and R2 indicated that leakages and door and window issues are typical defects found by the employer during the building inspection. Lastly, R2 ranked broken tiles in a 5 scale, as the very common defects in building inspection. The defects listed in Table 2 are supported by the common defect groups covered in the checklist of QLASSIC standards under architectural works.

Table 2. Summary of responses on category A – coding group 1

Category A: Contractors' perception on building inspection				
Coding Group 1: Type of defects		**Respondent**		
Themes	**Sub-Themes**	**R1**	**R2**	**R3**
Defects found by the employer (developer)	A3a-i Leakages	✓	✓	
	A3a-ii Hairline cracks	✓	✓	✓
	A3a-iii Door and window	✓	✓	
	A3a-iv Uneven paint	✓	✓	✓
	A3a-v Broken tiles		✓	
Rank the defects' common appearance	A3b-i Rank 1-not common			✓
	A3b-ii Rank 2-once common			
	A3b-iii Rank 3-occasionally common			
	A3b-iv Rank 4-often common	✓		
	A3b-v Rank 5-very common		✓	✓

Based on the responses of the respondents, the cost of rectification for each commonly mentioned defect by the respondents is listed as follows. First, the hairline cracks estimated rectification cost is RM10/m2 to RM30/m2. Second, uneven paint finishes estimated rectification cost is RM6/m2 to RM45/m2. Third, uneven or broken floor tiles estimated rectification cost is RM80/m2. Forth, the door or window estimated rectification cost is RM100/unit or may replace entirely new. Last, the leakage estimated rectification cost is RM20/m2. The data were extracted to fulfill the questionnaires for the house buyers regarding their perceptions on the worthiness of building inspection for a new house.

Table 3. Advantages of building inspection: legitimate rights

[*Level of Awareness: 5 = Extremely Aware; 4 = Moderately Aware; 3 = Somehow Aware; 2 = Slightly Aware; 1 = Not Aware At All]										
Advantages of Building Inspection towards New House Buyers		**Level of Awareness**					**TR**	**Remark**	**RII**	**Rank**
		EA	**MA**	**SHA**	**SA**	**NAAA**				
		5	**4**	**3**	**2**	**1**				
ADVANTAGES OF BUILDING INSPECTION – LEGITIMATE RIGHTS										
1	I aware of Housing Development (Control & Licensing) Act of 1966 (Act118) and Regulation enable house buyer to seek for remedy works of any defects discovered with the building during the Defect Liability Period.	16.67%	30%	29%	14%	11%	114	Somehow Aware	0.536	1
2	I aware that Professional Report by Tribunal for Homebuyer Claims (THC) can assess the quantum of building defects and enable home buyers to get quicker, easier and cheaper solutions to disputes with developers.	10%	22%	31%	18%	19%	114	Somehow Aware	0.464	2
									1.000	

Key Findings on Advantages of Building Inspection for New House Buyers

According to Table 3, the advantages of building inspection towards new house buyer regarding legitimate rights was tested for the level of awareness and ranked. There are mainly two legitimate rights that are compared. The mean score of both legitimate rights is very close to each other. House buyers' awareness of the Housing Development (Control & Licensing) Act of 1966 (Act118) and Regulation ranked first among the others, with a mean score of 3.281. Choong (2020) stressed multiple aspects of buyers' legitimate rights because he pointed out the most significant part of every legitimate right to ensure the buyers are aware of it. His finding proved that buyers are somehow aware of their rights to building inspection. Therefore, this finding is consistent with Choong (2020) regarding the less awareness of house buyers' legitimate rights on a building inspection.

Table 4. Advantages of building inspection: other aspects

[*Level of Agreement: 5 = Strongly Agree; 4 = Agree; 3 = Neither; 2 = Disagree; 1 = Strongly Disagree]									
Advantages of Building Inspection towards New House Buyers	SA 5	A 4	N 3	D 2	SD 1	TR	Remark	RII	Rank
ADVANTAGES OF BUILDING INSPECTION									
1 I agree that building inspection can help me to be accountable and transparent with my house defects' condition.	32%	39%	25%	4%	0%	114	Agree	0.109	8
2 I agree that accountability and transparency of building inspection towards my house defects' condition has secure my interest and rebuild confident towards my house.	30%	42%	23%	5%	0%	114	Agree	0.108	9
3 I agree that building inspection can help me to check and examines my house's building materials.	37%	42%	18%	3%	1%	114	Agree	0.112	3
4 I agree that building inspection can help me to check the workmanship and conditions of my house.	37%	43%	18%	1%	1%	114	Agree	0.113	2
5 I agree that building inspection can save my rectification cost if defects found before Defect Liability Period end.	42%	40%	15%	2%	1%	114	Strongly Agree	0.115	1
6 I agree that building inspection can ensure the house buyers understand each of the building element's usable life better to stay ahead of maintenance cost in the future.	31%	46%	19%	4%	1%	114	Agree	0.110	7
7 I agree that building inspector can save my time in building inspection part.	36%	39%	19%	4%	1%	114	Agree	0.111	6
8 I agree that building inspection report can save my time in understanding my building conditions and identifying defects.	36%	37%	25%	3%	0%	114	Agree	0.111	5
9 I agree that building inspection according to professional guidelines will ensure the environment safety of my house.	37%	39%	18%	4%	1%	114	Agree	0.111	4
								1.000	

According to Table 4, there are different aspects of the advantage of building inspection listed and ranked. Regarding financial aspects, saving defect rectification costs is the most vital element for house buyers to consider. The majority of respondents strongly agreed on this statement, with a mean score of

4.211. Most of the respondents strongly agreed that building inspection can save their rectification cost if the defects are detected before the DLP ends. The respondent's level of agreement causes this aspect to rank first place. This result is in line with the finding of Lawrence (n.d.). Additionally, the data analysed showed that only cost savings for defect rectification cost stand-alone with the result strongly agreed by the respondents. In contrast, the results of other aspects were shown as similar but ranked differently.

Furthermore, building inspection brings advantages to house buyers concerning quality checks and confirmation aspects. Buyers agreed that building inspection could help them to check the workmanship to ensure the conditions of houses. Besides, they also agreed that it could help to check and examine the building materials used. Both statements ranked second and third, respectively, with a mean score of 4.140 and 4.114. The result shows that buyers believe that building inspection can enhance the quality confirmation of the building purchased as the agreement level for both statements is more or less similar. As a result, it proved by Radzuan et al. (2011) was accurate and can be adopted in the context of this study.

Moreover, this study proves that building inspection can protect the house buyers' interest as much as the respondents are agreed to the statements raised in the survey. However, this statement has the lowest mean score, with 3.965. The result ranked at ninth place, which is the last one of the overall ranking, although the result of the data showed an "agree" status. The finding of this aspect is supported by Sulaiman et.al. (2012).

Key Findings on Advantages of Building Defect Rectification towards New House Buyers

Table 5. Advantages of building defect rectification: defect liability period

[*Level of Agreement: 5 = Strongly Agree; 4 = Agree; 3 = Neither; 2 = Disagree; 1 = Strongly Disagree]									
Advantages of Building Inspection for New House Buyers	**Level of Agreement**								
	SA	**A**	**N**	**D**	**SD**	**TR**	**Remark**	**RII**	**Rank**
	5	**4**	**3**	**2**	**1**				
ADVANTAGES OF BUILDING DEFECT RECTIFICATION									
1	I agree that I require a longer defect liability period to access the defects in my house.	33%	36%	28%	3%	0%	114	Agree	1.000	1
									1.000	

Table 5 shows the level of agreement regarding the house buyers requiring longer DLP to access the defects. There is no comparison between the data as there is only one data to analyse. However, we can see that most of the respondents agreed to have a longer defect liability period.

Since the respondents' results show that house buyers would like to have a more extended DLP, a follow-up question was asked in this survey. The responses reverted with multiple reasons. Most respondents opined that a longer period is needed as a guarantee as some defects tend to appear after years. They also explained that some shortcomings require a longer period to discover and the house buyers can find the defects easily when they stay in the unit. Meanwhile, some respondents stated that buyers could save costs if deficiencies were identified later due to high rectification costs for some elements. Some respondents pointed out that the house purchased is free of defects and in good condition for safety purposes.

Table 6. Advantages of building defect rectification: sales and purchase agreement

[*Level of Agreement: 5 = Strongly Agree; 4 = Agree; 3 = Neither; 2 = Disagree; 1 = Strongly Disagree]									
Advantages of Building Defect Rectification for New House Buyers	**Level of Agreement**								
	SA	**A**	**N**	**D**	**SD**	**TR**	**Remark**	**RII**	**Rank**
	5	**4**	**3**	**2**	**1**				
ADVANTAGES OF BUILDING DEFECT RECTIFICATION – SALES AND PURCHASE AGREEMENT									
1 I agree that the reasonable timeframe stated in the Sales and Purchase Agreement is sufficient for the contractor to rectify the defects.	17%	35%	32%	11%	5%	114	Agree	1.000	1
								1.000	

As shown in Table 6, the data analysed proves that 35% of the respondents, which is 40 of them, agreed that a reasonable timeframe is enough for the contractor to rectify the defects. REHDA Institute (2018) pointed out that the exact timeframe of the DLP still depends on the terms that the house buyer has signed in the SPA, which means the reasonable timeframe should be following the exact timeframe stated.

Table 7. Advantages of building defect rectification: latent defect

[*Level of Agreement: 5 = Strongly Agree; 4 = Agree; 3 = Neither; 2 = Disagree; 1 = Strongly Disagree]									
Advantages of Building Defect Rectification for New House Buyers	**Level of Agreement**								
	SA	**A**	**N**	**D**	**SD**	**TR**	**Remark**	**RII**	**Rank**
	5	**4**	**3**	**2**	**1**				
ADVANTAGES OF BUILDING DEFECT RECTIFICATION – LATENT DEFECT									
1 I agree that the latent defects can be identified in the limitation of six years from the date of the occurrence of latent defects and another extension of three years from the date of latent defects discovery, as well as action must be lodged within fifteen years of the occurrence of latent damages according to Section 24A Limitation Act.	19%	36%	42%	2%	1%	114	Agree	0.492	2
2 I agree that latent defects require a longer defect liability period to access the defects in my house.	26%	32%	39%	1%	1%	114	Agree	0.508	1
								1.000	

Table 7 demonstrates that 50.8% of respondents agreed that a longer DLP was required to access the latent defects. The mean score is 3.825. Besides, the remaining 49.20% of respondents agreed to statement 1. The mean score is 3.711. A follow-up question was asked in the questionnaire, in which the respondents are required to suggest or recommend the time frame of the limitation to access and rectify latent defects. Some responses indicated that the time frame should be extended from three to twenty years. However, according to the latest version of the Limitation Act 2018 in compliance with Section 24A, the current practice in the industry is up to fifteen years, unlike the six years of limitation given in the last version of the Limitation Act. Thus, the responses of fifteen years time frame are in line with Lai's (2021) finding.

Key Findings on Challenges of House Buyers on Building Defect Rectification

Table 8. Challenges of building defect rectification

[*Level of Agreement: 5 = Strongly Agree; 4 = Agree; 3 = Neither; 2 = Disagree; 1 = Strongly Disagree]									
Challenges of House Buyers on Building Defect Rectification	**Level of Agreement**					**TR**	**Remark**	**RII**	**Rank**
	SA	**A**	**N**	**D**	**SD**				
	5	**4**	**3**	**2**	**1**				
CHALLENGES OF BUILDING DEFECT RECTIFICATION									
1 I agree that the building defect rectification cost of my house has exceeded my budget.	24%	38%	32%	5%	2%	114	Agree	0.134	7
2 I agree that material price inflation will affect the cost of building defect rectification.	38%	42%	15%	4%	1%	114	Agree	0.147	1
3 I agree that the building height, area, and size will affect the cost of building defect rectification.	31%	35%	30%	4%	1%	114	Agree	0.139	6
4 I agree that the value of my house will be affected if there are many defects to be rectified during building defect rectification.	42%	32%	20%	4%	3%	114	Agree	0.145	4
5 I agree that the building defect rectification will affect the progress I move into my house.	39%	39%	19%	1%	3%	114	Agree	0.146	2
6 I agree that extreme weather will affect the productivity and workmanship of the contractor to proceed with building defect rectification for my house.	34%	43%	17%	5%	1%	114	Agree	0.144	5
7 I agree that building defect rectification will impact my health and safety conditions when the rectification works are carried out after I move into my house.	36%	41%	18%	4%	1%	114	Agree	0.145	3
								1.000	

As shown in Table 8, most of the respondents agreed that the challenges they faced in defect rectification. The result analysed all agree in Table 8. The only difference is the ranking of the challenges in building defect rectification. Inflation of material price is the respondents' biggest concern, influencing the cost of building defect rectification. It ranked first with a mean score of 4.114, the highest mean score among other challenges, although all of the results were shown to agree. This is in line with the finding of Wordsworth (2001).

Moving on, the progress of house buyers moving into their house is the challenge that ranked second in this study. It is displayed with a mean score of 4.096. This could be affected by the late response or delay in rectifying the defects by contractors. Narayan (2004) pointed out in her finding that delay in executing rectification works at the right time will cause a burden to the occupants.

Furthermore, the third challenge analysed is that building defect rectification will impact house buyer health and safety conditions when the reparation works are conducted after the house buyers move in. A mean score of 4.079 is presented. This is related to the finding of CDC (2013) as rectification works may produce biological pollutants, gases, airborne particles, particulate material and volatile organic compounds that may endanger the respiratory system of the occupants.

The last ranked challenge of building defect rectification is that the rectification cost exceeded the buyers' budget. This is because the developers and contractors will bear the rectification cost and expenses if the defect is reported during DLP. Thus, this aspect seems like not a huge challenge to the respondents compared to other challenges mentioned. It has the lowest mean score of 3.763.

Table 9. Worthiness of building inspection

[*Level of Worth: 5 = Extremely Worth; 4 = Moderately Worth; 3 = Somehow Worth; 2 = Slightly Worth; 1 = Not Worth At All]									
Worthiness of Building Inspection for a New House	**Level of Worth**					**TR**	**Remark**	**RII**	**Rank**
	EW	**MW**	**SHW**	**SW**	**NWAA**				
	5	**4**	**3**	**2**	**1**				
WORTHINESS OF BUILDING INSPECTION									
1 It is worth spending the cost on building inspection after vacant possession rather than spending the cost on rectifying plastering hairline cracks after the defect liability period. (Estimated rectification cost for plastering hairline cracks: RM10/m2 to RM30/m2)	19%	30%	38%	9%	4%	114	Moderately Worth	0.168	2
2 It is worth spending the cost on building inspection after vacant possession rather than spending the cost on rectifying uneven paint finishes after the defect liability period. (Estimated rectification cost for uneven paint finishes: RM6/m2 to RM45/m2)	12%	29%	37%	10%	12%	114	Somehow Worth	0.153	6
3 It is worth spending the cost on building inspection after vacant possession rather than spending the cost on rectifying uneven or broken floor tiles after the defect liability period. (Estimated rectification cost for uneven or broken floor tiles: RM80/m2)	17%	34%	31%	10%	9%	114	Moderately Worth	0.163	5
4 It is worth spending the cost on building inspection after vacant possession rather than spending the cost on rectifying door or window after the defect liability period. (Estimated rectification cost for door or window: RM100/unit or may replace entirely new)	20%	32%	30%	10%	9%	114	Moderately Worth	0.165	4
5 It is worth spending the cost on building inspection after vacant possession rather than spending the cost on rectifying piping leakage after the defect liability period. (Estimated rectification cost for piping leakage: RM20/m2 to RM50/m2)	19%	32%	34%	6%	9%	114	Moderately Worth	0.166	3
6 It is worth to have building inspection for a new house compared to the additional cost and time that will be incurred for defect rectification after defect liability period.	35%	33%	23%	5%	4%	114	Moderately Worth	0.187	1
								1.000	

Key Findings on Worthiness of Building Inspection for a New House

According to Table 9, the results of respondents are either moderately worth or somehow worth towards the level of the worthiness of building inspection for a new house. It shows that no specific item made the respondents think it is extremely worth having a building inspection. As an overall, the majority of respondents indicated that to have a building inspection for their new houses rather than incur additional cost and time for defect rectification after the DLP. This is moderately worthwhile from the respondents' perspective, with a mean score of 3.912, which ranked in first place.

Besides, according to Table 9, respondents thought it is moderately worth spending on building inspection for their residential buildings at VP rather than spending unnecessary costs to repair plastering hairline cracks. This is because if the defect spot after vacant possession, buyers can request the developer back to the site to rectify it, and the contractor will absorb the cost. There is no need for buyers to spend their expenses, and yet building inspection can be done for the whole building. It is moderately worthwhile in a sense from the respondents' perspective. It ranked second with a mean score of 3.509. A similar concept applies to other defects such as piping leakage, door and window, and uneven or broken floor tiles. The defects mentioned ranked third, fourth, and fifth, respectively, with a mean score of 3.456, 3.447, and 3.404. Lastly, uneven paint finishes ranked last with a mean score of 3.193. It is somehow worth it from the respondents' point of view to spend on building inspection if there is the only defect exists in the building. This is because uneven painting is extremely common and can easily be rectified. The respondents do not think it is much more worth having a building inspection if uneven painting finishes are the only defect.

CONCLUSION AND RECOMMENDATION

Limitations

The researcher faced a few limitations throughout this research journey. This study's main limitation is the lack of publications, journals, and past research studies in the industry regarding the chosen topic. In addition, the studied topic is too broad, and the researcher should choose one sub-topic to focus on. Besides, the data collection period is limited, resulting in the inadequate and quality sample size obtained. This research has only gathered approximately 35% of the required sample size, 143 respondents out of the required sample size of 384, before extracting valid and targeted responses. As mentioned, the research topic is too broad, which also results in the researcher's lack of sufficient time to analyse the data, especially if qualitative and qualitative research is carried out in a study.

Furthermore, obtaining the data and information for qualitative research was challenging. All the respondents requested to revert their responses via online social platforms due to their heavy-loaded working schedules. Based on the experience gained in this research journey, I believe that face-to-face interviews will be more effective and efficient, especially if there is follow-up clarification to the respondents.

Contribution of Study

This study drew out the worthiness of building inspection on house buyers' perceptions. By analysing and comparing the cost involvement of house buyers in building inspection and the cost involvement of building defect rectification from contractors' and house buyers' perceptions, it can show the public whether it is worth having a building inspection for a new house. Moreover, the findings of this study will empower house buyers to be aware of the advantages of building inspection and building defect rectification on a new house. House buyers will know their obligation as an owner of the housing property to maximize their benefits on building defect rectification during the DLP after VP. In addition, during the building inspection, house buyers will know more about the importance of the inspection and how it will impact them in the future. In addition, this research prepared house buyers for the challenges they may face during the rectification process of building deficiencies. This study will assist the attention of the developers and contractors on the negative impacts of building defects on house buyers. Seeing that rectification of building defects will cause unnecessary yet challenging trouble to the house buyers. Thus, the developers and contractors are responsible for mitigating the possibility of the deleterious impacts on house buyers caused by poor construction workmanship and the existence of building defects in the construction industry.

Recommendations

Future studies could focus either on building inspection or building defect rectification. As mentioned, the current scope of the study is too broad. Therefore, it is suggested that future research can explore both building inspection and building defect rectification individually. For building inspection, it is recommended to focus on QLASSIC inspection as well as the building inspector and building surveyor included as part of the targeted respondents. I believe there will be much insightful knowledge to be explored in future studies. Besides, it is also preferred that case study research on building defect rectification can be focused on as there are limited resources in the industry.

Conclusion

In a nutshell, both contractors' and house buyers' perspectives on building inspection and building defect rectification have been observed. The majority of the respondents have purchased their residential buildings, but not every buyer has put their attention on the advantages of having building inspection and building defect rectification. Undeniably, house buyers are also challenged when they opt for building defect rectification. However, house buyers more or less become more aware of their building purchaser rights and how they should abide by their buyers' obligations throughout this study. From this study, house buyers can better understand the cost involvement of the common defects and have their standard to measure the worthiness of building inspection.

REFERENCES

Ahmad, A. (2004). *Understanding Common Building Defects.*

Ahmad, H., Fadlie, M., Yahaya, N., & Abu, J. (2011). The Means of Escaping for Occupants for Renovation Works of Terrace Houses in Malaysia. *Procedia Engineering, 20,* 188–192. doi:10.1016/j.proeng.2011.11.155

Alejo, A. (2012). Comparative Study of Defects Liability Period Practice Between Nigeria and Malaysia. *IJMT.*

Ali, A., & Kam, H. (2011). *Building Defects: Possible Solution for Poor Construction Workmanship.* ResearchGate.

Ali, A., Kamaruzzaman, S., Sulaiman, R., & Yong, C. (2010). Factors Affecting Housing Maintenance Cost in Malaysia. *Journal of Facilities Management, 8*(4), 285–298. doi:10.1108/14725961011078990

BCA. (2022). *CONQUAS 21: The BCA Construction Quality Assessment System, Singapore.* Building and Construction Authority (BCA). https://www1.bca.gov.sg/buildsg/quality/conquas

Chan, C. (2002). *Commonwealth Construction Cases: The Singapore Perspective.* Singapore: Sweet & Maxwell Asia, A Thomson Company.

Chang, K. (2021). *Defects Turning New House Owners' Delight to Dismay [Blog].* Edge Prop. https://www.edgeprop.my/content/1899417/defects-turning-new-house-owners%E2%80%99-delight-dismay.

Chanter, B., & Swallow, P. (2008). *Building Maintenance Management.* John Wiley & Sons.

Che Ani, A., Mohd Tawil, N., Johar, S., Abd Razak, M., & Yahaya, H. (2014). Building Condition Assessment for New Houses: A Case Study in Terrace Houses. *Jurnal Teknologi, 70*(1). doi:10.11113/jt.v70.2812

Choong, S. (2020). *What Malaysian homebuyers should know about the Housing Development Act (HDA)?* iProperty.

Dai, J., Goodrum, P., & Maloney, W. (2009). Construction Craft Workers' Perceptions of the Factors Affecting Their Productivity. *Journal of Construction Engineering and Management, 135*(3), 217–226. doi:10.1061/(ASCE)0733-9364(2009)135:3(217)

Forcada, N., Macarulla, M., Fuertes, A., Casals, M., Gangolells, M., & Roca, X. (2012). Influence of Building Type on Post-Handover Defects in Housing. *Journal of Performance of Constructed Facilities, 26*(4), 433–440. doi:10.1061/(ASCE)CF.1943-5509.0000225

Forcada, N., Macarulla, M., Gangolells, M., & Casals, M. (2014). Assessment of Construction Defects in Residential Buildings in Spain. *Building Research & Amp. Information (Basel), 42*(5), 629–640.

Forcada, N., Macarulla, M., Gangolells, M., & Casals, M. (2015). Handover Defects: Comparison of Construction and Post-Handover Housing Defects. *Building Research &Amp. Information (Basel), 44*(3), 279–288.

Hong, C. (2016). *Investigation of Defects in New Buildings in Malaysia.* Eprints.utar.edu.my

Idrus, N., & Ho, C. (2008). *Affordable and Quality Housing Through the Low Cost Housing Provision in Malaysia.* Researchgate.

Ismail, I., Che-Ani, A., Abd-Razak, M., Mohd-Tawil, N., & Johar, S. (2015). Common Building Defects in New Terrace Houses. *Jurnal Teknologi, 75*(9), 83–88. doi:10.11113/jt.v75.5239

Josephson, P., & Hammarlund, Y. (1999). The Causes and Costs of Defects in Construction. *Automation in Construction, 8*(6), 681–687. doi:10.1016/S0926-5805(98)00114-9

Kang, J. (2019). *Performing A Building Defects Inspection During Vacant Possession.* Pegasus Work.

Lai, J. (2021). *Latent Defects: Beyond Defect Liability Period - Limitation Period for Latent Defects.* IPM.

Lateef, O. (2009). Building Maintenance Management in Malaysia. *Journal Of Building Appraisal, 4*(3), 207–214. doi:10.1057/jba.2008.27

Lau, Y. (2020). *Building Defect Assessment - Building Inspection Services Malaysia.* IPM.

Lawrence, J. (n.d.). *How a Property Inspection Can Save You Money.* Realestateinvestar.

Lopez, J. (n.d.). *Defects in Strata Buildings in Malaysia: Your Homebuyer Rights & How to Build a Legal Case.* Jmbmalaysia.org.

Macj. (n.d.). *How Home Inspection Can Save You Time & Money – Professional Home Inspection, India.* Professional Home Inspection, India.

Malaysia, C. I. D. B. (2017). *Quality Guidebook for Homeowners.* Canaan Building Inspector.

Meor-Hasan, M., Abd-Razak, N., Endut, I., Abu-Samah, S., Mohd-Ridzuan, A., & Saaidin, S. (2016). Minimizing Defects In Building Construction Project. *Jurnal Teknologi, 78* (5-2), 80.

Mills, A., Love, P., & Williams, P. (2009). Defect Costs in Residential Construction. *Journal of Construction Engineering and Management, 135*(1), 12–16. doi:10.1061/(ASCE)0733-9364(2009)135:1(12)

Mohit, M., Ibrahim, M., & Rashid, Y. (2010). Assessment of Residential Satisfaction in Newly Designed Public Low-Cost Housing in Kuala Lumpur, Malaysia. *Habitat International, 34*(1), 18–27. doi:10.1016/j.habitatint.2009.04.002

Mok, O. (2013). *New Buildings Could also Have Structural Defects.* Malay Mail.

Narayan, V. (2004). *Effective Maintenance Management: Risk and Reliability Strategies for Optimizing Performance.* Industrial Press Inc.

Pinsent, M. (2011). Defective Work. In *Construction Projects.* Pinsentmasons.

Radzuan, N., Hamdan, W., Hamid, M., & Abdullah-Halim, A. (2011). The Importance of Building Condition Survey Report for New House Buyers. *Procedia Engineering, 20,* 147–153. doi:10.1016/j.proeng.2011.11.149

REHDA Institute. (2018). *FAQ Common Property Defects Account – REHDA.* Rehdainstitute.

Reifenrath, P. (2020). Five Advantages Of Hiring A Building Inspector. *L'Essenziale. L'Essenziale - Interiors and Lifestyle Blog.*

Robert, B., Greene, L. & Craig-Gardei, L. (n.d.). *What Is a Building Condition Assessment and When Do You Need One?* GLE Associates, Inc.

Rotimi, F., Tookey, J., & Rotimi, J. (2015). Evaluating Defect Reporting in New Residential Buildings in New Zealand. *Buildings, 5*(1), 39–55. doi:10.3390/buildings5010039

Skinner, N. P. (1982). Local Authority House Maintenance – the Variation in Expenditure. *The Houston Review: History and Culture of the Gulf Coast*, *31*, 92–94.

Sommerville, J., Craig, N., & Bowden, S. (2004). The Standardisation of Construction Snagging. *Structural Survey*, *22*(5), 251–258. doi:10.1108/02630800410571562

Sufian, A., & Rozanah, A. (2008). Quality Housing: Regulatory and Administrative Framework in Malaysia. *IJEM*. upm.edu.my

Sulaiman, Z., Ali, A., & Ahmad, F. (2012). Abandoned Housing Project: Assessment On Resident Satisfaction Toward Building Quality. *Open House International*, *37*(3), 72–80. doi:10.1108/OHI-03-2012-B0008

Suttling, D. (2020). *Latent vs Patent Defects and How to Manage them*. C-Link.

Teoh, J. (2021). *Know Your Rights as a Homeowner: What Can a Homeowner Claim For From the Developer if the Property Has Defects? HHQ. IE (2015). Types of Residential Properties in Malaysia.* Insight Estate.

Wordsworth, P. (2001). *Lee's Building Maintenance Management* (4th ed.). Wiley.

Zolkafli, U., Yahya, Z., Zakaria, N., Akashah, F., Othman, M., Ali, A., & Salleh, H. (2014). Latent Defects: Approaches in Protecting House Buyers' Right in Malaysia. *MATEC Web Of Conferences, 15*, 01040.

Chapter 14
Key Criteria Affecting the Selection of Formwork Materials in Sarawak

Myzatul Aishah Kamarazaly
Taylor's University, Malaysia

Azrina Md Yaakob
Taylor's University, Malaysia

Tze Yee Angeline Tay
Taylor's University, Malaysia

Lam Tatt Soon
Taylor's University, Malaysia

Hasmawati Harun
Universiti Teknologi MARA, Malaysia

ABSTRACT

Choosing the proper formwork had become challenging, especially in the immediate aftermath of the Covid 19 pandemic. Various formwork materials, including wood, plastic, aluminium, steel, magnesium, and fabric, are available today. The purpose of each formwork is the same, but various properties are displayed. Formwork made of steel and timber is frequently used in Malaysia. Several factors, including resource availability, transportation, time constraints, and labour costs, influenced the contractors' preference for formwork materials. Therefore, this research aimed to determine whether contractors' preferred formwork was appropriate before and after the pandemic. Consequently, essential factors, including cost and preferences, were discussed when choosing formwork materials. Only steel and timber formwork were studied for this particular paper. The G7 contractors involved in various project types were interviewed as part of the qualitative methodology used in this study, which also included document analysis based on previous project reports. The cost was the determining factor before the pandemic, and resource availability held the top spot during the recovery stage, according to the first finding. The importance of transport remained at level 5 throughout both eras. In addition, the second finding revealed that all costs, including labour, transportation, and material, had increased for both timber and steel formwork, primarily as a result.

DOI: 10.4018/978-1-6684-8253-7.ch014

INTRODUCTION

Sawn formwork, as defined by JKR 2020, is formwork used to create concrete surfaces suitable for plastering or tiling. It is a temporary construction that creates a space where the structure elements (load transfer elements) that support the building by transmitting the load from the building to the ground can be built. Alternatively, formwork process expenses in reinforced concrete building account for 20% to 30% of total construction costs. In complex projects, the cost of the formwork process could exceed 40% to 60% of the total building cost (Sung et al., 2003). This evidence demonstrated that the formwork consumed nearly half the project's cost. Contractors may believe that selecting formwork is straightforward. However, many factors must be considered before making a decision. All factors that might affect the outcome of expenses, material waste, and the quality of the company's project are interconnected. There are not many studies that compare timber and steel formwork. Thus this study aims to ascertain the suitability of selected formwork in the construction industry. In addition, the importance of essential criteria in formwork selection will be determined in order. This study includes a discussion of material costs. Finally, the formwork material selection preferences of contractors were investigated. The objectives of the study are as follows,

1. To identify the importance of critical criteria in selecting formwork materials.
2. To analyse the cost of formwork materials.
3. To determine the preferences in selecting formwork materials.

PROBLEM STATEMENT

As technology advances, the market offers more options for consumers based on their preferences and practicability. This indirectly caused the dilemma while selecting appropriate formwork materials because the formworks perform the same function, but each material has distinct characteristics.

LITERATURE REVIEW

Formwork

Formwork is crucial in the initial construction phase (Rajeshkumar & Sreevidya, 2019). Load-bearing components such as columns, beams, and slabs cannot be constructed without formwork. In the absence of precast concrete or steelwork, the lack of formwork will significantly impact the on-site schedule of the project.

Key Criteria in Selecting Formwork Materials

Availability of Resources

Raw materials are the fundamental requirements for manufacturing primary products. In regard to the timber and steel formwork in Sarawak, it is evident that Sarawak had more timber as a raw material.

Table 1. Problem statement

Problem Statement	Explanation
Wastages created on site	The highest percentage of construction waste is timber (Foo et al., 2013). Although the practice of reuse was implemented, timber wastage still occupied the highest ranking of wastages due to sustainability.
Stereotype of contractor	Suppliers will always instil in consumers the notion that steel can save costs in the long term. In contrast, timber formwork requires a significant capital investment at the start of every project (Abhiyan et al., 2014).
Availability of resources	"There is more demand than supply" (Bota, 2021). In 2020, the price of material increased by 30% of wood and steel due to the pandemic.
Transportation	Throughout the construction period, the chosen or preferred mode of transportation must be available. The type of transportation used to transport the materials influences the distance. Material safety should also be considered (Sung et al., 2003).
Time	The construction period was included to compare the practicability of the formwork (Yip, 2008). The time required for transportation must also be considered, as stated in the contract.
Labour	The issue had arisen due to a lack of available labour. Different types of formwork were handled by different labourers (Akomah et al., 2020).
Cost	The maintenance costs, transportation costs and capital costs had influenced on the cost performance (Rajeshkumar et al, 2019)

The total land area of Sarawak is 12,4 million hectares, of which 7 million hectares (57%) are forested (Preferred, 2017). In addition, according to the report, the commercial director of the Sarawak-based Asteel Group, Fong Fui Yee, stated that domestic steel manufacturers were experiencing an influx of inquiries, but that steel allocation was limited in Malaysia. The words indicated that both raw materials are available locally, but only limited resources can be extracted.

Transportation

According to JKR Sarawak, the 'Schedule of Rates' specified the location factor explicitly. This serves as a guideline for the contractors to include the cost of the materials in their pricing. As a result of the stages of development in Sarawak, most materials are exported or imported to or from Kuching. On the other hand, the transportation cost includes transporting goods from the manufacturing facility to the construction site and their return to storage after the project's conclusion (Sung et al., 2003). The rental of vehicles and gasoline were the most costly aspects of transportation. The contractors will negotiate with the suppliers based on the provided packages and choose the optimal option to minimise transportation costs.

Time

Formwork installation necessitates a degree of expertise in cutting and connecting the formwork. The majority of construction workers are unable to comprehend drawings. The formwork installation will also be incorrect if the supervisor's instructions are incorrect. Simultaneously, it is possible that plants and machinery, as well as labour, were acquired before materials. The daily rate of equipment and labour was determined without regard to the work's progress. Therefore, to minimise loss, transportation time is a challenge to overcome.

Cost

The attributes of formwork material calculation include capital, labour, maintenance, and transportation expenses (Rajeshkumar, 2021). When more qualified people are involved in a project, these costs may affect the probability of winning the tender. Capital costs heavily influenced the estimation of formwork materials. Various formwork materials are purchased, and various expenses (capital costs) are incurred. Consequently, labour costs are affected by the number of workers hired and their status. Maintenance costs cannot be disregarded to extend the life of the plants and machines. The total cost of the project also includes transportation expenses. The project's expenditures were astronomical due to the gasoline and vehicle rental or purchase costs.

Labour

Since Sarawak relies on foreign labour for construction, it has attracted many foreigners, including Indonesians. About 122,075 foreign workers registered in the construction industry this year (Jalil, 2021). These statistics show that while there is a low demand for construction sector labour in Sarawak, employers can accept a certain number of foreign workers instead of local workers.

Costs of Formwork

Labour Costs

On-site workers are equipped with carpentry, bar-bending, and concrete work skills. Typically, the number of employees hired will impact the project's total cost (Pawar, 2014). As the economy recovers, Malaysia is experiencing a labor shortage (Network, 2021). The construction industry has a shortage of 800,000 to 1 million workers, resulting in a 30% increase in labor costs (Sin, 2021). Numerous individuals lost their jobs in 2019 due to the pandemic's effect on the global economy. In a single night, the unemployment rate has dramatically increased. However, after the "war", the economy and construction demand has recovered. Currently, abundant labour is on the market, which has led to a change in the cost of labour in this scenario.

Transportation Costs

According to Sung et al. (2003), the status of plants and equipment was the primary factor that needed to be revised in considering transportation costs. Heavy equipment, such as excavators and bulldozers, required transportation from the industry to the construction site. The equipment's initial cost is high, as are the required maintenance costs to extend its lifespan. In contrast, when renting heavy equipment, it is important to consider the site's accessibility, as this impacts transportation costs.

Materials Costs

The cost of materials is one of the classifications for analysing the overall cost of a project (Rahim, 2013). Due to the availability of raw materials, material costs can be obtained from different suppliers in various locations. Moreover, the market's demand and supply will impact the materials' prices. During the lockdown, most production is halted, resulting in a shortage of materials. After a few months of recovery, the contractors immediately resumed their work, resulting in a rise in demand. This increased material costs as the industry's supply fell short of demand. The Building Material Cost Index (BCI) in Sarawak increased by between 0.1 and 1.5% in 2020 (Bernama, 2020). This scenario demonstrated that the material costs in Sarawak had risen substantially, resulting in a burden for contractors.

Criteria Underpinning the Selection of Formwork

Timber Formwork

Pros of Timber Formwork

A.   Taking-off method

Standard Method of Measurement II (SMM2) clearly states the procedure for removing timber formwork (Yip & Poon, 2008). Section F, Concrete Work, of the SMM2, describes measure formwork. Units and voids were written clearly to ensure each subsection used the same unit.

B.   Availability of formwork replacement.

There is a risk of formwork splitting when cutting or constructing formwork due to poor workmanship. Nonetheless, it can easily replace the damaged section because the materials are readily accessible. As it is a common material, visiting the supplier's store for an extended time is unnecessary to obtain the broken part.

C.   Good thermal resistance

Timber formwork is good thermal resistance by preventing concrete damage in colder regions (Anupoju, 2018). Sarawak is an all-year-round rainy state. Similarly, timber is the most prevalent formwork material in the market.

Cons of Timber Formwork

A.   Quantities of material

Using their experience, Yip and Poon (2018) estimated the variety of uses for timber, including struts, side braces, and cutting waste. The only way to improve a quantity surveyor's measurement skills is to participate in various projects to reduce the variance in formwork quantity measurement.

B.   Wastages on site

The construction site had the greatest proportion of wood waste. The wood is discarded after a minimum of three times serving as formwork. According to the article, discarded wood formwork was strewn carelessly across the construction site. This demonstrates that the timber formwork has a significant detrimental effect on the construction site.

C.   Poor reuse of formwork

A layer of black oil is applied to the surface of the timber formwork to increase its durability. Due to corrosion on the surface, the timber formwork with black grease on the surface could only be used up to four times. Although the practice of reuse is possible, it is less frequent than other materials such as plastic, steel, metal, and magnesium. In addition, the workmanship must be supervised to ensure the timber formwork can be used multiple times.

Steel Formwork

Pros of Steel Formwork

A.   Requirement of labour

This study of 'Comparison of Timber and Metal Formwork Systems' reveals that the application of timber formwork required 16 carpenters, 10 semi-skilled helpers, and 5 unskilled workers. In contrast, applying steel formwork required 20 steel panel installers and 10 general workers. Evidently, skilled workers must be employed to install timber formwork, whilst more unskilled labour is needed to install steel formwork. Skilled labour requires particular expertise and experience to construct the formwork. In contrast, unskilled labour is readily available during the vacancy because they do not need to be trained in the installation.

B.   Practicality of reuse

Das et al., 2016) stated that steel formwork could be used more than 100 times. Steel formwork contains metal elements in the materials, making it more durable and stable while installing it on site. The durability of steel formwork allows the worker to reuse it in different projects if it achieves the dimension of the components.

C.   Concrete finishing surface

Constructing concrete in steel formwork allows the concrete to have a smooth surface as there are no nails or bracing between the formworks. The smooth surface can minimise labour work by reducing the time to improve the appearance of the concrete surface.

Disadvantages of steel Formwork

A.   Limited size or shape

Since steel formwork sizes are predetermined in the industry, only a limited number of shapes and sizes are available to the public. Therefore, the length of the formwork may not correspond to the engineer-specified size of the structure. In this instance, the extension of formwork is necessary to continue the concrete casting.

B.   Weight of formwork

Steel formwork is heavy and challenging for labourers to lift and move (Anupoju, 2018). Consequently, external plants and equipment, such as cranes, are necessary to transport the formwork around the construction site while the structure is being built. In the absence of plants and machinery, steel formwork requires more labour (compared to timber formwork) to be transported.

C.   Higher initial cost

Despite the fact that steel formwork can be reused multiple times, it must be purchased at a substantial initial cost. The contractors must not only consider the working cycle of formwork, but they must also prepare a storage area for the formwork if the company has no projects and prevent theft.

RESEARCH METHODOLOGY

The acquisition of qualitative data through questionnaires, interviews, or observation focuses on individuals' subjective experiences or meanings (Chetty, 2016). Moreover, qualitative data provides an in-depth analysis of the themes. The interview method was chosen for this paper to gain insight into the respondents' perspectives based on the circumstances they faced before and after the pandemic. In contrast, interviews were conducted using an online platform and an in-person interview. Converting the audio to text is additional work that must be performed. This study also used document analysis to determine which documents are interpreted to give voice and meaning to an assessment topic (Bowen, 2009). The cost of formwork was obtained from previous project reports and is used as evidence in this study.

Consequently, G7 contractors were the population of interest for this study, the highest grades for registrations issued by CIDB that permitted the contractor to have no limit on the value of work and tender. During the data collection process, 20 invitations were sent to contractors, but only 11 accepted the interview session. After completing the interviews, only five interviews met the study's requirements.

Figure 1. Research framework

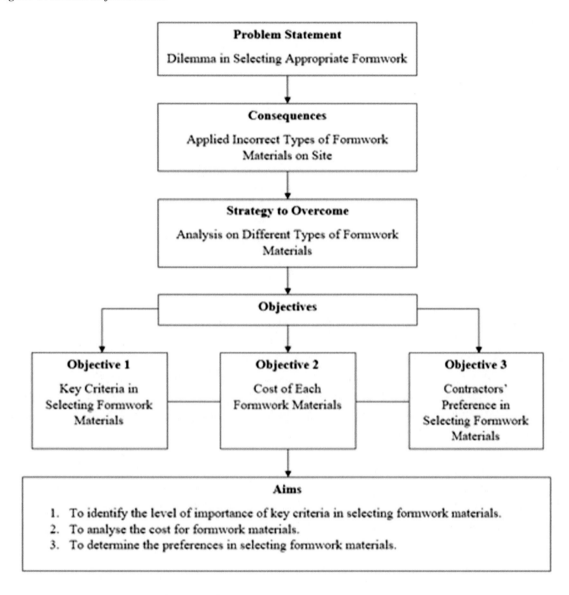

RESULTS AND DISCUSSIONS

1. Key Finding 1: Level of Importance of Key Criteria in Selecting Formwork Materials

Prior research titled "Performance Evaluation on Selection of Formwork Systems in High Rise Buildings Using Regression Analysis and Their Impacts on Project Success" concluded that the availability of resources ranked in the middle when compared to the quality, safety, adaptability, and project duration. Materials were the project's fundamental requirements. However, they were not always the contractor's top priority. This is due to the fact that availability was not an issue for industry participants.

Table 2. Coding for level of importance of availability of resources in selecting the formwork materials before pandemic

Key Criteria	Theme	Sub-Theme	Code
Availability of Resources	1. Raw Materials	a. Timber b. Steel	A1a A1b
	2. Location of Suppliers	a. Local (Sarawak) b. West Malaysia c. Oversea	A2a A2b A2c
	3. References for Resources	a. Tender documents b. Jabatan Kerja Raya Sarawak c. Forest Department Sarawak	A3a A3b A3c
	4. Relationship between the Suppliers	a. Cash flow b. Trust between parties	A4a A4b
	5. Purchasing Time Frame	a. Pre-contract b. Defect liability period	A5a A5b
	6. Supply of Resources	a. Easy to obtain b. Hard to obtain	A6a A6b

According to the respondents, Sarawak has abundant resources, particularly raw materials such as timber. The total land area of 12.4 million hectares is cited in the 'Sarawak Malaysia Timber Risk Profile' as supporting evidence. They can obtain the materials from the local supplier and deliver them to the construction site without considering other factors, such as the materials' demand. Clearly, before the pandemic, the supply was always greater than the demand. Although the authority was strict regarding logging activities, only certain areas could engage in logging with a license. Nonetheless, it continues to supply the market in Sarawak. This demonstrated that the availability of resources (wood) was a problem for local contractors.

On the other hand, steel formwork was the opposite of timber formwork. There were few suppliers in Sarawak but applied steel formwork was not as common as timber formwork. As a result, if there is a high demand from industry, steel formwork must be obtained from West Malaysia or from abroad, such as China, to meet the demand in Sarawak.

Table 3. Coding for level of importance of transportation in selecting the formwork materials before the pandemic

Key Criteria	Theme	Sub-Theme	Code
Transportation	1. Expenses	a. Fixed expenses b. Location factors	B1a B1b
	2. Types of Transportation	a. Land b. Sea	B2a B2b
	3. Schedule of Delivery	a. After issuance of purchasing order b. Alternate day	B3a B3b
	4. Consideration	a. Cost b. Types of formwork c. Location of site d. Types of vehicles e. Time	B4a B4b B4c B4d B4e

A previous study titled "Performance Evaluation on Selection of Formwork Systems in High Rise Buildings Using Regression Analysis and Their Impacts on Project Success" summarised the least important transportation factor. It was inadmissible, but the weight of this criterion was not as significant as others, such as price. According to the preceding discussion, respondents were more interested in Malaysian suppliers than those in West Malaysia or abroad. This is because local suppliers were able to reduce their delivery times to a level that does not delay the schedule on the construction site. In addition, the modes of transport, land and sea, affect the cost of transportation. It was necessary to implement additional procedures to prevent the types of transportation from violating the law.

Table 4. Coding for level of importance of time in selecting the formwork materials before the pandemic

Key Criteria	Theme	Sub-Theme	Code
Time	1. Time Consumes	a. Construction period	C1a
		b. Work carried on site	C1b
		c. Materials delivered	C1c
		d. Cure concrete	C1d
		e. Erect formwork	C1e
	2. Requirements	a. Construction timeframe	C2a
		b. Interim	C2b
	3. Benefits of on-time	a. Higher profit	C3a
		b. Cash flow	C3b
		c. Better reputation	C3c
	4. Causes of Delay	a. Poor workmanship	C4a
		b. Lack of workers	C4b
	5. Consequences of Delay	a. Extension of time	C5a
		b. Liquidated damages	C5b
		c. Delay of work	C5c

The study "Analysis of Factors Influencing Formwork Materials Selection in Construction Buildings" highlighted the inadequacy of handling instructions, which relate supervisor time to labour spent on formwork handling. In three of the five most recent interviews, the handling of materials by labourers necessitated the oversight of a site supervisor in three instances. If supervision is conducted regularly, the shoddy craftsmanship can be improved. Nonetheless, this necessitated a large number of on-site supervisors. Therefore, balancing cost and time had become a challenge for the contractor.

On the other hand, the labourers were given sufficient time to complete the work on-site. Understanding the labour involved in applying formwork is crucial because it affects the time spent on each component. Timber formwork required a carpenter to construct the structure, whereas steel formwork required a general labourer to install the panel. Steel formwork application was straightforward and needed less time than wood formwork application.

There are two significant factors that influence the selection of formwork materials. First, there is the waste of materials. Timber formwork had greater wastage than steel formwork because steel formwork was cast in the industry and shipped to the construction site. All panels were custom-made based on the blueprints, whereas the timber formwork was resized from standard-sized lumber to meet the structural specifications. This indirectly led to on-site waste.

Table 5. Coding for level of importance of cost in selecting the formwork materials before the pandemic

Key Criteria	Theme	Sub-Theme	Code
Cost	1. Types of Costs	a. Materials b. Transportation c. Labour d. Profit	D1a D1b D1c D1d
	2. Capital	a. Aesthetic building b. Complex building	D2a D2b
	3. Causes of Higher Expenses	a. Poor workmanship b. Wastages	D3a D3b
	4. Ways to Overcome the Overspent	a. Hired supervisor	D4a
	5. The Consequence of Managing Cost	a. Cash flow b. Tender project c. Cost fluctuation	D5a D5b D5c

Table 6. Coding for level of importance of labour in selecting the formwork materials before the pandemic

Key Criteria	Theme	Sub-Theme	Code
Labour	1. Types of Labour	a. Foreigner labour b. Skilled worker c. Unskilled worker	E1a E1b E1c
	2. Work Carried on Site	a. Plastering b. Bar bending c. Housekeeping d. Transferring materials	E2a E2b E2c E2d
	3. Familiarity towards the Application	a. Common skilled b. Familiar c. Brand-new technology	E3a E3b E3c
	4. Consequences of Poor Workmanship of Labour	a. Change sub-contractor b. Quality of work c. Time-consuming	E4a E4b E4c

The size of the steel formwork required on the construction site determined the order. After the construction of each floor, steel panels can be reused a few times, barring any intentional damage by the worker. Inadequate application of timber formwork, as demonstrated by the absence of a layer of black oil, reduces the formwork's durability after each construction. Therefore, a higher cost was incurred to acquire additional timber formwork on-site. In addition, the capital expenditures are mentioned in the literature review. In addition, labour, transportation, and material costs were discussed. As discussed by the respondents above, all costs were closely related.

The respondents did not mention semi-skilled labour because they identified skilled labour as the type of labour attained through training. The craftsmanship was then highlighted in these criteria to ensure that the quality of the work was guaranteed. Repeating the same work in stages creates workmanship obstacles for the on-site work. Not only does it delay the overall schedule, but it also increases the costs associated with specific elements. For instance, the formwork was improperly installed, forming a honeycomb upon disassembly. Hacking the defective component and redoing the work was required to fix the defect.

Table 7. Coding for level of importance of availability of resources in selecting the formwork materials during recovery phase

Key Criteria	Theme	Sub-Theme	Code
Availability of Resources	1. Consequences of Pandemic	a. Lack of resources	F1a
		b. Demand increase	F1b
		c. Cost fluctuation	F1c
		d. Lack of management	F1d
		e. Broken materials	F1e
	2. Actions of Contractors	a. Stored before pandemic	F2a
		b. Request from suppliers	F2b
		c. Find affordable resources	F2c
		d. Grabbed resources	F2d

The industry had a high demand, but the supply of resources was insufficient. According to the preceding interview, most contractors had limited resources due to the sudden work announcement. The contractors cannot prepare sufficient supplies and resources for the job site. As a result of the delayed completion of the project, they incurred a loss in revenue. The contractor's breach of contract necessitated that the employer receive compensation.

The contractor was not permitted to request an extension of time due to his negligence. Consequently, the loss incurred during the pandemic and the inability to complete any work during the period of the movement control order increased when a subsequent wave necessitated the expenditure of a substantial amount of money to acquire the necessary materials. Due to bankruptcy, a few small construction companies were forced to close their business.

Table 8. Coding for level of importance of transportation in selecting the formwork materials during recovery phase

Key Criteria	Theme	Sub-Theme	Code
Transportation	1. Consideration	a. Important	G1a
		b. Least important	G1b
		c. Commence to work	G1c
	2. Limitation of Movement	a. Movement control	G2a
		b. Project location	G2b
		c. Types of projects	G2c
	3. Obstacle Faced	a. Apply for permit	G3a
		b. Higher rate	G3b
		c. Delay of delivery	G3c

According to the preceding discussion, the greatest challenge for the contractors was delivering the materials to the construction site. Due to the movement restrictions, the community was not permitted to visit the other district without permission from the authority. Therefore, the remote construction site faced the difficulty of transporting labour and materials from Kuching to a rural location.

In addition, some respondents stated that the movement restriction does not affect the site's operations because the site is located within the restriction's boundaries. They do not have to travel far to the location, and most of the work can be resumed. They completed their tasks on time without delaying any progress.

Table 9. Coding for level of importance of time in selecting the formwork materials during recovery phase

Key Criteria	Theme	Sub-Theme	Code
Time	1. Priority to Control	a. Availability of resources b. Cost c. Labour d. Time	H1a H1b H1c H1d
	2. Construction Period	a. Extension of time b. Resume work	H2a H2b
	3. Work to be carried	a. Construct building b. Paperwork	H3a H3b
	4. Ways to Prevent Delay of Project	a. Work overtime b. Apply familiar materials	H3a H4b
	5. Obstacles Faced	a. Lack of materials b. Delay of delivery c. Lack of labour d. Loss and expenses	H5a H5b H5c H5d

According to the transcript in Table 9, contractors were more concerned with the factors that caused the delay than the time allotted to complete the project. Other factors, such as the delivery of materials and the on-site labour force, contributed to the time required to complete the project. These variables indirectly affected the proposed timeline for completing the project.

In addition, the contractor utilising direct labour is unconcerned with the time required to complete the work on-site. Materials and equipment are crucial as labourers cannot work without them. Consequently, this revealed that the contractors' schedules are impacted by the time required to deliver materials, plants, and machinery.

Table 10. Coding for level of importance of cost in selecting the formwork materials during recovery phase

Key Criteria	Theme	Sub-Theme	Code
Cost	1. Causes of Pandemic	a. Material cost increase b. Capital loss c. Higher demand for materials d. Broken cash flow	I1a I1b I1c I1d
	2. Element to ensure when Decreasing the Cost	a. Quality of work b. Attitudes of labour c. Cost management	I2a I2b I2c
	3. Substitute Materials	a. Sustainable	I3a
	4. Ways to Decrease the Extra Cost	a. Hired supervisor b. Highlight the wastages	I4a I4b

According to the preceding discussion, the primary concern of the contractors was the cash flow that would enable them to recover the loss during the movement control period. Due to the lack of profit during those few months, the fixed expenses had caused a substantial drain on their capital. Ineffective cost management resulted in the company's demise and bankruptcy.

In addition, the scenario described in the preceding interview was good to observe, as some contractors maintain their work quality. Even though they were experiencing cash flow issues, the quality of the construction work was maintained. On a long-term basis, they were guarding their reputation and assuming community responsibility.

Table 11. Coding for level of importance of labour in selecting the formwork materials during recovery phase

Key Criteria	Theme	Sub-Theme	Code
Labour	1. Skilled Labour	a. Carpenter b. Bar bender c. Plasterer	J1a J1b J1c
	2. Sub-Contractor	a. Permit labour b. Loyalty	J2a J2b
	3. Consequence of Pandemic	a. High demand for labour b. Delay of work c. Foreigner workers' status	J3a J3b J3c
	4. Ways to Hire Labour	a. Adjustment on the labour rate	J4a

According to the previously presented information, the contractors and contractors' quantity surveyors highlighted the market's supply and demand again. As a result of the pandemic, demand decreases as supply increases and vice versa. Everyone was concerned about the development of their respective construction sites due to this scenario. In contrast, the observation revealed that most skilled labourers were foreigners. It emphasises the extent to which Sarawak's construction industry depended on foreign workers.

Table 12. The costs of each formwork

Costs / Period	Before Pandemic	Recovery Phase	Difference
Timber Formwork			
Total Costs	RM 51.50	RM 57.50	RM 6.00
Labour Costs	RM 21.95	RM 27.07	RM 5.43
Transportation Costs	RM 1.96	RM 2.18	RM 0.22
Materials Costs	RM 12.88	RM 13.80	RM 0.93
Steel Formwork			
Total Costs	RM 68.50	RM 77.50	RM 9.00
Labour Costs	RM 24.81	RM 33.05	RM 8.42
Transportation Costs	RM 2.59	RM 2.93	RM 0.34
Materials Costs	RM 24.12	RM 25.41	RM 1.29

2.   Key Finding 2: Costs of Formwork Materials

The breakdown of average costs for formwork was provided in detail. According to Table 12, labour costs for timber formwork before the pandemic comprised nearly half of the total cost. The labour costs were high because the labour on site was foreign labour. It was necessary to prepare many budgets for the labour if they were to come to Sarawak for the first time, as many applications had to be submitted, and all associated costs had to be factored in. Compared to costs quoted before the pandemic, labour costs had increased. As a result of the pandemic's attack, the market's economy gradually decreased, and labour was compatible with the current situation (cost fluctuation). The authority adjusted the wage rate to balance living and gaining.

Transportation costs were factored into delivering resources to the construction sites. In practice, the greater the quantity ordered, the lower the shipping costs. This is because the materials were delivered using a single truck or lorry. Less fuel, labour, and delivery time are consumed. A minor additional cost was added to the transportation costs, resulting in the observed changes. The percentage of overall transportation costs did not change, but the estimated transportation costs increased. The adjustment of transportation costs was intended to compensate for the fluctuating price of gasoline. Fortunately, the authority had set a maximum gasoline price, as most construction vehicles were Diesel. The supplement of authority aided the contractor by lightening his financial load.

The difference between the highest and lowest material costs for timber formwork was RM2.50. The market's supply was sufficient to meet demand, and it could export. This allowed the materials costs to be quoted at a lower price, increasing the likelihood of winning the bid. Concurrently, the majority of respondents acquired their permanent supplier. As a result of their longstanding cooperation, they were offered a discount by negotiating a lower rate for the cost of materials. During the recovery phase, the same condition occurred with the material costs. There was an increase in the cost of materials. The contractors reduced the material cost by approximately RM1.00 per square meter. Because the authority supplemented the cost of materials, the increase in material costs is less than in other costs. The timber formwork was sourced locally. Hence the government charged a lower interest rate to allow the industry to return to normal before paying the interest rate. This was how the local government assisted the contractor during the recovery phase.

In addition, labour costs for applying steel formwork before the pandemic were presented in Table 12. Due to the involvement of skilled labour, a welder, in installing the steel formwork, these labour costs were estimated. Expenses associated with the application of steel formwork during the recovery phase. The increased estimated labor costs above RM30.00 indicated that the construction industry's labour supply was insufficient to meet demand. As a result of the economic downturn, the construction industry was compelled to increase labor costs to retain a sufficient number of workers on site. In addition, the installation of steel formwork necessitated the application of skilled labour, allowing the flow to return to the track at the construction site necessitating the expenditure of additional funds.

All respondents cited a range of RM2.00 to RM3.00 for the cost of transportation. Included in the transportation costs were the delivery of materials, vehicle rental, and gasoline. However, it does not account for a disproportionate amount of the total cost of steel formwork. As ordered formwork was required to be shipped to the construction site, transportation expenses and material costs were incurred. The estimated transportation costs rose by approximately 0.30 ringgit. Compared to before, there is a slight increase in transportation costs. When the pandemic severely damaged the economy, transportation costs also increased. Depending on the market's demand and supply, the cost fluctuation has caused every item used on the job site to increase by a certain percentage. However, transportation costs had the least impact compared to labour and material costs.

Before the pandemic, the cost of materials included one-third of the total price of steel formwork. A third of the total cost demonstrated that the materials costs were one of the most essential, as they had the average cost compared to labour and transportation costs. However, the timber formwork's reusability was not accounted for in the materials quoted at this price. Indirectly, this meant that the costs applied on-site had a lower rate since the costs divided by the number of times formwork was used were the most accurate cost of formwork. Compared to the period preceding the pandemic, the proportion of overall formwork costs attributable to materials had not changed significantly. The modest price increase for steel formwork was because the supply of materials was sufficient to meet demand. Due to the fact that steel formwork was not the contractor's first choice (due to capital constraints), particularly for G1 to G4 contractors, the industry's supply chain was not disrupted, and there was only a slight fluctuation in the cost of materials. As the price of steel's raw materials increased, costs continued to rise.

3. Key Finding 3: Preferences in Selecting Formwork Materials

Before the pandemic, every respondent selected timber formwork, which offers more advantages than steel formwork. The respondents agreed that timber formwork was widely known and utilised in Sarawak. Typically, the contractors do not change their habits or increase the risk of using different formwork material types. In addition, respondents R1, R4, and R5 stated that they understood the timber formwork better than the steel formwork. They can efficiently address issues such as the replacement of formwork, the mobility of formwork on the job site, and the plants and equipment used to cut and install formwork. Therefore, they chose not to take a greater risk by experimenting with a 'brand-new' formwork.

In contrast, respondents R2 and R3 shared steel formwork, which is believed to be more reusable than timber formwork, but only in certain circumstances. No other identical structure in the world was not constructed simultaneously. Therefore, the reuse of steel formwork was defined by constructing the same dimension of construction rather than on a structural component of a different size. However, there was a remote possibility that the customised steel formwork could be reused in another project. This is the reason why the majority of contractors refused to experiment with the use of steel formwork.

Table 13. Coding for preferences in selecting formwork materials before pandemic

Key Criteria	Theme	Sub-Theme	Code
Formwork Materials	1. Advantages of Timber Formwork	a. Familiarity b. Availability of replacement c. Good weather resistant d. Sustainability e. Lightweight	K1a K1b K1c K1d K1e
	2. Disadvantages of Timber Formwork	a. Wastage	K2a
	3. Disadvantages of Steel Formwork	a. Heavyweight b. Higher risk of accident c. Availability of replacement d. Limited size	K3a K3b K3c K3d
	4. Condition of State	a. Raining b. Tropical climate	K4a K4b

Table 14. Coding for preferences in selecting formwork materials during recovery phase

Key Criteria	Theme	Sub-Theme	Code
Formwork Materials	1. Advantages of Timber Formwork	a. Cheaper b. Reusability c. Familiarity d. Reduce the risk of delay in work e. Simple application f. Good weather resistant	L1a L1b L1c L1d L1e L1f
	2. Disadvantages of Timber Formwork	a. Wastages	L2a
	3. Disadvantages of Steel Formwork	a. Availability of replacement	L3a
	4. Consideration	a. Capital	L4a

Most respondents (R1, R3, R4, and R5) selected timber formwork because their familiarity with its application allowed them to expedite the work and submit it on schedule. This factor was closely related to the price of formwork and the amount of liquidated damages. This explained both the capital of the company and the project expenses. As the pandemic disrupted the economy, most contractors developed methods to cope with the crisis to maintain their positions in the field. Cost and expense management became their top priority for continuing their work.

On the other hand, respondent R2 voted for steel formwork with a contrasting, sustainable concept. A sustainable material, steel formwork, was suggested for use on-site to reduce the amount of waste generated. With a large amount of capital, the company can test the viability of 'new' materials in the market.

CONCLUSION

This study investigated the suitability of preferred formwork (timber and steel formwork) in the construction industry. The objectives of this paper were to examine the critical selection criteria for formwork materials, the costs of formwork, and the contractors' preferences. Following is an analysis and discussion of the key findings for each objective.

Table 15. Level of importance of key criteria before pandemic and during recovery phase

Key Criteria	Before Pandemic	Recovery Phase
Availability of Resources	2	5
Transportation	1	1
Time	4	4
Cost	5	3
Labour	3	2

Table 15 describes the relative significance of selecting both types of formwork (wood formwork and steel formwork). Before the pandemic, the economic cost of formwork was the most critical factor on the list, while transportation was the least. The remaining three criteria were time, labour, and then the availability of resources, in descending order. During the recovery phase, respondents emphasised the availability of resources, indicating a shift in the significance level. It had raised the level of importance from level 2, the second-to-last level, to the highest level. The significance level for transportation and time remained the same, whereas the significance level for cost and labour decreased by two levels. The supply and demand for resources were the most critical criterion among these five factors, as evidenced by a self-explanatory diagram. In addition, the concentration of time in construction has always been the foundation for on-time work completion.

Table 16. The condition of each cost

Formwork/Costs	Labour Costs	Transportation Costs	Materials Costs
Timber Formwork	Increase	Increase	Increase
Steel Formwork	Increase	Increase	Increase

All three costs had risen after the pandemic attack by transforming timber and steel formwork in terms of labour, transportation, and material costs. This demonstrated that the price fluctuations impacted all industry products, regardless of whether they were living or nonliving. Because market demand exceeds supply, labour and material costs for both types of formwork have increased. As market competition is intense, the market cannot recover its supply promptly, causing rising prices. Moreover, transportation costs increased because they were supplementary to materials. Without delivery of the materials to the job site, the work cannot continue as planned, and the contractors will suffer substantial loss and damage.

The third objective of the study was to investigate the preferences of contractors. As the market will always meet the needs of contractors, the trend of contractors influences the competition in the supplier industry. The respondents' opinion was interpreted by comprehending the contractors' justifications and considering the real-world application on the job site.

The contractors favoured wood formwork over steel formwork based on the collected data. This is because the application and practice of timber formwork were more familiar and conducive to the labour force. Despite the fact that it is not an eco-friendly material, the contractors will still prefer it because they will be less concerned. On-site waste will be the most significant consequence of using wood formwork. Nevertheless, taking precautionary measures can keep environmental damage to a minimum. Simultaneously, steel formwork could replace the disadvantage of timber formwork, but a substantial initial investment was required to implement steel formwork on the construction site. Despite this, the knowledge of labour toward the steel formwork necessitated the site supervisor devoting some time to preventing defects.

To summarise the abovementioned study, different types of companies experienced various challenges when selecting formworks. Steel formwork would be the ideal choice without regard to practicality because it is an eco-friendly material that complies with the country's mission of encouraging a sustainable industry. However, the company may experience a lack of capital, preventing them from investing a substantial amount of capital during the startup phase to purchase all sustainable materials. In addition, Sarawak has yet to develop an abundance of sustainable raw materials, which may be possible in the future. Therefore, if the company's capital is robust, steel formwork can be the material of choice. In contrast, the company can acquire sustainable formwork in bulk. A portion of timber formwork can be replaced with steel formwork to reduce the cost over the long term.

In brief, the application's timber and steel formwork performance was identical, but the materials' properties varied. Both formworks had advantages and disadvantages, but the market does not contain the ideal material. The selection may be influenced by the consideration of contractors, whose preferences were accommodated to the extent of their capacity.

Scope and Limitation

This study is limited by the fact that only two types of selected formwork materials, wood and steel, were examined. Due to the application of formwork in Sarawak, fewer forms of formwork were discussed. Although Sarawak is Malaysia's third wealthiest state, most suppliers will begin operations in Selangor, as it is the most developed state (Habibullah, 2018). The scope of this paper is limited to G7 contractors who performed work in Sarawak. This study focuses on Sarawak because it is a developed state located outside of East Malaysia. The uniqueness of transportation is highlighted because the materials cannot be transported on land. Therefore, the overall collected data might not be able to fulfil the criteria in other states as different states had different management of the formwork materials.

Future Recommendation

Further interpreting Objective 1's analysis makes it possible to conduct a specific investigation. The first objective of this paper was to examine only the most essential criteria affecting both materials. Specific criteria based on the various material types of formworks are lacking. Therefore, a more in-depth discussion can be conducted by reviewing the particular types of formworks to provide contractors with considerations for selection.

REFERENCES

Abhiyan, S.P., NeerajSharma, D., & Kashiyani, B.K. (2014). Selection Criteria of Formwork by Users in Current Age In South Gujarat Region. *International Journal of Innovative Research in Science, Engineering and Technology*, 3.

Akomah, B. B., Ahinaquah, L. K., & Mustapha, Z. (2020). Skilled labour shortage in the building construction industry within the Central Region. *Baltic Journal of Real Estate Economics and Construction Management*, 8(1), 83–92. doi:10.2478/bjreecm-2020-0006

Anupoju, S. (2018, August 4). Different materials used for formwork - advantages and disadvantages. *The Constructor*. https://theconstructor.org/building/materials-formwork-advantages-disadvantages/6188/

Bernama. (2021, November 11). DOSM: Building material cost index rises 0.1-2.3% in Oct 2021. *The Malaysian Reserve*. https://themalaysianreserve.com/2021/11/11/dosm-building-material-cost-index-rises-0-1-2-3-in-oct-2021/

Bota, P. (2021, September 30). Lack of raw materials causing problems in Construction Sector. *Majorca Daily Bulletin*. https://www.majorcadailybulletin.com/news/local/2021/10/01/90217/mallorca-construction-shortage-raw-materials.html

Das, R., Bhattacharya, I., & Saha, R. (2016). *Comparative Study between Different Types of Formwork, 1*(4), 173–175.

Foo, L. C., Rahman, I. A., Asmi, A., Nagapan, S., & Khalid, K. I. (2013). Classification and Quantification of Construction Waste at Housing Project Site. *International Journal of Zero Waste Generation, 1*, 1–4.

Habibullah, M. S., Sanusi, N. A., Abdullah, L., Kusairi, S., Golam Hassan, A. A., & Ghazali, N. A. (2018). Does the less developed states in Malaysia catching-up to the Richer State of Selangor? *Journal of Contemporary Issues and Thought, 8*, 29–40. doi:10.37134/jcit.vol8.4.2018

Jalil, A. (2021, November 2). Construction sector applies the highest number of foreign. *The Malaysian Reserve*. https://themalaysianreserve.com/2021/11/02/construction-sector-applies-the-highest-number-of-foreign-worker/

MySinchew. (2021). Construction sector short of 1M workers, labor cost up 30%. 星洲网 *Sin Chew Daily*. https://mysinchew.sinchew.com.my/20210414/construction-sector-short-of-1m-workers-labor-cost-up-30/

Network, A. N. (2021, October 21). Malaysia facing labour shortage as economy recovers. Malaysia facing labour shortage as economy recovers. *Phnom Penh Post*. https://www.phnompenhpost.com/international/malaysia-facing-labour-shortage-economy-recovers

Pawar, S. P., & Atterde, P. M.Sandip.P.Pawar. (2014). Comparative analysis of formwork in Multistory Building. *International Journal of Research in Engineering and Technology, 03*(21), 22–24. doi:10.15623/ijret.2014.0321006

Preferred by Nature. (2017, November 1). *Timber - malaysia - sarawak*. NEPCon - Preferred by Nature. https://preferredbynature.org/sourcinghub/timber/timber-malaysia-sarawak

Rajeshkumar, V., & Sreevidya, V. (2019). Performance evaluation on selection of formwork systems in high rise buildings using regression analysis and their impacts on project success. *Archives of Civil Engineering, 65*(2), 209–222. doi:10.2478/ace-2019-0029

Sung, W.-P., Chen, K.-S., Song, W., & Tsai, Y.-Y. (2003). Evaluation method for performance of formwork process of construction industry. *Journal of Asian Architecture and Building Engineering, 2*(2), 1–6. doi:10.3130/jaabe.2.b1

Yip, R., & Poon, C. S. (2008). Comparison of timber and metal formwork systems. *Proceedings of the Institution of Civil Engineers, 161*(1), 29–36. Waste and Resource Management. 10.1680/warm.2008.161.1.29

Section 5
Built Environment Wellbeing

Chapter 15
Impact of Restorative Environments Within the Office Developments on the Mental Wellbeing of Office Workers

TamilSalvi Mari

Taylor's University, Malaysia

Tan Wei Sen

Taylor's University, Malaysia

Ng Veronica

Taylor's University, Malaysia

Sujatavani Gunasagaran

Taylor's University, Malaysia

Sivaraman Kuppusamy

Reading University of Malaysia, Malaysia

ABSTRACT

The stress and mental health risks associated with living and working in cities have increased the importance of designing urban spaces. It is, therefore, crucial to prioritize the mental wellbeing of city residents. Research indicates that people's perception of their wellbeing is influenced by various factors, such as their environment and the people around them. Office workers spend significant time in their workspace, so a well-designed office can positively impact their wellbeing. Biophilic design, which incorporates natural elements into office spaces, has become increasingly popular, and studies have shown that workplace greenery can improve employees' wellbeing and job performance. A study conducted in Kuala Lumpur used a quantitative method to investigate whether incorporating restorative environments into offices could enhance employees' mental wellbeing. The study found that restorative environments within the office space were positively associated with office workers' self-perceived mental wellbeing.

DOI: 10.4018/978-1-6684-8253-7.ch015

INTRODUCTION

Approximately half of the world's population currently resides in cities, and it has been projected that by the year 2030, around three out of every five people will be living in urban areas (Fuller and Gaston, 2009). Healthy urban environments are becoming increasingly important because over 50% of the world's population resides in dense urban areas (Dye, 2007). The urban lifestyle is often associated with unsatisfactory working environments, heavy workloads, tight schedules, and extended working hours (Facey et al., 2015). Work-related stress is a significant challenge to both workers' and organizational health, leading to a decline in an individual's physical and mental health, as well as the effectiveness and performance of the organization (WHO, 2011).

White-collar workers, who bear psychosocial work stressors in their working environments, are at a higher risk of developing mental disorders (Stansfeld and Candy, 2006). Job or occupational stress is a harmful emotional and physical response that occurs when the job demands cannot meet the workers' needs or abilities (Centres for Disease Control and Prevention, 2014). In Kuala Lumpur, which is a constantly expanding city, the residents need thoughtfully designed spaces to balance their hectic daily routine, provide relief from mental fatigue and stress, recreation, and offset the negative psychophysiological consequences of living in densely built urban environments (Braubach et al., 2017; Lee et al., 2015; Zhang et al., 2015).

Mental Wellbeing

The Centers for Disease Control and Prevention (CDC) defines mental wellbeing as having positive emotions and moods, such as happiness and contentment and being free from depression, anxiety, or other negative emotions (CDC, 2020). Wellbeing is a multifaceted concept that includes various physical, social, emotional, psychological, and community aspects (Kreitzer, 2014). The definition of mental wellbeing encompasses the hedonic perspective of feeling satisfied and happy and the eudaimonic perspective of self-realization, good relationships with others, and personal growth (Ryan & Deci, 2001). The absence of negative feelings and thoughts and the ability to manage challenging situations are also integral components of mental wellbeing (CABA, n.d.). Good mental health involves not only the absence of mental illness but also the ability to cope with daily stressors, work productively, and contribute to the community (WHO, 2014).

Mental Health Issues Among Office Workers

The concept of restorative environments (RE) within office developments has gained traction in recent years as a potential solution to mitigate the negative effects of office work on mental wellbeing. A RE is a physical space that promotes relaxation, reduces stress, and enhances mental restoration (Ulrich et al., 1991). Features such as natural lighting, greenery, and access to nature have been found to have a positive impact on mental health and cognitive performance (Kaplan, 1995).

However, the COVID-19 pandemic has brought new challenges to the workplace, such as remote work, social isolation, and increased workloads. These challenges have made it difficult for employees to access RE and have increased their risk of developing mental health issues (Chen et al., 2020). As a result, employers must adapt their strategies to promote mental wellbeing in the new normal of remote work and hybrid work environments.

Furthermore, the COVID-19 pandemic has brought new challenges to the workplace, with many employees now working from home. This has resulted in increased social isolation and blurred boundaries between work and personal life, which can contribute to stress and anxiety (Maben & Bridges, 2020). The lack of access to RE within office spaces has also been highlighted as a potential issue, with some employees struggling to find ways to incorporate restorative elements into their home working environment (Bailenson et al., 2021).

Mental health issues among office workers are a significant concern that requires proactive measures from employers. The RE trend has been seen as a potential solution, although challenges have arisen after COVID-19. Employers need to continue to prioritize mental wellbeing in the workplace, whether employees are working from home or in the office, and to incorporate restorative elements where possible.

Problem Statement

The population growth of Malaysia is increasing at a rate of 1.1% per year, resulting in a rise in the workforce, with 15.6 million workers in 2019 and 15.7 million workers in 2020. Of the workers in 2020, 28.2% are highly skilled, while 59.9% are semi-skilled and primarily work in office or indoor environments (Department of Statistics, 2020). Space is becoming more valuable in densely populated urban areas such as Penang, Klang Valley, and Johor. As cities expand and more people work in office spaces, the negative impact of urban living and workplace stress increases exponentially. Office workers spend significant time in stressful environments, leading to deteriorating mental wellbeing.

Occupational stress is caused by a lack of support from colleagues and supervisors, a lack of control over work processes, and poor management practices (WHO). Designers play a vital role in creating workspaces that alleviate work stress and promote mental and physical wellbeing. Many studies have established guidelines and shown the positive impact of RE on mental wellbeing in interior spaces. However, the effects of RE within Malaysian office spaces have not been previously studied or documented (Department of Statistics, 2020). Thus, this study attempted to investigate the current state of workspaces for the presence of RE and their effects on the mental wellbeing of office workers in Malaysia.

Research Questions

1. What are the existing conditions and elements of restorative environments in office spaces within Malaysia?
2. How do the environments within the office space affect the perceived mental wellbeing of office workers in Malaysia?
3. What are the office workers' preferences for restorative environments in their workspace?

BACKGROUND

Indoor Environment Quality and Occupant Wellbeing

Indoor Environmental Quality (IEQ) is an important factor to consider in office spaces in Malaysia, as it can impact the wellbeing and health of occupants. Mallawaarachchi et al. (2012) explain that IEQ measures the performance of the indoor environment and its effects on occupants. Previous studies have shown that various indoor environmental factors, such as lighting, ventilation, acoustics, thermal conditions, furniture, and ergonomics, can positively affect the wellbeing of building occupants when properly designed and implemented (Salonen et al., 2012). To ensure safe and healthy indoor environments, the Centre for Disease Control (CDC) has published an "Indoor Environmental Quality Policy" providing guidelines and procedures for building occupants (CDC, n.d). Architects in Malaysia are also required to follow several clauses in the Malaysian Uniform Building By Law (UBBL), 1984, to ensure the health and safety of occupants (UBBL, 1984).

Restorative Environments (RE)

RE refer to environments, often in natural settings, that can help reduce emotional and psychophysiological stress and rejuvenate or restore depleted attention resources. Such environments are characterized by legibility and elements that offer a break from the daily routine. These environments are based on Attention Restoration Theory and the Psycho-evolutionary Theory, which state that viewing or immersing oneself in natural surroundings can help improve focus and cognitive fatigue (American Psychology Association). According to the Attention Restoration theories (ART) proposed by Kaplan (1989, 1995), the brain's capacity to focus on specific stimuli or tasks is limited, leading to "directed attention fatigue" and mental exhaustion. Mental fatigue can result in various adverse consequences, including irritability, inaccuracy, incivility, and impulsivity.

The COVID-19 pandemic has highlighted the importance of creating RE in office spaces; it promotes stress reduction, psychological restoration, and individual wellbeing (Cairns, 2020). The growing recognition of the link between the physical environment and mental health has fueled this trend. Studies have shown that the built environment can significantly impact individuals' mental health and wellbeing (Kjellgren & Buhrkall, 2010). For example, access to greenery and natural light has been found to reduce stress levels and promote relaxation (Cairns, 2020). Comfortable seating and ergonomic workstations have also been found to improve wellbeing and reduce physical discomfort among workers (Browning et al., 2014).

The COVID-19 pandemic has created new challenges for creating RE in office spaces. One of the main challenges is balancing health and safety concerns with creating welcoming and comfortable workspaces. For example, open-plan offices, which were popular in the past, may need to be redesigned to incorporate barriers or other safety measures (Holtzhausen, 2020). Despite these challenges, the trend towards creating RE in office spaces will likely grow in importance post-COVID-19. This is because the pandemic has highlighted the importance of mental health and wellbeing, and employers are recognizing the need to create supportive and restorative work environments. This trend is likely driven by a desire to attract and retain top talent and promote employee productivity and creativity (Stevenson, 2021).

Importance of Indoor Environment Quality in Workplaces

Previous research has demonstrated the relationship between indoor environmental quality and occupants' physical and psychosocial wellbeing (Dolan et al., 2016). Physical aspects of the indoor environment, such as lighting, noise control, and office furniture and layout, are directly linked to employee stress levels (Vischer, 2007). A field study of six different office spaces with varying features found that physical characteristics such as lighting, acoustics, and cubicle size in open-plan offices can impact work performance and satisfaction (Newsham et al., 2004; Haynes, 2008). There is also evidence that the indoor environment of a workplace can impact a company's operational costs (Heerwagen, 2000).

The indoor workplace environment directly impacts the wellbeing and health of occupants, and buildings that promote their prosperity and happiness contribute to healthy living (Croome, 2013). Architects and the construction industry should focus on creating built environments that foster occupants' health and wellbeing, rather than just meeting the minimum requirements of building regulations and maximizing cost efficiency for profit.

A well-designed and conducive interior work environment can lead to reduced staff turnover rates, fewer sick leaves, increased productivity and job satisfaction, and improved perceived health and wellbeing of the office staff (McGraw-Hill Construction, 2014; US Green Building Council, 2004). The past and current research findings highlight the impact of indoor environmental quality on employee productivity and underscore the importance of good Indoor Environment Quality (IEQ) for the occupants' productivity.

The Effect of Natural Environment on Health and Wellbeing of Individuals

According to Hartig et al. (1996), exposure to natural environments can positively impact the health and wellbeing of individuals compared to urban environments. Stigsdotter et al. (2010) also found empirical evidence of the positive relationship between green outdoor spaces and city dwellers. Studies conducted in the US by Kuo and Sullivan (2001a, 2001b) suggest that exposure to natural environments may reduce anger, frustration, and aggression, potentially leading to decreased aggressive behavior and criminal activity rates.

In addition, Berman et al. (2008) conducted multiple experiments with 50 adults with a mean age of 24.5 and found that short encounters with the natural environment could significantly increase cognitive control. The positive effects of nature on cognitive function and health have also been established by Sanchez et al. (2018). Furthermore, a study conducted in Sweden by Lottrup et al. (2013) found that there were significant relationships between visual and physical access to workplace greenery, decreased stress levels, and a positive workplace attitude among male respondents. These findings highlight the restorative qualities of exposure to nature in an outdoor setting, which have been extensively studied for decades and fall under the branch of study known as RE.

ELEMENTS OF RE AND THEIR BENEFITS

Windows and Views

Various studies have found windows and views of nature positively impact physical and psychological health (Velarde et al., 2007). Research conducted on nurses in hospitals with 12-hour shifts revealed that those with views of nature through windows experienced better stress recovery than those without non-nature views (Pati et al., 2007). In another study, workplaces with views of natural elements positively correlated with high view satisfaction, which correlated with high job satisfaction and work efficiency (Lottrup et al., 2013). A study conducted on a group of workers after a series of written tests and simulations of office workers found that those working in an office with a window view of nature experienced a more restorative heart rate recovery as compared to those without a view or with a nature view displayed through a flatscreen TV (Khan Jr et al., 2008).

Sounds and Sights of Simulated Nature

Using simulated nature, such as murals, paintings, videos, and sounds, has been found to have restorative benefits. Immersive and coherent depictions of nature in murals and paintings can give the observer a sense of being within the environment and increase their perception of being away from their current setting (de Kort et al., 2006). Natural landscapes depicted in murals are aesthetically pleasing and preferred for restoration (Purcell et al., 2001). Large nature murals have been found to provide restorative breaks for university students experiencing attentional fatigue (Flesten, 2009). The addition of natural sounds and large posters of natural landscapes to the waiting room of a student medical center was found to slightly lower the anxiety levels of patients compared to the waiting room with no changes, although the posters did not fully cover the walls (Watts et al., 2016).

Daylighting

Natural lighting has been identified as an essential element of RE. According to Heschong et al. (2002), natural lighting is one of the most important factors in enhancing workers' performance. Research has shown that individuals in urban settings spend 90% of their working hours indoors, leading to a lack of exposure to natural light-dark cycles (McCurdy & Graham, 2003). Office workers' productivity is linked to the distance from windows and the amount of daylight exposure in the workplace, as decreased exposure can lead to decreased productivity and increased sick leave (Boyce, 2006).

However, when workers in daylit, open-plan workplaces are exposed to highly correlated color temperature (CCT) fluorescent lamps, their subjective performance measures, sleep, and productivity improve (Viola et al., 2008). Natural lighting has also been found to be essential for wellbeing (Anderson et al., 2013). The California Energy Commission conducted a study that found workers' efficiency increases with natural lighting in workspaces (Heschong et al., 2003).

Real and Artificial Plants

Using real and artificial plants in indoor environments can have a restorative impact. Patients in a hospital waiting room exposed to real or fake plants reported lower stress levels than those in a control condition (Beukeboom & Dijkstra, 2012). Similarly, the presence of plants and exposure to nature has been positively associated with the productivity and wellbeing of workers, with outdoor plants having better results than indoor and potted plants (Grind & Patil, 2009). Adding green elements to a temporary site office led to better social benefits, such as cooperation and mentoring, and positive psychological effects, such as increased work satisfaction and higher morale, which enhanced users' productivity in handling work-related tasks (Grey & Birrel, 2014).

Timber Office Furniture

According to research, wooden furniture in indoor environments may reduce stress. Studies examining the psychophysiological effects of indoor timber have demonstrated a decrease in autonomic stress responses compared to spaces with little or no timber. In an office furnished with wood, participants showed lower stress levels throughout the study than those in a non-wood office (Bunard & Kutnar, 2015). Increasing the use of timber may be a cost-effective and sustainable way to connect building occupants with the natural environment, as it is perceived as more natural than other materials (Burnard et al., 2017).

METHODS

The study aimed to examine the current state of workspaces for the presence of RE and their effects on the mental wellbeing of office workers in Malaysia. A quantitative approach using survey instruments was used to collect the data from the respondents.

Instruments

In order to accomplish the objective of the study, a survey questionnaire was administered to office workers in office developments throughout Malaysia, utilizing a quantitative research methodology. A quantitative approach was deemed appropriate as the analysis and outcomes needed to be numerical for broader generalization to Malaysia's larger population of office workers. This method was well-suited for the study as it required a comparison among the target group, making any numerical discrepancies easily detectable (Sukamolson, 2007). The study participants were office workers, and the survey questionnaire was specifically created to elicit responses to the research questions.

An online survey questionnaire developed using Google Forms was used to collect data for the study. This method was chosen because it is efficient and time-saving, allowing for instant data collection and analysis through spreadsheets. Participants were briefly introduced to the RE and the study's aim. The survey was conducted over two months and distributed to individuals and their colleagues working in a high-rise or low-rise commercial office units across East and West Malaysia. The survey instrument comprised four main parts, as presented in Table 1.

Respondents of the Study

To ensure the study's accuracy, the participants were randomly selected from the target population of office workers who spend a considerable amount of time working in an office environment. Informed consent was obtained from the participants who met certain inclusion criteria, such as being of a particular age, having a specific level of education, or working full-time. This approach aimed to prevent potential bias in the sample selection (Kothari, 2004).

Part 2 of the questionnaire consists of 6 questions to understand the existing conditions of the respondent's office space and to identify the elements of RE in the office spaces. The elements used in the questionnaire were identified from the literature reviews (as shown in Table 2). Respondents were given a multiple-choice question to choose the variant for each element.

The third section of the questionnaire included the Warwick Edinburgh Mental Wellbeing Scale (WEMWBS) (Table 3), developed by the universities of Warwick and Edinburgh to assess an individual's mental wellbeing using a 5-point Likert scale. The Likert scale ranges from "1 - None of the time" to "5 - all of the time" and includes positively worded statements covering both functional and emotional aspects of mental wellbeing, making it easily understandable.

This tool has been widely used to evaluate programs and investigate determinants of mental wellbeing nationally and internationally. The WEMWBS scale is self-administered, and the total score is calculated

Table 1. Questionnaire survey aligned to the research questions of the study

Sections	Questions		Research Questions
Part 1	Q1-Q7	Demographics	-
Part 2	Q8-Q13	Identify the presence of elements of Restorative Environments within their current office space	What are the existing conditions or elements of restorative environments in office spaces within Malaysia?
Part 3	Q14-Q24	Assessment of respondents' mental wellbeing using the Warwick Edinburgh Mental Wellbeing Scale (WEMWBS) with a 5-point Likert Scale	How do the environments within the office space affect the perceived mental wellbeing of office workers in Malaysia?
Part 4	Q25-Q30	Preference of RE by respondents using a 5-point Likert scale questionnaire. Participants were to choose from a list of elements that they would prefer to have in future office development or a workplace	What are the office workers' preferences for restorative environments in their workspace?

Table 2. Elements of restorative environment identified from literature review.

	Part 2		
	Variant	**Element**	**Literature Review**
Q8	Presence of windows (views to nature, views to city, no views, no windows)	Windows	(Velarde et al., 2007) (Kaplan, 2001) (Pati et al., 2007) (Lottrup et al, 2013) (Khan Jr et al., 2008)
Q9	Presence of images of natural environments (Paintings/mural arts, photographs, wallpapers, none)	Painting/ Photographs of natural landscapes	(deKort et al., 2006) (Ulrich, 1993; Purcell et al, 2001) (Flesten, 2009) (Watts et al., 2016) (Beernink, 2017)
Q10	Presence of light (more natural light, more artificial light)	Natural light	(Sanchez et al., 2018) (Czeisler et al., 1999) (McCurdy & Graham, 2003) (P. Boyce, 2006) (Viola et al., 2008) (Heschong et al., 2003) (Anderson et al, 2013) (Joarder & Price, 2013)
Q11	Presence of plants (artificial /natural, none)	Plants (artificial / natural)	(Beukeboom & Dijkstra, 2012) (Grinde & Patil, 2009) (Grey & Birrel, 2014) (Sanchez et al., 2018)
Q12	Types of office furniture (timber, non-timber)	Timber furniture	(Bunard & Kutnar, 2015) (Fell, 2010) (Burnard et al., 2017)
Q13	Presence of sounds of nature (sounds of water feature, birds, none)	Sounds of nature	(Watts et al., 2016)

by adding up the scores of all 14 items, ranging from 14-70. The WEMWBS has been compared to the CES-D and has shown a high correlation (.84), with scores of 41-44 indicating possible/mild depression and scores below 41 indicative of probable clinical depression (Stewart-Brown, 2021; Warwick Medical School, n.d.).

Table 3. Warwick Edinburgh mental wellbeing scale

Part 3	
Q14	I am feeling optimistic towards the future
Q15	I have been feeling useful
Q16	I have been feeling relaxed
Q17	I have had the energy to spare
Q18	I have been dealing with problems well
Q19	I have been thinking clearly
Q20	I have been feeling good about myself
Q21	I have been feeling close to other people
Q22	I have been feeling confident
Q23	I have been able to make up my own mind about things
Q24	I have been feeling loved
Q25	I have been interested in new things
Q26	I have been feeling cheerful

(Source: https://warwick.ac.uk/fac/sci/med/research/platform/wemwbs/u
sing/howto/)

Part 4 of the questionnaire is related to the respondents' preferences on the individual elements of RE in their workspace using a 5-point Likert scale, which ranges from "1 - less important" to "5 - most important" (Table 4).

FINDINGS

To assess the potential influence of RE on the perceived mental wellbeing of office workers, the study intends to analyze the WEMWBS scores of each respondent according to the presence of RE elements in their office spaces. The mean and standard deviation of the WEMWBS scores for each variant will be calculated and compared to the average WEMWBS score of the entire target group. This approach aims to determine if the presence of RE elements in office spaces impacts the perceived mental wellbeing of office workers.

Table 4. Preferences of elements restorative environment

Part 4	
Q27	Natural light
Q28	Painting/Photo/Wallpaper of landscapes
Q29	Natural/Artificial plants
Q30	Timber/Wood Furniture
Q31	Windows with views
Q32	Sounds of water features/birds

• Presence of Windows

Respondents working within workplaces with 'Views towards cities' reported a higher mean WEMWBS score than 'Window views to nature'. Both items scored higher (48.28 and 36.50) than the average score of 35.14. As for 'Windows with no views (blocked or translucent glass)' and 'No windows' scored lower than average with 32.50 and 32.68, respectively (See Table 5)

• Presence of Images of Natural Environments

Meaning 'Painting/Mural' and 'Wallpaper of Natural Landscape' scored higher than the average score of 35.14 with 38.47 and 38 'Photographs' also scored relatively higher (35.53) than the average, while the item 'None' scored the least (32.93) (Table 5).

• Presence of Light

The item 'More natural light' was scored almost close (35.89) to the average, while 'More artificial light' was scored lower (34.55). However, the differences between the items are minimal.

• Presence of Plants

Within this RE element, the item 'Natural plants' and 'Artificial plants' were scored above the average with a mean of 36.60 and 35.76, respectively; meanwhile, item 'None' was scored lower (33.08) than average.

• Type of Office Furniture

Item 'Timber / wooden tables chairs and shelves' scored higher (38.50) than the average, while 'Non-timber / wooden tables chairs and shelves' scored lower (32.04) than the average.

• Presence of Sounds of Nature

Among these RE elements, 'Sounds of water feature/birds' is higher (38.50) than the average, and item 'None' scored lower (33.81) than the average.

The results presented in Table 6 demonstrate the restorative qualities of various elements and their impact on office workers' mental wellbeing. The elements were ranked in ascending order based on their mean WEMWBS score. The study found that 'Views to cities' had the highest mean WEMWBS score (48.28) among all the elements, followed by 'Sounds of water feature and birds' and 'Timber/ wooden tables, chairs, and shelves' with a mean score of 38.50. 'Painting/Mural' (38.47), 'Wallpaper of natural landscape' (38.00), 'Natural plants' (36.60), 'More natural light' (35.89), 'Artificial plants' (35.76), and 'Photographs' (35.53) also scored above average. However, the study found that seven elements scored lower than the average, including 'More artificial light' (34.55), 'No sounds of nature' (33.81), 'No plants' (33.08), 'No images of the natural landscape' (32.93), 'No windows' (32.68), 'Windows but with no views' (blocked or translucent glass) (32.50), and 'Non-timber/ wooden tables, chairs, and shelves' with the lowest mean score (32.04)

Table 5. Restorative elements, sum, Mean, and SD of WEMWBS score

Restorative Elements	Number of Respondents	Sum of WEMWBS Score	Mean of WEMWBS Score
	(N= 104)	(N=3655)	AVG: 35.14
Presence of Windows			
Window views of nature	34	1242	36.50 (8.04)
Views to Cities	25	1272	48.28 (7.52)
Windows with no views (blocked or translucent glass)	19	618	32.50 (8.80)
No windows	16	523	32.68 (9.02)
Presence of Images of Natural Environments			
Painting/Mural	19	731	38.47 (7.19)
Wallpaper of natural landscape	13	494	38.00 (6.89)
Photographs	15	553	35.53 (7.48)
None	57	1877	32.93 (8.67)
Presence of Light			
More natural light	46	1651	35.89 (8.67)
More artificial light	58	2004	34.55 (7.78)
Presence of Plants			
Natural plants	45	1647	36.60 (8.71)
Artificial plants	21	751	35.76 (8.08)
None	38	1257	33.08 (7.94)
Type of Office Furniture			
Timber / Wooden tables, chairs and shelves	50	1925	38.5 (6.51)
Non-timber / Wooden tables, chairs, and shelves	54	1730	32.04 (8.59)
Presence of Sounds of Nature			
Sounds of water feature / Birds	29	1119	38.5 (7.56)
None	75	2536	33.81 (7.99)

DISCUSSION

The study aimed to investigate whether incorporating RE in office spaces could improve the mental wellbeing of Malaysian office workers who spend significant time in stressful work environments. The study aimed to identify the presence of RE elements in current office spaces and assess their impact on the mental wellbeing of office workers. Furthermore, the study aimed to determine office users' preferences for RE features and elements in their workplace and identify potential improvements to current workspaces. Previous studies have shown that RE has been linked with allowing the brain to recover from low-stress situations.

The study aimed to investigate how RE in office spaces affects the perceived mental wellbeing of office workers by examining the current conditions of RE elements in office spaces and the preferences of office workers regarding RE. A quantitative method was employed to achieve this, and a survey questionnaire with four sections was distributed to participants using Google Forms. The sections were

Table 6. Elements of RE and mean WEMWBS score against the average score

Restorative Environments	Mean of WEMWBS Score
Views to Cities	48.28
Sounds of water feature / Birds	38.50
Timber / Wooden tables, chairs, and shelves	38.50
Painting/Mural	38.47
Wallpaper of natural landscape	38.00
Natural plants	36.60
Window views of nature	36.50
More natural light	35.89
Artificial plants	35.76
Photographs	35.53
Average	**35.14**
More artificial light	34.55
No sounds of nature	33.81
No plants	33.08
No images of the natural landscape	32.93
No windows	32.68
Windows but with no views (blocked or translucent glass)	32.50
Non-timber / wooden tables, chairs, shelves	32.04

demographics, identification of RE elements in current office spaces, the WEMWBS mental-wellbeing scale, and preferences. The data collected from 104 participants were analyzed using descriptive statistics.

The data on the characteristics of the respondents indicated that most of them were young professionals who had recently started working. Most respondents, 80 (76.9%), were aged between 21 and 30 years, and 71 (68.3%) had worked for less than two years. Less than half of the respondents, 49 (47.1%), worked five days a week, while 18 (17.3%) worked six days a week. This pattern is consistent with a previous study that identified unfavorable work conditions, heavy workloads, tight schedules, and long working hours as common features of urban workplaces (Facey et al., 2015).

The results of the data analysis revealed that respondents who worked in offices with RE (RE) had higher average scores on the WEMWBS mental wellbeing scale than those who worked in offices without RE. These findings support previous research that has suggested that exposure to RE can aid in the recovery from low-stress situations, allowing individuals to relax and unwind (Pati et al., 2007; Fell, 2010; Beukeboom & Dijkstra, 2012). This is because RE possess qualities such as "Being Away," which creates a sense of separation from one's thoughts and worries, and "Fascination," which holds an individual's attention effortlessly, facilitating relaxation and even introspection (Kaplan, 1989).

The presence of RE impacts the perceived mental wellbeing of office spaces, with the data collected indicating a strong correlation with visual qualities. Respondents with more natural lighting in their office spaces had higher WEMWBS scores than those with more artificial lighting (as shown in Table 7), which supports previous studies (Anderson et al., 2013; Joarder & Price, 2013). Natural light connects nature and the outside world, creating a sense of being away from the office space. It also provides good visual qualities and changes throughout the day, essential for regulating circadian rhythms. The importance of natural light to humans was also demonstrated in the study, as it was identified as the most preferred element (77.9%) by the respondents.

View plays an important role in increasing people's sense of wellbeing (Kaplan, 2001). As indicated in previous studies, office workers working in workspaces with views toward natural elements have higher satisfaction (Lottrup et al., 2013). In this study, 'Views toward cityscapes' was identified as having the most potent restorative effect compared to 'Views of nature' (Table 7). Interestingly, this finding correlates with a study that examined office workers from the US, which showed no differences between the wellbeing of office workers who have more natural or more man-made views through their windows.

View features are more important in affecting workers' wellbeing, such as views within a high-rise building overlooking the city or expansive views that offer long-range visibility (Esch et al., 2019). This finding contradicts the study conducted on university students within a campus, which reported that natural elements are more restorative than cityscapes (Fell, 2010). Findings show that artworks, mural arts, and nature photographs have strong restorative effects; however, the effect of these elements is lower compared to the view of real cityscapes from the window. Viewing outside a window, far away from the office space, evokes a sense of fascination and being away, losing one's thoughts and worries. Natural and artificial plant photographs have the same features that reflect outdoor space but are smaller. Therefore, their restorative effects are lower.

According to the data analysis (Table 7), elements of RE that provide immersion have a stronger restorative effect. These elements include views of cities, the sound of water features or birds, timber or wooden furniture, and paintings or murals of natural landscapes. These elements surround office workers spatially and align with the concept of RE, which emphasizes the need for elements that provide a break from routine and evoke fascination and a sense of being away from stressors (American Psychology Association, n.d.). These elements allow users to momentarily disconnect from their worries and concerns, which is a fundamental aspect of RE as proposed by the Kaplans. Even though physical distance is not necessary to achieve this effect, it can enhance it (Daniel, 2014).

RECOMMENDATIONS AND CONCLUSION

Windows and Views

The research indicates that for optimal employee wellbeing, it is recommended that workspaces should be positioned facing windows that avoid glare and excess solar radiation while providing views of wide-open spaces or features where human activities occur. To maximize natural light exposure throughout the day, the windows are suggested to face either North or South. Incorporating nearby public spaces such as parks can be beneficial in the design of office buildings.

Green Indoor Rest Spaces

To improve the quality of relaxation for employees, it is suggested that green spaces featuring plants or nature landscapes be incorporated into the office's rest areas, lounges, or dining areas. This addition will further enhance the restorative qualities of these areas, providing a space for workers to take a break from their work or enjoy their meals in a more relaxing environment.

Table 7. Identified patterns

Patterns	Natural light	Theme
P1	Office workers found to prefer natural lighting in their workspace as compared to artificial lighting	Light - Nature
P2	Natural lighting has a good effect on the mental wellbeing of office workers as compared to artificial lighting	Light - Nature
	Views	
P5	View towards cityscapes and nature have a good effect on the mental wellbeing of office workers	View
P6	Artwork and photographs of natural landscapes have a positive effect on the mental wellbeing of office workers	Views - Nature
P7	Murals and wallpapers of natural landscapes have a higher perceived wellbeing score than photographs and none.	Views - Immersion
P8	Office workers prefer artificial/natural plants compared to no plants at all in the office	Views - Nature
	Immersion	
P6	Artwork and photographs of natural landscapes have a positive effect on the mental wellbeing of office workers	Immersion - Views
P8	Sounds of nature have a positive effect on the perceived wellbeing of the office workers	Immersion - Nature
P10	Office workers prefer timber furniture compared to other materials	Immersion - Nature

Nature Sounds

In conclusion, the study recommends the installation of indoor water features in workplaces to produce soothing sounds during work hours and using speakers to play sounds of the forest or sea in office spaces. Based on the analysis of the mean WEMWBS scores and the elements of RE, there is a positive correlation between these elements and the mental wellbeing of office workers. These findings answer the research question: "How do restorative environments within office spaces impact the perceived mental wellbeing of office workers in Malaysia?"

A good RE for office workers is natural light, views and vistas, and a sense of immersion. These elements enable workers to shift their focus away from their tasks after prolonged periods of work (known as directed attention fatigue) and towards something else that requires less effort (known as effortless attention). This restoration process is based on the Attention Restoration Theory (ART) proposed by Kaplan in 1989 and 1995.

Natural light is important as it provides visual stimulation and allows for changing qualities throughout the day. Views and vistas, whether real or simulated, such as through wallpaper, mural art, or small plants, allow for effortless attention and a break from directed attention. Through mural art, wallpaper, sounds of nature, or timber furniture, immersion provides a sense of escape and relaxation, allowing for a break from work and the restoration of attention to continue focusing on tasks after a brief respite.

In conclusion, creating a RE in office spaces is essential for promoting the wellbeing of office workers. Elements such as natural light, views and vistas, and a sense of immersion can help workers recover from directed attention fatigue, which is common after long work periods. By implementing such features, workers can take breaks and shift their focus away from their tasks, allowing their minds to recharge and reducing stress. The benefits of RE are clear, with research demonstrating the positive correlation between these features and the mental wellbeing of office workers. Thus, employers should prioritize the creation of RE in the workplace to enhance the overall wellbeing of their workforce.

REFERENCES

American Psychology Association. (n.d.). *Restorative Environments.* APA. https://www.apa.org/monitor/2019/03/restorative-environments

Anderson, J., Wojtowicz, M., & Wineman, A. (2013). The impact of daylighting on human health. *Lighting Research & Technology, 45*(2), 159–175. doi:10.1177/1477153512457607

Anderson, M. D., Carson, D. C., & Grandy, J. (2013). Office light quality and alertness in two office environments. *Journal of Environmental Psychology, 36,* 94–101.

Bailenson, J. N., Yee, N., & Blascovich, J. (2021). Virtual restorative environments: An immersive technology for personal and planetary health. *Frontiers in Psychology, 11,* 3583.

Berman, M. G., Jonides, J., & Kaplan, S. (2008). The cognitive benefits of interacting with nature. *Psychological Science, 19*(12), 1207–1212. doi:10.1111/j.1467-9280.2008.02225.x PMID:19121124

Beukeboom, C. J., & Dijkstra, A. (2012). The effect of plants and fascia on stress-related symptoms and blood pressure in office workers: A randomized, controlled study. *Environmental Health Perspectives, 120*(3), 377–381.

Boyce, P. (2006). *Human factors in lighting* (2nd ed.). Taylor & Francis.

Braubach, M., Egorov, A. I., Mudu, P., Wolf, T., Ward Thompson, C., & Martuzzi, M. (2017). Effects of urban green space on environmental health, equity and resilience: A scoping review. *Urban Forestry & Urban Greening, 29,* 310–323.

Browning, W. D., Ryan, C. O., & Clancy, J. O. (2014). *14 Patterns of Biophilic Design.* Terrapin Bright Green LLC. https://www.terrapinbrightgreen.com/wp-content/uploads/2014/06/14-Patterns-of-Biophilic-Design-Terrapin-Bright-Green-2014.pdf

Bunard, D., & Kutnar, A. (2015). The effect of wood on stress responses in office workers. *Forests, 6*(7), 2336–2352.

Burnard, M., Fragiacomo, M., & Hozjan, T. (2017). Review of the perceptual qualities of timber and timber-based products relevant to sensory evaluation of indoor spaces. *Building and Environment, 124,* 52–63.

CABA. (n.d.). *What is mental wellbeing?* CABA. https://www.caba.org.uk/help-and-guides/information/what-mental-wellbeing

Cairns, T. (2020). *How to create a restorative environment in the office.* Raconteur. https://www.raconteur.net/sustainability/how-to-create-a-restorative-environment-in-the-office

Centers for Disease Control and Prevention. (2014). *Work-related stress.* National Institute for Occupational Safety and Health.

Centers for Disease Control and Prevention. (2020). *Mental health basics.* CDC. https://www.cdc.gov/mentalhealth/basics/index.htm

Chen, Y., McCabe, O. L., & Hyman, M. R. (2020). Workplace stress and mental health in the era of COVID-19: An urgent need for action. *International Journal of Environmental Research and Public Health, 17*(19), 7272. doi:10.3390/ijerph17197272 PMID:33027956

Croome, D. (2013). *Creating and managing healthy built environments*. Routledge.

Czeisler, C. A., Duffy, J. F., Shanahan, T. L., Brown, E. N., Mitchell, J. F., Rimmer, D. W., Ronda, J. M., Silva, E. J., Allan, J. S., Emens, J. S., Dijk, D.-J., & Kronauer, R. E. (1999). Stability, precision, and near-24-hour period of the human circadian pacemaker. *Science, 284*(5423), 2177–2181. doi:10.1126cience.284.5423.2177 PMID:10381883

Daniel, T. C. (2014). Contributions of psychology to an understanding of the restorative environment. In *Biophilic Cities* (pp. 19–31). Island Press.

de Kort, Y. A. W., Meijnders, A. L., Sponselee, A. A. G., & IJsselsteijn, W. A. (2006). What's wrong with virtual trees? Restoring from stress in a mediated environment. *Journal of Environmental Psychology, 26*(4), 309–320. doi:10.1016/j.jenvp.2006.09.001

Department of Statistics. (2020). *Malaysia Labour Force Statistics in Brief 2020*. DoSM. https://www.dosm.gov.my/v1/index.php?r=column/cthemeByCat&cat=155&bul_id=MGhZUTdVWXpveElUUld MYVhCRWlKQT09&menu_id=L0pheU43NWJwRWVSZklWdzQ4TlhUUT09

Dolan, M., Fullam, R., & Casey, E. (2016). The relationship between indoor environmental quality in Irish offices and occupant perceived health and productivity. *Building and Environment, 108*, 290–298.

Dye, C. (2007). Health and urban living. *Science, 318*(5852), 766–769. PMID:18258905

Esch, T., Kim, M. J., Stefano, G. B., Fricchione, G. L., Benson, H., & Kirschbaum, C. (2019). The city versus the country: A cross-sectional study of cortisol and depression in urban and rural areas. *BMC Psychiatry, 19*(1), 1–9. PMID:30606141

Facey, M. E., Middleton, J., & Griffiths, P. (2015). Managing Employee Stress and Wellness in the New Normal. In E. G. Carayannis & Y. H. Zhao (Eds.), *The Handbook of Stress and Health: A Guide to Research and Practice* (pp. 441–454). Springer. doi:10.1007/978-1-4939-3117-6_25

Facey, M. E., Rees, C. E., & Monrouxe, L. V. (2015). Being 'student-led': Challenging hierarchy in healthcare education and identifying solutions. *Journal of Further and Higher Education, 39*(2), 248–265.

Fell, D. (2010). *Nature, landscape and natural spaces in universities: Restorative qualities of familiar places for students*. University of Manchester.

Flesten, L. (2009). *The influence of natural views in an office environment on recovery from mental fatigue*. [Bachelor's thesis, Lund University, Lund, Sweden].

Fuller, R. A., & Gaston, K. J. (2009). The scaling of green space coverage in European cities. *Biology Letters, 5*(3), 352–355. doi:10.1098/rsbl.2009.0010 PMID:19324636

Grey, C. N., & Birrell, C. (2014). Green over grey: The importance of biophilic design in a temporary site office. *Indoor and Built Environment, 23*(6), 863–877.

Grind, C. C., & Patil, G. G. (2009). The effect of indoor foliage plants on health and discomfort symptoms among office workers. *HortTechnology*, *19*(2), 278–282.

Hartig, T., Evans, G. W., Jamner, L. D., Davis, D. S., & Gärling, T. (1996). Tracking restoration in natural and urban field settings. *Journal of Environmental Psychology*, *16*(2), 87–101.

Haynes, B. P. (2008). Workplaces and low carbon behaviour. *Building Research and Information*, *36*(2), 196–212.

Heerwagen, J. H. (2000). Green buildings, organizational success and occupant productivity. *Building Research and Information*, *28*(5-6), 353–367. doi:10.1080/096132100418500

Heschong, L., Heschong, M., & Wright, R. (2003). *Windows and offices: A study of office worker performance and the indoor environment*. California Energy Commission.

Heschong, L., Wright, R. L., Okura, S., & Moule, R. A. Jr. (2002). *Windows and Offices: A Study of Office Worker Performance and the Indoor Environment*. California Energy Commission.

Holtzhausen, D. (2020). Designing post-pandemic office spaces. *Engineering News*. https://www.engineeringnews.co.za/article/designing-post-pandemic-office-spaces-2020-07-10

Joarder, M. A., & Price, A. D. F. (2013). Factors influencing visual quality and occupants' preference in office buildings. *Architectural Science Review*, *56*(2), 146–155.

Kaplan, S. (1989). The restorative benefits of nature: Toward an integrative framework. *Journal of Environmental Psychology*, *15*(3), 169–182. doi:10.1016/0272-4944(95)90001-2

Kaplan, S. (1995). The restorative environment: Nature and human experience. In J. L. Nasar & A. S. G. Nasar (Eds.), *Environmental aesthetics: Theory, research, and application* (pp. 233–250). Cambridge University Press. doi:10.1017/CBO9780511525599.017

Kaplan, S. (2001). Meditation, restoration, and the management of mental fatigue. *Environment and Behavior*, *33*(4), 480–506. doi:10.1177/00139160121973106

Khan, M. M. Jr, Howe, E. T., Chu, A. H., & Nunamaker, J. F. Jr. (2008). *The impact of a nature view on stress reduction of users in a virtual reality simulated office environment*. 27th International Conference on Information Systems, Milwaukee, WI, USA.

Kjellgren, A., & Buhrkall, H. (2010). A comparison of the restorative effect of a natural environment with that of a simulated natural environment. *Journal of Environmental Psychology*, *30*(4), 464–472. doi:10.1016/j.jenvp.2010.01.011

Kothari, C. R. (2004). *Research methodology: Methods and techniques*. New Age International.

Kreitzer, M. J. (2014). Well-being concepts. In *Complementary and Integrative Therapies for Mental Health and Aging* (pp. 3–18). Oxford University Press.

Kuo, F. E., & Sullivan, W. C. (2001a). Aggression and violence in the inner city: Effects of environment via mental fatigue. *Environment and Behavior*, *33*(4), 543–571. doi:10.1177/00139160121973124

Kuo, F. E., & Sullivan, W. C. (2001b). Environment and crime in the inner city: Does vegetation reduce crime? *Environment and Behavior, 33*(3), 343–367. doi:10.1177/0013916501333002

Lee, A. C. K., Jordan, H. C., Horsley, J., & Value, E. (2015). The health benefits of urban green spaces: A review of the evidence. *Journal of Public Health, 38*(3), e450–e461. PMID:20833671

Lottrup, L., Stigsdotter, U. K., Meilby, H., & Claudi, A. G. (2013). The workplace window view: A determinant of office workers' work ability and job satisfaction. *Landscape Research, 38*(2), 259–267.

Lottrup, L., Stigsdotter, U. K., Meilby, H., & Claudi, A. G. (2013). The workplace window view: A determinant of office workers' work ability and job satisfaction. *Landscape Research, 38*(1), 19–34.

Lottrup, L., Stigsdotter, U. K., Meilby, H., Claudi, A. G., & Grahn, P. (2013). Workplace greenery and perceived level of stress: Benefits of access to a green outdoor environment at the workplace. *Landscape and Urban Planning, 110*, 5–11. doi:10.1016/j.landurbplan.2012.09.002

Maben, J., & Bridges, J. (2020). Covid-19: Supporting nurses' psychological and mental health. *Journal of Clinical Nursing, 29*(15-16), 2742–2750. doi:10.1111/jocn.15307 PMID:32320509

Mallawaarachchi, S., Jayasinghe, J., & Wijesooriya, W. (2012). Indoor environmental quality in green buildings. *Journal of Environmental Protection, 3*(03), 239–248. doi:10.4236/jep.2012.33032

McCurdy, L. E., & Graham, C. (2003). Living in the dark: A study of urban residents' environmental experience in a major North American city. *Journal of Environmental Psychology, 23*(4), 385–398. doi:10.1016/S0272-4944(02)00120-2

Mcgraw-Hill Construction. (2014). *The Drive Toward Healthier Buildings 2014: Tactical Intelligence to Transform Building Design and Construction.* SmartMarket Report.

Newsham, G. R., Veitch, J. A., Charles, K. E., & Huang, J. (2004). Effects of daylight and view of nature on office workers' well-being and performance. *Journal of Environmental Psychology, 24*(2), 417–435. doi:10.1016/j.jenvp.2004.08.009

Pati, D., Sahoo, S., & Sagar, R. (2007). Windows with a view: Nurses' stress relief at work. *Journal of Advanced Nursing, 60*(4), 427–432. PMID:17919164

Purcell, T., Peron, E., Berto, R., & Boyle, M. (2001). Why do preferences differ between scene types? *Environment and Behavior, 33*(1), 93–106. doi:10.1177/00139160121972882

Ryan, R. M., & Deci, E. L. (2001). On happiness and human potentials: A review of research on hedonic and eudaimonic well-being. *Annual Review of Psychology, 52*(1), 141–166. doi:10.1146/annurev.psych.52.1.141 PMID:11148302

Salonen, H. J., Lappalainen, S., & Kähkönen, E. (2012). Health and well-being in indoor spaces: A review of recent research. *Indoor and Built Environment, 21*(3), 335–351. doi:10.1177/1420326X11430862

Sanchez, C. A., Hedayati, M., Pielke, R. A. Jr, Anderson, C., & Steiner, A. L. (2018). The influence of greenness on the capacity of green infrastructure to provide multiple ecosystem services. *The Science of the Total Environment, 635*, 1175–1186.

Stansfeld, S. A., & Candy, B. (2006). Psychosocial work environment and mental health—A meta-analytic review. *Scandinavian Journal of Work, Environment & Health*, *32*(6), 443–462. doi:10.5271jweh.1050 PMID:17173201

Stevenson, F. (2021). *Restorative environments: the future of office design post-COVID-19*. The Guardian. https://www.theguardian.com/sustainable-business/2021/mar/25/restorative-environments-the-future-of-office-design-post-covid-19

Stewart-Brown, S. (2021). *Warwick Edinburgh Mental Wellbeing Scale (WEMWBS)*. Health and Wellbeing Services. https://warwick.ac.uk/fac/sci/med/research/platform/wemwbs/

Stigsdotter, U. K., Ekholm, O., Schipperijn, J., Toftager, M., Kamper-Jorgensen, F., & Randrup, T. B. (2010). Health promoting outdoor environments–Associations between green space, and health, health-related quality of life and stress based on a Danish national representative survey. *Scandinavian Journal of Public Health*, *38*(4), 411–417. doi:10.1177/1403494810367468 PMID:20413584

Sukamolson, S. (2007). *Research methodology and data analysis*. Srinakharinwirot University.

Ulrich, R. S., Simons, R. F., Losito, B. D., Fiorito, E., Miles, M. A., & Zelson, M. (1991). Stress recovery during exposure to natural and urban environments. *Journal of Environmental Psychology*, *11*(3), 201–230. doi:10.1016/S0272-4944(05)80184-7

Uniform Building By-Laws (UBBL) Malaysia. (1984). UBBL. *Lawnet*. http://www.lawnet.gov.my/act/akta-133/

US Green Building Council. (2004). *The business case for green building: A review of the costs and benefits for developers, investors and occupants*. US Green Building Council.

Velarde, M. D., Fry, G., & Tveit, M. (2007). Health effects of viewing landscapes – Landscape types in environmental psychology. *Urban Forestry & Urban Greening*, *6*(4), 199–212. doi:10.1016/j.ufug.2007.07.001

Viola, A. U., James, L. M., Schlangen, L. J., & Dijk, D. J. (2008). Blue-enriched white light in the workplace improves self-reported alertness, performance and sleep quality. *Scandinavian Journal of Work, Environment & Health*, *34*(4), 297–306. doi:10.5271jweh.1268 PMID:18815716

Vischer, J. C. (2007). The effects of the physical environment on job performance: Towards a theoretical model of workspace stress. *Stress and Health*, *23*(3), 175–184. doi:10.1002mi.1134

Warwick Medical School. (n.d.). *Warwick Edinburgh Mental Wellbeing Scale (WEMWBS) scoring*. Warwick. https://warwick.ac.uk/fac/sci/med/research/platform/wemwbs/using/wemwbs_scoring/

Watts, G., Mills, A. J., & Bullough, S. (2016). Adding nature back to the health service: An evaluation of a natural landscapes and sounds intervention in a student medical centre. *Health Environments Research & Design Journal*, *9*(3), 83–95. PMID:27733656

World Health Organization. (2011). Work-related stress. *Fact Sheet No. 331*. WHO.

World Health Organization. (2014). *Mental health: A state of well-being*. WHO. https://www.who.int/features/factfiles/mental_health/en/

Zhang, J., Wu, X., Chen, F., & Chen, Y. (2015). The effect of forest bathing on residents' perceived anxiety: Based on comparison of two forest types in Beijing. *Forests*, *6*(11), 4156–4170. doi:10.3390/f6114156

KEY TERMS AND DEFINITIONS

Attention Restoration Theory: A theory that suggests that mental fatigue and concentration can be improved by time spent in or looking at nature.

Mental Wellbeing: Mental wellbeing refers to a state of being in which an individual can cope with daily life's demands, work towards achieving their goals, and feel a sense of purpose and satisfaction. It is not simply the absence of mental health problems but rather a positive state of wellbeing.

Psycho-evolutionary Theory: the theoretical perspective that suggests that the human mind has evolved to adapt to the demands of the natural environment over time. It posits that the human mind has developed a set of psychological and cognitive mechanisms that have helped our ancestors to survive and reproduce in their specific ecological context.

Restorative Environments: Interior or exterior surroundings that have restorative capabilities.

Restorative Theory: the capacity for natural environments to replenish cognitive resources depleted by everyday activities and to reduce stress levels, according to the Attention Restoration Theory.

Warwick Edinburgh Mental Wellbeing Scale (WEMWBS): is a self-administered questionnaire with a 5-point Likert scale that measures an individual's mental wellbeing. The scale is intended for the general adult population and was developed in the United Kingdom.

Chapter 16
Architectural Challenges for Designing Social Interactive Spaces in Luxury High-Rise Residential Buildings in Kuala Lumpur

Xiang Loon Lee
Taylor's University, Malaysia

Sucharita Srirangam
Taylor's University, Malaysia

ABSTRACT

Affluent high-rise residential developments are booming in Mont Kiara and the City Centre of Kuala Lumpur, Malaysia. However, upscale high life subjects to social alienation issues. Research indicates that social spaces promote human health, but their integration in vertical living is still insignificant. This study investigates challenges with social space design in luxury high-rise buildings in Kuala Lumpur from designers' perspectives. Interviews were conducted with three architectural firms on the challenges they faced in implementation. Findings revealed challenges with synergistic relationships, architectural branding, spatial order, private-public articulation, space design, space optimisation, and space psychology. Subsequently, three characteristics of challenges on culture, impact, and communication were discussed for designers to respond to. On this basis, it is recommended that aspiring designers develop an awareness of these concerns in future designs and examine more challenges to identify tailored solutions to address these issues.

INTRODUCTION

Background

The demand for premium high-rise properties remains strong in hotspot areas in Kuala Lumpur, including Bangsar, Mont Kiara, and Cheras, due to their affordable entry price points (Bernama, 2019).

DOI: 10.4018/978-1-6684-8253-7.ch016

Other popular areas with a great supply include the Kuala Lumpur City Centre and Ampang Hilir (Ramachandran, 2018). Luxury high-rise residential buildings in Malaysia are commonly referred to as condominiums or serviced apartments owned by private entities and managed under the building community's landlord association. They are generally accompanied by private common facilities, such as sports courts, multipurpose halls, gymnasiums, barbecue areas, lush landscaping, and swimming pools. In contrast, multi-storey apartments and flats are typically owned by both public and private sectors. They tend to be low-end and affordable for the general public and have fewer facilities catering to the residents. Unlike condominiums and serviced apartments with gated and guarded security, apartments and flats are usually without such amenities, in exchange for a much smaller price tag.

Affluent Malaysians and expatriates prefer to reside in areas, such as Mont Kiara, Sri Hartamas, Damansara, KL City Centre, and Ampang due to their quiet districts, proximity to parks, and international institutions (The InterNations, 2019). With 56% of Mont Kiara's population comprising up to 7,540 expatriates, this expensive district is a prominent market for high-end lifestyle and exclusive living, with foreign cuisine eateries, branded grocery chains, and international schools (Chan, 2019). High-rise properties here are sold at an average price of MYR 680 to MYR 840 per square foot, compared to the state's average of MYR 396 per square foot (Knight Frank, 2019).

Occupants in high-rises have fewer friendships as they barely meet other residents on other floors, except in elevators and lobbies, compared to on streets. From the get-go, trips back home are optimised for efficient, personalised travel, from the car directly to the lifts and to individual dwellings, with little to no chance for any social relations whatsoever. In Malaysia, building owners in new gated and guarded condominiums prefer privacy to enjoy their privileged spaces away from the outside environment (Tedong, Grant & Abdul-Aziz, 2015). This leads to social polarisation, a term defined as the separation in a society into two distinctive groups on a spectrum between the rich and the poor (Castree, Kitchin & Rogers, 2013). The emerging premium high living often than not attracts expatriates or other affluent groups with money, contributing to the economy market. Such an expression of market power will likely change the urban character of the area and forces ethnic division (FL Sarayed, Zainol & Ahmad, 2017). Mont Kiara has showcased such migration of locals to other urban and suburban areas as buildings here turn into offices or expensive condominiums that serve as second homes or as an investment to the wealthy and expatriates. Daily and small businesses by the locals here do not work well, and the unlikelihood of locals who could not afford such extravagant living will eventually move out.

The Need to Investigate Architects' Challenges

Practice has shown that most important project decisions are conceived during the design stage, which significantly influences the subsequent stages of a project (Uher and Loosemore, 2004). A successful project delivery heavily depends on how well it is planned, designed, and documented during this stage. As decisions made by architects are of utmost significance, all efforts towards designing social spaces in luxury high-rise residential building to tackle social issues are vital.

The design breakthroughs to create residential towers to cater for families and to foster a sense of community oftentimes pose challenges to designers. Past literature has explored designer challenges for quality social spaces in high-rise living in cities such as Singapore and London (Evans, 2016; Modi, 2014; Quod, 2014) with relatively little research carried out in Malaysia. Past academia has examined the importance of social spaces in low to mid-cost high-rise housings, with a primary focus on the evaluation of spaces based on the perception of occupants. However, the growing number of expensive high-rises in Kuala Lumpur due to land scarcity and demand has resulted in social spaces in tower blocks receiving less spotlight. Therefore, the foregoing reasoning points to the need for in-depth investigation of designer challenges, which are worthy to be addressed.

This research thus aimed at understanding the scenarios of challenges faced by designers (i.e. architectural design firms) in the creation of social interactive spaces in luxury high-rise residential buildings in Kuala Lumpur by answering to the following questions:

1. What qualities do socially interactive spaces possess in high-rise residential designs?
2. What challenges must architects overcome to create effective social interactive spaces in upscale high-rise residential towers in Kuala Lumpur?
3. What are the defining characteristics of challenges that architects must respond to when designing socially interactive spaces?

In the sections that follow, a background literature review on high-rises, social interaction, and social spaces is discussed. Subsequently, the research method adopted for this study, and the resulting findings and conclusions are presented.

LITERATURE REVIEW

High-Rises and High-Rise Residential Typologies in Malaysia

The definition of a high-rise is subjective, but it considers the building's height in relation to its context, proportion, and technological incorporation. Craighead (2009) defined it as a multi-level built structure that requires lifts. In numbers, it is typically set at around 23 to 30 meters (i.e. seven to 10 storeys), where the available fire-fighting equipment is unreachable at the highest point of the building. The Malaysian Uniform Building By-Laws 1984 state that buildings, where the highest floor is beyond 18.3 meters above the fire appliance access level are deemed high-rises (Laws of Malaysia, 1984). This statement can also be supported by the Malaysian Green Building Index (GBI), which describes a high-rise building as a stratified building having the uppermost floor exceeding 18.3 meters above the ground level (Green Building Index (GBI), 2019).The emergence of high-rise housing in Malaysia dates back to the 1970s when the 17-storey low-cost Rifle Range Flats were built in Georgetown, Pulau Pinang.

With rapid urbanisation, soaring land prices and the introduction of Strata Title Act 1985 by the local government, high-density housing has become a prominent feature in urban regions (Seo & Omar, 2011). High-rise housing programs are developed by both public and private sectors. The public sector targets public and affordable housing schemes, which account for 40% of the overall high-rise dwellings in the country. The private sector, on the other hand, concentrates on medium and high-end housing programs, which make up the remaining 60% (Mat Noor & Eves, 2011). The boom of high-rise housing in Malaysia has paved way for other housing schemes in the market, such as serviced apartments and SOHOs, which are commonly built together as or near to shopping malls, offices, or hotels (Samad, Jalil & Anuar, 2018).

Cultivating Social Interaction

Social interaction, in sociology, is characterised as a social reciprocity between two or more persons who change their acts and responses based on the actions of their interaction partners. It is a "stimulus-response condition", an action-reaction experience between people (Farooq, 2014). Generally, the process where two or more individuals are in significant contact and their behaviours are altered to some extent is called social interaction (Merrill, 1969). Through such conditions of interrelating people among themselves, a social structure that leads to social groups is formed. In society, social interactions occur in four forms: between a person and a person, a person and a group, a group and a group, and people and cultures. The reciprocal process of social interaction between individuals and cultures is formed when people have social relationships with mass media, and social change in their lives is observed (Farooq, 2014).

Social relationships are crucial in determining the physical state and comfort of human beings, both mentally and physically, regardless of age, with positive outcomes in reducing health problems, stress, anxiety, depression, drug consumption, and alcohol abuse (Zuzana, 2012). In a community, social interaction between residents improves the security level of a neighbourhood. Neighbours maintain closer relationships with next-door neighbours if they are more ready to participate in informal supervision of the community's communal spaces (Bellair, 1997).

Public Spaces, Social Spaces in High-Rise Living in Malaysia

Public spaces emerge when all three types of activities are combined: necessary, optional, and social activities (Gehl, 1971). The primer form of a social space must allow for these embodied qualities: to meet, to see, and to hear other people as the basis. In a residential context, a hierarchy of social spaces is differentiated to show a structure of public versus private: a private space consists of a garden or balcony, while a public communal space offers semi-public characteristics. Public spaces that offer territoriality are perceived as a place of belonging and result in natural surveillance for children to play. Quality social spaces incorporate comfortable walking paths, intimate spaces with natural elements and lush greenery, physical structures for informal resting spots, an abundance of possible sitting areas, protection from vehicular traffic, favourable spaces, and climatic conditions through conducive cool weather and sun (Gehl, 1971; Whyte, 1980). Efficient sociable spaces with crowds result from the presence of diverse human activities or when people are looking at other people. For open spaces to work, they must be spacious, shaded, and unfenced to form undefined boundaries without any forms of rules that may limit people from using them (Whyte, 1980).

The Malaysian housing landscape, particularly condominiums and serviced apartments, are generally gated and guarded high-density housing typologies that are famous among urban dwellers (Seo & Omar, 2011). Traditional condominiums originated with three to four-storey buildings with proper landscape and minimal facilities, and transitioned to shared facilities like swimming pools, barbeque area, sports courts, and gymnasium in contemporary mid and high-rises known today due to the demand for higher quality of living environments. A typical high-rise housing in Malaysia consists of three classifications of common facilities: basic (i.e., religious, commercial, open recreation, building services and parking facilities); exclusive (i.e., security, closed recreation and open recreation facilities); and support facilities (i.e., education and community facilities) (Wahab, Chohan, Che-Ania, Tawil & Omar, 2016).

The planning guidelines for the Selangor state describe high-rise residential development schemes to allocate a minimum 10% of land area for open and recreational green space within the site boundary.

30% of this allocated space may be used for social spaces for football fields, swimming pools, courts for basketball and badminton, and jogging tracks. High-rise housing developments are required to offer common building facilities, including, but not limited to, shops or kiosks, gymnasium, library, multipurpose hall, reading area, and games room. The number and quality of facilities in high-density buildings are offered according to the exclusivity of the types of properties.

Theoretical Framework on Social Spaces

Space and Place

Social spaces function optimally when occupants interact positively with nature to sustain the vertical liveability in a high-rise. Blurring boundaries between communal spaces and private dwellings allows occupants to live in a visible way, promoting engagement with other individuals and nature (Scott, 2015). Active promotion of natural light and ventilation ultimately symbolises the integration of nature in architecture to form comforting spaces. Efficient social space that bridges a relationship to nature is closely associated with the use of locally available natural materials to introduce public realms in vertical living for a sense of place and community. (Gomez, 2016; Scott, 2015).

In addition to scenic spaces with a suitable choice of landscaping, water features, and sculptures, the growth of vertical public life counts on the careful planning of seating arrangements and undefined boundaries (Huang, 2006). In a setting where children's play areas are plenty, this affects the behaviour for social interaction among children and their supervisors. Undefined social spaces benefit children and the elderly in high-rises for natural surveillance (Hadi, Heath and Oldfield, 2014; Huang, 2006). Spatial elements, such as furniture and chairs, in common spaces further add to space conduciveness and increase the chance for social engagement compared to the size of a space (Ridwana, Prayitno & Hatmoko, 2018).

In summary, the character of social space and place is closely related to the dynamic relationship to the natural world, the availability and arrangement of physical elements, and the user experience of social spaces.

Space and People

Social communities flourish when participants interact through their basic senses in high-rise common spaces to sustain liveability. Occupants in Malaysian condominiums generally love to interact socially despite not knowing much about their respective neighbours (Fard, Sharif, Mohd Yunos & Mydin, 2015). They only engage in social activities when other functional activities take place or when they have views of people. For social participation to take place, a feeling of ownership on how a space is being used must be present without rules set by the building management (Hadi et al. 2014). Rules established for occupants to practice their social rights and limit social events result in uninteresting space. Social and environment liveability in high-rises is dependent on the psychological needs of the occupants. A perception of belonging can be developed by giving occupants responsibilities to look after the space and forming territoriality through space personalisation. A conducive environment for social relationships draws occupants to use a space if a satisfying quality is reached. Minimal interventions to the existing high-rise design by uplifting underused lift lobbies into small communities of social spaces foster passive contacts (Aw and Lim, 2016). Communal spaces are rarely utilised by occupants who choose to interact in areas outside the building over concerns about violating the privacy of others (Kennedy and

Buys, 2015). This leads to a preference for personal social space within respective dwelling spaces such as balconies as compared to a collective open area. Mid-block communal spaces may offer opportunities for chance encounters if they are designed for a larger number of occupants and activities.

The above discussion associates to the perception of liveability, the freedom to space preference and personalisation to meet the needs of high-rise occupants.

Space and Path

The design of efficient social spaces in high-rises involves connectivity and means of access to facilitate a socially-engaged community. One example is the Unité d'Habitation where communal spaces occurs interestingly on the large pilotis-supported volume on the ground level and rooftop instead of within the building (Ghazali, Bajunid and Peter Davis, 2014). Therefore, residents will need to access two vertical ends of the building for communal activities. The 1997 Commerzbank office building in Frankfurt is an ideal model for potential residential buildings with direct physical access for every occupant to one of ten four-storey sky-gardens (Wood, 2014). New apartment typologies that allow constant access to individual dwellings through courtyards encourage neighbourliness and ease of escape during a fire (Ghazali et al., 2014).

Universal design principles that prioritise unobstructed paths and the placement of social spaces within the building should be strongly focused on to cater to disabled groups and the elderly. It is vital that social spaces are conveniently distributed, with high accessibility and strong visual visibility for different user groups (Cao and Chye, 2017). In particular, elevated communal spaces have been shown to be less desirable for the elderly, who prefer conventional ground open spaces that offer higher accessibility, greater presence of other crowds, and close proximity to commercial and recreational functions.

Samad, Said and Rahim (2017) looked into the idea of 'design-for-all', which should not be limited to physically disabled individuals. Public spaces in Malaysia are often designed to appeal only to certain few demographics, neglecting the needs of a wider range of users. Moreover, some over-designed public spaces may fail due to inadequate infrastructure, attractions, or connections to existing economic and social networks.

In short, the principles of space and path are linked to the accessibility and connectivity of social spaces in high-rises, which can influence the safety of occupants. Lastly, attention to universal design principles that target disabled groups and a wider spectrum of economic groups is another quality of spaces that is required.

The domains of principles of place, people, and path form the basis to understand qualities of social spaces required in high-rise residential designs. Consequently, they help to identify respective architectural challenges to meet these qualities to be investigated in the sections that follow.

METHODOLOGY

The research aim of investigating the challenges of designing social space by architects requires an exploration of experiences, points of views and understanding within the industry. Qualitative research encompasses rich and comprehensive qualities of real-life prospects and has a flexible nature in its design and procedures (Groat & Wang, 2013). In the aspect of high-rise social space investigation, more qualitative approaches were employed to explore recent literatures aforementioned. For this study, qualitative semi-structured interviews were used to obtain data from the practitioners.

Figure 1. Three key frameworks of social spaces

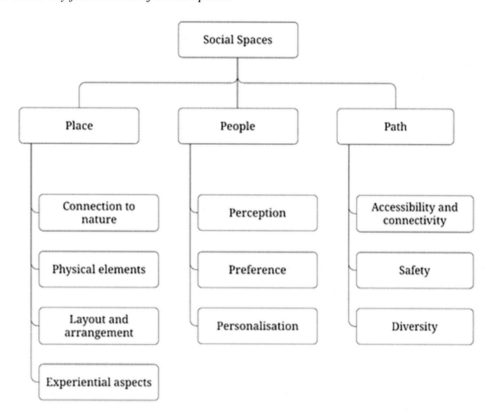

The sampling criteria involved narrowing down to representatives from top companies in Kuala Lumpur who possess extensive expertise, experience, and a portfolio of exclusive built high-rise housing designs that demonstrate successful socially interactive spaces specifically in the study areas of Mont Kiara and KL City Centre.

Three architectural firms were selected for participation, and interviews were conducted between November 2019 and April 2020. All the participants held top positions with authoritative powers over the design of their respective projects. Their direct involvement in designing projects and rich experience ensured a strong feedback and holistic representation of similar professionals in the industry. The profiles of the respondents are shown below:

Profiles of the respondents:

R1: Director and Architect, GDP Architects
R2: Associate Architect, Veritas Design Group
R3: Partner, Konzepte Asia

The interview questions, which focused on the architects' approach to designing social interactive spaces and the key challenges they faced, were formulated based on the thematic findings derived from the literature reviews, as shown in Figure 1. The interview-data collection also allowed "others" in the already pre-defined questions to allow for any additional views from the respondents. The interviews were tape-recorded and subsequently transcribed.

To identify the application of challenges in the built housing projects with successful socially interactive spaces, two developments designed by the selected respondents were observed through site visits to gain a further understanding of the interview results. The selected projects tackled the issues of social isolation in premium high-rise housing and were recognised for their significant contributions to building design. Arcoris Mont Kiara by GDP is a mixed-use development completed in 2019 with significant civic spaces that benefit the wider community and has received multiple international recognitions. Two parallel tower blocks are designed to allow for the formation of a green central plaza on the ground level and are highly permeable to the outside environment. Built in 2018, Tribeca Residences by Veritas in Jalan Imbi, Kuala Lumpur, is a twin residential tower merged into a single development through a central atrium. Five elevated double to triple volume sky pods form the main architectural facade of the development. The project features high-end facilities, including infinity pools on rooftop levels, and retail spaces on lower levels.

DATA FINDINGS AND ANALYSIS

The views of the respondents were summarised in Table 1. From this table, a total of 69 results emerged and the interviews substantiated most of their views on T1. Two additional issues that have not been explored previously in the literature were also revealed in T1 and T2.

The data were analysed to identify themes that emerged and were repeated in the interviews, revealing a range of challenges in designing socially interactive spaces. These challenges include synergistic relationship, architectural branding, spatial order, private-public articulation, space design, space optimisation, and space psychology. A summary of the analysed challenges is shown in Table 2.

Figure 2. Exterior perspectives of Arcoris Mont Kiara (left) and Tribeca residences (right)

Synergistic Relationship

An important challenge highlighted by the participants was decision-making and differences in project ideas and vision between designers and clients when planning for social spaces in luxury housing developments. R2 and R3 emphasised that social space design bounds to develop multi-perspective

Table 1. Summary of views of respondents based on frameworks of social spaces

Social Space Framework				Views of Respondents
Space and Place (T1)	Connection to nature	R1	1.	Sustainability in green design applications
			2.	Natural light and ventilation
			3.	Design as an extension of living rooms to outdoors
			4.	Blurring boundaries between private and public domains
			5.	Green building design requirements
		R2	6.	Weather
			7.	Natural light and ventilation
			8.	Use of technology and materials to counter rainwater
			9.	Wind load
			10.	Blurring boundaries between inside and outside
		R3	11.	Natural light and ventilation
	Physical elements	R1	12.	Interactive landscapes
		R3	13.	Bringing in furniture for interaction
	Experiential aspects	R1	14.	Memorable and experiential spaces
			15.	Vandalism and abuse of space
			16.	Views to outside landscapes
		R2	17.	Quality of social space
			18.	Space attractiveness
			19.	Connection between programmes
			20.	Space exclusivity through expensive products for marketing
		R3	21.	Space exclusivity
			22.	Experiential spaces
			23.	Views are overrated
	Others	R1	24.	Designing for the future
			25.	Designing differently from others
			26.	Designing to think outside the box
			27.	Marketing ploy
		R2	28.	Concept of building when introduce social spaces
			29.	Designing differently from other typologies and standard of operation of building
			30.	Marketing ploy
		R3	31.	Experiment beyond the standard typology

continued on following page

Table 1. Continued

Social Space Framework				Views of Respondents
Space and People (T2)	Perception	R1	32.	Looking into existing social issues
			33.	Social space awareness among people
			34.	Individualistic nature of residents
			35.	Social mindset consideration
			36.	Sustainable space to be used always
			37.	Cultural sensitivity
			38.	Fixed programmes by developers
		R2	39.	Social space awareness
			40.	Individualistic nature of residents
			41.	Social mindset consideration
		R3	42.	Individualistic nature of residents
			43.	Designing to fit other functions
			44.	Sustainable space for flexibility
	Preference	R1	45.	Provision of space usage regulations by architects to management bodies
			46.	Privacy
		R2	47.	Privacy
		R3	48.	Building operation by management bodies different from what it is intended
			49.	Privacy
	Personalisation	R2	50.	Size of space
			51.	Social responsibility of residents
		R3	52.	Design interventions for incidental opportunities for people
	Others	R2	53.	Conflicting ideas between designers and clients
			54.	Unwillingness for clients to take risks
		R3	55.	Compromising with developers on size of social spaces
Space and Path (T3)	Accessibility and connectivity	R1	56.	Intervals of social spaces across the building
		R2	57.	Intervals of social spaces across the building
		R3	58.	Visibility of social spaces from exterior building
			59.	Placement of space next to an important architectural element
	Safety	R1	60.	Privacy
			61.	Security when social spaces are fenceless environments
			62.	Small clusters of social spaces for convenience
		R2	63.	Safety concerning placement of children play areas within the building
			64.	Gated and guarded community
			65.	Privacy
		R3	66.	Privacy
	Diversity	R1	67.	Universal design practicality but not in Malaysia
			68.	Expensive high-rises targeted to rich individuals
			69.	Overly designed social spaces that are not interactive

Legends: R1: Respondent 1; R2: Respondent 2; R3: Respondent 3

Table 2. Summary of challenges to social interactive space design

List of Challenges	Categories of Challenges
Multi-perspective viewpoints in early stages of design process	Challenges on Synergistic Relationship
Decision-making and conflicting ideas between architects and clients	
Compromise and flexibility between designers and developers	
Social spaces as a means of exclusivity	Challenges on Architectural Branding
Design outcomes for social spaces driven by marketing schemes	
Provision of double and triple-volume spaces	Challenges on Spatial Order
Arrangement of social spaces on building facades	
Integration of social spaces on already existing architectural avenues	
Blurring boundaries between public and private domains for social cohesion	Challenges on Private-Public Articulation
Continuity from a private indoor living space to the outdoors	
Choice of landscapes to be incorporated	
Intervention by design to increase chance contacts	
Weather conditions for social spaces to function	Challenges on Space Design
Access to natural light and ventilation	
Space attractiveness	
Access to views to outside	
Green building design applications	Challenges on Space Optimisation
Designing for the future	
Distinct designs from other similar typologies	
Multifunctional and adaptive social space over time	
Practicality of universal design	
Social spaces associated with memory and experience of users	Challenges on Space Psychology
Negative mindsets of designers and occupants in buildings	
Awareness for social spaces in high-rise living	
Individualistic and private behaviours of high-rise communities	
Privacy concerns	
Security concerns	
Imposition of rules and regulations on communal spaces	

viewpoints during the design process. Reflecting on this, R2 revealed that the original intent of a green social space by the architect was eventually converted into utilitarian facility zones due to the client's change of vision. Projects also require a degree of compromise and flexibility between designers and developers to ensure a smooth project delivery. R3 acknowledged that the practice would negotiate with developers to propose smaller dwelling units in high-rises and use the accumulated extra living spaces to design larger communal spaces that populate throughout the building without affecting any construction costs.

Architectural Branding

With the growing urban political economy, designers are faced with the challenge of ensuring their buildings can be marketed and sold to local elites. The vast majority of social space design functions purely as a sales tool employed by project clients. International 'starchitects' are hired to stand out from other property developments, as described by R1. Glamourous building facilities, such as sky decks, sky bridges, infinity pools, and large gymnasium are some marketing tactics in luxury high-rises to attract prospective buyers, as experienced by R1 and R2. Elevated green pockets were transformed into facility spaces for commercial reasons. Designing exclusive social space in tall buildings is a common phenomenon in the industry. This is indicative as designers will include lavish products in social spaces "without addressing the real issue such as affordability, location and security," as acknowledged by R1. Furthermore, R3 claimed that tall residential developments are tailored to be luxurious and personal by clients and developers by limiting the number of dwellings per floor or offering private elevators.

Spatial Order

These challenges include the creative process of identifying, placing and arranging social spaces in skyrises for social activities. Elevated communal spaces must be thoroughly planned for maximum accessibility and convenience of occupants. While it is not easy for vertical living to support a single communal space that is easily accessible, architects have had to make alternative decisions for optimum convenience. For instance, R1 explained that smaller clusters of social spaces can be wedged between dwellings and distributed vertically in a building at different levels, which is unusual in other residential developments that have a single concentrated common area. R2 highlighted that, through this approach, designers must also study the overall building's façade for balance, hierarchy, and views. In view of this, R3 argued that social spaces are better integrated into existing architectural features instead, such as apartment corridors or building lift cores for a more impactful advantage, compared to designated areas.

Private-Public Articulation

There were challenges faced by designers that are specifically related to blurring boundaries between private and public domains in high-rises to foster social cohesion. As evident in typical high-rises with car park podiums and elevated green spaces, an invisible barrier is automatically established between the ground floor public scene and the dwellers above. It was felt that by softening this intangible boundary, buildings can be unfenced and opened up to the commons from neighbouring buildings. In addition, designers are challenged to devise a connection between the indoors and outdoors by providing green pocket zones in the building to spill into the central atrium as indoor elevated green platforms.

Another challenge is to look into different methods to introduce front gardens in landed housing developments which connect to the open streets in the high-rise scene. R1 highlighted that a social space should provide continuity from a private indoor living space to the outdoors. This grants occupants the opportunity to spend more time in shared common areas for socialisation rather than being confined to their bedrooms.

Another issue, according to R1, is the appropriate choice of landscapes to be incorporated in buildings. The incorporation of greenery must allow interactivity for communities to engage with them rather than for spatial aesthetics. As commented by the respondent, interactive landscapes that are reflective and well-suited to local culture, especially ones that grow naturally, nurture learning, and encourage high social engagement amongst children and adults.

Additionally, simple design interventions to building elements in high-rises are vital to build opportunities for social networks. The issue looks into where and how designers can intervene through design to increase chance contacts among dwellers. Reflecting on this, R3 felt that lift lobbies and corridors have potential for shared communal space where everyone has constant access, as opposed to dedicated homogenous social space uncelebrated by the community. Modifications to lift lobby and corridor dimensions with addition of appropriate seating areas can transform the spaces from empty passageways to semi-private functional zones.

Space Design

Designers in a country with harsh tropical climate face challenges in reconnecting social spaces with nature in tall projects. From an architect's point of view, natural light and ventilation in high-rises are of paramount importance for vertical communities to coexist, as expressed by R3. R1 highlighted that it is vital to use less energy and adopt sustainability in design without relying on mechanical ventilation or artificial lighting. This is also true when efforts to maintain sufficient natural wind and light in large expanse of social spaces in buildings are challenged by driving rain during windy days, as commented by R2. To overcome this, designers must plan for counteractive systems.

Space attractiveness was also viewed as another issue. According to R2, designers are required to take into account attractive social spaces to encourage people and families to stay, use and socialise, as reflected in the diverse programs introduced for the social spaces.

Another challenge is enriching social spaces with unobstructed and stunning skyline views to outside. Commenting on this, R1 criticised that while dwellings and social spaces are commonly designed with excellent outside views to entice potential homebuyers, it should not be regarded as a main space design principle. Likewise, R3 also disputed that panoramic views with a sightline to popular landmarks are questionably an odd reference point.

Space Optimisation

Dealing with energy and resource usage in high-rises is currently a pressing issue, and designers face a challenge in incorporating sustainability into social space design. One approach to addressing this problem is to effectively integrate green building strategies through passive design. As evident in projects by R1 and R2, large central atriums are created to promote stack effect from the ground floor and cross ventilation across apartment corridors through pockets of open elevated social spaces.

As new high-rises crop up urban cities, designers have to be forward-thinking and experiment beyond recognisable building typologies to pave the way for a sustainable future. In similar comments across the three respondents, R1 urged that current and future designers need to think unconventionally. Similarly, R2 had to construct programs distinctively from other tall typologies available in the current market. R3 also explored uncommon approaches by employing small interventions to lift lobbies and apartment corridors for social contact in high-rises.

Vertical social spaces need to cater to diverse roles and demographics to support social relations over time. R1 and R3 believed in designing spaces with a level of ambiguity to enable them to serve various purposes. Multifunctional and adaptive social spaces are more sustainable and effective without designers controlling how occupants use them, as opposed to homogeneous spaces.

Universally designed social spaces are difficult to accomplish in the Malaysian setting. R1 expressed that designers need to look holistically at the provision of greenery in communal and private spaces in high-rises to serve all occupants. It was felt that some occupants may maintain plants in their respective dwellings provided by designers, while others may not. Additionally, the respondent criticised the fact that luxury social spaces are typically designed to serve the richer population, but not the poor.

Space Psychology

A critical challenge highlighted by respondents is understanding human psychology, taking into account the memory and experience of a space, and social space awareness in vertical living. One issue is to accommodate social spaces with memory and experience for occupants. Communal spaces need to contribute meaningful experiences to younger demographics for their lifestyles and activities, as commented by R1 and R3. It was felt that the younger generation is more receptive to smaller dwelling spaces and prefers a large collective space for entertainment and hanging out as a way for experiential living.

Failed social spaces in high-rise residential designs are attributed to negative mindsets of designers and occupants. For social spaces to work, R1 believed that designers need to change their focus from promoting individualism among building occupants to designing for the masses. However, despite providing the best space for social engagement, R1 and R2 agreed that occupants themselves can also be an issue, as they may not interact with others. While it is not the norm for Malaysians to socialise with others in vertical housings, designers are presented with the challenge of shifting people's mindset to embrace change.

Awareness of social spaces in high-rise living may not be as great as in foreign lifestyle counterparts, as revealed by R1 and R2. Referring to this, both respondents acknowledged that social space design requires designers to study how occupants can be receptive to the spaces provided in tall buildings. For instance, this can be achieved through external façade design to highlight social spaces.

It is difficult to address individualistic and private behaviours of high-rise communities and encourage them to step out of their comfort zones and actively engage with others. All respondents agreed that occupants in high-rise living are often insensitive to others. Essentially, architects need to design spaces where people can interact inclusively, rather than providing the same common facilities in every residential development. This is because successful interaction between people has become a challenge since the experience of living has shifted from low-rise neighbourhoods to vertical living.

Malaysians value their privacy in high-rises, which poses another challenge for all respondents. This is particularly evident in average condominiums, which limit occupants from connecting with the external environment. R2 also discovered that some occupants living next to shared social spaces may be unhappy and feel interfered with when strangers from other floors use them. The provision of exclusive services for luxury lifestyles, such as private elevators in dwellings, encourages occupants to isolate themselves from their neighbours, as highlighted by R3. Additionally, occupants prefer luxury condominiums with a small number of dwellings per floor to maintain their privacy. While designing social spaces to be open to the outside for social participation, such an approach may lead to security problems. To counter this, landscapes and boom gates can provide the building with an invisible boundary and restrict vehicular traffic from entering the compound illegally.

High-rise residential typologies impose rules and regulations on communal spaces for occupants. Despite occupants not being able to personalise such spaces, R2 maintained that it is the social responsibility of people to abide by the rules as ownership of common spaces in tall residential buildings differs from low-rise developments.

DISCUSSION

Independent Challenges (Culture)

The findings have established independent challenges which are standalone and separated from the standard practice of design; encapsulating the culture, behaviour, mentality, and professional experience of designers, project clients, and building occupants. Without anticipating these events prior to any social space design in high-end residential projects, the subsequent stages in the design process may result in complications if not properly resolved beforehand.

To achieve successful design output, spatial psychology in high-rises plays a pivotal role. In the study, designers discovered that Malaysians are behaving more individualistic. This ever-changing lifestyle to live in a closed environment away from the outside world gives rise to problems where designers need to understand this way of living before incorporating social spaces in high-rises and innovate with new spatial typologies to respond to the people's new needs. In literature, however, Malaysians are found to be generally enthusiastic to interact with neighbours in high-rises despite not knowing them (Fard et al., 2015). This could imply that the mentality of occupants in a low and mid-cost housing is more receptive to getting to know others as compared to the attitude that wealthy occupants portray.

Designers need to deal with the privacy of occupants when providing social spaces in upscale high-rises. The implementation of interactive spaces and to open up housing developments to the public create uncertainties and worry to designers for violating the privacy of occupants. For example, the Arcoris and the Tribeca with gateless territories displayed issues on privacy since these attempts were uncommon in previous conventional high-rise typologies. Naturally, people have the impression about invading the privacy of others when using social spaces, which slowly develop a preference for a more personal social space within their dwellings (Kennedy & Buys, 2015). The provision of open social spaces ultimately forces occupants to engage with strangers and takes away their privilege of wanting a more private lifestyle (Ghazali et al., 2014). For the same reasons, public spaces may be less approachable to people than their private counterparts (Aw & Lim, 2016). That being said, it is difficult to design for such living concepts as they are a matter of preference for individuals. All participants in this study emphasised on the issue of privacy repetitively which suggests their respective encounters in their own homes.

Architects should expect rules and regulations in strata high-end properties to be applied when the buildings are fully constructed. The rules established by management bodies require occupants to adhere to them as their social responsibility. Common spaces in luxury tall buildings are maintained by these bodies and paid for by occupants as a collective. Compliance to rules aims to avert vandalism and to be constantly maintained for everyone. Social network in occupants faces a setback when a sense of entitlement towards the spaces is not present (Hadi et al., 2014). These rules discourage occupants from using them due to loss of ownership to the spaces (Fard et al., 2015). This hints that designers are to look into alternatives to provide occupants a level of ownership to these communal spaces by understanding the programmes people may require.

Focus should also be given on security problems when architects plan for interactive spaces. By designing a gateless development in effort to generate higher social interaction such as in the Arcoris, the safety of occupants in an open neighbourhood where anyone can roam freely is in question. Gateless neighbourhoods are becoming more prevalent in many Malaysian housing districts to naturally build a level of trust within the community. Despite not explicitly mentioned within literature, social spaces are focused as a place for ease of fire escape and not on the issue of protection (Ghazali et al., 2014).

The study also found new aspect of challenges where the effectiveness of social interactive spaces is influenced by memory and experience of users. This is evident where designers highlighted the need to accommodate spatial experience for frequent usage among younger population. However, prior studies have failed to evaluate memorable spaces as a technique to attract occupants.

Additionally, architects are expected to foresee the lack of spatial awareness in high-rises among occupants. Architects were challenged to develop a sense of awareness for social spaces by designing for the masses rather than encouraging individualism in high-rise living. Unaddressed by past studies, it is also important for architects to consider how social spaces can be made aware to occupants prominently through design and by adopting a changing mindset towards such spaces.

To achieve a workable interactive space, the study discovered additional challenges on synergistic relationship between architects and clients for a project. Designers faced constant conflict with multi-perspective viewpoints and disagreements with clients relating to social space design. This obstacle was contributed when two parties had different project visions. Therefore, the possibility of misunderstandings and disagreements with clients to deal with problems effectively should be anticipated by architects and fundamental communication skills are needed for negotiations. These findings were not addressed within literature.

Another social space design challenge is architectural branding. The implementation of social spaces was referred solely by participants as a marketing tactic for future homebuyers based on the clients' needs. Architects were forced to design for occupants with exclusivity in mind without providing for successful social interaction. Commenting on this, the designers were restricted to provide a quality social space design in high-rises which was not mentioned in literature.

Influential Challenges (Impact)

Based on the findings, influential challenges indicate actions of designers impacting other domains of building design and vice versa. Changes or efforts to address these challenges may interfere with the overall scheme, spatial form, and user experience of social interactive spaces in luxurious high-rises. Concurrently, they may also affect designers by prolonging their work time and the quality of design when undertaking these problems.

To foster social relationships, careful consideration of the placement and accessibility of interactive spaces in high-rises must be allowed. Every decision regarding the size, volume of space, and location within a building impacts the accessibility and convenience of occupants. Excellent accessibility to common areas in high-rises boosts the internal living environment (Wood, 2014). Efficient circulation paths that connect occupants from their dwellings to common spaces without interference demonstrate an attentive design decision. By allowing social spaces to be distributed in the building, as demonstrated in the findings, it helps to increase chance contacts among occupants for a friendly neighbourhood (Wood, 2014). Incorrect or poor judgment leading to failed social spaces will adversely affect architects and may require them to alter design drawings and consume resources and time.

Decisions to place social spaces at specific levels of a high-rise can influence the reception of spaces and the potential for social bonds. The study showed the importance of proposing a ground open plaza, which benefits the wider community by providing a link to other retail spaces and maximising social activities. Diverse programs and activities catering to a larger population increase the probability of passive contacts. This aligns with the literature, which emphasises the significance of ground social spaces for extensive engagement with people due to their closer proximity to other commercial and recreational areas (Cao & Chye, 2017).

In vertical buildings, architects are challenged to look into new models to bring back the typical front gardens of low-rise neighbourhoods that connect to open streets. Contemporary high-rises require designers to articulate and blur boundaries between private and public domains. This invites occupants to actively engage in social spaces, as explored in the findings. Designing to feel like an extension of personal living space to the outdoors generally allows occupants to live visibly to promote interaction with others and nature for unplanned communal activities and chance encounters (Gehl, 1971; Scott, 2015). Only when boundaries become undefined do communities in tall buildings spend less time cooped up in their respective homes (Whyte, 1980).

Efficient social spaces require engaging and interactive landscapes, where environmentally conscious architects design green spaces for socialization. As revealed in the study, landscapes that blend with the local culture, endemic and encourage interactivity help occupants lead healthier lives and socialise with others. Interactive plants offer favourable conditions for occupants to engage in social activities, thereby creating a stimulus for other events to occur in the same space, promoting a sustainable environment. Proposing interactive plants requires architects to collaborate intensively with landscape designers to set out technical information and documentation that can impact the outcome of built spaces. Scenic and attractive social spaces with carefully selected landscaping, water features, and sculptures motivate occupants to participate in conversations (Huang, 2006).

To meet the challenge of creating a seamless public and private domain, another high-rise design solution needs to consider providing physical elements to cultivate social life. Furniture, for instance, is excellent for incidental opportunities that allow people to make contact. Designers considered the arrangement of furnishings in areas that maximise social activities. Inappropriate furniture arrangement influences space quality, which subsequently impacts the social life of occupants. Providing a single large social space does not necessarily generate higher social connections in comparison with the presence of chairs, which significantly improve the comfortability of occupants to stay and exchange conversations with others (Gehl, 1971; Ridwana et al., 2018).

To create opportunities for social contact, architects rely on other plausible ways than planning for dedicated interactive spaces. Based on the findings, architects made minimal design changes to buildings to restore public life in vertical living by transforming lift lobbies into a communal garden and modifying the size of corridors. Uplifting lift lobbies with minimal interventions fosters passive contact among occupants (Aw and Lim, 2016). Despite all this, changes to the building elements may risk the adaptation of occupants who may be accustomed to the conventional way of living. By converting these grey domains into functional areas through expansion, clients may lose greater profits as common spaces are non-sellable areas and demand more resources to build them.

Social spaces need to be protected and conducive to climatic conditions. Tall developments have to deal with rough weather conditions in Malaysia's tropical climate with abundant sunshine and rain. The study revealed that designers were challenged with rainwater when designing for high-rises, so much so as to bridge a connection to outdoors through open spaces. While trying to promote sufficient natural ventilation and minimise air-conditioning supply to social spaces, the architects were troubled with rain-water splashing during windy days, particularly when such spaces have larger volume and span greater heights. Open spaces are paramount for social life; hence, architects intend to promote sunshine and wind into elevated social arenas. Only when occupants are connected to the natural world, a place for congregation can be formed (Scott, 2015). Natural lighting onto a space is important for it to function during daytime without mechanical applications (Whyte, 1980). As a result, human interaction can only work if comfortable spots with favourable climatic conditions are taken note of (Gehl, 1971).

Providing occupants with attractive, interactive spaces is a prerequisite for capturing their attention, encouraging them to stay, use, and socialise. By creating inviting spaces that offer diverse functional facilities suited for the occupants, they are given a choice to select and use them according to their preferences, as found in this study. This all-in-one attractive environment benefits occupants by improving social exchange (Huang, 2006). High-rise living with a homogenous setting can eventually lead to the abandonment and emptiness of open spaces, which hampers social liveability.

Designers are tasked with enriching social spaces in high-rises with open, panoramic skyline views to the outside, which is reported to mainly lure homebuyers and boost sales in the market. While designing with views fulfils the requirements set by project clients, it has not been highlighted in the literature as a benchmark for social interaction.

It was expressed that social space design needs to focus on successful optimization through green building applications that impact the use of energy and resources. In the findings, designers achieved passive design through open communal spaces that provided sufficient airflow. Without a sustainable effort, the space could negatively impact the well-being of its occupants and the social cohesion in a high-rise community. Establishing suitable design parameters to engage with nature improves the quality of life and social sustainability (Scott, 2015).

Optimising the quality of social space to serve multiple functions over time is known to have a direct positive impact on occupants. Thus, architects are presented with the challenge of designing flexible social spaces to support various roles. Confining spaces to a singular purpose diminishes occupants' productivity and satisfaction. Occupants are increasingly demanding a wider spectrum of activities in a space that can accommodate them. Flexible spaces stimulate beneficial social communication by increasing the number of occupants (Aw & Lim, 2016; Whyte, 1980).

The universal design approach to social spaces is difficult to achieve in the Malaysian scenario. A holistic design to serve all age and social groups in high-rises proved to be complex without the cooperation and respect given by occupants. In the study, it was found that luxury high-rises designed for the wealthy significantly exclude the underprivileged. User-friendly spaces deliver a harmonious way of living and place great emphasis on successful social life in high-rises. It is also indicated in the literature that the 'design-for-all' strategy is not limited to physically disabled individuals but to larger economic groups (Samad et al., 2017).

Architects need to commit to designing for a sustainable future. Designers in the study witnessed a paradigm shift in the way people interact in tall buildings. This calls for current and future designers to experiment beyond standard high-rise typologies. Building programs have to be distinctive from what other high-rises offer in the current property market. Predictable designs result in the way people use and behave with each other in social spaces. Despite not being mentioned in the literature, architects are expected to venture into new methods to deliver a thriving social cohesion in high-rises.

Dependent Challenges (Communication)

The findings show that dependent challenges require a two-way effort and reliance on others for support between designers and stakeholders in building design. Occasionally, the challenges address the demand for communication that corresponds to time.

When planning and designing lavish interactive spaces in a high-rise development, architects need to obtain proper communication from project clients to gather more information. Different architects exhibit different philosophies towards social space design in high-rises based on their varying professional experiences and attitudes. This requires properly acquiring credible and relevant information about the project from clients to ensure a project's success. Understanding is the mutual knowledge, beliefs, and assumptions that exist between parties. Without such reciprocal communication, conflicts, and disagreements with clients relating to social space design commonly occur, as manifested in the study. This leads to an extension of time to finish a project or a possible appointment of another architect by clients if a lack of understanding occurs between the two parties.

CONCLUSION

The study took off with the intention to establish an insight into the architectural challenges faced by professionals when designing social interactive space in response to the increasing development of luxury high-rise residential buildings in Kuala Lumpur, Malaysia. In addition, the study covered architects' perspectives, as previous studies have primarily focused on the perceptions of occupants in low to mid-cost high-rise housing. The challenges and their key characteristics have been presented and discussed. In doing so, it enables aspiring architects and designers to anticipate and identify tailored solutions to address these issues prior to their involvement in high-end property developments.

The study reported in this paper adopted a qualitative approach through semi-structured interviews with three professional architects who have been involved in high-end tall residential projects in Kuala Lumpur. Social spaces have been extensively explained under three domains of principles, namely place, people, and path. In addition, the paper provided evidence of seven challenges of social interactive space design in luxury high-rise residential developments, such as synergistic relationship, architectural branding, spatial order, private-public articulation, space design, space optimisation, and space psychology. Furthermore, these key findings lend support to the classification of characteristics of the findings, such as culture, impact, and communication.

In view of the criticality of social space implementation in luxury high-rise living, the study emphasises the importance of collaborative efforts among designers to promote social life in these environments. It is worth noting that the scarcity of literature on luxury high-rise residential developments in Malaysia posed a significant obstacle to understanding the research problem, as existing studies are inclined to low and mid-cost properties. This led to the generalisation of social space theories to be similarly applied to upscale high-rises. The qualitative approach allowed the participants to display receptive feedback on specific questions, without addressing the overall topic. As a consequence, some assumptions had to be made in evaluating the arguments presented in the study.

Finally, the study warrants future research directions on the performance of social interactive spaces in luxury high-rise living to verify and add to the findings. In addition to the presented social space design challenges, a potential study to look into detailed strategies or innovations which may help mitigate these issues. Another angle to explore may be a comparative study of social space design and challenges in western and eastern models of luxury high-rise living.

ACKNOWLEDGEMENT

The authors would like to acknowledge the support of Taylor's University and its research panellists for their guidance, as well as all the respondents who provided valuable insights and expertise in the research study.

REFERENCES

Aw, S. B., & Lim, P. I. (2016). The provision of vertical social pockets for better social interaction in high-rise living. *Planning Malaysia Journal, 14*(4). doi:10.21837/pmjournal.v14.i4.156

Bellair, P. E. (1997). Social interaction and community crime: Examining the importance of neighbor networks. *Criminology, 35*(4), 677–704. doi:10.1111/j.1745-9125.1997.tb01235.x

Bernama. (2019). *KL, Selangor, Penang, Johor remain top choices for properties.* Bernama. https://www.bernama.com/en/news.php?id=1684671

Cao, Y., Chye, H. K., & Chye, F. J. (2017). *The Impact of Elevated Neighborhood Open Spaces on the Elderly's Social Interactions in Singapore Public Housing. 14th International Congress of Asian Planning Schools Association*, Beijing, China.

Castree, N., Kitchin, R., & Rogers, A. (2013). *A dictionary of human geography.* Oxford University Press. doi:10.1093/acref/9780199599868.001.0001

Chan, J. (2019). Mont'Kiara: Still pulling in the expats. *The Edge Markets.* https://www.theedgemarkets.com/article/montkiara-still-pulling-expats

Craighead, G. (2009). *High-rise security and fire life safety.* Butterworth-Heinemann. doi:10.1016/B978-1-85617-555-5.00002-X

Evans, J. (2016). *Can high-rise buildings ever work as cohesive living spaces?* FT. https://www.ft.com/content/870e12f8-1d19-11e6-a7bc-ee846770ec15

Fard, P. A., Sharif, M. K. M., Mohd Yunos, M. Y., & Mydin, M. A. O. (2015). Preference on social spaces in high density condominiums in Malaysia. *Applied Mechanics and Materials, 747*, 165–167. doi:10.4028/www.scientific.net/AMM.747.165

Farooq, U. (2014). Social interaction, Definition, Elements, Types & Forms. *Study Lecture Notes.* http://www.studylecturenotes.com/basics-of-sociology/social-interaction-definition-elements-types-forms

Ghazali, M., Bajunid, A., & Davis, P. (2014). The "sky neighborhood" layout. *International Journal on Tall Buildings and Urban Habitat -. CTBUH Journal, II*, 40–47.

Ghel, J. (1971). *Life between buildings: Using public space.* Island Press.

Gomez, C. (2016). The socialscraper. In *Cities to Megacities*. Shaping Dense Vertical Urbanism.

Green Building Index (GBI). (2019). GBI Residential New Construction (RNC) Tool *V3.0*. https://new.greenbuildingindex.org/Files/Resources/GBI%20Tools/GBI%20RNC%20Residential%20Tool%20V3.0.pdf

Groat, L., & Wang, D. (2013). *Architectural research methods*. Wiley & Sons.

Hadi, Y., Heath, T., & Oldfield, P. (2014). Vertical public realms: Creating urban spaces in the sky. In *Future Cities: Towards Sustainable Vertical Urbanism–2014 Shanghai Conference Proceedings,* 112–119.

Huang, S. C. L. (2006). A study of outdoor interactional spaces in high-rise housing. *Landscape and Urban Planning, 78*(3), 193–204. doi:10.1016/j.landurbplan.2005.07.008

Kennedy, R. J., & Buys, L. (2015). The impact of private and shared open space on liveability in sub-tropical apartment buildings. In Global Interchanges: Resurgence of the Skyscraper City, 318–323.

Knight Frank. (2019). *Real Estate Highlights: 1ˢᵗ Half 2019*. Knight Frank. https://content.knightfrank.com/research/179/documents/en/ malaysia-real-estate-highlights-1h-2019-6532.pdf

Laws of Malaysia. (1984). *Uniform building by-laws 1984*. International Law Book Services.

Mat Noor, N. A., & Eves, C. (2011). *Malaysia high-rise residential property management: 2004-2010 trends and scenario*. In 17th Pacific Rim Real Estate Society Conference. Gold Coast, Australia.

Merrill, F. E. (1969). Society and culture: An introduction to sociology. Englewood Cliffs, NJ.

Modi, S. (2014). Improving the social sustainability of high-rises. *CTBUH Journal, 1*.

Quod. (2014). *Living in tall buildings*. Berkeley Group. https://www.berkeleygroup.co.uk/media/pdf/b/b/berkeley-group-report-living-in-tall-buidlings.pdf

Ramachandran, S. (2018). *Property hotspots for 2018*. Focus Malaysia. http://www.focusmalaysia.my/Property/property-hotspots-for-2018

Ridwana, R., Prayitno, B., & Hatmoko, A. U. (2018). The relationship between spatial configuration and social interaction in high-rise flats: A case study on the jatinegara barat in Jakarta. In *SHS Web of Conferences, 41*, 07003. 10.1051hsconf/20184107003

Samad, N. A. A., Jalil, R. A., & Anuar, N. A. N. K. (2018). Residents perception on strata property shared facilities potential for commercialisation. *International Journal of Real Estate Studies, 12*(2).

Samad, N. A. A., Said, I., & Rahim, A. A. (2017). Universally designed public spaces by enhancing accessibility and connectivity. *International Journal for Studies on Children, Women, Elderly And Disabled, 3*.

Sarayed, F. L. (2017). Exploring informality in a global south city: Issues of power and urban development in Kuala Lumpur. *Journal Of Design And Built Environment, 17*(1), 63–73. doi:10.22452/jdbe.vol17no1.4

Scott, P. (2015). Successful sky life. In Global Interchanges: Resurgence of the Skyscraper City.

Seo, R. J., & Omar, S. (2011). Housing typology of modern Malaysia. In *1st South East Asia Housing Forum of ARCH,* 6–7.

Tedong, P. A., Grant, J. L., Abdul-Aziz, W. N. A. W., Ahmad, F., & Hanif, N. R. (2014). Guarding the neighbourhood: The new landscape of control in Malaysia. *Housing Studies, 29*(8), 1005–1027. doi:10 .1080/02673037.2014.923089

The InterNations. (2019). *Living and Driving in Kuala Lumpur.* The Internations. https://www.interna-tions.org/kuala-lumpur-expats/guide/living-in-kuala-lumpur-15377/living-and-driving-in-kuala-lumpur-3

Uher, T. E., & Loosemore, M. (2004). *Essentials of construction project management.* UNSW Press.

Wahab, S. R. H. A., Chohan, A. H., Che-Ania, A. I., Tawil, N. M., & Omar, H. (2016). The classifica-tion of facilities to determine the management fund allocation at non-low cost of high-rise residential building. *Revista de la Facultad de Ingeniería, 31*(5), 9–18. doi:10.21311/002.31.5.02

Whyte, W. H. (1980). *The social life of small urban spaces.* Conservation Foundation.

Wood, A. (2014). *Rethinking the skyscraper in the ecological age: Design principles for a new high-rise vernacular.* Proceedings of the Council on Tall Buildings and Urban Habitat (CTBUH). Shanghai, China.

Zuzana (2012). The importance of social interaction to human health. *Hebio Feedback.* http://www.hebiofeedback.co.uk/hebf-latest/the-importance-of-social-interaction-to-human-health/

Chapter 17
Pragmatic Consideration on Eco–Friendly Building Materials for Healthy Homes

Siti Nuratirah Che Mohd Nasir

Universiti Malaysia Kelantan, Malaysia & Universiti Sultan Zainal Abidin, Malaysia

Nur Haizal Mat Yaacob Ariffin

Universiti Sultan Zainal Abidin, Malaysia

Najah Md Alwi

Sustainability and Urban Design Group, Faculty of Architecture and Ekistics, Universiti Malaysia Kelantan, Malaysia

Salmiah Aziz

Architectural Technology and Management Group, Faculty of Architecture and Ekistics, Universiti Malaysia Kelantan, Malaysia

Nur 'Izzati Mohd Amin

https://orcid.org/0000-0001-9395-4257

Human Centered Design Group, Faculty of Architecture and Ekistics, Universiti Malaysia Kelantan, Malaysia

Mohammed Fadzli Maharimi

Architectural Technology and Management Group, Faculty of Architecture and Ekistics, Universiti Malaysia Kelantan, Malaysia

ABSTRACT

The topic of health is becoming more of a crucial element in today's life particularly due to the COVID-19 crisis. This research was conducted to point out an eco-friendly building material focusing on interior environment towards better quality of life. The method adopted incorporates deeper literature study and interview sessions with expertise in the built environment mainly in eco-friendly and sustainable houses. The results show that there is a long list of available local eco-friendly material mainly timber,

DOI: 10.4018/978-1-6684-8253-7.ch017

brick, concrete, and bamboo that can be used in producing a healthy home. This research concludes that people need to gain more understanding of these materials and demand from our construction players will help to push more interest for these healthier options products. The data collected could be seen as important in the wake of recent endemic COVID-19 that involved wellbeing inside the house. This would be beneficial to the policy maker, enlightened building industry players and homeowners to highlight the significance of practicing a healthy environment.

INTRODUCTION

The built environment needs to find an equilibrium between economic growth and environmental sustainability as Malaysia continues to undergo rapid urbanization and development. Growing public awareness of how buildings affect both the environment and human health has boosted the need for eco-friendly building materials that can produce habitable places that are both healthier and more sustainable. In consideration of the hot tropical temperature and high humidity of the nation, choosing the appropriate building materials is essential to ensure the longevity and effectiveness of the structure while reducing its environmental impact. Specifically concentrating on their potential to enhance indoor air quality, lower energy use, and advance sustainable development, this paper explores the practical concerns of eco-friendly construction materials in the Malaysian home context.

Home is a dwelling where there is an assurance of complete mental and physical well-being, mainly for the residents and homeowner. Accordingly, housing has become a pivotal physical structure of shelter where it can influence people's daily activities such as sleeping, working, eating, playing, relaxing, and exercising (WHO, 2018). To support this, it is crucial to identify whether our homes are in a healthy housing context as it is supposed to give residents good indoor and outdoor vibes and a robust environment. People spend 90% of their time in buildings, (about 70% inside the house), thus it is certain that this healthy environment can have a big impact on our daily life, especially on health. Improved housing conditions including eco-friendly building materials can save lives, reduce disease, increase the nature of life, reduce poverty, help climate change, lower stress levels and the risk of injury (Che Mohd Nasir, 2022). This is in line with elements in the Sustainable Development Goals (SDG) in Malaysia that are known as the Global Goals which are embraced to protect the country and ensure that all people live peacefully and healthily by 2030 (Economic Planning Unit, 2021).

The COVID-19 outbreak has raised concerns about safe housing and the neighborhood. This situation forced lifestyle changes around the world at the end of 2019, which profoundly changed our daily life activities. Many countries, including Malaysia, have implemented lockdowns and this has led people to spend more time under quarantine at home, which affects employed adults and children who are subjected to home schooling (Hartini, 2020). Housing layout, space, safety, and indoor air quality, have been re-examined due to the pandemic and transpire to be a catalyst for healthy housing and sustainable building [19]. In conjunction with this, the design parameter for housing including the building materials should be redefined.

In this section, explanation and description of home in the context with respect to eco-friendly building materials for healthy home conditions, where several sides of interior spaces are presented. There are floor finishes, wall finishes, and ceiling finishes, also taking into account the finishing as an integral part of the interior building process. Through this research output, it will provide evidence-based recommendations on interventions that promote healthy living environments and facilitate the homeowner in enabling

Figure 1. Sustainable development goals
(Malaysia Economic Planning Unit, 2021)

healthy and safe considerations to underpin current housing regulations. The research questions that the present study tries to answer are: (a) What are effective interior building materials that can contribute to an environmentally friendly environment? and (b) How can housing be more sustainable? Therefore, this study aims to deepen understanding specifically on eco-friendly interior building materials from the perspective of producing healthy housing in Malaysia.

LITERATURE REVIEW

This section presents an array of studies which shows the scope of this paper which includes housing characteristics, components of eco-friendly building material, what they are, and how they are applied in interior design and interior architecture. This section also discusses precedent studies where the focus on eco-friendly materials integrates in home design.

Housing Characteristics

The evolution of housing characteristics in Malaysia is based on the most current lifestyle development. These characteristics are subdivided and subcategorized as terraces, semi-detached, bungalows, town-house, condominiums, service apartments, and the small office home office (SOHO), all showing great transformation of needs and requirements of users over the years. The design and materials that are used for houses are highly influenced by the socio-economic, cultural, and environmental needs. Air quality, temperature, ambience, light, noise, and several elements can affect the occupants' relationship with their home (Francesco Asdrubal, 2015). If the occupants feel vibrantly healthy and truly enjoy spending their time at home, then it is in good condition. Malaysia has a tropical climate and the temperature is in the range of 20°C to 30°C throughout the year. House design should provide the following points: 1) Ventilation for cooling and reducing humidity, 2) Use building materials that have a low environmental impact, 3) Control of direct solar radiation and glare from direct sunlight, and 4) Protection against the rain (Gür, 2020)

Healthy Housing Environment

Based on studies, more than 70% of our people times spent inside their home. In some places, the percentage is higher due to unemployment levels data are high. Children, elderly, disability people or someone who have chronic diseases were spending their time at home. Therefore, they are highly need in healthy housing condition.

Based on World Health Organization (WHO) Housing and Health guideline (HHGL), healthy housing is a shelter that provide feeling of home, including sense of belonging, security, good amenities, and facilities, and privacy. Healthy housing refers to physical structure of the home building that enable to provide and to facilitate comfortness, sufficient space, protect from pollution, injury and hazards.

A healthy home environment may be just as important as eating healthy and exercising to prevent disease and stay energized and healthy. Homes are the four places where people live, work, sleep or even work, which is a big factor that determines your health.

The air quality of the person breathing in the home must be fresh and free of toxins. Particles such as bacteria, mites, dust and light dirt if resident in our homes can be harmful to health even if our body's immune system is strong. It is important to understand that your home environment is one of the important elements that affect your overall health.

Following the current situation of the Covid-19 pandemic, no one thought that home conditions were a major factor in stopping the spread of the corona virus that was spreading recently. If you think logically, a dirty home condition can invite the reproduction of various types of germs. Therefore, home cleanliness is an important factor to prevent epidemic infections from occurring.

Those who do not clean the house regularly are at high risk of spreading the infection to other individuals, especially family members who also live in the same house. The more frightening thing is that the corona virus is easily transmitted to other individuals. Those living at home have the potential to become infected if there are individuals quarantined. This risk is multiplied if the cleanliness of the house is not maintained properly (WHO, 2018).

Our home place, affecting the location and the physical of the building itself, influence almost every aspect of our daily lives. Where it was from how well we rest and sleep, how often we meet family and friends, also how safe and secure we feel of the house. If we want to improve our family and community health and well-being, its were all started at home, where most of the people spend of their life.

WHO defines health as a great condition of complete physical, mental, and social well-being. Thus, the interpretation of health and well-being must include social, psychological, and physical factors. Mental health is about much more than just the absence of any mental illness, also enclose positive elements such as peace of mind, contentment, confidence, and social connection. Social well-being is related to individual relationships within their community (Nasir, 2021)

Figure 2. Health and wellbeing in homes
(United Kingdom Green Building Council, 2016)

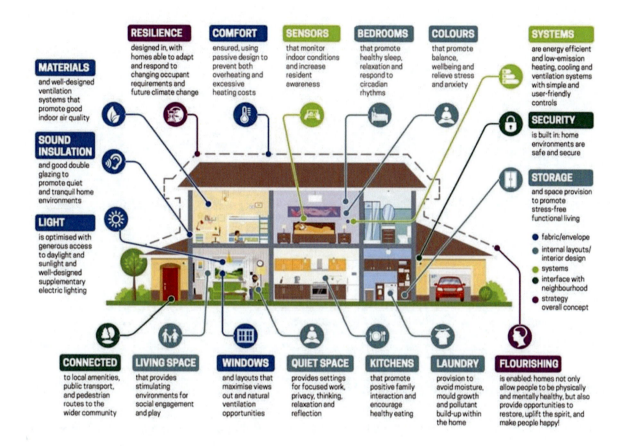

Housing in Healthy Community

Substandard housing that does not provide safe and adequate shelter may impact health, safety, and wellbeing for occupants. These can lead to chronic disease, asthma, and even mental health. For instance, improper material finishing or dampness may lead to asthma and even worse can cause cancer. Based on studies, poor mental health is also affected by housing that do not have structural quality where it acquired with pest infestation, dampness, cold, bad interior spatial planning and many more.

Thus, there are families living in a housing environment that are not optimally supportive for occupant health. For example, many houses and even residents fail to meet elements of healthy housing, that incorporate proper ventilation, good safety and security, cleanliness, accessibility, facilities and free from any injury.

Studies have found that there are components that need to be taken into consideration, the fundamental relationship between person's environment linked with behavior and health (WHO, 2018).

Figure 3. Social determinants of health
(Healthy Community, 2012)

Housing Standards That Promote Health

In the practice of creating a housing standard that meet the green building requirements are environmentally responsible and resource - efficient throughout building life-cycle. This applicable when designer starts to design, management, administration and operation, construction, maintenance, renovation, demolition and even refurbishment process happen.

Based on WHO housing and health guideline, the physical structure of housing plays an important part of built environment towards the occupants. Construction materials for outdoor and indoor give huge impact to human health as green materials approach were highlighted. Examples of unsuitable materials impact that we do not realize are: formaldehyde emissions from fibre board, asbestos from ceiling, fibres from glass insulation material, damp and mold from tiles and wood products where it all hazardous for human health. Damp housing also may lead to disturbed sleep and affect emotional upset especially for women and children.

Other than that, as we can see some designs of housing such high rise building often cause a problem especially for elder people to stay around, parents to carrying a shopping even to supervise their children playing outside.

Good housing design may naturally ventilate homes by entering or leaving windows open. Natural ventilation can supply energy efficiency also incorporate to bring in fresh air and get rid of stale air from inside house. Ventilation can come into buildings via several ways. There are from the doors and windows, opening at walls and floors, spot ventilation, and mechanical system ventilation. Poor ventilation may cause pollution made indoor, lead to mold growth, damp, humidity, and radon.

Figure 4. Different aspects in sustainable design of healthy housing environment
(Author)

Concepts such as sustainable development or sustainable design have emerged as a result of processes continuing for many years. The consequence of sustainable development is sustainable design based on the principles applied irrespective of the adopted formal aesthetics. There are numerous lists of principles and methods of assessing the sustainability of individual structures, whole complexes, or areas. Requirements that a healthy housing environment must meet in the context of human health are most comprehensively expressed for occupants and residents (WHO, 2018).

Based on the figure above, there are different aspect in sustainable housing design that may require for healthy housing environment. All aspects linked towards each other and incorporated not only personal residents but all surrounding environments.

Components of Eco-Friendly Building Material

The application of green building materials is a dominant strategy in designing a house or a building. This is subject to environmentally friendly materials that are obtained from recycled or sustainable natural sources. A thorough consideration of productivity and health of a building will reduce the maintenance cost of the building, as well as improve the occupants' health and productivity. The role of the construction players should be to confidently speak about constructing with sustainable materials that are not only good for the people, but also save money, preserve the heritage, and respond to construction policies (ArchDaily, 2013).

Definition and Importance of Eco-Friendly Building Materials

Eco-friendly building materials can be translated as a material that is harmless towards the environment even during production, when recycled or discarded. Most of these materials are composed of renewable resources such as reclaimed wood or bamboo. To design and construct a green building, it is important to implement efficient structures and building materials that are from an energy-efficient and eco-friendly environment. Contrary to conventional building, green building is regularly lower in operational expenditures and maintenance thus increasing the profitability for developers and owners (Sun et al., 2022).

Most developers, builders, and homeowners now use sustainable alternatives to reduce the projects' negative environmental effects. It is no longer something novel but something that will be made mandatory as it impacts social, economy and physical of all involved in a long term. Investing in this green building project can improve the health and productivity of the building's occupants while also reducing carbon emissions over the course of the structure's life.

Environment-Friendly Building Materials

The table below states several environmentally friendly building materials that are applicable for use in developing green homes or healthy homes.

Environmentally Friendly Implementation in Interior Building

The Malaysian Institute of Architects (PAM) created the Green Building Index (GBI), a non-governmental organization that serves as a recognized green rating system for assessing the environmental design and performance of Malaysian structures. There are over 300 listed green buildings and development projects in Malaysia that are certified by this body. What needs to be acknowledged is that these certified buildings are not only built in consideration of the natural environment but also to allow occupants and building users to live healthier, happier, and more productive lives as part of the design goals. As for the interior component, there are the GBI Interior Tools that have been developed by the Malaysian Green Building Confederation (MGBC) and Malaysian Institute of Interior Design (MIID). Based on Figure 2 below, the assessment of GBI incorporates six elements, they are energy efficiency, indoor environment quality, material resources, sustainable site planning and management, innovation, and water efficiency (A Nowotna, 2019; Alfuraty, 2020).

Presently, a significant problem in interior design practices that is influencing Environmentally Sustainable Interior Design (ESID) is where interior designers make sustainable choices in their project that are still insufficient, especially in the selection of materials (P. De Luca, 2017). While this study provides some insight into this issue, designers must also take into account the project's unique requirements as well as the regional context and the availability of sustainable materials. The entire lifecycle of the materials they select, from production and shipment through installation, maintenance, and disposal. By giving sustainability a higher priority when choosing materials, designers may create homes that are healthier and more environmentally friendly while reducing the negative consequences of interior design on the environment.

There are several features that should be incorporated into green homes. The most important of which is eco-friendly building materials, followed by LED lighting, solar panel, water system and conservation wind turbine, geothermal energy inside the house, sustainable insulation, energy efficiency appliances,

Table 1. Environment-friendly building materials

Types of material	Characteristics	Sources
1. Natural material		
• Concrete	Reduce urban heat, cool the building, durable material, low operational energy	(Ashraf, 2021) (Francesco Asdrubali, 2015)
• Timber – reclaimed timber	Durability, strong, good joining, aesthetic, many stain and color options, natural clean appearance, easy for maintenance, timeless, bold, versatile option.	(A Nowotna, 2019) (Francesco Asdrubali, 2015) (Green Building Action Plan, 2022) (Koca, 2017) (Patel, 2021)
• Brick	High thermal mass, absorb and stores heat, prevents penetration of moisture, re-used, reduce carbon dioxide emission,	(Sandy Halliday, 2016)
• Stone	Low maintenance, durable	(Green Building Action Plan, 2022) (Rousseau, n.d.)
• Cob	Energy efficient, Cost effective, and receive benefits from solar energy.	
• Bamboo	Durable, lightweight, can withstand compression, flexible material, atmospheric pollution and has an excellent water absorption capacity.	(P. De Luca, 2017) (Patel, 2021) (Penny Bonda, 2014)
• Cork	Thermal insulation, mold-resistant,	(Naglaa & Megahed, 2020)
• tiles	Durable, low maintenance, timeless beauty, long life span, variety of option, environmental friendly,	(Green Building Action Plan, 2022) (Francesco Asdrubali, 2015)
• Straw bales	excellent thermal insulation, very thick, lowers the cost of heating and cooling, fewer toxins,	(Green Building Action Plan, 2022)
• Cement	Sun resistant, low environmental impact, manufactured inexpensively, reducing greenhouse gas (GHG) emissions,	(Naglaa & Megahed, 2020)
• Ceramic	Easy to clean, solid and durable, chemically resistant, inexpensive, lightweight, smooth to the touch, environmentally compatible, do not stain and do not fade,	(Naglaa & Megahed, 2020)
• Sheep Wool	Natural insulation, provides thermal barrier, renewable resources, regulates humidity, stabilizes temperature, reacts to humidity, purifies the air, safe to touch, renewable, high nitrogen content.	(A Nowotna, 2019) (Matthias Richter, 2021)
• Plywood	Strength, flexibility, easily polished and painted, hold screws well, resistive to shrink, warp, twist and crack, economical, have many layers.	(Naglaa & Megahed, 2020) (Patel, 2021)
2. Salvaged material		
• Old crushed concrete	Viable for reuse, reduction of CO2 emissions associate with concrete production.	(Peiyu, 2022)
• Old clay brick	Good insulators, pest resistant, fireproof	(Peiyu, 2022)
• Recycle timber	Repairable, renewable and can be diverted from landfill	
• Recycle stonework	Help lower greenhouse gas emission, improve soil condition, energy usage is minimized.	(Umar, 2012)
3. Fibre glass insulation	Cost effective, strength, can be molded, corrosion resistant, low density, tensile, durable	(Naglaa & Megahed, 2020)
4. Paint – low VOC	Innovative product, water-based, non-toxic, durable, wide selection, cost effective, minimal environmental impact, biodegradable, safe for children, pregnant women, and elderly,	(Sandy Halliday, 2016) (Umar, 2012) Zebra, 2022)

water reuse, and the application of rainwater harvesting (*Recycling of Natural Stones,* 2020). Today technologies and innovative design have identified without a doubt that having a beautiful home can also be green and healthy (Patel, 2021)

Figure 5. Green building index (interior assessment criteria)
(Green building index, 2019)

PART	CRITERIA	ITEM	POINTS	SUBMITTER	GBI
	EE	**ENERGY EFFICIENCY**			
1	EE1	Engagement Of Qualified Professionals	2		
	EE2	Lighting & Plug Load	12		
	EE3	Air Conditioning System	6		
	EE4	Measurement, Verification & EE Performance	8		
	EQ	**INDOOR ENVIRONMENTAL QUALITY**			
	Air Quality				
	EQ1	Minimum IAQ Performance	2		
	EQ2	Indoor Air Pollutants	3		
	Thermal Comfort				
	EQ3	Thermal Comfort: Design & Controllability of Systems	2		
	EQ4	Carbon Dioxide Monitoring & Control	2		
	EQ5	Mould Prevention	2		
2	**Lighting, Visual & Acoustic Comfort**				
	EQ6	Daylighting	1		
	EQ7	Daylight Glare Control	1		
	EQ8	Electrical Lighting Levels	1		
	EQ9	High Frequency Ballasts	1		
	EQ10	External Views	1		
	EQ11	Internal Noise Levels	1		
	Verification				
	EQ12	IAQ Before & During Occupancy	1		
	EQ13	Post Occupancy Comfort Survey: Verification	1		
	SM	**SUSTAINABLE PLANNING & MANAGEMENT**			
	Site Planning				
	SM1	Building Selection	1		
	SM2	Refurbishment of Existing or Abandoned Interior Space	1		
	SM3	Public Transportation Access	1		
	SM4	Community Connectivity	1		
	Interior Space Design & Quality				
	SM5	Sustainable Space Design	10		
3	SM6	Indoor Greenscape & Indoor Water Feature	2		
	Construction Management				
	SM7	Sustainable Construction	1		
	SM8	Construction Pollution Control Policy	1		
	SM9	Storage & Collection of Recyclables	1		
	SM10	Construction Waste Management	1		
	SM11	Site Safety	1		
	Operation				
	SM12	Green Procurement & Operation Policy	2		
	SM13	Sustainable Maintenance & Green Office Guide	2		

PART	CRITERIA	ITEM	POINTS	SUBMITTER	GBI
	MR	**MATERIALS & RESOURCES**			
	Reused & Recycled Materials				
	MR1	Materials Reuse & Selection	2		
	MR2	Recycled Content Materials	4		
4	**Sustainable Resources**				
	MR3	Regional Materials	1		
	MR4	Rapidly Renewable Materials & Sustainable Timber	3		
	Green Products				
	MR5	Material Manufacture & Ingredients	2		
	MR6	Refrigerants & Clean Agents	2		
	WE	**WATER EFFICIENCY**			
	Increased Efficiency & Recycling				
5	WE1	Water Efficient Landscaping & Water Feature	1		
	WE2	Water Efficient Fittings	2		
	WE3	Drinking Water Quality	1		
	IN	**INNOVATION**			
6	IN1	Innovation in Design & Environmental Design Initiatives	9		
	IN2	Green Building Index Accredited Facilitator	1		
		TOTAL POINTS	**100**		

Figure 6. Criteria of eco-friendly home
(Ibiza, 2022)

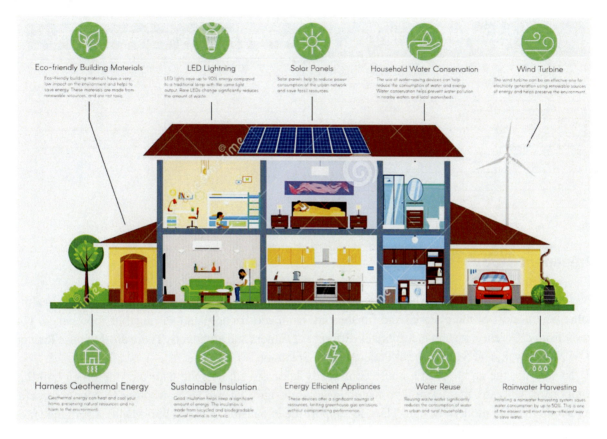

How do eco-friendly materials foster good health?

The utmost benefit of choosing eco materials is that they are free from harmful chemicals, and finishes have minimal effects on the surrounding environment. This makes them safer to build and creates a healthier home environment for occupants. Nevertheless, with current new technologies and construction techniques the concept of an eco-friendly home is continuously expanding. There are several elements that contribute to these concepts, where the home or building itself must be naturally amicable with the surrounding, the material used for construction is recyclable and non-pollutant which leads to less maintenance, also the electrical appliances should reduce energy consumption. The GBI approach aims to assist all the building players in attaining sustainable development. GBI environmental rating systems are developed to:

- Develop green buildings as a common standard in construction measurement;
- Encourage integration of the whole building design;
- Reconstruct the built environment to lessen environmental impact;
- To ensure that new construction remains relevant in the future and that the existing buildings can be upgraded appropriately to remain relevant (A Nowotna, 2019; Fadhil Muhammad, 2019)

Figure 7. Weightage of green building criteria/rating system
(Green Building Index, 2019)

PART	ITEM	MAXIMUM POINTS	SCORE
	ASSESSMENT CRITERIA OVERALL POINTS SCORE		
1	Energy Efficiency	23	
2	Indoor Environmental Quality	12	
3	Sustainable Site Planning & Management	37	
4	Material & Resources	10	
5	Water Efficiency	12	
6	Innovation	6	
	TOTAL SCORE	100	

POINTS	GBI RATING
GREEN BUILDING INDEX CLASSIFICATION	
86 to 100 points	Platinum
76 to 85 points	Gold
66 to 75 points	Silver
50 to 65 points	Certified

Precedent Study

Two (2) precedent studies have been selected based on their design, which has the elements of a healthy home where most of the material and finishes are from eco-friendly and sustainable approaches. The study from different state and incorporates different designers and architects. There are T-House located at Miri, Sarawak, and S11 House at Petaling Jaya, Selangor.

To sum up, the architect of a house continually learns to support the nature of the green building component, whereby the desire is to feature a good design that has value in order to have a forceful impact on tropical modern design. Thus, to support the expansion of green building as a component of the whole construction market, and to provide a criterion in quantifying future changes in our industry, the houses are organized around the personality of both the owners - which involves the qualities of a humble, free from interference and intrusive design and the proximity to their family members. The architecture portrays stories between space, material, texture, light, and sight. It tells an owner's journey and evolution in their personal career (Choo, 2022; Seyed Meysam Khoshnava, 2020).

Green design elements that are implemented by the architect are very successful and can minimize the degradation of the environment, reduce greenhouse emission, promote healthy housing, and improve the environment for all forms of life. By evolving the method to apply eco-materials in the planning, the architect also conserves energy in promoting renewable resources. Both houses combine energy-saving technology into every aspect of their planning, construction, and maintenance (Che Mohd Nasir, 2022)

However, in Malaysia, the number of green constructions that are carried out is small compared to the overall projects that have been constructed. Thus, this case study of houses that have won the platinum-rated GBI residential building is the ultimate GBI rating, and can serve as an excellent example in promoting green construction (Green Building, 2019).

Challenges in Implementing Green Construction

In Malaysia, sustainability has been expanding in favor by global construction industry all around the world cause of minimizing industry adverse impact. Many studies have investigated construction industry

Table 2. Home features between two precedent studies (Choo, 2022; ArchDaily, 2013)

	T-House	S11 House
Exterior View		
Architect	Ar. William Khoo Boo Chuan, Design Network Architects (DNA) Sdn. Bhd, Sarawak.	Ar. Dr. Tan Loke Mun, Archicentre Sdn. Bhd, Subang Jaya, Selangor
Owner	Teresa Ling	Dr. Tan Loke Mun & Chew May-Ann
Year	**2019**	**2012**
Award	Gold, Malaysia Institute of Architects (PAM) 2022 Awards: Single Residential	Malaysia's first Green Building Index (GBI) Platinum (CVA) RM224, 297.73 GBI Green Cost Sustainable Design Award ● Asia Pacific Interior Design Awards for Elite APDC Awards 2011 – Residential Category
Area	Total build-up of 764 sqm Land size of about 3193 sqm	Total site area 1, 240 sq m Total built up area 1, 100 sq m cost of works approximately RM2.1m
Level	**2**	**3**
Interior photos		
Concept/style	Modern tropical with green sustainability. Cultural heritage inspired by traditional Chinese courtyard houses.	Green tropical inspired by dream resort home.

continued on following page

Table 2. Continued

	T-House	S11 House
Material/ Eco friendly material	● Staircase: Bespoke steel and wood – from the fern garden leads to upper floor. ● 7 pockets garden – water courtyard, central courtyard, garden boulevard, secret garden, franji court, outer garden, and fern garden. ● Warm material palette with extensive use of timber ● Glass roof: aluminium screen ● Interior landscape: timber, marble, and stone – original tactile quality ● Floor: stone and marble ● Cladding: concrete surfaces and fair face stone ● Staircase: steel mesh and timber	● Roof tiles: old crushed concrete for gravel fill ● Feature wall: old clay bricks ● Formwork strutting and propping: roofing timbers ● Yards: old steel ● Backfilling: cement aprons ● Wall: cement plastered without paint ● Brickwork: natural faced common red clay ● Bathrooms: Stone ● Driveway: stone, cement render and timber ● Living areas: stone and timber, and recycle wood pallets. ● Ground floor decks: old recycled chengal ● Flooring: timber – Forest Stewardship Council (FSC) certified
How the material supporting healthy home	● Green or eco materials can make occupant calm emotionally and mentally where tranquility of nature world can reduce harmful gases, leading to our health for a long term. For example, biophilic design approaches can protect the body, mind, and heart for years to come.	● Natural materials are off gas less and positively can affect occupant mental and emotional health by rooting the residents in nature, good ventilation, fine spatial planning and treatment with water feature.
Finishing	● 68% of the interior finishes are using timber including ceiling panels and flooring. ● Safety glass to provide adequate privacy and security ● Steel and screens components are used for furniture	● Most of all surfaces painted with low Volatile Organic Compound (VOC) ● Joinery for internal has low VOC content and from water-based glue ● Wall and ceiling: bare natural finishes
Extra features	● Small gaps at the interface, between glass roof and glass wall to allow air to infiltrate in promoting natural ventilation. ● Contemporary timber louvers to add distinct identity and touch of avant garden. ● Belian hardwood screens are pivoted to allow privacy and sun shading assistance. ● Fern garden inspired by flora of Sarawakian rainforest	● Roof: 15 turbines are driven both by wind along with convection glass pyramids heat as the results of greenhouse out-turn. ● Solar hot water heaters
Lighting	Secondary aluminum screens to articulate sunlight into the interior to reduce heat.	T5 tubes, LED, and compact fluorescent for energy savings.

will face the challenge of green building implementation. There are economic issues, attitude and market, management and government, product information and sourcing, and lastly technology and training.

There are an issue of many developers going green with the cost inflation in all development. Despite of that fact, developers today must change their mindsets, and should not only go for cheapest level but have in view for the best long-term condition and solution. Green buildings are valued higher than conventional buildings where it may go for higher rentals. Other than that, these building not only give commercial benefit satisfaction, but also incorporate social and environmental advantages where it does not have tangible value.

Every step of the construction process should have holistic top-to toe approach that need to consider required by green buildings. Thus, these buildings are designed to decrease their impact on environment and surrounding community, energy, and water efficient, uses materials that are recyclable and non-toxic. The other outcome of these design is focusing on increasing the efficiency of resources on energy, water and materials where it can reduce building impacts especially towards human health and environment building lifecycle through better design, construction, and maintenance.

The government, owners, designers, and contractor should embrace the concept of going green to make it work.

At other side, even with support from government to build green building and global awareness on environmental issues, only small number of developers and designer are willing to go for it instead still maintaining conventional method in construction.

Based on studies, housing is one of the main sectors that contribute to Malaysian economic growth. These industries cater career opportunities for 800,000 people in Malaysia. Adding to this, housing can be referred as an industry with activities that supply buildings and structures with the objective to provide human shelter, protect from danger and place for rest. Besides that, the population in Malaysia are growing year by year as well as demand for housing development. Along with that, housing development also should complement with healthy environment, basic amenities, and adequate facilities to improve people well-being.

Based on research done by Esa, (2011), the main obstacle in developing green buildings in Malaysia is to build a paradigm shift in the environmental issues of our Malaysians, especially construction players. Architects, designers, consultants, and client highlighted that lack of awareness is the main issues involving this development. Minimal investments and contribution from Government and private company in green building approach also create an obstacle to building players in designing and building effectively.

Malaysian government and Malaysia Institute of Architect (PAM) can provide a competent training to our construction players especially to publics as well as to give awareness on the environmentally friendly buildings so that more demand on this development can be achieved. Other than that, PAM and Public Works Department Malaysia (JKR) can play a big role in making it as a compulsory for all Malaysian architects and designers to understand and attend the training for them to acknowledge and studies more about green building. Finally, the government also can start to administer all the developers to incorporate some of green building elements in all future developments before they give the approvals. Then by this implementation, client and architects have no alternative but to attach to the requirements (Nordin, 2021).

Other studies done by Nordin (2020), also related to this green building implementation, the main challenge in implementing this development is higher capital upfront. There are green assessment fees, design, material cost and professional fees. Minimal financial incentives from government also one of the issues. Besides, the same issues with above studies mentioned that lack of in-depth knowledge among construction players. However, the studies revealed there is an improvement in green materials in the current market. Thus, government should play an important role by not only spread awareness on green campaign but also enhance the enforcement on the guideline and requirement of green building developments in Malaysia.

An intent in making green practices as an essential for all developers to secure for their future projects can be a great start. Thus, the government also can consider preparing financial incentives for construction players as a booster element for them in developing and designing green design practices (Esa, 2011).

METHOD

The study aimed to identify eco-friendly building materials for a healthy interior environment. To achieve this, two strategies will be adopted, the first stage is to conduct a research study of the literature on topics that are related to the green and sustainable material approach, the implementation towards interior environments is also two precedent studies of green houses that have won awards, which subsequently yield the criteria and objective of this research. The second stage is to conduct an interview session with three experts who are building construction players (architects and interior designers). The structured questions have been given to the experts with five questions that are related to the objective of this research.

Data Analysis

This section presents the data analysis procedures followed conducting the interviews, including participant selection, interview design, data collection, and analysis. It also discusses the ethical considerations considered throughout the research process.

There are a few indicators that can be used to gauge the acceptance and demand for eco-friendly building materials in Malaysia. Examining the increase in such materials' market share is one approach to do this. This can be accomplished by looking at the country's market patterns and sales numbers for environmentally friendly building materials over a given time frame.

Furthermore, by keeping track of the number of projects that have utilized these materials, the utilization of ecologically friendly building materials may be quantified. In this study for example, the Green Building Index (GBI), a grading system for evaluating the environmental performance of buildings in Malaysia, is used as an indicator to examine building permits or certificates.

From Table 3, we can understand that eco-friendly building materials are getting popular in the market, demanded among construction professionals, and actively implemented in Malaysia. Experts understand that the advantages of using green material can reduce human errors that cause wastage, are harmful to the environment, decrease injury, shorten the construction time, and that can save the ecosystem as well as give good benefits to the occupants Furthermore, there is the need to increase suppliers of green

Table 3. Interview with experts in construction professionals

Participants, State	Definition of eco–friendly building material	Materials closely relate to sustainable design	Malaysia Current approach	Advantages of using sustainable materials	Future planning
A, Johor Bharu	Extending building life and protect human life consideration,	Wide coverage – roof, wall, floor, slab, and interior products. Timber and concrete are highlighted. Paint with low VOC.	Raise awareness of strategic sustainability consideration – materials, technology	Reduce risk of future adaptations to meet changing regulations	Have positive impact on health, well-being, and productivity – individuals, community, and organisation.
B, Kuala Lumpur	Secure occupant health, less harmful for environment	Bamboo without any doubt – easy to harvest, minimal damage, biodegradable and reusable.	Arising now, initiate lot of innovation. This is due to incentives reward to developer to build more green building.	Minimise pollution, give good environment to occupants.	A thorough review on building materials to meet the sustainability goals.
C, Selangor	Vital contribution to people experiences the house/ building	Certified by experts-timber, bricks, fiberglass insulation, plaster ceiling (gypsum board)	Green building Index (GBI) limit the production and method (contractor) such materials that can cause pollution or high energy consumptions	Create healthy environments, enhance biodiversity, should not cause pollution to river, sea, drain, landfill waste.	Sustainability goals in terms of material should embed with business strategic plan and fully commitment by project team.

building materials in our country. Without any doubt, the approach in developing a healthy home can be achieved (Installation & Finishing, 2022).

DISCUSSION

The results of this study indicate that environmentally friendly building materials are becoming more popular in Malaysia, with rising demand from industry professionals in construction and active application in building projects. This approach is consistent with global initiatives to support sustainable growth and lessen the negative environmental effects of the construction sector.

Sustainable development has gradually become a new important agenda at both local and national levels. This can be seen through the SDG that the government has always highlighted. The construction industry is one of the productive sectors that constantly contribute to the economy in Malaysia (Sun et. al, 2022). As an integral part of this effort, in the field of architecture and interior design, a large number of materials are used in large quantities. Building and construction operations in the world annually consume approximately 3 billion tons of raw materials which represent 40% of the total resource consumption (Alfuraty, 2020).

Based on the study, materials can be classified according to their sources. There are natural materials, converted materials, salvaged materials, and artificial materials. Hence, natural materials are the endure as a lowest environmental impact (Alfuraty, 2020). The selection of materials for the interior design process is a crucial part, where it incorporates the functionality and performance of the houses or buildings. The definition of sustainable interior design is interior spaces that have systems and materials that are designed to minimize negative impacts- especially for the occupants, and to maximize the positive impacts on the environment, social system, and economy (Amirhossein Balali, 2020).

To answer the research questions of this study it can be concluded that there is a long list of available local eco-friendly materials that can be used in producing a healthy home; above all, designers are encouraged to use these materials creatively and must include them in the early design planning and components. Moreover, the interior designer also needs to step up the solution to raise the performance level of the sustainable materials approach in terms of material and furniture selection. This is to raise the environmental sustainability of the interior spaces to achieve good well-being and build a better sustainable future for the occupants (Alfuraty, 2020).

CONCLUSION

There has been a shift in recent years in the world of design and construction towards a more sustainable approach. In order to improve building efficiency, save costs, and reduce environmental effects, designers, architects, and developers are suddenly realizing the value of incorporating natural components into contemporary buildings. This study has brought to light the crucial part that knowledge and research play in increasing sustainability in the built environment. The conclusions and suggestions in this section can be used for more research in the future.

This research has emphasized the new attitude of designers, architects, and developers who propose innovative modern buildings in compliance with the elements of nature and the built environment. This is to upgrade the comfort of buildings, higher performance, to lower the cost and to limit environmental impact. Thus, it is crucial to emphasize the accountability of research and information in the field of sustainability. The purpose of this paper is to bring to the forefront newly developed materials that are generally unconventional, not only for architecture students and academics, but also for built environment professionals, construction professionals, and project teams pursuing sustainability goals (ArchDaily, 2013).

Through alternative ideas for new buildings, energy savings can be achieved by using new methods that use fuel consumption where can improve human health. Finally, raising the level of environmental sustainability for any interior spaces, including houses, commercial spaces, and office buildings builds a better future.

This would be beneficial to the policymaker, enlighten building industry players as well as homeowners by highlighting the significance of practicing a healthy environment. This research is also more inclined towards any space and building, and not necessarily the 'home'.

REFERENCES

Alfuraty, A. B. (2020). Sustainable Environment in Interior Design: Design by Choosing Sustainable Materials. *IOP Conference Series. Materials Science and Engineering, 1-2*(1), 4–8. doi:10.1088/1757-899X/881/1/012035

Amirhossein Balali, A. V. (2020). Identification and selection of building façade's smart materials according to sustainable development goals. *Sustainable Materials and Technologies, 1*, 3.

ArchDaily. (2013, January 2). S11 House / ArchiCentre. *ArchDaily*. https://www.archdaily.com/313041/s11-house-archicentre

Che Mohd Nasir, D. W. (2022). Housing as an Integral Development For Health categories that deliver a healthy housing in Malaysia. *International Journal of Accounting, Finance and Business*, 391

Choo, J. (2022, July 14). *Home Tour: A Multi-Generational Family Home In Miri, Sarawak*. Tatler. https://www.tatlerasia.com/homes/home-tours/home-tour-a-multi-generational-family-home-in-miri-sarawak

P. De Luca, I. C. (2017). Green building materials: A review of state-of-the-art studies of innovative materials. *Journal of Green Building, 151*, 160.

Economic Planning Unit. (2021). *Sustainable Development Goals*. Economic Planning Unit, Prime Minister's Department: https://www.epu.gov.my/en/sustainable-development-goals

Esa, M. R. (2011). Obstacles in implementing Green Building projects in Malaysia. *Australian Journal of Basic and Applied Sciences*, 1806–1812.

Fadhil Muhammad, S. W. (2019). Building Material in The Perspective of Energy Efficiency and Thermal Environment in TOD Area. *IOP Conference Series. Earth and Environmental Science*, 2–6.

Francesco Asdrubali, F. D. (2015). A review of unconventional sustainable building insulation materials. *Sustainable Materials and Technologies, 1*.

Green Building Action Plan. (2022). The University of British Columbia. https://sustain.ubc.ca/campus/green-buildings/green-building-action-plan#:~:text=OVERVIEW,to%20human%20and%20natural%20systems

Green Building Index. (2019). Green Building Index INTERIORS - Design reference guide & submission format. GBI.

Gür, M. (2020). Post-pandemic lifestyle changes and their interaction with resident behavior in housing and neighborhoods: Bursa, Turkey. *Journal of Housing and the Built Environment*, 823–828. PMID:34512216

Hartini, L. B. W. (2020). Sustainable Materials and Technologies with Environmentally Sustainability Materials. *IOP Conference Series. Materials Science and Engineering*, 1–5.

Installation & Finishing. (2022). *Elmwood Reclaimed Timber*. Elmwood Reclaimed Timber. https://www.elmwoodreclaimedtimber.com/resources/installation-finishing/

Koca, G. (2017). Interior Finishing Materials. *Research Gate*, 606-617.

Matthias Richter, W. H. (2021, January 5). *Natural Building Materials for Interior Fitting and Refurbishment—What about Indoor Emissions?* pp. 1-2.

Naglaa, A., & Megahed, E. M. (2020). Antivirus-built environment: Lessons learned from Covid-19 pandemic. *Sustainable Cities and Society*, 1-4, 7.

Nasir, S. N. (2021). Information on creating a healthy home environment in Malaysia. AIP Conference Proceedings 2347 (pp. 020100 - 020100-8). Malaysia: AIP Publishing. doi:10.1063/5.0053683

Nordin, R. M. (2020). Challenges in the implementation of Green Home Development in Malaysia. *IOP Publishing Conf. Series. Materials Science and Engineering*, 291.

Nowotna, B. P. (2019). Eco-Friendly Building Materials. *IOP Conference Series. Earth and Environmental Science*, 2-4, 7.

Patel, P. P., & Patel, A. (2021). Use of sustainable green materials in construction of green buildings for sustainable development. *IOP Conference Series. Earth and Environmental Science*, 785(1), 2–8. doi:10.1088/1755-1315/785/1/012009

Peiyu Xu, J. Z. (2022). Are bamboo construction materials environmentally friendly? A life cycle environmental impact analysis. *Science Direct*, *1*, 3.

Penny Bonda, K. S. (2014). *Sustainable Commercial Interiors*. John Wiley & Sons, Inc., Hoboken, New Jersey.

Recycling of Natural Stones, Management and Benefits. (2020, October 6). Work-Tops. https://www.work-tops.com/blogs/stone/recycling-of-natural-stones-management-and-benefits

Rousseau, D. (n.d.). Environmentally Friendly Building Materials. *Sustainable Built Environment*, *3-6*, 8.

Sandy Halliday, R. A. (2016). *RIBA Plan of Work 2013 Guide Sustainability*. RIBA Publishing.

Seyed Meysam Khoshnava, R. R. (2020). The Role of Green Building Materials in Reducing Environmental and Human Health Impacts. *International Journal of Environmental Research and Public Health*, 6, 11.

Sun, H., Mao, W., Dang, Y., & Xu, Y. (2022). Optimum path for overcoming barriers of green construction supply chain management: A grey possibility Dematel-Nk approach. *Computers & Industrial Engineering*, *164*, 107833. doi:10.1016/j.cie.2021.107833

UK Green Building Council. (2015). *Health & Wellbeing in Homes*. UK Green Building Council. 08453 UKGBC Healthy Homes FINAL WEB.pdf (biid.org.uk)

Umar, U. A. (2012). Sustainable Building Material for green building construction, conservation, and refurbishing. *Research Gate*, 1-4.

WHO Housing and health guidelines. (2018, November 23). World Health Organization. https://www. who.int/publications/i/item/9789241550376

Zebra, T. (2022, August 11). 15 Green building materials for an eco-conscious home. *The Zebra*. https:// www.thezebra.com/resources/home/green-building-materials/

Section 6

Culture, Place Experience, and the Everyday Spaces

Chapter 18
Architecture and the Everyday:
Analysing the Malaysian Cross-Cultural Coffee Spaces

Najah Md. Alwi
Universiti Malaysia Kelantan, Malaysia

Ida Marlina Mazlan
UCSI University, Malaysia

ABSTRACT

Although Malaysia is traditionally a tea-drinking nation, the global coffee culture has become an integral part of a "third" space in the country's urban and rural areas. The study highlights the shared qualities and cultural elements that shape the design and atmosphere of Malaysian coffee places, providing insights into their role as important social tools in the country. By exploring the spatial design and social meaning of these coffee places, this research contributes to a deeper understanding of the relationship between architecture, cultural identity, and everyday life experiences in Malaysia. However, this study focuses on a limited number of selected coffee houses in specific regions of Malaysia. The findings should be interpreted within this context and may not capture the full diversity of coffee places across the country. The findings contribute to the growing body of knowledge on the intersection of architecture, culture, and social interactions, serving as a foundation for further exploration and appreciation of Malaysia's unique coffee culture.

BACKGROUND OF THE RESEARCH

There is a growing interest in researching the design and construction of coffee shops and eateries in Malaysia, as they have become an integral part of the social fabric of Malaysian communities and have the potential to significantly impact the cultural and urban development of the areas they serve. The culture revolving around food is essential to Malaysians and is often considered a "third" space – where social environments beyond the home and workplace are where people gather, relax, and engage in meaningful conversations. As such, coffee shops have become a focal point for researchers interested in the inter-

DOI: 10.4018/978-1-6684-8253-7.ch018

section of placemaking, social connection, and urban development. While the current post-pandemic research in placemaking and social connection focuses majorly on cities with a bigger population where the impact may be more significant, there are still benefits in studying the ways smaller townships and rural areas in Malaysia revitalise and strengthen communities that may be struggling with economic or social challenges due to rapid changes occurring globally.

Several theories discuss the significance of placemaking from different stakeholders' perspectives (as shown in Figure 1). These theories overlap with a query to explore the other ways architecture, through creating spaces and place-making, builds social connections and celebrations of local culture and even fosters a sense of ownership and attachment to the place. What is worth noting is how the emphasis on bringing communities and finding ways to enforce personal or placement attachment are the core characteristics of the success of meaningful places. By taking a more detailed interest in this topic of meaning, this project builds on exploring the Malaysian version of "The Practice of Everyday Life" by Michel De Certeau and the works of Ray Oldernberg on that "third space" between home (first) and work (second space) in its reflection of the timeless ways a social space can be in fostering communities (Oldernberg, 1999).

As De Certeau defined the concept of "cultural practice" as a "...coherent assemblage of elements that are concrete and every day...once coming from a tradition (that of a family or social group) and re-actualised from day to day across behaviours", this study attempts to translate the fragments of this

Figure 1. Different theories pertaining to third places and place-making
(Source: Author Compilation)

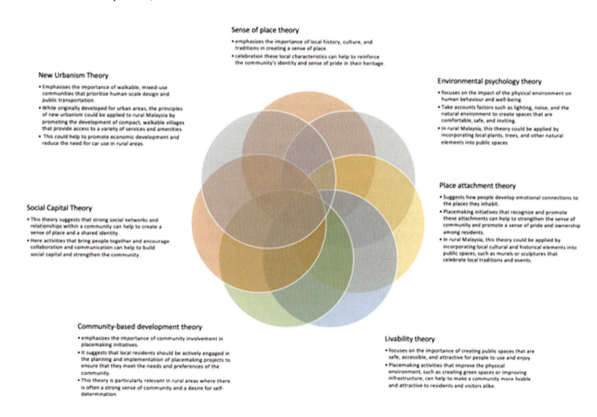

cultural device into social visibility for spatial use and architecture design. A "practice" of "everyday-ness" such as coffee drinking can be what is decisive for the identity of a dweller or a group in so far as this identity allows him or her to take up a position in the network of social relations inscribed in the environment." (De Certeau, 1998. pg.9). Furthermore, investigating the architecture of social spaces in the more rural patriarchal societies, particularly in the East Coast region, allows for a closer examination of gendered spatial practices and how they shape social interactions for the people. It opens avenues for discussions on issues of privacy, visibility, and the negotiation of power within these spaces.

At the level of communal "third" spaces, such as local cafes and eateries, food and beverage can serve as identity markers and act as unifying or divisive agents. They can define community identity based on shared interests, ethnicity, religion, locality, and nationality. In the context of everyday life, food and beverage have a range of roles and functions, depending on the specific situation and context in which they are consumed. The love for a particular cuisine or beverage can foster social cohesion, creating bonds and lifelong friendships. Conversely, dietary preferences, gender roles and religious restrictions can lead to divisions within communities.

By studying the design and construction of coffee shops in Malaysia, researchers can gain valuable insights into how these spaces contribute to Malaysian communities' cultural and urban fabric. Moreover, investigating coffee-drinking culture and the role of coffee shops as third spaces can help researchers better understand how these spaces shape and influence social interactions, community identity, and urban development. In highlighting the importance of spaces dedicated to small mundane day-to-day activities, such as talking or sitting while enjoying a beverage or a meal, this study intends to contribute towards place-making a socially resilient future for the multicultural, multi-ethnic and gender-equal Malaysia.

DESCRIPTION OF THE RESEARCH

This project explores the link between cultural resources in architecture and the spatial use of space and place. The selected focus of interest is within the Malaysian social context and design of spaces that respond to the overall local café culture of the people. The study seeks what can be revealed in the spatial patterns of the local coffee premises through different narratives of local use and how it can share a representation of everydayness. For example, a coffee shop that is designed with comfortable seating, welcoming decor, and a layout that encourages conversation and interaction can serve as a third place where people from the community can gather, socialise, and form connections. Here, the case study method of collecting data and studying the spaces presents a valuable tool to reveal the non-conceptual yet meaningful embedded aspects of human culture in Malaysia. It is worth noting that placemaking and the concept of the "third" place focus on creating and improving public spaces that foster social interaction, community engagement, and a sense of belonging. By understanding how these two contribute to one another, recreating similar approaches can help create vibrant and resilient communities that can better address social and economic challenges.

COFFEE PLACES AS THIRD SPACES

This section elaborates on the different styles of coffee-drinking spaces used as third spaces in Malaysia and the development of the urban culture. In many Asian cities, drinking coffee outside of the home or in a café as part of the social experience only became more of a lifestyle trend for the generation of diaspora Malaysians starting in the 1990s when they returned after studying or working overseas. It was mostly assumed that only those who had had the privilege to have been exposed to a more developed "Westernised" consumption culture would continue this social trend. What is observed by studies, however, is that the link between coffee consumption and daily social activity continues to rise with the increasing affluence of social media and the internet in the early millennial. However, what is even lesser known is that research in the fields of history and sociology (Aljunied (2014), Akbar, P., & Edelenbos, J. (2020) & Beh, M.T. (2022) have long suggested the development of cafes or coffee shops in Southeast Asia is also rooted around its social and ethnic daily practices during the transition of colonial to independent stages of the country.

The consumption of coffee and its association with social "third" space further expanded among adolescents and the generation of millennials as they spend more time commuting between home and work in their daily life. The Malaysian coffee culture also has flourished in line with the needs and demands of consumers, causing the mushrooming of coffee outlets in Malaysian cities and towns in recent years (Lee, 2014a, 2014b). There have been suggestions that speciality outlets that attract younger consumers provide different spatial configurations from the conventional coffee shops or Kopitiams that serve unbranded, strong bitter and black coffee frequented by the older generations (Ravagan, n.d.). However, there are limited studies focusing on the architectural perspective of these establishments. The following section provides some local typologies of Malaysian local coffee shops in the study and why it was chosen to be included in this project.

The Kopitiam

The Kopitiam is an excellent example of a generational "third space" for coffee nationwide in Malaysia. Kopitiam is traditionally known as the popular Chinese-owned coffee shop with a culinary ethnic heritage (Jess, 2013) cited in Duruz, J.J., & Khoo, G.C. (2014). The word itself is derived from the Chinese dialect, Hokkien, whereby Kopi means "coffee" and Tiam means "shop" (Zwain, A., Bahauddin, A.,2021). The restaurant concept serves not only Chinese cuisine but also Malay and Indian cuisines, representing the multiracial groups of Malaysian society (Eng., 2010). Lim (2013) added other popular Malaysian dishes, including Curry Laksa, Char Kuey Teow and Nasi Lemak. Currently, Kopitiam is still frequented not only due to the arrays of dishes offered under one roof but also to indulge in the combined history and eating culture that comes with it (T). Yazam and Hamid (2011) state that Kopitiam offers more than just coffee but also is a place to socialise, organise business meetings, and indulge in other activities. New customers of Kopitiam are usually introduced by Kopitiam's regular customers (Foo et al., 2013). These studies have repeatedly demonstrated the different ways social standards operate and how the establishment earns the trust of the locals.

The Kopitiam has been debated by different scholars from multi-disciplinary perspectives (Beh, M.T. (2022), Khoo, G. C. (2009), Aljunied, K. (2014) & Perry, M.S (2017)) as a place of a social centre where families would indulge in eating, meeting, and conversations on anything that comes to mind, light or serious. From an architectural point of view, studying a sociological perspective helps understand the implication of space use and how it engages the social interaction which happens in the space. While it can be common for regulars of Kopitiam to refer to the source of information as "coffee shop talk", the context of these conversations also shows the kind of social dynamics in the spaces they take place in. In Malaysia, it is the Malaysian Hainanese, Hokkien-speaking descendants that predominantly own the establishment of Kopitiam. Studies have shown that Kopitiam's strategic site location is also usually on the main street of the township they are located in. The main mealtimes for the Kopitiam are predominantly at breakfast due to the historical past of the previously employed Colonial Chinese working early in the town centres. This favourite timeline of traffic continues to this day, albeit even earlier and for longer hours where the weekend brunch takes place. The Hainanese skill in the food-making and beverage industry ties also close to their regional identity as the skills are passed from generation to generation through early experiences of working in a European household and progressing towards opening the Kopitiams, as a bakery, and of course for coffee processing.

Many studies have shown that availability of placemaking activities, such as adding outdoor seating or hosting community events, helps to enhance further the coffee shop's role as a third place and strengthen the sense of community in the area. In their works, Aljunied (2014) and Duruz, J.J., & Khoo, G.C. (2014) claim that coffee drinking culture is just as much of a colonial inheritance as tea drinking. Despite many studies on the specifics of Singaporean colonial roots, the association with coffee also links with the use of public spheres when the nation's identity was taking shape during independence with old Malaya. There was substantial evidence to show why eateries and beverage shops also link to political studies due to their potential link to creating familiar and local spaces. A study by Waxman later (2006) explored coffee shops' physical and social characteristics in the U.S., showing evidence that third spaces can encourage people to gather and become emotionally attached to their frequented places. His study also revealed that coffeehouses mainly serve as a "third place" to interact with other community members regularly.

Warung and Kedai Kopi Kampung

Community trust is still vital to security and unity for many rural areas, or "kampung" of Malaysia. There has been observation in rural areas where the entity of local coffee shops becomes a means of surveillance. This was especially essential for the community of men in the rural areas of Malaysia, as patriarchal society remains the way of life in many parts of rural Asia, as reported in the thesis by Akbar, P., & Edelenbos, J. (2020). These locally owned coffee shops act as gathering spaces and are informally used as a space for reconnaissance and social announcement of news for residents and the villages surrounding the context. The convenience and practicality of this depended on the location of the coffee shops or warungs, which are commonly placed along the streets, and at corners (Figure 2). This informal system of surveillance and news dissemination is particularly vital in patriarchal societies, where social structures rely on communal monitoring.

The following section describes the places chosen for this study and the limitation of scope conducted for this expedition. While these locations provide valuable insights into the informal surveillance system and community dynamics within patriarchal societies, they do not represent the full spectrum of social spaces or architectural variations within Malaysia or other regions. The findings and conclusions drawn from this study should be interpreted within the context of the specific places and communities under investigation.

METHODS

A combination of qualitative methods, as suggested by Creswell (2013), offers an effective way of studying each community's specific needs and characteristics in this study. The case study approach,

Figure 2. A sketch of security use of coffee spaces in rural Kampungs
(Source: Author Observation in Kota Bharu, 2019)

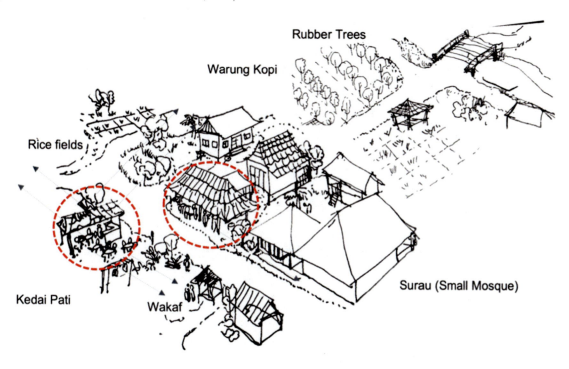

together with a period of ethnographic data collection (semi-structured interviews, sketches, and photographic observation), was conducted between January to August 2019 and again between March to September 2022. To be able to analyse the spatial use of each case study, notes and observations are noted on the layout of floor plans, elevations, and selected sections, which illustrate the everyday use and spatial importance.

The selection of case study sites was important to showcase the geographic diversity of Malaysia and compare the urban-rural continuum each place offers (See Figure 3). Klang is in the central part of Peninsular Malaysia, Kota Bharu is in the northeastern part, and Penang is located on the northwest coast. All three cities chosen for this study have a long history of the "Peranakan" Chinese-Malay population that is unique to the state and provided samples for everyday "multiculturalism" in the Malaysian context, as explained by Khoo, G. C. (2009). The focus of the study from the multitude of perspectives of sociology, culture and architecture influences the design of local eateries and the spaces that social interactions occupy. The terminology "Peranakan" specifically refers to the descendants of Chinese traders that had settled in Malaysia during the colonial era. In all chosen case studies in the township of Klang, Kota Bharu, and Penang, each implemented various placemaking initiatives in recent years before the start of the Covid-19 pandemic in 2020.

The aim for each of the case studies selected was to shed light on the rich historical and cultural significance of the place, which displays different types of social connections unique to the everyday life of the community there. All sites also represent different economic contexts, with Klang being a predominantly industrialised region, Kota Bharu being a predominantly agricultural region, and Penang being a more urbanised and industrialised region. Unknowingly, this project has allowed for the

Figure 3. Map of case study locations of two Kopitiam in Klang (South), two Kedai Pati Kota Bharu (East Coast) and one Kopitiam in Penang (West Coast) of Peninsula Malaysia

opportunity to analyse the updated place-making initiatives led by the owners of the coffee places by recording, observing, and making comparative notes with the use of third spaces function in different community settings.

While efforts have been made by authors to ensure the accuracy and reliability of the information collected through ethnographic data collection methods, there may be limitations and biases inherent in the research process for this type of study. The data collected through semi-structured interviews, sketches, and photographic observation may be subjective and influenced by the perspectives and experiences of the participants and researchers involved. These limitations should be taken into consideration when interpreting the findings and drawing strong conclusions.

FINDINGS AND DISCUSSION OF THE RESEARCH

To fully appreciate the unique attributes of the timeless "third places" in Malaysia, there is a need to comprehend the dynamic narratives of the local demographics in Malaysia and the history behind the architectural approach adopted for this region. The selected cities of Kuala Lumpur, Penang and Kota Bharu are all three different sites, each representing specific strength and criteria which provides further discourse in seeking an understanding of meaningful place-making approaches for urban and rural areas of the Peninsula Malaysia. This section discusses the observed emerging social patterns recorded and observed in the case study spaces in the order of coffee shop type and site.

Data from observation and interviews were analysed thematically according to groups of people that came at different times, their self-identified social groups, gender, community, and the types of activities engaged in the spaces. Detailed preferences of each group using different spaces, such as indoor or outdoor seating, were also noted and studied.

Case Study in Klang, Selangor: Chong Kok Kopitiam

Chong Kok Kopitiam has a long history that dates well into the early 1940s. It is part of a three-storey building consisting of a hotel, restaurant and Kopitiam. The family decided to cease the other operations in the 1970s and focus only on the Kopitiam. Until today Chong Kok has remained a family business. Chong Kok Kopitiam's physical characteristics maintain what is shown here (Figure 4), but it has gradually been renovated and adapted to suit its primary function as a coffee place throughout the different generations of family owners.

The first physical characteristic one might notice how narrow the façade is and how it is elongated towards the back. It might appear narrow from the front facade, but the planning of spaces is elongated towards the back. The planning is divided into a few spaces: a five-foot walkway, main dining area, secondary dining area, preparation space and the toilet, which is placed at the rear of the building (Figure 4). All living spaces are on the 2nd and 3rd floor, clearly separating the public and private zoning vertically.

In addition to the main dining area, Chong Kok Kopitiam also features a secondary dining area. This additional space provides flexibility in seating arrangements and can be used to accommodate overflow during peak hours or for hosting private gatherings. The separation of the dining areas allows for different types of customers and social groups to find suitable seating options based on their preferences.

There is a designated preparation space located in the dining areas, where the skilled staff of Chong Kok Kopitiam diligently brew and prepares the coffee and other beverages. It can be assumed that this space division is crucial to the functioning of Kopitiam, as it ensures that the beverages are made with precision and expertise, maintaining the quality that Chong Kok Kopitiam is known for.

Furthermore, the toilet facilities are located at the rear of the building, ensuring that they are easily accessible to customers without intruding upon the main dining areas. This thoughtful placement enhances the overall comfort and convenience of visitors.

The five-foot walkway, a prominent feature in traditional shophouses, was initially designed by the British to provide shelter from the tropical heat and downpours (Changsong W. et al.,2021.) However, as shown in Figure 5, the breakfast traffic often spills out of the shop, blurring the inside-outside design boundary and obstructing the five-foot walkway. These images also show the diversity of their customers during peak hours. This was not the same in the past due to limited public knowledge of the distinct food requirement practices for Muslims and Non-Muslims customers. However, Chong Kok Kopitiam has included areas for food stalls managed by Muslims selling the local favourite rice known as Nasi Lemak for extra options, while its Non-Muslim Chinese owner continues to serve usual Kopitiam food such as bread, soft-boiled eggs, and coffee.

Chong Kok Kopitiam has also been observed to implement a more intimate multiracial community with its seating arrangements and ushering for sharing tables which encourage cross-cultural mingling among the customers (Figure 7). Overall, the atmosphere recorded was positive and socially jovial.

A Case Study in Penang: Bee Hwa Kopitiam, Georgetown

The Bee Hwa Kopitiam is located in the town of Georgetown, Penang, within the walls of a UNESCO heritage area and is the only halal-serving option for Kopitiam establishment that the local Malay Muslims could eat in. Unlike Chong Kok Kopitiam in Klang, the food preparation in this establishment is placed in the front section of the Kopitiam, indicating probability to show transparency in food preparation for the Muslim customers. Although when interviewed, the owners were vague to officially confirm this,

Figure 4. Too, K (2020), Axonometric layout of the traditional shophouse, series of drawings of traditional shophouses

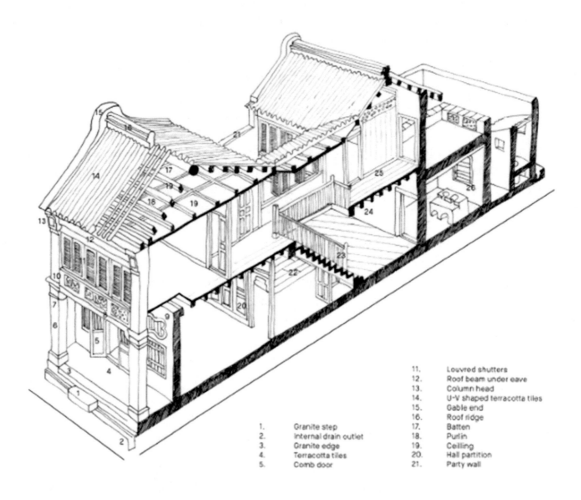

11.	Louvred shutters
12.	Roof beam under eave
13.	Column head
14.	U-V shaped terracotta tiles
15.	Gable end
16.	Roof ridge
1. Granite step	17. Batten
2. Internal drain outlet	18. Purlin
3. Granite edge	19. Ceiling
4. Terracotta tiles	20. Hall partition
5. Comb door	21. Party wall

other Muslim customers spoken to during the observation had suggested how they were at ease when some food-making practices were shown publicly, as Non-Muslim Chinese Malaysians predominantly populate Penang. On the table, the usual condiments presented in the area are chopsticks and ceramic spoons (Figure 8).

Case Study in Kota Bharu, Kelantan: The Kedai Pati

The type of coffee place in Kelantan is of the lesser-known coffee spaces in Malaysia as these social spaces are more rooted in the locals of the region of East Coast Malaysia. Two different premises of this style were visited and studied, one at Jalan Pos Ofis Lama and another at Jalan Bayam, both in the centre of Kota Bharu township. Research by Anuar et al. (2022) described this social eatery as another food place that is much a shorter stopping point for breakfast, known as Kedai Pati.

Kedai Pati is an urban phenomenon unique to the town of Kota Bharu, the capital of Kelantan, Malaysia and has taken root from Indian migrant communities that still reside in these parts of the country.

Figure 5. A sketch of the layout plan of Chong Kok Kopitiam
(Source: Author, observed and recorded in August 2019)

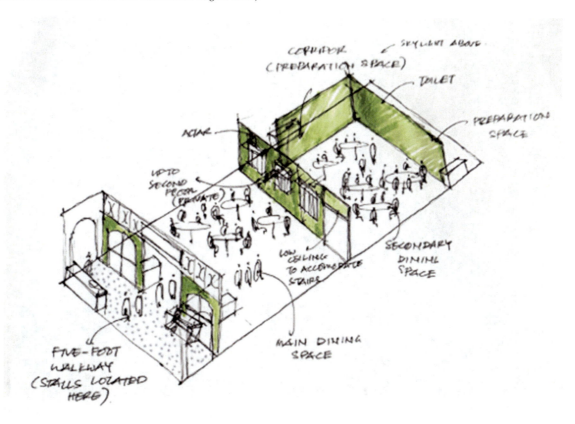

They are inexpensive and usually open only during the early hours of the day, very similar to Kopitiams in catering to the breakfast and starting hours of the day. Anuar et al. (2022) suggested that the local name came about in two ways: first, the habit of customers stopping by for a snack before "flying" elsewhere, and second, the physical resemblance of the stall's aesthetics to the structure of pigeon coops. This distinctive physical characteristic and name set Kedai Pati apart within the local culinary landscape of East Coast Malaysia.

The spatial layout of this coffee shop resembles a box that is pierced so that the tops of the walls can be opened. Much of this flexibility is to allow for the shop owner to interact with customers and still have some structural separation (and much-needed privacy to perform daily prayers, for the Muslim owners particularly) when he pulls back the flap for any temporary break or closure. The shop itself is a simple structure but one that serves the needs of the end user very well. In this study, many of the locals interviewed agreed that the owners of the shop are part of the appeal of this location; they have a good relationship with their regular customers and are reliable sources for local conversation. The venues also bear some resemblance to social clubs in that the seating arrangements allow strangers to become friends through the lively exchange of news and stories, sitting next to or across from one another.

While Kedai Pati specifically caters to individuals on the move and is typically open during the early hours of the day, Warung and Kedai Kopi, on the other hand, is a broader term that encompasses various types of local shops or stalls. Both Warung and Kedai Pati share similar functions as social gathering

Figure 6. Business spills over to the five-foot walkway
(Source: Author, observed and recorded in August 2019)

Figure 7. Multiracial table sharing
(Source: Author, observed recorded August 2019)

Figure 8. Condiments display (left), open kitchen area (middle), eating/social space (right)
Source: Author (2019)

Figure 9. A sectional sketch by the author during data collection (left), A picture of a hectic morning in Jalan Pos Ofis Lama, Kota Bharu (right)
Source: Author (2019)

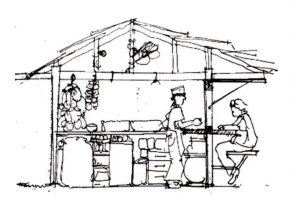

places, and o,f they offer a space for residents and villagers to connect, exchange news, and maintain a sense of community, the "third" space between home and work. The strategic placement of these establishments, often along streets and at corners, enhances their accessibility and visibility within the local context, making them convenient hubs for social interaction and surveillance.

Recognising the rising numbers of air-conditioned and modern cafes in the urban areas of Kota Bharu in recent years, pre-global pandemic, the appeal of Kedai Pati has not waned for many reasons. They are accessible, cheap, and casual and serve simple flavours, often promoting loyalty from the lar customers. While the interviews with the owners revealed how Kedai Pati traditionally and originally only catered for working men in between their daily city routines (a symbol of patriarchy society in Asia), the evolving changes to Kota Bharu in recent years have also welcomed women, children, and much younger crowds as part of the ongoing local community. This shift highlights the evolving nature of these establishments and their ability to adjust to changing societal dynamics while still retaining their core appeal.

CONCLUSION

Findings from all case studies conclusively demonstrate the different roles that coffee shops have as "third" places that foster social interaction and community engagement. Each township, local ethnic, and diverse community groups of different demographics have been shown to have established strong spatial dominance for specific food-preparation areas and beverages in the places observed. The overarching similarities of conviviality show how these places are both physical and social infrastructures that strengthen their role as community hubs and promote social and economic resilience. It is sufficient to say how much happiness and joy these "third" spaces bring to the community they serve.

This research contributes to a step towards further understanding the significance of traditional coffee places and eateries as communal spaces that bring together individuals from different walks of life, fostering social interactions and reflecting the country's diverse cultural heritage and evolving social dynamics. The research findings continuously highlight the intriguing nature of locally selected coffee places as social hubs that bring together individuals from different walks of life. Exploring norms and values in the artefacts of different cultural practices in local-owned Malaysian coffee places such as Kedai Pati and Kopitiam is intriguing and is a worthwhile pursuit to study and conserve. They have value as meeting points where people can gather, connect, and engage in meaningful conversations but also have an active role for equality and power in use space. This aspect is particularly important in a country like Malaysia, known for its rich multicultural heritage, as these coffee places serve as spaces where diverse cultural backgrounds converge.

While the style and spatial design will adapt to changing times and locations of the place, it is unlikely that the coffee culture and its root in ethnic and social importance will diminish. However, the research findings also acknowledge how the quality of social space and the "third" space network may also have been affected in the post-pandemic era.

Suggestions towards future work might consider extending the scope of analysis for different types of café styles in Malaysia that have been re-adapted or comparing space between use during and after the Covid-19 pandemic. An in-depth study of spatial use utilising space syntax for a more accurate socio-behavioural pattern study may potentially add more understanding of social space in the context of Malaysia.

ACKNOWLEDGEMENT

A photo essay version of this paper was presented at the *Slices of Everyday Life Conference* at the University of Cambridge, Cambridgeshire, held on 6-7 September 2019, with data collected the same year. New data were collected during the pandemic period of 2020-2022, and this project was continued. The research and presentation of this research were supported and funded externally by the authors: the School of Architecture and Built Environment, UCSI University and the Faculty of Architecture & Ekistics of the University Malaysia Kelantan. The authors are grateful to the participants at the conference for their helpful comments and suggestions in improving this paper.

REFERENCES

Akbar, P., & Edelenbos, J. (2020). Social Impacts of Place-Making in Urban Informal Settlements: A Case Study of Indonesian Kampungs. *Social Sciences (Basel, Switzerland)*, *9*(6), 104. doi:10.3390ocsci9060104

Aljunied, K. (2014). Coffee-shops in Colonial Singapore: Domains of Contentious Publics. *History Workshop Journal*, *77*(1), 65–85. doi:10.1093/hwj/dbt011

Anuar, N., Alwi, N., Hanafi, N., Mohamad, J., & Faudzi, Y. (2022). *Revitalisation Of Kedai Pati: An Exercise in Architectural Heritage Studies*. Faculty Of Creative Technology and Heritage, Universiti Malaysia Kelantan.

Beh, M. T. (2022). The Urban Middle-Class Consumer Identity in Malaysia's Socio-political Coffee House Culture. *Anthropological Forum*, *32*(2), 109–124. doi:10.1080/00664677.2022.2042189

Changsong, W., Rahman, T., Sadat, A. A., Amalia, A., & Sudiwijajaya, E. (2021). *Digital Representation of the Coffee Culture and Cultural Heritage by Chinese Indonesian and Malaysian Coffee Brands*. GATR Journal of Management and Marketing Review. http://gatrenterprise.com/GATRJournals/JMMR/vol6_2021_issue2.html

Creswell, J. W. (2013). *Research Design: Qualitative, Quantitative, and Mixed Methods Approaches* (4th ed.). SAGE Publications, Inc.

De Certeau, M. (1998). *Living and Cooking* (Vol. 2). University of Minnesota Press.

Duruz, J. J., & Khoo, G. C. (2014). *Eating Together: Food*. Space, and Identity in Malaysia and Singapore.

Khoo, G. C. (2009). Kopitiam: Discursive cosmopolitan spaces and national identity in Malaysian culture and media. In Everyday Multiculturalism. doi:10.1057/9780230244474

Klemmer, R. S., Thomsen, M., Phelps-Goodman, E., Lee, R., & Landay, J. A. (2002). Where do websites come from? Capturing and interacting with design history. In *Proc. CHI 2002* (pp. 1-8). ACM Press.

Langgat, J., Pawan, M. T., Fabeil, N. F., & Pazim K. H. (2020). Green Kopitiam and Local Intentions to Visit. *Asian Journal of Entrepreneurship*, 72-82.

Oldenburg, R. (1999). *The Great Good Place* (3rd ed.). Marlowe & Company.

Omar, S. R., & Omar, S. N. (2018). Malaysian Heritage Food (MHF): A Review on Its Unique Food Culture, Tradition and Present Lifestyle. *International Journal of Heritage, Art and Multimedia, 1*(3), 01-15.

Waxman, L. (2006). The Coffee Shop: Social and Physical Factors Influencing Place Attachment. *Journal of Interior Design*, *31*(3), 35–53. doi:10.1111/j.1939-1668.2006.tb00530.x

Zwain, A., & Bahauddin, A. (2021). *Malacca's "Straits Chinese traditional courtyard eclectic style shophouses"*:

Chapter 19
Re-Imagining Kedai Pati:
Local Third Places, Kota Bharu, Kelantan

Nor Hafizah Anuar
Universiti Malaysia Kelantan, Malaysia

Najah Md. Alwi
Universiti Malaysia Kelantan, Malaysia

Nik Nurul Hana Hanafi
Universiti Malaysia Kelantan, Malaysia

Juliza Mohamad
Universiti Malaysia Kelantan, Malaysia

Siti Nuratirah Che Mohd Nasir
Universiti Malaysia Kelantan, Malaysia

ABSTRACT

This chapter attempts to rediscover and envision the revitalization idea of Kedai Pati, a gastronomic urban node in Kota Bharu, Kelantan. More than 50 years ago, Kedai Pati likely existed and acted as a local third place, whereby people tend to drop in for a quick snack before going to work or elsewhere. Kedai Pati is perceived as a valuable space for the local working men to informally attend on the regular or irregularly. At the present day, Kedai Pati still survives with its signature theatrical-service pantry operation, and seller-buyer social setting, which is part of a unique ambiance considered Kelantan's cultural heritage. These nodal gastronomic places around Kota Bharu town have been mapped to indicate their current location and studies on reimagining and rebranding the Kedai Pati itself have been made to promote and reintroduce its existence. Varieties of design proposals have then been put forward as it may indicate a new pop-up cart style for Kedai Pati.

INTRODUCTION

Kelantan is a state strategically located in an eastern coastal state of the peninsula of Malaysia. It is known for its unique way of life and nationwide fame, where its traditional heritage is expressed through

DOI: 10.4018/978-1-6684-8253-7.ch019

its local dishes. The blending of Malay, Thailand, or Chinese influences gave exquisite exclusivity to their unique combinations of its ingredients due to their geographical location. Food is often used to increase the authenticity of a visit by bringing tourists closer to the locals. The richness of its heritage, which includes numerous culinary spots, has potentially contributed to the income and development of the local creative economy. According to Marzuki et al. (2011) and Aziz et al. (2012), despite its remote location from Peninsular Malaysia's main attractions, Kelantan is well known for its natural environments and distinct cultural heritage, which have influenced the development of the tourism industry in terms of generating local revenue.

The culinary experience is distinguished not only by its culinary variety but also through its local setting and hospitality service. As the expression 'eating out' or 'dining out' has become a part of the local customs in Kelantan as the increasing number of places scattered in the city centres and much of its smaller towns reflects much of this phenomenon. This situation is largely attributable to the local population's preference for eating outside at food stalls as well as the efforts of food industry entrepreneurs to boost their revenue. In the pricing category, the adjectives 'affordable', 'inexpensive', and 'reasonable' create a favourable impression of Malaysian cuisine as one that delivers excellent value for money (Kamarulbaid & Mustapha, 2021). Kedai Pati offers a wide range of culinary varieties from the local food palette; the culinary experience and modest design are significant attractions that might facilitate and encourage today's local entrepreneurship culture as well as the creative industry of 'Culinary Tourism'.

According to urban sociologist Ray Oldenburg, a 'third place' is any location other than a person's home or place of employment where they frequently congregate and interact with people they do not know very well. A third place is defined as a friendly and comfortable place frequented by regulars and ideal for reconnecting with old acquaintances, where making new ones is the primary theme of Oldenburg's treatise on the topic. Third places are also often related to small businesses, cafes, coffee shops, bars, pubs, restaurants, community centres, general stores, and so on. Even though such destinations are called third places, Oldenburg discusses only a few physical aspects of third places, such as their proximity and easy access from home or work, and highlights that these places are likely to offer food and drinks (Oldenburg, 1991). It can be concluded that a "Third Place" is a public place where people gather on their own, informally, and often that is not their home or place of work. One of the things that makes a "Third Place" is that it feels like home and is a place where people can relax, recharge, feel at ease, and meet new people. They are neutral places that are easy to get to and usually in buildings that don't stand out in the community. They are democratic and social, with a place to sit and a focus on talking. The mood is playful, and everyone is treated the same.

In the case of Kedai Pati, which is normally located in the suburbs of a town, it has become a place for workers to hang out between their homes and their offices. The long-seating benches and the bar-like designed setting of the kedai pati create a friendly atmosphere between the customer-owner as well as the customer-customer, to just mingle and talk freely with one another (see Figure 3). Ultimately, whether "kedai pati" can be considered a local third place depends on various factors, including its significance within the community and the extent to which it facilitates social interactions and community building. The concept of the local third place emphasizes the importance of public spaces in fostering social interactions, community engagement, and a sense of belonging. Public spaces are shared areas accessible to all members of the community, where people can gather, interact, and develop relationships beyond their private homes and workplaces. These public spaces can take various forms, such as parks, community centres, libraries, cafes, and local shops like "kedai pat'. The key aspect is that they provide a welcoming environment that encourages socializing, conversation, and the formation of social bonds among community members. In the context of "kedai pati" if it serves as a gathering place for workers and locals, it can be seen as fulfilling the role of a local third place. It offers a public space where individuals can meet, engage in conversations, share experiences, and establish connections with others from the community. These public spaces play a vital role in community development, promoting social cohesion and enhancing overall well-being. They contribute to the sense of place, identity, and pride within a local community, fostering a sense of belonging and collective ownership. In short, the concept of the local third place emphasizes the significance of public spaces as communal hubs that facilitate social interactions and community building. "Kedai pati" can be seen as an example of a local third place if it provides an environment that promotes social connections, engagement, and a sense of community among its visitors.

Urban heritage revitalization can be viewed as a new awareness in Malaysia. It includes multidisciplinary parties such as the authorities, private sectors, and members of the public or communities in the designated area. Strategies to ensure the continuity of this local cultural heritage are required so that future generations can enjoy the ambience of a culinary experience or perhaps just the atmosphere of bartending that Kedai Pati provides. Knowledge transmission from educational and training programs is critical for future generations to take or propose specific safeguarding measures (Karakul, 2015). Kedai pati for urban revitalization by incorporating other local cultural elements can offer exciting and new life to these spaces, which will contribute to the urban development and communities. It is important to focus on preserving the original kedai pati which is also associated with cultural heritage. The idea of incorporating cultural heritage that showcases local arts, crafts, music, and traditions might infuse the rebranding of kedai pati with fresh and appealing identities. It is important to have a long-term plan for the economic sustainability of its local communities in the revitalization efforts, including ongoing maintenance, monitoring of community needs, and adaptation to changing cultural dynamics. Kedai pati can be revitalized into thriving cultural hubs that attract tourists, instil a sense of community pride, and add to the area's overall cultural and economic vitality.Top of Form

Kedai 'Burung Merpati'

Kedai Pati, an abbreviation of 'Kedai Burung Merpati', is said to have gotten its name from its resemblance to a typical pigeon coop, which can be found in Malaysia's rural and small towns in the state of Kelantan. The appeal of a 'modest' food stall for the working-class men in the town centre is a concept similar to that of a pigeon coop as a place "to drop in for a snack before 'flying' off elsewhere". This is a welcoming and significant characteristic model for a 'third' place—a place to go between work and home. Kedai Pati can be said to be like a social club by providing its bartender with coffee and tea servings and a pleasant, informal setting to sample the local dishes. The theatrical-like service pantry places the strangers at ease, and strangers can be friends with each other and have a lively conversation by exchanging news, stories, and nostalgia. As Raji M. has mentioned, much of the food culture of the past is still present in the current operations (Raji, Ab Karim, Ishak & Arshad, 2017). Therefore, there is a lot of information about the small number of Kedai Pati's that are still around today, running their modest, theatrical-service pantry business, which is part of Kelantan's cultural heritage.

In the case of Kedai Pati, interviews had shown that these stalls had been around for more than fifty years and that most of the original owners came from a village in North India and moved to Malaya during the time when the British ruled the area. They have now gained resident status (Figure 1). Some of the present owners are now the third and fourth generations who have inherited the kedai pati from their ancestors. Even though they have permanent residency in Malaysia, they still return to their home country to see their families, as most of them live alone in Malaysia. During their absence, the kedai pati will be managed by their subordinates amongst the kedai patis' sellers in Kelantan. During the interview sessions with some of the owners, they claim that the concept of kedai pati in Kelantan is very akin to the concept he kedai pati in their home country. They also claimed that they brought a similar building design concept of kedai pati to Kelantan. They are normal served common breakfast such as *roti canai*, half boiled egg and drink (their famous pulled tea or commonly known as *teh tarik* drink) which is prepared by the Kedai Pati seller, together with varieties of local food that are nicely put and placed in a small basket send by the locals to be sold at the premises. The packed food is normally sent by the local community especially the housewives, who are helping the economic growth of their families. There are opportunities for this study to contribute to addressing poverty issues in Kelantan, as Rosenbaum's research (2006) has shown that many third places can help with the quality of life and support the local community.

Figure 2 exhibits an example showing the two side elevations, its facade, and an overview of a typical Kedai Pati that is modelled 3-dimensionally. When observed closely, the model reveals the interactive social focus in the design decision of having three-sided openings surrounding three-quarters of the small stall. It must be noted that the location is orientated towards the street and is also a form of representation of a time in the urban space of Kota Bharu's old city, where the relationship between private and public spaces is represented and is openly expressive in the embrace of the working men.

Figure 3 depicts the basic layout plan for Kedai, Pati which consists of four distinct areas: a preparation area where trading and food ordering take place- this space is usually attached to a secondary smaller storage or kitchenette, which also serves as a rest area for the attending trader because it is more private.

Figure 1. Owners of the third or fourth generations

Figure 2. Kedai Pati on 3D model showing the different angles of the stall and a photograph of the daily routine
(Source: Junaidi, 2016)

Figure 3. Plan layout
(Source: Junaidi, 2016)

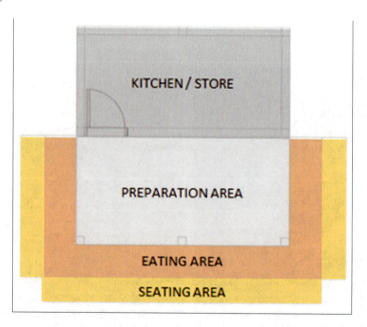

The third component is a tabletop counter for placing food and beverages, and the final component is the seating area, which is typically equipped with a type of long bench for seating.

Mentioned on Kedai Pati

There has been a very limited source or mention that has been found on Kedai Pati in Kelantan. The latest mentioned by Anuar identified some of the locations of surviving kedai pati in the suburbs of Kota Bharu town (Anuar et. al, 2021). This research investigates into the physical presence and distribution of Kedai Pati, providing insights into their spatial aspects and shedding light on their historical and cultural context. Meanwhile, Zaidi focused on the past and current situations of social interactions place - kedai pati for communities (Zaidi, 2018). This study discovers the social dynamics and significance of Kedai Pati as a gathering space. It may delve into their role in fostering community interactions, social connections, and cultural practices. This research could provide valuable insights into the social fabric of Kelantan and the role of Kedai Pati in community building. Later, Ismail interviewed one of the Kedai Pati owners and recorded Kedai Pati as a Malaysian street food documentary (Ismail, 2016). A nature-based tourism corridor, the kedai pati as an authentic local service has been identified by Hamzah and Ismail as a pilot project at Kelantan Darul Naim (Hamzah & Ismail, 2008). This research explores the potential of Kedai Pati as an attraction within a tourism context. It may delve into how these establishments contribute to the local culture and enhance tourism experiences in Kelantan. The study also may offer insights into the ways Kedai Pati serves as a unique and authentic element of the local tourism industry. Winzeler made the mention in a small chapter of a book titled, Ethnic Differences and Economic Change in a Local Malaysian Setting. Lastly, while discussing the economic growth of Malaysia's ethnic races, Winzeler made a few remarks about Kedai Pati in Kelantan and how it influenced the local economic situation in 1950 (Winzeler, 1976). Winzeler's articles basically touch on Kedai Pati in Kelantan while discussing ethnic differences, economic change, and local economic situations. These works likely provide historical and sociological insights into Kedai Pati's role in the local economy, its influence on the social fabric of Kelantan, and the relationship between ethnic communities and economic development. By examining Kedai Pati's impact on the local economic situation, these publications contribute to a broader understanding of its socio-economic significance. Together, these mentioned sources provide a multifaceted understanding of Kedai Pati in Kelantan. They offer insights into its physical presence, spatial distribution, social dynamics, cultural significance, economic role as a local hanging out place for interactions in communities, and potential as a tourism attraction. By exploring Kedai Pati from different angles, these sources contribute to preserving and re-imagining Kedai Pati's cultural heritage.

Methodology

This study implemented a historical research method by collecting data through the literature review, field studies which include interviews with Kedai Pati owners, and building surveying and mapping. This research was conducted in the vicinity of the Kota Bharu historic area. Cultural mapping is a research method that involves mapping various cultural assets and locations within a specific area or community. In the case of locating "kedai pati" in a town, cultural mapping can be used to identify and map the physical locations of these establishments. Mapping will involve identifying the location of Kedai Pati which is in the vicinity of the historic area of old Kota Bharu. Locations of "kedai pati" are pinpointed on the Google map. Once the mapping is complete, the data is analyzed to understand the spatial distribution and arrangement of "kedai pati" within the town. The findings are then presented in a report and visual representation, which shows clear distribution on mapped locations of kedai pati.

Meanwhile, the material of this study also includes design proposals for kedai pati re-imagination as an innovative method of revitalization that has cultural and historical significance. It has been carried out by the students who are taking the Architectural Heritage II subject. The aim of the project is to familiarise the student with methods and practices of conservation. To regenerate and re-imagine a new fresh outlook for a Kedai Pati proposal, students were to work in pairs and given a basic Kedai Pati typology drawing as a starting point. Briefings and information were given on how to regenerate the kedai pati by suggesting to them to include other local heritage arts and culture (food, coffee shop, batik, *keris* and spinning top) wit of bringing to bring back the livelihood of the urban context of the area. The students were encouraged to expand their proposal beyond the norm of traditional kedai pati.

Through their design proposals, the students sought to strike a balance between preserving the traditional charm of Kedai Pati and introducing innovative elements that would appeal to contemporary sensibilities. They considered factors mainly on their façade including signage, interior design, functionality, and integration of local heritage elements to create a cohesive and engaging environment. The aim of the project was not only to provide the students with a hands-on experience in conservation methods but also to encourage them to think creatively and critically about the revitalization of cultural spaces. Overall, this study provided the students with a unique opportunity to re-imagine Kedai Pati as a revitalized space that honours its cultural and historical significance while embracing new elements that can bring it to life in the contemporary urban context. The design proposals developed by the students showcase their creativity, critical thinking, and commitment to preserving and promoting local heritage arts and culture through the regeneration of Kedai Pati.

RESULTS AND DISCUSSION

Mapping Urban Areas

During the data collection process conducted amidst the global pandemic, where the Malaysian Government has implemented the Recovery Movement Control Order (RMCO), a total number of thirteen Kedai Patis have been identified. Despite the limitations and challenges imposed by the pandemic, efforts were made to gather information and identify these significant cultural spaces.

The identification of these thirteen Kedai Patis highlights their resilience and enduring presence within the community. It showcases their ability to withstand challenging circumstances and continue serving as important social hubs. Despite the restrictions and uncertainties brought about by the pan-

Table 1. Several identified Kedai Pati

Street Locations	Number of stalls/shops
Jalan Atas Banggol Jalan Kelochor Jalan Belakang Istana	5 1 1
Jalan Pengkalan Chepa	1
Jalan Pos Ofis Lama	4
TOTAL	13

demic, these Kedai Patis have managed to maintain their operations, albeit with necessary adaptations and precautions in place.

The data collection process itself may have been restricted due to the limitations imposed by the RMCO, which may have affected the ability to access and survey a larger number of Kedai Patis. Nevertheless, the identification of these thirteen establishments is important to acknowledge and provides valuable insights into the continued existence and significance of Kedai Patis within the local community. Understanding their resilience and continued existence can provide valuable insights and inspiration for preserving and promoting the unique characteristics and contributions of Kedai Patis within the local context.

Figure 4 depicts a visual representation of the distribution of Kedai Patis along several streets, which includes Jalan Atas Banggol, Jalan Kelochor, Jalan Belakang Istana, Jalan Pengkalan Chepa, and Jalan Pos Ofis Lama in Kota Bharu town, where the remaining stalls are still open (Listed in Table 1). Many of these stalls continue to serve as breakfast stalls, opening shortly after sunrise, catering to early risers and closing shortly before, if not immediately after, lunch, providing a much-needed start to the day for locals. This aligns with their traditional role as a quick stop for a morning snack or light meal. The mapping of the kedai pati around the urban settings of Kota Bharu town is interesting because it indicates the strategic positioning of nodal gastronomic places. These Kedai Patis serve as crucial stopping points for the public, allowing them to take a break before heading to work or simply for leisure purposes.

Figure 4. Mapping of Kedai Pati
(Source: Anuar et al, 2020)

The preferred construction method for the kedai pati establishment is also what makes it notable for its type. It is a simple post-and-beam approach with an extended roof overhang structure towards the front part of the stall. Timber materials were used for the wall frames, panels, columns, and roof rafters. Looking at the photographs in Figure 5, it seems that the original roof tiles have been placed with a sheet of zinc as a cheaper material cost. Some of these structures were built together with another small part of the area, i.e., mostly at the back, which was used for residences. The three long benches provided for the eating area were normally swamped with working men indicating the proximity between the seller-customer interactions, which expressed the social needs.

Re-Imagine Revitalization Proposals

In the context of an ongoing Architectural Heritage course, a small group of third-year Architecture students from Universiti Malaysia Kelantan were given the task of proposing revitalization ideas for kedai pati in Kelantan. These proposals became a part of the final project in the course as a design practice of safeguarding this intangible culture from an architectural perspective. Students were also asked to re-imagine future entrepreneurial possibilities for the kedai pati in whatever way they think possible, including suggesting different ways for the local cultural heritage to help boost the economies of other similar places that might become the potential third place to drop by in Kelantan.

From this urban revitalization and re-imagination project, the students have been given the freedom to choose the category according to their preferences. The preferences would be divided into two categories: food and local arts and handicrafts. Under the food category, it is encouraged to suggest and select the local culinary traditions, maybe by showcasing traditional Kelantanese dishes can promote local ingredients and preserve Kelantan's food heritage.

Figure 5. Kedai Pati
(Source: Anuar et al, 2020)

Besides the local food, the student is also encouraged to suggest and select local traditional arts and handicrafts as part of the revitalization efforts. They are free to opt for local traditional handicrafts and games such as *gasing* (spinning top), silverware, batik, and *mengkuang* weaving. By showcasing and promoting these local crafts, the revitalized Kedai Pati becomes a platform for preserving and promoting Kelantan's artistic heritage. It creates opportunities for local artisans and craftsmen to showcase their skills and generate income. By allowing students to choose their preferred category for revitalization the course encourages creativity and allows for a diverse range of proposals. This approach ensures that the revitalization of Kedai Pati is not limited to a single perspective but explores multiple dimensions of Kelantan's cultural heritage. The proposed revitalization projects have the potential to transform Kedai Pati into vibrant and dynamic spaces that celebrate the local identity, boost the local economy, and serve as potential "third places" for the community to gather and interact.Top of FormBottom of Form

To realizethe project, the student was given input and a drawing on the typology and plan of kedai pati. This is as a guidance for the students to develop their proposals for the revitalization project. The student proposals were divided into two categories, each with four groups resulting in eight groups of various revitalization projects.

Local Traditional Food

Gastronomy is an enormous intangible culture that defines Malaysia. This heritage and traditional cuisines have been passed down through generations, forming one of the national identities that must be preserved and valued for future generations. Notably, the kedai pati has been one of Kelantan's culinary hotspots since the 1950s, serving local traditional cuisine. In the local food category, four groups chose to focus on showcasing the well-known and popular local cuisine within the community. These proposals aimed to create Kedai Pati spaces that celebrate the rich culinary heritage of Kelantan. The student groups envisioned spaces that would evoke the senses and provide an authentic experience for visitors.

Four revitalization proposal groups have chosen to concentrate on the local food, which is well-known and popular in the community. Two of the proposals show that they are attempting to use vernacular design elements such as gable end (*tebar layar*) and decorative fascia board on their roofs (*papan cantik*) as shown in Figure 6. On the other hand, the other two have simply used metal zinc on their roofs. Figure 7 depicts decorative wall panels being used on the Laksa and the kedai patis.

Local Traditional Art

Tangible cultural heritage includes not only buildings and artefacts, but also the traditional arts and crafts of the local community in that area or location. This includes the traditional arts and crafts that are deeply rooted in the area or location. The students undertaking this task were given the option to explore something beyond local food by focusing on local traditional handicrafts and games, allowing for a more comprehensive representation of the cultural heritage of Kelantan. The students showcase a diverse range of local cultural practices by incorporating traditional handicrafts and games such as *gasing* (spinning top), silverware, batik, and *mengkuang* weaving. Through their proposals, the students aim to preserve and promote these traditional crafts, ensuring they continue to be cherished and passed down to future generations.

Another four groups of revitalization proposals in this scope have focused on local traditional games, arts, and handicrafts because this local heritage is well known in the community. Three of the proposals

Figure 6. Kedai Pati for local dishes; nasi tumpang and roti canai
(Source: Anuar, 2021)

Figure 7. Kedai Pati for local dishes, laksa and local coffee brand, Richiamo
(Source: Anuar, 2021)

demonstrate how they use simple and modest vernacular design; rather than embellishing with other ornamental design elements, they use earthy colours to achieve vernacular looks. In Figure 9, decorative wall panels have also been adopted, where three of the four designs use metal zinc on their roofs. Meanwhile, one of the proposals improves its appearance by employing glass as its roof.

These student revitalization proposals showcase the diverse perspectives and creative approaches taken towards re-imagining how to revitalize kedai pati. By providing alternatives other than their norm, the students were able to explore various aspects of Kelantan's cultural identity. Through their innovative and thoughtful designs, they contribute to the preservation and re-imagining of Kedai Pati as spaces that celebrate local traditions, foster economic growth, and serve as hubs of cultural exchange and community engagement.

Figure 8. Kedai Pati for local arts and handicraft; spinning top and mengkuang
(Source: Anuar, 2021)

Figure 9. Kedai Pati for local silversmith and batik
(Source: Anuar, 2020)

CONCLUSION

This study contributes to a deeper understanding of the elements that lead to this sort of eating establishment's cultural relevance in Kelantanese society. To sum up, the essential role of this simple third location that attracts the Kota Bharu audience is precisely its simplicity in design and structure, its core commercial purpose. This gastronomic cultural heritage that is already a part of Kelantan's urban fabric should be known and addressed properly by the communities where food experience plays a crucial role in tourism. Although the purpose for travelling is not gastronomy related, the local food experience gives a significant effect and memorable experiential value to the tourist. Hence, preserving kedai pati should be taken seriously. The unique characteristics of urban areas are also lost as they adopt global standards. It has always been challenging to revitalize cultural and historical buildings. Likewise, retrofitting public spaces as well as experimenting with innovative architecture and space utilization equally important. By introducing a new approach to revitalization, it is critical for the proposal of a contemporary method of architectural heritage preservation to consider its key principles. As a clear definition of conservation, minimal intervention, and preservation, Kedai Pati's existing ambience and context are important and as such, must be perceived as an endeavor, to be preserved for its authenticity.

In this light, culture can be seen as a strategic asset for tackling urban development challenges and preserving urban cultural identities, with culture-based strategies providing the means towards more sustainable, inclusive, and equitable urban development. Meanwhile, it may not align perfectly with all the characteristics of a traditional "Third Place," such as the feeling of being a neutral and easily accessible space, it does serve as a gathering place for individuals to relax, recharge, and interact with others in a social setting. The fact that the local keep visiting "kedai pati" during their transition between home and work indicates its potential as a space where individuals can unwind, socialize and establish connections with others from the local community. This suggests that it may fulfil the role of a local third place by providing a space for informal, social interactions outside of the structured environments of home and work. Ultimately, the classification of "kedai pati" as a local third place would depend on how it is perceived and utilized the community members who frequent it. If it serves as a meaningful social space for individuals to relax, socialize and build relationships during their daily routines, then it can indeed be considered a local third place in that specific context.

These educational exercises will serve as a catalyst for generating innovative ideas and prove valuable to a diverse range of stakeholders who have a vested interest in the development of such enterprises. The aim is to foster a collaborative approach where the knowledge and insights gained from these exercises can inform future planning and decision-making processes. This collaborative effort has the potential to generate practical and sustainable solutions that align with the needs and aspirations of the local community. The results derived from these exercises can be a valuable resource for all stakeholders. Shop owners can share the idea and inspiration put forth by the students for improving their own kedai pati. Thus, this paper has consequently explored how kedai pati engages the communities with the support of human–place interactions and with the process of fostering the younger generations with one of many ways how conservation can do more towards sustainable communities. With the hope that these educational exercises will aid in the future generation of ideas and be beneficial to a wide range of stakeholders, including local Town planning officials, shop owners, and community members who are interested in this type of company.

REFERENCES

Anuar, N. H., Mohd Faudzi, Y., Md Alwi, N., Mohd Nasir, S. N. A., Mohd Nasir, M. R., & Mhd Zain, M. H. K. (2021). Rediscovering local 'third places' of Kota Bharu, Kelantan Malaysia: The study of Kedai Pati. *AIP Conference Proceedings, 2347*, 020220. doi:10.1063/5.0051986

Aziz, Y., Awang, K., & Zaiton, S., (2012). Challenges Faced by Micro, Small, and Medium Lodgings in Kelantan, Malaysia. *International Journal of Economics and Management 6*(1), 167–190.

Kamarulbaid, A. M., & Mustapha, N. A. (2021). The Role of Food Image in Promoting Domestic Tourism. *International Journal of Academic Research in Business & Social Sciences*, *11*(16). doi:10.6007/IJARBSS/v11-i16/11226

Karakul, Ö. (2015). An Integrated Methodology for the Conservation of Traditional Craftsmanship in Historic Buildings. *International Journal of Intangible Heritage*, *10*, 136–144.

Marzuki, A., Hussin, A. A., Mohamed, B., Othman, A. G., & Mat Som, A. P. (2011). Assessment of Nature-Based Tourism in South Kelantan, Tourismos. *An International Multidisciplinary Journal of Tourism*, *6*(1), 281–295.

Oldenburg, R. (1991). *The great good place*. Paragon House.

Raji, M., Ab Karim, S., Ishak, F., & Arshad, M. (2017). Past and present practices of the Malay food heritage and culture in Malaysia. *Journal Of Ethnic Foods*, *4*(4), 221–231. doi:10.1016/j.jef.2017.11.001

Rosenbaum, M. (2006). Exploring the Social Supportive Role of Third Places in Consumers' Lives. Journal of Service Research -. *Journal of Service Research*, *9*(1), 59–72. doi:10.1177/1094670506289530

Winzeler, R. L., (1976). Ethnic Differences and Economic Change in a Local Malaysian Setting. 東南アジア研究, *14*(3), 309-333.

Zaidi, A. S. (2018). *Kedai Pati Sebagai Wadah Interaksi Sosial Masyarakat Dahulu dan Sekarang: Kajian Kes di Kota Bharu Kelantan*. Universiti Malaysia Kelantan.

Chapter 20
A Phenomenological Study of Learner's Virtual Place Experience

Jing Hao Koh
Taylor's University, Malaysia

Nurul Alia Ahamad
ⓘ https://orcid.org/0000-0002-6714-2455
Taylor's University, Malaysia

ABSTRACT

This study investigates the virtual place experience (VPE) approach, using 360° images in Google Street View (GSV), to help learners attain a sense of place. It examines their experience and attitude in the virtual setting of the place of knowledge inquiry. Interpretive phenomenological analysis (IPA) was adopted to examine learners' cognitive learning of place identity, interpretation of place meanings, and attitudes toward the place. Findings indicate that learners developed their sense of presence in VPE through visual elements reflecting the place identity. Place attribute learning requires additional research to understand place identity. Place meanings in the virtual setting were interpreted through the sense of community and historical evidence. Positive affection towards the place was identified, leading to motivation to visit the real place. The study provides insight into how learners' experience with the virtual place phenomenon may contribute to constructing their sense of place, which shall guide their design cognition in future design exercises.

INTRODUCTION

Place-based learning is a crucial component of architectural education, as it allows learners to understand a place's physical, historical, philosophical, cultural, and social dimensions (Johnson, 2012; Zandvliet, 2014). According to Baker (2014), this type of learning involves establishing a connection between the learner and the place by exploring its unique qualities and expressing personal perceptions and responses.

DOI: 10.4018/978-1-6684-8253-7.ch020

Nikezić and Marković (2015) emphasize the importance of place-based learning in expanding students' spatial-cultural knowledge and promoting environmental literacy and responsibility.

Traditionally, architectural education utilizes site visits and academic trips to facilitate knowledge dissemination. Site visits involve investigating a specific location with a defined problem to provide the basis for problem-solving exercises (Yusoff, Ja'afar, & Mohammad, 2019). During these visits, learners analyse the site's physical attributes (such as the environment and topography) and non-physical attributes (such as demographics, culture, and history), allowing them to relate their understanding to the real world.

However, physical visits to a site may be affected by various factors such as accessibility, safety, mobility, resource limitations, and environmental distractions, according to Fiorillo, Rizzi, & Achille (2021); Langran & DeWitt (2020); and Zhao et al. (2020). Due to the COVID-19 pandemic, these challenges have intensified, prompting researchers to explore alternative approaches like virtual place-based learning, as Squire (2022) and Wallgrün et al. (2022) suggested. Connolly (2020) believes that this alternative method allows educators to create significant lessons by utilizing the local context, history, culture, and environment while adapting to the current educational situation. Koh et al. (2022) argue that during the COVID-19 pandemic, the virtual learning environment has enhanced students' problem-solving, analytical, design-thinking, and communication abilities.

A virtual place is a setting created through a computer-generated environment that represents real places using symbols (Ghani, Rafi, & Woods, 2016). Janz (2018) proposes that a virtual place is convincing enough to make users believe they exist in a computer-generated space, allowing for meaningful interaction. Šašinka et al. (2019) suggest that learning in a virtual place goes beyond the limitations of time and space. It offers an alternative to navigating geospatial learning activities when physical access to a location is difficult (Carbonell-Carrera & Saorín, 2017).

According to this research, "virtual place experience" (VPE) refers to the phenomenological attainment of interacting with a virtually simulated place. VPE is a crucial element of virtual place-based learning, allowing users to "feel" their presence or sense of being in the virtual location. Previous studies have indicated that virtual place-based learning has a positive impact on learners' place cognition, as noted by Christofi et al. (2018), Hillstrom (2019), Fiorillo et al. (2021), Park (2019), Zhao et al. (2020). Therefore, the potential of VPE as an effective learning approach should be recognized and further investigated.

ATTAINMENT OF THE SENSE OF PLACE FROM THE VIRTUAL PLACE EXPERIENCE

The concept of "place" can be interpreted in various ways, including a physical space with a specific location or a person's existence in a spatial setting (Champion, 2019; Krummel, 2018; Seamon, 2000; Tuan, 1975). It may be associated with the emotional aspect of place cognition (Arora & Khazanchi, 2010). "Sense of place" refers to an individual's understanding and interpretation of their experience in a particular place, involving multiple dimensions such as cognitive, affective, and evaluative aspects that are developed through various mechanisms (Ardoin, 2006; Relph, 2007). Arora and Khazanchi (2014) describe "sense of place" as a person's perception of how a place fulfils their functional and socio-emotional needs. It represents a person's attachment, unique human experience, and emotional connection to a particular place, contributing to their self-identity (Ghani et al., 2016, p.1; Tuan, 2001). Existing literature suggests that "sense of place" may be classified into three categories: place identity, place meaning, and place attachment.

Place identity refers to the perception of the significance of a spatial setting, which is determined by the physical environment and the associated values of the human relationship with the place (Chen, Wang & Xu, 2017). It also involves a sense of distinctiveness that helps differentiate one place from another, with significant continuity of self-conceptualisation developed over time. Place identity knowledge may be assessed through the physical fabric of the site, such as building facades and architectural styles, historical events associated with the place, and traditional businesses and trades. History, daily activities, and shared memories also contribute to the cognitive understanding of a place's identity (Morel-EdnieBrown, 2012).

Place meaning involves identifying the experiential, interactive and relational components of a place where one may relate to the place (Sebastien, 2020). It is derived from the living experiences that are connected to the environment and activities of a particular place setting (Relph, 2007, p.18).

Place attachment encompasses the feelings and emotions associated with a place, forming the attitude towards the place (Sebastian, 2020, p.207). It also involves the association of emotional and symbolic meanings to places in developing one's affinity (Alasli, 2019). Personal attachments to a place result from the emotive and symbolic meanings associated with the place.

These sense of place dimensions may serve as measures to understand how one acknowledges consciousness, cognition and affect from experiencing a place. As Arora and Khazanchi (2010) allude, a virtual environment may be seen as a faithful re-creation of the natural environments, and the sense of place dimensions might be observed in a virtual place setting. The premise of this study holds that sense of place attained by learners in virtual settings of place phenomena may be studied from their personal experience.

GOOGLE STREET VIEW (GSV)

In virtual place-based learning, the virtual place representation is a crucial component, and simulated places can be fully immersive using Virtual Reality (VR) systems like the Cave Automatic Virtual Environment (CAVE) or partially immersive or non-immersive experiences through computers and mobile devices with or without a VR headset (Google Earth, n.d.). Google Street View (GSV) is a non-immersive VR platform that captures virtual content as images in multiple directions, which are then developed into 360° images called treks. These images are commonly used in GSV to provide a human viewing experience in a virtual environment, allowing users to rotate viewing angles in multiple directions to create a sense of "looking" at objects projected in VR. GSV is linked to Google Maps and Google Earth to provide a three-dimensional view of places, and users can navigate around to identify visual cues such as buildings and landmarks for orientation. Studies have shown that GSV is a beneficial educational tool for disseminating knowledge (Choi et al., 2018; Huh, 2020; Pham et al., 2018; Violante et al., 2019). In GSV, 360° imagery can be viewed as interactive or passive media, depending on whether users interact with the contents of the virtual simulation. Google treks may include interactive features that allow users to extract information by clicking on visual cues.

As mentioned by Carbonell-Carrera and Saorin (2017) and Sasinka et al. (2019), GSV is a valuable tool for virtual place learning even though it is commonly used for navigation. Nugroho et al. (2021) suggest that GSV has potential uses in streetscape evaluation, place visual characteristics study, and architectural conservation, thereby proving the potential of GSV for virtual place-based learning. Despite existing studies investigating the sense of place in physical and virtual environments, there is a lack of focus on virtual place learning with GSV in architectural education. This research addresses this gap by studying the VPE approach using 360° images in GSV to help learners attain a sense of place. It also investigates their experience and attitude in the virtual setting of the place of knowledge inquiry.

RESEARCH METHODS

This study examines how undergraduate students in an architecture program approach virtual place-based learning and how it impacts their sense of place. The study uses phenomenology to evaluate how learners personally experience the virtual environment and acquire a sense of place. Specifically, it evaluates learners' sense of place acquisition of cognitive learning, interpretation of place meaning, and emotion and attitude towards the place, using the module "Theories of Asian Architecture" as the basis for inquiry. The research questions are addressed through the framework outlined in Figure 1:

- To what extent do learners understand place identity in a virtual place setting? (Cognitive learning of the place identity)
- What place meanings do learners interpret from the virtual place experience? (Interpretation of the place meaning)
- To what extent do they show affection towards the place? (Emotion and attitude towards the place)

Historical streets in Kuala Lumpur and Malacca were selected as the cohort's study sites before the Covid-19 outbreak due to their historical significance, urban development, and accessibility. The selection of the two sites was also based on the amount of well-documented information available online. This provides learners with valuable learning opportunities throughout the restriction of movement. The students were assigned to observe the streets' tangible and intangible contexts to develop their interpretations of the place. However, due to the pandemic-related restrictions, the learners in this study had to conduct virtual site visits to selected streets in Kuala Lumpur and Malacca using 360° photos in

Figure 1. Research framework
Source: Authors (2022)

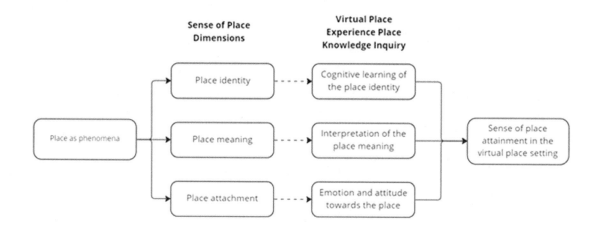

GSV, as shown in Figure 2. The previous cohorts' findings on the physical place setting could serve as a reference for examining the learners' virtual place experience of the exact locations.

In GSV, learners may employ different methods, such as stationary viewing (observing from one point), navigation (moving along a path), or wayfinding (exploring an open environment), to identify the contexts. The duration of virtual presence in GSV varies based on the individual, the simulated environment type, and the immersion intensity. Learners were recommended to navigate in GSV for 15-40 minutes to provide for adequate cognitive building and to decrease the adverse effects of long-term virtual environment exposure as reported in existing studies (Kennedy, Stanney, & Dunlap, 2000; Smith & Burd, 2019; Yoon et al., 2021).

The contexts shown in Table 1 represent the visual cues in GSV. Interpretations of these contexts were shown in sketches and a written summary (Figure 3).

Interpretative Phenomenological Analysis (IPA)

The interpretive phenomenological analysis (IPA) was employed in this study to investigate the learners' cognitive learning of place identity, their interpretation of place meanings, and their attitudes towards the place in a virtual environment. The IPA approach examines the lived experiences of individuals and the meaning they assign to these experiences in the context of a particular phenomenon (Eatough & Smith, 2008; Šašinka et al., 2019; Smith & Osborn, 2003). According to Smith and Osborn (2003, p.55), IPA is an appropriate method for exploring how individuals perceive and rationalize their personal and social worlds. Researchers agree that IPA aims to understand how individuals make sense of a phenomenon from their first-person perspective (Larkin et al., 2006, p.110; Pietkiewicz & Smith, 2012, p.367; Smith, 2019, 2011). Alase (2017) claims that IPA is the most participant-oriented qualitative research approach, which values and acknowledges the participants' lived experiences. This approach enables the researchers to recognize "the individuals' experiences, understandings, perceptions and accounts" as the objective truth about their lived experiences (Reid et al., 2005, as cited in Symeonides & Childs, 2015).

Table 1. Place contexts descriptions

Category	Contexts	Description
Tangible	Religious buildings	Suggest the society and culture of the community residing within the street boundary
	Shophouses	Accommodate business activities that form an essential part of a community.
	Architecture façade and styles	Provide references to time and may reflect the affluence of the community.
	Market	Reflects the community lifestyle through the groceries and merchandise sold
Intangible	Traditional trades/businesses	Reflect the community lifestyle and form part of the social memories
	Historical events/ festivals	Reflect collective social memories of the community
	Local/ traditional cuisines	Reflect the food traditions and culture of the community
	Social institutions	Provide references to the social groups who witnessed the development of the community, e.g., clan associations.

Source: Authors (2022)

Figure 2. Google Street View showing views of Jalan Tun H.S. Lee, Kuala Lumpur (top left); Lorong Pangung, Kuala Lumpur (bottom left); Jalan Tokong, Malacca (top right) and Jalan Kampung Kuli, Malacca (bottom right)
Source: Google Earth (n.d.)

Figure 3. Project outcomes
Source: Authors (2022)

Data Collection

The study used purposive homogenous sampling to obtain a closely defined group of 11 architecture undergraduate learners for a focus group interview, as the research question was experiential in nature.

Semi-structured interviews were conducted to collect data, which allowed participants to voice their opinions and produced rich data. The small sample size was deemed acceptable for IPA, which involves an intensive and in-depth analysis of each participant's account. Before the interview, the researchers established the key topics, including learners' cognitive learning of place identity, interpretation of place meanings, and attitude towards the place. The researchers moderated the focus group interview, and participants were encouraged to express their thoughts in their own words. The session was conducted using Microsoft Teams online video meeting and recorded with participants' knowledge and permission to ensure all subjects discussed were captured for future transcription (Abdullah, 2013; Cooper et al., 2012; Hefferon & Gil-Rodriguez, 2011; Larkin et al., 2006; Smith & Osborn, 2003).

Data Analysis

Coding the Collected Data

The research employed a coding procedure to identify patterns of participant response and categorise them after transcribing the data (Alase, 2017). This approach involved reading and listening to the interview transcript multiple times, distilling and coding information to gain a general understanding of the data (Abdullah, 2013; Alase, 2017; Smith & Osborn, 2003). To analyse the data, the researchers were able to recall and immerse themselves in the interview environment (Pietkiewicz & Smith, 2012). The coded transcript was then organised into a spreadsheet based on the sense of place dimensions for subsequent data analysis.

The Analysis Processes

The researchers used a cycle inquiry approach that includes analysing well-structured coded transcripts to acquire insight into participants' personal experiences in the virtual environment (Smith & Osborn, 2003; Abdullah, 2013). The exploratory comments and remarks made on the coded transcripts helped the researchers identify key phrases, repetitive elements, and explanations, which were used to capture emergent themes (Cooper et al., 2012; Symeonides & Childs, 2015). The researchers interpreted the data and selected themes based on the participants' descriptive, linguistic, and conceptual comments (Cooper et al., 2012). Through this process, six major themes were identified.

Table 2. Interview questions

Learners' Cognitive Learning of Place Identity	Learners' Interpretation of Place Meanings	Learners' Attitude Towards the Place
Did you feel like 'being there' at the street?	What does the street mean to you?	Did you like or dislike the place?
Were you able to identify the tangible attributes that made up the identity of the street?	Which contexts help you to generate your interpretation of the place meanings?	Which context you like/dislike the most?
How did you learn about the intangible attributes that construct the identity of the street?	How did you develop a sense of place during your virtual visit?	Would you like to visit the actual place?
What attribute do you think best represents the identity of your selected studied street?	How do the place attributes represent the sense of place?	Would you feel or experience the same way by physically visiting the place?

Source: Authors (2022)

FINDINGS

Upon analysing the interview transcripts of participants, six significant themes were identified concerning learners' attitudes and experiences towards the virtual place setting in GSV. These themes include the association of the virtual place with real places, difficulties in comprehending intangible place attributes, the ability to understand physical contexts, a strong sense of community in VPE, positive attachment to the place, and the motivation to visit the real place. Table 3 illustrates the correlation of these themes with the dimensions of a sense of place.

Associations With Real Places

This theme indicates how learners associate virtual settings with real places with similar contexts. Learners may identify similarities between the settings in GSV and places they are familiar with or have previously visited. Drawing on prior experiences of different real places with similar contexts, learners may construct their understanding of place identity in the virtual setting, as exemplified by the following excerpt from the interview transcript.

It reminds me of Penang. The place is quite similar, so I can quite relate. It's kind of close in terms of the contexts. Yeah, I haven't been there, but there is quite a lot of information to obtain. The virtual visit allows you to be more focused and more detail oriented. (Learner 1)

Learner 1 connected her childhood experiences in George Town, Penang, and her virtual visit to Jalan Tukang Besi in Malacca. She noticed that both cities share similar historical development, which helped her to identify similar contexts between the two places. Although she had not visited Jalan Tukang Besi in person, she learned about the place through a virtual visit and by researching information online. Learner 1 expressed that the virtual visit provided a concentrated way of exploring and learning about the place.

I have been to the location before. The first time I visited the site, the experience of the five senses created a map in my mind. When I went to Google Street View to study the site, it was just overlaying these details onto this map that I created of the space. For the sense of being there, I wouldn't say Google Street View would be able to give you that. I feel that the sense of being related to this map you created of the experience can only be found when you're in the space. But in terms of completing the assignment, I think it did help to add to this map that I had. (Learner 6)

Learner 6 had previously visited the selected place when he was younger. He tries to connect his previous experience with the VPE by referring to the "five senses map" he created during his first visit. He believes the VPE creates an additional sense of presence that supplements his perception of the place.

Challenges in Understanding Intangible Place Attributes

The analysis has revealed a theme related to learners' cognitive learning of intangible place attributes, specifically those related to social activities. The findings indicate that learners had a limited understanding of these intangible attributes and needed further research to enhance their cognitive understanding.

During the virtual visit in Google Street View, I couldn't see any blacksmith shops because they appeared to be closed, and I can't really identify them. The place is very hidden, and sometimes the view in Google Street View is a bit distorted, so I can't really identify the blacksmith shops. The only way I was able to find out was I had to search really hard, and then I eventually visited a Chinese website which provides such information. (Learner 1)

Learner 1 studied Jalan Tukang Besi in Malacca, which has a significant historical context related to blacksmiths. However, this intangible context was not visible in the GSV as the view was limited. Therefore, the learner had to use external sources such as websites to understand the intangible context of the place.

We can't interview the locals. We don't really know about the history of the place and what happened before. All of that can only be gathered from online information. (Learner 9)

Learner 9 emphasised the difficulty in understanding the intangible place contexts, particularly the historical and societal aspects of VPE. This was attributed to the lack of human interaction in the virtual setting, which precludes the possibility of conducting interviews with community members.

Ability to Grasp an Understanding of Physical Contexts

This theme demonstrates learners' experiences understanding physical place contexts such as building facades, architectural styles, building typologies, and marketplaces. The findings reveal that general tangible attributes may be identified to a limited extent as there were constraints in obtaining detailed information.

If you only look through Google Street View, you can't really find the information that you want; you can only find the general information. You can only see the building exteriors; you can't really see what's inside, like the intangible contexts in specific. (Learner 4)

I saw a very old shop during my virtual site visit. I know that they sell either gold or silver or something, but I don't really know exactly. The name of the shop was not even visible. I think we need to go to the site to understand what they do over there. There's a bit of limitation to learning about the tangible contexts; it's even more challenging if online information about the place is limited. I remember when I was searching for the wooden bucket craftsman using Google Street View; there were some limitations of view angles in the navigation. The location of the subject that I intended to identify might be somewhere not visible. (Learner 11)

Learner 4 claims that the general understanding of tangible contexts is achievable through VPE. Learner 11 affirms this by highlighting the challenges in identifying the physical contexts due to constraints of view angle in virtual navigation. Human activities were not clearly shown in GSV, making it more challenging to understand the relevant, tangible contexts.

Strong Sense of Community in VPE

This theme relates to learners' interpretation of place meanings. It exemplifies learners' perception through the sense of community and historical evidence reflecting the place's origin, evolution, development, and transformation over time. Traditional trades and cultural activities contribute to giving meaning to a place.

For me, it is the mixture of historical contexts and traditional trades. The place used to have many blacksmiths back in the past along Blacksmith Street as the major traditional trade, thus forming the meaning of the place. (Learner 10)

For Jalan Tun Tan Cheng Lock, it was a street where the elite Baba and Nyonya communities resided. So, for me, I think this street is very important to us. It shows the history of Baba Nyonya, like where they originated and how their traditions have evolved and how they assimilate into our local culture. I think an important feature of this street is also the architecture....it's mainly about the architecture and the history of the street, it's very important as the identity of the place, it's crucial for the future generation to remember the history of Baba and Nyonya. (Learner 7)

Learner 10's understanding of the place meanings was based on the history and traditional trade of the blacksmiths in Jalan Tukang Besi, Malacca. Learner 7's interpretation of Jalan Tun Tan Cheng Lock, Malacca, was based on historical evidence of community and architecture.

Positive Attachment to the Place

This theme refers to learners' attitudes towards the place they visited with GSV. The analysis reveals that learners' positive emotional attachment to the place was identified.

I think like the street even more than I did before because before this, even like going to the place physically, I didn't know about its interesting contexts. It's the little quirks that make it interesting. After knowing all this information, I think the street appears more interesting to me. (Learner 3)

I went to the street just for food previously. After going through the virtual experience using Google Street View, I notice seeing things differently, particularly the architectural contexts. It's not just about food... I like the place for its culture like how the religious buildings of different faiths are placed along the street. (Learner 8)

I really like the place. I wouldn't have liked it that much if I haven't done the virtual visit. After understanding all the things about the street, it is really that interesting. Particularly the blacksmiths carry a lot of sentimental emotions and feelings from the past till now, as well as the old shophouses. I remember there is a dim sum shop that has been operating for decades. I also like the religious buildings of different faiths coexisting in one place. If I ever go to Malacca, that would be the first place I will visit because it really carries various attributes which make that place so meaningful. (Learner 1)

Most learners exhibited a positive attitude towards the places they studied using VPE, as they discovered place attributes that interested them. Learners with previous experience with the place could develop new perspectives and interpretations of the place's meanings.

Motivation to Visit the Real Place

This theme demonstrates that most learners are motivated to visit the real place compared to their virtual experience.

I expect to have the same feeling as my virtual visit, and I want to verify it because the place seems interesting. (Learner 5)

I would want to go to the real place to experience it and then have my own opinion about the place. (Learner 9)

I think Google Street View cars might not capture conditions at different times on the street. So, you might not see the real condition virtually. I'd like to go there to see if it's really like what I feel in the virtual setting. (Learner 11)

I would absolutely love to go there. The first thing I would do is check out the abandoned mansion because we couldn't get much information about it on the Internet, so I could see it myself and ask the locals about its history. (Learner 7)

The learners in the study expressed a desire to visit the places they had studied using VPE, citing various motivations. Some, such as Learner 5, Learner 9, and Learner 11, wish to confirm their understanding of the place in person as they believe VPE may not provide a complete representation of the place at different times of the day. Others, like Learner 7, are intrigued by discoveries made in the VPE, such as an abandoned mansion, and are motivated to learn more about the place by conducting further research and interviews in a real-world setting.

DISCUSSIONS

Cognitive Learning of Place Identity

Montello, Waller, Hegarty, & Richardson (2004) explain that place learning may be achieved through direct and indirect sources. Direct sources involve experiencing the environment through sensorimotor capabilities, while indirect sources refer to simulated environments that use external representation. In a physical environment, one may experience stimuli and receive spatial information through sensory methods, including vestibular and kinesthesis, alongside sight, sound, smell, taste, and touch. However, in virtual settings, the stimuli experience may be limited, and navigation methods may involve little or no vestibular and kinaesthetic senses.

It is important to highlight that experience in a virtual environment may be influenced by the memory of previous places, as demonstrated by the findings where learners' experience in the virtual setting

Table 3. Summary of findings

Sense of Place Dimension	Themes	Descriptions
Learners' cognitive learning of place identity	Association with real places	Learners relate VPE with real places of similar contexts
	Challenges in understanding intangible place attributes	Understanding intangible attributes were limited and required additional research to construct learners' cognitive understanding.
	Ability to grasp an understanding of physical contexts	General tangible attributes may be identified to a limited extent as there were constraints in obtaining detailed information.
Learners' interpretation of place meanings	Strong sense of community in VPE	Interpretation of place meanings was generated through the sense of community and historical evidence reflecting the place's origin, evolution, development, and transformation over time. Traditional trades and cultural activities contribute to giving meaning to a place.
Learners' attitude towards the place	Positive attachment to the place	Positive emotional attachment to place was identified.
	Motivation to visit the real place	Most learners are motivated to visit the real place to compare it with their virtual experience.

Source: Authors (2022)

reminded them of a real place with similar contexts. This factor is unimportant; rather, it emphasises the importance of place memory in shaping learners' VPE. The sense of presence in a virtual place may be influenced by familiarity with a similar real place, as it affects learners' behaviour and interaction in the virtual environment (Saunders, Rutkowski, Genuchten van, Vogel, & Orrego, 2011). This familiarity may influence how learners navigate and seek information, just as they would in a physical environment. However, the limitations of virtual representation in GSV may result in limited identification of tangible attributes (Montello et al., 2004). In addition, the lack of human interaction and the use of human sensory perception in virtual environments may limit the sense of presence (Saunders et al., 2004).

The use of GSV for navigation is restricted to a certain area of street or place. While GSV provides some visual cues for intangible aspects, it may not be sufficient in communicating comprehensive information to users. Due to its limitations, GSV does not adequately depict the actual context of a place, and learners need to conduct additional research to develop their cognitive understanding.

Learners' Interpretation of Place Meanings

According to Hashem, Abbas, Akbar, & Nazgol, (2013), a person's perceived meaning of a place is influenced by the activities and interactions that take place within it. These interactions may take two forms: the individual's correspondence with the place through movement and exploration, and communication with others in the place through social activities. However, real-time computer-simulated environments achieve a similar effect by responding to the user's locomotion and movement control (Montello et al., 2004, p. 256). Avatars are used for social engagement in this environment, allowing for real-time communication between users (Ghani et al., 2016).

This study is concerned with how learners derive meanings of place through the activities and interactions associated with it in VPE. However, GSV's interaction with the place is limited to movement control and changes of views, providing learners with only an observational view of the depicted activities. Furthermore, social interaction within the setting is absent, as human figures featured in GSV are static images. Despite these limitations, learners still gained a sense of community by observing the street's history, culture, and architecture. The findings show that community living forms the place meaning through learners' interpretation of traditional trades and social and cultural activities. They understood how the streets show history layers that inform the place's origin, evolution, and development. Learners are aware of misinterpretation of place meanings due to inaccurate representation in social media. This reflects their level of critical thinking in the learning process. The interpretation of place meanings was developed and influenced by learners' prior knowledge and experience. Past experiences and memories of similar places may help learners relate better in a virtual environment to derive place meanings (Ghani et al., 2016, p.4).

Learners' Attitude Towards the Place

Learners' emotional connection with the place in VPE is closely related to their attitude towards the place. This emotional correspondence results from establishing symbolic relationships and meanings with the place, which increases their place awareness and positive affection towards it (Hashem et al., 2013, p.112). Physical factors, social factors, cultural factors, personal factors, memories and experiences, place satisfaction, interaction and activity features, and time factor are all significant determinants of place attachment. (Hashem et al., 2013, p.113). Although not all of these factors fully explain learners' experiences in this study, they provide helpful insights into understanding their attitude towards the place.

Findings indicate that physical place attributes such as architecture and space settings allow the discovery of significant contexts that may foster a favourable attitude towards the place. One participant highlighted how discovering an abandoned old mansion motivated her to explore the area further.

Physical and social factors may elicit learners' memories and experiences of similar places and contribute to their emotional attachment to the virtual place. Learners may relate the virtual place to their hometown or other places they have visited based on shared architectural styles, physical environment, traditional trades, and cultural activities.

Personal factors refer to how an individual aligns with the place setting to develop specific attitudes and opinions. The expectation gap may affect attitude towards the place when one's anticipation about the place experience is not aligned with the experience. It depends on their place expectation developed from previous experience and cognitive processes, which influence place satisfaction (Hashem et al., 2013, p.114). This is observed in learners without prior knowledge or experience of the studied place. Each expresses different feelings and opinions about their experience in GSV, reflecting how individuality affects their attitude towards the space.

Interaction and activities are essential elements in place experience of both real and virtual settings. Interaction in a simulated environment enhances the experience of users (Mahdjoubi, Koh & Moobela, 2014). However, the static navigation and absence of interactions in GSV may not be sufficient to evoke learners' emotions towards the place. Using multimedia tools such as videos to showcase the place attributes, positive attitudes may be strengthened.

FUTURE RESEARCH DIRECTIONS

The study's limitations primarily relate to the sample of data, which only consisted of students from one school within a single institution. Architecture students from other institutions may have different experiences with virtual learning, resulting in different responses. Further investigation with a different sample from various institutions may be done to discover and assess architecture students' virtual learning experiences in greater depth.

CONCLUSION

Findings indicate that learners' sense of place in a virtual setting can be attained but requires further research or assistive tools to improve cognitive learning of the place attributes. Learners establish positive affection towards the place. They also develop the motivation to visit the real place. The study provides insight into how learners' experience with the virtual place phenomenon may contribute to constructing their sense of place, which will guide their cognitive design in future design exercises. It also offers references in guiding the virtual place-based education pedagogical design. However, the research identifies the need to address GSV's lack of interaction and activities. Users' experience in a virtual simulation may be enhanced by social presence, where interactions happen (Mahdjoubi et al., 2014, p.34). As such, a VPE system designed with interaction and activity capabilities may positively affect learners' attitudes and behaviour in the virtual place phenomenon. This feature may also contribute to engaging learners and improving their cognitive learning. Future research to evaluate potential enhancing functions such as videos, real-time chat, interactive games, avatars, etc., may be required to improve VPE as a virtual place-based learning approach.

ACKNOWLEDGMENT

This research received no specific grant from any funding agency in the public, commercial, or not-for-profit sectors. The authors would like to thank all the students involved in this research.

REFERENCES

Abdullah, F. (2013). Phenomenological Approach for Evaluating Problem Based Learning in Architectural Education. *Methodologies In Architectural Research*, 4.

Alase, A. (2017). The interpretative phenomenological analysis (IPA): A guide to a good qualitative research approach. *International Journal of Education and Literacy Studies*, 5(2), 9. doi:10.7575/aiac. ijels.v.5n.2p.9

Alasli, M. (2019). Toponyms' contribution to identity: The case study of Rabat (Morocco). *Proceedings of the ICA*, 2(July), 1–7. doi:10.5194/ica-proc-2-3-2019

Ardoin, N. M. (2006). Toward an Interdisciplinary Understanding of Place: Lessons for Environmental Education. [CJEE]. *Canadian Journal of Environmental Education*, 11(1), 1.

Arora, V., & Khazanchi, D. (2010). Sense of Place in Virtual World Learning Environments: A Conceptual Exploration. *Proceedings of the Fifth Midwest Association for Information Systems Conference*. Fifth Midwest Association for Information Systems Conference.

Arora, V., & Khazanchi, D. (2014). Sense of place in virtual learning environments. *Proceedings of the Ninth Midwest Association for Information Systems Conference*. Ninth Midwest Association for Information Systems Conference.

Baker, K. (2014). Sense of Place: Understanding Architectural and Landscape Design through a Layering of Visual Representations. *Journal of Learning Design*, 7(1), 74–83. doi:10.5204/jld.v7i1.138

Carbonell, C., & Saorín, J. (2017). Geospatial Google Street View with Virtual Reality: A Motivational Approach for Spatial Training Education. *ISPRS International Journal of Geo-Information*, 6(9), 261. doi:10.3390/ijgi6090261

Champion, E. (2019). Norberg-Schulz: Culture, Presence, and a Sense of Virtual Place. In E. Champion (Ed.), *The Phenomenology of Real and Virtual Places* (pp. 144–163). Routledge.

Champion, E. M. (2006). *Evaluating cultural learning in virtual environments* [Doctoral thesis, The University of Melbourne].

Chen, S., Wang, S., & Xu, H. (2017). Influence of place identity on residents' attitudes to dark tourism. *Journal of China Tourism Research*, 13(4), 338–356. doi:10.1080/19388160.2017.1401023

Choi, K., Yoon, Y. J., Song, O. Y., & Choi, S. M. (2018). Interactive and immersive learning using 360° virtual reality contents on mobile platforms. *Mobile Information Systems*, 2018, 2018. doi:10.1155/2018/2306031

Christofi, M., Kyrlitsias, C., Michael-Grigoriou, D., Anastasiadou, Z., Michaelidou, M., Papamichael, I., & Pieri, K. (2018). A Tour in the Archaeological Site of Choirokoitia Using Virtual Reality: A Learning Performance and Interest Generation Assessment. In M. Ioannides (Ed.), *J.*

Clark, S., & Maher, M. L. (2003). The effects of a sense of place on the learning experience in a 3D virtual world. *Communities of Practice. Research Proceedings of the 10th Association for Learning Technologies Conference (ALT-C2003)*, 82–101.

Connolly, F. (2020, November 5). *Integrating Place-based Education Into Classroom or Distance Learning During the COVID-19 Pandemic*. U.S. Department of Education. https://ies.ed.gov/ncee/edlabs/regions/pacific/blogs/blog33_integrating-place-based-education-into-classroom.asp

Cooper, R., Fleischer, A., & Cotton, F. A. (2012). Building Connections: An Interpretative Phenomenological Analysis of Qualitative Research Students' Learning Experiences. *Qualitative Report*, 17, 1–16.

Dalgarno, B., & Lee, M. J. W. (2010). What are the learning affordances of 3-D virtual environments? *British Journal of Educational Technology*, 41(1), 10–32. doi:10.1111/j.1467-8535.2009.01038.x

Eatough, V., & Smith, J. A. (2008). Interpretative phenomenological analysis. In *The Sage handbook of qualitative research in psychology* (pp. 179–194). SAGE Publications. doi:10.4135/9781848607927.n11

Fiorillo, F., Rizzi, G., & Achille, C. (2021). Learning through virtual tools: Visit a place in the pandemic era. *The International Archives of the Photogrammetry, Remote Sensing and Spatial Information Sciences, XLVI-M-1-2021*, 225–232.

Ghani, I., Rafi, A., & Woods, P. (2016). Sense of place in immersive architectural virtual heritage environment. *2016 22nd International Conference on Virtual System & Multimedia (VSMM)*, 1–8.

Google Earth. (n.d.). *Street View*. Google. https://www.google.com/earth/education/tools/street-view/

Hashem, H., Abbas, Y. S., Akbar, H. A., & Nazgol, B. (2013). Comparison the concepts of sense of place and attachment to place in Architectural Studies. *Malaysia Journal of Society and Space*, *9*(1), 107–117.

Hefferon, K., & Gil-Rodriguez, E. (2011). Reflecting on the rise in popularity of interpretive phenomenological analysis. *The Psychologist*, *24*(10), 756–759.

Hillstrom, J. E. (2019). Virtual Place-Based Learning in Interdisciplinary Contexts: A Psychological Perspective and a Meta-analytic Review. In R. D. Lansiquot & S. P. MacDonald (Eds.), *Interdisciplinary Perspectives on Virtual Place-Based Learning* (pp. 13–34). Springer International Publishing. doi:10.1007/978-3-030-32471-1_2

Huh, Y. (2020). 360 Virtual Reality Project to Inspire Future Educators to be Creators. *Journal of Education for Teaching*, *46*(3), 421–423. doi:10.1080/02607476.2020.1766833

Janz, B. B. (2018). Virtual Place and Virtualized Place. In *The Phenomenology of Real and Virtual Places*. Routledge. doi:10.4324/9781315106267-6

Johnson, J. T. (2012). Place-based learning and knowing: Critical pedagogies grounded in Indigeneity. *GeoJournal*, *77*(6), 829–836. doi:10.100710708-010-9379-1

Kennedy, R., Stanney, K., & Dunlap, W. (2000). Duration and exposure to virtual environments: Sickness curves during and across sessions. *Presence (Cambridge, Mass.)*, *9*(5), 463–472. doi:10.1162/105474600566952

Koh, K., Kusnadi, Y., Pan, G., & Shankararaman, V. (2022). Making virtual project-based learning work during the COVID-19 pandemic. [IJE]. *International Journal of Education*, *10*(02), 1–14. doi:10.5121/ije.2022.10201

Krummel, J. W. (2018). The Kyoto School Philosophy on Place: Nishida and Ueda. *The Phenomenology of Real and Virtual Places*, 141.

Langran, E., & DeWitt, J. (2020). Facilitating Student Learning. In *Navigating Place-Based Learning: Mapping for a Better World* (pp. 91–115). Springer. doi:10.1007/978-3-030-55673-0_4

Larkin, M., Watts, S., & Clifton, E. (2006). Giving voice and making sense in interpretative phenomenological analysis. *Qualitative Research in Psychology*, *3*(2), 102–120. doi:10.1191/1478088706qp062oa

Mahdjoubi, L., Koh, J. H., & Moobela, C. (2014). Effects of Interactive Real-Time Simulations and Humanoid Avatars on Consumers' Responses in Online House Products Marketing. *Computer-Aided Civil and Infrastructure Engineering*, *29*(1), 31–46. doi:10.1111/j.1467-8667.2012.00775.x

Montello, D. R., Waller, D., Hegarty, M., & Richardson, A. E. (2004). Spatial memory of real environments, virtual environments, and maps. In G. L. Allen (Ed.), *Human spatial memory: Remembering where* (pp. 251–285). Lawrence Erlbaum Associates, Inc.

Morel-Edniebrown, F. (2012). Wither Genius Loci? The City, Urban Fabric and Identity in Perth, Western Australia. In H. Casakin & F. Bernardo (Eds.), *The Role of Place Identity in the Perception, Understanding, and Design of Built Environments* (pp. 275–299). Bentham Science Publishers. doi:10 .2174/9781608054138112010102009

Moysey, S. M. J., & Lazar, K. B. (2019). Using Virtual Reality as a Tool for Field-Based Learning in the Earth Sciences. In R. D. Lansiquot & S. P. MacDonald (Eds.), *Interdisciplinary Perspectives on Virtual Place-Based Learning* (pp. 99–126). Springer International Publishing. doi:10.1007/978-3-030-32471-1_7

Nikezić, A., & Marković, D. (2015). Place-based education in the architectural design studio: Agrarian landscape as a resource for sustainable urban lifestyle. *Sustainability (Basel)*, *7*(7), 9711–9733. doi:10.3390u7079711

Nugroho, S., Rizqiyah, F., Bararatin, K., Mahendra, A. S., Kharismawan, R., & Soemardiono, B. (2021). Pemanfaatan Google-Street-View untuk Observasi Kota di Tengah Pandemi Covid-19. *ATRIUM: Jurnal Arsitektur*, *7*(1), 1–12. doi:10.21460/atrium.v7i1.111

Park, L. (2019). Virtual Reality as a Pedagogical Tool for Interdisciplinarity and Place-Based Education. In R. D. Lansiquot & S. P. MacDonald (Eds.), *Interdisciplinary Perspectives on Virtual Place-Based Learning* (pp. 35–51). Springer International Publishing. doi:10.1007/978-3-030-32471-1_3

Pham, H. C., Dao, N., Pedro, A., Le, Q. T., Hussain, R., Cho, S., & Park, C. (2018). Virtual field trip for mobile construction safety education using 360-degree panoramic virtual reality. *International Journal of Engineering Education*, *34*(4), 1174–1191.

Pietkiewicz, I., & Smith, J. A. (2014). A practical guide to using interpretative phenomenological analysis in qualitative research psychology. *Psychological Journal*, *20*(1), 7–14.

Relph, E. (2007). Spirit of Place and Sense of Place in Virtual Realities. *Techné: Research in Philosophy and Technology*, *10*(3), 17–25.

Šašinka, Č., Stachoň, Z., Sedlák, M., Chmelík, J., Herman, L., Kubíček, P., Šašinková, A., Doležal, M., Tejkl, H., Urbánek, T., Svatoňová, H., Ugwitz, P., & Juřík, V. (2018). Collaborative immersive virtual environments for education in geography. *ISPRS International Journal of Geo-Information*, *8*(3), 3. doi:10.3390/ijgi8010003

Saunders, C., Rutkowski, A. F., Genuchten van, Vogel, & Orrego. (2011). Virtual space and place: Theory and test. *Management Information Systems Quarterly*, *35*(4), 1079–1098. doi:10.2307/41409974

Seamon, D. (2000). Phenomenology, place, environment, and architecture: A review of the literature. *Phenomenology Online*, *36*, 1–29.

Sebastien, L. (2020). The power of place in understanding place attachments and meanings. *Geoforum*, *108*, 204–216. doi:10.1016/j.geoforum.2019.11.001

Smith, J. A. (2011). Evaluating the contribution of interpretative phenomenological analysis. *Health Psychology Review*, *5*(1), 9–27. doi:10.1080/17437199.2010.510659

Smith, J. A. (2019). Participants and researchers searching for meaning: Conceptual developments for interpretative phenomenological analysis. *Qualitative Research in Psychology*, *16*(2), 166–181. doi:10.1080/14780887.2018.1540648

Smith, J. A., & Osborn, M. (2003). Interpretative Phenomenological Analysis. In J. A. Smith (Ed.), *Qualitative Psychology: A Practical Guide to Research Methods* (pp. 53–80). SAGE.

Smith, S. P., & Burd, E. L. (2019). Response activation and inhibition after exposure to virtual reality. *Array (New York, N.Y.)*, *3–4*, 100010. doi:10.1016/j.array.2019.100010

Squire, K. D. (2022). From virtual to participatory learning with technology during COVID-19. *E-Learning and Digital Media*, *19*(1), 55–77. doi:10.1177/20427530211022926

Symeonides, R., & Childs, C. (2015). The personal experience of online learning: An interpretative phenomenological analysis. *Computers in Human Behavior*, *51*, 539–545. doi:10.1016/j.chb.2015.05.015

Tuan, Y.-F. (1975). Place: An Experiential Perspective. *Geographical Review*, *65*(2), 151–165. doi:10.2307/213970

Tuan, Y.-F. (2001). *Space And Place: The Perspective of Experience by Yi-Fu Tuan | Goodreads*. University of Minnesota Press.

Violante, M. G., Vezzetti, E., & Piazzolla, P. (2019). Interactive virtual technologies in engineering education: Why not 360° videos? [IJIDeM]. *International Journal on Interactive Design and Manufacturing*, *13*(2), 729–742. doi:10.100712008-019-00553-y

Wallgrün, J. O., Chang, J. S.-K., Zhao, J., Trenham, P., Sajjadi, P., Simpson, M., & Klippel, A. (2022). Place-based education through immersive virtual experiences—Preparing biology students for the field. *Journal of Biological Education*, *0*(0), 1–24. doi:10.1080/00219266.2022.2067580

Yoon, H. J., Moon, H. S., Sung, M. S., Park, S. W., & Heo, H. (2021). Effects of prolonged use of virtual reality smartphone-based head-mounted display on visual parameters: A randomised controlled trial. *Scientific Reports*, *11*(1), 1–9. doi:10.103841598-021-94680-w PMID:34321504

Yusoff, W. F. M., Ja'afar, N. H., & Mohammad, N. (2019). Perception of Architecture Students on Factors Influencing the Selection of Locations for Academic Trip and Site Visit. *Journal of Technical Education and Training*, *11*(3), 22–31.

Zandvliet, D. B. (2014). PLACES and SPACES: Case studies in the evaluation of post-secondary, place-based learning environments. *Studies in Educational Evaluation*, *41*, 18–28. doi:10.1016/j.stueduc.2013.09.011

Zhao, J., Lafemina, P., Carr, J., Sajjadi, P., Wallgrun, J. O., & Klippel, A. (2020). Learning in the Field: Comparison of Desktop, Immersive Virtual Reality, and Actual Field Trips for Place-Based STEM Education. *Proceedings - 2020 IEEE Conference on Virtual Reality and 3D User Interfaces, VR 2020*, 893–902. IEEE.

ADDITIONAL READING

Arslan, F., & Kaysi, F. (2013). Virtual Learning Environments. *Journal of Teacher Education, 2*(4), 57–65.

Georgiou, Y., Tsivitanidou, O., Eckhardt, C., & Ioannou, A. (2020). Work-in-progress—a learning experience design for immersive virtual reality in physics classrooms. *2020 6th International Conference of the Immersive Learning Research Network*. IEEE. 10.23919/iLRN47897.2020.9155097

Huang, H.-M., & Liaw, S.-S. (2018). An analysis of learners' intentions toward virtual reality learning based on Constructivist and technology acceptance approaches. *International Review of Research in Open and Distance Learning, 19*(1). doi:10.19173/irrodl.v19i1.2503

Huang, H.-M., Rauch, U., & Liaw, S.-S. (2010). Investigating learners' attitudes toward virtual reality learning environments: Based on a constructivist approach. *Computers & Education, 55*(3), 1171–1182. doi:10.1016/j.compedu.2010.05.014

Marinovic, G. I. (2021). Belonging to place: Interpretative phenomenological analysis of incremental housing. *ACE: Architecture. City and Environment, 16*(46). doi:10.5821/ace.16.46.9706

Rudd, J. W. (1985). Architecture and ideas: A phenomenology of interpretation. *Journal of Architectural Education (1984-), 38*(2), 9. doi:10.2307/1424812

Sun, Y., Albeaino, G., Gheisari, M., & Eiris, R. (2020). Virtual collaborative spaces for online site visits: A plan-reading pilot study. *EPiC Series in Built Environment*. doi:10.29007/d14v

Whateley, G., & Manly, A. (2021). The transition to online teaching and learning. *Advances in Human and Social Aspects of Technology*, 188–196. doi:10.4018/978-1-7998-6772-2.ch011

KEY TERMS AND DEFINITIONS

Cognitive: The process of being conscious of intellectual activity such as thinking, reasoning, remembering, etc.

Genius Loci: It refers to the essence of a place.

Geolocation: The process of determining the actual geographical location of electronic devices.

Kinesthesis: The experiences that happen during movement from sensory organs.

Phenomenology: A philosophical inquiry into human beings' existence and lived experience.

Place-based learning: A learning approach that engages learners in the place through the physical environment, local culture, history, and society.

Sensorimotor: It refers to an ability to process external information through our senses and to respond to it.

Vestibular: It relates to the experience of body position and movement.

Chapter 21
Public Perception of a Public Participation Exercise in Designing Public Parks in Malaysia

Ungku Norani Sonet

https://orcid.org/0000-0003-4144-150X

Taylor's University, Malaysia

ABSTRACT

The design of public parks is a vital aspect of urban planning. To ensure that public parks are designed to cater to the needs and preferences of communities, it is important to consider public perception and participation. Therefore, the aim of this study is to evaluate people's perception of public participation in designing public parks in Malaysia. The questionnaire design is mainly derived from the theories of public awareness of public participation exercises in designing public parks in Malaysia. This study adopted quantitative survey questionnaire method. The respondents of the study are users of two public parks in Johor Bahru. In total, there were 383 data collected and analysed. The findings show that civil society in general has a collective interest in participating in public participation exercises in designing public parks in Malaysia.

INTRODUCTION

Public parks are an essential aspect of urban planning, providing spaces for residents to engage in recreational activities and socialise with one another. Moreover, urban parks need to be studied since their presence in urban areas directly impacts the population's quality of life. The relationship between urban parks and the public's perception of their participation in designing these public spaces is a critical area for investigation. Understanding the public's perception of public participation in designing public parks is essential, as it can provide insights into how communities perceive and value urban green spaces. Through such research, valuable information can be obtained on how to improve the design of public parks to best

DOI: 10.4018/978-1-6684-8253-7.ch021

meet the needs and preferences of residents. People's perception is one of the most interesting parts of human-geographic research, and accommodating public participation in urban public spaces such as a park can develop healthy communities and promote the equity of economic, social, and environmental aspects in urban areas. Furthermore, understanding citizens' needs and their perception of urban parks has an important role in planning and providing public services to different parts of a city. Research conducted by Halkos revealed that the availability of public spaces and green open spaces is crucial in meeting the needs and expectations of residents regarding their living environment.

Background

Local government policies (such as democratic governance, sustainable development goals, and local agenda 21) are a major driver of the concept of public participation around the world, and the initiative taken by local governments to publicly state their position on public participation encourages other government agencies to deliver the agenda through suitable platforms. As a result, we describe the connection and correlation between public engagement and three major local governance strategies in Malaysia: Democratic Governance (DG), Sustainable Development Goals (SDG), and Local Agenda 21 (LA21).

Democratic nations encourage their citizens to take an active role in shaping public policy so that it more effectively meets the needs of the populace (Johnson, 2014). Bottom-up development frameworks are evident in this sort of public policy, as are widespread public participation and citizen engagement (Eckerd & Heidelberg, 2020; Feng et al., 2020). Many people view public involvement as a novel approach to governance that leverages the expertise and experience of a wide range of stakeholders to inform decision-making and foster consensus at every stage (Sondermann & Ulbert, 2021). The policymaking process, the way in which citizens' concerns are heard and taken into consideration, determines whether or not a democracy produces more responsive governments, yet this political system stays more inclusive overall (Putra, 2019). Therefore, the local populace must be included in the government's deliberations on civil policy if they are to help promote democracy in the country. Additonally, public input into government policymaking has been shown to have a positive effect on democracy's development (Manaf et al., 2016; Sondermann & Ulbert, 2021; Yaakob, 2012). The strategic use of detention orders and other legal and emergency powers, along with other restrictions on the exercise of civil and political liberties, have led to Malaysia being labelled as a "semi-democratic" regime (Welsh, 1996). Therefore, a major shift is required in Malaysian democracy, with the people playing a far larger role in policymaking (Kamaruddin & Rogers, 2020). In addition, it is thought to encourage openness in government by encouraging citizen engagement. Therefore, public infrastructure planning may change and evolve in accordance with the changing demands of the public.

Public Participation

Lawson and Kearns (2010), and Sondermann and Ulbert (2020) all agree that public engagement fosters a spirit of collaboration within civic society. Participation in public decision making also serves an educational purpose by teaching citizens how to work together effectively, and it fosters civic virtues and a sense of community (Lawson & Kearns, 2010; Michels, 2019). The public now has a new way to communicate with government officials (Creighton, 2005). Furthermore, it allows for the identification of socially-acceptable solutions, aids in determining the conflict's trajectory, and protects local authorities from being marginalised (Zaczna, 2018). Different phrases are sometimes used interchangeably, and there is no universally accepted meaning of "public participation." Terms like "citizen engagement," "citizen/civil/public participation," "public involvement," "citizen consultation," "public dialogue," and "participatory democracy" can be found in scholarly and international publications. Deliberative mini-publics require the involvement of specialists during public engagement (Michels, 2019). Lawson and Kearns (2010) argue that when the public takes part in an exercise, they should feel like they have a say in the results. At the same time, stakeholders have a say in how buildings are evaluated, with their input shaping developments towards more open and accessible methods of assessing building performance that take into account not only environmental but also social and economic concerns throughout a structure's entire lifecycle (Brophy, 2014).

Table 1 shows the advantages and disadvantages of public participation exercise. The advantages of public participation include indirectly educating the public and being able to receive direct input from them, enhancing the relationship between the government and the public, breaking gridlock and being able to achieve the outcomes and public participation will create inclusivity and better policy and implementations, representatives of the needs and priorities of the community. The disadvantages of public participation include, is time consuming, costly and may backfire, losing control over decision-making by government, public participation is risky with the possibility of bad decisions being made and the resources devoted to public participation will not be available to the actual projects for other use. Even though the public participation exercise has its significant downside, the benefits of integrating public and local authorities would produce interactive and responsible publics.

Table 2 shows the advantages and disadvantages of public participation as listed by Irvin and Stansbury (2004). The advantages of public participation include education – learning from citizens and helping to enhance their knowledge, building trust and relationships between government and the public, breaking gridlocks and achieving positive outcomes, and more inclusive and better policy and implementation, representative of the needs and priorities of the community. On the other hand, the disadvantages of public participation include time-consuming - costly and may backfire, government fears and/or experience loss of decision-making control, risky – with the possibility of bad decisions being made and resources devoted to public participation will not be available to the actual projects for other uses.

The wisdom of public involvement itself in its application in public policy has been further illuminated by this study thanks to the topic of public participation in general. Discussion about public engagement

Table 1. Comparison of integrated design process (IDP) and conventional design process (CDM)

Integrated Design Process	Conventional Design Process
Inclusive from the outset	Involves team members only when essential
Front-loaded – time and energy invested early	Less time, energy, and collaboration exhibited in early stages
Decisions influenced by broad team	More decisions made by fewer people
Iterative process	Linear process
Whole-systems thinking	Systems often considered in isolation
Allows for full optimisation	Limited to constrained optimisation
Seek synergies	Diminished opportunity for synergies
Life-cycle costing	Emphasis on up-front costs
Process continues through post-occupancy	Typically finished when construction is complete

Source: (Grimmer & Wille, 2020)

Table 2. Advantages and disadvantages of public participation

Advantages of Public Participation	Disadvantages of Public Participation
Education – learning from citizens and helping to enhance their knowledge	Time consuming, costly, and may backfire
Builds trust and relationships between government and the public	Government fears and/ or experience loss of decision-making control
Breaks gridlock and achieves outcomes	Risky, with the possibility of bad decisions being made
More inclusive and better policy and implementation, representative of the needs and priorities of the community	Resources devoted to public participation will not be available to the actual projects for other uses

Source: (Irvin & Stansbury, 2004)

followed by a debate on how the local authority, in its role as event planner, should handle anticipated problems. As a result, the authors of this study dig deeper into the mitigation strategy for dealing with the pros and cons of public engagement in Malaysia. Its potential for use and its advantages carry considerable weight in the direction of environmentally and socially responsible growth. Therefore, it is crucial in establishing a suitable public involvement framework in Malaysia.

Public engagement in Malaysia is still below the threshold of acceptability (Ali & Arifin, 2019; 2020; Dola & Mijan, 2006; Nurudin et al., 2015). Several factors have been identified as contributing to this phenomenon (Ali & Arifin, 2019; Dola & Mijan, 2006), including a general lack of public understanding and familiarity with the local authority's public involvement system. Citizens' belief that their input makes no impact or difference at all discourages them from taking part in public deliberation in the future (Ali & Arifin, 2019). Social well-being and community work are two of the most important components of life in Malaysia, and both are directly influenced by public engagement (Gopal et al., 2021). Individuals, families, and communities all have a vested interest in fostering social well-being, and community service is a strategy for fostering that objective (Gopal et al., 2021). To encourage community engagement, it is crucial to understand the factors that contribute to people's social well-being. By addressing their fundamental needs and promoting social mobility, you can effectively foster participation and involvement in your community. Therefore, people in the community are free to grow into their full potential, participate in communal activities, and make positive contributions to the well-being of all members (Gopal et al., 2021).

Table 3 shows the success and weakness factors of public participation in Malaysia, which Ali and Arifin (2019) suggested, based on their studies on the factors contributing to the success and weakness of public participation in local plans at local authority in Malaysia. Furthermore, Ali and Arifin (2019) suggested that these findings, both success and weakness factors, should be further considered in proposing and measuring the framework model of public participation by the local authorities in Malaysia.

According to Creighton (2005), no one can design a public participation programme without being clear on which interpretation applies in their particular programme. Therefore, there are four major categories to describe the continuum of participation. Figure 2.4 shows the continuum of participation formulated by Creighton (2005), which is also widely used and referred to research conducted in the public participation niche. The continuum of participation formulated includes; inform the public, listen to the public, engage in problem solving and develop agreements.

The continuum of participation is further elaborated in the IAP2 spectrum of public participation (see Table 4). IAP2's spectrum of public participation is designed to assist the selection of the level

Table 3. Success and weakness factors of public participation in Malaysia.

Success Factors of PPE	Weakness Factors of PPE
Communication	Motivation
Process Management	Support
Social Learning	Lack of Trust
Publicity	Publicity
	Knowledge

Source: (Ali & Arifin, 2019)

Figure 1. Continuum of participation
Source: (Creighton, 2005)

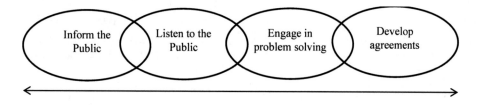

Table 4. IAP2 spectrum of public participation

	Inform	Consult	Involve	Collaborate	Empower
Public Participation Goal	To provide the public with balanced and objective information to assist them in understanding the problem, alternatives, opportunities and/or solutions.	To obtain public feedback on analysis, alternatives and/or decisions.	To work directly with the public throughout the process to ensure that public concerns and aspirations are consistently understood and considered.	To partner with the public in each aspect of the decision, including the development of alternatives and the identification of the preferred solution.	To place final decision making in the hands of the public.
Promise to the Public	We will keep you informed	We will keep you informed, listen to and acknowledge concerns and aspirations, and provide feedback on how public input influenced the decision.	We will work with you to ensure that your concerns and aspirations are directly reflected in the alternatives developed and provide feedback on how public input influenced the decision.	We will look to you for advice and recommendations into the decisions to the maximum extent possible.	We will implement what you decide.

Source: (IAP2, 2019)

of participation that defines the public's role in any public participation process. The spectrum is used widely, and it is found in public participation worldwide.

By laying out the commitment given to the public at each level of engagement, the spectrum demonstrates that varying degrees of participation are appropriate based on the decision's objectives, timeline, available resources, and level of concern (IAP2, 2019). Even though it is seen as a necessary first step towards complete public involvement, 'inform', the lowest level, contemplates only one-way contacts and is thus not considered public participation in any meaningful sense. As a result, from the outset of the process (during the 'consult' phase), public engagement is a two-way street, and citizens can expect to get real replies to their comments (Manroth et al., 2014).

Figure 2 shows a model proposed by Arnstein (1969): A ladder of Citizen Engagement. The ladder metaphor is eight-level (or rungs) from the lowest, which is 'manipulation', in which there is no participation; through 'consultation', in which involves some engagement; to the highest, 'citizen control', where citizens gain the highest degree of power over decision-making. Arnstein (1969) classifies the 'consultation' as tokenism; although this form allows the government to seek civil society's opinion on a specific issue, it retains full discretion to consider or ignore those opinions.

The observed models frame public engagement as a sort of civil society participation that lies between fully decentralised decision-making by local governments and complete result control by the latter. Local authorities, who are familiar with the constraints and rules that apply to them, should be given ultimate decision-making authority, as proposed by Creighton (2005). The genuine output of discussing an issue with stakeholder groups to enhance the quality of a decision, ensure an inclusion of the opinion of people affected by the policy, and so on, is what makes public participation meaningful (Arnstein, 1969). Therefore, when sufficient effort is made to involve key stakeholders, actively seek citizen feedback, and ensure participant contributions to the conclusion, public participation can be regarded as a powerful technique for citizen engagement.

This study also elaborated on the Public Consultation Index (PCI), which is primarily used to evaluate the process of public consultation, as well as to assess the success or failure of public participation and the degree to which it converges with best international practises and appropriate local standards (Jibladze et al., 2021). PCI is meant to assist relevant authorities and stakeholders in establishing public

Figure 2. Arnstein's ladder of citizen engagement
Source: (Arnstein, 1969)

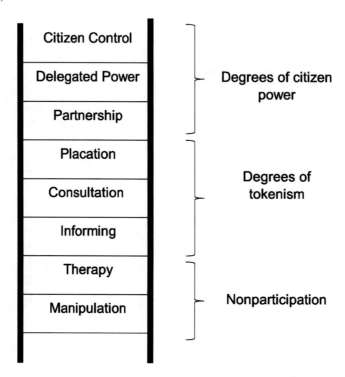

involvement best practices, and it facilitates comparison across policy documents and assessment of the behaviour of the coordinating agencies.

PCI is composed of six criteria, including accessibility, openness, the effectiveness of the public consultation process, accountability, diversity of participants, and public engagement/interest, as shown in Table 5.

According to Creighton (2005), the organiser, the landscape department, in this case, should play the prominent role as the organiser and the primary decision-maker. This is mainly because the landscape department is well-versed in the present restriction and obligation of the public parks project in Malaysia. Therefore, the role of the landscape department is undoubtedly essential and crucial in ensuring that the outcome of the PPE is rational and possible for its implementation. However, the PPE consists of four main factors, including the stages of development, public participation technique or format, group of public or stakeholders and concerns. In this research, the intention is to achieve a higher level of public involvement, as suggested by Arnsteins (1969) and IAP2 (2019), to empower the civil society in the decision-making process by determining the indicators on each of these four main factors of PPE. Consequently, this will affect the public motivation to be involved in the actual public participation for a future project of public parks in Malaysia on top of the benefits of first-hand exposure to the public in establishing a public participation process.

Table 5. The criteria of public consultation index (PCI)

Criteria	Aspect
1. Accessibility	• Announcement disseminated was accessible for diverse groups (language accessibility, clarity, etc.) • Announcement and/or policy brief were disseminated through multiple channels • Policy document/brief was accessible for diverse groups (language accessibility, clarity, etc.) • The process was adapted to the needs of diverse groups (pwd, ethnic minority, etc)
2. Openness	• Announcement on public consultations was openly available. • Policy document/brief was publicly available • Everyone involved / registered had an opportunity to provide feedback on a policy document • Everyone involved / registered had an opportunity to provide feedback on a policy document
3. Effectiveness of public consultation process	• The announcement was disseminated reasonably (one week) early before the event • Information in the announcement is sufficient • Public consultations were conducted in at least two formats (the document was sent on emails, discussions organised, posted online) • The multiple was of feedback mechanism were ensured • Sufficient time (minimum one week) was provided for feedback on policy document/brief • Public consultation was conducted at least at three different stages of policy development
4. Accountability	• Summary report on public consultation correspond to the requirement of AoG • Justified explanations of the accepted/ rejected feedback provided
5. Diversity of participants	• Equal representation of different genders among participants • Equal representation of minorities among participants • Concrete measures were taken to ensure diversity
6. Public engagement/interest	• Number of CSO/ individuals engaged (announcement) • Number of unique feedback contributors • Coordinating agencies' evaluation of CSO engagement • Feedback was provided within the set deadline

Source: (Jibladze et al., 2021)

Public Parks

Gibberd (1982) defines a public park as "an enclosed plot of land within or near a city or town that is ornamentally laid out and dedicated for public recreation." Cities are experiencing a rise in the need for public open spaces as their populations live longer, become more mobile, and spend more time relaxing. Adiati et al. (2018) write that public parks and green spaces are crucial for people to unwind and have fun. Collective memory and cultural memory are intrinsically linked to urban areas like public parks (Grilli et al., 2020; Tomlinson, 2021; Ujang et al., 2015). In addition, Ujang et al. (2015) explain that the concept of place attachment is situated within the psychological (emotion and sensation) and functional (dependence) domains of environmental experience, linking place attachment with the longing to remain in close proximity to the object attachment and the special feeling towards a specific location. People have indirect associations with these places because of their recollections and experiences there. Urban spaces have social-cultural importance because of the individuals who participated in the physical or verbal activities held there and the architecture and design aspects that made people feel welcome and at home there (Tomlinson, 2021).

It has been established that exposure to nature has a positive effect on people's mental and physical health, and this is especially true for those who live in or near densely populated areas. Therefore, it was proposed that public park designs of the future incorporate a variety of design variables and adapt to suit the changing demands of the public (Adiati et al., 2018). It is important that everyone be able to freely enter and move about in the public park (Adiati et al., 2018). According to Ahmad (2006), public parks have three main parts: the park itself, the park's services, and the park's landscape and architecture. Despite their close links to open space and recreational activities, these three parts are often treated separately. Public parks, as mentioned by Grilli et al. (2020), provide a number of health-enhancing benefits. It is possible that the public might respond similarly to the green areas seen in parks. Planners and policymakers might benefit from evidence of the precise qualities and design variables that support or encourage public usage of greenspaces (Grilli et al., 2020).

Public parks and other open places for recreation and amusement are thus crucial to the long-term viability of a city (Khaza et al., 2020). Ridings and Chitrakar (2020) state that the old urban design framework prioritised the dissemination of ideas and values through artistic expression. According to Ridings and Chitrakar (2020), this was accomplished through the use of conditioning and control strategies such emphasising the significance of central, civic, and sacred structures through the use of scale, decoration, and geometry. The National Landscape Department of Malaysia has developed a planned development framework (JLN, 2020) to guide the design of urban public spaces like public parks. Successful urban public space design relies heavily on the development framework, which plays a pivotal role in the collection, analysis, and synthesis of the necessary data. The designated landscape architect consultant uses this data while planning municipal green spaces. However, Ridings & Chitrakar (2020) argue that the numerous public space frameworks established in conventional cities are no longer relevant. The absence of active participation from the public in the established framework is a major contributing element. It was also discovered that the current planning framework for public parks in Malaysia does not adequately account for this scenario.

Research Method

The study on public perception of public participation exercises in designing public parks in Malaysia employed a quantitative research method, specifically utilising a survey questionnaire. The study gathered data from respondents who have visited either one of two public parks in Johor Bahru, Malaysia (Hutan Bandar Johor Bahru and Taman Merdeka). The sample size consisted of 393 participants from different age groups, genders and ethnic backgrounds. The data collected through the survey questionnaire was analysed using descriptive statistics to gain insight into the level of public participation exercise in designing public parks in Malaysia.

Unit Analysis and Respondents

The unit of analysis refers to the focus of the investigation to be carried out (Zikmund et al., 2013). For the purpose of this study, the unit of analysis refers to the individual, particularly the visitor or used the public parks in Johor Bahru, Malaysia. Each visitor who used the public parks located in Johor Bahru formed a respondent for this study. This study only considered the respondent that visited and/or individuals that used two different public parks located in Johor Bahru, which are Hutan Bandar Johor Bahru and Taman Merdeka. Visitors of public parks located in Johor Bahru are best positioned to observe and evaluate the essential factors in developing the framework for public participation in designing public parks in Malaysia.

RESULT AND FINDING

Demographic Detail

In these demographic details, the five dependent variables are also presented in its frequency value for each variable, followed by the frequency details of public participation exercise in public parks design, method for local authority to disseminate the public participation activity to the public and public preference in receiving the outcomes of the public participation activity from the local authority.

Table 6 shows the summary of the demographic characteristic of the sample. Each of these items is discussed in the subsequent topic.

Respondents of Public Participation Awareness in Designing Public Park in Malaysia

There are five indicators in public participation awareness in designing public park in Malaysia: (1) it creates awareness among public on sustainable development, (2) it demonstrates democratic governance, (3) it allows interaction between the public and the local authorities, (4) it promotes social leadership among the public, and (5) it encourages public involvement in public events.

The following are the discussion of the frequency tabulation of data received for each variable from the public participation awareness in designing public parks in Malaysia, which is also the dependent variable of this research. The results show in percentage tabulation are discussed in the following subtopics which are divided into five subtopics.

Table 6. Descriptive statistics of sample (N=393)

Item	Frequency	Percentage (%)
1. Age		
18-24	73	18.6
25-34	101	25.7
35-44	71	18.1
45-54	73	18.6
Above 54	75	19.1
Total	393	100
2. Gender		
Male	203	51.7
Female	187	47.6
Prefer not to say	3	8.0
Total	393	100
3. Nationalities		
Malaysian	393	99.99
Non-Malaysian	1	0.01
Total	393	100
4. Race / Ethnicity		
Malay / Bumiputra	275	70
Chinese	85	21.6
Indian	33	8.4
Total	393	100
5. Academic Qualification		
No formal education	20	5.1
SPM	138	35.1
STPM	25	6.4
Certificate	10	2.5
Diploma	45	11.5
Bachelor Degree	142	36.1
Master's Degree	7	1.8
Doctorate (PhD)	3	0.8
Others	3	0.8
Total	393	100
6. Frequency Visiting Public Parks		
Less than once a month	83	21.1
1-3 days a month	60	15.3
Once a week	62	15.8
2-3 days a week	63	16.0
4-7 days a week	125	31.8
Total	393	100

continued on following page

Table 6. Continued

Item	Frequency	Percentage (%)
7. Accompany to Public Parks		
Alone	94	30
With family	214	54.5
With friend	84	21.4
Others	1	0.3
Total	393	100
8. Time Visiting Public Parks		
6.00 am to 11.59 am	227	57.8
12.00 pm to 5.59 pm	36	9.2
6.00 pm to 7.59 pm	121	30.8
8.00 pm to 5.59 am	9	2.3
Total	393	100
9. Method to Go to Public Parks		
Car	237	60.3
Motorcycle	50	12.7
Taxi / E-hailing	9	2.3
Bus	2	0.5
Bicycle	6	1.5
Walking	89	22.6
Total	393	100

It creates awareness among the public on sustainable development.

Figure 3 displays one of the indicators, "it creates awareness among the public on sustainable development." The results indicate that 67.7% strongly agreed with the statement, followed by 23.9% who agreed, and 6.6% who moderately agreed. In total, 98.2% of respondents agreed with the statement, with the majority strongly agreeing. The public participation is an exercise that allow the public to directly contributes towards the decision-making process, therefore, the public participation in local development projects will expose the public on the knowledge of sustainable development hence enhance their awareness and it will also inject in public to caring for the maintaining of the development in the future (Feng et al., 2020; Yuliani et al., 2020). The exposure of the knowledge of sustainable development to the public will indirectly educate a public (Santé et al., 2019). This will result in a better public community, as the knowledge will lead to a better understanding and a betterment in awareness (Feng et al., 2020). In implementing any future policy which enhances the sustainable level of the country, an educated public will ease the process and it will affect an increase of percentage among the public in supporting the sustainable movement development.

It demonstrates democratic governance.

Figure 4 depicts one of the indicators that demonstrate democratic governance. The results show that, of 393 respondents, 50.4% strongly agree to the statement, followed by 24.7% agree, 18.3% moderately agree, 4.5% disagree and 2% strongly disagree. In general, it can be concluded that respondents agreed to the statement and majority of it is strongly agreed. Public participation strongly associated with the

Figure 3. It creates awareness among public on sustainable development

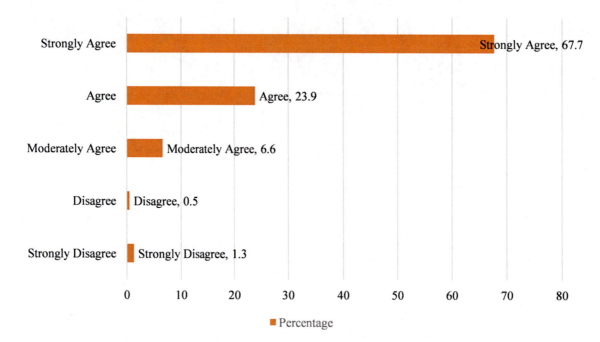

democratic governance and public participation is seen as a game changer in terms of decision making, shifting from top-down to bottom-up which to more participatory processes involving diversified actors (Feng et al., 2020; Liu et al., 2020; Pløger, 2021; Santé et al., 2019) and an ideal democratic is the public have a right to influence the decisions that affect them or the things they value (Bidwell & Schweizer, 2021). Therefore, public participation is proven to be a good exercise in enhancing the democratic governance and expanding its horizon by creating a bigger opportunity for the public to engage in the decision-making process by shifting the present top-down framework policy development to more participatory processes which involve the public.

It allows interaction between the public and the local authorities.

Figure 5 showcases one of the indicators that facilitate interaction between the public and local authorities. The results indicate that out of 393 respondents, 53.2% strongly agree with the statement, followed by 28.8% who agree, 14% who moderately agree, 3.1% who disagree, and 1% who strongly disagree. Therefore, the majority of respondents strongly agreed with the statement, indicating a significant level of agreement overall. The public participation activity facilitates interaction between the public and local authorities, enabling the exchange of knowledge and contributing to the decision-making process. This includes sharing knowledge about the local context, technical data, as well as public values and preferences (Bidwell & Schweizer, 2021; Liu et al., 2020; Pløger, 2021). The interaction between the public and the local authorities is important as the future local development will affect the local public in many aspects including identifying issues and conflict (Liu et al., 2020; Santé et al., 2019). Therefore, a good relationship between the public and the local authorities will also affect the better outcomes of the future projects involve (Liu et al., 2020; Pløger, 2021).

It promotes social leadership among the public

Figure 4. It demonstrates democratic governance

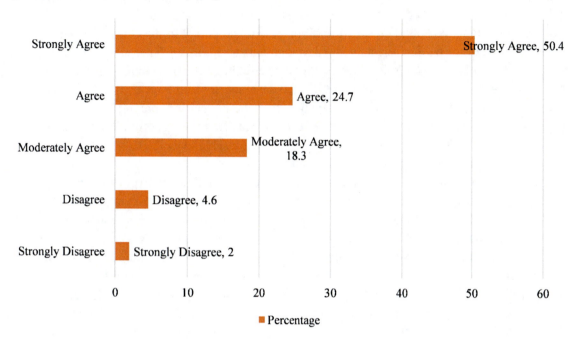

Figure 5. It allows interaction between the public and the local authorities

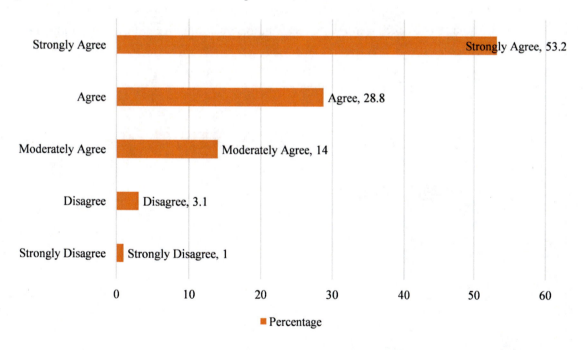

Figure 6 illustrates one of the indicators that promote social leadership among the public. The results reveal that out of 393 respondents, 60.1% strongly agree with the statement, followed by 24.9% who agree, 10.7% who moderately agree, 3.3% who disagree, and 1% who strongly disagree. This demonstrates that

Malaysians strongly agree on the significance of public participation in enhancing the role of the public as a driving force for sustainable development. Social leadership skills are reflecting the responsibility and awareness among the public towards the development and policy in the country. The importance and essential role of the public in sustainable development are discussed. Therefore, it is crucial to accurately identify and define the role of the public to ensure their effective contribution (Yuliani et al., 2020). Thus, the public participation exercise in local development framework will be able to create an opportunity for the public in Malaysia to actively participate in decision making and also to have the sense of responsibility in contributing in future development. This will benefit in promoting the social leadership among the public (Feng et al., 2020; Fry & Egel, 2021; Pløger, 2021).

It encourages public involvement in public events.

Figure 7 illustrates an indicator that focuses on "encouraging public involvement in public events." The results reveal that out of 393 respondents, 63.1% strongly agree with the statement, followed by 24.9% who agree, 8.7% who moderately agree, 2% who disagree, and 1.3% who strongly disagree. The majority of respondents agreed with the statement, with the highest percentage strongly agreeing. The public participation activity enhances public engagement in the decision-making process, resulting in a greater inclination for the public to participate in other public events. Active participation in public events organized by local government and authorities is crucial, as it serves as an initiative to foster and establish connections between the local authorities and the public (Liu et al., 2020; Pløger, 2021).

Furthermore, regarding public participation awareness, one respondent provided their perspective, stating that *'in Malaysia there is totally no or very minimal public participation arrangement by local authority. The local authority does what they think is good for them only'*. This response somehow reflects a gesture of frustration and hope for a public participation activity to take place in the development framework in Malaysia. The roles played by the local authority is to represent the public and to ensure

Figure 6. It promotes social leadership among the public

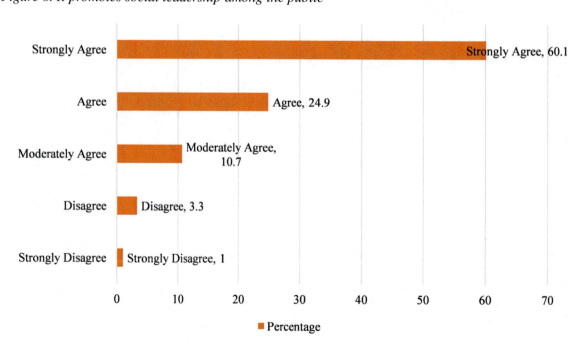

Figure 7. It encourages public involvement in public events

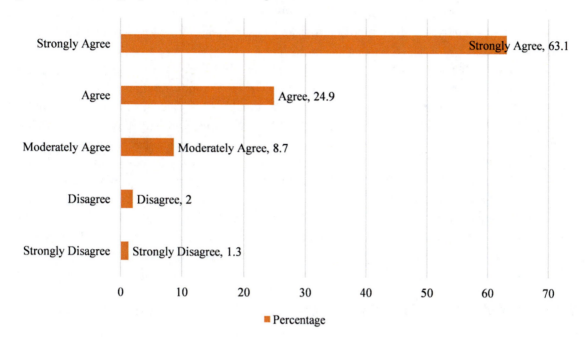

the public facility meeting the needs of the public, hence, the local authority has certain weightage in the scope of work to meet the needs of the public while planning and designing public infrastructure and facilities development including public park in Malaysia.

The percentage presented of each indicator shows that Malaysians in general have strong awareness of the importance and how essential public participation activities are. This also demonstrates Malaysia's readiness to incorporate public participation exercises in its future development. The positive response from the public supports the statement and highlights the beneficial outcomes of public participation. These include raising sustainable development awareness among the public, enhancing democratic governance, providing a platform for systematic interaction between the public and local authorities, fostering social leadership among the public, and promoting increased public involvement in public events. The public participation activity symbolizes a shared space, and its outcomes encompass self-discipline rooted in morals, ethics, and a shared understanding of the current situation in the local development context (Pløger, 2021). Acknowledging the need for public participation in landscape planning and management, it is recognized as essential (Santé et al., 2019).

Furthermore, the results validate the existence and significance of public participation awareness in Malaysia. As a result, this research delves deeper into the findings regarding the relationship between the independent variables and dependent variables.

Public Opinion on PPE Implementation Onto Public Parks Design

Public opinion was gathered regarding the implementation of public participation exercises (PPE) in the design of public parks in Malaysia. The perspective was assessed based on three main criteria, namely: (1) the significance of the role of residents/community associations in organising the PPE, (2) the significance of the role of residents or community members in participating in the association's implementation of the PPE, and (3) the significance of input from the PPE to the local authority in public parks projects. The questionnaire employed a five-point Likert scale measurement, ranging from "strongly disagree" to "strongly agree".

Table 7 presents the significance of various factors related to public participation exercises (PPE) in public park design, as perceived by the respondents. The results indicate that the role of resident's/community association in organizing the PPE has a mean value of 4.45, a median value of 5.00, and the highest percentage (61.6%) strongly agreeing with the statement. Similarly, the role of residents or community members in participating in the association's implementation of the PPE has a mean value of 4.39, a median value of 5.00, and the highest percentage (56.5%) strongly agreeing with the statement. Additionally, the input from the PPE to the local authority in public park projects has a mean value of 4.49, a median value of 5.00, and the highest percentage (63.1%) strongly agreeing with the statement. From these findings, it can be concluded that the collected data strongly support the three perspectives regarding PPE, including the significance of residents/community associations organizing PPE for public park projects, the importance of active public participation in the association's activities, and the essentiality of public feedback during the PPE for the local authority's consideration in designing public parks.

PPE is Essential to be Organised by the Resident's / Community Association

In Figure 8, the graph illustrates the significance of the role of resident's or community association in organizing public participation activities (PPE) for public park projects. The question asked was, "Is organizing public participation activities by the residents or community association essential for public park projects?" The data collected revealed that 61.6% of the respondents strongly agreed with the statement, followed by 26.7% who agreed, 8.1% who moderately agreed, 2% who disagreed, and 1.5% who strongly disagreed.

Public park projects serve as essential public facilities and infrastructure, designed to cater to various recreational activities and provide common amenities for the community. These parks are regarded as valuable community assets, and their presence in residential areas contributes to an increase in the value of nearby properties (Hayes & Dockerill, 2020). There is also a requirement on green area allocation of 15% out of total development area for residential masterplan required by the Town Planning in Malaysia. This 15% green area is mostly converted to public parks for the residents. Thus, these public park projects are highly related to the public as the end user rather than a single user, therefore, the public participation activity will allow an improvement of the public park design.

Table 7. Public opinion on PPE implementation onto public parks design

Item	N	Mean	Median	Highest Percentage %
Organisation of public participation activities by the residents or community association is essential for public parks projects	393	4.45	5.00	61.6% Strongly Agree
Becoming an active member for the residents or community association is essential to public participation activity	393	4.39	5.00	56.5% Strongly Agree
Public feedback during public participation activity is essential for the local authority consideration in designing g public parks projects	393	4.49	5.00	63.1% Strongly Agree

Figure 8. Graph of the significant of the role resident's / community association in organising the PPE

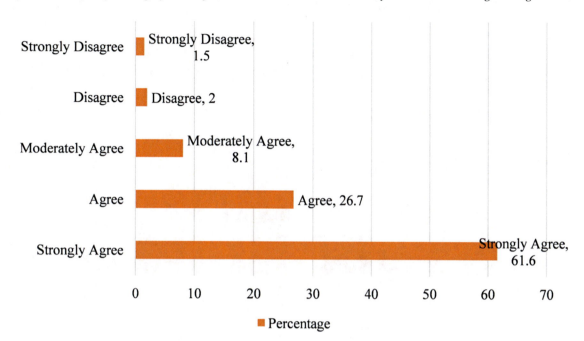

Becoming an Active Member in Residents Association is Essential for Public Participation.

In Figure 9, the graph illustrates the significance of the role of residents or the community in actively participating in the implementation of public participation activities. The respondents were asked about their opinion on the statement "Becoming an active member of the residents or community association is essential for public participation activity." The results indicate that the majority, with 56.5%, strongly agree with the statement. This is followed by 29.3% who agree, 11.5% who moderately agree, 2% who disagree, and 0.8% who strongly disagree.

This shows that the public do relate the importance of public participation activity and its significance to residents or community association. Hence, public participation will also enhance the engagement in residents' association and community association of a place and this will lead to a strong development of social capital. A strong social capital is associated with a better health society and an active engagement among the public is also encouraged to strengthen the social trust in a society (Saville, 2021).

Public Feedback is Essential in Designing Public Parks

Figure 10 presents the graph depicting the significance of input from public participation exercises (PPE) to the local authority in public parks projects. The question posed was "Is public feedback during public participation activity essential for the local authority's consideration in designing public parks projects?" The results of the frequency test indicate that the highest percentage, with 63.1%, strongly agreed with the statement. This is followed by 26.2% who agree, 8.4% who moderately agree, 1.3% who strongly disagree, and 1% who disagree.

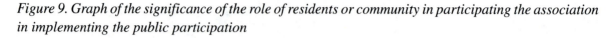

Figure 9. Graph of the significance of the role of residents or community in participating the association in implementing the public participation

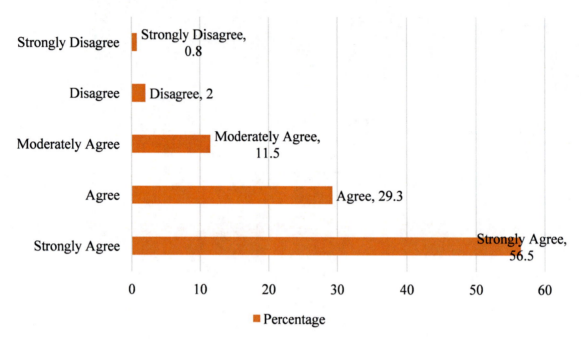

Figure 10. Graph of the significance of input from PPE to the local authority in public parks project

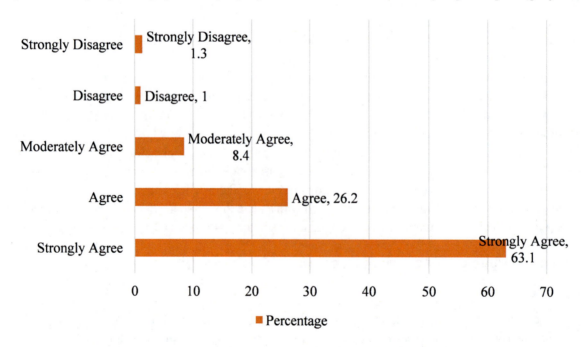

In this research, the Department of Landscape Architect, which is responsible for public park projects in Malaysia, is identified as the relevant local authority. The results indicate that the public believes that the local authorities should gather input from the public and synthesise the data before undertaking public park projects. There is strong support for involving the public as stakeholders in the decision-making process of designing public parks. This aligns with the trend observed over the past 50 years, where policy makers and environmental managers in democratic governance have embraced public participation in decision-making processes (Bidwell & Schweizer, 2021). Therefore, it is recommended for Malaysia's local authorities to implement a systematic public participation exercise in physical development projects across the country. Additionally, this research proposes an integrated design framework for public park design in Malaysia.

Despite the widespread support for public participation from scholars, policy makers, and practitioners, as well as the existence of laws and policies mandating its use, there remains a lack of consensus regarding the purpose of engaging the public in decision making. Different individuals and groups involved in a decision, whether as conveners or affected parties, may have varied justifications for advocating public participation, based on their underlying values or perceived stakes in the decision. These inconsistencies in goals among participants can potentially lead to conflicts or dissatisfaction with participatory processes. In order to improve decision processes and ultimately the outcomes, it is crucial for conveners and facilitators of such processes to strive towards better understanding and addressing the diverse goals of participants (Bidwell & Schweizer, 2021).

Thus, in proposing the public participation integrated design framework for public park design in Malaysia, the forthcoming analysis and findings are the proposed indicators for the integrated design framework. A public participation strategy is designed with the aim of ensuring that public opinions was taken into account from the beginning of the process and included in the final results (Santé et al., 2019). The public participation activity consists of: (1) integrating scientific knowledge and public participation, (2) including participation in every stage of the process, (3) involving stakeholder and relevant participants from the community and particularly, (4) incorporating the results of public participation in the results and content of the inventory in an explicit, direct and transparent manner (Santé et al., 2019).

Announcement of PPE

Figure 11 presents the results indicating the preferred methods for local authorities to disseminate public participation activities to the public. Out of 393 respondents, the highest percentage of 38% favored social media announcements, followed by 31% for traditional media, 12% for email, 9% for face-to-face communication, 7% for postage mail, and 3% for phone calls.

Therefore, based on the results it can be concluded that the most relevant methods to disseminate the public participation activity in designing public parks are through social media announcement, media, and email, as these three methods have the highest percentages. The remaining methods, namely face-to-face communication, postage mail, and phone calls, exhibited the lowest percentages, indicating a lesser preference among respondents. This could be attributed to the prevalence of modern communication technologies, particularly smartphones, which make the other three methods, namely social media announcements, traditional media, and email, more easily accessible and widely available.

Furthermore, postage mail, face-to-face interactions, and phone calls are not only time-consuming and energy-consuming for government servants but also more costly compared to the other three methods. According to the Malaysian Communications and Multimedia Commission, there are 19.2 million internet users in Malaysia, with 15.6 million of them being active Facebook users. Additionally, the majority of Malaysians have access to smartphones, with more than 85% of the population having such

Figure 11. Method for local authority to disseminate the public participation activity to the public

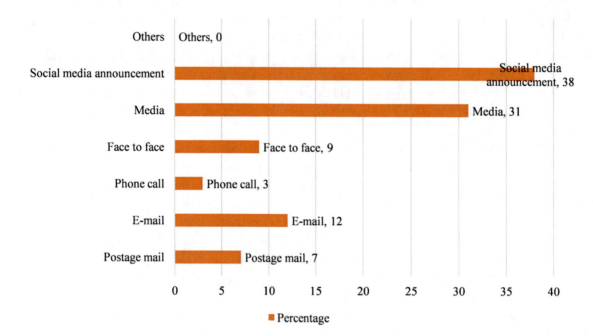

access. Internet data provided by telecommunication providers is also considered affordable, and approximately 64% of Malaysians are actively engaged in social media (Kumar et al., 2020). Therefore, the high availability of smartphones among Malaysians allows for a broader reach and accessibility.

Announcement of PPE Outcome

In Figure 12, the results indicate the public's preference for receiving the outcomes of the public participation activity from the local authority. Among the 393 respondents, the highest percentage, 70.2%, preferred online announcements through platforms such as websites and social media. This was followed by 19.3% who preferred receiving reports from resident's associations, 10.2% who preferred reports directly from the local authority, and a small percentage of 0.3% who opted for other methods.

Therefore, the preference in distributing the outcome of the public participation can be concluded by three main methods which are; (1) online announcement (website and social media), (2) resident's association report and (3) report by the local authority. Even though there are three main distribution methods, these three methods may inter-cross one another. The online announcement platform appears to be the most viable option, considering the high level of smart phone and internet accessibility among Malaysians. As a result, the reports from resident's associations and the local authority can also be disseminated through these online announcement platforms, such as official websites or social media accounts. However, it is important to acknowledge that different age groups have varying needs and capacities, particularly among the elderly population who may face difficulties in handling smartphones or accessing the internet. In such cases, the traditional method of providing printed reports by the resident's association and the local authority becomes necessary to cater to their requirements.

Figure 12. Public preference in receiving the outcomes of the public participation activity from local authority.

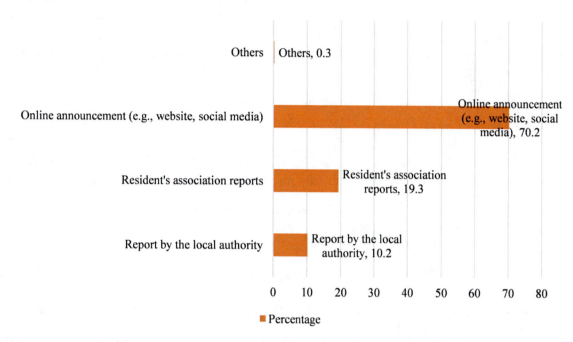

The resident's association report should be available and accessible at the resident's association resource centre, or should be exhibited on the wall mounted information wall. Similar to the local authority's report, the report should be accessible by the public. The report should be placed in a resource centre or archive which allows access to the public. The transparency, and the efficiency in managing the outcome is crucial, as the outcome of the public participation activity and its impact on the project involved will encourage the public in engaging more public participation activity. The local authority must ensure that the outcome of public participation as documented in the report does affect the projects involved.

CONCLUSION

The design and development of public parks have a significant impact on the well-being of communities. Therefore, understanding public perceptions and participation in designing these parks is crucial. It has been observed that the level of public participation in Malaysia is quite low, which highlights the need for increased awareness and better communication between stakeholders and the public. Perception plays a crucial role in understanding citizens' needs and their overall satisfaction with urban parks. To ensure the provision of effective and satisfactory public services, it is crucial to involve park user groups in the planning process, taking into account their views and opinions. In conclusion, future research should focus on understanding the factors that contribute to low public participation in Malaysia's park planning process. Additionally, more emphasis should be placed on creating and implementing strategies that promote increased community participation in park design. This will not only result in better parks but also in healthier and more engaged communities that value public spaces. Furthermore, assessing and understanding the public's sentiment about public spaces can be strengthened through extensive citizen consultation and engagement strategies such as walking tours and mobile stations for community input. Overall, it can be said that by creating opportunities for public participation in the development of public spaces such as parks, Malaysia can create a sense of empowerment amongst its citizens, improve the social and environmental aspects of its urban areas, and ultimately contribute to the creation of healthy, equitable communities.

REFERENCES

Abidin, N. I., Zakaria, R., Aminuddin, E., Saar, C. C., Munikanan, V., Zin, I. S., & Bandi, M. (2016). Malaysia's Local Agenda 21: Implementation and approach in Kuala Lumpur, Selangor and Johor Bahru.

Acuti, D., Bellucci, M., & Manetti, G. (2020). Company disclosures concerning the resilience of cities from the Sustainable Development Goals (SDGs) perspective. *Cities (London, England)*, *99*, 102608. doi:10.1016/j.cities.2020.102608

Adiati, M., Lestari, N., & Wiastuti, R. (2018). Public parks as urban tourism in Jakarta. IOP Conference Series: Earth and Environmental Science, Ahmad, M. H. (2006). The Architecture of Public Park: Fading the Line between Architecture and Landscape. *Jurnal Alam Bina, 8*. 10.1088/1755-1315/126/1/012063

Ahmadi, D., Rachmiatie, A., & Nursyawal. (2019). Public Participation Model for Public Information Disclosure. *Jurnal Komunikasi: Malaysian Journal of Communication*, *35*(4), 305–321. doi:10.17576/JKMJC-2019-3504-19

Ali, M. A. M., & Arifin, K. (2019). Factors contributing to the success and weakness of public participation in local plans at local authority malaysia: a review. *Asian Journal of Environment, History and Heritage 3*(2).

Ali, M. A. M., & Arifin, K. (2020). Penglibatan Awam Sebagai Pembuat Keputusan Dalam Rancangan Tempatan Pihak Berkuasa Tempatan (Public Participation as a Decision Maker in Local Plans at Local Authority). *Akademika, 90*(1).

Anuar, M. I. N. M., & Saruwono, M. (2018). Obstacles of public participation in the design process of public parks. *Journal of Asian Behavioural Studies*, *3*(6), 147–155. doi:10.21834/jabs.v3i6.247

Arnstein, S. (1969). A ladder of citizen participation. [In.]. *Journal of the American Institute of Planners*, *35*(4), 216–224. doi:10.1080/01944366908977225

Aziz, N. A. A., Mokhtar, M. D. M., Raman, T. L., Saikim, F. H., & Nordin, N. M. (2020). Use Of Urban Green Spaces: A Case Study In Taman Merdeka. Johor Bahru.

Bakar, J. A. (2002). *A design guide of public parks in Malaysia*. Penerbit UTM.

Bhandari, P. (2020). A guide to operationalization. *Scribbr, 1*(03), 2021.

Bidwell, D., & Schweizer, P. J. (2021). Public values and goals for public participation. *Environmental Policy and Governance*, *31*(4), 257–269. doi:10.1002/eet.1913

Brophy, V. (2014). Building environmental assessment—a useful tool in the future delivery of holistic sustainability. The 2014 world sustainable building conference, Barcelona: Paper, Castillo-Villar, R. G. (2020). Identifying determinants of CSR implementation on SDG 17 partnerships for the goals. *Cogent Business & Management, 7*(1), 1847989. doi:10.1080/23311975.2020.1847989

Chear, S. L. S., Hamzah, S. H., Yusof, N. M., & Nordin, N. (2021). Parents and neighbourhood engagement to enhance the quality of maintenance and safety of playgrounds in private kindergartens. *Jurnal Pendidikan Awal Kanak-kanak Kebangsaan, 10*(1), 1–15.

Christoffersen, S. E., & Sarkissian, S. (2009). City size and fund performance. *Journal of Financial Economics, 92*(2), 252–275. doi:10.1016/j.jfineco.2008.06.001

Cooper, D., & Schindler, P. (2014). Business Research Methods.© The McGraw– Hill Companies.

Creighton, J. L. (2005). *The public participation handbook: Making better decisions through citizen involvement.* John Wiley & Sons.

Dola, K., & Mijan, D. (2006). Public participation in planning for sustainable development: Operational questions and issues. *International Journal on Sustainable Tropical Design Research & Practice, 1*(1), 1–8.

DOSM. (2021). *Department of Stastistics Malaysia Official Portal.* Malaysia's Official Statistics. https://www.dosm.gov.my/v1/index.php?r=home/index&menu_id=dHVYa1N5WVZPeTU2cXF6dHNZYVRtdz09

Eckerd, A., & Heidelberg, R. L. (2020). Administering Public Participation. *American Review of Public Administration, 50*(2), 133–147. doi:10.1177/0275074019871368

Feng, L., Wu, Q., Wu, W., & Liao, W. (2020). Decision-maker-oriented vs. collaboration: China's public participation in environmental decision-making. *Sustainability (Basel), 12*(4), 1334. doi:10.3390u12041334

Fonseca, L. M., Domingues, J. P., & Dima, A. M. (2020). Mapping the Sustainable Development Goals Relationships. *Sustainability (Basel), 12*(8), 3359. doi:10.3390u12083359

Fry, L. W., & Egel, E. (2021). Global Leadership for Sustainability. *Sustainability (Basel), 13*(11), 6360. doi:10.3390u13116360

Fu, Y., & Ma, W. (2020). Sustainable urban community development: A case study from the perspective of self-governance and public participation. *Sustainability (Basel), 12*(2), 617. doi:10.3390u12020617

Ghiasi, S., Hassanzadeh, M., & Forghanifar, B. (2015). Role of public participation in Sustainable City.

Gibberd, F. (1982). Harlow: The design of a new town. *The Town Planning Review, 53*(1), 29. doi:10.3828/tpr.53.1.m44nk27n01w15383

Gopal, P. S., Tamizi, N. E. A., Shaed, M. M., Malek, N. M., & Yahaya, M. H. (2021). Kesejahteraan dalam Pembangunan Komuniti Program Perumahan Rakyat (PPR): Suatu Pemerhatian Awal. [MJSSH]. *Malaysian Journal of Social Sciences and Humanities, 6*(10), 292–302. doi:10.47405/mjssh.v6i10.1065

Grilli, G., Mohan, G., & Curtis, J. (2020). Public park attributes, park visits, and associated health status. *Landscape and Urban Planning, 199*, 103814. doi:10.1016/j.landurbplan.2020.103814

Grimmer, A., & Wille, R. (2020). Integrated Design Process. In *Designing Droplet Microfluidic Networks* (pp. 127–133). Springer. doi:10.1007/978-3-030-20713-7_9

Hajmirsadeghi, R. S., Shamsuddin, S., Bin Lamit, H., & Foroughi, A. (2013). Design's factors influencing social interaction in public squares. *European Online Journal of Natural and Social Sciences*, 2(4), 556–564.

Hassan, A. M., & Lee, H. (2015). The paradox of the sustainable city: Definitions and examples. *Environment, Development and Sustainability*, 17(6), 1267–1285. doi:10.100710668-014-9604-z

Hayes, S. J., & Dockerill, B. (2020). A Park for the People: Examining the creation and refurbishment of a public park. *Landscape Research*, 1–14.

Humphreys, D., Singer, B., McGinley, K., Smith, R., Budds, J., Gabay, M., Bhagwat, S., de Jong, W., Newing, H., & Cross, C. (2019). *SDG 17: Partnerships for the Goals-Focus on Forest Finance and Partnerships*.

IAP2. (2000). *International Association of Public Participation*. IAP2. https://www.iap2.org/404.aspx?404;http://iap2.org:80/practitionertools/index.shtml]

IAP2. (2019). *IAP2 Public Participation Spectrum*. Internation Association for Public Participation. https://www.iap2.org.au/resources/spectrum/

Irvin, R. A., & Stansbury, J. (2004). Citizen participation in decision making: Is it worth the effort? *Public Administration Review*, 64(1), 55–65. doi:10.1111/j.1540-6210.2004.00346.x

Jekabsone, I., & Sloka, B. (2017). The role of municipality in promotion of well-being: development of public services. *Economic and Social Development: Book of Proceedings*, 713-721.

Jibladze, G., Romelashvili, E., Chkheidze, A., Modebadze, E., & Mukeria, M. (2021). *Assessing public participation in policymaking process*.

Jiménez-Aceituno, A., Peterson, G. D., Norström, A. V., Wong, G. Y., & Downing, A. S. (2020). Local lens for SDG implementation: Lessons from bottom-up approaches in Africa. *Sustainability Science*, 15(3), 729–743. doi:10.100711625-019-00746-0

JLN. (2020). *Pelan Induk Lanskap Majlid Perbandaran dan Majlis Daerah Malaysia*. JLN. http://www.jln.gov.my/resources/index/user_1/TextDocuments/DokumenPenerbitan/ManualPIL/Manual_Pelan_Induk_Landskap_1.pd

Johnson, C. (2014). *Local civic participation can help reinforce the legitimacy of the democratic system*. Democratic Audit Blog.

JPBD. (2016). *Perancang Bandar Dan Desa*. JPBD. https://www.townplan.gov.my/index.php?option=com_docman&view=flat&layout=table&category%5B0%5D=48&category_children=1&own=0&Itemid=427&lang=ms&limit=20&limitstart=20

Kamaruddin, N., & Rogers, R. A. (2020). Malaysia's democratic and political transformation. *Asian Affairs: An American Review*, 47(2), 126–148. doi:10.1080/00927678.2020.1715046

Khaza, M. K. B., Rahman, M. M., Harun, F., & Roy, T. K. (2020). Accessibility and service quality of public parks in Khulna City. *Journal of Urban Planning and Development*, *146*(3), 04020024. doi:10.1061/(ASCE)UP.1943-5444.0000589

Krejcie, R. V., & Morgan, D. W. (1970). Determining sample size for research activities. *Educational and Psychological Measurement*, *30*(3), 607–610. doi:10.1177/001316447003000308

Kumar, J., Konar, R., & Balasubramanian, K. (2020). The impact of Social Media on Consumers' purchasing behaviour in Malaysian Restaurants. *Journal of Spatial and Organizational Dynamics*, *8*(3), 197–216.

Kumar, V., Jones, E., Venkatesan, R., & Leone, R. P. (2011). Is market orientation a source of sustainable competitive advantage or simply the cost of competing? *Journal of Marketing*, *75*(1), 16–30. doi:10.1509/jm.75.1.16

Lanang, W. N. W. W., & Hassan, M. S. (2021). Crime Prevention Program in Perak through the Role of the Royal Malaysian Police (PDRM) and the Community. *Perspektif: Jurnal Sains Sosial Dan Kemanusiaan*, *13*(1), 85–101.

Larco, N. (2016). Sustainable urban design–a (draft) framework. *Journal of Urban Design*, *21*(1), 1–29. doi:10.1080/13574809.2015.1071649

Lawson, L., & Kearns, A. (2010). Community engagement in regeneration: Are we getting the point? *Journal of Housing and the Built Environment*, *25*(1), 19–36. doi:10.100710901-009-9168-7

Liu, L., Chen, J., Cai, Q., Huang, Y., & Lang, W. (2020). System Building and Multistakeholder Involvement in Public Participatory Community Planning through Both Collaborative-and Micro-Regeneration. *Sustainability (Basel)*, *12*(21), 8808. doi:10.3390u12218808

Liu, Z. (2007). *Internet Based PPGIS for Public Involved Spatial Decision Making*. ProQuest.

Madanipour, A. (2011). Sustainable development, urban form, and megacity governance and planning in Tehran. In *Megacities* (pp. 67–91). Springer. doi:10.1007/978-4-431-99267-7_4

Magis, K. (2010). Community resilience: An indicator of social sustainability. *Society & Natural Resources*, *23*(5), 401–416. doi:10.1080/08941920903305674

Manaf, H. A., Mohamed, A. M., & Lawton, A. (2016). Assessing public participation initiatives in local government decision-making in Malaysia. *International Journal of Public Administration*, *39*(11), 812–820. doi:10.1080/01900692.2015.1035788

Manroth, A., Hernandez, Z., Masud, H., Zakhour, J., Rebolledo, M., Mahmood, S. A., Seyedian, A., Hamad, Q., & Peixoto, T. (2014). *Strategic framework for mainstreaming citizen engagement in World Bank Group Operations: Engaging with citizens for improved results*. World Bank.

Marzukhi, M. A., Omar, D., & Leh, O. L. H. (2012). Re-appraising the framework of planning and land law as an instrument for sustainable land development in Malaysia. *Procedia: Social and Behavioral Sciences*, *68*, 767–774. doi:10.1016/j.sbspro.2012.12.265

MBJB. (2016a). *Info Bandar*. MBLB. https://www.mbjb.gov.my/ms/pelawat/info-bandar

MBJB. (2016b). *Sukan dan Rekreasi.* MBJB. https://www.mbjb.gov.my/ms/rakyat/perkhidmatan/sukan-rekreasi

Mehmet, O. (2013). *Development in Malaysia (Routledge Revivals): Poverty, Wealth and Trusteeship.* Routledge. doi:10.4324/9781315823416

Michels, A. (2019). Participation in citizens' summits and public engagement. *International Review of Administrative Sciences, 85*(2), 211–227. doi:10.1177/0020852317691117

MMC. (2016). *Local Agenda 21 (LA21) Program.* MMC. https://www.mpm.gov.my/en/mpm/program-local-agenda-21-la21

Moten, A. R. (2019). The 14th general elections in Malaysia: Ethnicity, party polarization, and the end of the dominant party system. *Asian Survey, 59*(3), 500–520. doi:10.1525/as.2019.59.3.500

Muhamad Khair, N. K., Lee, K. E., & Mokhtar, M. (2020). Sustainable City and Community Empowerment through the Implementation of Community-Based Monitoring: A Conceptual Approach. *Sustainability (Basel), 12*(22), 9583. doi:10.3390u12229583

Mustafa, M. (2019). *Environmental law in Malaysia.* Kluwer Law International BV.

Ngah, K., Mustaffa, J., Zakaria, Z., Noordin, N., & Sawal, M. Z. H. M. (2011). Formulation of Agenda 21 process indicators for Malaysia. *Journal of Management and Sustainability, 1*(1), 82. doi:10.5539/jms.v1n1p82

Ngesan, M. R., Karim, H. A., Zubir, S. S., & Ahmad, P. (2013). Urban community perception on night-time leisure activities in improving public park design. *Procedia: Social and Behavioral Sciences, 105,* 619–631. doi:10.1016/j.sbspro.2013.11.065

Nurudin, S. M., Hashim, R., Rahman, S., Zulkifli, N., Mohamed, A. S. P., & Hamik, S. A. (2015). Public participation process at local government administration: A case study of the Seremban Municipal Council, Malaysia. *Procedia: Social and Behavioral Sciences, 211,* 505–512. doi:10.1016/j.sbspro.2015.11.067

Payne, S. R., Mackrill, J., Cain, R., Strelitz, J., & Gate, L. (2015). Developing interior design briefs for health-care and well-being centres through public participation. *Architectural Engineering and Design Management, 11*(4), 264–279. doi:10.1080/17452007.2014.923288

Pløger, J. (2021). Politics, planning, and ruling: The art of taming public participation. *International Planning Studies, 26*(4), 1–15. doi:10.1080/13563475.2021.1883422

Putra, F. (2019). Examining the link between democracy, social policy, and inclusive development in South-East Asia. *Asian Social Work and Policy Review, 13*(3), 226–241. doi:10.1111/aswp.12175

Putra, F., & Aminuddin, M. F. (2020). Democracy and Social Policy in Southeast Asia: A Comparative Process Tracing Analysis. *The Journal of Politics, 5*(2), 221–258.

Rao, T., & Mustapa, S. I. (2020). A review of climate economic models in Malaysia. *Sustainability, 13*(1), 325.

Ridings, J., & Chitrakar, R. M. (2020). Urban design frameworks, user activities and public tendencies in Brisbane's urban squares. *URBAN DESIGN International,* 1–17.

Ridings, J., & Chitrakar, R. M. (2021). Urban design frameworks, user activities and public tendencies in Brisbane's urban squares. *URBAN DESIGN International*, *26*(3), 272–288. doi:10.105741289-020-00113-x

Sakip, S. R. M., Akhir, N. M., & Omar, S. S. (2015). Determinant factors of successful public parks in Malaysia. *Procedia: Social and Behavioral Sciences*, *170*, 422–432. doi:10.1016/j.sbspro.2015.01.003

Sakip, S. R. M., Akhir, N. M., & Omar, S. S. (2018). The Influential Factors of Successful Public Parks in Malaysia. *Asian Journal of Behavioural Studies*, *3*(12), 195–205. doi:10.21834/ajbes.v3i12.135

Salleh, N. H. (2009). *Kesanggupan Membayar Oleh Pengunjung Terhadap Hutan Bandar Di Daerah Johor Bahru*.

Santé, I., Fernández-Ríos, A., Tubío, J. M., García-Fernández, F., Farkova, E., & Miranda, D. (2019). The Landscape Inventory of Galicia (NW Spain): GIS-web and public participation for landscape planning. *Landscape Research*, *44*(2), 212–240. doi:10.1080/01426397.2018.1444155

Saville, C. W. (2021). Not belonging where others do: A cross-sectional analysis of multi-level social capital interactions on health and mental well-being in Wales. *Journal of Epidemiology and Community Health*, *75*(4), 349–356. doi:10.1136/jech-2020-215188 PMID:33161384

Sekaran, U., & Bougie, R. (2019). *Research methods for business: A skill building approach*. John Wiley & Sons.

Sondermann, E., & Ulbert, C. (2021). Transformation through 'Meaningful' Partnership? SDG 17 as Metagovernance Norm and Its Global Health Implementation. *Politics and Governance*, *9*(1), 152–163. doi:10.17645/pag.v9i1.3656

Spijkers, O., & Honniball, A. (2015). Developing Global Public Participation (1): Global Public Participation at The United Nations. *International Community Law Review*, *17*(3), 222–250. doi:10.1163/18719732-12341305

Szabó, M., Csete, M. S., & Pálvölgyi, T. (2018). Resilient Regions From Sustainable Development Perspective. *European Journal of Sustainable Development*, *7*(1). doi:10.14207/ejsd.2018.v7n1p395

Tajuddin, Z., Sum, S. M., Zainol, R. M., & Jusoh, H. (2019). Penentu Sosial Penglibatan Komuniti Dalam Projek Kebun Komuniti Bandar: Social Determinants of Community Involvement In Urban Community Garden Projects. *Sarjana*, *34*(1), 56–68.

Tibbalds, F. (2012). *Making people-friendly towns: Improving the public environment in towns and cities*. Taylor & Francis. doi:10.4324/9780203469521

Tomlinson, C. (2021). City of culture, city of transformation: Bringing together the urban past and urban present in The Hull Blitz Trail. *Urban History*, *48*(2), 351–363. doi:10.1017/S0963926819001172

Too, L., & Bajracharya, B. (2015). Sustainable campus: Engaging the community in sustainability. *International Journal of Sustainability in Higher Education*, *16*(1), 57–71. doi:10.1108/IJSHE-07-2013-0080

Ujang, N., Moulay, A., & Zakariya, K. (2015). Sense of well-being indicators: Attachment to public parks in Putrajaya, Malaysia. *Procedia: Social and Behavioral Sciences, 202*, 487–494. doi:10.1016/j. sbspro.2015.08.195

UN. (2015). *Sustainable Development Goals.* UN. https://sdgs.un.org/goals

UNDP. (2020). *Human Development Report 2020.* UN. https://report.hdr.undp.org/

Vallance, S., Perkins, H. C., & Dixon, J. E. (2011). What is social sustainability? A clarification of concepts. *Geoforum, 42*(3), 342–348. doi:10.1016/j.geoforum.2011.01.002

Wampler, B., & Touchton, M. (2019). Designing institutions to improve well-being: Participation, deliberation and institutionalisation. *European Journal of Political Research, 58*(3), 915–937. doi:10.1111/1475-6765.12313

Welsh, B. (1996). Attitudes toward democracy in Malaysia: Challenges to the regime? *Asian Survey, 36*(9), 882–903. doi:10.2307/2645537

Yaakob, H. (2012). Penyertaan awam: kejayaan dan kegagalannya dalam perancangan pembangunan. *Jurnal Pengurusan Awam*, 67-84.

Yuliani, S., Hardiman, G., & Setyowati, E. (2020). Green-roof: The role of community in the substitution of green-space toward sustainable development. *Sustainability (Basel), 12*(4), 1429. doi:10.3390u12041429

Zal, W. A. (2018). The practice of community potential mapping as a guideline for community development in Malaysia. *Community Development Journal: An International Forum, 53*(2), 321–339.

Załęczna, M. (2018). Public participation in land use planning and the building of a civil society. *Real Estate Management and Valuation, 26*(2), 23–32. doi:10.2478/remav-2018-0013

Zalite, K. A. (2002). *Understanding a theory of public participation in park planning for Nunavut.* University of Guelph.

Zikmund, W. G., Carr, J. C., & Griffin, M. (2013). *Business Research Methods (Book Only).* Cengage Learning.

Chapter 22
Local People's Participation in Cultural Heritage Conservation and Management

Ahmad Nasrolahi
University of Turin, Italy

ABSTRACT

Public participation in cultural heritage, with particular regard to conservation, has been a concern ever since the Venice Charter, and it still is to this day. This approach has also been highlighted in World Heritage documents. The Faro Convention adopted a shift in focus from the conservation of cultural heritage values to the value of cultural heritage for society. Accordingly, cultural heritage institutions inevitably have to apply a participatory approach in order to achieve sustainable conservation. Moreover, a number of papers have focused on the importance of public participation in heritage conservation and tourism management. This chapter studies the concept of people's participation in cultural heritage conservation and management in international charters and documents. It also takes into account various methods and approaches in Human-Computer Interaction studies, which have valuable resources for user engagement in designing services by people for people, in order to propose an effective, applicable people-participation approach to cultural heritage management.

INTRODUCTION

Public participation in cultural heritage, with particular regard to conservation, has been a concern ever since the Venice Charter (1964) and it still is to this day (Europe, 2017). This approach has also been highlighted in World Heritage Documents. The Faro Convention (Europe, 2005)adopted a shift in focus from the conservation of cultural heritage values to the value of cultural heritage for society. In this case, it is necessary to engage the public and local people in all stages of cultural heritage conservation and management (Dian & Abdullah, 2013). According to this convention, cultural heritage institutions inevitably have to apply a public participatory approach. Moreover, several papers have focused on the importance of public participation in heritage conservation and tourism management (Kong & Yeoh, 1994; Steinberg, 1996).

DOI: 10.4018/978-1-6684-8253-7.ch022

The term 'public participation' refers to a variety of formal processes that incorporate public concerns, needs, and values into governmental decisions. Public participation consists of identifying public concerns and preferences and addressing them during decision-making through techniques such as public meetings and hearings, advisory committees, interactive workshops, interviews, questionnaires, focus groups, and other methods (Creighton, 2018). Public participation applies different values and aspects for reaching the best results.

According to the core values provided by the International Association for Public Participation-IAP2, it is widely accepted that people who are affected by a decision have the right to be involved in the decision-making process. This public participation must assure that the people's concern will affect the decision. In addition, "public participation promotes sustainable decisions by recognizing and communicating the needs and interests of all participants, including decision-makers" (IAP2, 2019). The engagement of those affected by, or interested in, a decision must be facilitated by interactive methods for achieving maximum participation. In this respect, useful and trustworthy information will help people to participate in a meaningful way. Finally, the results of participation must be published for communicating to participants how their input affected the decision.

People's Participation in Cultural Heritage-Global Context

The Operational Guideline for the Implementation of the World Heritage Convention (Operational Guideline) encourages the state parties to involve local people and national populations in various stages of cultural heritage conservation and management. It states that the state parties must adopt an effective method of public participation to ensure the maximum engagement of a wide variety of stakeholders in a sustainable approach. This concept may be interpreted differently. Like Iran's cultural heritage associations established by the Ministry of Cultural Heritage, Handicrafts, and Tourism, the role of the people has been completely removed from its constitution. They assume it is possible to replace the people's participation with the local authorities' participation.

The latest version of the Operational Guidelines (2021) encourages state parties to adopt a gender-equity and human-rights-based participation approach in the identification, nomination, conservation, and management processes of world heritage properties. It declares that a wide variety of rights holders and stakeholders, including local and regional governments, site managers, local communities, indigenous peoples, NGOs, and other interested parties should be involved in all stages of the conservation process. World Heritage properties can support ecosystem benefits and biological and cultural diversity to enhance environmental and cultural sustainability. This ability is also capable of improving the quality of life and well-being of local communities by encouraging and promoting equitable, inclusive, and effective community-based participation that engages indigenous peoples and stakeholders. This community-based participation aims to enhance capacity building and research; increase public awareness, understanding, and appreciation of the need to preserve cultural and natural heritage; improve the role of World Heritage in community life; and increase the equitable, inclusive, and effective participation of local and national populations, including indigenous peoples in the protection and presentation of heritage (Committee, 2021).

The concept of community participation in cultural heritage issues dates back to the ratification of the World Heritage Convention in 1972. Although the Convention did not make a direct reference to this term, it adopts a general policy aimed at giving cultural and natural heritage a function in community life. This idea has been enhanced over time in charters and international documents (Srijuntrapun,

Fisher, & Rennie, 2018). In 1975, the Amsterdam Declaration (ICOMOS, 1975) was probably the first international consensus on community engagement in cultural heritage management.

The Amsterdam Declaration concerned the social dimensions of heritage management as the main principle. It mentioned that considering social factors is the key to successfully integrating conservation. The declaration also stated that conservation is not a matter just for experts; the support of public opinion is a vital element for the effective management of cultural heritage. It was explicitly stated that people should take an active role in every stage of the work, from design to decision-making, by helping them to understand the situation, clarifying values, and publishing the entire plan. The declaration suggests that the local authorities should call for citizens' participation. They should provide a meeting place for the public to consult together. Furthermore, the decisions of local authorities should be put in the public eye for learning, discussing, and assessing the purposes of the local communities in the form of exhibitions, opinion polls, and the use of mass media. They also should facilitate the formation and efficient functioning of voluntary associations for conservation. In addition, it stated that one of the most important requirements for effective heritage management is the education of young people on environmental issues and their involvement in conservation.

Later on, in 1987, the Washington Charter (ICOMOS, 1987) recommended that to encourage people to participate and to be involved, it is necessary to set up an information program for all residents, including children of school age. The Charter is concerned that the participation and involvement of local inhabitants and their support are essential for the success of the conservation program and that the locals, first of all, should be taken into account. After that, in 1990, the Lausanne Charter (Elia, 2020) repeatedly recommended that the participation of indigenous people and local cultural groups is essential for the protection and conservation of cultural heritage based upon access to the knowledge necessary for decision-making, which is an important element in integrated protection. It is therefore defined that local participation should be actively encouraged insofar as the protection and management of cultural heritage should be entrusted to the local people.

In 2003, the Convention for the Safeguarding of the Intangible Cultural Heritage (UNESCO, 2003) recognized the importance of indigenous communities in the safeguarding, maintenance, and re-creation of intangible cultural heritage. It emphasized that the state parties should encourage the widest possible participation of communities, groups, and relevant non-governmental organizations in identifying and defining the various types of intangible cultural heritage as well as in its management.

Two years later, the Faro Convention (2005) mainly focused on people and human values at the heart of an expanded and multidisciplinary concept of the cultural heritage (Fojut, 2018). As highlighted in the Universal Declaration of Human Rights (Assembly, 1948), the rights related to cultural heritage are inherent in the right to participate in cultural life, in all aspects of the interaction between people and the environment through time. It defined the heritage community as the people who value specific aspects of cultural heritage which they wish to sustain and transmit to future generations. The Convention emphasizes lifelong education and training, unlimited access to information, shared responsibilities, and cooperation in the monitoring of the process of cultural heritage management and conservation. The table shows the concept of people's participation in international documents and charters (Table 1).

Although people's participation in cultural heritage management is relatively a new concept, it has been well-developed in other interdisciplinary and multidisciplinary sciences that cultural heritage studies can borrow and implement. Human-Computer Interaction (HCI) provides valuable experience in user engagement in designing a system or service that is applicable to people's participation in cultural

Table 1. Public's participation in international documents

Types of Participation	Level of Participation	1964 Venice Charter	1972 Heritage Convention	1975 Amsterdam Declaration	1987 Washington Charter	1990 Lausanne Charter	1996 Underwater Heritage ICOMOS	2001 Underwater Heritage UNESCO	2002 Budapest Declaration	2003 Intangible Heritage	2003 E.C.C.O Professional Guidelines	2005 Faro Convention	2005 European Cultural Heritage	2018 New European Agenda for Culture
Real Participation	Citizen Control											✓	✓	✓
	Delegation													
	Partnership			✓						✓	✓			
Symbolic Participation	Placation													
	Consultation					✓		✓	✓					
	Informing				✓		✓							
Non-participation	Therapy		✓											
	Manipulation	✓												

heritage management. Why not use the HCI approach in cultural heritage if people are the true users of cultural heritage and cultural heritage management and conservation is a service for people?

Before the emergence of Web 2.0, public participation was based on face-to-face communication in the forms of interviews, meetings, workshops, voting, etc. (Agency, 2022). In 2011, The Recommendation on the Historic Urban Landscape (The HUL Recommendation) highlights the implementation of traditional and innovative tools adapted to local contexts, including civic engagement tools, knowledge, and planning tools, regulatory systems, and financial tools. HUL also emphasizes the integration of cultural heritage conservation, management, and planning strategies into local development processes at a local level to bring about effective protection of natural and cultural heritage. These tools aim to engage a diverse cross-section of stakeholders to empower them; protect the integrity and authenticity of attributes; reflect social, environmental, and cultural values; and support innovative income-generating development (UNESCO, 2011).

Methods in People Participation

The importance of the strong voices of citizens in social issues drove researchers to think about the meaning of unheard voices in the decision-making process. It started in the 1960s within the political context and spread out to other disciplines such as industry, urban planning, computer sciences, human rights, etc. in different parts of the world, simultaneously. In computer science until the late 1980s, most programs were influenced by management principles that controlled the process of program design. The method they used was called the waterfall model, which means the management designed a program with no input from those we today call users.

The concept of users has emerged with the appearance of micro, mini, and desktop computers. In the early 1980s, when Computer-Human Interaction attempted to find how user interfaces could be designed, HCI was established on traditional programming, including a set of procedures to help designers think about users' thoughts. Instead of involving users in the process, they asked users to test out an interface, and they focused on eye movement or keystrokes.

This concept developed when new technologies were introduced in the workplace, for instance, using computers in companies based on knowledge-based strategies focused on standardizing and simplifying interfaces. Although the management procedures were widespread, the Scandinavian workers' movement led to workers' rights to information and codetermination over the work conditions. Consequently, different action projects have been launched to bridge the gap between new technologies and users (Kensing & Greenbaum, 2013).

Human-Computer Interaction and People Participation

HCI includes a wide variety of methods and processes for the involvement of users in designing a system, such as action research, cooperative system design, user-centered design, codesigning, experience-centered design, participatory design, socially engaged art practice, community-based participatory design, and human-centered design, respectively. The concept of involving the users in the design phase originally dated back to the 1970s, when Scandinavian countries encountered a worker movement to deal with the problems raised by utilizing new technologies in the industry. Since then, researchers have attempted to involve the final users in the design process as early as possible to empower workers (Bødker, Ehn,

Sjögren, & Sundblad, 2000). There are various methods of involving people in cultural heritage conservation and management including:

Action Research

According to Kurt Lewin (1890–1947), action research is a study that compares the circumstances and results of various types of social action and research that supports social action, which is an iterative process of planning, action, and fact-finding about the result of the action. He argued that planning in general terms begins with a general idea that must be examined in the first place by a fact-finding process. Consequently, the next two steps will be identified; the overall plan and how to execute the first step of the plan. He highlighted that in social management, planning, action, and fact-finding must proceed in a spiral of steps (Lewin, 1946). Later on, action research was widely used in HCI.

Action research in HCI refers to a set of actions to be executed within a community engagement to enhance the quality of life and social well-being. During this community collaboration, the research questions, data analysis, and processes have been created, which needs people's commitment to be involved equally in all stages of the research (Hayes, 2011). Similar to grounded theory, knowledge and learning emerged through the research. Action research is typically action-focused and its method is participatory. In grounded theory, the researcher theorizes but the actions are left to the people. Action research requires establishing a relationship cycle between the researcher and the participant (Dick, 2003). Some researchers argue that action research is research with people rather than for or about people. However, it is effective in specific contexts and at local levels (Heitlinger, 2017).

Cooperative System Design

Cooperative or participatory design is looking for a way to establish a collaboration of people with various skills in designing a system by highlighting workplace activities from multiple viewpoints. It requires users and designers to actively work together. It tried to combine the Scandinavian and American philosophies in participatory design to support and promote users' interests through an interdisciplinary study, including humanities, social sciences, and computer science. They indeed emphasized human actors rather than human factors.

Co-Designing

Although communication with the potential users to understand their real needs and wishes was a goal, they were also looking for active engagement of users in the design process. The results showed that there are probably different meanings from system designers' perspectives as outsiders and people involved in day-to-day activity. In addition, engaging people to take part creatively in design activities is completely new to users and is not easy. The users and designers are not able to entirely understand each other, thereby it requires them to close their experiences together. Greenbaum and Kyng provided several ideas to bridge the gap between users and designers, including mutual learning; using familiar tools for the users in the design process; considering the users' experience and the effect of using new designs on work practice; and starting "the design process in the practice of the users" (Greenbaum & Kyng, 2020).

User-Centered Design

In the United States, user-centered design emerged in the 1970s when people were allowed to participate in the informing, ideating, and conceptualizing activities in the design phase, which led to the evolution of the co-designing process. The co-design process emphasized that user-centered design from an expert's perspective was the central purpose. This approach tries to involve trained researchers in collecting data from passive users who participate in instructed tasks and/or provide their opinions on product ideas that were primarily created by others. The method is distinguishable from the expertise and attitudes of the practitioners. The users have been modified as the customers, and the focus has been shifted from product and service to personalized consumer experiences. This method allowed people to customize their own goods or services. The participants were carefully selected among elite groups, and the roles of user, researcher, and designer have changed.

The users in the user-centered design were passive. The researchers extracted knowledge from theories, observations, and interviews. Then the designers added their technological knowledge to the design process. In co-designing, the users sometimes become co-designers based on their skills and creativity. The researchers, who acted as translators between the users and the designers, became facilitators. The researchers facilitated the different levels of creativity by leading, guiding, and providing frameworks to encourage people to participate in the process. Designers were responsible for undertaking creative processes, filling in the gaps left by lacking information and being able to make critical decisions in the absence of all the information they needed (Sanders & Stappers, 2008). These changing roles raise various issues. For instance, participants have different levels of creativity; thereby, they need appropriate tools to express their creativity. In this case, it is required to involve a specific group of people who may not represent the majority. Moreover, it is not possible to listen to the voices of marginalized people who are deliberately ignored. The researchers require a high level of social skills to lead, guide and frame the participants in the different levels of creativity. Although user-centered design became widespread in the 1990s, it was not able to address the complexity of design in the next decades. However, it has driven the design process in the new landscape such as interaction design, service design, and transformation design based on applying traditional design techniques to social and economic challenges (Sanders & Stappers, 2008).

Experience-Centered Design

Peter Wright and John McCarthy (2010) expanded on user-centered design and codesigning to include the ethical and political ideals of democracy, equality, and choice in the design process. They emphasized the richness of human experiences with available technologies as new technologies like mobile computing, social media, and localized-customized applications emerged. Because of the widespread use of computers in family, social, community, and leisure life, experience-centered design is more focused on people's lived and felt experiences that are mediated by digital media and new ways of communication and information. The approach concerned "giving people the chance to have a richer life, including people who might otherwise feel excluded, and ensuring that everybody has a chance to have their say, especially those who often feel voiceless" to make new technologies accessible and usable for everybody.

This method attempted to reflect people's desires, values, and feelings in the design process to create a usable, effective, efficient, satisfying, and easy-to-learn product. In this respect, it requires developing a transparent and simple computer interface. The designers and developers also need to have a deep understanding of what end-users really want; how they currently get their work done; and whether they understand and use the system that will be designed for them. Some scholars in experience-centered design highlighted the importance of the user experience by considering the fact that "all experiences grow out of previous experiences and help shape future experiences; that is that experience as a process is both continuous and cumulative." This method is applicable in diverse disciplines, ranging from social actions, health, and cultural heritage to the education system, art galleries, and museums.

The key points in human and HCI's interactions are: concentrating on how individuals interpret their experiences; recognizing the user and the designer as co-creators of the experience; recognizing the individual as a component of a social network of relationships (self-other) through which experience is co-constructed; and recognizing the individual as a caring agent, imagining opportunities, making original decisions, and acting. Although experience-centered design provides a valuable discourse in considering human values, desires, and real needs in the design process, the problem is that there is no clear and straightforward approach to implementing the method, which makes it more complicated. Each researcher has to design their own research approach and style (Wright & McCarthy, 2010).

Participatory Design

According to the Routledge International Handbook of Participatory Design, participatory design is defined as "a process of investigating, understanding, reflecting upon, establishing, developing, and supporting mutual learning between multiple participants in collective reflection-in-action. The participants typically undertake the two principal roles of users and designers, where the designers strive to learn the realities of the users' situation while the users strive to articulate their desired aims and learn appropriate technological means to obtain them" (Simonsen & Robertson, 2013). The participatory design approach is looking for genuine participation in design. It believes that former traditional user empowerment methods such as user-centered design and one-way data gathering are not able to achieve genuine participation (Kensing & Greenbaum, 2013). Participatory design is a comprehensive series of research, methods, and theories on the inclusion of affected people by a system in the decision-making processes.

The epistemology and methodology of action research, participatory design, and community-based participatory design have been merged to establish socially engaged art practice by emphasizing the ethics and aesthetics of sociocultural interaction in the form of social events including workshops, performance arts, and involving communities. Based on the nature of this approach, it provides a method for better understanding the current and future complex challenges, including climate change, environmental sustainability, immigration, and population issues, aimed at improving public awareness about sociocultural problems (Clarke, Briggs, Light, Heitlinger, & Crivellaro, 2014).

Community-Based Participatory Design

One of the relatively recent themes in participatory design is community-based participatory design, which focuses on designing for, with, and by communities. There is an ongoing trend of producing lower cost, smaller size, improved capacity, stronger connectivity, and deeper penetration into everyday life, providing the potential to apply participatory design approaches in community contexts. This technological trend, accompanied by the importance of social services and civil society, is able to address societal issues including sustainable development, environmental protection, cultural heritage preservation, medical service, and so forth. According to DiSalvo et al., this approach went out of context and addressed issues of the formal organizational workplace, such as factories, offices, hospitals, etc. (DiSalvo, Clement, & Pipek, 2012).

The internet of things and new media provide an opportunity to implement an innovative approach to effective user interaction. Through human-centered design, museums and cultural heritage institutions are also seeking a way to engage visitors in their exhibitions. The human-centered design aims at designing an exhibition or art gallery based on visitor needs and interests. This method extensively applies new, innovative, and interactive technologies such as video walls, touchscreens, interactive flipbooks, and video components to encourage visitors to engage (Hanlee, 2019). Unfortunately, museums and cultural heritage institutions prefer to work on visitor interpretation and visitor engagement to attract more visitors rather than community and local people participating in the conservation and management processes. This is unfortunate not for encouraging more visitors but for ignoring the affected people who are living in or around the cultural heritage institutions.

For example, community-based participatory research is one of the approaches extracted from community-based participatory design. Like the community-based participatory design, this process is a collaborative method of research driven by equitable partnerships of community members, academic researchers, and organizational representatives. This partnership framework aims to increase "the value of the research product for all parties." This approach facilitates the translation of research and leads to positive and sustainable community improvement. Even though community-based participatory research has been extensively applied in the public health research (Coughlin, Smith, & Fernandez, 2017), it is capable of being implemented in other cultural and social contexts. These terms are also defined as synonyms of community participation, including "citizen oversight; citizen participation and bottom-up planning; civil society; collaboration; community deliberation; community development; community empowerment; deliberative democracy; open government; public participation; public policy" (Lachapelle & Austin, 2014).

Digital Platforms and Cultural Heritage Institutions

In the digital and social media age, people are accustomed to using portable internet devices instead of desktops. Smartphones and their applications are a new and rapidly expanding industry and they have a global positive impact. They are running on small hand-held mobile devices which are transportable, simple to use, and accessible from anywhere and at any time. Consequently, a large number of people use mobile applications for contacting friends, browsing the internet, file management, document creation, entertainment, and so on (Islam, Islam, & Mazumder, 2010).

Today, the current world population is 7.937 billion. While 7.26 billion have mobile phones (including both features and smartphones), around 6.648 billion are using smartphones. It means that 83% of people around the world have access to smartphones. Surprisingly, the mobile connections rate is 10.57 billion, which means "there are 2.64 billion more mobile connections than people worldwide" (Group, 2020). There is 1.8 billion active iOS (Warren, 2022) and 2.5 billion active Android mobiles in the world (InMobi, 2021). According to Statista, more than two billion users are world widely using Android. More than 230 billion mobile applications have been globally downloaded in 2021, and a little bit more than 90% of users used chat applications in the third quarter of the same year. On average, consumers spent around 8 Euro on mobile applications in the second quarter of 2021 (Statista, 2021).

In Iran itself, among the total population (84.52 million in January 2021), less than 60 million have access to and are using the internet. In addition, more than 131 million mobiles have been officially registered by the end of 2020 which is equivalent to around 155% of the total population (Kemp, 2021). While Facebook, YouTube, Telegram, Twitter, Blogger, Snapchat, Netflix, Hulu, and Medium are fully blocked, but still 36 million are using these social media. In 2020, individuals using the internet are 84.11% of the total population (Group, 2020).

A mobile application, more usually abbreviated as an app, is a form of application software created specifically to run on mobile devices like smartphones and tablets. Users of mobile applications frequently receive services that are comparable to those obtained through personal computers. Apps are often small, discrete software modules with constrained capabilities. The App Store, which houses thousands of programs for the iPhone, iPad, and iPod Touch, is where this use of app software first gained popularity. A mobile application may also be referred to as an iPhone app, a smartphone app, a web app, or an online app (Techopedia, 2020).

Web 2.0 (participatory Wen, people-centered Web, Social Web, and read/write Web) provides a more interactive collaboration in engaging the users more effectively in user-generating content. It consequently formed social media such as Myspace, Flicker, YouTube, Wikipedia, Facebook, and other sorts of social applications (Murugesan, 2007). Onward, many cultural heritage professionals, institutions, and scholars are using social media as a tool for public participation to have a community-based platform for facilitating users' interaction with cultural heritage. Social media likewise works as crowd-sourcing and big data resources. A large number of museums and cultural heritage institutions are using social media. Typically, users can upload and share their images and stories or comment on a specific post (Ginzarly, Roders, & Teller, 2019).

According to the International Telecommunication Union (ITU) report, it is estimated that 4.1 billion people (more than 53%) have connected to the internet by the end of 2019 (ITU, 2021) and the COVID-19 situation in early 2020 has increased the number of users during the block out time. In order to avoid the Coronavirus, more than 85,000 cultural heritage institutions worldwide (around 90%) closed their doors and nearly 13% of museums may never reopen their doors. Besides the economic impact of these closures, it has particularly affected social life. The museums are playing a vital role in promoting education, inspiration, and dialogue. They also enhance social cohesion, foster creativity, and are conveyors of collective memory. In addition, they are a key driver in the sustainable economic development (UNESCO, 2020).

During the quarantine, mostly between February and July 2020, the cultural heritage institutions inevitably brought their life to the internet. The main "real" activities of the museums have had to transform into the 'virtual'; online collections, 360° tours, virtual museums, online publications, digital exhibitions, remote participation, etc. Consequently, museums have increased their activity on the internet to keep interacting with their users. In Canada for instance, according to Ontario Museums Associations' website (Association, 2020), there are more than 650 cultural heritage organizations in Ontario itself. Among them, 642 organizations are accessible via the internet, and a bit more than 80% are utilizing social media platforms, according to their websites. Based on this online survey, the most favorable platforms for those organizations are Facebook, Twitter, Instagram, YouTube, LinkedIn, Pinterest, and Flicker, consecutively. A bit less than four out of five have an institutional page on Facebook, 64% on Twitter, and half of them are available via Instagram. The proportion of YouTube and LinkedIn are approximately 35 and 10 percent, respectively. The ratio of other social media platforms like Pinterest, TripAdvisor, and Flicker is just 5%. While around one-fifth of cultural heritage organizations do not appear on the internet, 82% have more than one profile on social media and again Facebook is at the top. The majority of organizations have more than three links to their social networks.

Although cultural heritage organizations are increasingly using social media as a tool for community engagement purposes over the world, the problem is that mentioned social media are not able to meet the demands of the community engagement approach. The Royal Ontario Museum has 118,848 followers on the Facebook page (royalontariomuseum-ROM, 2020), for example. By considering the last one hundred posts between March 27th and August 12th, 2020, the midpoint of likes and comments are 90 and 6 per post respectively, and the engagement rate is 0.08. On Twitter, the situation is even worse. More than 205,400 people are following the ROM Twitter page (ROMtoronto, 2020), surprisingly, the average number of comments on the last hundred Tweets, between May 5th and August 12th, 2020, is 0.85, not even a single comment for each Tweet. The midpoint of likes is around 22 per Tweet. The engagement rate is 0.01 per tweet.

This situation is not related to the size and fame of the cultural heritage organizations. For instance, more than 2.5 million people have followed the Louvre Museum page on Facebook (museedulouvre, 2020). The average like and comments are 3141 and 100 per post and the interaction rate is 0.12%. This museum has also more than 1.4 million followers on Twitter (MuseeLouvre, 2020). The midpoint of likes and comments are 177 and 0.22 respectively. The interaction rate is 0.012!

Another example is the Guelph Museums in Ontario, Canada. The Guelph Museums profiles are accessible through Facebook and Twitter (guelphmuseums, 2020). The average of likes and comments per post (the last hundred posts between April 18th and August 16th, 2020) on Facebook with 2,409 followers are 12 and 0.6 respectively. The ratio of interaction is 0.49 with 4,017 followers on Twitter, and the proportion of likes and comments is 7.8 and 0.27 percent, for the last hundred tweets between March 31st and August 16th, 2020. Here, the interaction ratio is 0.19%, much higher than the average (Table 2).

The interaction rate (or engagement rate) is the number of interactions (like, comment and share) divided by the account size which is the number of followers (Garmur, 2020). According to Statista, during the second quarter of 2020, the average Facebook page fan engagement with posts on a page was 0.21. Video posts drew the highest level of engagement from page fans, having an interaction rate of 0.26 percent (statista, 2020). In general, the engagement rate on Twitter is 0.08 (Table 3).

Despite the growing use of online tools to engage the public, in many cases, the number of participants is too low, most participants engage infrequently and the connection between participation and

Table 2. Engagement rate of three museums on Facebook

Cases	Facebook Followers	Average Likes	Average Comments	Engagement Rate	Average Rate
Royal Ontario Museum (CA)	118,848	90	6	∇0.08	0.21
Louvre Museum (FR)	2,569,076	3141	100	∇0.12	0.21
Guelph Museums (CA)	2,409	12	0.6	Δ0.49	0.21

Table 3. Engagement rate of three museums on Twitter

Cases	Twitter Followers	Average Likes	Average Comments	Engagement Rate	Average Rate
Royal Ontario Museum (CA)	205,400	22	0.85	∇0.011	0.08
Louvre Museum (FR)	1,400,000	177	0.26	∇0.012	0.08
Guelph Museums (CA)	4,017	8	0.27	Δ0.19	0.08

authorities is unclear. There are also important concerns regarding the level of participation, unequal power among participants and between participants and authorities, and lack of online civic engagement skills (Lyons, 2017). Moreover, these so-called social media are not originally designed for community engagement purposes (Dollarhide, 2019). Thereby, they are not able to be used as a comprehensive tool in different steps of community engagement. These steps mostly are informing the community, exploring and explaining the projects or issues, opening a discussion room, obtaining feedback, collecting data, building capacity, developing collaboration, and making a clear decision. Internet-based engagement enhances the techniques utilized to engage the community, it is not a replacement (Lyons, 2017). Undeniably, it must not be forgotten that the values of social media lie in improving users' knowledge and understanding of cultural heritage as well as raising public awareness, which is an effective medium in a social, cultural, and political campaign functioning as a virtual public space. Thus, it is clear that social media are inappropriate technology for achieving the purposes of a people-centered approach in cultural heritage management because these platforms are not able to meet the needs and interests of involved stakeholders in cultural heritage issues.

Stakeholders Analysis

The engaged stakeholders in a given cultural heritage site are divided into three main categories; community of place, community of interest, and community of practice. In each category, the stakeholders are:

- Community of place, namely local people living in the core zone, buffer zone, and other urban areas as public;
- Community of interest, namely local cultural heritage NGOs (Non-Governmental Organizations), media, and private sectors;
- Community of practice, namely Cultural Heritage Research Institutions, Municipality, experts, Governmental Cultural Heritage Organizations, and Administration of World Heritage Protection.

Community of place refers to a group of people who share a common connection to a specific geographic location. This includes people who live, work, or otherwise spend time in a particular place and who have developed a sense of identity, belonging, and attachment to that place. Community of place is important when it comes to people's participation in managing cultural heritage because it can help make sure that decisions about how to manage cultural heritage sites and artifacts take into account the needs and points of view of the people who are most directly affected by them. Effective engagement of a community of place in cultural heritage management involves recognizing and respecting their unique experiences, values, and perspectives. This means working together with local people, businesses, and community groups to find out their priorities and concerns and come up with ways to manage cultural heritage that are in line with their goals and dreams.

Involving a community of place in cultural heritage management can also help to build a sense of ownership and pride in cultural heritage sites and artifacts and promote a greater understanding and appreciation of the cultural significance of these resources. It also helps make cultural heritage conservation and management more sustainable and fairer by involving those who have the most direct connection to and impact on these resources.

Community of interest refers to a group of people who share a common interest or concern, often related to a particular issue or topic. It means a group of people, organizations, or other stakeholders who all care about the management and preservation of cultural heritage sites and artifacts. This is in the context of people taking part in managing cultural heritage. Engaging a community of interest in cultural heritage management can be valuable for a number of reasons. These groups often have specialized knowledge or expertise related to cultural heritage management and can offer important insights and perspectives that can inform decision-making and management strategies. Also, these groups may have a stake in how cultural heritage resources are managed and may be able to offer help and resources for efforts to protect cultural heritage.

Engagement with a community of interest can involve a range of activities, including consultation, collaboration, and co-creation. This could mean asking for feedback on plans for managing cultural heritage, giving people chances to help make these plans, and building partnerships to help with the conservation and management of cultural heritage. Involving a community of interest in cultural heritage management can also help to build a sense of shared responsibility and accountability for the preservation of cultural heritage resources. By recognizing how important these resources are and getting different groups involved in their management and preservation, we can make cultural heritage conservation more inclusive, sustainable, and fair.

Community of practice refers to a group of individuals who share a common expertise in a particular field and who engage in ongoing learning, knowledge exchange, and collaboration to improve their collective knowledge and practice. Community of practice is a term for a group of professionals, experts, or practitioners who have specialized knowledge and skills related to cultural heritage management. This term is used in the context of people taking part in managing cultural heritage. Engaging a community of practice in cultural heritage management can be valuable for a number of reasons. These individuals often have significant expertise and knowledge related to cultural heritage conservation and management and can provide valuable insights and guidance on best practices, standards, and new developments in the field.

Also, these people may have worked on similar cultural heritage projects or sites in the past and can share their knowledge about the unique challenges and opportunities of managing cultural heritage resources. Engagement with a community of practice can involve a range of activities, including professional development, training, mentorship, and knowledge sharing. It means giving training and education on how to protect and manage cultural heritage; holding conferences or workshops to help people share knowledge and work together; or creating online communities and resources for people to keep learning and sharing. Involving a community of practice in cultural heritage management can also help promote the professionalization of the field and build a strong and sustainable network of professionals and practitioners in the field. By including people with different backgrounds and levels of experience in decision-making and management, we can help protect cultural heritage in a way that is more informed, creative, and effective.

These three main stakeholders can be divided into two main categories, internal and external: internal stakeholders are those people susceptible to the direct effect of a decision; external stakeholders are those indirectly involved with the cultural heritage site. Internal stakeholders are living within (or by) the site and external stakeholders are engaged in coordination, funding, resourcing, and publication of the issues related to related heritage sites. Figure 1 shows an example of a stakeholder analysis of people participating in cultural heritage conservation and management

Figure 1. Example of stakeholder analysis for recognizing the main and secondary sectors in a participatory approach

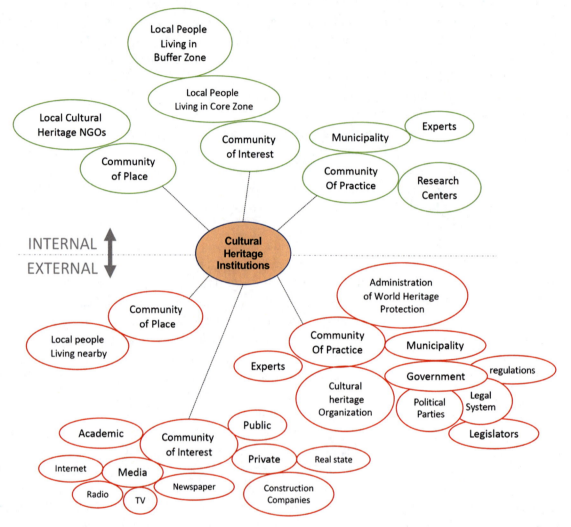

Planning in People Participation

There are different approaches to public participation, which started with Arnstein's Ladder of Citizen Participation (Arnstein, 1969). The ladder of participation defines the differentiation between participation and involvement. According to Arnstein, there are different levels of participation, ranging from manipulation to citizen control. This model casts doubt on whether each stage of public participation (for example, informing) can be considered a form of participation in and of itself. Later on, the ladder was transformed into the wheel of participation by the South Lanarkshire Council and Scott Davidson in 1998 (Davidson, 1998). Then it was developed and adapted for different sciences and fields.

It must not be forgotten that the wheel of participation is not a selective plan. The wheel of participation proposes a master planning system that must be applied as a whole and is based on information, consultation, participation, and empowerment. This approach minimizes the problems of the ladder by providing a responsive approach to achieving clear objectives without needing to climb to the top of the ladder. The entire process of public participation is depending on building trust and capacity, which are both long-term projects (Figure 2).

In the context of public awareness, indirect training could refer to a form of public education or communication that seeks to indirectly influence people's attitudes, beliefs, or behaviors. This could involve providing accurate information or experiences that indirectly impact people's perceptions or

Figure 2. Adopted wheel of participation for cultural heritage management, based on the South Lanark-shire Council model
(Davidson, 1998)

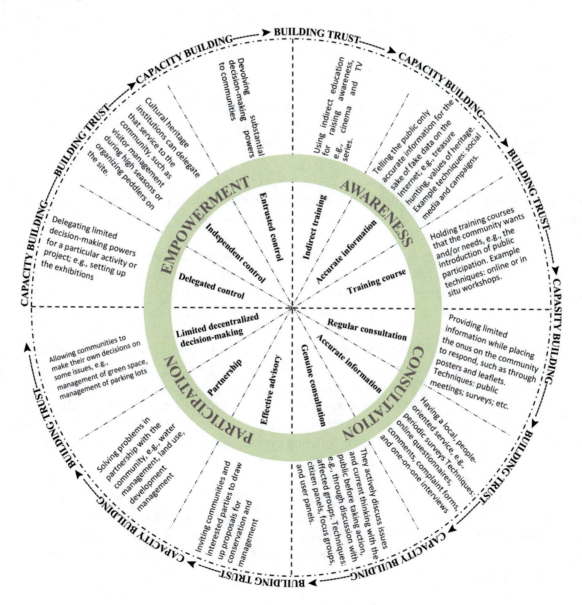

understanding of cultural heritage conservation and management rather than directly instructing them on what to think or do. It can be an effective approach for cultural heritage conservation, as it can help foster a deeper understanding of and appreciation for heritage sites and artifacts. For example, a cultural heritage institution might use an indirect training approach by hosting an educational event that showcases the value of local cultural resources rather than explicitly telling attendees what actions to take to protect those resources.

Some examples of indirect education in cultural heritage conservation and management are as follows:

- Storytelling: sharing stories about the history and significance of cultural heritage sites and artifacts can help to create a connection between people and these places or objects. By weaving in details about the culture and values of the people who created or used the heritage sites, storytellers can help to convey a deeper sense of meaning and importance.

- Artistic expression: creative works like paintings, sculptures, or music can be used to indirectly educate people about cultural heritage. By incorporating themes or motifs from cultural heritage sites or artifacts, artists can help to create a sense of connection and appreciation for these important pieces of history.

- Interactive experiences: providing hands-on or interactive experiences can be an effective way to indirectly educate people about cultural heritage. For example, a museum exhibit might allow visitors to touch or handle replicas of artifacts, which can help convey a sense of the materials, textures, and craftsmanship involved in creating the original pieces.

Indirect education approaches like these can be effective because they engage people on an emotional or experiential level rather than simply presenting information or facts. By creating a deeper sense of connection and appreciation, these approaches can help inspire people to take action to protect and preserve cultural heritage sites and artifacts.

Consultation is an important aspect of engaging people in cultural heritage management. It can help to ensure that the perspectives and needs of the local community are taken into account when making decisions about the management of cultural heritage sites and artifacts. The following are a few crucial factors to take into account for effective public participation in cultural heritage management and consultation:

- Timing: consultation should occur early enough in the process to allow for meaningful input but not so early that it is unclear what the specific issues or decisions are that need to be discussed. It's also important to provide sufficient notice and time for people to prepare and participate.

- Accessibility: consultation should be accessible to all members of the community, including those with limited English proficiency, disabilities, or other barriers to participation. Making sure everyone can take part can be helped by offering translation services, sign language interpretation, or other accommodations as needed.

- Engagement: consultation should be designed to engage people in meaningful discussion rather than simply presenting information or gathering feedback. Giving people a chance to talk, ask questions, and give feedback can help them feel like they own the project and support it.

- Follow-up: it is important to provide feedback to the community about how their input was incorporated into the decision-making process and to follow up with any actions or decisions that were made. This can help build trust and accountability and encourage ongoing engagement and participation.

Overall, consultation can be a powerful tool for engaging people in cultural heritage management. By involving the community in decision-making processes and building relationships based on trust and mutual respect, consultation can help to ensure that cultural heritage sites and artifacts are managed in a way that is respectful and responsive to the needs and perspectives of the people who care about them.

Participation is a critical component of people's participation in cultural heritage management. It involves actively involving individuals and communities in the planning, implementation, and evaluation of cultural heritage management initiatives. Here are a few key considerations for effective participation in cultural heritage management:

- Inclusivity: participation should be open and inclusive, with opportunities for a broad range of people to contribute. This could mean getting rid of language barriers, making accommodations for people with disabilities, and creating safe spaces for groups that aren't as popular or well-known.
- Empowerment: participation should involve empowering individuals and communities to take an active role in decision-making rather than simply providing input or feedback. This may involve providing training or capacity-building opportunities and sharing decision-making power and responsibilities.
- Collaboration: participation should be collaborative and involve working together with communities to develop shared goals and objectives. This could mean building trust and relationships over time and looking for different points of view and expertise.
- Transparency: participation should be transparent and involve sharing information openly and honestly. This may involve providing clear explanations of decision-making processes and sharing data and other information related to cultural heritage management.

Generally, effective participation in cultural heritage management aims to build more sustainable and equitable approaches to cultural heritage conservation and management. We can help make sure that cultural heritage is valued, protected, and celebrated for generations to come if we include communities in decision-making and give them the power to take an active role in managing cultural heritage.

Empowerment is another critical aspect of people's participation in cultural heritage management. It involves enabling individuals and communities to take an active role in decision-making and to have a say in the management of cultural heritage sites and artifacts. Key factors to keep in mind when giving people agency over cultural heritage include the following:

- Capacity-building: empowerment involves building the capacity of individuals and communities to take an active role in cultural heritage management. This could mean teaching people how to protect and manage cultural heritage as well as how to be leaders and get things done.
- Shared decision-making: empowerment involves sharing decision-making power and responsibilities with individuals and communities. This may involve establishing collaborative decision-making processes that involve a range of stakeholders and providing opportunities for communities to set their own goals and priorities.
- Advocacy and representation: empowerment involves advocating for the needs and perspectives of communities and individuals and ensuring that they are represented in decision-making processes. This could mean forming partnerships with community-based organizations and people who want to protect cultural heritage and giving support to grassroots efforts to do so.

- Access to resources: empowerment involves ensuring that individuals and communities have access to the resources they need to participate in cultural heritage management. This could mean giving money and other resources to community-based cultural heritage projects and giving people access to the tools and equipment they need to preserve and manage cultural heritage.

Therefore, empowerment is essential for effective public participation in cultural heritage management. By building the capacity of individuals and communities, sharing decision-making power and responsibilities, and advocating for their needs and perspectives, we can create more sustainable and equitable approaches to cultural heritage conservation and management.

Building trust and capacity building are the two main pillars on which the wheel of participation is based. Building trust is an important factor in fostering people's participation in cultural heritage conservation and management. Trust is essential to ensuring that people are motivated to participate, are engaged in the process, and are willing to work together towards a common goal. Some key approaches to building trust for people's participation in cultural heritage conservation and management are:

- Open Communication: effective communication is essential to building trust between stakeholders. Open communication can help to ensure that everyone is informed about the decision-making process, the progress of the project, and the potential impacts of conservation and management strategies. Communication should be open, clear, and respectful, with the goal of encouraging dialogue and collaboration.
- Inclusion and Diversity: creating an inclusive and diverse environment can help build trust among different groups of people. Involving people from different backgrounds, cultures, and points of view can help create a sense of ownership and empowerment and make sure that everyone's voice is heard and respected.
- Transparency and Accountability: being transparent and accountable in decision-making processes is key to building trust. This can involve sharing information about the conservation and management strategies, the expected outcomes, and the potential risks and benefits. Accountability can be shown through regular reporting, monitoring, and evaluation, as well as feedback and problem-solving systems.

Thus, building trust in people's participation in cultural heritage conservation and management is essential to ensuring that everyone is engaged and committed to the process. Stakeholders can work together to reach common goals and protect cultural heritage for future generations by promoting open communication, inclusion and diversity, transparency and accountability, and capacity building.

Capacity building involves equipping individuals and communities with the necessary knowledge, skills, and resources to effectively contribute to the preservation, protection, and management of cultural heritage sites and resources. This can include a range of activities, such as training programs, workshops, community engagement, and educational initiatives. Some important ways to make it easier for people to take part in preserving and managing cultural heritage are:

- Education and awareness-raising: educational programs can help individuals and communities better understand the value of cultural heritage and the importance of its preservation. Bringing attention to cultural heritage also helps people feel like they own it and are responsible for keeping it safe.

- Training and Skills Development: developing practical skills in conservation and management techniques can help individuals become effective stewards of cultural heritage. Training programs can give people hands-on experience and information about the best ways to protect and manage resources.
- Community Engagement: engaging with local communities is essential for successful heritage conservation. This can involve developing relationships with local stakeholders, encouraging their participation and consultation, and incorporating their perspectives into decision-making processes.
- Collaborative partnerships: bringing together different groups and organizations, like government agencies, non-governmental organizations (NGOs), academic institutions, and local communities, can help protect and manage cultural heritage in the best way possible.

CONCLUSION

There are various methods of involving the local community in cultural heritage conservation and management that must be designed and implemented on a local scale, depending on the specific socio-cultural context. Although it is extremely difficult to answer the question of how we must apply people's participation in cultural heritage management, it is clear that each cultural heritage institution is able to design and apply its own participatory approach by considering the ways and valuable experiences in Human-Computer Interaction approaches. This difficulty is not because of the complexity of cultural heritage problems but because of the social interaction that occurs when people and cultural heritage mix within a participatory approach. Cultural heritage conservation methods and practices are determinedly established in multidisciplinary studies, which are a combination of archaeology, architecture, urban planning, museum studies, etc. They are aimed at implementing a set of typically complicated actions for protecting cultural heritage. In fact, by adding a participatory approach, we are applying a series of complicated procedures to sustain the process of cultural heritage conservation. Here is a set of ideal people participation including:

- Public participation is a set of retrieval activities that must be implemented entirely as a master plan throughout all projects and activities in a given cultural heritage institution. The backbone of this master plan is capacity building and building trust between local people and cultural heritage institutions.
- Effective and sustainable cultural heritage conservation and management requires full public participation in all stages of identification, documentation, diagnosis, protection, assessment, monitoring, and management. This requires training and active public participation.
- Cultural heritage should enhance the quality of life and social well-being of the local people and communities who are living within or around a cultural heritage property.
- The people participation approach is a tool for facilitating the engagement of different stakeholders in cultural heritage management; thereby, this tool needs to be designed in a way that is under the control of the people using it. It also must be flexible and modifiable to deal with new issues in the future.

- Different groups of stakeholders have different needs and wishes. Cultural heritage managers who want to apply a participatory approach have a different attitude from the people who want to participate. Conflicts are inevitable in the process (Greenbaum & Kyng, 2020).
- Public participation, like other social phenomena, is an extraordinary long-term, open-ended project. The cultural heritage authorities are always pushing things to the side or ignoring them in their rush to come up with instantaneously tangible outcomes, which is absolutely impossible.

ACKNOWLEDGMENTS

This project has received funding from the European Union's Horizon 2020 research and innovation programme under the Marie Skłodowska-Curie grant agreement No 754511 in the frame of the Ph.D. Program Technologies for Cultural Heritage (T4C) held by the University of Torino. The author would like to express his sincere gratitude to his research supervisors, Vito Messina and Cristiana Gena, for their guidance, patience, and encouragement.

REFERENCES

EPA. (2022). *Public Participation Guide: Tools to Generate and Obtain Public Input*. EPA. https://www.epa.gov/international-cooperation/public-participation-guide-tools-generate-and-obtain-public-input

Arnstein, S. R. (1969). A ladder of citizen participation. *Journal of the American Institute of Planners*, *35*(4), 216–224. doi:10.1080/01944366908977225

Assembly, U. G. (1948). Universal declaration of human rights. *UN General Assembly*, *302*(2), 14–25.

Ontatio Museum Association. (2020). Discover-Ontario Museums. Museums Ontatio. https://www.museumsontario.ca/

Bødker, S., Ehn, P., Sjögren, D., & Sundblad, Y. (2000). *Co-operative Design—perspectives on 20 years with 'the Scandinavian IT Design Model'*. Paper presented at the proceedings of NordiCHI.

Clarke, R. E., Briggs, J., Light, A., Heitlinger, S., & Crivellaro, C. (2014). Socially engaged arts practice in HCI. In CHI'14 Extended Abstracts on Human Factors in Computing Systems (pp. 69-74). doi:10.1145/2559206.2559227

World Heritage Committee. (2021*). Operational guidelines for the implementation of the World Heritage Convention*. World Heritage Committee.

Coughlin, S. S., Smith, S. A., & Fernandez, M. E. (2017). *Handbook of community-based participatory research*. Oxford University Press. doi:10.1093/acprof:oso/9780190652234.001.0001

Creighton, J. L. (2018). Public Participation. In Public Participation. Encyclopedia.com.

Davidson, S. (1998). Community Planning: Spinning the wheel of empowerment. *Planning (Chicago, Ill.)*, *3*, 14–15.

Dian, A. M., & Abdullah, N. C. (2013). Public participation in heritage sites conservation in Malaysia: Issues and challenges. *Procedia: Social and Behavioral Sciences, 101,* 248–255. doi:10.1016/j.sbspro.2013.07.198

Dick, B. (2003). Robust processes for learning, change and action research. Retrieved from http://bobdick.com.au/DLitt/index.html

DiSalvo, C., Clement, A., & Pipek, V. (2012). Communities: Participatory Design for, with and by communities. In Routledge international handbook of participatory design (pp. 202-230): Routledge.

Dollarhide, M. (2019). Social media definition. *Investopedia.* http://billscomputerpot. com/menus/windows/SocialMedia. pdf

Elia, R. J. (2020). Charter for the Protection and Management of the Archaeological Heritage (1990). In Encyclopedia of Global Archaeology (pp. 2184-2186): Springer International Publishing Cham.

COE. (2005). *Convention on the Value of Cultural Heritage for Society (Faro Convention, 2005).* COE. https://www.coe.int/en/web/culture-and-heritage/faro-convention

COE. (2017). *Faro Convention Action Plan Handbook 2018-2019* (pp. 30). RM. https://rm.coe.int/faro-convention-action-plan-handbook-2018-2019/168079029c

Fojut, N. (2018). *The Encyclopedia of Archaeological Sciences,* 1-4. Faro Convention.

Garmur, M. (2020). *How do you calculate overperforming scores.*

Ginzarly, M., Roders, A. P., & Teller, J. (2019). Mapping historic urban landscape values through social media. *Journal of Cultural Heritage, 36,* 1–11. doi:10.1016/j.culher.2018.10.002

Greenbaum, J., & Kyng, M. (2020). *Design at work: Cooperative design of computer systems.* CRC Press. doi:10.1201/9781003063988

Group, W. B. (2020). *Individuals using the Internet (% of population) - Iran.* World Bank. https://data.worldbank.org/indicator/IT.NET.USER.ZS?locations=IR

Hanlee, I. (2019). Human-centred design in digital media. In *The Routledge international handbook of new digital practices in galleries, libraries, archives, museums and heritage sites* (pp. 319–325). Routledge. doi:10.4324/9780429506765-28

Hayes, G. R. (2011). The relationship of action research to human-computer interaction. [TOCHI]. *ACM Transactions on Computer-Human Interaction, 18*(3), 1–20. doi:10.1145/1993060.1993065

Heitlinger, S. (2017). *Talking Plants and a Bug Hotel: Participatory Design of ludic encounters with an urban farming community.*

IAP2. (2019). *IAP2 Core Values.* IAP2. https://www.iap2.org.au/About-Us/About-IAP2-Australasia-/Core-Values/

ICOMOS. (1975). *The Declaration of Amsterdam.* ICOMOS. https://www.icomos.org/en/and/169-the-declaration-of-amsterdam

ICOMOS. (1987). *Washington Charter: Charter on the Conservation of Historic Towns and Urban Areas (1987)*. ICOMOS. https://www.icomos.org/images/DOCUMENTS/Charters/towns_e.pdf

InMobi. (2021). *Understanding Android Users Worldwide*. InMobi. https://www.inmobi.com/blog/understanding-android-users-worldwide

Islam, R., Islam, R., & Mazumder, T. (2010). Mobile application and its global impact. *IACSIT International Journal of Engineering and Technology*, *10*(6), 72–78.

ITU. (2021). *Statistics*. ITU. https://www.itu.int/en/ITU-D/Statistics/Pages/stat/default.aspx

Kemp, S. (2021). Digital 2021: Iran. Retrieved from https://datareportal.com/reports/digital-2021-iran

Kensing, F., & Greenbaum, J. (2013). In J. Simonsen, & T. Robertson. Heritage: Having a say. Routledge international handbook of participatory deisgn, 21e36.

Kong, L., & Yeoh, B. S. (1994). Urban conservation in Singapore: A survey of state policies and popular attitudes. *Urban Studies (Edinburgh, Scotland)*, *31*(2), 247–265. doi:10.1080/00420989420080231

Lachapelle, P., & Austin, E. (2014). Community participation. In J. B. Metzler (Ed.), *Encyclopedia of Quality of Life and Well-Being Research* (pp. 1073–1078). doi:10.1007/978-94-007-0753-5_471

Lewin, K. (1946). Action research and minority problems. *The Journal of Social Issues*, *2*(4), 34–46. doi:10.1111/j.1540-4560.1946.tb02295.x

Lyons, S. H. (2017). *Digital Engagement, Social Media & Public Participation*. International Association for Public Participation.

Murugesan, S. (2007). Understanding Web 2.0. *IT Professional*, *9*(4), 34–41. doi:10.1109/MITP.2007.78

Sanders, E. B.-N., & Stappers, P. J. (2008). Co-creation and the new landscapes of design. *CoDesign*, *4*(1), 5–18. doi:10.1080/15710880701875068

Simonsen, J., & Robertson, T. (2013). *Routledge international handbook of participatory design* (Vol. 711). Routledge New York.

Srijuntrapun, P., Fisher, D., & Rennie, H. G. (2018). Assessing the sustainability of tourism-related livelihoods in an urban World Heritage Site. *Journal of Heritage Tourism*, *13*(5), 395–410. doi:10.1080/1743873X.2017.1373779

Statista. (2020). *Global Facebook pages fan engagement rate 2020, by type of post*. Statista. https://www.statista.com/statistics/934749/average-facebook-page-user-engagement-rates-selected-posts-worldwide/#:~:text=Global

Statista. (2021). *Mobile app usage - Statistics & Facts*. Statista. https://www.statista.com/topics/1002/mobile-app-usage/#dossierKeyfigures

Steinberg, F. (1996). Conservation and rehabilitation of urban heritage in developing countries. *Habitat International*, *20*(3), 463–475. doi:10.1016/0197-3975(96)00012-4

Techopedia. (2020). *Mobile Application (Mobile App)*. Techopedia. https://www.techopedia.com/definition/2953/mobile-application-mobile-app

UNESCO. (2003). *Convention for the Safeguarding of the Intangible Cultural Heritage.* UNESCO. https://ich.unesco.org/en/convention

UNESCO. (2011). *Recommendation on the Historic Urban Landscape.* UNESCO. https://whc.unesco. org/uploads/activities/documents/activity-638-98.pdf

UNESCO. (2020). *Museums around the world in the face of COVID-19.* UNESCO.

Warren, T. (2022). Apple now has 1.8 billion active devices. *The Verge.* https://www.theverge. com/2022/1/28/22906071/apple-1-8-billion-active-devices-stats

Wright, P., & McCarthy, J. (2010). Experience-centered design: designers, users, and communities in dialogue. *Synthesis lectures on human-centered informatics, 3*(1), 1-123.

Chapter 23
Investigation of the Effect of Kastamonu Historical Bazaar Area on Urban Morphology

Filiz Karakuş

Ankara Yıldırım Beyazıt University, Turkey

ABSTRACT

The most important step in the tendency of human beings to change their natural environment is urbanization. Cities are in constant change with re-adaptation of different parts, which developed spontaneously or consciously planned under different socio-economic, natural, religious, and political conditions. Anatolian cities are the simplest and most modest reflections of traditional Turkish-Islamic life. Kastamonu, one of these cities, blends its structure built on this Turkish-Islamic life system with the topography of the region, climatic data, cultural layers, lifestyle, and architectural features of the local people and becomes original with its own internal dynamics. In this study, urbanization, and settlement features of Kastamonu city in the historical process are discussed. Kastamonu historical city center and historical bazaar area were examined by discussing how the main axes shaped in line with unchangeable natural data became subjectivized by human hands and the components of the traditional urban texture in the context of the border, and the morphological inputs of these components were mentioned.

INTRODUCTION

Cities are formed when cultural traditions and socio-economic values affect many independent groups over time and these components come together (Moudon, 1997). Cities, which are living organisms, have hosted many events, cultures, and social values in every corner of the world from the past to the present, and will continue to transfer these values to future generations as well as to the present.

The reason why cities are evaluated based on concepts such as Hellenistic city, medieval city and Renaissance city is the result of the reflection of the values of the societies living in these areas to the cities. Cities have acquired their present forms because of religion, culture, economic or political interactions in societies from the past to the present. Culture is a value that defines all the values and concepts

DOI: 10.4018/978-1-6684-8253-7.ch023

that a society has from past to present. Depending on the lands people live in or their way of life, culture has had an impact on society and every element around it from past to present.

The study of the physical form, structure and components of the city and the relationship between them is called urban morphology (Wilkinson & Willoughby, 1962). Urban morphology is an approach that allows understanding the form, formation and transformation processes of human settlements, their spatial structure and character, by analyzing the historical development processes and the component parts that make up the settlements. It is used as an important evaluation method in determining the change-transformation processes of urban textures, making sense of the historical roots of spatial and functional structures, and transferring them to the present.

Traditional settlements have built environments with unique characteristics, shaped by the accumulation of mutual interaction and where different cultures have lived together throughout history. The unique combination of natural (topography, climate), social (lifestyle) and socio-cultural (local traditions, cultural structure) data, which is determinant in the formation of these environments, shapes the unique textural character of that settlement (Yücel, 1981).

Within the scope of this study, firstly, the formation of the city in Turkish-Islamic cities and the effect of trade areas on the city was briefly discussed. Afterwards the history of Kastamonu city and the urbanization and settlement features in the historical process were examined. In this urbanization process, the morphological features of the city and the effects of structures such as Nasrullah Mosque, Yılanlı Mosque, İsmail Bey (Kurşunlu Khan), Karanlık Bedesten (Covered Bazaar), Frenkşah Hamam (Bath), Yakup Ağa Kulliye (Complex) on the city and its morphology, which are located in the urban protected area, are emphasized. By making use of the 1924/1925 city plan, the 1970 and 1990 Conservation Development Plans, it has been tried to explain how these structures and the historical bazaar area shaped the urban morphology of Kastamonu and the effects of the physical characteristics of the city on the settlement in the city.

THE FORMATION OF THE CITY IN TURKISH-ISLAMIC CITIES AND THE EFFECT OF TRADE AREAS ON THE CITY

While the Roman Empire influenced urban structuring, this feature disappeared in Islamic states and the city began to be built by the user. As a result, culde sac (dead end streets) emerged that do not directly associate the buildings with the street due to an organic texture and perception of privacy. In addition, a street system with narrow roads and away from the main street phenomenon has been formed (Kubat et al., 2001). When the building typologies in Turkish cities are examined, the most important building can be considered as the mosque. While mosques were built as an identification method at first, this act of gaining identity continued with the construction of mosques in the direction desired for the development of the city. Thus, mosques were first built in the place where the city was wanted to be established, and then the system of the city developed with a mosque in the center and cities were established around mosques (Tanyeli, 1987). Other important structures were the külliyes[1] (complexes) where the city's trade took place and various functions were housed.

In Islamic cities, the splendor of the mosque and the length of the marketplace have always been related to the prosperity of the cities. Marketplaces were created as a space used for talks and meetings. Apart from the conversations of the visitors about their private lives, the marketplace, where social and political thoughts are shared, has been used as a platform where news and thoughts such as the Roman city forum are shared and not just for commercial purposes (Nazemi, 2013).

The fact that a significant part of the İpekyolu (Silk Road) and Baharat Yolu (Spice Road) passed through Anatolian lands brought both commercial and strategic importance to the Seljuk and Ottoman states that ruled in the region. The statesmen, who realized the importance of international trade, gave importance to the safe, easy, and comfortable realization of commercial activities. For this reason, countries have created important commercial areas such as ranges and caravanserais on commercial road routes, and khans, covered bazaars and bazaars in cities (Tabakoğlu, 1985). The most important of these commercial areas are the bazaars, which are the heart of the city's economy, and the units that support their function.

Seljuk and later Ottoman period bazaars were shaped by the influence of traditional Turkish and Islamic urban culture and were in certain parts of the cities. Factors such as the castle or city walls within the city, trade routes, proximity to social and cultural areas were important in this positioning (Kejanlı, 2010). In the Islamic urban culture, it is seen that cities develop around commercial areas, usually around a central mosque (Ergenç, 1978; Saoud, 2002). In the center of the bazaar system, covered bazaars were in the Seljuk and Ottoman periods, and shops were designed in a row around the covered bazaars. As the value of the product sold increases, the shop is positioned closer to the covered bazaar (Cezar, 1983; Aktüre, 1987).

In the Seljuk city structure, the "mosque, pazar (market), hamam (bath)" elements that make up the Islamic city type, such as the caravanserai, were also adopted and they were combined with the "citadel, şehristan (city), and rabad[2] " elements that formed the Central Asian city type. Other important urban components, namely "neighborhoods, covered bazaars and bazaars", formed the other parts of the city, which are the most distinctive features of post-Islamic Turkish cities (Kuban, 1968; Yenen, 1987). During the Seljuk period, the bazaars were extending from the city center of the city, "şehristan[3]" or "batin-ul medina", to the city walls (Barthold, 1963). There are three basic elements in the spatial and functional organization of bazaars and markets, which serve as commercial activity centers in Anatolian Seljuk cities:

- As the religious buildings assumed the function of meeting centers of the city, bazaars were generally formed near these structures.
- The bazaars are located near the city gates that determine the entry-exit points of the cities.
- Various bazaars were established as a result of the spatial requirements arising from any traded goods and product combinations (Özcan, 2005).

The fact that there are bazaars such as blacksmiths, coppersmiths, shoemakers, cutlers, cooks, and attars[4] in the vakıf (foundation)[5] records of the Seljuk period, as well as bazaars devoted to certain fields of activity such as wheat or horse markets, shows that tradesmen and craftsmen engaged in the same activities in Anatolian Seljuk cities could organize in common places (Özcan, 2010).

According to Ottoman law, for a place to be considered a city, it must have a place of commerce and a mosque where Friday prayers are performed (Kejanlı, 2010). Therefore, the increase and development of permanent and organized commercial areas gained importance in the Ottoman period. In the Ottoman period, a certain order was observed in the distribution of bazaars and markets according to occupation, and there were mostly mosques or covered bazaars in the center of the bazaars (Ülgener, 1991). During the Ottoman period, the "old core", which was surrounded by Byzantine walls on one side, overflowed the walls because of the expansion of the city area. On the other hand, a "new urban core", which is not close to the existing main residential area, has begun to form. The growth and development of the city was realized by the intensification of these new cores and their addition to the old urban area (Aktüre, 1987). The formation periods of non-agricultural activities and commercial production in the early Ottoman period formed a gradation in the traditional spatial organization of the city. This stratification can be listed as 4 regions (Tekeli, 1985):

- The central region where the urban management and control activity is focused,
- The business district where the activities of artisans and tradesmen are focused next to or in the vicinity of the center,
- Residential area,
- The region where some economic activities of groups outside the current commercial system take place.

The center, where mosques and bazaars, which formed the first core in Ottoman cities, were located, were the main places where traders carried out their social and economic activities. This central region, where commercial activities take place, was built close to the castle settlement of the cities. The most important reason why the bazaar was built close to the castle was to ensure the safety of this place, which is the economic heart of the city (Kejanlı, 2010). In the Ottoman city structure, in addition to commercial activities, the places where industrial activities took place and the public spaces that were used extensively were positioned according to the relationship between the bazaar and the castle (Tanyeli, 1986). The introversion in the lifestyle of the Turkish-Ottoman society and the dominant political systems in this society did not require the design of large city squares (Kuruyazıcı, 1998). People used mosques (Aktüre, 1978) or marketplaces (Kuruyazıcı, 1998) in Ottoman cities for gathering and meeting, rather than squares, which were the center of the neighborhood, in small groups. While the markets established at the city gates most of the time constitute the first phase of the establishment of the bazaar (Tanyeli, 1986), it would be wrong to argue that the commercial center was always built next to the city walls of the Ottoman period, within the open morphology of the Ottoman city (Faraqhi, 2000; Yılmazçelik, 1995). The bazaar is the center of the city that grew around it (Yılmazçelik, 1995; Tanyeli, 1986). Khans/inns formed the first circle in the center of the bazaar, followed by shops, craft districts, and leather workshops and markets (Faroqhi, 2000; Yılmazçelik, 1995). Because religion was the center of urban formation, as in Ottoman daily life, religious buildings were both urban benchmarks and places that shape the city itself. In addition to transportation axes, the formation of the surrounding building blocks and similar features, they also shaped the city socially.

The important natural elements that shape the Anatolian city are the topographical thresholds such as direction, streams and steep slopes and valleys. There is a river in every Anatolian city since the settlement was established near the water. Except for Seljuk cities such as Kayseri and Sivas, which were established on the plain and surrounded by walls, the Anatolian city, which generally developed on sloping slopes, is in the form of settlements extending to the plain with its trade center (Cerasi, 1999).

A city with an ancient core has undergone a transformation with the Turkization-Islamization periods, and a mosque, khan, and bath, as well as a madrasah, were established in the bazaar area or in the most suitable place of the city for development. In the 12th and 13th centuries, there are three different types of cities in Anatolia: the closed city, the open city, and the edge city. In the closed city model, a large part of the settlement area is surrounded by walls that loosely surround the city, while it also has an inner castle. Cities such as Kastamonu, Antalya, Sinop, Malatya, Diyarbakir, and Mardin set an example for a closed city (Aktüre, 1987). While the other closed-plan Anatolian cities were made by the Turks, Kastamonu, which is the subject of this study, is a castle city from the Byzantine period (Eyüpgiller, 1995).

THE KASTAMONU CITY AND URBANIZATION CHARACTERISTICS IN HISTORY

The city, which is within the borders of the Western Black Sea Region, was established on the rugged area formed by the mountain ranges in the inner and coastal parts of the North Anatolian Mountains. Kastamonu is located on a plain at an altitude of 790 meters above sea level, along the valley of the stream called "Karaçomak" or "Kastamonu Stream" descending from the northern slopes of Ilgaz Mountain (Figure 1).

There is no definite information about where the name Kastamonu came from and what it means. Yaman (1935) attributes the name "Kastamonu" to the Gasgas, one of the first peoples of the region, and to the city of "Tumanna", which is stated to exist in the region (Yaman, 1935). The region in which Kastamonu was in ancient times was called "Paphlagonia". Strabon gives the boundaries of this region as follows: The western border is Bartın Stream, the eastern border is Kızılırmak, the southern border is Phrygia and Galatia, the northern border is the region that ends in the Black Sea (Strabon, 1989).

Figure 1. The map of Kastamonu
Source: Lafsozluk (2009)

There are also various assumptions about the name of the city in the Byzantine period. It has been suggested that the city (Artuk, 1971), which is called "Kastamon" in the late Byzantine works, could be used in this way due to the word "Kastra Komnen(os)" because Emperor Alexios had a castle (kastra) built here during the Komnenian period (Tanyeli, 1986).

In Kastamonu, which came under the domination of the Turks after the 1071 Malazgirt Victory, a principality was established by Emir Karatekin, who captured Sinop in 1084, including Kastamonu and Çankırı (Turan, 1965; Kankal, 2004). The city changed hands as a result of the struggles between the Byzantines and the Turks during the 11th and 12th centuries (Bilici, 1991). Kastamonu and its surroundings came under the rule of the Çobanoğulları Principality, founded by Emir Hüsamettin Çoban, who was the margrave of the Anatolian Seljuks, at the end of the 12th century (Yücel, 1980). This domination, which lasted for about a century, ended when the Çobanoğulları lands were captured by the Candaroğulları Principality, which was established around Kastamonu and Sinop in the early 14th century. After a while, Kastamonu became the center of the principality. The city was the capital of the principality called Candaroğulları or İsfendiyaroğulları (Tevhid, 1911) for about 150 years (Darkot, 1977). The city was annexed to the Ottoman lands by Mehmet the Conqueror in 1461 (Tansel, 1953) and was made the center of a sanjak of the Anatolian Province (Darkot, 1977).

Kastamonu city structure is very important in terms of Anatolian city architecture. Although there are 3 rock tombs thought to have been built in the 1st BC- 2nd AD, within the boundaries of the settled area of the city, it is accepted that the foundation of the city started with the Castle, which is thought to have been built in the Byzantine period. It is possible that the city structure of Kastamonu was built in the form of an inner castle on the hill and a residential area spreading towards the slopes and the outer fortifications surrounding it (Figure 2) (Leonhard, 1915; Kuban, 2001). The only remnant in Kastamonu, which is estimated to be Byzantine artifacts, is the castle (Leonhard, 1915). Although it is not fully understood when it was built, it is estimated that the castle belongs to the Komnenian period (Baydil, 1990). İçkale and its surroundings formed the first core of the settlement in Kastamonu. Although the city is thought to have appeared as a medieval city surrounded by outer walls in the 13th century, no trace of these walls can be found today. On the other hand, according to some verbal information about the city walls, some conclusions can be reached about the city walls, city gates and road structure, considering the topography of the city, the locations and chronology of the buildings, and the names of the old roads and neighborhoods. During the Seljuk period, when the city was ruled by the Çobanoğulları, the castle, which was surrounded by an outer wall on the north, south and east and was strengthened by making new additions, should have been in the south-west corner of the city in the form of an "İçkale". It is thought that the city is surrounded by water as a natural boundary from these three directions (Figure 3). There is no trace of the stream beds surrounding the city from the north and south, apart from the Karaçomak Stream, which separates the two sides of the city today. However, it was possible to determine these limits in line with the information conveyed by the people living in the said regions.

Kastamonu City Development in the Cobanogullari and Candarogullari Periods

The city of Kastamonu has not undergone a significant change in the early periods of the Turkish era. All structures (mosque, madrasah, bath, etc.) in the 13th and 14th centuries were built in the inner-city walls. The oldest known structure is the Frenkşah Hamamı (Bath) (Figure 4), which is known to have been built in 1262, and it is understood from its charter that it was built as Çifte Hamam (Behçet, 1922; Eyüpgiller, 1995). Among the other buildings whose construction date is known, Yılanlı Darüşşifa

Figure 2. Kastamonu Citadel and its surroundings

Figure 3. The creeks surrounding the inner castle and outer walls of Kastamonu city

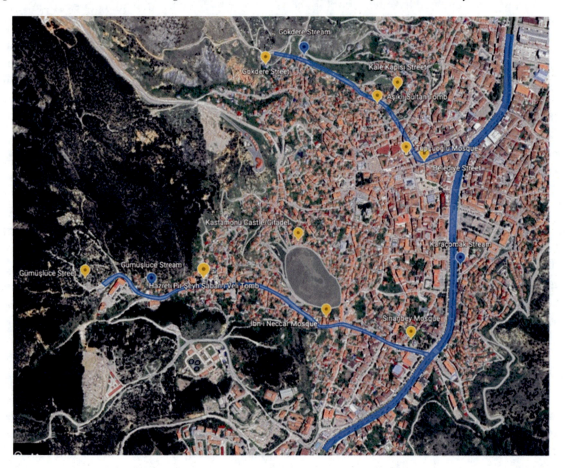

(Hospital) is dated 1272 and Atabey Mosque (Figure 4) is dated 1273. The fact that two structures such as the Frenkşah Bath and Yılanlı Darüşşifa are very close to the stream shows that the city center was within the current borders in this century. In the Frenkşah Foundation Charter[6], it is stated that the person who built the bath dedicated nine shops around the bath (Behcet, 1923). This shows that the bazaar at that time was also in its present place. The Vakıf Hamam (Bath) and the Atabey Madrasa, which has completely disappeared, are among the foundations of the Atabey Mosque. Therefore, it is thought that they were built on the same date as the mosque. The first construction of the Kale Hamam (Bath), near the Atabey Mosque, is dated to the 13th century. The Tomb of Yaman bin Mehmet, which is understood to have been built in 1289, only has an inscription today. It is thought that the "Kale Masjid", which is mentioned in the 18th century registry records but no trace of it has survived, was built in the 13th century.

It is estimated that the city had two gates in the 13th century. Starting in front of the Vakıf Hamam and following Atabey Street, you can reach the Arabapazarı Çifte Hamam, the Acem Khan, which does not exist today, and the bazaar, from the side of the Yakup Ağa Complex. It is thought that the road that connects to Kale Kapısı Street, a little below the structure called Aşıklı Sultan Tomb by turning to the north-east from here, is the main road connecting the two gates of the city (Kuban, 1967). It is noteworthy that the buildings of the 13th century are located on this main road close to the city gates. Accordingly, structures such as Vakıf Hamam, Karanlık Evliya Tomb, Atabey Mosque and Tomb, and İsa Dede Tomb and Kale Hamam (Bath) are located on both sides of the main road in the east of the Citadel and in the south-west corner of the city.

It is thought that the Great Mosque was influential in the formation of the city center, but there is no structure called "Cami-i Kebir (grand mosque)" or "Cami-i Atik" in written sources. However, when factors such as Frenkşah Bath, Yılanlı Darüşşifa, shops and bazaar are considered, it can be said that a great mosque built in the first half of the 13th century played a role in the city center (Tanyeli, 1987). It is possible that there is a great mosque in the place of today's Nasrullah Mosque, which was built near the Frenkşah Hamam (Bath) at a time before the bath.

Kastamonu, which was under the rule of Çobanoğulları for about a century, was captured by Süleyman Pasha at the beginning of the 14th century and thus the Candarogullari period began in the city. With the city being the capital of the principality, the settlement movements accelerated, the population

Figure 4. Frenkşah Hamam (Bath) and Atabey Mosque
Source: Rıfat Ilgaz Cultural Center Archive

of the city increased, and as a result, new settlements emerged. The city became one of the important cultural centers in this period (Figure 5) (Yurt encyclopedia, 1983).

The "Ibn Neccar Mosque" (Figure 6), dated 1353, is the only work that has survived from the 14th century. The building, which was changed to a great extent later, is in the north of the 13th century Vakıf Hamam (Figure 6). This may mean that a new settlement started around the city gate to the south in the mid-14th century. Because of the Ibn Neccar Mosque, this part of the city was named as Ibn Neccar Neighborhood as it was in the 17th century (Tanyeli, 1987).

Figure 5. Çobanoğulları and Candarogullari period structures

Figure 6. İbn Neccar Mosque and Vakıf Hamam (Bath)
Source: Photo archive of the author

Ahi Şorve Zaviye, which was learned to have been built by a sheikh named Ahi Şorve from its charter dated 1304 (Kastamonu Şeriyye Sicilleri[7] (Court Records Book) No.411/I- Number 209, registration date 1689-90), has not survived. The Ahi Şorve Tomb, located in the Beyçelebi Neighborhood, just behind the current Sports Hall, shows that the city overflowed from the walls in the south.

The Daya Sultan Zaviye, which was built in the 14th century and has not survived, was located in the west of the city, outside the walls and adjacent to the Daya Sultan Tomb. This means that in the 14th century there was a third city gate on the wall to the west of the city. As a matter of fact, the presence of a street called the "Cracked Door" around the Acem Khan, which has been destroyed today, is due to this door. Ibn Batuta (Kopraman, 1989) writes for the Dede Emir Zawiya, which is not standing today, as near the "At Pazarı (Horse Bazaar)", but there is currently no place with this name in the city.

It is seen that the city developed in the west, north-west, north-east directions of the castle and on the east side of the stream during the Candarogullari period, which is considered to be the most important era in the history of the city (Avcı, 2004). It can be said that İsfendiyar Bey played a leading role in the expansion of the city towards the east side of the creek and its spread from across the present museum to the Aktekke District. There is a third city gate in the city, which is mentioned in the registry records dated M.1726-27. The oldest known structures on the eastern side of the city are İsfendiyar Bey Mosque (Figure 7), Madrasa and Hamam (Bath), built between 1392 and 1439. At the time these structures were built, there was another important building community in this vicinity. Only the Hatun Sultan Tomb has survived from these structures. It is possible that the other structures in question were built in 1436-37 like the tomb. At least 5 neighborhoods are known to have been inhabited during the reign of Isfendiyar Bey and where there are settlements: These are Honsalar, Şadi Bey and Musa Fakih Neighborhoods on the side of the castle, and İsfendiyar Bey and Deveciler Neighborhoods on the eastern part of Karaçomak Creek (Kankal, 2004).

This new settlement, which is still known as Aktekke Mahallesi (Neighbourhood) today due to the mosque called Aktekke and the imaret (soup kitchen) that once stood next to it, shows that a certain part of the eastern side of the city was inhabited towards the middle of the 15th century. In order to connect the city with the new settlement in the east, it was necessary to open a door in the eastern fortification walls.

Only two of the buildings outside the walls in the west have survived. Of these, the Honsalar Mosque (Figure 7) is to the west of the Daya Sultan Zaviye and Tomb. The "masjid built by Hamza Ağa", which is learned to be in the center of Kastamonu, Beyoğlu District and Yukarı Pazar from the foundation charter dated 1446-47, is at the southern end of the western settlement.

While the Daya Sulan Zawiyah and Tomb, Honsalar Mosque and Hamam are located very close to the city gate in the west, they are in the opposite direction of the mosque built by Hamza Ağa and in the place called "Yukarı Pazar (Upper Market)". This situation shows that towards the middle of the 15th century, the settlement here spread as far as the Inner Castle.

In addition to the Halife Sultan Mosque, built in the middle of the 15th century in the north, close to the city gate, İsmail Bey Kulliye (Complex) (Figure 8), the most monumental building group of the period, added striking dimensions to the city's silhouette. It also shows how big a role the sultan played in the formation of the new core. Two structures from this period are known within the walled city. One of these is the Kubbeli Mescit on Atabey Street, which is thought to have been built in the first half of the 15th century, and the other is the İsmail Bey (Kurşunlu) Khan, which was dedicated to the complex built by İsmail Bey (Figure 9). This monumental structure, which we learned from İsmail Bey's endowment charter that it was in the "Attarlar Bazaar" (Yaman, 1935), shows the dimensions of the commercial activities of the city towards the middle of the 15th century.

Kastamonu City Development in the Ottoman Period

In the city, which came under Ottoman rule in 1461, only two buildings from the 15th century have survived. Among these, the Bedesten (Karanlık Bedesten) built by Sultan Cem when he was the Sanjakbey of Kastamonu, and the Balkapı[8] (Penbe) Khan, built by Beyazıt the 2nd at the end of the century, are important in terms of the commercial life of the city.

From all this information about the 15th century, it is understood that the city expanded and grew to the east, west and north outside the walls. This situation occurred as a result of the individual preferences of the rulers, especially the sultans. The zawiyas, which played a major role in urbanization in the 14th century, were replaced by social complexes consisting of buildings of different qualities such

Figure 7. İsfendiyar Bey Mosque and Honsalar Mosque

Figure 8. Ismail Bey Complex site plan and general view

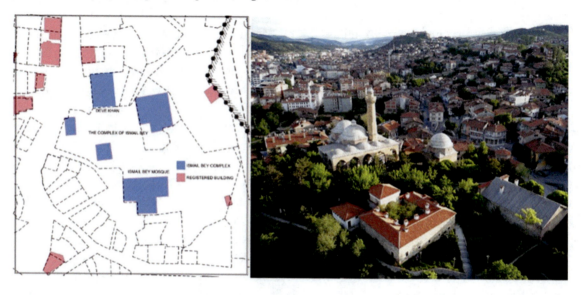

Figure 9. İsmail Bey (Kurşunlu) Khan

as mosques, imarets (hospice), masjids, madrasahs and hamams (baths) in this century. In addition, it is possible to understand that the city has a highly developed commercial potential. Thus, it is understood that the neighborhoods that cluster around these buildings and gradually form a texture relate to each other as a result of the increase in the city population and physically integrated with residences, gardens and bazaars.

In the 16th century, many more buildings were added to the series of monumental constructions that started with the Nasrullah Mosque (Figure 10), with the Sinan Bey Mosque and the Ferhat Pasha Mosque, a work of Mimar Sinan. The Nasrullah Mosque, which was built in 1506, should probably have been built on the site of the Seljuk period "Ulucami (Grand Mosque)" that was here before. To the north of the Kadı Nasrullah Mosque, a fountain, a madrasa (no traces of it today), a bridge (Figure 10) and a Çifte (Double) Hamam were dedicated to the mosque. The bridge is located in front of the eastern city gate. It is understood that the Double Hamam was built near the western gate of the city and next to the trade center called "Aşağı Pazar (Lower Bazaar)", "Attarlar Bazaar" or "Horse Bazaar".

This development in the center of the city gained even more activity with a social complex built towards the middle of the century. Yakup Ağa Complex (Figure 11), built on the side of the main road that forms the backbone of the city, on the road connecting Atabey Mosque and Arabapazarı Double Bath, and on a hill overlooking the city center, adds striking dimensions to the 16th century city panorama. It also contributed to the growth of the neighborhood here. In the lower parts of this complex, in the southeast "Mahkemealtı Street", there is a Çifte Hamam (Mahkemealtı Hamam) built by Halimi Çelebi in 1514.

Sinan Bey Mosque was built in the third quarter of the 16th century, inside the city surrounded by walls. It is surprising that the mosque was built in this part, which was not inhabited until then, and next to the walls. In this case, it is certain that the walls surrounding this part of the city disappeared in the 16th century, or at least a door was opened here. The "Acem Khan", which was demolished, and a new office building was built in its place, was from the foundation of the Sinan Bey Mosque and was located close to the city gate in the west, opposite the Araba Pazarı Double Bath. Another building belonging to this period within the walls is the Topçuoğlu Mosque, which is located on the road that reaches Nasrullah Square from Kale Kapısı Street and gives its name to the neighborhood here. Another structure in this vicinity is the Hasan Efendi Mosque (Karanlık Mosque) built in 1588-89. One of the remarkable developments in the 16th century was the new settlements formed in the south-east and south-west of the city, apart from the walls, and the new buildings added to the east side of the stream. The structures that

Figure 10. Nasrullah Mosque and Nasrullah Bridge (two spans of the bridge have not survived due to road construction works)
Source: Photo archive of the author and Kastamonu Archive

Figure 11. Yakup Ağa Complex and its surroundings

determine the settlement in the south-east are the Mevlevihane and the Turkish bath. It can be said that the settlement in the south-west is clustered around the Musa Fakih Mosque. As a matter of fact, there is a neighborhood with the same name here. The neighborhood here became larger with the construction of the Sheikh Şabani Veli Dervish Lodge and Mosque after a short while, and an important texture spread from the city gate in the south to here (Figure 12).

One of the suhte (madrasah students) uprisings that affected Anatolia from the mid-16th century to the beginning of the 17th century was also seen in Kastamonu. The Suhte revolt was suppressed with great difficulty, but then, in 1581, the Celali revolts broke out. When the Celali revolts were bloodily suppressed, a heavily damaged city remained. It can be said that both these events and the earthquake that occurred in 1675 (Kastamonu Şeriyye Sicilleri Notebook No 13-row number 93) damaged many buildings in the city. For this reason, the number of buildings from the 17th century in the city is small. The construction date of Sheikh Saban-i Veli Tomb is 1611-12. It is also learned from the sources that there was a madrasa, dar'ül kurra and dar'ül hadis and a hamam (bath) built by Kara Mustafa Pasha in the city. Today, the bath is active in the Topçuoğlu District Jewelers' Bazaar, under the name of Yeni Hamam. There is no trace of the other buildings that are known to be in the area where the museum and the garden of the school opposite are located.

In the 18th century, many buildings were repaired because of the earthquake in 1675 and the fire in 1718. One of the few buildings known to have been built in the 18th century is the "Urgan Khan (Aşir Efendi Khan, Reis'ül Küttab Hacı Mustafa Efendi Khan)", which was built in 1748. According to the foundation charter dated 1748, the founder of the Turşucu Khan in the Topçuoğlu District was Hacı

Figure 12. Ottoman period buildings

Mustafa Efendi. No trace of this building remains today. Other structures built in this period in the city are the "Yanık Han", which is dated to the end of the 17th or the beginning of the 18th century, on the current Belediye Street and the Münire Madrasa dated 1714.

RELATIONSHIP BETWEEN NEIGHBORHOOD AND BAZAAR IN KASTAMONU CITY CENTER

According to the city plan of 1924/1925[9] (Figure 13), which was examined and combined by Emin Baydil and Ünal İbret to better understand the physical development of the city, the development areas of the city were determined as follows:

When the buildings/monuments on the plan of the city of 1924/1925 are followed, it is seen that the Frenkşah Hamam (Bath) and Yılanlı Dar'ül Şifası, which were built before 1262, descended to the valley floor during the Çobanoğulları period. During the Candaroğulları Period, the city of Kastamonu spread to the eastern side of the stream bed and many mosques and tombs were built in this area. Some of these are the Isfendiyar Mosque, the Kalender Mosque, which is in the place of today's Imam Hatip

High School, the Ahi Ali (Tekke Altı) Mosque, which is understood to be in the place of today's Public Education building, and the İsfendiyarbey Madrasa, where the current Pancar Cooperative is located. Therefore, during the Çobanoğulları period of the city of Kastamonu, it descends to the east and north of the hill where the castle is located (between Atabey Mosque and Yılanlı Hospital), and during the Candaroğulları period, it descends to Gökdere in the north and extends to İsmail Bey Mosque, by following the Vakıf Street along the Kerpiçlik Stream and into the bed of the Karaçomak Stream. It is seen that the valley is spread over a wider area with mosques and tombs built in places on the eastern side of the valley. During the Ottoman period, the city witnessed more construction. However, it is possible to say that this development did not exceed the area in the Candarogullari period, and it was mostly concentrated in the empty fields in the same area. During the Ottoman period, a commercial center developed in and around the Nasrullah Mosque, whose core was formed in previous periods. This section has become prominent as the center of the city with a large mosque, social complex, inns, covered bazaar, madrasahs, and workplaces.

While the Turks were developing their cities, they did not consider it necessary to connect the settlement to any street system. However, cities were divided into zones in terms of the functioning of the city, the safety, health and comfort of the citizens, and the residential areas were isolated from all kinds of disturbing functions (Eldem, 1987). Accordingly, the effective functional areas in Anatolian Turkish cities consist of castle, residential areas, bazaar and market area, service structures, roads, and open areas.

In Kastamonu, commercial structures played a major role in the development of the city center. This center, which was formed in the Seljuk period, grew gradually with the khans/inns, bazaars and marketplaces built during the Principalities period and the Ottoman period and approached its present form at the end of the 18th century. The fact that there were nine shops near the hamam (bath) built by the person in the second half of the 13th century in the foundation charter of Frenkşah Cemalettin is an indication that the bazaar was in this vicinity. Ibn Batuta, who traveled around the city in the 14th century, says that "he has never seen a place with prices cheaper than this city in any country" and talks about a marketplace called "At Pazarı (Horse Bazaar)" (Kopraman, 1989). This market, whose exact location cannot be determined, is thought to be in the outer part of the city (Bilici, 1991). In the 15th century, during the Candaroğulları Principality, the "caravanserai-khan" built by İsmail Bey was in the Attarlar Bazaar. The Sultan had donated a shop and a garden in the Wheat Bazaar with all his income to the newly built complex (Behcet, 1923). It is possible that the bazaar in question was the same place as the "Grain Bazaar", which was mentioned in the foundation charter prepared by Yakup Ağa in the 16th century and which coincides with the current Arabapazarı Double Bath. The Hamza Ağa foundation charter dated 1446-47 shows that there was a market called "Yukarı Pazar (Up Market)" in the Beyoğlu District, outside the city walls, to the west of the city (Behcet, 1923). The "Karanlık Bedesten" and "Balkapanı Khan (Penbe Khan)" belonging to the first years of the Ottoman rule were built right next to the "Ismail Bey (Kurşunlu) Khan", which was the key structure of the commercial center of the city, and in the Attarlar Bazaar. After the construction of the Karanlık Bedesten (Covered Bazaar) and then the Balkapı Khan, a very large and interconnected business center was formed around these structures. With the Reis'ül-Küttab Hacı Mustafa Efendi Khan, madrasah and library built in the 18th century, the city gained its current shape (Figure 14), and even spread to the north and west. While this center was connected to the south by the Mahkemealtı Street and its continuation streets, the road entering the city with the Nasrullah Bridge in the east opened to this bazaar in front of the mosque. It is noteworthy that this settlement is clustered in bazaars that host very different occupational groups and marketplaces where various products are bought and sold. For example, it is known that there is the "Tailor's Bazaar"

Figure 13. Kastamonu city plan dated 1924/1925
Source: Baydil & İbret (1999)

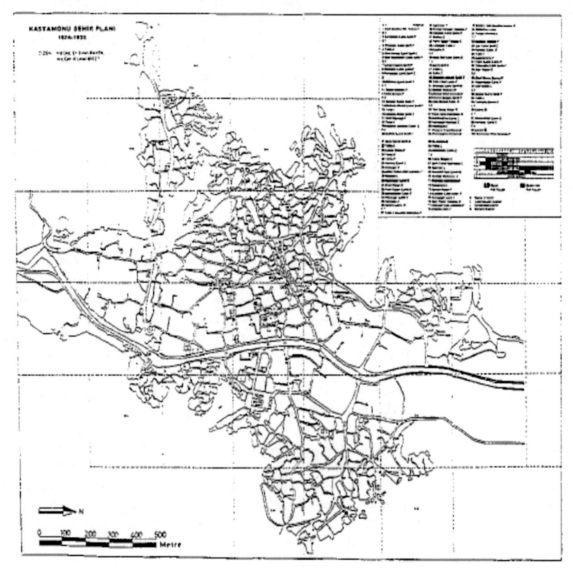

on the east of the Bedesten, on the street that runs parallel to the current Belediye Street and bounded by the Ismail Bey Khan on the south (VGM Archive, Notebook No: 204, row No: 1548). Apart from this, Jewellers' Bazaar, Yemeniciler's Bazaar, Locksmith's Bazaar, Iplikciler Bazaar, Coppersmith's Bazaar, Tannery Bazaar, and Rice Bazaar also have an important place in the commercial life of the city.

In 1842, Ainsworth recorded the existence of wool and cotton weaving/textile, printing, dyeing and leatherworking industries in the city (Ainsworth, 1842). In 1862, Texier states that weaving /textile and coppersmithing were two industries in the city (Texier, 1862). Trade agreements made with England and other European countries in 1838-1841 and 1860-1862 negatively affected Kastamonu like the whole country. The city became one of the regions where foreign goods attacked and production decreased, but the number of sales establishments increased. According to the 1892 Kastamonu Provincial Year-

Figure 14. The bazaar area by the end of the 18th century (processed over the Conservation Development Plan dated 1990)

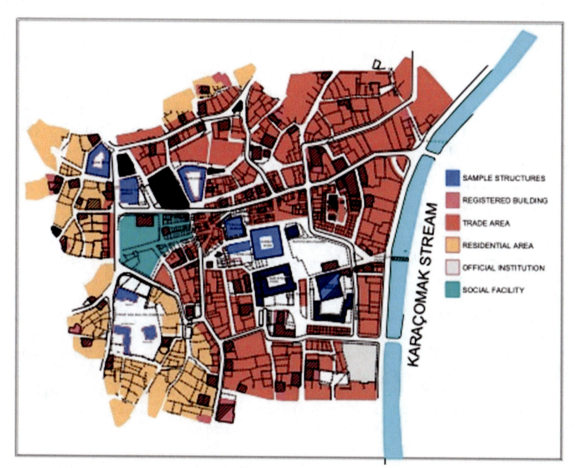

book, in the city of Kastamonu at the end of the 19th century, there were 3585 houses, 1 Government Office, 1 Military Service, 2 barracks, 2 warehouses, 4 police stations, 1 telegraph office, 1769 shops and stores, 45 inns, 15 hamams (baths), 9 coffee houses, 17 madrasas, 21 warehouses, 4 tile making houses, 26 ovens and 1 flour trap.

Information about the districts of the city during the Seljuk period consists of Atabey District (Kastamonu Şeriyye sicilleri (Court Registers), Notebook No 411/I, Number 56, registry dated 1689-90). The information for the 14th century is scarce, and it is thought that the district referred to as "İbn Neccar Neighborhood" (Kastamonu Şeriyye Sicilleri, Notebook No 411/I Serial No 56, dated 1689-90) dates from the Candaroğulları period. Until the middle of the 15th century, when the Candaroğulları Principality was the capital, the city grew gradually, and new settlements emerged thanks to the monuments built in this period. It is thought that the names of some of the neighborhoods we encountered in the records of the 17th century represent new settlements dating back to the Candaroğulları Principality. It can be said that the districts of Halife Sultan, Aktekke, Hamza Ağa, Beyçelebi, İsmail Bey, Honsalar, Cemal Ağa, İsfendiyar, Cebrail, İbn Süle, Kırkçeşme, İbn Sadi and Arız (Kastamonu Şeriyye Registers) preserved their names from this period. As the names they bear indicate, most of the neighborhoods were formed around the foundation works built by the people who managed Kastamonu. Sometimes they were called by the name of their founder or the building, and sometimes the name of the place where they were located.

It is understood that Kırkçeşme, İsfendiyar, Halife Sultan, Cebrail and Aktepe neighborhoods are on the east bank of Kastamonu (Karaçomak) Stream, Beyçelebi neighborhood is in the south of the city and outside the walls, Hamza Ağa and Honsalar neighborhoods are in the west, and İsmail Bey neighborhood is in the north and outside the walls. The Cemalağa neighborhood is located under the castle, where the present Musa Fakih District is located, while the İbn Süle and Arız Districts are within the city. In this case, it is understood that the unit called "neighborhood" formed spontaneously around buildings such as mosques, masjids, or social complexes, and these, in time, were connected to each other and formed the urban texture. The settlements outside the city walls were originally based on the rural urban system. The population, which was clustered around the zawiyas, masjids and kulliyes, grew in time by merging with new neighborhoods and streets. In the meantime, a very important religious center, which is respected even today, was formed with the Seyh Şaban-ı Veli Lodge in the south-west.

The historical part of the city, which has a bowl-shaped macroform, includes the southern parts of Ibn Neccar, İsfediyar, Hepkebirler, Cebrail, Topçuoğlu, Kırkçeşme, Honsalar, Akmescit, Atabeygazi, Hisarardı and İsmailbey and Aktekke neighborhoods and the northern part of Beyçelebi neighborhoods (Figure 15).

In the Turkish city, the residential texture is an organic texture that fits the topography, and therefore, developed in a free order, consisting of roads that follow the slope by bending rather than linear axes. Aru (1998) calls these types of textures rhythmic textures. Traditional residential areas in Kastamonu have developed around the traditional center on the slopes of the east and west sides of the Karaçomak Stream.

The houses in this structure are positioned parallel to the slope without forcing the topography. It is possible to see the residential texture and the monumental structures in between, especially in Joillier's photographs (Figure 16) documenting 100 years ago. When these photographs taken at the beginning of the 20th century are compared with the current situation, there is not much change, but it is seen that the buildings in some parcels of traditional housing pattern were demolished and multi-storey buildings were built in their place (Erkan Biçer, 2002).

The 20th century and the Republican era brought the western concept of square to Kastamonu. In this direction, various buildings were demolished to open the Nasrullah and Government squares on the west and east sides of the city (Figure 17) (Eyüpgiller, 1995). Although there are no major differentiations in the historical urban texture of Kastamonu, in the first years of the Republic, some of the dead-end streets were connected to each other. It was not possible for the city to develop in the east and west directions, and the city showed a development in the north-south direction, where the physical structure was more suitable.

The urban land use of the city of Kastamonu in 1925 is quite sparse along the Karaçomak Stream. As a result of the creek overflowing in certain periods (1939, 1947, 1948, 1954, 1957 and 1963), many residences and workplaces were flooded. After the Karaçomak dam was built in 1976, it is seen that the city has spread to the valley floor and multi-storey buildings have been built in the area covered with orchards (Baydil & İbret, 1999).

Figure 15. Kastamonu city historical section neighborhoods
Source: Erkan Biçer (2002)

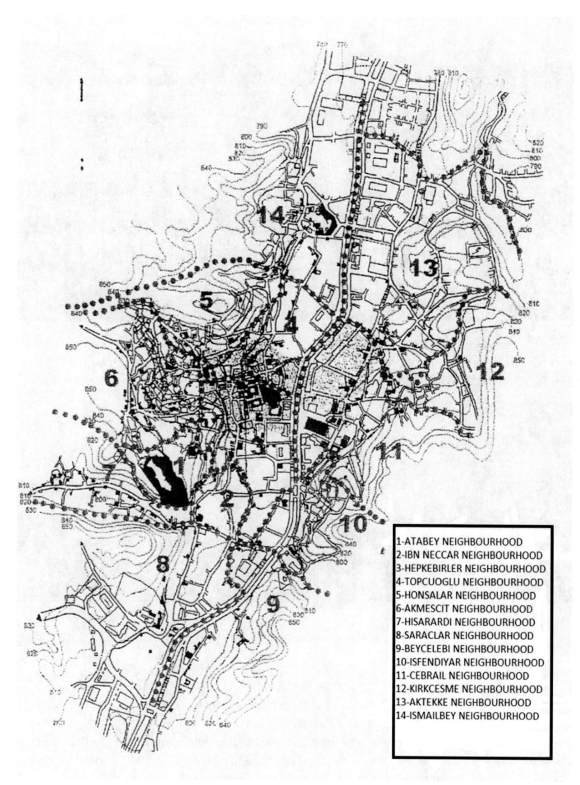

1-ATABEY NEIGHBOURHOOD
2-IBN NECCAR NEIGHBOURHOOD
3-HEPKEBIRLER NEIGHBOURHOOD
4-TOPCUOGLU NEIGHBOURHOOD
5-HONSALAR NEIGHBOURHOOD
6-AKMESCIT NEIGHBOURHOOD
7-HISARARDI NEIGHBOURHOOD
8-SARACLAR NEIGHBOURHOOD
9-BEYCELEBI NEIGHBOURHOOD
10-ISFENDIYAR NEIGHBOURHOOD
11-CEBRAIL NEIGHBOURHOOD
12-KIRKCESME NEIGHBOURHOOD
13-AKTEKKE NEIGHBOURHOOD
14-ISMAILBEY NEIGHBOURHOOD

Figure 16. Kastamonu Traditional residential texture[10]
Source: Erkan Biçer (2002)

Figure 17. Nasrullah Square before some buildings were demolished and after the square was opened
Source: Rıfat Ilgaz Cultural Center Archive

CONCLUSION

It is seen that the first settlement of the city of Kastamonu was concentrated in the castle and its surroundings, and the borders of this settlement were determined by the streams that also bordered the walls. Especially Karaçomak Stream divides the city into two as east and west today, and it significantly affects the development aspects of the city. However, in the following periods, the physical characteristics of the city were changed by human hands by covering the Gümüşlüce and Gökdere Streams and asphalting them. Another issue affecting the development of the city is the bazaar and its surroundings, where commercial life developed, which is an important element in the formation of Anatolian Turkish cities. It is seen that the bazaar, which forms the core of the city in Kastamonu, is separated from the residential areas with definite borders. It is seen that the formation of the neighborhoods also developed around a mosque or a small mosque. Another type of building that has an impact on the structuring of the city is the kulliyes. Especially İsmail Bey Complex and Yakup Ağa Complex constitute the important focal points of the city and add striking dimensions to the silhouette of the city. These structures also show how big a role the sultans played in the formation of the city's new settlement areas. During the development period, the city continued to develop around the traditional texture, especially in the south and north, as the topography allowed. This situation has resulted in the intensification of the settlement, especially on the west bank of Kastamonu Stream. Because there are more habitable areas on the west coast than on the east coast. The historical bazaar, which forms the core of Kastamonu's central texture, is also located on the west side of the city. However, today, the central function is developing along the streets following the creek, provided that it is more intense on the west side of the city. With the Development Plan made in 1985, the city developed towards the partially flat areas at the end of the valley in the north. The central function developed in the north direction along the two main streets, which are the backbone of the settlement.

REFERENCES

Ainsworth, W. F. (1842). *Travels and Research in Asia Minor*. Academic Press.

Aktüre, S. (1978). *19. Yüzyılın Sonunda Anadolu Kenti Mekansal Yapı Çözümlenmesi*. ODTÜ Yayınları.

Aktüre, S. (1987). Mimarbasi Sinan and the Building Policies of the Ottoman State. Environmental Design: Journal of the Islamic Environmental Design Research Centre, 1-2, 98-105.

Artuk, İ., & Artuk, C. (1971). *İstanbul Arkeoloji Müzeleri Teşhirdeki İslami Sikkeler Kataloğu* (Vol. 1). MEB Eski Eserler ve Müzeler Genel Müdürlüğü Yayınları.

Aru, K. A. (1998). *Türk Kenti*. Yapı Endüstri Merkezi Yayınları.

Avcı, F. F. (2004). Ondokuzuncu Yüzyıl Kastamonu Konutları Değişim Süreci. Yüksek Lisans Tezi, İzmir: Dokuz Eylül Üniversitesi, Fen Bilimleri Enstitüsü.

Barthold, V. V. (1963). *İslam Medeniyeti Tarihi* (2nd ed.). (M. Fuad Köprülü, Trans.). Diyanet İşleri Başkanlığı Yayınları.

Baydil, E. (1990). *Kastamonu Şehri Coğrafyası*. Yüksek Lisans Tezi, İstanbul Üniversitesi Sosyal Bilimler Enstitüsü.

Baydil, E., & İbret, B., Ü. (1999). Kastamonu Şehrinin Tarihi Gelişimi ve 1924/1925 Şehir Planı Üzerine Bir Değerlendirme. *Kastamonu Eğitim Dergisi*, 7(1), 3–18.

Behcet, M. (1923). *Kastamonu Asar-ı Kadimesi*. Matbaa-i Amire.

Bilici, Z. K. (1991). *Kastamonu'da Türk Devri mimarisi ve şehir dokusunun gelişimi (18. yüzyıl sonuna kadar)* [PhD thesis]. Ankara Üniversitesi Sosyal Bilimler Enstitüsü.

Investigation of the Effect of Kastamonu Historical Bazaar Area

Cerasi, M. M. (1999). *Osmanlı Kenti*. Yapı Kredi Yayınları.

Cezar, M. (1983). *Typical Commercial Buildings of The Ottoman Classical Period And The Ottoman Construction System*. Türkiye İş Bankası Kültür Yayınları.

Darkot, B. (1977). *Kastamonu maddesi, Encyclopedia of Islam (vol. 6)*. Milli Eğitim Bakanlığı Yayınları.

Eldem, S. H. (1987). *Türk Evi: Osmanlı Dönemi:III*. Türkiye Anıt Çevre Turizm Değerlerini Koruma Vakfı.

Ergenç, Ö. (1978). Osmanlı Şehrinde Esnâf Örgütlerinin Fizik Yapıya Etkileri, I. In Uluslararası Türkiye'nin Sosyal ve Ekonomik Tarihi Kongresi Tebliğleri, 103-109.

Erkan Biçer, N. Ç. (2002). Kastamonu Kent Örneğinde Anadolu Kenti İmaj Öğeleri ve Değişim Süreci. Doktora Tezi, Yıldız Teknik Üniversitesi Fen Bilimleri Enstitüsü, İstanbul.

Eyüpgiller, K., Topçubaşı, M., & Polat, I. (2008). Kastamonu'da 19. yüzyıl Ticaret Yapıları. *METU JFA*, 25(2), 1–20.

Eyüpgiller, K. (1995). *Kastamonu Kent Tarihi*. Yayımlanmamış Doktora Tezi, İstanbul: İstanbul Teknik Üniversitesi Fen Bilimleri Enstitüsü.

Faroqhi, S. (2000). *Osmanlı'da Kentler ve Kentliler*. Tarih Vakfı Yurt Yayınları.

Gökoğlu, A. (1952). *Paphlagonia*. Doğrusöz Matbaası.

Kankal, A. (2004). *Türkmen'in Kaidesi Kastamonu (XV-XVIII. Yüzyıllar Arası Şehir Hayatı)*. Zafer Matbaa.

Kejanlı, D. (2010). Anadolu'da Selçuklu ve Osmanlı Dönemlerinde Kent. *E-Journal of New World Sciences Academy*, 5(3), 287–303.

Kopraman, K. Y. (1989). Memluk Kaynaklarına Göre XV. yüzyılda Kastamonu ve Çevresi. Türk Tarihinde ve Kültüründe Kastamonu, Tebliğler.

Kuban, D. (1967). Kastamonu'nun Tarihi Yapısı ve Bu Yapının İmar Planında Değerlendirilmesiyle İlgili Rapor. Academic Press.

Kuban, D. (1968). Anadolu-Türk Şehri, Gelişmesi, Sosyal ve Fiziki Özellikleri Üzerine Bazı Gözlemler. *Vakıflar Dergisi*, (7), 53–73.

Kubat, A. S., Asami, Y., & İstek, İ. C. (2001). Characterization of Street Networks in Turkish – Islamic Urban Form. *Proceedings 3rd International Space Syntax Symposium*.

Kuruyazıcı, H. (1998). Cumhuriyet'in İstanbul'daki Simgesi Taksim Cumhuriyet Meydanı, 75 Yılda Değişen Kent ve Mimarlık Bilanço'98, Tarih Vakfı Yayınları, İstanbul.

Lafsozluk. (2009). Retrieved January, 20, 2023, from https://www.lafsozluk.com/2009/04/kastamonu-ilinin-ilceleri-ve-nufus-sayilari.html

Leonhard, R. (1915). *Paphlagonia*. Buch, Reimer.

Moudon, A. V. (1997). Urban Morphology as an emerging interdisiplinary field. *Urban Morphology*, 1(1), 3–10. doi:10.51347/jum.v1i1.4047

460

Nazemi, P. (2013). A Comparison Between Beauty in Islamic Urban Textures and European Historic Cities: Differences in Urban Conservation Strategies. *Conservation Science in Cultural Heritage, 13,* 193–211.

Özcan, K. (2005). Anadolu'da Selçuklu Dönemi Yerleşme Sistemi ve Kent Modelleri (Yayımlanmamış doktora tezi). Selçuk Üniversitesi Fen Bilimleri Enstitüsü, Konya.

Özcan, K. (2010). Erken Dönem Anadolu–Türk Kenti Anadolu Selçuklu Kenti ve Mekânsal Ögeleri. *Bilig, 55,* 193–220.

Tabakoğlu, A. (1985). *Gerileme Devrine Girerken Osmanlı Maliyesi.* Dergâh Yayınları.

Tansel, S. (1953). *Osmanlı Kaynaklarına Göre Fatih Sultan Mehmed'in Siyasi ve Askeri Faaliyeti.* Türk Tarih Kurumu Basımevi.

Tanyeli, U. (1986). Anadolu-Türk Kentinde Fiziksel Yapının Evrim Süreci (XI.-XV. Yüzyıllar) (Yayımlanmamış doktora tezi). İstanbul Teknik Üniversitesi Fen Bilimleri Enstitüsü, İstanbul.

Tanyeli, U. (1987). *Anadolu Türk Kentinde Fiziksel Yapının Evrim Süreci: 11-15. yüzyıl.* İTÜ Yayını.

Tekeli, İ. (1985). Tanzimat'tan Cumhuriyet'e Kentsel Dönüşüm, Türkiye Ansiklopedisi. İletişim Yayınları.

Tevhid, A. (1911). Kastamoni ve Sinobda İsfendiyaroğulları veyahut Kızıl Ahmedliler. *Tarih-i Osmani Encümeni Mecmuası, 6,* 252–257.

Texier, C. (1862). *Asie Mineure, description géographique, historique et archéologique des provinces et des villes de la Chersonnése d'Asie.* Firmin Didot.

Turan, O. (1965). *Selçuklular Tarihi ve İslam Medeniyeti.* Türk Kültürünü Araştırma Enstitüsü Yayınları.

Ülgener, S. (1991). *İktisadî Çözülmenin Ahlak ve Zihniyet Dünyası.* Der Yayınları.

Yaman, T., M. (1935). *Kastamonu Tarihi.* Ahmed İhsan Matbaası.

Yenen, Z. (1987). Vakıf Kurumu İmaret Sistemi Bağlamında Osmanlı Dönemi Türk Kentlerinin Kuruluş ve Gelişim İlkeleri (Yayımlanmamış Doktora Tezi). İstanbul Teknik Üniversitesi Fen Bilimleri Enstitüsü, İstanbul.

Yılmazçelik, İ. (1995). *XIX. Yüzyılın İlk Yarısında Diyarbakır (1790-1840).* Türk Tarih Kurumu Yayınları.

Yücel, A. (1981). *Mimarlıkta Biçim ve Mekânın Dilsel Yorumu Üzerine.* Doktora Tezi, İstanbul Teknik Üniversitesi.

Yücel, Y. (1980). *XIII-XV. Yüzyıllar Kuzey-Batı Anadolu Tarihi Çobanoğulları Candaroğulları Beylikleri.* Türk Tarih Kurumu Yayınları.

Yurt Ansiklopedisi. (1983). *Kastamonu maddesi.* Anadolu Yayıncılık.

KEY TERMS AND DEFINITIONS

Candaroğulları Principality: Candaroğulları Principality was a Turkmen principality established in and around Kastamonu after the collapse of the Anatolian Seljuk Empire.

City: A city is a multi-populated settlement center with a population of over 10,000 with clear boundaries prepared according to a certain plan, where most of the working population is in the trade, industry and service sector.

Çobanoğulları Principality: Çobanoğulları Principality is one of the Anatolian principalities that ruled in and around Kastamonu between 1211-1309.

Conservation Plan: A conservation plan is a document which explains why a site is significant and how that significance will be retained in any future use, alteration, development, or repair.

Kastamonu: Kastamonu is the city in the Black Sea Region of the Republic of Turkey.

Urban Morphology: Urban morphology can be defined as 'the study of the conditions under which the formal and structural elements that define the physical fabric of cities come together and the processes and actors that cause the formation, change and metamorphosis of the fabric'.

Yakup Ağa Külliyesi (Complex): Yakup Aga Complex is one of the most beautiful examples reflecting the power and wealth of the Ottoman Empire in Kastamonu.

ENDNOTES

[1] All the structures such as madrasah, imaret, public fountain, library, hospital built around a mosque.

[2] These are large areas outside the city walls where commercial activities are carried out in Turkish cities after Islam.

[3] City, big city.

[4] Spice seller.

[5] A vakıf-foundation is an institution formed by the allocation of real and legal persons with a specific property and right for a specific and permanent purpose.

[6] Foundation Charter (Waqfiyye), which means "the deed that shows what charity a donated property will be used for and how it will be managed", has an important place in the history of Islamic civilization.

[7] Şer'iyye Sicili: These are the books in which lawsuits are filed on all matters related to the administrative, financial, military, economic, social, and architectural activities of the state.

[8] Balkapanı is a shop that sells honey and oil-type foods.

[9] The plan, which consists of a total of 39 layouts, has 24 layouts today, but some of the missing layouts have been completed by interpolation.

[10] Edited by Erkan Biçer based on the photograph taken by Sebah and Joailler between 1901-1908.

Compilation of References

101 Blockchains. (2022). *10 Best Metaverse Platforms That You Can Try In 2022.* 101Blockchains. https://101blockchains.com/best-metaverse-platforms/

Aathaworld. (2019). *Green building materials Malaysia, design and install.* Aatha World. https://www.aathaworld.com/single-post/Green-Building-Materials-Malaysia-Design-Install

Abdullah, F. (2013). Phenomenological Approach for Evaluating Problem Based Learning in Architectural Education. *Methodologies In Architectural Research*, 4.

Abhiyan, S.P., NeerajSharma, D., & Kashiyani, B.K. (2014). Selection Criteria of Formwork by Users in Current Age In South Gujarat Region. *International Journal of Innovative Research in Science, Engineering and Technology*, 3.

Abidin, N. I., Zakaria, R., Aminuddin, E., Saar, C. C., Munikanan, V., Zin, I. S., & Bandi, M. (2016). Malaysia's Local Agenda 21: Implementation and approach in Kuala Lumpur, Selangor and Johor Bahru.

Abrami, P. C., Bernard, R. M., Bures, E. M., Borokhovski, E., & Tamim, R. M. (2012). Interaction in distance education and online learning: Using evidence and theory to improve practice. In *The next generation of distance education* (pp. 49–69). Springer. doi:10.1007/978-1-4614-1785-9_4

Acer for Education. (2017, July 5). *How Technology Can Empower Students' Peculiarities.* Acer for Education. https://acerforeducation.acer.com/education-trends/inclusive-education/how-technology-can-empower-students-peculiarities/

Acuti, D., Bellucci, M., & Manetti, G. (2020). Company disclosures concerning the resilience of cities from the Sustainable Development Goals (SDGs) perspective. *Cities (London, England)*, 99, 102608. doi:10.1016/j.cities.2020.102608

Adedoyin, O. B., & Soykan, E. (2020). Covid-19 pandemic and online learning: The challenges and opportunities. *Interactive Learning Environments*, 1–13.

Adiati, M., Lestari, N., & Wiastuti, R. (2018). Public parks as urban tourism in Jakarta. IOP Conference Series: Earth and Environmental Science, Ahmad, M. H. (2006). The Architecture of Public Park: Fading the Line between Architecture and Landscape. *Jurnal Alam Bina*, 8. 10.1088/1755-1315/126/1/012063

Agarwal, S., & Kaushik, J. S. (2020). Student's perception of online learning during covid pandemic. *Indian Journal of Pediatrics*, 87(7), 554–554. doi:10.100712098-020-03327-7 PMID:32385779

Ahmad Arzlee, H., Hamimah, A., Abdul Izz, M. K., & Noor Aisyah, A. M. (2019). *Challenges against Adjudication Decisions on Payment Disputes within the Construction Industry.* IOP. doi:10.1088/1755-1315/233/2/022035

Ahmad, A. (2004). *Understanding Common Building Defects.*

Ahmad, A., Ibrahim Kulliyyah, A., & Ahmad Ibrahim Kulliyyah, M. (n.d.). *Alternative Dispute Resolution in the Malaysian Construction Industry.*

Ahmad, H., Fadlie, M., Yahaya, N., & Abu, J. (2011). The Means of Escaping for Occupants for Renovation Works of Terrace Houses in Malaysia. *Procedia Engineering*, *20*, 188–192. doi:10.1016/j.proeng.2011.11.155

Ahmadi, D., Rachmiatie, A., & Nursyawal. (2019). Public Participation Model for Public Information Disclosure. *Jurnal Komunikasi: Malaysian Journal of Communication*, *35*(4), 305–321. doi:10.17576/JKMJC-2019-3504-19

Ahmad, Z., & Ismail, I. Z. (2013). Utilization of hybrid learning in accomplishing learning satisfaction as perceived by university student. International Journal of e-Education, e-Business, e-. *Management Learning*, *3*(2), 98.

Aigbavboa, C. O., & Thwala. (2014). *An Exploratory Study of the Major Causes of Construction Disputes in the South African Construction Sector*, 311–318.

Ainsworth, W. F. (1842). Travels and Research in Asia Minor. Academic Press.

Aixia, D., & Wang, D. (2011). Factors influencing learner attitudes toward e-learning and development of e-learning environment based on the integrated e-learning platform. International Journal of e-Education, e-Business, e-. *Management Learning*, *1*(3), 264.

Akbar, P., & Edelenbos, J. (2020). Social Impacts of Place-Making in Urban Informal Settlements: A Case Study of Indonesian Kampungs. *Social Sciences (Basel, Switzerland)*, *9*(6), 104. doi:10.3390ocsci9060104

Akçay Kavakoğlu, A. G.-C., Güleç Özer, D., Domingo-Callabuig, D., & Bilen, Ö. (2022). Architectural design communication (ADC) in online education during COVID-19 pandemic: A comparison of Turkish and Spanish universities. *Open House International*, *47*(2), 361–384. doi:10.1108/OHI-07-2021-0144

Akçayır, M., & Akçayır, G. (2017). Advantages and challenges associated with augmented reality for education: A systematic review of the literature. *Educational Research Review*, *20*, 1–11. doi:10.1016/j.edurev.2016.11.002

Akinyode, B. F., & Khan, T. H. (2018). View of Step by step approach for qualitative data analysis. *International Journal Of Built Environment And Sustainability*. https://ijbes.utm.my/index.php/ijbes/article/view/267/130

Akomah, B. B., Ahinaquah, L. K., & Mustapha, Z. (2020). Skilled labour shortage in the building construction industry within the Central Region. *Baltic Journal of Real Estate Economics and Construction Management*, *8*(1), 83–92. doi:10.2478/bjreecm-2020-0006

Aktüre, S. (1987). Mimarbasi Sinan and the Building Policies of the Ottoman State. Environmental Design: Journal of the Islamic Environmental Design Research Centre, 1-2, 98-105.

Aktüre, S. (1978). *19. Yüzyılın Sonunda Anadolu Kenti Mekansal Yapı Çözümlenmesi*. ODTÜ Yayınları.

Al Ansi, A. M., & Al-Ansi, A. (2020). Future of education post covid-19 pandemic: Reviewing changes in learning environments and latest trends. *Solid State Technology*, *63*(6), 201584–201600.

Al Najdi, S. (2014, March). Hybrid learning in higher education. *In Society for Information Technology & Teacher Education International Conference* (pp. 214-220). Association for the Advancement of Computing in Education (AACE).

Alam, I., Khusaro, S., & Naeem, M. (2017, December). A review of smart TV: Past, present, and future. In *2017 International Conference on Open Source Systems &Technologies (ICOSST)* (pp. 35-41). 10.1109/ICOSST.2017.8279002

Alase, A. (2017). The interpretative phenomenological analysis (IPA): A guide to a good qualitative research approach. *International Journal of Education and Literacy Studies*, *5*(2), 9. doi:10.7575/aiac.ijels.v.5n.2p.9

Alasli, M. (2019). Toponyms' contribution to identity: The case study of Rabat (Morocco). *Proceedings of the ICA*, *2*(July), 1–7. doi:10.5194/ica-proc-2-3-2019

Albee, B. L. (2019). *The Malaysian forest and timber industry: Policies and strategies for sustainable growth.* Routledge.

Alejo, A. (2012). Comparative Study of Defects Liability Period Practice Between Nigeria and Malaysia. *IJMT.*

Alfuraty, A. B. (2020). Sustainable Environment in Interior Design: Design by Choosing Sustainable Materials. *IOP Conference Series. Materials Science and Engineering, 1-2*(1), 4–8. doi:10.1088/1757-899X/881/1/012035

Ali, A. (2004). Issues & challenges in implementing e-learning in Malaysia.

Ali, M. A. M., & Arifin, K. (2019). Factors contributing to the success and weakness of public participation in local plans at local authority malaysia: a review. *Asian Journal of Environment, History and Heritage 3*(2).

Ali, M. A. M., & Arifin, K. (2020). Penglibatan Awam Sebagai Pembuat Keputusan Dalam Rancangan Tempatan Pihak Berkuasa Tempatan (Public Participation as a Decision Maker in Local Plans at Local Authority). *Akademika, 90*(1).

Ali, P. T. (2013). *Issues and Challenge in Implementing E-Learning in Malaysia.* Open University Malaysia Knowledge Repository. http://library.oum.edu.my/repository/145/1/issues_and_challenges.pdf

Ali, A., Kamaruzzaman, S., Sulaiman, R., & Yong, C. (2010). Factors Affecting Housing Maintenance Cost in Malaysia. *Journal of Facilities Management, 8*(4), 285–298. doi:10.1108/14725961011078990

Ali, A., & Kam, H. (2011). *Building Defects: Possible Solution for Poor Construction Workmanship.* ResearchGate.

Aljunied, K. (2014). Coffee-shops in Colonial Singapore: Domains of Contentious Publics. *History Workshop Journal, 77*(1), 65–85. doi:10.1093/hwj/dbt011

Al-Sibai, N. (2022, February 1). Virtual reality users keep suffering horrible injuries. *Futurism.* https://futurism.com/neoscope/vr-injuries

Alsop, T. (2022). *Reported price of leading consumer VR headsets 2019.* Statista. https://www.statista.com/statistics/1096886/reported-price-of-leading-consumer-vr-headsets-by-device/

Alvanchi, A., & Seyrfar, A. (2020). Improving facility management of public hospitals in Iran using building information modeling. *Scientia Iranica, 27*(6), 2817–2829.

Alvarado, S., Kanter-Braem, B., Manz, K., Masciopinto, P., Mckenna, E., Nelson, D., & Wozniak, W. (2011). *SENSATION AND PERCEPTION a unit lesson plan for high school psychology teachers.* TOPSS of the American Psychological Association.

American Psychology Association. (n.d.). *Restorative Environments.* APA. https://www.apa.org/monitor/2019/03/restorative-environments

Amgad, M., Hamood, A., Suliman, M. (2020). A Smart fire detection system using IoT Technology with Automatic Water Sprinkler. *International Journal of Electrical and Computer Engineering.*

Amirhossein Balali, A. V. (2020). Identification and selection of building façade's smart materials according to sustainable development goals. *Sustainable Materials and Technologies, 1,* 3.

Amri, Y., & Setiawan, M. A. (2018). Improving smart home concept with the internet of things concept using raspberrypi and nodemcu. []. IOP Publishing.]. *IOP Conference Series. Materials Science and Engineering, 325*(1), 012021. doi:10.1088/1757-899X/325/1/012021

Anderson, J., Wojtowicz, M., & Wineman, A. (2013). The impact of daylighting on human health. *Lighting Research & Technology, 45*(2), 159–175. doi:10.1177/1477153512457607

Anderson, M. D., Carson, D. C., & Grandy, J. (2013). Office light quality and alertness in two office environments. *Journal of Environmental Psychology*, *36*, 94–101.

Andreas, J., Joseph, B., & Paul, D. (2016). On Privacy and Security Challenges in Smart Connected Homes. *European Intelligence and Security Informatics Conference*. IEEE. https://ieeexplore.ieee.org/document/7870217

Ansary, N., Balogun, O. A., & Thwala, W. D. (2017). *Adjudication and arbitration as a technique in resolving construction industry disputes A literature review View project*. Seek. doi:10.15224/978-1-63248-139-9-55

Anuar, M. I. N. M., & Saruwono, M. (2018). Obstacles of public participation in the design process of public parks. *Journal of Asian Behavioural Studies*, *3*(6), 147–155. doi:10.21834/jabs.v3i6.247

Anuar, N. H., Mohd Faudzi, Y., Md Alwi, N., Mohd Nasir, S. N. A., Mohd Nasir, M. R., & Mhd Zain, M. H. K. (2021). Rediscovering local 'third places' of Kota Bharu, Kelantan Malaysia: The study of Kedai Pati. *AIP Conference Proceedings*, *2347*, 020220. doi:10.1063/5.0051986

Anuar, N., Alwi, N., Hanafi, N., Mohamad, J., & Faudzi, Y. (2022). *Revitalisation Of Kedai Pati: An Exercise in Architectural Heritage Studies*. Faculty Of Creative Technology and Heritage, Universiti Malaysia Kelantan.

Anupoju, S. (2018, August 4). Different materials used for formwork - advantages and disadvantages. *The Constructor*. https://theconstructor.org/building/materials-formwork-advantages-disadvantages/6188/

Appleton, J. V. (1995). Analysing qualitative interview data: Addressing issues of validity andreliability. *Journal of Advanced Nursing*, *22*(5), 993–997. doi:10.1111/j.1365-2648.1995.tb02653.x PMID:8568076

ArchDaily. (2013, January 2). S11 House / ArchiCentre. *ArchDaily*. https://www.archdaily.com/313041/s11-house-archicentre

Ardoin, N. M. (2006). Toward an Interdisciplinary Understanding of Place: Lessons for Environmental Education. [CJEE]. *Canadian Journal of Environmental Education*, *11*(1), 1.

Arnstein, S. (1969). A ladder of citizen participation. [In.]. *Journal of the American Institute of Planners*, *35*(4), 216–224. doi:10.1080/01944366908977225

Arora, V., & Khazanchi, D. (2010). Sense of Place in Virtual World Learning Environments: A Conceptual Exploration. *Proceedings of the Fifth Midwest Association for Information Systems Conference*. Fifth Midwest Association for Information Systems Conference.

Arora, V., & Khazanchi, D. (2014). Sense of place in virtual learning environments. *Proceedings of the Ninth Midwest Association for Information Systems Conference*. Ninth Midwest Association for Information Systems Conference.

Artuk, İ., & Artuk, C. (1971). *İstanbul Arkeoloji Müzeleri Teşhirdeki İslami Sikkeler Kataloğu* (Vol. 1). MEB Eski Eserler ve Müzeler Genel Müdürlüğü Yayınları.

Aru, K. A. (1998). *Türk Kenti*. Yapı Endüstri Merkezi Yayınları.

Asmah, L., Basarudin, N., Yusoff, Z., Dahlan, N. (2018). smart home Users Perception on Sustainable Urban Living and Legal Challenges in Malaysia. *The Journal of Social Sciences Research*.

Assembly, U. G. (1948). Universal declaration of human rights. *UN General Assembly*, *302*(2), 14–25.

Atkinson, D. (2000). The challenges facing statutory adjudication. *Construction News*. https://www.constructionnews.co.uk/archive/the-challenges-facing-statutoryadjudication-30-03-2000/

Avcı, F. F. (2004). Ondokuzuncu Yüzyıl Kastamonu Konutları Değişim Süreci. Yüksek Lisans Tezi, İzmir: Dokuz Eylül Üniversitesi, Fen Bilimleri Enstitüsü.

Aw, S. B., & Lim, P. I. (2016). The provision of vertical social pockets for better social interaction in high-rise living. *Planning Malaysia Journal*, *14*(4). doi:10.21837/pmjournal.v14.i4.156

Ayob, N. H., Aziz, M. A., & Ayob, N. A. (2022). Bridging the Digital Divide: Innovation Policy and Implementation in Malaysia. *International Journal of Academic Research in Business & Social Sciences*, *12*(8), 1373–1389. doi:10.6007/IJARBSS/v12-i8/14554

Azhar, S. (2011, June 15). Building Information Modeling (BIM): Trends, benefits, risks, and challenges for the AEC industry. *Leadership and Management in Engineering: 11*(3). https://ascelibrary.org/doi/10.1061/%28ASCE%29LM.1943-5630.0000127

Aziz, N. A. A., Mokhtar, M. D. M., Raman, T. L., Saikim, F. H., & Nordin, N. M. (2020). Use Of Urban Green Spaces: A Case Study In Taman Merdeka. Johor Bahru.

Aziz, Y., Awang, K., & Zaiton, S., (2012). Challenges Faced by Micro, Small, and Medium Lodgings in Kelantan, Malaysia. *International Journal of Economics and Management 6*(1), 167–190.

Azizan, F. Z. (2010). Blended learning in higher education institution in Malaysia. In *Proceedings of regional conference on knowledge integration in ICT* (Vol. 10, pp. 454-466). Scientific Research Publishing.

Azman, N., & Abdullah, D. (2021). A Critical Analysis of Malaysian Higher Education Institutions' Response towards COVID-19: Sustaining Academic Program Delivery. *Journal of Sustainability Science and Management*, *16*(1), 70–96. doi:10.46754/jssm.2021.01.008

Baba, H. D. (2010, December). *Building information modeling in local construction industry*. UTM. http://eprints.utm.my/id/eprint/15311/4/HammadDaboBabaMFKA2010.pdf

Badenko, V., Fedotov, A., & Zotov, D. (2018). Extracting features from laser scanning point cloud. SHS Web of Conferences, Baiker-Sørensen, M., Herlaar, K., Keereweer, I., Pauw-Vugts, P., & Visser, R. (2020). Interpol review of shoe and tool marks 2016-2019. *Forensic Science International. Synergy*, *2*, 521–539.

Bahji, S., Lefdaoui, Y., & El Alami, J. (2013). Enhancing motivation and engagement: A top-down approach for the design of a learning experience according to the S2P-LM. [iJET]. *International Journal of Emerging Technologies in Learning*, *8*(6), 35–41. doi:10.3991/ijet.v8i6.2955

Bailenson, J. N., Yee, N., & Blascovich, J. (2021). Virtual restorative environments: An immersive technology for personal and planetary health. *Frontiers in Psychology*, *11*, 3583.

Bakar, J. A. (2002). *A design guide of public parks in Malaysia*. Penerbit UTM.

Baker, K. (2014). Sense of Place: Understanding Architectural and Landscape Design through a Layering of Visual Representations. *Journal of Learning Design*, *7*(1), 74–83. doi:10.5204/jld.v7i1.138

Ball, M. (2022). The Metaverse and how it will revolutionize everything. In *Liveright Publishing Corporation*. Liveright. doi:10.1080/15228053.2022.2136927

Bang, M., Wohn, K., & Shi, C. (2014). The Establishment of an e-Learning System Based on SDT. *Olnline Journals*, *9*(4), 43-49.

Barbour, M. K., & Unger, K. L. (2014). Strategies For Overcoming Common Obstacles In The Online Environment. *RealLife Distance Education: Case Studies in Practice*, 21.

Barnard, D. (2020, November 10). *Guide for training employees in VR (from 1000s of hours of experience)*. Virtual Speech. https://virtualspeech.com/blog/guide-training-employees-vr

Barreh, K. A., & Abas, Z. W. (2015). A Framework for Mobile Learning for Enhancing Learning in Higher Education. *Malaysian Online Journal of Educational Technology, 3*(3), 1–9.

Barthold, V. V. (1963). *İslam Medeniyeti Tarihi* (2nd ed.). (M. Fuad Köprülü, Trans.). Diyanet İşleri Başkanlığı Yayınları.

Basaglia, B., Lewis, K., Shrestha, R., & Crews, K. (2015). A comparative life cycle assessment approach of two innovative long span timber floors with its reinforced concrete equivalent in an Australian context. In *Proceedings of the Second International Conference on Performance-based and Lifecycle Structural Engineering (PLSE 2015)*. eSpace. https://espace.library.uq.edu.au/view/UQ:399256 doi:https://doi.org/10.14264/uql.2016.714

Battalio, J. (2007). Interaction online: A re-evaluation. *Quarterly Review of Distance Education, 8*(4), 339–352.

Battle Infinity (IBAT). (2023). *Home*. IBAT. https://battleinfinity.io/

Baydil, E. (1990). *Kastamonu Şehri Coğrafyası*. Yüksek Lisans Tezi, İstanbul Üniversitesi Sosyal Bilimler Enstitüsü.

Baydil, E., & İbret, B., Ü. (1999). Kastamonu Şehrinin Tarihi Gelişimi ve 1924/1925 Şehir Planı Üzerine Bir Değerlendirme. *Kastamonu Eğitim Dergisi, 7*(1), 3–18.

BCA. (2022). *CONQUAS 21: The BCA Construction Quality Assessment System, Singapore*. Building and Construction Authority (BCA). https://www1.bca.gov.sg/buildsg/quality/conquas

Behcet, M. (1923). *Kastamonu Asar-ı Kadimesi*. Matbaa-i Amire.

Beh, M. T. (2022). The Urban Middle-Class Consumer Identity in Malaysia's Socio-political Coffee House Culture. *Anthropological Forum, 32*(2), 109–124. doi:10.1080/00664677.2022.2042189

Bejo, L. (2017). Operational vs. Embodied Energy: A Case for Wood Construction. *Drvna Industrija, 68*(2), 163–172. doi:10.5552/drind.2017.1423

Bekele, T. A. (2010). Motivation and satisfaction in Internet-supported learning environments: A review. *Journal of Educational Technology & Society, 13*(2), 116–127.

Bellair, P. E. (1997). Social interaction and community crime: Examining the importance of neighbor networks. *Criminology, 35*(4), 677–704. doi:10.1111/j.1745-9125.1997.tb01235.x

Berman, M. G., Jonides, J., & Kaplan, S. (2008). The cognitive benefits of interacting with nature. *Psychological Science, 19*(12), 1207–1212. doi:10.1111/j.1467-9280.2008.02225.x PMID:19121124

Bernama, N. S. T. (2019, March 18). CIDB recommends mandatory use of BIM in certain private sector projects. *New Straits Time*. https://www.nst.com.my/news/nation/2019/03/470468/cidb-recommends-mandatory-use-bim-certain-private-sector-projects

Bernama. (2019). *KL, Selangor, Penang, Johor remain top choices for properties*. Bernama. https://www.bernama.com/en/news.php?id=1684671

Bernama. (2021, November 11). DOSM: Building material cost index rises 0.1-2.3% in Oct 2021. *The Malaysian Reserve*. https://themalaysianreserve.com/2021/11/11/dosm-building-material-cost-index-rises-0-1-2-3-in-oct-2021/

Bernheim, B., Bongshin, L., Ratul, M., & Sharad, A. (2016). *Home Automation in the Wild*. Challenges and Opportunities.

Bestoun, S., & Miroslav, B. (2019). Testing of Smart TV Applications. *Key Ingredients, Challenges and Proposed Solutions.* https://www.researchgate.net/publication/325102886_Testing_of_Smart_TV_Applications_Key_Ingredients_Challenges_and_Proposed_Solutions

Beukeboom, C. J., & Dijkstra, A. (2012). The effect of plants and fascia on stress-related symptoms and blood pressure in office workers: A randomized, controlled study. *Environmental Health Perspectives, 120*(3), 377–381.

Bhandari, P. (2020). A guide to operationalization. *Scribbr, 1*(03), 2021.

Bhandari, P. (2020). What is Qualitative Research? *Methods & Examples.* https://www.scribbr.com/methodology/qualitative-research/

Bhandari, P. (2022). *What is qualitative research? Methods & examples.* Scribbr. https://www.scribbr.com/methodology/qualitative-research/

Bhat, A. (2021, December 17). *Qualitative Research: Definition, Types, Methods and Examples.* QuestionPro. https://www.questionpro.com/blog/qualitative-research-methods/

Bidwell, D., & Schweizer, P. J. (2021). Public values and goals for public participation. *Environmental Policy and Governance, 31*(4), 257–269. doi:10.1002/eet.1913

Bilici, Z. K. (1991). *Kastamonu'da Türk Devri mimarisi ve şehir dokusunun gelişimi (18. yüzyıl sonuna kadar)* [PhD thesis]. Ankara Üniversitesi Sosyal Bilimler Enstitüsü.

Birbal, R., Ramdass, M., & Harripaul, M. C. (2018). Student teachers' attitudes towards blended learning. *Journal of Education and Human Development, 7*(2), 9–26. doi:10.15640/jehd.v7n2a2

Biruk, S., Jakowski, P., Czarnigowska, A., Jiang, W., Wu, W., Wei, M., Hadi, N. A., Othman, K. F., & Dadi, A. M. (2018). The Perception on the Importance of Construction Industry Payment and Adjudication Act (CIPAA) 2012 Towards Remedying Payment Disputes: A Research on Subcontractors in Kuching, Sarawak. *IOP Conference Series. Materials Science and Engineering, 429*(1), 012105. doi:10.1088/1757-899X/429/1/012105

Bødker, S., Ehn, P., Sjögren, D., & Sundblad, Y. (2000). *Co-operative Design—perspectives on 20 years with 'the Scandinavian IT Design Model'.* Paper presented at the proceedings of NordiCHI.

Bomia, L., Beluzo, L., Demeester, D., Elander, K., Johnson, M., & Sheldon, B. (1997). The impact of teaching strategies on intrinsic motivation. Champaign, IL: ERIC Clearinghouse on Elementary and Early Childhood Education.

Bönsch, J., Elstermann, M., Kimmig, A., & Ovtcharova, J. (2022). A subject-oriented reference model for Digital Twins. *Computers & Industrial Engineering, 172*, 108556. doi:10.1016/j.cie.2022.108556

Bota, P. (2021, September 30). Lack of raw materials causing problems in Construction Sector. *Majorca Daily Bulletin.* https://www.majorcadailybulletin.com/news/local/2021/10/01/90217/mallorca-construction-shortage-raw-materials.html

Bouchrika, I. (2020, June 30). *50 Online Education Statistics: 2020/2021 Data on Higher Learning & Corporate Training.* Research.Com. https://research.com/research/online-education-statistics

Bourreau, D., Aimene, Y., Beauchêne, J., & Thibaut, B. (2013). (n.d) Feasibility of glued laminated timber beams with tropical hardwoods. *Holz als Roh- und Werkstoff, 71*(5), 653–662. doi:10.100700107-013-0721-4

Bourreau, M., Aimene, Y., Beachene, S., & Thibaut, B. (2013). From GLT to GLVL: Developing new products for tropical hardwoods. In *Proceedings of the International Conference on Civil, Environmental and Construction Engineering (ICCECE'13)* (pp. 34-38). Paris, France.

Boyce, P. (2006). *Human factors in lighting* (2nd ed.). Taylor & Francis.

BQSM. (2021). *Accrediation Manual For Online Quantity Surveying Programmes*. BQSM. https://www.bqsm.gov.my/reference-documents/category/19-accreditation-manual.html

Brand, M. C., & Davenport, P. (n.d.). *A proposal for a "Dual Scheme" of statutory adjudication for the building and construction industry in Australia.*

Braubach, M., Egorov, A. I., Mudu, P., Wolf, T., Ward Thompson, C., & Martuzzi, M. (2017). Effects of urban green space on environmental health, equity and resilience: A scoping review. *Urban Forestry & Urban Greening, 29*, 310–323.

Brenčič, M., Bukovec, P., Kryžanowski, A., Kuzman, M. K., & Pavlič, M. (2017). Sustainability aspects of cross-laminated timber facade systems. *Energy and Building, 151*, 228–237.

Briggs, A. (2015). *Ten ways to overcome barriers to student engagement online*. Online Learning Consortium. https://onlinelearningconsortium.org/news_item/tenways-overcomebarriers-student-engagement-online/

Brophy, V. (2014). Building environmental assessment—a useful tool in the future delivery of holistic sustainability. The 2014 world sustainable building conference, Barcelona: Paper, Castillo-Villar, R. G. (2020). Identifying determinants of CSR implementation on SDG 17 partnerships for the goals. *Cogent Business & Management, 7*(1), 1847989. doi:10.1080/23311975.2020.1847989

Browning, W. D., Ryan, C. O., & Clancy, J. O. (2014). *14 Patterns of Biophilic Design*. Terrapin Bright Green LLC. https://www.terrapinbrightgreen.com/wp-content/uploads/2014/06/14-Patterns-of-Biophilic-Design-Terrapin-Bright-Green-2014.pdf

Bryan, C. Leighton, & Paisner. (2014). *The continued growth of statutory adjudication is good news for a global construction industry*. BCL Plaw. https://www.bclplaw.com/en-US/insights/the-continued-growth-of-statutoryadjudication-is-good-news-for-a-global-construction-industry.html

Buchanan, A. H., & Honey, T. J. (2020). *Timber: a global survey of mass-timber architecture, engineering and construction*. Thames & Hudson.

Building Research Establishment. (2018). *Barriers to the uptake of innovative construction products and processes in the UK*. BE Group. https://www.bregroup.com/wp-content/uploads/2018/08/Barriers-to-the-uptake-of-innovative-construction-products-and-processes-in-the-UK.pdf

Buisness2Community. (2022). *12 Best Metaverse Platforms to Play & Invest in February 2023*. Buisness2Community. https://www.business2community.com/cryptocurrency/best-metaverse-platforms

Bujang, S. D., Selamat, A., Krejcar, O., Maresova, P., & Nguyen, N. T. (2020, April 30). Digital Learning Demand for Future Education 4.0—Case Studies at Malaysia Education Institutions. *Informatics (MDPI), 7*(13), 11. doi:10.3390/informatics7020013

Bunard, D., & Kutnar, A. (2015). The effect of wood on stress responses in office workers. *Forests, 6*(7), 2336–2352.

Burnard, M., Fragiacomo, M., & Hozjan, T. (2017). Review of the perceptual qualities of timber and timber-based products relevant to sensory evaluation of indoor spaces. *Building and Environment, 124*, 52–63.

CABA. (n.d.). *What is mental wellbeing?* CABA. https://www.caba.org.uk/help-and-guides/information/what-mental-wellbeing

Cabrelles, M., Galcerá, S., Navarro, S., Lerma, J. L., Akasheh, T., & Haddad, N. (2009). Integration of 3D laser scanning, photogrammetry and thermography to record architectural monuments. Proc. of the 22nd International CIPA Symposium, .

Cairns, T. (2020). *How to create a restorative environment in the office*. Raconteur. https://www.raconteur.net/sustainability/how-to-create-a-restorative-environment-in-the-office

Cameron, L. (2006). Teaching with technology: Using online chat to promote effective in-class discussions. In *Proceedings of the 23rd Annual Conference of the Australasian Society for Computers in Learning in Tertiary Education: Who's Learning*. Ascilite.

Cannon, S., & Black, I. (2014). *Statutory Adjudication*. Chartered Institute of Arbitrators.

Cao, L. (2020, March). What to Expect from Interiors of the Future. *Archdaily.com*. https://www.archdaily.com/935089/what-to-expect-from-interiors-of-the-future

Cao, Y., Chye, H. K., & Chye, F. J. (2017). *The Impact of Elevated Neighborhood Open Spaces on the Elderly's Social Interactions in Singapore Public Housing*. 14th International Congress of Asian Planning Schools Association, Beijing, China.

Carbonell, C., & Saorín, J. (2017). Geospatial Google Street View with Virtual Reality: A Motivational Approach for Spatial Training Education. *ISPRS International Journal of Geo-Information*, *6*(9), 261. doi:10.3390/ijgi6090261

Castell, N., Dauge, F. R., Schneider, P., Vogt, M., Lerner, U., Fishbain, B., & Broday, D. M. (2016). Smartphone-based environmental sensing for personal exposure assessment. *Environmental Science & Technology*, *50*(21), 11507–11515.

Castree, N., Kitchin, R., & Rogers, A. (2013). *A dictionary of human geography*. Oxford University Press. doi:10.1093/acref/9780199599868.001.0001

Cejudo-Ruíz, J. P., García-Pérez, A., González-Velasco, H. M., & García-Zubía, J. (2019). Smartphone-based measurements of light and sound for environmental monitoring applications. *Sensors (Basel)*, *19*(19), 4253. PMID:31575009

Centers for Disease Control and Prevention. (2014). *Work-related stress*. National Institute for Occupational Safety and Health.

Centers for Disease Control and Prevention. (2020). *Mental health basics*. CDC. https://www.cdc.gov/mentalhealth/basics/index.htm

Cerasi, M. M. (1999). *Osmanlı Kenti*. Yapı Kredi Yayınları.

Cezar, M. (1983). *Typical Commercial Buildings of The Ottoman Classical Period And The Ottoman Construction System*. Türkiye İş Bankası Kültür Yayınları.

Chad, D., & Mohammad, A. (2019). Design and Implementation of an IoT- Based smart home Security System. *Atlantis Press SARL*. https://www.researchgate.net/publication/332667088_Design_and_Implementation_of_an_IoTBased_Smart_Home_Security_System

Chaiprasurt, C., Esichaikul, V., & Wishart, J. (2011). Designing mobile communication tools: A framework to enhance motivation in an online learning environment, *Proceedings of the 10th World Conference on Mobile and Contextual Learning*, (p. 112–120). Semantic Scholar.

Champion, E. M. (2006). *Evaluating cultural learning in virtual environments* [Doctoral thesis, The University of Melbourne].

Champion, E. (2019). Norberg-Schulz: Culture, Presence, and a Sense of Virtual Place. In E. Champion (Ed.), *The Phenomenology of Real and Virtual Places* (pp. 144–163). Routledge.

Chan, C. (2002). *Commonwealth Construction Cases: The Singapore Perspective*. Singapore: Sweet & Maxwell Asia, A Thomson Company.

Chan, J. (2019). Mont'Kiara: Still pulling in the expats. *The Edge Markets*. https://www.theedgemarkets.com/article/montkiara-still-pulling-expats

Chan, D. W. M., & Kumaraswamy, M. M. (2002). Compressing construction durations: Lessons learned from Hong Kong building projects. *International Journal of Project Management*, *20*(1), 23–35. doi:10.1016/S0263-7863(00)00032-6

Chandra, Y., & Leenders, M. A. A. M. (2012). User innovation and entrepreneurship in the virtual world: A study of Second Life residents. *Technovation*, *32*(7–8), 464–476. doi:10.1016/j.technovation.2012.02.002

Chang, K. (2021). *Defects Turning New House Owners' Delight to Dismay [Blog]*. Edge Prop. https://www.edgeprop.my/content/1899417/defects-turning-new-house-owners%E2%80%99-delight-dismay.

Chang, E., Kim, H. T., & Yoo, B. (2020). Virtual reality sickness: A review of causes and Measurements. *International Journal of Human-Computer Interaction*, *36*(17), 1658–1682. doi:10.1080/10447318.2020.1778351

Chang, J., Ren, Q., Han, H., & Xu, L. (2018). Integration and Service Strategy of VR/AR in practical teaching. *IOP Conference Series. Materials Science and Engineering*, *466*, 012109. doi:10.1088/1757-899X/466/1/012109

Changsong, W., Rahman, T., Sadat, A. A., Amalia, A., & Sudiwijajaya, E. (2021). *Digital Representation of the Coffee Culture and Cultural Heritage by Chinese Indonesian and Malaysian Coffee Brands*. GATR Journal of Management and Marketing Review. http://gatrenterprise.com/GATRJournals/JMMR/vol6_2021_issue2.html

Chanter, B., & Swallow, P. (2008). *Building Maintenance Management*. John Wiley & Sons.

Chartered Institute of Arbitrators. K. (n.d.). *Adjudication*. CIArb Kenya. https://ciarbkenya.org/adjudication/

Che Ani, A., Mohd Tawil, N., Johar, S., Abd Razak, M., & Yahaya, H. (2014). Building Condition Assessment for New Houses: A Case Study in Terrace Houses. *Jurnal Teknologi*, *70*(1). doi:10.11113/jt.v70.2812

Che Mohd Nasir, D. W. (2022). Housing as an Integral Development For Health categories that deliver a healthy housing in Malaysia. *International Journal of Accounting, Finance and Business*, 391

Chear, S. L. S., Hamzah, S. H., Yusof, N. M., & Nordin, N. (2021). Parents and neighbourhood engagement to enhance the quality of maintenance and safety of playgrounds in private kindergartens. *Jurnal Pendidikan Awal Kanak-kanak Kebangsaan*, *10*(1), 1–15.

Chemoxy. (2017). *What is low VOC and what are the benefits?* Chemoxy. https://www.chemoxy.com/about-2/knowledge-hub/what-is-low-voc/

Chen, S., & Lu, Y. (2013, June). The negative effects and control of blended learning in university. In *2013 the International Conference on Education Technology and Information*. Atlantis Press. 10.2991/icetis-13.2013.7

Chen, T. L., Eng, P. E. C., Ashrae, F., & Izdihar, A. (2013). *High performing buildings*. Malaysia energy commission headquarters (Diamond Building). HPB Magazine. https://www.hpbmagazine.org/malaysia-energy-commission-headquarters-putrajaya-malaysia

Cheng, J. C. P., Lu, Q., & Phil, M. (2015, October). *A Review of the Efforts and Roles of the Public Sector for BIM Adoption Worldwide*. ITcon. https://www.itcon.org/papers/2015_27.content.01088.pdf

Cheng, X., & Jin, W. (2006). Study on reverse engineering of historical architecture based on 3D laser scanner. *Journal of Physics: Conference Series*.

Chen, S., Wang, S., & Xu, H. (2017). Influence of place identity on residents' attitudes to dark tourism. *Journal of China Tourism Research*, *13*(4), 338–356. doi:10.1080/19388160.2017.1401023

Chen, W., Chen, J. Z., & So, R. H. Y. (2011). Visually induced motion sickness: Effects of translational visual motion along different axes. *Proceedings of the International Conference on Ergonomics & Human Factors*, (pp. 281–287). IEEE.

Chen, Y., & He, W. (2013). Security risks and protection in online learning: A survey. *International Review of Research in Open and Distance Learning*, *14*(5), 108–127. doi:10.19173/irrodl.v14i5.1632

Chen, Y., McCabe, O. L., & Hyman, M. R. (2020). Workplace stress and mental health in the era of COVID-19: An urgent need for action. *International Journal of Environmental Research and Public Health*, *17*(19), 7272. doi:10.3390/ijerph17197272 PMID:33027956

Cheshmehzangi, A. (2021). Revisiting the built environment: 10 potential development changes and paradigm shifts due to COVID-19. *Journal of Urban Management*, *10*(2), 166–175.

Chian, L. K., Tunku, U., & Rahman, A. (2016). *Benefits Of The Construction Industry Payment And Adjudication Act 2012 (Cipaa) And Its Impacts To Payment Problem In Construction*. Cipaa.

Choi, K., Yoon, Y. J., Song, O. Y., & Choi, S. M. (2018). Interactive and immersive learning using 360° virtual reality contents on mobile platforms. *Mobile Information Systems*, *2018*, 2018. doi:10.1155/2018/2306031

Choi, S.-H., Koh, K., Lee, K.-J., Hwang, C.-J., & Cha, J.-Y. (2018). Analysis of the morphological characteristics of the palatal rugae for three-dimensional superimposition of digital models in Korean subjects. *BioMed Research International*, *2018*, 2018. doi:10.1155/2018/3936918 PMID:30598994

Choo, J. (2022, July 14). *Home Tour: A Multi-Generational Family Home In Miri, Sarawak*. Tatler. https://www.tatlerasia.com/homes/home-tours/home-tour-a-multi-generational-family-home-in-miri-sarawak

Choong, S. (2020). *What Malaysian homebuyers should know about the Housing Development Act (HDA)?* iProperty.

Christoffersen, S. E., & Sarkissian, S. (2009). City size and fund performance. *Journal of Financial Economics*, *92*(2), 252–275. doi:10.1016/j.jfineco.2008.06.001

Christofi, M., Kyrlitsias, C., Michael-Grigoriou, D., Anastasiadou, Z., Michaelidou, M., Papamichael, I., & Pieri, K. (2018). A Tour in the Archaeological Site of Choirokoitia Using Virtual Reality: A Learning Performance and Interest Generation Assessment. In M. Ioannides (Ed.), *J*.

Chu, W. (2022, February 24). VR Setup 101: Building a functional room for VR. *Newegg Insider*. New Egg. https://www.newegg.com/insider/vr-setup-101-building-a-functional-room-for-vr/

Circuit stream. (2021, January 12). *VR locomotion: How to move in VR environment*. Circuit Stream. https://circuitstream.com/blog/vr-locomotion/

Clark, S., & Maher, M. L. (2003). The effects of a sense of place on the learning experience in a 3D virtual world. *Communities of Practice. Research Proceedings of the 10th Association for Learning Technologies Conference (ALT-C2003)*, 82–101.

Clarke, R. E., Briggs, J., Light, A., Heitlinger, S., & Crivellaro, C. (2014). Socially engaged arts practice in HCI. In *CHI'14 Extended Abstracts on Human Factors in Computing Systems* (pp. 69-74). doi:10.1145/2559206.2559227

Clemens, A. (2022). *Metaverse For Beginners A Guide To Help You Learn About Metaverse, Virtual Reality And Investing In NFTs*.

Clifford, N. J., French, S., & Valentine, G. (2010). *Key methods in geography*. 545.

COE. (2005). *Convention on the Value of Cultural Heritage for Society (Faro Convention, 2005)*. COE. https://www.coe.int/en/web/culture-and-heritage/faro-convention

COE. (2017). *Faro Convention Action Plan Handbook 2018-2019* (pp. 30). RM. https://rm.coe.int/faro-convention-action-plan-handbook-2018-2019/168079029c

Coles, J. (2021, September 13). *What causes motion sickness in VR, and how can you avoid it?* Space.com. https://www.space.com/motion-sickness-in-vr

Coman, C., Ţîru, L. G., Meseşan-Schmitz, L., Stanciu, C., & Bularca, M. C. (2020). Online teaching and learning in higher education during the coronavirus pandemic: Students' perspective. *Sustainability (Basel)*, *12*(24), 10367. doi:10.3390u122410367

Connolly, F. (2020, November 5). *Integrating Place-based Education Into Classroom or Distance Learning During the COVID-19 Pandemic*. U.S. Department of Education. https://ies.ed.gov/ncee/edlabs/regions/pacific/blogs/blog33_integrating-place-based-education-into-classroom.asp

Cook, M., Lischer-Katz, Z., Hall, N., Hardesty, J., Johnson, J., McDonald, R., & Carlisle, T. (2019). Challenges and strategies for Educational Virtual reality. *Information Technology and Libraries*, *38*(4), 25–48. doi:10.6017/ital.v38i4.11075

Coomer, N., Bullard, S., Clinton, W., & Williams-Sanders, B. (2018). Evaluating the effects of four VR locomotion methods. *Proceedings of the 15th ACM Symposium on Applied Perception*. ACM. 10.1145/3225153.3225175

Cooper, D., & Schindler, P. (2014). Business Research Methods.© The McGraw– Hill Companies.

Cooper, R., Fleischer, A., & Cotton, F. A. (2012). Building Connections: An Interpretative Phenomenological Analysis of Qualitative Research Students' Learning Experiences. *Qualitative Report*, *17*, 1–16.

Corporate Affairs Division, Malaysia Digital Economy Corporation (MDEC). (2022, July 4). *Malaysia Digital is Set To Accelerate Growth of Digital Economy*. MDEC. https://mdec.my/news: https://mdec.my/news/malaysia-digital-is-set-to-accelerate-growth-of-digital-economy

Cort, K. A. (2013). *Low-e Storm Windows: Market Assessment and Pathways to Market Transformation*. Pacific Northwest National Laboratory. doi:10.2172/1095439

Coughlin, S. S., Smith, S. A., & Fernandez, M. E. (2017). *Handbook of community-based participatory research*. Oxford University Press. doi:10.1093/acprof:oso/9780190652234.001.0001

Cover, V. R. (2022, August 16). Ways to make your meta quest 2 more comfortable. *VR Cover*. https://vrcover.com/ways-to-make-your-meta-oculus-quest-2-more- comfortable/

Craighead, G. (2009). *High-rise security and fire life safety*. Butterworth-Heinemann. doi:10.1016/B978-1-85617-555-5.00002-X

Crawford, C., Barker, J., & Seyam, A. A. (2014). The promising role of hybrid learning in community colleges: Looking towards the future.

Creighton, J. L. (2018). Public Participation. In Public Participation. Encyclopedia.com.

Creighton, J. L. (2005). *The public participation handbook: Making better decisions through citizen involvement*. John Wiley & Sons.

Creswell, J. W. (2013). *Research Design: Qualitative, Quantitative, and Mixed Methods Approaches* (4th ed.). SAGE Publications, Inc.

Criminale, A., & Langar, S. (2017). *Challenges with BIM implementation: A review of literature*. ResearchGate. https://www.researchgate.net/profile/Sandeep-Langar/publication/317842173_Challenges_with_BIM_Implementation_A_Review_of_Literature/links/594db74caca27248ae3436c2/Challenges-with-BIM-Implementation-A-Review-of-Literature.pdf

CRL. (2018). *7 Sustainable Construction Materials.* CRL. https://c-r-l.com/content-hub/article/sustainable-constructi on-materials/

Croome, D. (2013). *Creating and managing healthy built environments.* Routledge.

Cunneen, W. (2021, May 4). 5 problems with virtual reality training they don't want you to know. *Roundtable Learning.* https://roundtablelearning.com/5 -problems-with-virtual- reality-training-they-dont-want-you-to-know/

Cyon Research. (2003, February 19). *Architectural automation: Facing the challenges of work-culture.* (A Cyon Research White Paper). http://www.cyonresearch.com/portals/0/files/whitepapers/Cyon%20Research%20white%20paper %20 on%20Work-Culture%20030218%20-%20final%20form.pdf

Czeisler, C. A., Duffy, J. F., Shanahan, T. L., Brown, E. N., Mitchell, J. F., Rimmer, D. W., Ronda, J. M., Silva, E. J., Allan, J. S., Emens, J. S., Dijk, D.-J., & Kronauer, R. E. (1999). Stability, precision, and near-24-hour period of the human circadian pacemaker. *Science, 284*(5423), 2177–2181. doi:10.1126cience.284.5423.2177 PMID:10381883

Dai, J., Goodrum, P., & Maloney, W. (2009). Construction Craft Workers' Perceptions of the Factors Affecting Their Productivity. *Journal of Construction Engineering and Management, 135*(3), 217–226. doi:10.1061/(ASCE)0733-9364(2009)135:3(217)

Dalgarno, B., & Lee, M. J. W. (2010). What are the learning affordances of 3-D virtual environments? *British Journal of Educational Technology, 41*(1), 10–32. doi:10.1111/j.1467-8535.2009.01038.x

Daniel, D. (2021, February 9). *What Is Hybrid Learning?* ViewSonic Library. https://www.viewsonic.com/library/education/what-is-hybrid-learning/#What_Is_Hybrid_Learning

Daniel, T. C. (2014). Contributions of psychology to an understanding of the restorative environment. In *Biophilic Cities* (pp. 19–31). Island Press.

Daniotti, B., Gianinetto, M., & Della Torre, S. (Eds.). (2020). Digital Transformation of the Design, Construction and Management Processes of the Built Environment. Open Acces (Publishing in European Networks). doi:10.1007/978-3-030-33570-0

Darko, A. (2019). *Adoption of green building technologies in Ghana: Development of a model of green building technologies and issues influencing their adoption.* The Hong Kong Polytechnic University. https://ira.lib.polyu.edu.hk/handle/10397/80543.

Darko, A., Zhang, C., & Chan, A. (2017). Drivers for green building: A review of empirical studies. *Habitat International, 60*, 34–49. doi:10.1016/j.habitatint.2016.12.007

Darkot, B. (1977). *Kastamonu maddesi, Encyclopedia of Islam (vol. 6).* Milli Eğitim Bakanlığı Yayınları.

Das, R., Bhattacharya, I., & Saha, R. (2016). *Comparative Study between Different Types of Formwork, 1*(4), 173–175.

Davidson, S. (1998). Community Planning: Spinning the wheel of empowerment. *Planning (Chicago, Ill.), 3*, 14–15.

Davies, L. (2018). *Adjudication versus other approaches to construction disputes.* Pinset Masons. https://www.pinsent-masons.com/out-law/guides/adjudication-construction-disputes

Davis, F. D. (1989). Perceived usefulness, perceived ease of use, and user acceptance of information technology. *Management Information Systems Quarterly, 13*(3), 319–340. doi:10.2307/249008

De Certeau, M. (1998). *Living and Cooking* (Vol. 2). University of Minnesota Press.

de Kort, Y. A. W., Meijnders, A. L., Sponselee, A. A. G., & IJsselsteijn, W. A. (2006). What's wrong with virtual trees? Restoring from stress in a mediated environment. *Journal of Environmental Psychology*, *26*(4), 309–320. doi:10.1016/j.jenvp.2006.09.001

Dean. (2021, July 16). *The Pros and Cons of Hybrid Learning*. Dean College. https://www.dean.edu/news-events/dean-college-blog/story/the-pros-and-cons-of-hybrid-learning/#:%7E:text=Limited%20Internet%20Access%20Can%20Be,a%20long%20time%20to%20download

Debajyoti, P., Tuul, T., & Suree, F. (2017). smart homes and Quality of Life for the Elderly. *IEEE International Symposium*. IEEE.

Deli, R., Galantucci, L. M., Laino, A., D'Alessio, R., Di Gioia, E., Savastano, C., Lavecchia, F., & Percoco, G. (2013). Three-dimensional methodology for photogrammetric acquisition of the soft tissues of the face: A new clinical-instrumental protocol. *Progress in Orthodontics*, *14*(1), 1–15. doi:10.1186/2196-1042-14-32 PMID:24325783

Deng, J., Deng, Y., & Cheong, K. H. (2021). Combining conflicting evidence based on Pearson correlation coefficient and weighted graph. *International Journal of Intelligent Systems*. https://onlinelibrary.wiley.com/doi/abs/10.1002/int.22593

Department of Standards Malaysia. (2013). *MS 544:2013 Portland cement*. Department of Standards Malaysia.

Department of Statistics. (2020). *Malaysia Labour Force Statistics in Brief 2020*. DoSM. https://www.dosm.gov.my/v1/index.php?r=column/cthemeByCat&cat=155&bul_id=MGhZUTdVWXpveElUUldMYVhCRWlKQT09&menu_id=L0pheU43NWJwRWVSZklWdzQ4TlhUUT09

Department of Statistics. (2020). *Malaysia Labour Force Statistics in Brief 2020*. DOSM. https://www.dosm.gov.my/v1/index.php?r=column/cthemeByCat&cat=155&bul_id=MGhZUTdVWXpveElUUldMYVhCRWlKQT09&menu_id=L0pheU43NWJwRWVSZklWdzQ4TlhUUT09

Desai, N., & Kageni, E. (2022). *Arbitration procedures and practice in Kenya: overview*. Practical Law. https://uk.practicallaw.thomsonreuters.com/5338955?transitionType=Default&contextData=(sc.Default)&firstPage=true

Dezeen. (2023). *Metaverse*. Dezen. https://www.dezeen.com/tag/metaverse/

Dian, A. M., & Abdullah, N. C. (2013). Public participation in heritage sites conservation in Malaysia: Issues and challenges. *Procedia: Social and Behavioral Sciences*, *101*, 248–255. doi:10.1016/j.sbspro.2013.07.198

Dick, B. (2003). Robust processes for learning, change and action research. Retrieved from http://bobdick.com.au/DLitt/index.html

Dincelli, E., & Yayla, A. (2022). Immersive virtual reality in the age of the Metaverse: A hybrid-narrative review based on the technology affordance perspective. *The Journal of Strategic Information Systems*, *31*(2), 101717. doi:10.1016/j.jsis.2022.101717

DiSalvo, C., Clement, A., & Pipek, V. (2012). Communities: Participatory Design for, with and by communities. In Routledge international handbook of participatory design (pp. 202-230): Routledge.

Dixson, M. D. (2010). Creating Effective Student Engagement in Online Courses: What Do Students Find Engaging? *The Journal of Scholarship of Teaching and Learning*, *10*(2), 1–13.

Dola, K., & Mijan, D. (2006). Public participation in planning for sustainable development: Operational questions and issues. *International Journal on Sustainable Tropical Design Research & Practice*, *1*(1), 1–8.

Dolan, M., Fullam, R., & Casey, E. (2016). The relationship between indoor environmental quality in Irish offices and occupant perceived health and productivity. *Building and Environment*, *108*, 290–298.

Dollarhide, M. (2019). Social media definition. *Investopedia*. http://billscomputerpot. com/menus/windows/SocialMedia. pdf

Dona, E., & Elvitigalage Dona, A. (2008). *Women's career advancement and training & development in the construction Industry*. Salford. http://usir.salford.ac.uk/id/eprint/9822/

Dorst, K. (2011, November). The core of 'design thinking' and its application. *Design Studies, 32*(6), 521–532. doi:10.1016/j.destud.2011.07.006

DOSM. (2021). *Department of Stastistics Malaysia Official Portal*. Malaysia's Official Statistics. https://www.dosm. gov.my/v1/index.php?r=home/index&menu_id=dHVYa1N5WVZPeTU2cXF6dHNZYVRtdz09

Dozio, N., Marcolin, F., Scurati, G. W., Ulrich, L., Nonis, F., Vezzetti, E., Marsocci, G., La Rosa, A., & Ferrise, F. (2022). A design methodology for affective Virtual reality. *International Journal of Human-Computer Studies, 162*, 102791. doi:10.1016/j.ijhcs.2022.102791

Drennan, J., Kennedy, J., & Pisarski, A. (2005). Factors affecting student attitudes toward flexible online learning in management education. *The Journal of Educational Research, 98*(6), 331–338. doi:10.3200/JOER.98.6.331-338

Duggal, S. K. (2008). *Building Materials*. New Age International.

Dunleavy, M., Dede, C., & Mitchell, R. (2009). Affordances and limitations of immersive participatory augmented reality simulations for teaching and learning. *Journal of Science Education and Technology, 18*(1), 7–22. doi:10.100710956-008-9119-1

Duruz, J. J., & Khoo, G. C. (2014). *Eating Together: Food*. Space, and Identity in Malaysia and Singapore.

Dwivedi, Y. K., Hughes, D. L., Coombs, C., Constantiou, I., Duan, Y., Edwards, J. S., Gupta, B., Lal, B., Misra, S., Prashant, P., Raman, R., Rana, N. P., Sharma, S. K., & Upadhyay, N. (2020). Impact of COVID-19 pandemic on information management research and practice: Transforming education, work and life. *International Journal of Information Management, 55*, 102211. doi:10.1016/j.ijinfomgt.2020.102211

Dwivedi, Y. K., Hughes, L., Baabdullah, A. M., Ribeiro-Navarrete, S., Giannakis, M., Al-Debei, M. M., Dennehy, D., Metri, B., Buhalis, D., Cheung, C. M. K., Conboy, K., Doyle, R., Dubey, R., Dutot, V., Felix, R., Goyal, D. P., Gustafsson, A., Hinsch, C., Jebabli, I., & Wamba, S. F. (2022). Metaverse beyond the hype: Multidisciplinary perspectives on emerging challenges, opportunities, and agenda for research, practice and policy. *International Journal of Information Management, 66*, 102542. Advance online publication. doi:10.1016/j.ijinfomgt.2022.102542

Dye, C. (2007). Health and urban living. *Science, 318*(5852), 766–769. PMID:18258905

Dziuban, C., Moskal, P., Thompson, J., Kramer, L., DeCantis, G., & Hermsdorfer, A. (2015). Student Satisfaction with Online Learning: Is It a Psychological Contract. *Online Learning : the Official Journal of the Online Learning Consortium, 19*(2), n2. doi:10.24059/olj.v19i2.496

Eastman, C., Teicholz, P., Sacks, R., & Liston, K. (2008). *BIM Handbook*. BIM. doi:10.1002/9780470261309

Eatough, V., & Smith, J. A. (2008). Interpretative phenomenological analysis. In *The Sage handbook of qualitative research in psychology* (pp. 179–194). SAGE Publications. doi:10.4135/9781848607927.n11

Eckerd, A., & Heidelberg, R. L. (2020). Administering Public Participation. *American Review of Public Administration, 50*(2), 133–147. doi:10.1177/0275074019871368

Economic Planning Unit. (2021). *Sustainable Development Goals*. Economic Planning Unit, Prime Minister's Department: https://www.epu.gov.my/en/sustainable-development-goals

Education Destination Malaysia. (2018, June 29). *5 Benefits of Extracurricular Activities*. Education Destination Malaysia. https://educationdestinationmalaysia.com/blogs/5-benefits-of-extracurricular-activities

Education Times. (2009, March 16). Importance of guidance. Career, Higher Education & Study Abroad. *Education Times*. https://www.educationtimes.com/article/editors- pick/69574156/importance-of-guidance

Ehsan Che Munaaim, M. (2019). *Five years on: A review of statutory adjudication in Malaysia*. HKA. https://www.hka.com/review-of-statutory-adjudication-inmalaysia/

El Said, G. R. (2021). How did the COVID-19 pandemic affect higher education learning experience? An empirical investigation of learners' academic performance at a university in a developing country. *Advances in Human-Computer Interaction, 2021*, 1–10. doi:10.1155/2021/6649524

Eldeeb, I. (2020, November 16). *Online Learning: 6 Threats Schools and Students Should be Prepared for*. GAT Labs. https://n.gatlabs.com/blogpost/6-online-learning-threats-for-schools/

Eldem, S. H. (1987). *Türk Evi: Osmanlı Dönemi:III*. Türkiye Anıt Çevre Turizm Değerlerini Koruma Vakfı.

Elia, R. J. (2020). Charter for the Protection and Management of the Archaeological Heritage (1990). In Encyclopedia of Global Archaeology (pp. 2184-2186): Springer International Publishing Cham.

El-Seoud, M. A. S., El-Khouly, M., & Taj-Eddin, I. A. T. F. (2015). Strategies to enhance learner's motivation in e-learning environment. In *Proceedings of 18th International Conference on Interactive Collaborative Learning* (pp. 944–949). 10.1109/ICL.2015.7318154

Emmitt, S., & Yeomans, D. T. (2008). *Specifying buildings: a design management perspective* (2nd ed.). Elsevier. doi:10.4324/9780080569710

Environmental Defense Fund. (2019). *Measuring air quality with smartphone sensors: A practical guide for citizen scientists*. EDF. https://www.edf.org/health/measuring-air-quality-smartphone-sensors-practical-guide-citizen-scientists

EPA. (2022). *Public Participation Guide: Tools to Generate and Obtain Public Input*. EPA. https://www.epa.gov/international-cooperation/public-participation-guide-tools-generate-and-obtain-public-input

Ergenç, Ö. (1978). Osmanlı Şehrinde Esnâf Örgütlerinin Fizik Yapıya Etkileri, I. In Uluslararası Türkiye'nin Sosyal ve Ekonomik Tarihi Kongresi Tebliğleri, 103-109.

Erkan Biçer, N. Ç. (2002). Kastamonu Kent Örneğinde Anadolu Kenti İmaj Öğeleri ve Değişim Süreci. Doktora Tezi, Yıldız Teknik Üniversitesi Fen Bilimleri Enstitüsü, İstanbul.

Esa, M. E., Marhani, M. A., Yaman, R., Hassan, A. A., Rashid, N. H. N., & Adnan, H. (2011). Obstacles in Implementing Green Building Projects in Malaysia. *Australian Journal of Basic and Applied Sciences, 10*, 1806–1812.

Esa, M. R. (2011). Obstacles in implementing Green Building projects in Malaysia. *Australian Journal of Basic and Applied Sciences*, 1806–1812.

Esch, T., Kim, M. J., Stefano, G. B., Fricchione, G. L., Benson, H., & Kirschbaum, C. (2019). The city versus the country: A cross-sectional study of cortisol and depression in urban and rural areas. *BMC Psychiatry, 19*(1), 1–9. PMID:30606141

Essiet, I. O., Sun, Y., & Wang, Z. (2019). Optimized energy consumption model for smart home using improved differential evolution algorithm. *Energy, 172*, 354–365. https://www.researchgate.net/publication/322201732_Smart_Homes_and_Quality_of_Life_for_the_Elderly_A_Systematic_Review. doi:10.1016/j.energy.2019.01.137

Evans, J. (2016). *Can high-rise buildings ever work as cohesive living spaces?* FT. https://www.ft.com/content/870e12f8-1d19-11e6-a7bc-ee846770ec15

Experience Crew. (2019, June 28). *Why is price of VR so high?: Blog: Experience AR/VR Company.* Experience. https://4experience.co/why-is-price-of-vr-so-high

Eyüpgiller, K. (1995). *Kastamonu Kent Tarihi.* Yayımlanmamış Doktora Tezi, İstanbul: İstanbul Teknik Üniversitesi Fen Bilimleri Enstitüsü.

Eyüpgiller, K., Topçubaşı, M., & Polat, I. (2008). Kastamonu'da 19. yüzyıl Ticaret Yapıları. *METU JFA, 25*(2), 1–20.

Fabi, V., Spigliantini, G., & Corgnati, S. P. (2017). Insights on smart home concept and occupants' interaction with building controls. *Energy Procedia, 111*, 759–769. doi:10.1016/j.egypro.2017.03.238

Facey, M. E., Middleton, J., & Griffiths, P. (2015). Managing Employee Stress and Wellness in the New Normal. In E. G. Carayannis & Y. H. Zhao (Eds.), *The Handbook of Stress and Health: A Guide to Research and Practice* (pp. 441–454). Springer. doi:10.1007/978-1-4939-3117-6_25

Facey, M. E., Rees, C. E., & Monrouxe, L. V. (2015). Being 'student-led': Challenging hierarchy in healthcare education and identifying solutions. *Journal of Further and Higher Education, 39*(2), 248–265.

Fadhil Muhammad, S. W. (2019). Building Material in The Perspective of Energy Efficiency and Thermal Environment in TOD Area. *IOP Conference Series. Earth and Environmental Science*, 2–6.

Falk, B., Duinker, P., & Vailshery, L. (2020). Barriers to using cross-laminated timber and glue-laminated timber in North America. *Forests, 11*(9), 933.

Fard, P. A., Sharif, M. K. M., Mohd Yunos, M. Y., & Mydin, M. A. O. (2015). Preference on social spaces in high density condominiums in Malaysia. *Applied Mechanics and Materials, 747*, 165–167. doi:10.4028/www.scientific.net/AMM.747.165

Farooq, U. (2014). Social interaction, Definition, Elements, Types & Forms. *Study Lecture Notes.* http://www.studylecturenotes.com/basics-of-sociology/social-interaction-definition-elements-types-forms

Faroqhi, S. (2000). *Osmanlı'da Kentler ve Kentliler.* Tarih Vakfı Yurt Yayınları.

Fell, D. (2010). *Nature, landscape and natural spaces in universities: Restorative qualities of familiar places for students.* University of Manchester.

Feng, L., Wu, Q., Wu, W., & Liao, W. (2020). Decision-maker-oriented vs. collaboration: China's public participation in environmental decision-making. *Sustainability (Basel), 12*(4), 1334. doi:10.3390u12041334

Fiorillo, F., Rizzi, G., & Achille, C. (2021). Learning through virtual tools: Visit a place in the pandemic era. *The International Archives of the Photogrammetry, Remote Sensing and Spatial Information Sciences, XLVI-M-1-2021*, 225–232.

Firmansyah, R., Putri, D. M., Wicaksono, M. G. S., Putri, S. F., & Arif, A. (2021, July). The University Students' Perspectives on the Advantages and Disadvantages of Online Learning Due to COVID-19. In *Journal of College Science Teaching, 40*(1), 34–40.

Fisher. (2017). *What Are The Benefits And Risks Of Adjudication?* Fisher Cogginswaters. https://www.fisherscogginswaters.co.uk/blog/article/248/what-are-the-benefits-andrisks- of-adjudication

Flesten, L. (2009). *The influence of natural views in an office environment on recovery from mental fatigue.* [Bachelor's thesis, Lund University, Lund, Sweden].

Fojut, N. (2018). *The Encyclopedia of Archaeological Sciences*, 1-4. Faro Convention.

Fonseca, L. M., Domingues, J. P., & Dima, A. M. (2020). Mapping the Sustainable Development Goals Relationships. *Sustainability (Basel)*, *12*(8), 3359. doi:10.3390u12083359

Foo, L. C., Rahman, I. A., Asmi, A., Nagapan, S., & Khalid, K. I. (2013). Classification and Quantification of Construction Waste at Housing Project Site. *International Journal of Zero Waste Generation*, *1*, 1–4.

Forcada, N., Macarulla, M., Fuertes, A., Casals, M., Gangolells, M., & Roca, X. (2012). Influence of Building Type on Post-Handover Defects in Housing. *Journal of Performance of Constructed Facilities*, *26*(4), 433–440. doi:10.1061/(ASCE)CF.1943-5509.0000225

Forcada, N., Macarulla, M., Gangolells, M., & Casals, M. (2014). Assessment of Construction Defects in Residential Buildings in Spain. *Building Research & Amp. Information (Basel)*, *42*(5), 629–640.

Forcada, N., Macarulla, M., Gangolells, M., & Casals, M. (2015). Handover Defects: Comparison of Construction and Post-Handover Housing Defects. *Building Research &Amp. Information (Basel)*, *44*(3), 279–288.

Forest and Wood Products Australia (FWPA). (2017). *WoodSolutions: Cross Laminated Timber (CLT) and Glue Laminated Timber (GLT)*. Wood Solutions. https://www.woodsolutions.com.au/articles/cross-laminated-timber-clt-and-glue-laminated-timber-glt

Francesco Asdrubali, F. D. (2015). A review of unconventional sustainable building insulation materials. *Sustainable Materials and Technologies*, *1*.

Francisco, L. S., Marcel, Z., & Rolando, D. L. (2022). The Interaction of Product Attractiveness and Decision-Making Style on ConsumerPurchase Intention: A Cultural Moderation Perspective. Journal of International Consumer Marketing.

Franzoni, E. (2011). Materials selection for green buildings: Which tools for engineers and architects? *545. Procedia Engineering*, *21*, 883–890. doi:10.1016/j.proeng.2011.11.2090

Froese, A. D., Carpenter, C. N., Inman, D. A., Schooley, J. R., Barnes, R. B., Brecht, P. W., & Chacon, J. D. (2012). Effects of classroom cell phone use on expected and actual learning. *College Student Journal*, *46*(2), 323–332.

Froese, T. M. (2010). The impact of Emerging Information Technology on project management for Construction. *Automation in Construction*, *19*(5), 531–538. doi:10.1016/j.autcon.2009.11.004

Fry, K. (2001). E-learning markets and providers: Some issues and prospects. *Education + Training*, *43*(4/5), 233–239. doi:10.1108/EUM0000000005484

Fry, L. W., & Egel, E. (2021). Global Leadership for Sustainability. *Sustainability (Basel)*, *13*(11), 6360. doi:10.3390u13116360

Fu, Q. K., & Hwang, G. J. (2018). Trends in mobile technology-supported collaborative learning: a systematic review of journal publications from 2007 to 2016. *Computers and Education*, *119*(2017), 129–143.

Fuller, R. A., & Gaston, K. J. (2009). The scaling of green space coverage in European cities. *Biology Letters*, *5*(3), 352–355. doi:10.1098/rsbl.2009.0010 PMID:19324636

Furrer, C., & Skinner, E. (2003). Sense of relatedness as a factor in children's academic engagement and performance. *Journal of Educational Psychology*, *95*(1), 148–162. doi:10.1037/0022-0663.95.1.148

Fu, Y., & Ma, W. (2020). Sustainable urban community development: A case study from the perspective of self-governance and public participation. *Sustainability (Basel)*, *12*(2), 617. doi:10.3390u12020617

Gamage, A. (2020). *Alternative Dispute Resolution in Construction Contracts*. Sihela Consultants. https://sihelaconsultants.com/alternative-dispute-resolution-inconstruction/

Garmur, M. (2020). *How do you calculate overperforming scores.*

Gautam, P. (2020, October 10). *Advantages And Disadvantages Of Online Learning.* ELearning Industry. https://el-earningindustry.com/advantages-and-disadvantages-online-learning

GBI. (2004). *What and why green buildings?* Green Building Index. https://www.greenbuildingindex.org/what-and-why-green-buildings

Ghani, I., Rafi, A., & Woods, P. (2016). Sense of place in immersive architectural virtual heritage environment. *2016 22nd International Conference on Virtual System & Multimedia (VSMM)*, 1–8.

Gharechelou, S., Tateishi, R., & Johnson, A. (1711). B. (2018). A simple method for the parameterization of surface roughness from microwave remote sensing. *Remote Sensing, 10*(11). Advance online publication. doi:10.3390/rs10111711

Ghazali, M., Bajunid, A., & Davis, P. (2014). The "sky neighborhood" layout. *International Journal on Tall Buildings and Urban Habitat -. CTBUH Journal, II*, 40–47.

Ghel, J. (1971). *Life between buildings: Using public space.* Island Press.

Gherheş, V., Stoian, C. E., Fărcaşiu, M. A., & Stanici, M. (2021). E-Learning vs. Face-To-Face Learning: Analyzing Students' Preferences and Behaviors. *Sustainability (Basel), 13*(8), 4381. doi:10.3390u13084381

Ghiasi, S., Hassanzadeh, M., & Forghanifar, B. (2015). Role of public participation in Sustainable City.

Giarla, A. (2021, December 29). *The Benefits Of Blended Learning.* TeachThought. https://www.teachthought.com/technology/benefits-of-blended-learning/

Gibberd, F. (1982). Harlow: The design of a new town. *The Town Planning Review, 53*(1), 29. doi:10.3828/tpr.53.1.m44nk27n01w15383

Gill, P., Stewart, K., Treasure, E., & Chadwick, B. (2008). Methods of data collection in qualitative research: interviews and focus groups. *British Dental Journal 2008, 204*(6), 291–295. doi:10.1038/bdj.2008.192

Ginzarly, M., Roders, A. P., & Teller, J. (2019). Mapping historic urban landscape values through social media. *Journal of Cultural Heritage, 36*, 1–11. doi:10.1016/j.culher.2018.10.002

Goff, J., Ervin, J., Lorentz, M., & Ring, R. (2016). There's no such thing as Perfect Technology. There's No Such Thing As Perfect Technology.| *Theology of Technology - A Camp Infinity Blog.* https://campinfinity.com/blog/2016/09/05/truth-3/

Gökoğlu, A. (1952). *Paphlagonia.* Doğrusöz Matbaası.

Gomez, C. (2016). The socialscraper. In *Cities to Megacities.* Shaping Dense Vertical Urbanism.

Google Earth. (n.d.). *Street View.* Google. https://www.google.com/earth/education/tools/street-view/

Google for Education. (n.d.). *Future of the Classroom: Emerging trends in classroom education.* Google for Education. https://edu.google.com/future-of-the-classroom/

Gopal, P. S., Tamizi, N. E. A., Shaed, M. M., Malek, N. M., & Yahaya, M. H. (2021). Kesejahteraan dalam Pembangunan Komuniti Program Perumahan Rakyat (PPR): Suatu Pemerhatian Awal. [MJSSH]. *Malaysian Journal of Social Sciences and Humanities, 6*(10), 292–302. doi:10.47405/mjssh.v6i10.1065

Gould, N. (n.d.). *Adjudication in Malaysia.* Fenwick Elliott. www.fenwickelliott.co.uk

Green Building Action Plan. (2022). The University of British Columbia. https://sustain.ubc.ca/campus/green-buildings/green-building-action-plan#:~:text=OVERVIEW,to%20human%20and%20natural%20systems

Green Building Index (GBI). (2019). GBI Residential New Construction (RNC) Tool *V3.0*. https://new.greenbuildingindex.org/Files/Resources/GBI%20Tools/GBI%20RNC%20Residential%20Tool%20V3.0.pdf

Green Building Index. (2019). Green Building Index INTERIORS - Design reference guide & submission format. GBI.

Green Pages Malaysia. (2020). *Directory*. Green pages Malaysia. http://www.greenpagesmalaysia.com/directory/

Greenbaum, J., & Kyng, M. (2020). *Design at work: Cooperative design of computer systems*. CRC Press. doi:10.1201/9781003063988

Grey, C. N., & Birrell, C. (2014). Green over grey: The importance of biophilic design in a temporary site office. *Indoor and Built Environment, 23*(6), 863–877.

Grilli, G., Mohan, G., & Curtis, J. (2020). Public park attributes, park visits, and associated health status. *Landscape and Urban Planning, 199*, 103814. doi:10.1016/j.landurbplan.2020.103814

Grimmer, A., & Wille, R. (2020). Integrated Design Process. In *Designing Droplet Microfluidic Networks* (pp. 127–133). Springer. doi:10.1007/978-3-030-20713-7_9

Grind, C. C., & Patil, G. G. (2009). The effect of indoor foliage plants on health and discomfort symptoms among office workers. *HortTechnology, 19*(2), 278–282.

Groat, L., & Wang, D. (2013). *Architectural research methods*. Wiley & Sons.

Grondzik, W. T., & Kwork, A. G. (2014). *Mechanical and Electrical Equipment for Buildings*. Wiley. doi:10.5860/CHOICE.29-6058

Group, W. B. (2020). *Individuals using the Internet (% of population) - Iran*. World Bank. https://data.worldbank.org/indicator/IT.NET.USER.ZS?locations=IR

Gunasagaran, S., & Mari, M. (2014). Using Digital Simulation as an E-Learning Tool to Create Dynamic Learning in Architecture Students. *Global Journal of Business and Social Science Review, 2*(3), 61–68. doi:10.35609/gjbssr.2014.2.3(10)

Gunasagaran, S., Mari, M. T., Srirangam, S., & Kuppusamy, S. (2019). Adoption of social media by architecture students in fostering community SERVICE initiative using technology acceptance model. []. IOP Publishing.]. *IOP Conference Series. Materials Science and Engineering, 636*(1), 012015. doi:10.1088/1757-899X/636/1/012015

Gunay, H. B., O'Brien, W., Beausoleil-Morrison, I., & Cui, Y. (2017). Smartphone sensor-based building energy auditing. *Building and Environment, 123*, 152–162.

Günel, H., & Ilgın, H. (2014). *Tall Buildings Structural Systems and Aerodynamic Form*. Routledge. https://doi.org/https://doi.org/10.4324/9781315776521 doi:10.4324/9781315776521

Gupta, S. (2017, November 11). *9 Benefits Of eLearning For Students*. ELearning Industry. https://elearningindustry.com/9-benefits-of-elearning-for-students

Gür, M. (2020). Post-pandemic lifestyle changes and their interaction with resident behavior in housing and neighborhoods: Bursa, Turkey. *Journal of Housing and the Built Environment*, 823–828. PMID:34512216

Habibullah, M. S., Sanusi, N. A., Abdullah, L., Kusairi, S., Golam Hassan, A. A., & Ghazali, N. A. (2018). Does the less developed states in Malaysia catching-up to the Richer State of Selangor? *Journal of Contemporary Issues and Thought, 8*, 29–40. doi:10.37134/jcit.vol8.4.2018

Hadi, Y., Heath, T., & Oldfield, P. (2014). Vertical public realms: Creating urban spaces in the sky. In *Future Cities: Towards Sustainable Vertical Urbanism–2014 Shanghai Conference Proceedings,* 112–119.

Haidawati, N., Fuead, A., Kushsairy, K., & Sheroz, K. (2018). The Implementation of IoT Based Smart Refrigerator System. *International Conference on Smart Sensors and Application.* IEEE.

Hajmirsadeghi, R. S., Shamsuddin, S., Bin Lamit, H., & Foroughi, A. (2013). Design's factors influencing social interaction in public squares. *European Online Journal of Natural and Social Sciences, 2*(4), 556–564.

Hamdan, K., & Ben-Chabane, Y. (2013) An interactive mobile learning method to measure students' performance. *QScience Proceedings, 12th World Conference on Mobile and Contextual Learning* (mLearn 2013). Qatar.

Hamzah, A. B. (2006). *Guide to fire protection in Malaysia. Kuala Lumpur: The Institute of Fire Engineers.* Malaysia Branch.

Hanlee, I. (2019). Human-centred design in digital media. In *The Routledge international handbook of new digital practices in galleries, libraries, archives, museums and heritage sites* (pp. 319–325). Routledge. doi:10.4324/9780429506765-28

Hannay, M., & Newvine, T. (2006). Perceptions of distance learning: A comparison of online and traditional learning. *Journal of Online Learning and Teaching, 2*(1), 1–11.

Hargreaves, T., Wilson, C., & Hauxwell-Baldwin, R. (2018). Learning to live in a smart home. *Building Research and Information, 46*(1), 127–139. doi:10.1080/09613218.2017.1286882

Harlan, H., Badara, A., & Kamaluddin, K. (2019). The use of hand phone application to increase student's ability in learning English vocabulary. *Journal Pendidikan Bahasa, 8*(2), 106–107.

Harold. (2017). *Statutory Adjudication 101.* HLP Lawyers. https://hlplawyers.com/statutory-adjudication-101/

Haron, N. A., Soh, R. P. Z. A. R., & Harun, A. (2017). *Implementation of building information modelling (Bim) in malaysia: A review.* ResearchGate. https://www.researchgate.net/publication/318266244_Implementation_of_building_information_modelling_Bim_in_malaysia_A_review

Harper James Solicitors. (2020). *A Guide To The Adjudication Process.* Harper James Solicitors. https://hjsolicitors.co.uk/article/guide-to-adjudication-in-construction-disputes/

Harrison, R., Flood, D., & Duce, D. (2013). Usability of mobile applications: Literature review and rationale for a new usability model. *Journal of Interaction Science, 1*(1), 1–16. doi:10.1186/2194-0827-1-1

Harshal, S., Rpalundarkar, V., Surve,S., Biswas, B. (2018). Internet of Things Based smart home Automation. *International Journal of Scientific Research & Engineering Trends, 4*(1).

Hartig, T., Evans, G. W., Jamner, L. D., Davis, D. S., & Gärling, T. (1996). Tracking restoration in natural and urban field settings. *Journal of Environmental Psychology, 16*(2), 87–101.

Hartini, L. B. W. (2020). Sustainable Materials and Technologies with Environmentally Sustainability Materials. *IOP Conference Series. Materials Science and Engineering,* 1–5.

Hashem, H., Abbas, Y. S., Akbar, H. A., & Nazgol, B. (2013). Comparison the concepts of sense of place and attachment to place in Architectural Studies. *Malaysia Journal of Society and Space, 9*(1), 107–117.

Hassan, A. M., & Lee, H. (2015). The paradox of the sustainable city: Definitions and examples. *Environment, Development and Sustainability*, *17*(6), 1267–1285. doi:10.100710668-014-9604-z

Hassanein, K., Head, M., & Wang, F. (2010). Understanding student satisfaction in a mobile learning environment: the role of internal and external facilitators. *2010 Ninth International Conference on Mobile Business and 2010 Ninth Global Mobility Roundtable* (ICMB-GMR), (pp.289–296). IEEE. 10.1109/ICMB-GMR.2010.38

Hattingh, V., & Maritz, M. J. (n.d.). *Should the application and practice of construction adjudication be underpinned by legislative intervention in the South African construction industry?* SCL. www.scl.org.uk

Hayes, G. R. (2011). The relationship of action research to human-computer interaction. [TOCHI]. *ACM Transactions on Computer-Human Interaction*, *18*(3), 1–20. doi:10.1145/1993060.1993065

Hayes, S. J., & Dockerill, B. (2020). A Park for the People: Examining the creation and refurbishment of a public park. *Landscape Research*, 1–14.

Haynes, B. P. (2008). Workplaces and low carbon behaviour. *Building Research and Information*, *36*(2), 196–212.

Headspace. (n.d.). Face To Face Vs. Online Learning Options. *headspace*. https://headspace.org.au/explore-topics/for-young-people/face-to-face-vs-online-learning/

Heerwagen, J. H. (2000). Green buildings, organizational success and occupant productivity. *Building Research and Information*, *28*(5-6), 353–367. doi:10.1080/096132100418500

Hefferon, K., & Gil-Rodriguez, E. (2011). Reflecting on the rise in popularity of interpretive phenomenological analysis. *The Psychologist*, *24*(10), 756–759.

Heitlinger, S. (2017). *Talking Plants and a Bug Hotel: Participatory Design of ludic encounters with an urban farming community*.

Heschong, L., Heschong, M., & Wright, R. (2003). *Windows and offices: A study of office worker performance and the indoor environment*. California Energy Commission.

Heschong, L., Wright, R. L., Okura, S., & Moule, R. A. Jr. (2002). *Windows and Offices: A Study of Office Worker Performance and the Indoor Environment*. California Energy Commission.

Hidayati, W., Mokhtar, W., & Ismail, A. (2018). Adoption of smart home Technologies Features Among the Homeowners in Hulu Hangat, Selangor. *International Journal of Real Estate Studies*. https://www.utm.my/intrest/

Hietanen, J., & Drogemuller, R. (2008, January). *Approaches to university level BIM education*. ResearchGate. https://www.researchgate.net/publication/233604171_Approaches_to_university_level_BIM_education

Hillstrom, J. E. (2019). Virtual Place-Based Learning in Interdisciplinary Contexts: A Psychological Perspective and a Meta-analytic Review. In R. D. Lansiquot & S. P. MacDonald (Eds.), *Interdisciplinary Perspectives on Virtual Place-Based Learning* (pp. 13–34). Springer International Publishing. doi:10.1007/978-3-030-32471-1_2

Hiltz, S. R., & Turoff, M. (2002). What makes learning networks effective? *Communications of the ACM*, *45*(4), 56–59. doi:10.1145/505248.505273

Hinkle, D. E., Wiersma, W., & Jurs, S. G. (2003). *Applied statistics for the behavioral sciences* (Vol. 663). Houghton Mifflin College Division.

Ho, L. (2019, November 15). *13 Reasons Why Online Learning Is an Effective Way to Learn*. Lifehack. https://www.lifehack.org/856820/online-learning-effective

Hodgson, C. (2015, December 5). *4 Tips To Create High Quality Content In eLearning*. ELearning Industry. https://elearningindustry.com/4-tips-create-high-quality-content-elearning

Holley, D., & Oliver, M. (2010). Student engagement and blended learning: Portraits of risk. *Computers & Education*, *54*(3), 693–700. doi:10.1016/j.compedu.2009.08.035

Holtzhausen, D. (2020). *Designing post-pandemic office spaces*. Engineering News. https://www.engineeringnews.co.za/article/designing-post-pandemic-office-spaces-2020-07-10

Hong, C. (2016). *Investigation of Defects in New Buildings in Malaysia*. Eprints.utar.edu.my

Hrastinski, S. (2008). Asynchronous and synchronous e-learning. *EDUCAUSE Quarterly*, *31*(4), 51–55.

Huang, S. C. L. (2006). A study of outdoor interactional spaces in high-rise housing. *Landscape and Urban Planning*, *78*(3), 193–204. doi:10.1016/j.landurbplan.2005.07.008

Huang, W., Zhang, Y., & Zeng, W. (2022). Development and application of digital twin technology for integrated regional energy systems in smart cities. *Sustainable Computing: Informatics and Systems*, *36*, 100781. doi:10.1016/j.suscom.2022.100781

Huang, Y., Tu, M., Wang, S., Chen, S., Zhou, W., Chen, D., Zhou, L., Wang, M., Zhao, Y., Zeng, W., Huang, Q., Xu, H., Liu, Z., & Guo, L. (2020). Clinical characteristics of laboratory confirmed positive cases of SARS-CoV-2 infection in Wuhan, China: A retrospective single center analysis. *Travel Medicine and Infectious Disease*, *36*, 101606. doi:10.1016/j.tmaid.2020.101606 PMID:32114074

Hua, W., Qiao, Y., & Hou, M. (2020). The great wall 3d documentation and application based on multi-source data fusion– a case study of no. 15 enemy tower of the new guangwu great wall. *The International Archives of the Photogrammetry, Remote Sensing and Spatial Information Sciences*, *43*, 1465–1470. doi:10.5194/isprs-archives-XLIII-B2-2020-1465-2020

Huber, D., Akinci, B., Tang, P., Adan, A., Okorn, B., & Xiong, X. (2010). Using laser scanners for modeling and analysis in architecture, engineering, and construction. 2010 44th Annual Conference on Information Sciences and Systems (CISS). ISS.

Huerta, O., Unver, E., Aslan, R., Kus, A., & Chotrov, D. (2019). Application of VR and AR Tools for Technical Drawing Education. *Proceedings of CAD'19*. CAD Solutions. 10.14733/cadconfP.2019.363-366

Hugh. (2017). *Construction Adjudication*. Hugh James. https://www.hughjames.com/service/construction/construction-adjudication

Huh, Y. (2020). 360 Virtual Reality Project to Inspire Future Educators to be Creators. *Journal of Education for Teaching*, *46*(3), 421–423. doi:10.1080/02607476.2020.1766833

Humphreys, D., Singer, B., McGinley, K., Smith, R., Budds, J., Gabay, M., Bhagwat, S., de Jong, W., Newing, H., & Cross, C. (2019). *SDG 17: Partnerships for the Goals-Focus on Forest Finance and Partnerships*.

Hunt, V. (2016, December 18). *Pros And Cons Of Blended Learning At College*. ELearning Industry. https://elearningindustry.com/pros-cons-blended-learning-at-college

Hu, P. J., Chau, P. Y. K., Sheng, O. R. L., & Tam, K. Y. (1999). Examining the technology acceptance model using physician acceptance of telemedicine technology. *Journal of Management Information Systems*, *16*(2), 91–112. doi:10.1080/07421222.1999.11518247

Huynh-The, T., Pham, Q.-V., Pham, X.-Q., Nguyen, T. T., Han, Z., & Kim, D.-S. (2022). Artificial Intelligence for the Metaverse. *Survey (London, England)*. doi:10.1016/j.engappai.2022.105581

Hwang, B. G., & Tan, J. S. (2010). Green building project management: Obstacles and solutions for sustainable development. *Sustainable Development*. Advance online publication. doi:10.1002d.492

Hydes, K., & Creech, L. (2000). Reducing mechanical equipment cost: The economics of green design. *Building Research and Information*, 28(5/6), 403–407. doi:10.1080/096132100418555

IAP2. (2000). *International Association of Public Participation*. IAP2. https://www.iap2.org/404.aspx?404;http://iap2.org:80/practitionertools/index.shtml]

IAP2. (2019). *IAP2 Core Values*. IAP2. https://www.iap2.org.au/About-Us/About-IAP2-Australasia-/Core-Values/

IAP2. (2019). *IAP2 Public Participation Spectrum*. Internation Association for Public Participation. https://www.iap2.org.au/resources/spectrum/

Ibáñez, L. A. H., & Naya, V. B. (2012). Cyberarchitecture: A Vitruvian approach. *Proceedings of the 2012 International Conference on Cyberworlds, Cyberworlds 2012*, 283–289. 10.1109/CW.2012.48

Ibrahim, M. (2007). *The challenge of integrating BIM based CAD in today's architectural curricula*. Papers.cumincad.org. http://papers.cumincad.org/data/works/att/ascaad2007_051.content.pdf

ICOMOS. (1975). *The Declaration of Amsterdam*. ICOMOS. https://www.icomos.org/en/and/169-the-declaration-of-amsterdam

ICOMOS. (1987). *Washington Charter: Charter on the Conservation of Historic Towns and Urban Areas (1987)*. ICOMOS. https://www.icomos.org/images/DOCUMENTS/Charters/towns_e.pdf

Idrus, N., & Ho, C. (2008). *Affordable and Quality Housing Through the Low Cost Housing Provision in Malaysia*. Researchgate.

Immersion, V. R. (2022) *VR for education - the future of education*. Immersion VR. https://immersionvr.co.uk/about-360vr/vr- for-education/

Indeed. (2021). *What Is Research Methodology and Why Is it Important?* Indeed.com. https://www.indeed.com/career-advice/career-development/researchmethodology

InMobi. (2021). *Understanding Android Users Worldwide*. InMobi. https://www.inmobi.com/blog/understanding-android-users-worldwide

Installation & Finishing. (2022). *Elmwood Reclaimed Timber*. Elmwood Reclaimed Timber. https://www.elmwoodreclaimedtimber.com/resources/installation-finishing/

Irvin, R. A., & Stansbury, J. (2004). Citizen participation in decision making: Is it worth the effort? *Public Administration Review*, 64(1), 55–65. doi:10.1111/j.1540-6210.2004.00346.x

Iryani Mohamed Nasir, N. I., Ismail, Z., & Muhd Fadhlullah Ng, N. K. (2018). *View of Comparative Analysis On Construction Adjudication Systems Towards Effective Implementation Of Statutory Adjudication In Malaysia*. UTM Journals. https://journals.utm.my/mjce/article/view/16025/7499

Islam, R., Islam, R., & Mazumder, T. (2010). Mobile application and its global impact. *IACSIT International Journal of Engineering and Technology*, 10(6), 72–78.

Ismail S., Muhammad N., and Ahmad Z. (2020), Bending properties of Mengkulang Gluedlaminated (glulam) timber and laminated veneer lumber (LVL). *International Journal of Basic and Applied Sciences*, 20(02).

Ismail, I., Che-Ani, A., Abd-Razak, M., Mohd-Tawil, N., & Johar, S. (2015). Common Building Defects in New Terrace Houses. *Jurnal Teknologi*, *75*(9), 83–88. doi:10.11113/jt.v75.5239

It, P. (2020, November 17). [*Advantages of Traditional Education*. University of the Potomac. https://potomac.edu/top-advantages-of-traditional-education/]. *Top (Madrid)*, *6*,.

ITU. (2021). *Statistics*. ITU. https://www.itu.int/en/ITU-D/Statistics/Pages/stat/default.aspx

Ivan. (2022, June 2). *What graphics card do you need for VR in 2022? A short guide*. KommandoTech. https://kommandotech.com/guides/what-graphics-card-do-you-need-for- vr/

Jacob, K. (2018). *It's really complicated to connect the Home of the Future*. The Verge.

Jaggars, S. S., & Xu, D. (2016). How do online course design features influence student performance? *Computers & Education*, *95*, 270–284. doi:10.1016/j.compedu.2016.01.014

Jalil, A. (2021, November 2). Construction sector applies the highest number of foreign. *The Malaysian Reserve*. https://themalaysianreserve.com/2021/11/02/construction-sector-applies-the-highest-number-of-foreign-worker/

Jamal, K. A. A., Mohammad, M. F., Hashim, N., Mohamed, M. R., & Ramlil, M. A. (2019). Challenges of Building Information Modelling (BIM) from the Malaysian Architect's Perspective. *Sci.* https://sci-hub.hkvisa.net/https://doi.org/10.1051/matecconf/201926605003

James, C. (2020). What is a smart home? *Investopedia*. https://www.investopedia.com/terms/s/smart-home.asp

Janz, B. B. (2018). Virtual Place and Virtualized Place. In *The Phenomenology of Real and Virtual Places*. Routledge. doi:10.4324/9781315106267-6

Japheth, L. (2013). *St Diamond Building: The green building landmark in Southeastasia*. JAPHET LIM. http://blog.japhethlim.com/index.php/2013/10/15/st-diamond-building-the-green-building-landmark-in-southeast Asia.

Jekabsone, I., & Sloka, B. (2017). The role of municipality in promotion of well-being: development of public services. *Economic and Social Development: Book of Proceedings*, 713-721.

Jia, Y., Liu, B., Jiang, W., Wu, B., & Wang, C. (2020). Poster: Enhancing Remote Healthiness Attestation for Constrained IoT Devices. In *2020 IEEE 28th International Conference on Network Protocols (ICNP)* (pp. 1-2). IEEE.

Jiang, L., Liu, D. Y., & Yang, B. (2004, August). Smart home research. In Proceedings of 2004 international conference on machine learning and cybernetics (IEEE Cat. No. 04EX826) (*Vol. 2*, pp. 659-663). IEEE. 10.1109/ICMLC.2004.1382266

Jibladze, G., Romelashvili, E., Chkheidze, A., Modebadze, E., & Mukeria, M. (2021). *Assessing public participation in policymaking process*.

Jiménez-Aceituno, A., Peterson, G. D., Norström, A. V., Wong, G. Y., & Downing, A. S. (2020). Local lens for SDG implementation: Lessons from bottom-up approaches in Africa. *Sustainability Science*, *15*(3), 729–743. doi:10.100711625-019-00746-0

JLN. (2020). *Pelan Induk Lanskap Majlid Perbandaran dan Majlis Daerah Malaysia*. JLN. http://www.jln.gov.my/resources/index/user_1/Text Documents/Dokumen Penerbitan/Manual PIL/Manual_Pelan_Induk_Landskap_1.pd

Joarder, M. A., & Price, A. D. F. (2013). Factors influencing visual quality and occupants' preference in office buildings. *Architectural Science Review*, *56*(2), 146–155.

Johnson. N. (2021, August 12). *The effects of blended learning on students in higher education*. Software2. https://www.software2.com/resource-centre/remote-learning/blended-learning-effects

Johnson, C. (2014). *Local civic participation can help reinforce the legitimacy of the democratic system*. Democratic Audit Blog.

Johnson, J. T. (2012). Place-based learning and knowing: Critical pedagogies grounded in Indigeneity. *GeoJournal*, *77*(6), 829–836. doi:10.100710708-010-9379-1

Joseph, P. S., & Tretsiakova-McNally, S. (2010). Sustainable non-metallic building materials. *Sustainability (Basel)*, *2*(2), 400–427. doi:10.3390u2020400

Josephson, P., & Hammarlund, Y. (1999). The Causes and Costs of Defects in Construction. *Automation in Construction*, *8*(6), 681–687. doi:10.1016/S0926-5805(98)00114-9

JPBD. (2016). *Perancang Bandar Dan Desa*. JPBD. https://www.townplan.gov.my/index.php?option=com_docman&view =flat&layout=table&category%5B0%5D=48&category_children=1&ow n=0&Itemid=427&lang=ms&limit=20&limitstart=20

Jusufi, I., & Capra, B. (2019). Energy consumption in building materials: Comparison between traditional and innovative materials. *Energy Procedia*, *158*, 2094–2099. doi:10.1016/j.egypro.2019.01.550

Kamara, J. M., Anumba, C. J., & Evbuomwan, N. F. O. (2002). Capturing Client Requirements in Construction Projects. In Capturing Client Requirements in Construction Projects. doi:10.1680/ccricp.31036

Kamaruddin, N., & Rogers, R. A. (2020). Malaysia's democratic and political transformation. *Asian Affairs: An American Review*, *47*(2), 126–148. doi:10.1080/00927678.2020.1715046

Kamarulbaid, A. M., & Mustapha, N. A. (2021). The Role of Food Image in Promoting Domestic Tourism. *International Journal of Academic Research in Business & Social Sciences*, *11*(16). doi:10.6007/IJARBSS/v11-i16/11226

Kang, J. (2019). *Performing A Building Defects Inspection During Vacant Possession*. Pegasus Work.

Kankal, A. (2004). *Türkmen'in Kaidesi Kastamonu (XV-XVIII. Yüzyıllar Arası Şehir Hayatı)*. Zafer Matbaa.

Kaplan, S. (1989). The restorative benefits of nature: Toward an integrative framework. *Journal of Environmental Psychology*, *15*(3), 169–182. doi:10.1016/0272-4944(95)90001-2

Kaplan, S. (1995). The restorative environment: Nature and human experience. In J. L. Nasar & A. S. G. Nasar (Eds.), *Environmental aesthetics: Theory, research, and application* (pp. 233–250). Cambridge University Press. doi:10.1017/CBO9780511525599.017

Kaplan, S. (2001). Meditation, restoration, and the management of mental fatigue. *Environment and Behavior*, *33*(4), 480–506. doi:10.1177/00139160121973106

Karakul, Ö. (2015). An Integrated Methodology for the Conservation of Traditional Craftsmanship in Historic Buildings. *International Journal of Intangible Heritage*, *10*, 136–144.

Kazaz, B., Poddar, S., Arabi, S., Perez, M. A., Sharma, A., & Whitman, J. B. (2021). Deep Learning-Based Object Detection for Unmanned Aerial Systems (UASs)-Based Inspections of Construction Stormwater Practices. *Sensors (Basel)*, *21*(8), 2834.

Ke, F., & Kwak, D. (2013). Constructs of student-centered online learning on learning satisfaction of a diverse online student body: A structural equation modeling approach. *Journal of Educational Computing Research, 48*(1), 97-122. doi: . e doi:10.2190/EC.48.1

Keaton, W., & Gilbert, A. (2020). Successful Online Learning: What Does Learner Interaction with Peers, Instructors and Parents Look Like? *Journal of Online Learning Research*, *6*(2), 129–154.

Kedzierski, M., Wierzbicki, D., Fryskowska, A., & Chlebowska, B. (2016). Analysis Of The Possibilities Of Using Low-Cost Scanning System In 3d Modeling. *The International Archives of the Photogrammetry, Remote Sensing and Spatial Information Sciences*, 41.

Keengwe, J., & Kidd, T. T. (2010, June 2). *Towards Best Practices in Online Learning and Teaching in Higher Education*. Merlot. https://jolt.merlot.org/vol6no2/keengwe_0610.pdf

Keith, J., & Topping, W. D. (2022, May 10). Effectiveness of online and blended learning from schools: A systematic review. *Review of Education*, 10(2), 1–41. doi:10.1002/rev3.3353

Kejanlı, D. (2010). Anadolu'da Selçuklu ve Osmanlı Dönemlerinde Kent. *E-Journal of New World Sciences Academy*, 5(3), 287–303.

Kemp, S. (2021). Digital 2021: Iran. Retrieved from https://datareportal.com/reports/digital-2021-iran

Keng, T. Z., & Kah, S. (2018). Effectiveness Of Construction Industry Payment And Adjudication Act (CIPAA) In Remedying Payment Issues Among Sub-Contractors. INTI JOURNAL-BUILT ENVIRONMENT Faculty of Engineering and Quantity Surveying, 2(5).

Kennedy, R. J., & Buys, L. (2015). The impact of private and shared open space on liveability in subtropical apartment buildings. In Global Interchanges: Resurgence of the Skyscraper City, 318–323.

Kennedy, P. (2006). Progress of statutory adjudication as a means of resolving disputes in construction in the United Kingdom. *Journal of Professional Issues in Engineering Education and Practice*, 132(3), 236–247. doi:10.1061/(ASCE)1052-3928(2006)132:3(236)

Kennedy, R., Stanney, K., & Dunlap, W. (2000). Duration and exposure to virtual environments: Sickness curves during and across sessions. *Presence (Cambridge, Mass.)*, 9(5), 463–472. doi:10.1162/105474600566952

Kensing, F., & Greenbaum, J. (2013). In J. Simonsen, & T. Robertson. Heritage: Having a say. Routledge international handbook of participatory deisgn, 21e36.

Khalil, H., Suha Ibrahim, A. (2019). Security Challenges and Limitations in IoT Environments. *International Journal of Computer Science and Network Security*.

Khalil, A., & Stravoravdis, S. (2019). H-BIM and the domains of data investigations of heritage buildings current state of the art. 2nd International Conference of Geomatics and Restoration (GEORES 2019), .

Khan, A., Egbue, O., Palkie, B., & Madden, J. (2017). Active learning: Engaging students to maximize learning in an online course. *Electronic Journal of e-Learning*, 15(2), 107–115.

Khan, M. M. Jr, Howe, E. T., Chu, A. H., & Nunamaker, J. F. Jr. (2008). *The impact of a nature view on stress reduction of users in a virtual reality simulated office environment. 27th International Conference on Information Systems*, Milwaukee, WI, USA.

Khaza, M. K. B., Rahman, M. M., Harun, F., & Roy, T. K. (2020). Accessibility and service quality of public parks in Khulna City. *Journal of Urban Planning and Development*, 146(3), 04020024. doi:10.1061/(ASCE)UP.1943-5444.0000589

Khoo, G. C. (2009). Kopitiam: Discursive cosmopolitan spaces and national identity in Malaysian culture and media. In Everyday Multiculturalism. doi:10.1057/9780230244474

Kim, D.-H., & Gratchev, I. (2021). Application of optical flow technique and photogrammetry for rockfall dynamics: A case study on a field test. *Remote Sensing*, 13(20), 4124.

Kirsten, G., & Sarah, J. (2017). "Home is where the smart is?" Evaluating smart home research and approaches against the concept of home. *Energy Research & Social Science, 37*, 94–101.

Kjellgren, A., & Buhrkall, H. (2010). A comparison of the restorative effect of a natural environment with that of a simulated natural environment. *Journal of Environmental Psychology, 30*(4), 464–472. doi:10.1016/j.jenvp.2010.01.011

Klemmer, R. S., Thomsen, M., Phelps-Goodman, E., Lee, R., & Landay, J. A. (2002). Where do websites come from? Capturing and interacting with design history. In *Proc. CHI 2002* (pp. 1-8). ACM Press.

Knight Frank. (2019). *Real Estate Highlights: 1st Half 2019*. Knight Frank. https://content.knightfrank.com/research/179/documents/en/ malaysia-real-estate-highlights-1h-2019-6532.pdf

Koca, G. (2017). Interior Finishing Materials. *Research Gate*, 606-617.

Koh, K., Kusnadi, Y., Pan, G., & Shankararaman, V. (2022). Making virtual project-based learning work during the COVID-19 pandemic. [IJE]. *International Journal of Education, 10*(02), 1–14. doi:10.5121/ije.2022.10201

Koksal, I. (2020, May 2). *The Rise Of Online Learning*. Forbes. https://www.forbes.com/sites/ilkerkoksal/2020/05/02/the-rise-of-online-learning/?sh=125b1ff72f3c

Kong, L., & Yeoh, B. S. (1994). Urban conservation in Singapore: A survey of state policies and popular attitudes. *Urban Studies (Edinburgh, Scotland), 31*(2), 247–265. doi:10.1080/00420989420080231

Kopraman, K. Y. (1989). Memluk Kaynaklarına Göre XV. yüzyılda Kastamonu ve Çevresi. Türk Tarihinde ve Kültüründe Kastamonu, Tebliğler.

Kothari, C. R. (2004). *Research methodology: Methods and techniques*. New Age International.

Kreitzer, M. J. (2014). Well-being concepts. In *Complementary and Integrative Therapies for Mental Health and Aging* (pp. 3–18). Oxford University Press.

Krejcie, R. V., & Morgan, D. W. (1970). Determining Sample Size for Research Activities. *Educational and Psychological Measurement, 30*(3), 607–610. doi:10.1177/001316447003000308

Krummel, J. W. (2018). The Kyoto School Philosophy on Place: Nishida and Ueda. *The Phenomenology of Real and Virtual Places*, 141.

Kuban, D. (1967). Kastamonu'nun Tarihi Yapısı ve Bu Yapının İmar Planında Değerlendirilmesiyle İlgili Rapor. Academic Press.

Kuban, D. (1968). Anadolu-Türk Şehri, Gelişmesi, Sosyal ve Fiziki Özellikleri Üzerine Bazı Gözlemler. *Vakıflar Dergisi*, (7), 53–73.

Kubat, A. S., Asami, Y., & İstek, İ. C. (2001). Characterization of Street Networks in Turkish – Islamic Urban Form. *Proceedings 3rd International Space Syntax Symposium*.

Kulkarni, M. (2019). *10 Things architects learn about in environmental studies in college*. Rethinking The Future. https://www.re-thinkingthefuture.com/rtf-fresh-perspectives/a1693-10-things-architects-learn-about-in-environmental-studies-in-college/

Kumar, J., Konar, R., & Balasubramanian, K. (2020). The impact of Social Media on Consumers' purchasing behaviour in Malaysian Restaurants. *Journal of Spatial and Organizational Dynamics, 8*(3), 197–216.

Kumar, V., Jones, E., Venkatesan, R., & Leone, R. P. (2011). Is market orientation a source of sustainable competitive advantage or simply the cost of competing? *Journal of Marketing, 75*(1), 16–30. doi:10.1509/jm.75.1.16

Kuo, F. E., & Sullivan, W. C. (2001a). Aggression and violence in the inner city: Effects of environment via mental fatigue. *Environment and Behavior, 33*(4), 543–571. doi:10.1177/00139160121973124

Kuo, F. E., & Sullivan, W. C. (2001b). Environment and crime in the inner city: Does vegetation reduce crime? *Environment and Behavior, 33*(3), 343–367. doi:10.1177/0013916501333002

Kuo, Y. C., Walker, A. E., Belland, B. R., & Schroder, K. E. (2013). A predictive study of student satisfaction in online education programs. *International Review of Research in Open and Distance Learning, 14*(1), 16–39. doi:10.19173/irrodl.v14i1.1338

Kuruyazıcı, H. (1998). Cumhuriyet'in İstanbul'daki Simgesi Taksim Cumhuriyet Meydanı, 75 Yılda Değişen Kent ve Mimarlık Bilanço'98, Tarih Vakfı Yayınları, İstanbul.

Kymmell, W. (2008, January). *Building Information Modeling: Planning and managing construction projects with 4D CAD and simulations (McGraw-Hill Construction Series)*. Access Engineering. https://www.accessengineeringlibrary.com/content/book/9780071494533

Laal, M. (2011). Lifelong learning: What does it mean? *Procedia: Social and Behavioral Sciences, 28*, 470–474. doi:10.1016/j.sbspro.2011.11.090

Laal, M., Laal, M., & Kermanshahi, Z. K. (2012). 21st century learning; learning in collaboration. *Procedia: Social and Behavioral Sciences, 47*, 1696–1701. doi:10.1016/j.sbspro.2012.06.885

Lachapelle, P., & Austin, E. (2014). Community participation. In J. B. Metzler (Ed.), *Encyclopedia of Quality of Life and Well-Being Research* (pp. 1073–1078). doi:10.1007/978-94-007-0753-5_471

Lafsozluk. (2009). Retrieved January, 20, 2023, from https://www.lafsozluk.com/2009/04/kastamonu-ilinin-ilceleri-ve-nufus-sayilari.html

Lai, J. (2021). *Latent Defects: Beyond Defect Liability Period - Limitation Period for Latent Defects*. IPM.

Lanang, W. N. W. W., & Hassan, M. S. (2021). Crime Prevention Program in Perak through the Role of the Royal Malaysian Police (PDRM) and the Community. *Perspektif: Jurnal Sains Sosial Dan Kemanusiaan, 13*(1), 85–101.

Lang, B. (2021, December 3). *How to tell if your PC is VR ready*. Road to VR. https://www.roadtovr.com/how-to-tell-pc-virtual-reality-vr-oculus- rift-htc-vive-steam-vr-compatibility-tool/

Langbehn, E., Lubos, P., & Steinicke, F. (2018). Evaluation of locomotion techniques for room-scale VR. *Proceedings of the Virtual Reality International Conference*. Laval Virtual. 10.1145/3234253.3234291

Langgat, J., Pawan, M. T., Fabeil, N. F., & Pazim K. H. (2020). Green Kopitiam and Local Intentions to Visit. *Asian Journal of Entrepreneurship*, 72-82.

Langran, E., & DeWitt, J. (2020). Facilitating Student Learning. In *Navigating Place-Based Learning: Mapping for a Better World* (pp. 91–115). Springer. doi:10.1007/978-3-030-55673-0_4

Larco, N. (2016). Sustainable urban design–a (draft) framework. *Journal of Urban Design, 21*(1), 1–29. doi:10.1080/13574809.2015.1071649

Larkin, M., Watts, S., & Clifton, E. (2006). Giving voice and making sense in interpretative phenomenological analysis. *Qualitative Research in Psychology, 3*(2), 102–120. doi:10.1191/1478088706qp062oa

Lateef, O. (2009). Building Maintenance Management in Malaysia. *Journal Of Building Appraisal, 4*(3), 207–214. doi:10.1057/jba.2008.27

Latiffi, A., Mohd, S., & Rakiman, U. (2015, October). *Potential Improvement of Building Information Modeling (BIM) Implementation in Malaysian Construction Projects.* ResearchGate. https://www.researchgate.net/publication/290443821_Potential_Improvement_of_Building_Information_Modeling_BIM_Implementation_in_Malaysian_Construction_Projects

Laurell, C., Sandström, C., Berthold, A., & Larsson, D. (2019). Exploring barriers to adoption of Virtual Reality through Social Media Analytics and Machine Learning–An assessment of technology, network, price and trialability. *Journal of Business Research*, *100*, 469–474. doi:10.1016/j.jbusres.2019.01.017

Lauren, L., Nasibeh, Z., & Sherif, A. (2019). *Health Monitoring in smart homes Utilizing Internet of Things.* Department of Electrical and Computer Engineering.

Lau, Y. (2020). *Building Defect Assessment - Building Inspection Services Malaysia.* IPM.

Lawrence, J. (n.d.). *How a Property Inspection Can Save You Money.* Realestateinvestar.

Laws of Malaysia. (1984). *Uniform building by-laws 1984.* International Law Book Services.

Laws of Malaysia. (1984). *Uniform building by-laws 1984. Kuala Lumpur: International Law Book.* Services Malaysian Timber Council.

Lawson, L., & Kearns, A. (2010). Community engagement in regeneration: Are we getting the point? *Journal of Housing and the Built Environment*, *25*(1), 19–36. doi:10.100710901-009-9168-7

Learning and Education Center. (n.d.). *NSU Florida.* Learning and Education Center. https://www.nova.edu/lec/This-Week-in-the-LEC/2019/August/Benefits%20of%20Blogging%20in%20Education.html#:~:text=Blogging%20develops%20students'%20analytical%20thinking,their%20thoughts%20about%20the%20subject

Lee, A. C. K., Jordan, H. C., Horsley, J., & Value, E. (2015). The health benefits of urban green spaces: A review of the evidence. *Journal of Public Health*, *38*(3), e450–e461. PMID:20833671

Lee, J., Ahn, S. C., & Hwang, J.-I. (2018). A walking-in-place method for virtual reality using position and orientation tracking. *Sensors (Basel)*, *18*(9), 2832. doi:10.339018092832 PMID:30150586

Leeraphong, A., Papasratorn, B., & Chongsuphajaisiddhi, V. (2016). A study on the Factors Influencing Elderly Intention to use smart home in Thailand. *10th International Conference INCEB2016.* IEEE.

Leonard, E., & Gardiner, H. (2017). *Statutory adjudication of construction contracts in the UK.* Womble Bond Dickinson. https://www.womblebonddickinson.com/uk/insights/articles-and-briefings/statutoryadjudication-construction-contracts-uk

Leonhard, R. (1915). *Paphlagonia.* Buch, Reimer.

Lerma, J. L., Navarro, S., Cabrelles, M., Seguí, A. E., Haddad, N., & Akasheh, T. (2011). Integration of laser scanning and imagery for photorealistic 3D architectural documentation. *Laser scanning, theory and applications*, 414-430.

Lewin, K. (1946). Action research and minority problems. *The Journal of Social Issues*, *2*(4), 34–46. doi:10.1111/j.1540-4560.1946.tb02295.x

Life, S. (2023). Retrieved 27 February 2023, from https://secondlife.com/

Lim, C. F. (2016). *Resolution Of Construction Industry Disputes: Arbitration, Statutory Adjudication Or Litigation In The Construction Court?* Mondaq. https://www.mondaq.com/constructionplanning/467878/resolution-of-construction-industry-disputes-arbitration-statutoryadjudication-or-litigation-in-the-construction-court

Liu, L., Chen, J., Cai, Q., Huang, Y., & Lang, W. (2020). System Building and Multistakeholder Involvement in Public Participatory Community Planning through Both Collaborative-and Micro-Regeneration. *Sustainability (Basel)*, *12*(21), 8808. doi:10.3390u12218808

Liu, Z. (2007). *Internet Based PPGIS for Public Involved Spatial Decision Making.* ProQuest.

Li, X., Wu, P., Shen, G. Q., Wang, X., & Teng, Y. (2017). Mapping the knowledge domains of Building Information Modeling (BIM): A bibliometric approach. *Automation in Construction, 84*(July), 195–206. doi:10.1016/j.autcon.2017.09.011

Li, X., Yi, W., Chi, H.-L., Wang, X., & Chan, A. P. C. (2018). A critical review of virtual and augmented reality (VR/AR) applications in Construction Safety. *Automation in Construction, 86*, 150–162. doi:10.1016/j.autcon.2017.11.003

Loizides, F., El Kater, A., Terlikas, C., Lanitis, A., & Michael, D. (2014). Presenting cypriot cultural heritage in virtual reality: A user evaluation. *Progress in Cultural Heritage: Documentation, Preservation, and Protection, 572*–579. Digital Heritage. doi:10.1007/978-3-319-13695-0_57

López Peláez, A., Erro-Garcés, A., Pinilla García, F. J., & Kiriakou, D. (2021). Working in the 21st Century. The coronavirus crisis: A driver of digitalization, teleworking, and innovation, with unintended social consequences. *Information (Basel), 12*(9), 377. doi:10.3390/info12090377

Lopez, J. (n.d.). *Defects in Strata Buildings in Malaysia: Your Homebuyer Rights & How to Build a Legal Case.* Jmb-malaysia.org.

Lottrup, L., Stigsdotter, U. K., Meilby, H., & Claudi, A. G. (2013). The workplace window view: A determinant of office workers' work ability and job satisfaction. *Landscape Research, 38*(2), 259–267.

Lottrup, L., Stigsdotter, U. K., Meilby, H., Claudi, A. G., & Grahn, P. (2013). Workplace greenery and perceived level of stress: Benefits of access to a green outdoor environment at the workplace. *Landscape and Urban Planning, 110*, 5–11. doi:10.1016/j.landurbplan.2012.09.002

Love, P., Irani, Z., Li, H., Tse, R., & Cheng, E. W. L. (2001, March). *An empirical analysis of the barriers to implementing e-commerce in small-medium sized construction contractors in the state of Victoria, Australia.* Emerald Insight.

Lunce, L. M. (2006). Simulations: Bringing the benefits of situated learning to the traditional classroom. *Journal of Applied Educational Technology, 3*(1), 37–45.

Lv, Z., Qiao, L., Li, Y., Yuan, Y., & Wang, F. Y. (2022). BlockNet: Beyond reliable spatial Digital Twins to Parallel Metaverse. *Patterns (New York, N.Y.), 3*(5), 100468. Advance online publication. doi:10.1016/j.patter.2022.100468 PMID:35607617

Lynch, G. (2021, September 13). *How to set up your room for VR.* Space.com. https://www.space.com/how-to-set-up-your-room-for-vr

Lyons, S. H. (2017). *Digital Engagement, Social Media & Public Participation.* International Association for Public Participation.

Maben, J., & Bridges, J. (2020). Covid-19: Supporting nurses' psychological and mental health. *Journal of Clinical Nursing, 29*(15-16), 2742–2750. doi:10.1111/jocn.15307 PMID:32320509

MacCallum, K. (2009) 'Student characteristics and variables that determine mobile adoption: An initial study', *Proceedings of the Universal College of Learning: Teaching and Learning Conference*, (pp. 1–8). IEEE.

Macj. (n.d.). *How Home Inspection Can Save You Time & Money – Professional Home Inspection, India.* Professional Home Inspection, India.

Madanipour, A. (2011). Sustainable development, urban form, and megacity governance and planning in Tehran. In *Megacities* (pp. 67–91). Springer. doi:10.1007/978-4-431-99267-7_4

Magis, K. (2010). Community resilience: An indicator of social sustainability. *Society & Natural Resources*, *23*(5), 401–416. doi:10.1080/08941920903305674

Magomadov, V. S. (2020). Examining the potential of VR and AR Technologies for Education. *Journal of Physics: Conference Series*, *1691*(1), 012160. doi:10.1088/1742-6596/1691/1/012160

Mah, R. (2016). *Construction Adjudication in Malaysia: Faster and Cheaper Dispute Resolution*. Mahwengkwai. https://mahwengkwai.com/construction-adjudication-inmalaysia-faster-andcheaper/? utm_source=Mondaq&utm_medium=syndication&utm_campaign=Linked In-integration

Mah, R., & Woo, M. (2013). *Construction adjudication in malaysia*. Mahwengkwai. https://mahwengkwai.com/construction-adjudication-in-malaysia/

Mahdjoubi, L., Koh, J. H., & Moobela, C. (2014). Effects of Interactive Real-Time Simulations and Humanoid Avatars on Consumers' Responses in Online House Products Marketing. *Computer-Aided Civil and Infrastructure Engineering*, *29*(1), 31–46. doi:10.1111/j.1467-8667.2012.00775.x

Maheswari, C., Priyanka, E. B., Thangavel, S., Vignesh, S. R., & Poongodi, C. (2020). Multiple regression analysis for the prediction of extraction efficiency in mining industry with industrial IoT. *Production Engineering*, *14*(4), 457–471. doi:10.100711740-020-00970-z

Makarova, E. (2021). Effectiveness of traditional and online learning: comparative analysis from the student perspective. In *SHS Web of Conferences* (Vol. 99, p. 01019). EDP Sciences. 10.1051hsconf/20219901019

Makewa, L. N., Kuboja, J. M., Yango, M., & Ngussa, B. M. (2014). ICT-integration in higher education and student behavioral change: Observations at university of Arusha, Tanzania. *American Journal of Educational Research*, *2*(11A), 30–38. doi:10.12691/education-2-11A-5

Malaysia, C. I. D. B. (2017). *Quality Guidebook for Homeowners*. Canaan Building Inspector.

Mali, D., & Lim, H. (2021). How do students perceive face-to-face/blended learning as a result of the Covid-19 pandemic? *International Journal of Management Education*, *19*(3), 100552. doi:10.1016/j.ijme.2021.100552

Mallawaarachchi, S., Jayasinghe, J., & Wijesooriya, W. (2012). Indoor environmental quality in green buildings. *Journal of Environmental Protection*, *3*(03), 239–248. doi:10.4236/jep.2012.33032

Manaf, H. A., Mohamed, A. M., & Lawton, A. (2016). Assessing public participation initiatives in local government decision-making in Malaysia. *International Journal of Public Administration*, *39*(11), 812–820. doi:10.1080/0190069 2.2015.1035788

Manroth, A., Hernandez, Z., Masud, H., Zakhour, J., Rebolledo, M., Mahmood, S. A., Seyedian, A., Hamad, Q., & Peixoto, T. (2014). *Strategic framework for mainstreaming citizen engagement in World Bank Group Operations: Engaging with citizens for improved results*. World Bank.

Mao, W., Zhu, Y., & Ahmad, I. (2007, July 3). *Applying metadata models to unstructured content of construction documents: A view-based approach*. Automation in Construction. https://www.sciencedirect.com/science/article/pii/S092658050 6000203

Marco, B. (2018). *Sensors in smart homes: A new way of living*. Digital Innovation.

Maritz, M. J. (2003). *Adjudication of disputes in the construction industry.* AC. https://www.up.ac.za/media/shared/Legacy/sitefiles/file/44/2163/8121/innovate3/inn bl7879.pdf

Maritz, M. J., & Hattingh, V. (2015a). Adjudication in South African construction industry practice: Towards legislative intervention. *Journal of the South African Institution of Civil Engineering, 57*(2), 45–49. doi:10.17159/2309-8775/2015/v57n2a6

Marsh, J. (2018). *What are the main disadvantages of fossil fuels?* Solar News. https://news.energysage.com/disadvantages-fossil- fuels/

Martinko, M. J., Zmud, R. W., & Henry, J. W. (2011). *An attributional explanation of individual resistance to the introduction of information technologies in the Workplace.* Taylor & Francis. https://www.tandfonline.com/doi/abs/10.1080/014492996120085a

Marzukhi, M. A., Omar, D., & Leh, O. L. H. (2012). Re-appraising the framework of planning and land law as an instrument for sustainable land development in Malaysia. *Procedia: Social and Behavioral Sciences, 68*, 767–774. doi:10.1016/j.sbspro.2012.12.265

Marzuki, A., Hussin, A. A., Mohamed, B., Othman, A. G., & Mat Som, A. P. (2011). Assessment of Nature-Based Tourism in South Kelantan, Tourismos. *An International Multidisciplinary Journal of Tourism, 6*(1), 281–295.

Maslow, A. H. (Abraham H., & Frager, R. (1987). Motivation and personality. Harper and Row.

Mat Noor, N. A., & Eves, C. (2011). *Malaysia high-rise residential property management: 2004-2010 trends and scenario.* In 17th Pacific Rim Real Estate Society Conference. Gold Coast, Australia.

Matende-Omwoma, R. (n.d.). *The Story of Land Adjudication in Kenya: Paradoxes, Uncertainties and Reversionary Tendencies. – Institution of Surveyors of Kenya.* ISK. https://isk.or.ke/2021/01/26/the-story-of-landadjudication-in-kenya-paradoxes-uncertainties-and-reversionary-tendencies/

Matipa, W. M., Kelliher, D., & Keane, M. (2008). How a quantity surveyor can ease cost management at the design stage using a building product model. *Construction Innovation, 8*(3), 164–181. doi:10.1108/14714170810888949

Matthias Richter, W. H. (2021, January 5). *Natural Building Materials for Interior Fitting and Refurbishment—What about Indoor Emissions?* pp. 1-2.

Mayouf, M., Gerges, M., & Cox, S. (2019, February 18). *5D BIM: an investigation into the integration of quantity surveyors within the BIM process.* Emerald Insight. https://sci-hub.se/

Mazani, Q. A., Sahab, S. S., & Ismail, Z. (2019). *Trends of Adjudication Cases in Malaysia.* doi:10.1051/matecconf/2019

MBJB. (2016a). *Info Bandar.* MBLB. https://www.mbjb.gov.my/ms/pelawat/info-bandar

MBJB. (2016b). *Sukan dan Rekreasi.* MBJB. https://www.mbjb.gov.my/ms/rakyat/perkhidmatan/sukan-rekreasi

McClone, M. C. (2019, September 25). *Top 4 technology challenges in the construction industry.* McClone Insurance Group. https://www.mcclone.com/blog/top-4-technology-challenges-in-the-construction-industry

McCurdy, L. E., & Graham, C. (2003). Living in the dark: A study of urban residents' environmental experience in a major North American city. *Journal of Environmental Psychology, 23*(4), 385–398. doi:10.1016/S0272-4944(02)00120-2

Mcgraw-Hill Construction. (2014). *The Drive Toward Healthier Buildings 2014: Tactical Intelligence to Transform Building Design and Construction SmartMarket Report.* McGraw-Hill.

Mcgraw-Hill Construction. (2014). *The Drive Toward Healthier Buildings 2014: Tactical Intelligence to Transform Building Design and Construction*. SmartMarket Report.

McNulty, N. (2021, November 24). *Online education vs traditional education – which one is better and why*. Niall McNulty. https://www.niallmcnulty.com/2021/04/what-is-the-difference-between-online-education-and-traditional-education/#htoc-what-are-the-advantages-of-traditional-education

MDA Law. (n.d.). *South Africa won't meet the demand for adjudicators in the construction sector*. MDA Law. https://mdalaw.co.za/southafrica-wont-meet-the-demand-for-adjudicators-in-the-construction-sector/

Medelyan, A. (2021). Coding Qualitative Data: How to Code Qualitative Research. *InSights*. https://getthematic.com/insights/coding-qualitative-data/

Mehmet, O. (2013). *Development in Malaysia (Routledge Revivals): Poverty, Wealth and Trusteeship*. Routledge. doi:10.4324/9781315823416

Memon, A. H., Rahman, I. A., Memon, I., & Azman, N. I. A. (2014, August 5). BIM in Malaysian Construction Industry: Status, Advantages, Barriers and Strategies to Enhance the Implementation Level. *Research Journal of Applied Sciences, Engineering and Technology*. https://www.airitilibrary.com/Publication/alDetailedMesh?docid=20407467-201408-201502170022-201502170022-606-614

Menachem, D. (2019). *smart home Systems Based on IoT*. Automated and Smart Appliances.

Meor-Hasan, M., Abd-Razak, N., Endut, I., Abu-Samah, S., Mohd-Ridzuan, A., & Saaidin, S. (2016). Minimizing Defects In Building Construction Project. *Jurnal Teknologi, 78* (5-2), 80.

Merrill, F. E. (1969). Society and culture: An introduction to sociology. Englewood Cliffs, NJ.

Mewomo, M., & Maritz, M. (2017). The Experts' Views On Factors Influencing The Effective Implementation Of Statutory Adjudication. *Journal of Construction Project Management and Innovation, 7*(1), 1877–1892.

Miao, G. (2012). Interactive design and realization of mobile learning resources through 3G mobile phones, *International Conference on Information Management, Innovation Management and Industrial Engineering* (ICIII), (pp. 56–59). IEEE.

Michels, A. (2019). Participation in citizens' summits and public engagement. *International Review of Administrative Sciences, 85*(2), 211–227. doi:10.1177/0020852317691117

Mike, A. (2017). *The SAGE Encyclopedia of Communication Research Methods*. Sage.

Miller, H. B., & Cuevas, J. A. (2017). Mobile Learning and its Effects on Academic Achievement and Student Motivation in Middle Grades Students. *International Journal for the Scholarship of Technology Enhanced Learning, 1*(2), 91–110.

Mills, A., Love, P., & Williams, P. (2009). Defect Costs in Residential Construction. *Journal of Construction Engineering and Management, 135*(1), 12–16. doi:10.1061/(ASCE)0733-9364(2009)135:1(12)

Ministry of Finance Malaysia. (2021). *Budget Speech 2022*. Ministry of Finance Malaysia. Percetakan Nasional Malaysia Berhad. https://budget.mof.gov.my/pdf/2022/ucapan/bs22.pdf

Ministry of Finance Malaysia. (2021). *Touchpoints Budget 2022 Measures*. Ministry of Finance Malaysia. Ministry of Finance Malaysia. https://budget.mof.gov.my/pdf/2022/ucapan/bs22.pdf

MITEC. (2020). *MITEC awarded green building index certification*. MITEC. https://mitec.com.my/press/gbi/

MMC. (2016). *Local Agenda 21 (LA21) Program*. MMC. https://www.mpm.gov.my/en/mpm/program-local-agenda-21-la21

Modi, S. (2014). Improving the social sustainability of high-rises. *CTBUH Journal*, 1.

Mohamed Nasir, N. I. I., Ismail, Z., & Muhd Fadhlullah Ng, N. K. (2018). Comparative Analysis on Construction Adjudication Systems Towards Effective Implementation of Statutory Adjudication in Malaysia. *Malaysian Journal of Civil Engineering*, *30*(2), 202–216. doi:10.11113/mjce.v30n2.475

Mohammad, M., Yousef, J., Manasrah, A., & Ismael, J. (2019). Sensors of Smart Devices in the Internet of Everything (IOE) Era. *Big Opportunities and MassiveDoubts*. Hindawi. https://www.hindawi.com/journals/js/2019/6514520/

Mohd Nawi, M. N., Mohd Sani, M. R., Md Din, M. F., & Roslan, N. (2018). The potential of traditional timber construction in Malaysia: A review. *Journal of Advanced Research in Materials Science*, *44*(1), 9–21.

Mohit, M., Ibrahim, M., & Rashid, Y. (2010). Assessment of Residential Satisfaction in Newly Designed Public Low-Cost Housing in Kuala Lumpur, Malaysia. *Habitat International*, *34*(1), 18–27. doi:10.1016/j.habitatint.2009.04.002

Mok, O. (2013). *New Buildings Could also Have Structural Defects*. Malay Mail.

Montello, D. R., Waller, D., Hegarty, M., & Richardson, A. E. (2004). Spatial memory of real environments, virtual environments, and maps. In G. L. Allen (Ed.), *Human spatial memory: Remembering where* (pp. 251–285). Lawrence Erlbaum Associates, Inc.

Monton, A. L. (2022, March 22). *Difference and Similarities: Digitization, Digitalization, and Digital Transformation.* Globalsign by GMO. https://www.globalsign.com/en-sg/blog/difference-and-similarities-digitization-digitalization-and-digital-transformation

Mora, C. E., Martín-Gutiérrez, J., Añorbe-Díaz, B., & González-Marrero, A. (2017). Virtual Technologies Trends in education. *Eurasia Journal of Mathematics, Science and Technology Education*, *13*(2), 469–486. doi:10.12973/eurasia.2017.00626a

Morel-Edniebrown, F. (2012). Wither Genius Loci? The City, Urban Fabric and Identity in Perth, Western Australia. In H. Casakin & F. Bernardo (Eds.), *The Role of Place Identity in the Perception, Understanding, and Design of Built Environments* (pp. 275–299). Bentham Science Publishers. doi:10.2174/9781608054138112010010209

Morison, J. (2018, February 24). *8 ways technology improves education.* eLearning Industry. https://elearningindustry.com/technology-improves-education-8-ways

Morrison, C. (2010, October). *Bim 2010: The benefits and barriers for construction contractors in Auckland.* Research Bank Home. https://www.researchbank.ac.nz/handle/10652/1778

Moten, A. R. (2019). The 14th general elections in Malaysia: Ethnicity, party polarization, and the end of the dominant party system. *Asian Survey*, *59*(3), 500–520. doi:10.1525/as.2019.59.3.500

Moudon, A. V. (1997). Urban Morphology as an emerging interdisiplinary field. *Urban Morphology*, *1*(1), 3–10. doi:10.51347/jum.v1i1.4047

Mouzakitis, G. S., & Tuncay, N. (2011). E-learning and lifelong learning. *Turkish Online Journal of Distance Education*, *12*(1), 166–173.

Moysey, S. M. J., & Lazar, K. B. (2019). Using Virtual Reality as a Tool for Field-Based Learning in the Earth Sciences. In R. D. Lansiquot & S. P. MacDonald (Eds.), *Interdisciplinary Perspectives on Virtual Place-Based Learning* (pp. 99–126). Springer International Publishing. doi:10.1007/978-3-030-32471-1_7

Muhamad Khair, N. K., Lee, K. E., & Mokhtar, M. (2020). Sustainable City and Community Empowerment through the Implementation of Community-Based Monitoring: A Conceptual Approach. *Sustainability (Basel)*, *12*(22), 9583. doi:10.3390u12229583

Muigua, K. (2011). *Dealing with Conflicts in Project Management.*

Muigua, K. (2018). *Traditional Dispute Resolution Mechanisms Under Article 159 Of The Constitution Of Kenya 2010 Kariuki Muigua.* Idea. https://www.idea.int/africa/conflict_management_en.cfm,

Muigua, K. (n.d.). *Heralding a New Dawn: Achieving Justice through effective application of Alternative Dispute Resolution Mechanisms (ADR) in Kenya.* Metros.. http://www.metros.ca/amcs/international.htm

Muraleedharan, K., & Reiterer, A. (2017). Glue laminated timber (GLT) as an alternative construction material in the tropics. *International Journal of Sustainable Built Environment, 6*(1), 7–17. doi:10.1016/j.ijsbe.2017.02.001

Murugesan, S. (2007). Understanding Web 2.0. *IT Professional, 9*(4), 34–41. doi:10.1109/MITP.2007.78

Musarat, M. A., Alaloul, W. S., Irfan, M., Sreenivasan, P., & Rabbani, M. B. A. (2022). Health and safety improvement through Industrial Revolution 4.0: Malaysian construction industry case. *Sustainability (Basel), 15*(1), 201. doi:10.3390u15010201

Mustafa, M. (2019). *Environmental law in Malaysia.* Kluwer Law International BV.

MySinchew. (2021). Construction sector short of 1M workers, labor cost up 30%. 星洲网 *Sin Chew Daily.* https://mysinchew.sinchew.com.my/20210414/construction-sector-short-of-1m-workers-labor-cost-up-30/

Nachimuthu, K. (2012). *Need of e-content developments in education. Education Today, An International Journal Of Education & Humanities.* APH Pub.

Naglaa, A., & Megahed, E. M. (2020). Antivirus-built environment: Lessons learned from Covid-19 pandemic. *Sustainable Cities and Society, 1-4,* 7.

Nagrale, P. (2019, October 13). *Advantages and Disadvantages of Distance Education.* Sure Job. https://surejob.in/advantages-and-disadvantages-of-distance-education.html

Nanou, E. (2021, November 14). *The 8 pros and cons to VR Fitness Technology.* MUO. https://www.makeuseof.com/pros-cons-vr-fitness-technology

Napolitano, R., Blyth, A., & Glisic, B. (2018). Virtual environments for visualizing structural health monitoring sensor networks, data, and metadata. *Sensors (Basel), 18*(1), 243. doi:10.339018010243 PMID:29337877

Narayan, V. (2004). *Effective Maintenance Management: Risk and Reliability Strategies for Optimizing Performance.* Industrial Press Inc.

Nasir, S. N. (2021). Information on creating a healthy home environment in Malaysia. AIP Conference Proceedings 2347 (pp. 020100 - 020100-8). Malaysia: AIP Publishing. doi:10.1063/5.0053683

Nazemi, P. (2013). A Comparison Between Beauty in Islamic Urban Textures and European Historic Cities: Differences in Urban Conservation Strategies. *Conservation Science in Cultural Heritage, 13,* 193–211.

Network, A. N. (2021, October 21). Malaysia facing labour shortage as economy recovers. Malaysia facing labour shortage as economy recovers. *Phnom Penh Post.* https://www.phnompenhpost.com/international/malaysia-facing-labour-shortage-economy-recovers

Neufert, E. (2019). *Arhitects' data.* John Wiley & Sons Ltd.

Newsham, G. R., Veitch, J. A., Charles, K. E., & Huang, J. (2004). Effects of daylight and view of nature on office workers' well-being and performance. *Journal of Environmental Psychology, 24*(2), 417–435. doi:10.1016/j.jenvp.2004.08.009

Ng Tee Wei. (2019). smart home in Malaysia. *Dissertation. University Tunku Abdul Rahman*

Ngah, K., Mustaffa, J., Zakaria, Z., Noordin, N., & Sawal, M. Z. H. M. (2011). Formulation of Agenda 21 process indicators for Malaysia. *Journal of Management and Sustainability, 1*(1), 82. doi:10.5539/jms.v1n1p82

Ngesan, M. R., Karim, H. A., Zubir, S. S., & Ahmad, P. (2013). Urban community perception on nighttime leisure activities in improving public park design. *Procedia: Social and Behavioral Sciences, 105*, 619–631. doi:10.1016/j.sbspro.2013.11.065

Nguyen, W. (2022, May 14). *How to make the quest 2 more comfortable (zero pressure).* VR Heaven. https://vrheaven.io/how-to-make-the-oculus-quest-more-comfortable/

Nigam, M., Dixit, A., & Sachan, K. K. (2016). Bim vs traditional quantity surveying and its future mapping. *IJEDR.* https://www.ijedr.org/papers/IJEDR1602222.pdf

Nikezić, A., & Marković, D. (2015). Place-based education in the architectural design studio: Agrarian landscape as a resource for sustainable urban lifestyle. *Sustainability (Basel), 7*(7), 9711–9733. doi:10.3390u7079711

Nikyema, G. A., & Blouin, V. Y. (2020). Barriers to the adoption of green building materials and technologies in developing countries: The case of Burkina Faso. *IOP Conference Series. Earth and Environmental Science, 410*(1), 1–10. doi:10.1088/1755-1315/410/1/012079

Nordin, R. M. (2020). Challenges in the implementation of Green Home Development in Malaysia. *IOP Publishing Conf. Series. Materials Science and Engineering, 291.*

Nowotna, B. P. (2019). Eco-Friendly Building Materials. *IOP Conference Series. Earth and Environmental Science, 2-4, 7.*

Ntiyakunze, J., & Inoue, T. (2023). Segmentation of Structural Elements from 3D Point Cloud Using Spatial Dependencies for Sustainability Studies. *Sensors (Basel), 23*(4), 1924. doi:10.339023041924 PMID:36850520

Nugroho, S., Rizqiyah, F., Bararatin, K., Mahendra, A. S., Kharismawan, R., & Soemardiono, B. (2021). Pemanfaatan Google-Street-View untuk Observasi Kota di Tengah Pandemi Covid-19. *ATRIUM: Jurnal Arsitektur, 7*(1), 1–12. doi:10.21460/atrium.v7i1.111

Nurudin, S. M., Hashim, R., Rahman, S., Zulkifli, N., Mohamed, A. S. P., & Hamik, S. A. (2015). Public participation process at local government administration: A case study of the Seremban Municipal Council, Malaysia. *Procedia: Social and Behavioral Sciences, 211*, 505–512. doi:10.1016/j.sbspro.2015.11.067

NVIDIA. (2023). *Omniverse.* NVIDIA. https://www.nvidia.com/en-us/omniverse/

O'Leary, R., & Ramsden, A. (2002). *Virtual learning environments. Learning and Teaching Support Network Generic Centre/ALT Guides.* LTSN.

Odacc.ca. (n.d.). *Adjudication Process.* ODACC. https://odacc.ca/en/adjudication-process/

Ogunnusi, M., Hamma-Adama, M., Salman, H., & Kouider, T. (2020). COVID-19 pandemic: the effects and prospects in the construction industry. *International journal of real estate studies, 14*(Special Issue 2).

Oldenburg, R. (1991). *The great good place.* Paragon House.

Oldenburg, R. (1999). *The Great Good Place* (3rd ed.). Marlowe & Company.

Omar, S. R., & Omar, S. N. (2018). Malaysian Heritage Food (MHF): A Review on Its Unique Food Culture, Tradition and Present Lifestyle. *International Journal of Heritage, Art and Multimedia, 1*(3), 01-15.

Ong Et Al, J. (2020, December 2). *7 missing pieces: why students prefer in-person over online classes.* University Affairs. https://www.universityaffairs.ca/features/feature-article/7-missing-pieces-why-students-prefer-in-person-over-online-classes/

Ontatio Museum Association. (2020). Discover-Ontario Museums. Museums Ontatio. https://www.museumsontario.ca/

Opoku, D. G. J., Ayarkwa, J., & Agyekum, K. (2019). Barriers to environmental sustainability of construction projects. *Smart and Sustainable Built Environment, 8*(4), 292–306. doi:10.1108/SASBE-08-2018-0040

Orb, A., Eisenhauer, L., & Wynaden, D. (2001). Ethics in qualitative research. *Journal of Nursing Scholarship, 33*(1), 93–96. doi:10.1111/j.1547-5069.2001.00093.x

Osaily, N. Z. (2010). *The key barriers to implementing sustainable construction in West Bank.* Prifysgol Cymru University of Wales.

Otter, R. R., Seipel, S., Graeff, T., Alexander, B., Boraiko, C., Gray, J., & Sadler, K. (2013). Comparing student and faculty perceptions of online and traditional courses. *The Internet and Higher Education, 19*, 27–35. doi:10.1016/j.iheduc.2013.08.001

Oweis, T. I. (2018, November 4). *Effects of Using a Blended Learning Method on Students' Achievement and Motivation to Learn English in Jordan: A Pilot Case Study.* Hindawi. https://www.hindawi.com/journals/edri/2018/7425924/

Özcan, K. (2005). Anadolu'da Selçuklu Dönemi Yerleşme Sistemi ve Kent Modelleri (Yayımlanmamış doktora tezi). Selçuk Üniversitesi Fen Bilimleri Enstitüsü, Konya.

Özcan, K. (2010). Erken Dönem Anadolu–Türk Kenti Anadolu Selçuklu Kenti ve Mekânsal Ögeleri. *Bilig, 55*, 193–220.

P. De Luca, I. C. (2017). Green building materials: A review of state-of-the-art studies of innovative materials. *Journal of Green Building, 151*, 160.

Palaha, J. (2022). 22 Best Metaverse Platforms To Watch Out For in 2022. *Jatinderpalaha.* https://www.jatinderpalaha.com/metaverse-platforms/

Pandey, N., & Pal, A. (2020). Impact of digital surge during Covid-19 pandemic: A viewpoint on research and practice. *International Journal of Information Management, 55*, 102171. doi:10.1016/j.ijinfomgt.2020.102171 PMID:32836633

Panith, A. (2020, July 10). *Digital Transformation is the New Normal of Construction.* Construction Plus Asia. https://www.constructionplusasia.com/my/digital-transformation-is-the-new-normal-of-construction/

Papapicco, C. (2020). Informative contagion: The coronavirus (COVID-19) in Italian journalism. *Online Journal of Communication and Media Technologies, 10*(3), e202014. doi:10.29333/ojcmt/7938

Pappas, C. (2016, October 5). *Top 8 eLearning Barriers That Inhibit Online Learners Engagement With eLearning Content.* ELearning Industry. https://elearningindustry.com/top-elearning-barriers-that-inhibit-online-learners-engagement-elearning-content

Park, L. (2019). Virtual Reality as a Pedagogical Tool for Interdisciplinarity and Place-Based Education. In R. D. Lansiquot & S. P. MacDonald (Eds.), *Interdisciplinary Perspectives on Virtual Place-Based Learning* (pp. 35–51). Springer International Publishing. doi:10.1007/978-3-030-32471-1_3

Parra-Serrano, J., Komatsu, K., Inoue, M., Lee, S. H., & Kawai, S. (2018). Performance of glued-laminated timber made from rubber tree and oil palm lumber. *BioResources, 13*(4), 8545–8557.

Patel, P. P., & Patel, A. (2021). Use of sustainable green materials in construction of green buildings for sustainable development. *IOP Conference Series. Earth and Environmental Science, 785*(1), 2–8. doi:10.1088/1755-1315/785/1/012009

Pati, D., Sahoo, S., & Sagar, R. (2007). Windows with a view: Nurses' stress relief at work. *Journal of Advanced Nursing*, *60*(4), 427–432. PMID:17919164

Patil, M. (n.d.). *How is digitalization taking over architecture*. Rethinking The Future. https://www.re-thinkingthefuture.com/technology-architecture/a2561-how-is-digitalization-taking-over-architecture/

Paul, J. (2020, May 20). *Why AR and VR are struggling to break into the classroom*. eLearning Industry. https://elearningindustry.com/ar-and-vr-are-struggling-break-into- classroom.

Pawar, S. P., & Atterde, P. M.Sandip.P.Pawar. (2014). Comparative analysis of formwork in Multistory Building. *International Journal of Research in Engineering and Technology*, *03*(21), 22–24. doi:10.15623/ijret.2014.0321006

Payne, S. R., Mackrill, J., Cain, R., Strelitz, J., & Gate, L. (2015). Developing interior design briefs for health-care and well-being centres through public participation. *Architectural Engineering and Design Management*, *11*(4), 264–279. doi:10.1080/17452007.2014.923288

Pedagoo. (2020, June 20). *What are the uses of ICT in education?* Pedagoo. https://pedagoo.com/uses-of-ict-in-education/?lang=en

Peiyu Xu, J. Z. (2022). Are bamboo construction materials environmentally friendly? A life cycle environmental impact analysis. *Science Direct*, *1*, 3.

Pejić, P., Krasić, S., Krstić, H., Dragović, M., & Akbiyik, Y. (2017). 3D virtual modelling of existing objects by terrestrial photogrammetric methods-Case study of Barutana. *Tehnicki Vjesnik (Strojarski Fakultet)*, *24*(Supplement 1), 233–239.

Penny Bonda, K. S. (2014). *Sustainable Commercial Interiors*. John Wiley & Sons, Inc., Hoboken, New Jersey.

Pham, H. C., Dao, N., Pedro, A., Le, Q. T., Hussain, R., Cho, S., & Park, C. (2018). Virtual field trip for mobile construction safety education using 360-degree panoramic virtual reality. *International Journal of Engineering Education*, *34*(4), 1174–1191.

Philips, R. O. (1965). Climate as an Influence of Building Design. *Architectural Science Review*, *8*(4), 125–128. doi:10.1080/00038628.1965.9696152

Pickavance, J. (2015). *A Practical Guide to Construction Adjudication*. 768. https://books.google.com/books/about/A_Practical_Guide_to_Construction_Adjudi.html?id=ieHNCgAAQBAJ

Pietkiewicz, I., & Smith, J. A. (2014). A practical guide to using interpretative phenomenological analysis in qualitative research psychology. *Psychological Journal*, *20*(1), 7–14.

Pinsent, M. (2011). Defective Work. In *Construction Projects*. Pinsentmasons.

Pløger, J. (2021). Politics, planning, and ruling: The art of taming public participation. *International Planning Studies*, *26*(4), 1–15. doi:10.1080/13563475.2021.1883422

PLP Architecture. (2022). *PLP Architecture and Verse Prop Join Forces to Launch NFT Collection*. PLP Architecture. https://plparchitecture.com/plp-architecture-and-verseprop-join-forces-to-launch-nft-collection/

Poore, S. (2021, October 23). *5 reasons you can't use your VR headset outside (and how to overcome them)*. ShaunPoore.com. https://www.shaunpoore.com/vr -headset-outside/

Poore, M. (2015). Using social media in the classroom: A best practice guide. *Sage (Atlanta, Ga.)*.

Potter, L. E., Carter, L., & Coghlan, A. (2016). Virtual reality and nature based tourism. *Proceedings of the 28th Australian Conference on Computer-Human Interaction - OzCHI '16*. ACM. 10.1145/3010915.3011854

Poudel, D. (2019, September 26). *Pros and Cons of Traditional Schools*. Honest Pros and Cons. https://honestproscons.com/pros-and-cons-of-traditional-schools/

Preferred by Nature. (2017, November 1). *Timber - malaysia - sarawak*. NEPCon - Preferred by Nature. https://preferredbynature.org/sourcinghub/timber/timber-malaysia-sarawak

Prep, U. (n.d.). *Introducing Online Education*. Uni-Prep. https://www.uni-prep.com/online-education/introducing-online-education/

Priego, R. G., & Peralta, A. G. (2013, November). Engagement factors and motivation in e-Learning and blended-learning projects. In *Proceedings of the first international conference on technological ecosystem for enhancing multiculturality* (pp. 453-460). IEEE. 10.1145/2536536.2536606

Prout, T. (2021, June 15). *Weighing the Pros and Cons of Online vs. In-Person Learning*. National University. https://www.nu.edu/resources/weighing-the-pros-and-cons-of-online-vs-in-person-learning/

Pulselli, R. M., Simoncini, E., Pulselli, F. M., & Bastianoni, S. (2007). Energy analysis of building manufacturing, maintenance and use: Building indices to evaluate housing sustainability. *Energy and Building*, *39*(5), 620–628. doi:10.1016/j.enbuild.2006.10.004

Purcell, T., Peron, E., Berto, R., & Boyle, M. (2001). Why do preferences differ between scene types? *Environment and Behavior*, *33*(1), 93–106. doi:10.1177/00139160121972882

Putra, F. (2019). Examining the link between democracy, social policy, and inclusive development in South-East Asia. *Asian Social Work and Policy Review*, *13*(3), 226–241. doi:10.1111/aswp.12175

Putra, F., & Aminuddin, M. F. (2020). Democracy and Social Policy in Southeast Asia: A Comparative Process Tracing Analysis. *The Journal of Politics*, *5*(2), 221–258.

QuestionPro. (2022, October 13). *What is research - definition, types, methods & examples*. QuestionPro. https://www.questionpro.com/blog/what-is-research/

Quod. (2014). *Living in tall buildings*. Berkeley Group. https://www.berkeleygroup.co.uk/media/pdf/b/b/berkeley-group-report-living-in-tall-buidlings.pdf

Qureshi, A. H., Alaloul, W., Murtiyoso, A., Hussain, S., Saad, S., & Oad, V. K. (2022). Evaluation of 3D model of rebar for quantitative parameters. *The International Archives of the Photogrammetry, Remote Sensing and Spatial Information Sciences*, *48*, 215–220. doi:10.5194/isprs-archives-XLVIII-2-W1-2022-215-2022

Radianti, J., Majchrzak, T. A., Fromm, J., & Wohlgenannt, I. (2020). A systematic review of immersive virtual reality applications for higher education: Design elements, lessons learned, and research agenda. *Computers & Education*, *147*, 103778. doi:10.1016/j.compedu.2019.103778

Radzuan, N., Hamdan, W., Hamid, M., & Abdullah-Halim, A. (2011). The Importance of Building Condition Survey Report for New House Buyers. *Procedia Engineering*, *20*, 147–153. doi:10.1016/j.proeng.2011.11.149

Rajeshkumar, V., & Sreevidya, V. (2019). Performance evaluation on selection of formwork systems in high rise buildings using regression analysis and their impacts on project success. *Archives of Civil Engineering*, *65*(2), 209–222. doi:10.2478/ace-2019-0029

Raji, M., Ab Karim, S., Ishak, F., & Arshad, M. (2017). Past and present practices of the Malay food heritage and culture in Malaysia. *Journal Of Ethnic Foods*, *4*(4), 221–231. doi:10.1016/j.jef.2017.11.001

Rajoo, P. D. S. (2014). *Dispute Boards & Adjudication in Malaysia: An Insight into the Road Ahead by Professor Datuk Sundra Rajoo*. AIAC. https://www.aiac.world/news/108/Dispute-Boards-&-Adjudication-in-Malaysia-:- An-Insight-into-the-Road-Ahead-by-Professor-Datuk-Sundra-Rajoo

Ramachandran, S. (2018). *Property hotspots for 2018*. Focus Malaysia. http://www.focusmalaysia.my/Property/property-hotspots-for-2018

Ranta-Maunus, A. (2021). Glue-laminated timber in architecture: a review of recent research. *Architectural Engineering and Design Management*, 1-15.

Rao, T., & Mustapa, S. I. (2020). A review of climate economic models in Malaysia. *Sustainability*, *13*(1), 325.

Razali, M., Idris, A., Razali, M., & Syafuan, W. (2022). Quality Assessment of 3D Point Clouds on the Different Surface Materials Generated from iPhone LiDAR Sensor. *International Journal of Geoinformatics*, *18*(4), 51–59.

Recycling of Natural Stones, Management and Benefits. (2020, October 6). Work-Tops. https://www.work-tops.com/blogs/stone/recycling-of-natural-stones-management-and-benefits

Reddy, B. V. V. (2009). *Sustainable materials for low carbon buildings*. Journal International of Low Carbon Technologies.

REHDA Institute. (2018). *FAQ Common Property Defects Account – REHDA*. Rehdainstitute.

Reifenrath, P. (2020). Five Advantages Of Hiring A Building Inspector. *L'Essenziale. L'Essenziale - Interiors and Lifestyle Blog*.

Relph, E. (2007). Spirit of Place and Sense of Place in Virtual Realities. *Techné: Research in Philosophy and Technology*, *10*(3), 17–25.

Renaissance. (n.d.). *What is digital literacy and why does it matter?* Renaissance. https://www.renaissance.com/2019/02/08/blog-digital-literacy-why-does-it-matter/

Research and Markets. (n.d.). Global Glue Laminated Timber Market 2018-2022. *Research and Markets*. https://www.researchandmarkets.com/reports/4618201/global-glue-laminated-timber-market-2018-2022

Revere, L., & Kovach, J. V. (2011). ONLINE TECHNOLOGIES FOR ENGAGED LEARNING A Meaningful Synthesis for Educators. *Quarterly Review of Distance Education*, *12*(2).

Rhumbix. (2021, August 25). *How Technology in Construction is Revolutionizing the Industry*. Rhumbix.com. https://www.rhumbix.com/blog/how-technology-in-construction- is-revolutionizing-the-industry

Richardson, J. C., & Newby, T. (2006). The role of students' cognitive engagement in online learning. *American Journal of Distance Education*, *20*(1), 23–37. doi:10.120715389286ajde2001_3

Ridings, J., & Chitrakar, R. M. (2020). Urban design frameworks, user activities and public tendencies in Brisbane's urban squares. *URBAN DESIGN International*, 1–17.

Ridwana, R., Prayitno, B., & Hatmoko, A. U. (2018). The relationship between spatial configuration and social interaction in high-rise flats: A case study on the jatinegara barat in Jakarta. In *SHS Web of Conferences*, *41*, 07003. 10.1051hsconf/20184107003

Robert, B., Greene, L. & Craig-Gardei, L. (n.d.). *What Is a Building Condition Assessment and When Do You Need One?* GLE Associates, Inc.

Robertson, A., Lam, F., & Cole, R. (2012). A Comparative Cradle-to-Gate Life Cycle Assessment of Mid-Rise Office Building Construction Alternatives: Laminated Timber or Reinforced Concrete. *Buildings.*, *2*(3), 245–270. doi:10.3390/buildings2030245

Robertson, A., Lam, F., & Cole, R. (2012). A review of the sustainability of wood buildings in North America. *Wood and Fiber Science*, *44*(1), 1–1.

Roopa, S., & Rani, M. (2012). Questionnaire Designing for a Survey. *The Journal of Indian Orthodontic Society*, *46*(4_suppl1), 273–277. doi:10.1177/0974909820120509S

Rosenbaum, M. (2006). Exploring the Social Supportive Role of Third Places in Consumers' Lives. Journal of Service Research -. *Journal of Service Research*, *9*(1), 59–72. doi:10.1177/1094670506289530

Rotimi, F., Tookey, J., & Rotimi, J. (2015). Evaluating Defect Reporting in New Residential Buildings in New Zealand. *Buildings*, *5*(1), 39–55. doi:10.3390/buildings5010039

Rousseau, D. (n.d.). Environmentally Friendly Building Materials. *Sustainable Built Environment*, *3-6*, 8.

Rovai, A. P., & Jordan, H. M. (2004). Blended learning and sense of community: A comparative analysis with traditional and fully online graduate courses. *International Review of Research in Open and Distance Learning*, *5*(2), 1–13. doi:10.19173/irrodl.v5i2.192

Ryan, R. M., & Deci, E. L. (2001). On happiness and human potentials: A review of research on hedonic and eudaimonic well-being. *Annual Review of Psychology*, *52*(1), 141–166. doi:10.1146/annurev.psych.52.1.141 PMID:11148302

Sa'ar, D. C. (2017, December 29). *Digitalisation in Built Environment*. IPM. https://ipm.my: https://ipm.my/digitalisation-built-environment/

Sa'ed, H. Z., Koni, A., Al-Jabi, S. W., Amer, R., Shakhshir, M., Al Subu, R., Salameh, H., Odeh, R., Musleh, S., & Abushamma, F. (2022). Current global research landscape on COVID-19 and cancer: Bibliometric and visualization analysis. *World Journal of Clinical Oncology*, *13*(10), 835–847. doi:10.5306/wjco.v13.i10.835 PMID:36337308

Sacks, R., Eastman, C., Lee, G., & Teicholz, P. (2018, July 27). *Bim handbook: A guide to building information modeling for owners, designers, engineers, contractors, and facility managers, 3rd Edition*. Wiley. https://www.wiley.com/en-sg/BIM+Handbook:+A+Guide+to+Building+Information+Modeling+for+Owners,+Designers,+Engineers,+Contractors,+and+Facility+Managers,+3rd+Edition-p-9781119287537

Said, A. S., & Syafik, E. (2016). The development of online tutorial program design using problem-based learning in open distance learning system. *Journal of Education and Practice*, *7*(18), 222–222.

Sakip, S. R. M., Akhir, N. M., & Omar, S. S. (2015). Determinant factors of successful public parks in Malaysia. *Procedia: Social and Behavioral Sciences*, *170*, 422–432. doi:10.1016/j.sbspro.2015.01.003

Sakip, S. R. M., Akhir, N. M., & Omar, S. S. (2018). The Influential Factors of Successful Public Parks in Malaysia. *Asian Journal of Behavioural Studies*, *3*(12), 195–205. doi:10.21834/ajbes.v3i12.135

Salleh, N. H. (2009). *Kesanggupan Membayar Oleh Pengunjung Terhadap Hutan Bandar Di Daerah Johor Bahru.*

Salonen, H. J., Lappalainen, S., & Kähkönen, E. (2012). Health and well-being in indoor spaces: A review of recent research. *Indoor and Built Environment*, *21*(3), 335–351. doi:10.1177/1420326X11430862

Samad, N. A. A., Said, I., & Rahim, A. A. (2017). Universally designed public spaces by enhancing accessibility and connectivity. *International Journal for Studies on Children, Women, Elderly And Disabled, 3.*

Samad, N. A. A., Jalil, R. A., & Anuar, N. A. N. K. (2018). Residents perception on strata property shared facilities potential for commercialisation. *International Journal of Real Estate Studies*, *12*(2).

Sanchez, C. A., Hedayati, M., Pielke, R. A. Jr, Anderson, C., & Steiner, A. L. (2018). The influence of greenness on the capacity of green infrastructure to provide multiple ecosystem services. *The Science of the Total Environment*, *635*, 1175–1186.

Sanders, E. B.-N., & Stappers, P. J. (2008). Co-creation and the new landscapes of design. *CoDesign*, *4*(1), 5–18. doi:10.1080/15710880701875068

Sandy Halliday, R. A. (2016). *RIBA Plan of Work 2013 Guide Sustainability*. RIBA Publishing.

Sanpanich, N. (2021). Investigating Factors Affecting Students' Attitudes toward Hybrid Learning. *Reflections: The SoL Journal*, *28*(2), 208–227.

Santé, I., Fernández-Ríos, A., Tubío, J. M., García-Fernández, F., Farkova, E., & Miranda, D. (2019). The Landscape Inventory of Galicia (NW Spain): GIS-web and public participation for landscape planning. *Landscape Research*, *44*(2), 212–240. doi:10.1080/01426397.2018.1444155

Sarayed, F. L. (2017). Exploring informality in a global south city: Issues of power and urban development in Kuala Lumpur. *Journal Of Design And Built Environment*, *17*(1), 63–73. doi:10.22452/jdbe.vol17no1.4

Šašinka, Č., Stachoň, Z., Sedlák, M., Chmelík, J., Herman, L., Kubíček, P., Šašinková, A., Doležal, M., Tejkl, H., Urbánek, T., Svatoňová, H., Ugwitz, P., & Juřík, V. (2018). Collaborative immersive virtual environments for education in geography. *ISPRS International Journal of Geo-Information*, *8*(3), 3. doi:10.3390/ijgi8010003

Saunders, C., Rutkowski, A. F., Genuchten van, Vogel, & Orrego. (2011). Virtual space and place: Theory and test. *Management Information Systems Quarterly*, *35*(4), 1079–1098. doi:10.2307/41409974

Saville, C. W. (2021). Not belonging where others do: A cross-sectional analysis of multi-level social capital interactions on health and mental well-being in Wales. *Journal of Epidemiology and Community Health*, *75*(4), 349–356. doi:10.1136/jech-2020-215188 PMID:33161384

SBCI. (2007). Buildings and climate change- status, challenges and opportunities. United Nations Environment Programme.

Sch¨oggl, J. P., Baumgartner, R. J., & Hofer, D. (2017). Improving sustainability performance in early phases of product design: A checklist for sustainable product development tested in the automotive industry. *Journal of Cleaner Production*, *140*, 1602–1617. doi:10.1016/j.jclepro.2016.09.195

Schiavi, B., Havard, V., Beddiar, K., & Baudry, D. (2022). Bim data flow architecture with AR/VR Technologies: Use Cases in architecture, engineering and construction. *Automation in Construction*, *134*, 104054. doi:10.1016/j.autcon.2021.104054

Schoof, U. (2018). *From shacks to skyscrapers: Timber towers hit new heights*. DW Made for Minds. https://www.dw.com/en/from-shacks-to-skyscrapers-timber-towers-hit-new-heights/a-43775847

Schurman, K. (2019, September 25). *Where is wall padding used and what kind?* Greatmats. https://www.greatmats.com/where-should-i-use-wall-padding.php

Scott, P. (2015). Successful sky life. In Global Interchanges: Resurgence of the Skyscraper City.

Seamon, D. (2000). Phenomenology, place, environment, and architecture: A review of the literature. *Phenomenology Online*, *36*, 1–29.

Sebastien, L. (2020). The power of place in understanding place attachments and meanings. *Geoforum, 108*, 204–216. doi:10.1016/j.geoforum.2019.11.001

Sekaran, U., & Bougie, R. (2019). *Research methods for business: A skill building approach.* John Wiley & Sons.

Seo, R. J., & Omar, S. (2011). Housing typology of modern Malaysia. In *1st South East Asia Housing Forum of ARCH,* 6–7.

Seyed Meysam Khoshnava, R. R. (2020). The Role of Green Building Materials in Reducing Environmental and Human Health Impacts. *International Journal of Environmental Research and Public Health, 6*, 11.

Sha, L., Looi, C. K., Chen, W., Seow, P., & Wong, L. H. (2012). Recognizing and measuring self-regulated learning in a mobile learning environment. *Computers in Human Behavior, 28*(2), 718–728. doi:10.1016/j.chb.2011.11.019

Shamsy, J. (2014, May). *elearn Magazine: A Balancing Act Part I: Technical Support and the Online Instructor.* ELearnmagazine. https://elearnmag.acm.org/featured.cfm?aid=2627756

Shankar, S. S. & Jain, S. P. (2021). Blended Learning is the future of Education. *The Asian Conference on Education (ACE2021).* Research Gate. https://www.researchgate.net/publication/356557242_Blended_Learning_is_the_future_of_Education

Sharen, K. (2020). *MITEC Awarded Green Building Index Certification.* New Straits Times. https://www.nst.com.my/property/2020/04/586627/mitec-awarded-green-building-index-certification

Shearing, M. (2018a). *A guide to adjudication in construction...* Burnetts Solicitors. https://www.burnetts.co.uk/blog/a-guide-to-adjudication-in-constructioncontracts

Shearing, M. (2018b). *A guide to adjudication in construction contracts.* Burnetts. https://www.burnetts.co.uk/blog/a-guide-to-adjudication-in-construction-contracts

Siddiqui, F., Abdekhodaee, A., & Thaheem, M. (2022). *Taxonomy of Digital Skills Needed in the Construction Industry: A Literature Review.*

Sika Malaysia. (2017). *Malaysia International Trade And Exhibition Centre (MITEC).* Sika Malaysia. https://mys.sika.com/en/project-references/local-projects/malaysia-international-trade-and-exhibition-centre-mitec.html

Simonsen, J., & Robertson, T. (2013). *Routledge international handbook of participatory design* (Vol. 711). Routledge New York.

Singh, D. & Zaitun A. B. (2006, August). Mobile Learning in Wireless Classrooms [MOJIT]. *Malaysian Online Journal of Instructional Technology, 3*(2), 26–42.

Singh, D., Psychoula, I., Kropf, J., Hanke, S., & Holzinger, A. (2018, July). Users' perceptions and attitudes towards smart home technologies. In *International Conference on smart homes and Health Telematics* (pp. 203-214). Springer. 10.1007/978-3-319-94523-1_18

Sit, J. W., Chung, J. W., Chow, M. C., & Wong, T. K. (2005). Experiences of online learning: Students' perspective. *Nurse Education Today, 25*(2), 140–147. doi:10.1016/j.nedt.2004.11.004 PMID:15701540

Skaik, S. (2016). *(PDF) Taking statutory adjudication to the next level: a proposal for review mechanism of erroneous determinations.* Research Gate. https://www.researchgate.net/publication/305223084_Taking_statutory_adjudication_to_the_next_level_a_proposal_for_review_mechanism_of_erroneous_determinations

Skinner, N. P. (1982). Local Authority House Maintenance – the Variation in Expenditure. *The Houston Review: History and Culture of the Gulf Coast, 31*, 92–94.

Smith, D., & Tardif, M. (2009, March). *Building Information Modeling: A Strategic Implementation Guide for Architects, Engineers, Constructors, and Real Estate Asset Managers*. ResearchGate. https://www.researchgate.net/publication/319088001_Building_Information_Modeling_A_Strategic_Implementation_Guide_for_Architects_Engineers_Constructors_and_Real_Estate_Asset_Managers

Smith, P. (2015, September). *BIM & Automated quantities – Implementation Issues for the Australian Quantity Surveying Profession*. icoste.org. https://www.icoste.org/wp-content/uploads/2015/09/Smith-PAQS-Paper.pdf

Smith, J. A. (2011). Evaluating the contribution of interpretative phenomenological analysis. *Health Psychology Review*, *5*(1), 9–27. doi:10.1080/17437199.2010.510659

Smith, J. A. (2019). Participants and researchers searching for meaning: Conceptual developments for interpretative phenomenological analysis. *Qualitative Research in Psychology*, *16*(2), 166–181. doi:10.1080/14780887.2018.1540648

Smith, J. A., & Osborn, M. (2003). Interpretative Phenomenological Analysis. In J. A. Smith (Ed.), *Qualitative Psychology: A Practical Guide to Research Methods* (pp. 53–80). SAGE.

Smith, S. P., & Burd, E. L. (2019). Response activation and inhibition after exposure to virtual reality. *Array (New York, N.Y.)*, *3–4*, 100010. doi:10.1016/j.array.2019.100010

Sommerville, J., Craig, N., & Bowden, S. (2004). The Standardisation of Construction Snagging. *Structural Survey*, *22*(5), 251–258. doi:10.1108/02630800410571562

Sondermann, E., & Ulbert, C. (2021). Transformation through 'Meaningful' Partnership? SDG 17 as Metagovernance Norm and Its Global Health Implementation. *Politics and Governance*, *9*(1), 152–163. doi:10.17645/pag.v9i1.3656

Spagler, B. (2003). Adjudication. *Beyond Intractability*. https://www.beyondintractability.org/essay/adjudication

Spijkers, O., & Honniball, A. (2015). Developing Global Public Participation (1): Global Public Participation at The United Nations. *International Community Law Review*, *17*(3), 222–250. doi:10.1163/18719732-12341305

Squire, K. D. (2022). From virtual to participatory learning with technology during COVID-19. *E-Learning and Digital Media*, *19*(1), 55–77. doi:10.1177/20427530211022926

Srijuntrapun, P., Fisher, D., & Rennie, H. G. (2018). Assessing the sustainability of tourism-related livelihoods in an urban World Heritage Site. *Journal of Heritage Tourism*, *13*(5), 395–410. doi:10.1080/1743873X.2017.1373779

Stanley, R., & Thurnell, D. (2013, November). *Current and anticipated future impacts of BIM on cost modelling in Auckland*. Research Bank Home. https://www.researchbank.ac.nz/handle/10652/2450

Stanley, R., & Thurnell, D. (2014). *The benefits of, and barriers to, implementation of 5D BIM for quantity surveying in New Zealand*. Search.informit.org. https://search.informit.org/doi/epdf/10.3316/informit.200817347855487

Stansfeld, S. A., & Candy, B. (2006). Psychosocial work environment and mental health—A meta-analytic review. *Scandinavian Journal of Work, Environment & Health*, *32*(6), 443–462. doi:10.5271jweh.1050 PMID:17173201

Statista. (2020). *Global Facebook pages fan engagement rate 2020, by type of post*. Statista. https://www.statista.com/statistics/934749/average-facebook-page-user-engagement-rates-selected-posts-worldwide/#:~:text=Global

Statista. (2021). *Mobile app usage - Statistics & Facts*. Statista. https://www.statista.com/topics/1002/mobile-app-usage/#dossierKeyfigures

Stegner, B. (2021, July 7). *5 common PC gaming problems (and how to fix them)*. MUO. https://www.makeuseof.com/tag/5 -common-pc-gaming-problems-and- how-to-fix-them/

Steinberg, F. (1996). Conservation and rehabilitation of urban heritage in developing countries. *Habitat International*, *20*(3), 463–475. doi:10.1016/0197-3975(96)00012-4

Stephenson, P., & Blaza, S. (2001). *Implementing technological change in construction organisations*. ITC. https://itc.scix.net/pdfs/w78-2001-66.content.pdf

Stevenson, F. (2021). Restorative environments: the future of office design post-COVID-19. *The Guardian*. https://www.theguardian.com/sustainable-business/2021/mar/25/restorative-environments-the-future-of-office-design-post-covid-19

Stewart-Brown, S. (2021). *Warwick Edinburgh Mental Wellbeing Scale (WEMWBS)*. Health and Wellbeing Services. https://warwick.ac.uk/fac/sci/med/research/platform/wemwbs/

Stigsdotter, U. K., Ekholm, O., Schipperijn, J., Toftager, M., Kamper-Jorgensen, F., & Randrup, T. B. (2010). Health promoting outdoor environments–Associations between green space, and health, health-related quality of life and stress based on a Danish national representative survey. *Scandinavian Journal of Public Health*, *38*(4), 411–417. doi:10.1177/1403494810367468 PMID:20413584

Stone, P. (2022, May 19). *5 Key Trends For Digitalization In The Construction Industry*. FlowForma. https://www.flowforma.com/blog/5-key-trends-for-digitalization-in-the-construction-industry

Strang, T., & Leardini, P. (2019). Opportunities for tropical hardwood glulam in Australia. *International Wood Products Journal*, *10*(2), 58–66.

Sufian, A., & Rozanah, A. (2008). Quality Housing: Regulatory and Administrative Framework in Malaysia. *IJEM*. upm.edu.my

Sukamolson, S. (2007). *Research methodology and data analysis*. Srinakharinwirot University.

Sulaiman, Z., Ali, A., & Ahmad, F. (2012). Abandoned Housing Project: Assessment On Resident Satisfaction Toward Building Quality. *Open House International*, *37*(3), 72–80. doi:10.1108/OHI-03-2012-B0008

Sulastiningsih, I., Purwanto, A., & Sudjadi, U. (2019). Energy analysis of glue-laminated timber (GLT) production for sustainable building material. *International Journal of Energy Economics and Policy*, *9*(1), 132–137. https://www.econjournals.com/index.php/ijeep/article/view/7276/4172

Sung, W.-P., Chen, K.-S., Song, W., & Tsai, Y.-Y. (2003). Evaluation method for performance of formwork process of construction industry. *Journal of Asian Architecture and Building Engineering*, *2*(2), 1–6. doi:10.3130/jaabe.2.b1

Sun, H., Mao, W., Dang, Y., & Xu, Y. (2022). Optimum path for overcoming barriers of green construction supply chain management: A grey possibility Dematel-Nk approach. *Computers & Industrial Engineering*, *164*, 107833. doi:10.1016/j.cie.2021.107833

Sun, H., Xu, Z., Yao, L., Zhong, R., Du, L., & Wu, H. (2020). Tunnel monitoring and measuring system using mobile laser scanning: Design and deployment. *Remote Sensing (Basel)*, *12*(4), 730. doi:10.3390/rs12040730

Suruhjaya Tenaga. (2013). *The energy commission diamond building*. Suruhjaya Tenaga. https://www.st.gov.my/en/details/aboutus/9

Suttling, D. (2020). *Latent vs Patent Defects and How to Manage them*. C-Link.

Swan, K. (2002). Building learning communities in online courses: The importance of interaction. *Education Communication and Information*, *2*(1), 23–49. doi:10.1080/1463631022000005016

Symeonides, R., & Childs, C. (2015). The personal experience of online learning: An interpretative phenomenological analysis. *Computers in Human Behavior*, *51*, 539–545. doi:10.1016/j.chb.2015.05.015

Szabó, M., Csete, M. S., & Pálvölgyi, T. (2018). Resilient Regions From Sustainable Development Perspective. *European Journal of Sustainable Development, 7*(1). doi:10.14207/ejsd.2018.v7n1p395

Tabakoğlu, A. (1985). *Gerileme Devrine Girerken Osmanlı Maliyesi*. Dergâh Yayınları.

Tailor, J. (2022, February 9). *How 3D Modeling can Benefit Construction Industry?* GharPedia. https://gharpedia.com/blog/how-3d-modeling-can-benefit-construction-industry/

Tajuddin, Z., Sum, S. M., Zainol, R. M., & Jusoh, H. (2019). Penentu Sosial Penglibatan Komuniti Dalam Projek Kebun Komuniti Bandar: Social Determinants of Community Involvement In Urban Community Garden Projects. *Sarjana, 34*(1), 56–68.

Takewaki, I. (2020). New architectural viewpoint for enhancing society's resilience for multiple risks including emerging COVID-19. *Frontiers in Built Environment, 6*, 143. doi:10.3389/fbuil.2020.00143

Tamm, S. (2022). *10 Biggest Disadvantages of E-Learning*. E-Student. https://e-student.org/disadvantages-of-e-learning/.

Tansel, S. (1953). *Osmanlı Kaynaklarına Göre Fatih Sultan Mehmed'in Siyasi ve Askeri Faaliyeti*. Türk Tarih Kurumu Basımevi.

Tanyeli, U. (1986). Anadolu-Türk Kentinde Fiziksel Yapının Evrim Süreci (XI.-XV. Yüzyıllar) (Yayımlanmamış doktora tezi). İstanbul Teknik Üniversitesi Fen Bilimleri Enstitüsü, İstanbul.

Tanyeli, U. (1987). *Anadolu Türk Kentinde Fiziksel Yapının Evrim Süreci: 11-15. yüzyıl*. İTÜ Yayını.

Tao, F., Xiao, B., Qi, Q., Cheng, J., & Ji, P. (2022, July 1). Digital twin modeling. *Journal of Manufacturing Systems, 64*, 372–389. Elsevier B.V. doi:10.1016/j.jmsy.2022.06.015

Tawafak, R. M., Romli, A. B., & Arshah, R. B. A. (2018). Continued intention to use UCOM: Four factors for integrating with a technology acceptance model to moderate the satisfaction of learning. *IEEE Access : Practical Innovations, Open Solutions, 6*, 66481–66498. doi:10.1109/ACCESS.2018.2877760

Tawafak, R., Malik, S., Mathew, R., Ashfaque, M., Jabbar, J., AlNuaimi, M., ElDow, A., & Alfarsi, G. (2021). A Combined Model for Continuous Intention to Use E-Learning System. *International Journal of Interactive Mobile Technologies, 15*(3), 113–129. doi:10.3991/ijim.v15i03.18953

Team, B. (n.d.). *4 Ways to Improve Adoption of Your Digital Education Program*. BenchPrep. https://blog.benchprep.com/4-ways-to-improve-adoption-of-your-digital-education-program

Team, G. (2020, October 5). *Why instructional design is so critical for effective e-learning classes*. Gamelearn: Game-Based Learning Courses for Soft Skills Training. https://www.game-learn.com/en/resources/blog/why-instructional-design-is-so-critical-for-effective-e-learning-classes/

Techopedia. (2020). *Mobile Application (Mobile App)*. Techopedia. https://www.techopedia.com/definition/2953/mobile-application-mobile-app

Teddy, S., & Rahmithul, I. (2017). Prototype Design of smart home System using Internet of Things. *Indonesian Journal of Electrical Engineering and Computer Science*, 107–115.

Tedong, P. A., Grant, J. L., Abdul-Aziz, W. N. A. W., Ahmad, F., & Hanif, N. R. (2014). Guarding the neighbourhood: The new landscape of control in Malaysia. *Housing Studies, 29*(8), 1005–1027. doi:10.1080/02673037.2014.923089

Tee Wei, Ng., Baharudin, A., Hussein, L., & Hilmi, M. (2019). Factors Affecting User's Intention to Adopt smart home in Malaysia. *International Journal of Interactive Mobile Technologies*. https://online-journals.org/index.php/i-jim/article/view/11083

Tee, Y. Y., & Kamal, E. M. (2021, May 18). The Revolution of Quantity Surveying Profession in Building Information Modelling (BIM) Era: The Malaysian Perspective. *Journals of universiti tun hussein onn Malaysia.* https://publisher. uthm.edu.my/ojs/

Tekeli, İ. (1985). Tanzimat'tan Cumhuriyet'e Kentsel Dönüşüm, Türkiye Ansiklopedisi. İletişim Yayınları.

Teng, J. (2015, January 1). *The effectiveness of video tutorial and preview on self-efficacy, task performance and learning: An experimental study conducted at a middle school in Shanghai, China.* [Thesis, University Of Twente]. https:// essay.utwente.nl/69309/

Teoh, J. (2021). *Know Your Rights as a Homeowner: What Can a Homeowner Claim For From the Developer if the Property Has Defects? HHQ. IE (2015). Types of Residential Properties in Malaysia.* Insight Estate.

Tevhid, A. (1911). Kastamoni ve Sinobda İsfendiyaroğulları veyahut Kızıl Ahmedliler. *Tarih-i Osmani Encümeni Mecmuası, 6,* 252–257.

Texier, C. (1862). *Asie Mineure, description géographique, historique et archéologique des provinces et des villes de la Chersonnése d'Asie.* Firmin Didot.

Tey, J. S., Goh, K. C., Seow, T. W., & Goh, H. H. (2013). Challenges in adopting sustainable materials in Malaysian construction industry. *International conference on sustainable building asia.* IEEE.

Thakkar, V. (2018, June 11). *Benefits of VR in Education.* fotonVR. https://fotonvr.com/benefits-of-vr-in- education/

The Economic Times. (2020). *What Is Solar Panel? Definition Of Solar Panel, Solar Panel Meaning.* The Economic Times. https://economictimes.indiatimes.com/definition/solar-panel

The Engineered Wood Association. (2020). *The Rise of Mass Timber Construction.* APA Wood. https://www.apawood. org/the-rise-of-mass-timber-construction

The InterNations. (2019). *Living and Driving in Kuala Lumpur.* The Internations. https://www.internations.org/kuala-lumpur-expats/guide/living-in-kuala-lumpur-15377/living-and-driving-in-kuala-lumpur-3

The Star. (2011). Diamond Building: A shining example of energy efficiency. *The Star.* https://www.thestar.com.my/ lifestyle/features/2011/07/05/diamond-building-a-shining-example-of-energy-efficiency

The World Bank. (2021, September 24). *Digital Technologies in Education: The use of information and communication technologies in education can play a crucial role in providing new and innovative forms of support to teachers, students, and the learning process more broadly.* World Bank. https://www.worldbank.org/en/topic/edutech

Thompson, D. B., & Miner, R. G. (2007). *Building information modeling—BIM: Contractual risks are changing with technology.* Aepronet. http://www.aepronet.org/ge/no35.html

Thorne, S. (2000). Data analysis in qualitative research. *Evidence-Based Nursing, 3*(3), 68–70. doi:10.1136/ebn.3.3.68

Tibbalds, F. (2012). *Making people-friendly towns: Improving the public environment in towns and cities.* Taylor & Francis. doi:10.4324/9780203469521

Tomlinson, C. (2021). City of culture, city of transformation: Bringing together the urban past and urban present in The Hull Blitz Trail. *Urban History, 48*(2), 351–363. doi:10.1017/S0963926819001172

Ton, B., Ahmed, F., & Linssen, J. (2022). Semantic Segmentation of Terrestrial Laser Scans of Railway Catenary Arches: A Use Case Perspective. *Sensors (Basel), 23*(1), 222. doi:10.339023010222 PMID:36616820

Too, L., & Bajracharya, B. (2015). Sustainable campus: Engaging the community in sustainability. *International Journal of Sustainability in Higher Education*, *16*(1), 57–71. doi:10.1108/IJSHE-07-2013-0080

Tru, Q. C. (n.d.). *Digitization vs. digitalization: Differences, definitions and examples*. TruQC. https://www.truqcapp.com/digitization-vs-digitalization-differences-definitions-and-examples/

Truong, P., Hölttä-Otto, K., Becerril, P., Turtiainen, R., & Siltanen, S. (2021). Multi-user virtual reality for remote collaboration in construction projects.

Tsai, S., & Machado, P. (2002). E-learning, online learning, web based learning, or distance learning: Unveiling the ambiguity in current terminology. *Association for Computer Machinery eLearn Magazine*, (7), 3-5.

Tuan, Y.-F. (1975). Place: An Experiential Perspective. *Geographical Review*, *65*(2), 151–165. doi:10.2307/213970

Tuan, Y.-F. (2001). *Space And Place: The Perspective of Experience by Yi-Fu Tuan | Goodreads*. University of Minnesota Press.

Tulenheimo, R. (2015, May 13). *Challenges of implementing new technologies in the world of BIM – case study from construction engineering industry in Finland*. ScienceDirect. https://www.sciencedirect.com/science/article/pii/S2212567115002014

Turan, O. (1965). *Selçuklular Tarihi ve İslam Medeniyeti*. Türk Kültürünü Araştırma Enstitüsü Yayınları.

Uher, T. E., & Loosemore, M. (2004). *Essentials of construction project management*. UNSW Press.

Uhive. (2023). *Oasis*. Uhive. https://www.uhive.com/oasis

Ujang, N., Moulay, A., & Zakariya, K. (2015). Sense of well-being indicators: Attachment to public parks in Putrajaya, Malaysia. *Procedia: Social and Behavioral Sciences*, *202*, 487–494. doi:10.1016/j.sbspro.2015.08.195

UK Green Building Council. (2015). *Health & Wellbeing in Homes*. UK Green Building Council. 08453 UKGBC Healthy Homes FINAL WEB.pdf (biid.org.uk)

Ülgener, S. (1991). *İktisadî Çözülmenin Ahlak ve Zihniyet Dünyası*. Der Yayınları.

Ullah, O., Khan, W., & Khan, A. (2017). Students' attitude towards online learning at tertiary level. *PUTAJ–Humanities and Social Sciences*, *25*(1-2), 63–82.

Ulrich, R. S., Simons, R. F., Losito, B. D., Fiorito, E., Miles, M. A., & Zelson, M. (1991). Stress recovery during exposure to natural and urban environments. *Journal of Environmental Psychology*, *11*(3), 201–230. doi:10.1016/S0272-4944(05)80184-7

Umar, U. A. (2012). Sustainable Building Material for green building construction, conservation, and refurbishing. *Research Gate*, 1-4.

UN. (2015). *Sustainable Development Goals*. UN. https://sdgs.un.org/goals

UNDP. (2020). *Human Development Report 2020*. UN. https://report.hdr.undp.org/

UNESCO. (2003). *Convention for the Safeguarding of the Intangible Cultural Heritage*. UNESCO. https://ich.unesco.org/en/convention

UNESCO. (2011). *Recommendation on the Historic Urban Landscape*. UNESCO. https://whc.unesco.org/uploads/activities/documents/activity-638-98.pdf

UNESCO. (2020). *Museums around the world in the face of COVID-19*. UNESCO.

Uniform Building By-Laws (UBBL) Malaysia. (1984). UBBL. *Lawnet.* http://www.lawnet.gov.my/act/akta-133/

Uniform Building By-Laws (UBBL) Malaysia. (1984). *Uniform Building By-Laws.* Lawnet. http://www.lawnet.gov.my/act/akta-133/

United Nations Educational, Scientific, and Cultural Organization (UNESCO). (2020). *COVID-19 Educational Disruption and Response.* UNESCO. https://en.unesco.org/themes/education-emergencies/coronavirus-school-closures

United Nations. (2012). *Report of the United Nations Conference on Sustainable Development.* United Nations.

US Green Building Council. (2004). *The business case for green building: A review of the costs and benefits for developers, investors and occupants.* US Green Building Council.

USCRossier. (n.d.). *What Will Education Look Like in 20 Years?* USCRossier. https://rossieronline.usc.edu/blog/education-20-years/

Vallance, S., Perkins, H. C., & Dixon, J. E. (2011). What is social sustainability? A clarification of concepts. *Geoforum, 42*(3), 342–348. doi:10.1016/j.geoforum.2011.01.002

Valle, G. (2021, June 25). *8 benefits of 3D modeling in construction.* BuilderSpace. https://www.builderspace.com/benefits-of-3d-modeling-in-construction

Vance, L. K. (2012). Do students want web 2.0? An investigation into student instructional preferences. *Journal of Educational Computing Research, 47*(4), 481–493. doi:10.2190/EC.47.4.g

Vasilakos, C., Chatzistamatis, S., Roussou, O., & Soulakellis, N. (2018). Terrestrial photogrammetry vs laser scanning for rapid earthquake damage assessment. *The International Archives of the Photogrammetry, Remote Sensing and Spatial Information Sciences, 42*(W4), 527–533. doi:10.5194/isprs-archives-XLII-3-W4-527-2018

Vasiljević, I., Obradović, R., Đurić, I., Popkonstantinović, B., Budak, I., Kulić, L., & Milojević, Z. (2021). Copyright protection of 3D digitized artistic sculptures by adding unique local inconspicuous errors by sculptors. *Applied Sciences (Basel, Switzerland), 11*(16), 7481. doi:10.3390/app11167481

Velarde, M. D., Fry, G., & Tveit, M. (2007). Health effects of viewing landscapes – Landscape types in environmental psychology. *Urban Forestry & Urban Greening, 6*(4), 199–212. doi:10.1016/j.ufug.2007.07.001

Venkatarama, R. B. (2009). Sustainable materials for low carbon buildings. *The International Journal of Low Carbon Technologies, 4*(3), 175–181. doi:10.1093/ijlct/ctp025

Venkatarama-Reddy, B. V., & Jagadish, K. S. (2003). Embodied energy of common and alternative building materials and technologies. *Energy and Building, 35*(2), 129–137. doi:10.1016/S0378-7788(01)00141-4

VertigoVisual. (2021, August 4). *Wondering: VR is so expensive? here is why.* VertigoVisual. https://vertigovisual.com/why-is-vr-so-expensive/

Victoria. (2018, June 12). *7 Benefits to Blogging in the Classroom.* Techstarter. https://www.teachstarter.com/us/blog/7-benefits-blogging-classroom-us/

Vikas, S. N. (2019). Evaluating Privacy and Security Threats in IoT-based smart home Environment. International *Journal of Applied Engineering Research.* https://www.ripublication.com/ijaerspl2019/ijaerv14n7spl_18.pdf

Viner, R. M., Russell, S. J., Croker, H., Packer, J., Ward, J., Stansfield, C., Mytton, O., Bonell, C., & Booy, R. (2020). School closure and management practices during coronavirus outbreaks including COVID-19: A rapid systematic review. *The Lancet. Child & Adolescent Health, 4*(5), 397–404. doi:10.1016/S2352-4642(20)30095-X PMID:32272089

Viola, A. U., James, L. M., Schlangen, L. J., & Dijk, D. J. (2008). Blue-enriched white light in the workplace improves self-reported alertness, performance and sleep quality. *Scandinavian Journal of Work, Environment & Health, 34*(4), 297–306. doi:10.5271jweh.1268 PMID:18815716

Violante, M. G., Vezzetti, E., & Piazzolla, P. (2019). Interactive virtual technologies in engineering education: Why not 360° videos? [IJIDeM]. *International Journal on Interactive Design and Manufacturing, 13*(2), 729–742. doi:10.100712008-019-00553-y

Vischer, J. C. (2007). The effects of the physical environment on job performance: Towards a theoretical model of workspace stress. *Stress and Health, 23*(3), 175–184. doi:10.1002mi.1134

Vishwakarma, S. K., Upadhyaya, P., Kumari, B., & Mishra, A. K. (2019, April). Smart energy efficient home automation system using iot. In *2019 4th international conference on internet of things: Smart innovation and usages (IoT-SIU)* (pp. 1-4). IEEE. 10.1109/IoT-SIU.2019.8777607

Vogel, D., Kennedy, D., Kuan, K., Kwok, R., & Lai, J. (2007). Do mobile device applications affect learning? *40th Annual Hawaii International Conference on System Science*s (HICSS'07). IEEE.

Wahab, S. R. H. A., Chohan, A. H., Che-Ania, A. I., Tawil, N. M., & Omar, H. (2016). The classification of facilities to determine the management fund allocation at non-low cost of high-rise residential building. *Revista de la Facultad de Ingeniería, 31*(5), 9–18. doi:10.21311/002.31.5.02

Wallagher, M. (2015, September 8). *How Blogging is Being Used in the Classroom Today: Research Results*. EmergingEdTech. https://www.emergingedtech.com/2015/09/the-state-of-blogging-in-the-classroom/

Wallgrün, J. O., Chang, J. S.-K., Zhao, J., Trenham, P., Sajjadi, P., Simpson, M., & Klippel, A. (2022). Place-based education through immersive virtual experiences—Preparing biology students for the field. *Journal of Biological Education, 0*(0), 1–24. doi:10.1080/00219266.2022.2067580

Wampler, B., & Touchton, M. (2019). Designing institutions to improve well-being: Participation, deliberation and institutionalisation. *European Journal of Political Research, 58*(3), 915–937. doi:10.1111/1475-6765.12313

Wang, X., & Love, P. E. (2012, March). *Bim + ar: Onsite information sharing and communication via advanced*. Research Gate. https://www.researchgate.net/publication/254039790_BIM_AR_Onsite_information_sharing_and_communication_via_advanced_visualization

Wang, P., Wu, P., Wang, J., Chi, H.-L., & Wang, X. (2018). A critical review of the use of virtual reality in Construction Engineering Education and training. *International Journal of Environmental Research and Public Health, 15*(6), 1204. doi:10.3390/ijerph15061204 PMID:29890627

Wang, W.-C., Weng, S.-W., Wang, S.-H., & Chen, C.-Y. (2014). Integrating building information models with construction process simulations for Project Scheduling Support. *Automation in Construction, 37*, 68–80. doi:10.1016/j.autcon.2013.10.009

Wang, X., Zhou, J., Li, X., Li, S., & Gao, Y. (2020). Barriers to promoting the application of CLT (cross-laminated timber) in China. *Forests, 11*(4), 414.

Wang, Y., Kang, X., & Chen, Z. (2022). A Survey of Digital Twin Techniques in Smart Manufacturing and Management of Energy Applications. *Green Energy and Intelligent Transportation, 1*(2), 100014. doi:10.1016/j.geits.2022.100014

Warren, T. (2022). Apple now has 1.8 billion active devices. *The Verge*. https://www.theverge.com/2022/1/28/22906071/apple-1-8-billion-active-devices-stats

Warwick Medical School. (n.d.). *Warwick Edinburgh Mental Wellbeing Scale (WEMWBS) scoring*. Warwick Medical School. https://warwick.ac.uk/fac/sci/med/research/platform/wemwbs/using/wemwbs_scoring/

Warwick Medical School. (n.d.). *Warwick Edinburgh Mental Wellbeing Scale (WEMWBS) scoring*. Warwick. https://warwick.ac.uk/fac/sci/med/research/platform/wemwbs/using/wemwbs_scoring/

Wasunna, M. K. (n.d.). Kenya has a massive skills gap: how it can fix the problem. *The Conversation*. https://theconversation.com/kenya-has-a-massiveskills-gap-how-it-can-fix-the-problem-91170

Watson, D., Perez, L., & Wing, I. S. (2015). Environmental Monitoring with Smartphones. In Smartphones as Locative Media (pp. 59-73). Palgrave Macmillan, London.

Watts, G., Mills, A. J., & Bullough, S. (2016). Adding nature back to the health service: An evaluation of a natural landscapes and sounds intervention in a student medical centre. *Health Environments Research & Design Journal*, 9(3), 83–95. PMID:27733656

Waxman, L. (2006). The Coffee Shop: Social and Physical Factors Influencing Place Attachment. *Journal of Interior Design*, 31(3), 35–53. doi:10.1111/j.1939-1668.2006.tb00530.x

Welsh, B. (1996). Attitudes toward democracy in Malaysia: Challenges to the regime? *Asian Survey*, 36(9), 882–903. doi:10.2307/2645537

White, I., & Che, Y. (2011). 3 Is GRC a "Green" Building Material? *Proc.Of The 16th Int. Congress of the GRCA*. Whole Building Design Guide (WBDG). *Evaluating and Selecting Green Products*. https://www.wbdg.org/resources/evaluating-and-selecting-green-products

WHO Housing and health guidelines. (2018, November 23). World Health Organization. https://www.who.int/publications/i/item/9789241550376

Whyte, W. H. (1980). *The social life of small urban spaces*. Conservation Foundation.

Williams, K., & Dair, C. (2007). What is stopping sustainable building in England? Barriers experienced by stakeholders in delivering sustainable developments. *Sustainable Development (Bradford)*, 15(3), 135–147. doi:10.1002d.308

Winzeler, R. L., (1976). Ethnic Differences and Economic Change in a Local Malaysian Setting. 東南アジア研究, 14(3), 309-333.

Wood Products Council. (2017). *Building Tall with Wood: Opportunities and Challenges for 21st Century Wood Construction*. AWC. https://www.awc.org/pdf/education/BUILDING_TALL_WITH_WOOD.pdf

Wood, A. (2014). *Rethinking the skyscraper in the ecological age: Design principles for a new high-rise vernacular*. Proceedings of the Council on Tall Buildings and Urban Habitat (CTBUH). Shanghai, China.

Wordsworth, P. (2001). *Lee's Building Maintenance Management* (4th ed.). Wiley.

World Health Organization (WHO). (2020). *WHO Director-General's opening remarks at the media briefing on COVID-19*. WHO. https://www.who.int/director-general/speeches/detail/who-director-general-s-opening-remarks-at-the-media-briefing-on-covid-19---20-march-2020

World Health Organization. (2011). Work-related stress. *Fact Sheet No. 331*. WHO.

World Health Organization. (2014). *Mental health: A state of well-being*. WHO. https://www.who.int/features/factfiles/mental_health/en/

World Heritage Committee. (2021*). Operational guidelines for the implementation of the World Heritage Convention.* World Heritage Committee.

Wright, P., & McCarthy, J. (2010). Experience-centered design: designers, users, and communities in dialogue. *Synthesis lectures on human-centered informatics, 3*(1), 1-123.

Wu, Z., Jiang, M., Cai, Y., Wang, H., & Li, S. (2019). What hinders the development of green building? An investigation of China. *International Journal of Environmental Research and Public Health, 16*(17), 3140. doi:10.3390/ijerph16173140 PMID:31466403

Yaakob, H. (2012). Penyertaan awam: kejayaan dan kegagalannya dalam perancangan pembangunan. *Jurnal Pengurusan Awam*, 67-84.

Yaman, T., M. (1935). *Kastamonu Tarihi*. Ahmed İhsan Matbaası.

Yang, J., Wang, X., Wu, C., & Bai, C. (2019). Regularized reconstruction of grid system for traditional chinese timber structure building in HBIM. *The International Archives of the Photogrammetry, Remote Sensing and Spatial Information Sciences, 42*(W15), 1229–1233. doi:10.5194/isprs-archives-XLII-2-W15-1229-2019

Yenen, Z. (1987). Vakıf Kurumu İmaret Sistemi Bağlamında Osmanlı Dönemi Türk Kentlerinin Kuruluş ve Gelişim İlkeleri (Yayımlanmamış Doktora Tezi). İstanbul Teknik Üniversitesi Fen Bilimleri Enstitüsü, İstanbul.

Yılmazçelik, İ. (1995). *XIX. Yüzyılın İlk Yarısında Diyarbakır (1790-1840)*. Türk Tarih Kurumu Yayınları.

Yip, R., & Poon, C. S. (2008). Comparison of timber and metal formwork systems. *Proceedings of the Institution of Civil Engineers, 161*(1), 29–36. Waste and Resource Management. 10.1680/warm.2008.161.1.29

Yong, L. C., Aziz, N. M., & Mohd-Rahim, F. A. (2022, December 10). Adapting To A New Normal During COVID-19: Leveraging The Smart Building System With BIM Integration for Lifecycle Sustainability. *Planning Malaysia Journal, 20*(5), 209–222. doi:10.21837/pm.v20i24.1198

Yoon, H. J., Moon, H. S., Sung, M. S., Park, S. W., & Heo, H. (2021). Effects of prolonged use of virtual reality smartphone-based head-mounted display on visual parameters: A randomised controlled trial. *Scientific Reports, 11*(1), 1–9. doi:10.103841598-021-94680-w PMID:34321504

Yu, C. (2008). *Environmentally sustainable acoustics in urban residential areas.* [Ph.D. dissertation, University of Sheffield, UK: School of Architecture].

Yuce, B., & Turk, R. (2019). Embodied energy and carbon footprint of building materials in Turkey. *Journal of Building Engineering, 26*, 100824. doi:10.1016/j.jobe.2019.100824

Yücel, A. (1981). *Mimarlıkta Biçim ve Mekânın Dilsel Yorumu Üzerine*. Doktora Tezi, İstanbul Teknik Üniversitesi.

Yücel, Y. (1980). *XIII-XV. Yüzyıllar Kuzey-Batı Anadolu Tarihi Çobanoğulları Candaroğulları Beylikleri*. Türk Tarih Kurumu Yayınları.

Yudelson, J. (2008). *The green building revolution*. Island Press.

Yuliani, S., Hardiman, G., & Setyowati, E. (2020). Green-roof: The role of community in the substitution of green-space toward sustainable development. *Sustainability (Basel), 12*(4), 1429. doi:10.3390u12041429

Yurt Ansiklopedisi. (1983). *Kastamonu maddesi*. Anadolu Yayıncılık.

Yusoff, S. (2007). *Sustainable solid waste management: incorporating life cycle assessment as a decision support tool* (Vol. 34). The Ingeniur Board of Engineer Malaysia.

Yusoff, W. F. M., Ja'afar, N. H., & Mohammad, N. (2019). Perception of Architecture Students on Factors Influencing the Selection of Locations for Academic Trip and Site Visit. *Journal of Technical Education and Training*, *11*(3), 22–31.

Zahrizan, Z., Ali, N., Haron, A., Marshall-Ponting, A., & Hamid, Z. (2013, December 20). *Exploring the Barriers and Driving Factors in Implementing Building Information Modelling (BIM) in the Malaysian Construction Industry: A Preliminary Study*. MOAM. https://moam.info/exploring-the-barriers-and-driving-factors-in-implementing-building-_599c2a961723dd09401ad760.html

Zaidi, A. S. (2018). *Kedai Pati Sebagai Wadah Interaksi Sosial Masyarakat Dahulu dan Sekarang: Kajian Kes di Kota Bharu Kelantan*. Universiti Malaysia Kelantan.

Zainon, N. Mohd-Rahim, F. Azli, & Salleh, H. (2016, January). *The Rise Of BIM in Malaysia And Its Impact Towards Quantity Surveying Practices*. ResearchGate. https://www.researchgate.net/publication/305309677_The_Rise_Of_BIM_in_Malaysia_And_Its_Impact_Towards_Quantity_Surveying_Practices

Zainon, N., Rahim, F., Aziz, N. M., Kamaruzzaman, S., & Puidin, S. (2018, June). *Catching Up With Building Information Modelling: Challenges and Opportunities for Quantity Surveyors*. researchgate. https://www.researchgate.net/publication/329920573_CATCHING_UP_WITH_BUILDING_INFORMATION_MODELING_CHALLENGES_AND_OPPORTUNITIES_FOR_QUANTITY_SURVEYORS

Zainul, A. N. (2010). Investigating the awareness and application of sustainable construction concept by Malaysian developers. *Habitat International*, *34*(4), 421–426. doi:10.1016/j.habitatint.2009.11.011

Załęczna, M. (2018). Public participation in land use planning and the building of a civil society. *Real Estate Management and Valuation*, *26*(2), 23–32. doi:10.2478/remav-2018-0013

Zalite, K. A. (2002). *Understanding a theory of public participation in park planning for Nunavut*. University of Guelph.

Zallio, M., & John Clarkson, P. (2022). Designing the Metaverse: A study on Inclusion, Diversity, Equity, Accessibility and Safety for digital immersive environments. *Telematics and Informatics*, *101909*, 101909. Advance online publication. doi:10.1016/j.tele.2022.101909

Zal, W. A. (2018). The practice of community potential mapping as a guideline for community development in Malaysia. *Community Development Journal: An International Forum*, *53*(2), 321–339.

Zandvliet, D. B. (2014). PLACES and SPACES: Case studies in the evaluation of post-secondary, place-based learning environments. *Studies in Educational Evaluation*, *41*, 18–28. doi:10.1016/j.stueduc.2013.09.011

Zang, Y., Yang, B., Liang, F., & Xiao, X. (2018). Novel adaptive laser scanning method for point clouds of free-form objects. *Sensors (Basel)*, *18*(7), 2239. doi:10.339018072239 PMID:29997374

Zappia, S. (n.d.). *Pros & Cons of Hybrid Courses*. Seattlepi. https://education.seattlepi.com/pros-cons-hybrid-courses-3288.html

Zebra, T. (2022, August 11). 15 Green building materials for an eco-conscious home. *The Zebra*. https://www.thezebra.com/resources/home/green-building-materials/

Zhai, X., Li, M., & Chen, S. (2019). Examining the uses of student-led, teacher-led, and collaborative functions of mobile technology and their impacts on physics achievement and interest. *Journal of Science Education and Technology*, *28*(4), 310–320. doi:10.100710956-019-9767-3

Zhai, X., & Shi, L. (2020). Understanding how the perceived usefulness of mobile technology impacts physics learning achievement: A pedagogical perspective. *Journal of Science Education and Technology*, *29*(6), 743–757. doi:10.100710956-020-09852-6

Zhang, C., & Chen, B. (2019). Enhancing Learning and Teaching for Architectural Engineering Students Using Virtual Building Design and Construction. *Higher Education Studies, 9*(2), 45–56. doi:10.5539/hes.v9n2p45

Zhang, J., Wu, X., Chen, F., & Chen, Y. (2015). The effect of forest bathing on residents' perceived anxiety: Based on comparison of two forest types in Beijing. *Forests, 6*(11), 4156–4170. doi:10.3390/f6114156

Zhang, X., Platten, A., & Shen, L. (2011). Green property development practice in China: Costs and barriers. *Building and Environment, 46*(11), 2153–2160. doi:10.1016/j.buildenv.2011.04.031

Zhao, J., Lafemina, P., Carr, J., Sajjadi, P., Wallgrun, J. O., & Klippel, A. (2020). Learning in the Field: Comparison of Desktop, Immersive Virtual Reality, and Actual Field Trips for Place-Based STEM Education. *Proceedings - 2020 IEEE Conference on Virtual Reality and 3D User Interfaces, VR 2020,* 893–902. IEEE.

Zhao, Y., Jiang, J., Chen, Y., Liu, R., Yang, Y., Xue, X., & Chen, S. (2022). Metaverse: Perspectives from graphics, interactions and visualization. *Visual Informatics, 6*(1), 56–67. doi:10.1016/j.visinf.2022.03.002

Zheng, S., Apthorpe, N., Chetty, M., & Feamster, N. (2018). User perceptions of smart home IoT privacy. *Proceedings of the ACM on human-computer interaction, 2(CSCW),* (pp. 1-20). ACM. 10.1145/3274469

Zhineng, T. (2017). Review of the application of green building and energy saving technology. *IOP Conference Series. Earth and Environmental Science, 100,* 1–4.

Zhou, Y., Yang, Y., & Yang, J.-B. (2019). Barriers to BIM implementation strategies in China. *EmeraldInsight.* https://sci-hub.se/https://doi.org/10.1108/ECAM-04-2018-0158

Zhu, C. (2017). University student satisfaction and perceived effectiveness of a blended learning course. *International Journal of Learning Technology, 12*(1), 66–83. doi:10.1504/IJLT.2017.083996

Zhu, Y., Au, W., & Yates, G. C. (2013). *University Students' Attitudes toward Online Learning in a Blended Course.* Australian Association for Research in Education.

Zikmund, W. G., Carr, J. C., & Griffin, M. (2013). *Business Research Methods (Book Only).* Cengage Learning.

Zolkafli, U., Yahya, Z., Zakaria, N., Akashah, F., Othman, M., Ali, A., & Salleh, H. (2014). Latent Defects: Approaches in Protecting House Buyers' Right in Malaysia. *MATEC Web Of Conferences, 15,* 01040.

Zuo, J., & Zhao, Z. (2014). Green building research–current status and future agenda: A review. *Renewable & Sustainable Energy Reviews, 30,* 271–281. doi:10.1016/j.rser.2013.10.021

Zuzana (2012). The importance of social interaction to human health. *Hebio Feedback.* http://www.hebiofeedback.co.uk/hebf-latest/the-importance-of-social-interaction-to-human-health/

Zwain, A., & Bahauddin, A. (2021). *Malacca's "Straits Chinese traditional courtyard eclectic style shophouses":*

About the Contributors

Foong Peng Ng is currently the Head of School of Architecture, Building & Design, Taylor's University (Malaysia). Anchored by her PhD thesis titled "Re-thinking Place", her research focusses on the notion of place and place-making, and contemporary Malaysian architecture. She is currently engaged in the institutional initiative on purpose learning, while leading a research project on socio-spatial framework for temporary migrant worker housing in Malaysia and developing a design pedagogy framework for post-covid architecture education. She authors books and contributes to architecture magazines such as World Architecture, Architecture Asia, Architecture Malaysia, Architecture Australia, and d+a. Her active role in the Malaysian Institute of Architects through the Education, Media and Publication committees has landed her numerous appointments as convenor and moderator of international and national events.

Ungku Norani Sonet is an architecture and urbanism senior lecturer at Taylor's University. After several years of architectural practice, she opted to pursue postgraduate studies and finished her PhD research. Her primary area of interest in architecture education is the responsive architectural design approach to local context and identity. In addition to the responsive design approach, she is particularly interested in doing research on public participation exercises in development frameworks. Her current research delves deeper to increase public involvement toward a holistic approach of sustainable built environment.

* * *

Nurul Alia Ahamad is a Senior Lecturer at Taylor's University, Malaysia. She is also a registered architect with the Lembaga Arkitek Malaysia (Board of Architects Malaysia) and a registered Professional Technologist with the Malaysia Board of Technologists. She serves as an education committee member for the Pertubuhan Akitek Malaysia (Malaysian Institute of Architects). Prior to joining Taylor's University, she worked in the consulting industry for several years, designing residential and commercial buildings. Her research primarily focuses on Architectural Education and Place Identity. She holds a Master of Architecture and a Bachelor of Applied Science (Architectural Science) from Curtin University of Technology, Australia.

Khairool Aizat Ahmad Jamal is a Certified Autodesk Revit Professional and an avid advocator of Building Information Modelling (BIM). He is registered as Graduate Architect with Malaysia Board of Architects (LAM) and Professional Technologist with Malaysia Board of Technologist (MBOT). Currently a PhD candidate in Built Environment studies, he holds an M.Sc degree in Integrated Construction

Project Management from Universiti Teknologi MARA (UITM) and Bachelor of Architecture (Hons.) from Universiti Teknologi Malaysia (UTM). He also obtained a Post-Graduate Certificate of Teaching and Learning with Taylor's University. Prior academia, he has over 6 years experience as an architect working with several local and international firms. His teaching roles involves working with students from different disciplines and background within the built environment, hence this unique experience has enhanced his knowledge of the whole construction process from a diverse perspectives, inspiring him to explore BIM and Integrated Project Delivery (IPD) as a game-changing approach to transform the architecture and construction industry. He is currently active in research and supervision activities with several on-going research projects. He had also presented in numerous workshop and conferences and have published research books, articles in indexed journals and proceedings as well as magazines.

Nor Hafizah Anuar is an academician and a traveller at heart. She received her PhD in Architecture Theory and History from Yildiz Technical University, Turkey in 2018. She graduated respectively in Bachelor of Science Architecture in 2006, Bachelor of Construction Management in 2009 and Master of Science in Heritage and Conservation in 2012 from MARA University of Technology, Shah Alam Selangor. Now she is an academic at the Architecture Department of Faculty of Architecture and Ekistics, Universiti Malaysia Kelantan. She is an active member of the Malaysian Institute of Architects (PAM) and her research interest are architecture heritage and conservation (tangible and intangible), colonial architecture, sustainable architecture and design.

Ekrem Bahadır Çalışkan received his B.Arch in Architecture from Middle East Technical University, Faculty of Architecture (2005). His M.Sc. and Ph.D. degrees are in building science from Middle East Technical University. Currently, he works as an Instructor at Ankara Yıldırım Beyazıt University. Major research interests include knowledge management, virtual environments, and construction methods. Besides his academic background, he has designed many buildings since 2007.

Siti Nuratirah Che Mohd Nasir embarked on her higher education journey at Academia International College in Taiping, Perak. She then pursued her Diploma studies in Interior Design at Universiti Teknologi Mara (UiTM) in Sri Iskandar, Perak. she furthered her studies by enrolling in a Bachelor of Interior Architecture with Honours program at Universiti Teknologi Mara (UiTM) in Shah Alam. Following that, she proceeded to pursue a Postgraduate degree in MSc in Facilities Management at the same university. While pursuing her Master's degree on a part-time basis, she worked at Pavilion Project Sdn Bhd for five years as a Design Coordinator. In October 2017, she was offered and accepted a position as a lecturer at the Faculty of Architecture and Ekistics, Universiti Malaysia Kelantan. Currently, doing her PhD studies in Design and Technology at Universiti Sultan Zainal Abidin (UniSZA) in Kuala Terengganu. Her research interests encompass a wide range of topics, including creating healthy home environments, exploring the Internet of Things, designing furniture, studying anthropometric and ergonomic factors, developing sustainable design practices, managing facilities in commercial buildings, and specializing in interior architecture spatial planning. Over the years, she has secured several research grants totalling approximately RM50,000 from the university. Through these grants, she has made significant contributions to the community since 2018. She actively engages in volunteer work at both university and state levels. Additionally, she enjoys undertaking design projects and providing consultations, often collaborating with industries and the private sector.

Kai Kong Chow is a student at Taylor's University who recently completed his last semester of the Bachelor of Quantity Surveying degree. He has spent 3.5 years at Taylor's University studying subjects relating to quantity surveying, and his current cumulative grade point average (CGPA) is 3.26. He truly like modern technologies and studied information technology in his foundation.

Hsien Shien Goh is a final year student from Taylor's University who is currently doing her degree in Bachelor of Quantity Surveying (Hons). She started her degree since the year 2019 and had gone through her 6-month internship. Her interest of being a quantity surveyor grows deeper throughout the 3 and a half year journey of being a quantity surveying student at Taylor's University. She has good leadership skills and is also a team player. She is enthusiastic to expand her knowledge in the field, build connections, develop business acumen and be an all-rounder.

Sujatavani Gunasagaran is a Programme Director and Senior Lecturer at the School of Architecture, Building and Design, Taylor's University. She received BSc (Architecture) from University of Malaya, MSc in Building Technology from University Science of Malaysia, and Doctor of Education from University of Selangor. She is a member of Malaysian Institute of Architects (PAM) Education, Malaysia Green Building Council (malaysiaGBC), Society of Building Science Educators (SBSE) and a Green Building Index (GBI) Facilitator. She has won several awards for her innovation in teaching architecture. Her teaching and research emphasize sustainability, creativity, BIM, digital simulation, and technology. She supervises students from undergraduate, masters and PhD programme. Her administrative work concentrates in designing new programmes and auditing existing programmes as a member of Committee for Curriculum, Design, Assessment and Delivery. Currently, she is engaged as an Editor for a journal publication.

Nik Nurul Hana Hanafi is an academician at Universiti Malaysia Kelantan. Prior to that, she has involved in various projects as Project Architect where she develops research interest in relationships between human behavior and the natural and built environment. Her research includes housing issues, post-disaster housing intervention, and placemaking. She has also collaborated actively with researchers in various disciplines of Built Environment.

W. T. (Ashley) Hong is an Assistant Professor in Quantity Surveying & Construction Project Management at Heriot-Watt University Malaysia. Prior to her academic positions, she accumulated extensive quantity surveying experience and skills from the construction industry. She is also a registered Professional QS with the Board of Quantity Surveyors Malaysia. Ashley holds a Ph.D. in Sustainable Design, a Master of Science (Building), and an honors degree in Quantity Surveying from the University of Malaya. She is experienced in research and teaching at both the undergraduate and postgraduate levels, for more than 15 years. She is actively involved in Learning and Teaching, Research and Knowledge Transfer, Administration, Management, and Leadership roles. Her research area of expertise is Sustainable Design and Development in the Built Environment, Construction Project Management, etc.

Habizah Ilmi has a degree in Quantity Surveying and a master in Integrated Project Management and Construction. She is a member of Royal Institution of Surveyors Malaysia (RISM) and Royal Institution of Chartered Surveyors (RICS) and also a registered Consultant Quantity Surveyor with Board of Quantity Surveyors Malaysia (BQSM). She has 13 years experiences in the construction industry before joining the education industry and has been teaching quantity surveying program for more than 13 years.

Kenn Jhun Kam has a Degree in Building Technology, a Master's Degree in Building Technology, and a Ph.D. in Building Quality and Assessment. He is a Chartered Surveyor from the Royal Institution of Chartered Surveyors (RICS), a registered Professional Technologist with the Malaysian Board of Technologists (MBOT) and a registered Engineering Technologist with the Board of Engineers Malaysia (BEM). He has experience in construction for 5 years and has completed 2 high rises projects from IJM before joining the education industry. He has almost 10 years of experience in academia. He also held a management position such as Associate Dean at his current institution. Most of the subjects that he has been teaching are construction-related subjects such as Construction Technology, Building Services, Research Methodology and Dissertation.

Filiz Karakuş received her B.Arch in Architecture from Middle East Technical University, Faculty of Architecture (2002). She earned her M.Sc. and PhD. degree in architecture from Gazi University, Faculty of Architecture (2012-2017). Currently works as an Associate Professor at Ankara Yıldırım Beyazıt University. Major research interests include conservation and restoration.

Jing Hao Koh is a lecturer in the School of Architecture, Building & Design at Taylor's University, Malaysia. His research and publication interests include traditional Chinese architecture, heritage architecture documentation, and Malaysian Chinese culture and society. He is currently pursuing doctoral studies at the Institute of Chinese Studies of Universiti Tunku Abdul Rahman, focusing on the aesthetic philosophy, historical, social, and cultural investigations of the timber frame structure of traditional Chinese temples in Malaysia.

Sivaraman Kuppusamy is a lecturer in University of Reading, Malaysia. Dr. Siva has many years of industrial and academic experience. Dr Siva has successfully supervised more than 35 undergraduate Quantity Surveying students and co-supervised 10 Masters in Architecture students. Dr Siva is a certified Green Building Index Facilitator and an active member in the Association of Project Management (APM-UK). His research interests include environmental architecture, sustainability in built env. education for 4IR, AR/VR in built environment, BIM, and building technology and design approaches.

Xiang Loon Lee received his Master of Architecture and Bachelor of Science (Honours) in Architecture from Taylor's University, Malaysia in 2020 and 2017, respectively. His research interests cover high-rise typologies, flexible architecture and market designs. His final year architectural thesis focused on reinventing urban market typology through a flexible hybrid paradigm in Klang, Malaysia. Other interests of his include typography, graphic design and photography.

Yee Lin Lee received her Ph.D. in Project & Construction Management from University of Malaya in year 2016. She was currently with Tunku Abdul Rahman University of Management and Technology and taught several courses on construction technology and measurement to quantity surveying students. Her research interest includes innovation and technology applications, small & Medium sized construction companies, project management.

Tze Shwan Lim has a degree in Quantity Surveying and a Master's Degree in Construction Contract Management. She is a member of the Royal Institution of Surveyors Malaysia (RISM) and a registered Professional Quantity Surveyor with the Board of Quantity Surveyors Malaysia (BQSM). She has experience in the construction industry specializing in quantity surveying for 6 years before joining the education industry. Most of the subjects that she had been teaching are quantity surveying subjects such as Measurement, Software Application for Quantity Surveying, Price Analysis, Construction economics, Industrial Training and Integrated Project.

TamilSalvi Mari is a Senior lecture in Architecture, Taylor's University. Salvi's research area revolves around investigating the humane design-the interaction between humans, built environment, and natural environment, focusing on current societal and environmental needs. Thus, she is interested in exploring ways in the process of designing a better living/working environment to accommodate the elements of humane design and tapping into nature not only for the resources but also as the inspiration. Her research interests are also shaped by the emerging trends of sustainability in multi-storey residential/office buildings in urban areas focusing on wellbeing, carbon footprint, alternative building materials, and exploring the potential of vertical/urban farming to mitigate urban heat island issues, operational energy and to promote social sustainability.

Ida Marlina Mazlan received the Bachelor of Architecture from Victoria University of Wellington, New Zealand in 2007. She went into education in 2010 and has not looked back since then. Currently a PhD. candidate in a local university, she is also a lecturer at the School of Architecture and Built Environment UCSI University, Kuala Lumpur, specialising in Architectural Pedagogy and Cultural History.

Najah Md. Alwi is an Academic at the newly Part I LAM accredited Faculty of Architecture & Ekistics at Universiti Malaysia Kelantan, East Coast Peninsula Malaysia. She has been registered as a Graduate architect at the Malaysian Board of Architects (LAM) since 2008, an active member of the Malaysian Institute of Architects (PAM) since 2010, and working as Project Architect and Designer in firms in Malaysia, New Zealand and the UK since 2007. Besides teaching and research, she works closely in PAM sub-committees such as Graduate, Youth, Housing & Urban Wellbeing, and Gender & Equality in Architecture.

Juliza Mohamad received the Bachelor of Architecture and Master of Science in Heritage and Conservation Management degrees from the MARA University of Technology in 2009 and 2011, respectively. In June 2012, she became a lecturer at the Department of Creative Technology and Heritage, Universiti Malaysia Kelantan (UMK), Malaysia. In 2016, she joined the Department of Architecture at UMK as a lecturer. Her research interests are building heritage & conservation, mosque design studies, traditional Malay architecture and construction.

Nur 'Izzati Mohd Amin is currently working as a lecturer in University Malaysia Kelantan in Interior Architecture Department. Experienced teaching for 7 years in local universities. Previously was an interior designer. Was graduated from International Islamic University Malaysia in Bachelor of Applied Arts and Design, majoring in Interior Design in 2011. Masters qualification from University Malaysia Kelantan (UMK) in Masters of Arts. Reasearch interest are Interior Architecture and Design, Green and Sustainable Design, and Heritage Architecture. Have vast teaching experience especially in Interior Architecture including retail design, hospitality design, residential design, rehab design and many more.

Nor Diyana Mustapa is a lecturer at Faculty of Architecture & Ekistics, Universiti Malaysia Kelantan since 2018. She received her PhD from Universiti Sains Malaysia with specialization on children's connectedness to nature. Her major research interest includes children's environment and human and nature connection related to interior and landscape architecture.

Ahmad Nasrolahi is a conservator-restorer in the field of historical buildings and sites. He received his bachelor's and master's degrees in "Restoration and Renovation of Historical Cities and Buildings" in Iran. After graduating, he has been working for the Iranian Cultural Heritage Organization at Bam and Soltaniyeh World Heritage Sites. He has also done several types of research on different aspects of heritage protection as well as using new technologies in the management of cultural heritage sites. Ahmad gradually changed his focus from the conservation of architectural materials to the engagement of the local community in the preservation process. He has also completed a second master's (dual degree) in "International Cooperation in Urban Development and Planning" at the University of Darmstadt (Germany) and the Grenoble University Alpes (France). Now, he is working on local people's participation in cultural heritage management by using technologies to achieve maximum participation in his research project. In fact, he is applying urban planning and human-computer interaction approaches to cultural heritage management through new technologies such as smartphone apps.

Nik Syazwan Nik Ab. Wahab is currently a lecturer at the School of Architecture, Building, and Design at Taylor's University since 2019. He was educated at Universiti Teknologi Malaysia (UTM) in Bachelor Degree in Architecture (Part I and II). He obtained his MA degree in Design Technology from Universiti Teknologi MARA (UiTM). He currently pursuing his PHD in Philosophy and Urbanism in UTM. He co-wrote a book The Architectural Touch of Hijjas Kasturi. He specializes in Theory and History of Architecture and Design.

Sucharita Srirangam, also known as Dr Suchi, works as a Senior Lecturer at the School of Architecture, Building & Design of Taylor's University, Malaysia. Her research focus is primarily on urban design, where a synergy between space and user is understood as sustainability, with specific expertise in the themes of sense of place, urban resilience, sustainable cities, smart cities and urban digital representation. Her contributions consist of recommendations and effective space planning with environmental simulation tools such as space syntax, GIS, digital twins for smart cities and digital modelling; with a succinct exploration on the social aspects of urban resilience, inclusivity, marginalisation, public realm and safety. Dr Suchi is also explorative in research on architectural teaching and practice. For this, her contributions are in the form of designing new pedagogies, innovative social projects and practice-led design studio-based learning, SBL.

Azim Sulaiman is a lecturer in the School of Architecture, Building, and Design at Taylor's University, Malaysia, where he teaches and researches architectural heritage and conservation. His recent research in Malacca and Johor Bahru included the traditional shophouse at 120, Jalan Bunga Raya, Harbour Kuli Culture Gallery, and Hilltop Private School. He is currently co-writing a book on Kedah's architectural heritage. He is an associate member of ICOMOS Malaysia and a committee member of the Sungai Buloh Settlement Heritage Society. Recently he completed his second post-graduate study in Heritage and Conservation Management at MARA University of Technology Shah Alam.

Index

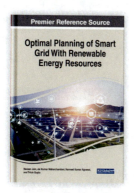

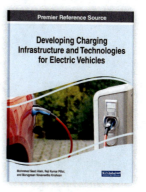
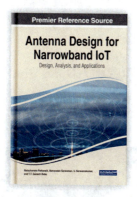
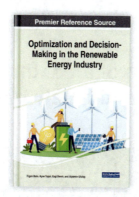
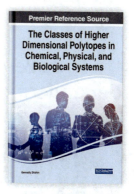

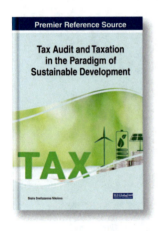
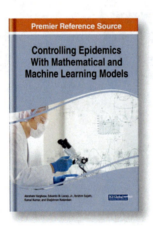
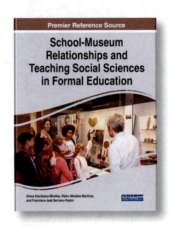
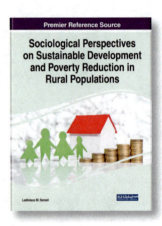

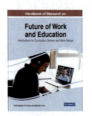

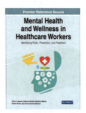